500 BREAD RECIPES

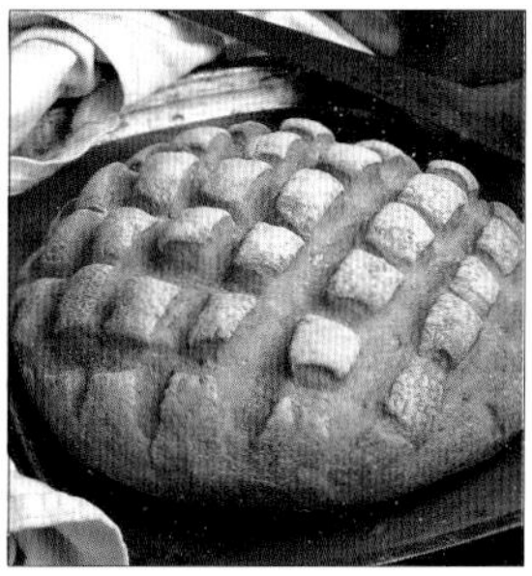

500 BREAD RECIPES

An irresistible collection of bread recipes from around the world, made both by hand and in a bread machine, shown in 500 tempting photographs

EDITOR JENNIE SHAPTER

LORENZ BOOKS

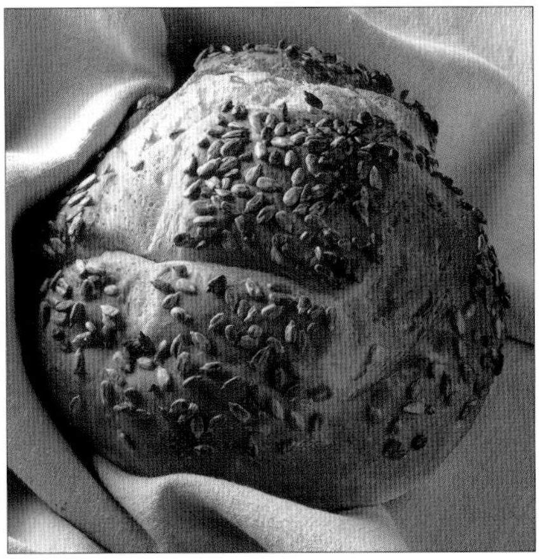

This edition is published by Lorenz Books,
an imprint of Anness Publishing Ltd,
108 Great Russell Street,
London WC1B 3NA;
info@anness.com

www.lorenzbooks.com; www.annesspublishing.com;
twitter: @Anness_Books

A CIP catalogue record for this book is available from the British Library.

Publisher: Joanna Lorenz
Senior Editor: Felicity Forster
Production Controller: Rosanna Anness

COOK'S NOTES

Bracketed terms are intended for American readers.
For all recipes, quantities are given in both metric and imperial measures and, where appropriate, in standard cups and spoons. Follow one set of measures, but not a mixture, because they are not interchangeable.
Standard spoon and cup measures are level. 1 tsp = 5ml, 1 tbsp = 15ml, 1 cup = 250ml/8fl oz.
Australian standard tablespoons are 20ml. Australian readers should use 3 tsp in place of 1 tbsp for measuring small quantities.
American pints are 16fl oz/2 cups. American readers should use 20fl oz/2.5 cups in place of 1 pint when measuring liquids.
Electric oven temperatures in this book are for conventional ovens. When using a fan oven, the temperature will probably need to be reduced by about 10–20°C/20–40°F. Since ovens vary, you should check with your manufacturer's instruction book for guidance.
The nutritional analysis given for each recipe is calculated per portion (i.e. serving or item), unless otherwise stated. If the recipe gives a range, such as Serves 4–6, then the nutritional analysis will be for the smaller portion size, i.e. 6 servings. The analysis does not include optional ingredients, such as salt added to taste.
Medium (US large) eggs are used unless otherwise stated.
Main front cover image shows *Three Cheeses Bread* – for recipe, see page 204.

Contents

Introduction

There is something undeniably special about bread. The flavour of a good loaf and the texture of the soft crumb contrasting with the crispness of the crust is almost a sensual experience. Who can walk home with a fresh baguette without slowly, almost absent-mindedly breaking off pieces to eat en route? Or resist the promise of a slice of a soft white farmhouse loaf, spread simply with butter? Most people have their own favourite: ciabatta, rich with olive oil; dark, malty rye; honeyed challah or a Middle Eastern bread, freshly baked and redolent of herbs and spices.

Whatever the shape or texture, bread has a special place in our affections, and this book shows how to make your own at home. After an introduction section on ingredients and techniques, the book is divided into two main sections: Hand-made Breads, and Bread Machine Breads.

BREAD INGREDIENTS

The simplest breads are a mixture of flour and water and some type of leavening agent. Beyond that narrow definition, however, lies an infinite number of possibilities. The flour is most likely to come from wheat, but may be derived from another type of grain or even, in the case of buckwheat, from another source entirely. The liquid may be water, but could just as easily be milk, or a mixture. Yeast is the obvious raising agent, but there are other options. Salt is normally essential, fats are often added, and other ingredients range from sweeteners like sugar or molasses to dried fruit, spices and savoury flavourings.

Plain White Flour

This flour, also called all-purpose flour, contains about 75 per cent of the wheat grain, with most of the bran (the outer layer) and the wheat germ (the grain's embryo) extracted. Self-raising (self-rising) flour is plain flour with a raising agent.

Strong White/White Bread Flour

For almost all bread making, the most suitable flour is one made from high-protein wheat. It is usually described as 'strong' flour and is often labelled 'bread flour'. The proteins in the flour, when mixed with water, combine to make gluten, and it is this that gives dough its elasticity when kneaded, and allows it to trap the bubbles of carbon dioxide given off by the yeast.

Wholemeal (Whole-wheat) Flour

This flour is made from the whole of the wheat germ and is sometimes called 100 per cent extraction flour, meaning nothing is added and nothing is taken away. If milled between rollers, the bran and wheat germ are separated from the white inner portion and then added back at the end. If stoneground in the traditional process between two millstones, there is no separation of the wheat grain, helping the resulting flour to retain more flavour.

Brown Flour

This low-gluten flour contains about 85 per cent of the original grain, with some of the bran and wheat germ removed. It produces a lighter loaf than 100 per cent wholemeal flour, while still containing a high percentage of wheat germ, which gives bread much of its flavour.

Left: Flour is the largest single ingredient used in bread.

Cornmeal

This meal is made from white or yellow corn and is normally available in coarse (also known as polenta), medium or fine grinds. There are numerous corn breads that originated in the Americas. Cornmeal contains no gluten so needs to be blended with wheat flour to make bread, adding a pleasant flavour and colour.

Rye Flour

This flour comes from the only other grain besides wheat to be widely used in bread making. It has a good gluten content, although different to the gluten in wheat, creating dough that can be sticky and difficult to handle. It is usually blended with other flours to make the dough more manageable. Rye grows better in colder, wetter climates, explaining the traditional use of rye flours in breads from Scandinavia, Russia and Germany.

Yeast

This is the most popular leavening agent for bread making. It is simple to use, more reliable than a natural leaven and considerably quicker to activate. Active dried yeast, which resembles small pellets, and easy-blend (rapid-rise) dried or fast-action yeast, which is more powdery and generally sold in small packets, are both produced for the convenience of making bread at home. Almost all bakers prefer fresh yeast, since it is considered to have a superior flavour and to be more reliable.

There are several ways of adding yeast to flour. Fresh yeast is usually blended with lukewarm water before being mixed into the flour; active dried yeast is first reconstituted in warm water and left until frothy; and easy-blend dried yeast is added directly to the flour – which makes it ideal for using in bread machines.

Baking Powder

This is made up of a mixture of acid and alkaline chemicals. When these come into contact with moisture, as in a dough, the reaction of the chemicals produces tiny bubbles of air so the dough rises and becomes spongy, as it does with yeast. It is important to work fast, as the carbon dioxide will quickly escape and the loaf will collapse.

Above: Sourdough is made using a natural leaven in a long period of fermentation.

Above: Sweet loaves, rolls and buns are often made using milk, butter and eggs.

Above: Dried fruits are used in teabreads such as Bara Brith and Panettone.

Bicarbonate of Soda
Also called baking soda, this is another leavening agent used, for example, in traditional Irish soda bread. It is an alkaline chemical compound (sodium bicarbonate) which, when mixed with an acid in a moist environment, reacts to produce carbon dioxide. Cream of tartar, an acid that is made from fermented grapes, is commonly used in conjunction with bicarbonate of soda for soda breads, or else the soda is combined with another acidic substance, such as soured milk or buttermilk.

Natural Leavens
Sourdoughs are breads based on a natural leaven. An authentic sourdough relies entirely on the wild yeasts that exist in the air. Given the right conditions, any dough of flour and water or batter of vegetable origin will ferment spontaneously and will continue if starch or sugar is fed to it.

There are all sorts of sourdough breads available. All of them begin with a 'starter', which can take anything up to a week to ferment and become established. This 'starter', or leaven, is used daily by bakers, or less frequently by home bakers, for the day's bread. A small amount of the dough is kept back and used for the next batch. Each time part of the starter is used, the remaining starter is refreshed with equal amounts of flour and water. In this way, some starters have been known to survive for many years.

Water or Milk
As a general rule, savoury loaves are made using water; teabreads and sweeter breads with milk. Breads made with milk are softer in both the crumb and the crust than those using water.

Salt
Almost all bread recipes add salt at the beginning. It is one of the few essential ingredients in bread making, important for both flavour and the effect on the yeast and dough. Essentially, it slows down the yeast's action – which is why it should not be added directly to the yeast. Take care when measuring salt – too little and the loaf will stale more quickly; too much and the crust will harden.

Sugar
Once added to all breads, sugar is no longer necessary for savoury breads as modern yeasts can be activated without it. Some bakers still prefer to add a little, contending that it gives better results. White and brown sugar, honey, treacle (molasses) and golden (light corn) syrup can be used to sweeten teabreads and fruit loaves.

Butter and Eggs
Enriched breads that use butter and eggs have a cake-like texture and soft crust. Butter is either melted or diced and the eggs beaten before being worked into other ingredients to make a sticky batter.

Fruit
Almost any dried fruit can be added to bread. Raisins, sultanas (golden raisins), currants and mixed (candied) peel are popular choices for fruit loaves. Others include chopped dates, apricots and prunes, or more exotic fruits such as dried mango or papaya.

Fats
Butter, oil, lard, or white cooking fat, and vegetable fats are sometimes added to savoury loaves. They add flavour and help to preserve the freshness of the loaf. The Italians particularly love adding olive oil to their breads.

Flavourings
Some of the most popular breads are flavoured with herbs, nuts, seeds, vegetables and other ingredients. The Italians add olives or sun-dried tomatoes to their ciabatta, while walnut bread is to be found in many countries around the world. These savoury additions should be roughly chopped before being kneaded into the dough after the first rising.

There are also various spices that impart a delicious flavour to many breads. Cinnamon, nutmeg, cloves and ginger are good for sweet loaves, while for savoury breads try cumin, fennel, caraway and anise. Mace, pepper and coriander seeds can be used for both sweet and savoury breads. Spices can be added with the flour, or kneaded in with fruit and nuts.

Making Bread by Hand

Making bread requires little more than a pair of hands, some time, an oven and a few basic ingredients – just flour and water in its simplest form. Add yeast and a sprinkling of salt to control the yeast, mix with the flour and water to a dough, shape and leave it to rise, and on baking it will transform into a deliciously aromatic and crusty loaf.

Many people enjoy the artistry of a hand-shaped loaf, as well as the satisfaction that comes from kneading the dough. The ritual of kneading, proving and shaping bread dough is a very personal activity, which is why many people still get great pleasure from kneading by hand.

Using Fresh Yeast

Pale beige and with a sweet and fruity smell, fresh yeast should crumble easily. It can be stored in the refrigerator, wrapped in clear film (plastic wrap), for up to 2 weeks or can be frozen for up to 3 months. A quantity of 15g/½oz fresh yeast should be sufficient for 675–900g/1½–2lb/6–8 cups flour, although this will depend on the recipe.

1 Put the yeast in a small bowl. Using a spoon, mash or 'cream' it with a little of the measured water until smooth.

2 Pour in the remaining measured liquid, which may be water, milk or a mixture of the two. Mix well. Use as directed in the recipe.

Using Active Dried Yeast

The dehydrated form of yeast needs to be blended with lukewarm liquid before use. Once mixed in a bowl, cover with clear film (plastic wrap) and leave in a warm place for about 15 minutes until frothy. Stir will and use as directed.

Using Easy-Blend/Rapid-Rise Dried Yeast

Convenient because they can be added directly into the flour, most of these yeasts come in 7g/¼oz packets. Do not store opened packets, as the yeast deteriorates.

Mixing Dough

The easiest way to mix dough is by hand, or you can start with a spoon.

1 If using fresh or regular dried yeast, mix it with lukewarm water or milk as described in the recipe. Sift the flour, salt and any other dry ingredients, including easy-blend (rapid-rise) dried yeast, into a large, warm mixing bowl.

2 If using butter or lard, rub it in. Make a well in the centre of the flour mixture and pour in the yeast mixture with the remaining lukewarm water. If oil is being used, add it now.

3 Mix the liquid with your hand, stirring the mixture so that all the dry ingredients are evenly incorporated and a dough forms. Knead lightly in the bowl.

Kneading

This is something you just cannot skip in bread making. If you do not have strong wrists, or simply do not enjoy it, you will have to resort to using the food processor, which takes all the effort – and much of the time – out of kneading. Better still, though, learn to love it.

1 Place the mixed dough on a floured surface and flour your hands generously.

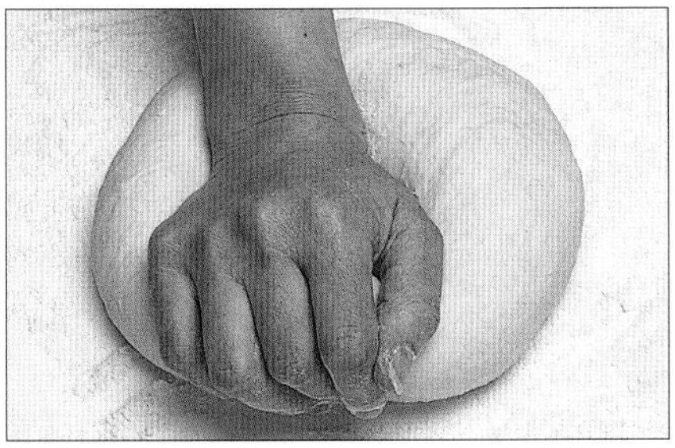

2 Press the heel of your hand firmly into the centre of the dough, then curl your fingers around the edge of the dough.

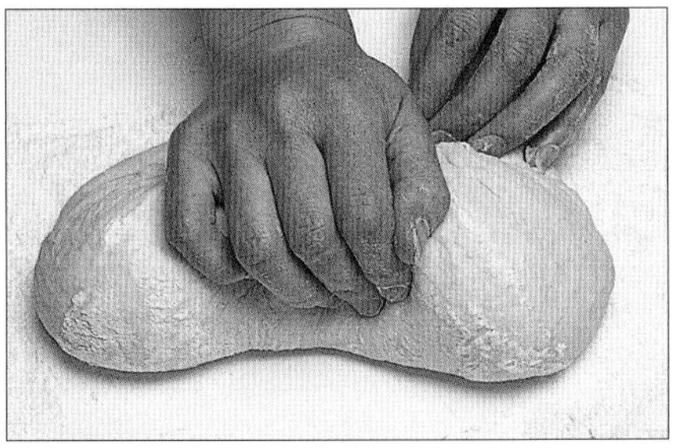

3 Pull and stretch the dough towards you and press down again, giving the dough a quarter turn as you do so.

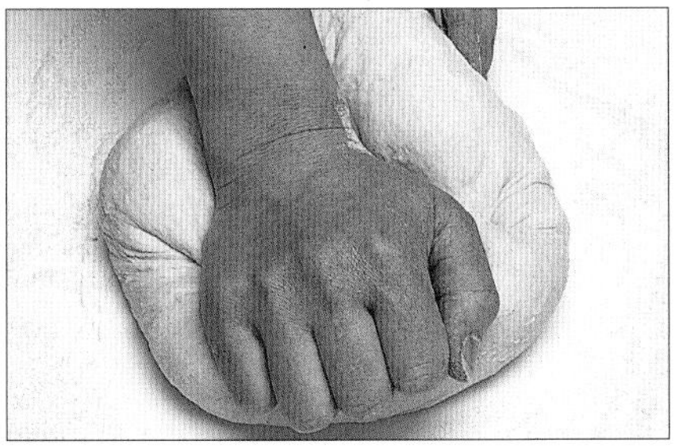

4 Continue pressing and stretching the dough, making quarter turns so that it is evenly kneaded. After about 10 minutes the dough should be supple and elastic; however, some breads need more kneading, so do check the recipe.

Rising

This is the easy part of bread making – all you need now is to give the dough the right conditions, and nature and chemistry will do the rest. While kneading works and conditions the gluten in the flour, during rising the yeast does the work. The fermentation process creates carbon dioxide, which is trapped within the dough by the elastic gluten. This process also has the effect of conditioning the flour, improving the flavour and texture of the eventual loaf.

The number of times you leave your bread to rise will depend on the yeast you are using and the recipe. An easy-blend yeast needs no first rising, but dough using fresh yeast and active dried yeast normally requires two risings, with some recipes calling for even more. Generally, dough should be left to rise in a warm place, such as near a warm oven.

1 Place the kneaded dough in a bowl that has been lightly greased. This will prevent the dough from sticking. Cover the bowl with a damp dish towel or a piece of oiled clear film (plastic wrap), to prevent a skin from forming on top.

2 Leave to rise until the dough has doubled in bulk. At room temperature, this should take 1½–2 hours – less if the temperature is warmer; more if the room is cool. It can even be left to rise in the refrigerator for about 8 hours.

Knocking Back

This process, also called punching down, not not only redistributes the gases in the dough, it also reinvigorates the yeast.

1 Knock back (punch down) the risen dough with your knuckles. Place it on a floured work surface and knead lightly for a couple of minutes. Shape the dough, depending on the bread being made.

Shaping

There are several ways to shape dough.

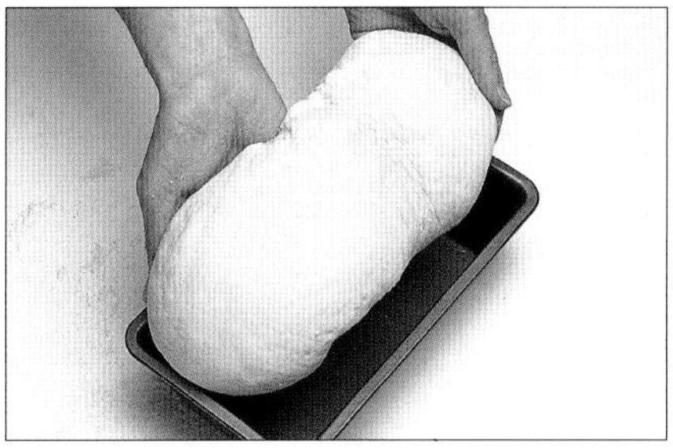

1 To make a loaf, shape the dough roughly into an oval and place it in the tin, with the smooth side on top.

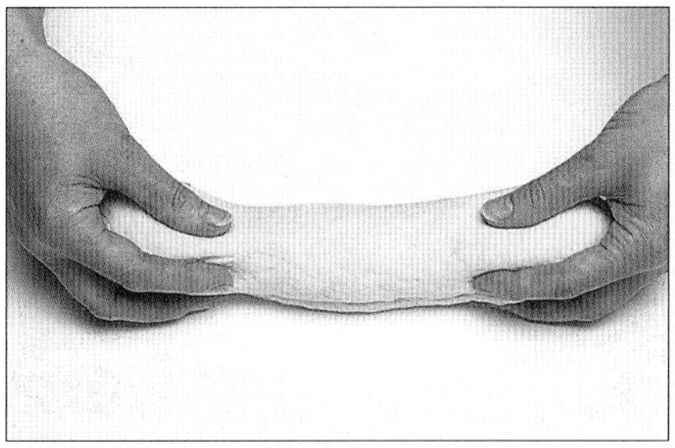

2 To make a baguette, divide the dough into equal pieces. Shape each piece into a ball and then into a rectangle measuring 15 × 7.5cm/6 × 3in. Fold the bottom third up and the top third down lengthways. Press the edges together to seal them. Repeat twice, then stretch each piece to a 33–35cm/13–14in loaf.

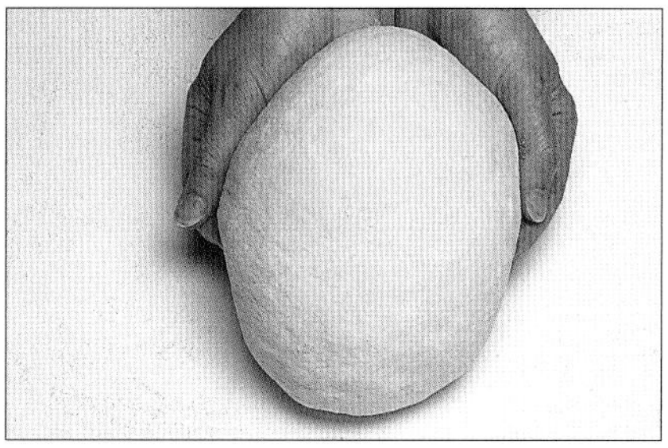

3 To make a cob loaf, shape the dough into a round, then press along the centre with your hand. Turn the dough over, so that the smooth side is uppermost. Shape the dough into a round or oval, and place it on a baking sheet.

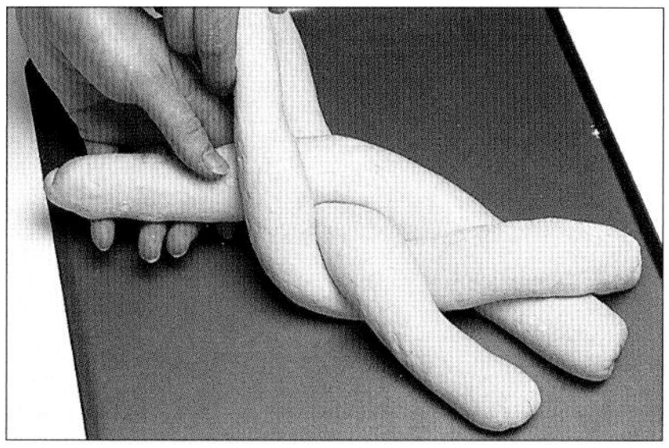

4 To make a plait (braid), divide the dough into three equal pieces. Roll each piece into a 25cm/10in sausage about 4cm/1½in thick. Place the three 'sausages' on a greased baking sheet. Either start the plait in the centre, plaiting to each end in turn, or pinch the pieces firmly together at one end then plait. When you have finished, pinch the ends together, and turn them under.

Cook's Tips

- *Always knock back the dough after the first rising and knead lightly to redistribute the yeast and the gases formed by fermentation, otherwise you may end up with large holes in the loaf or the crust may lift up and become detached from the crumb.*
- *Rising the dough in a warm place is not always necessary – it is simply a method of speeding up the process. Dough will rise (albeit slowly) even in the refrigerator. But wherever you decide to rise your dough, the temperature must be constant. Avoid draughts or hot spots, as both will spoil the bread and may cause it to bake unevenly.*

Using a Bread Machine

A bread machine is the perfect addition to home baking. It still allows you to create your own bread with the ingredients you wish to use, but with the minimum of effort and time. It will mix together the ingredients for a loaf of bread, then knead it, leave it to rise and finally bake it, all within a self-contained unit.

All machines have a choice of programmes, offering options to bake a wide variety of breads, from basic white breads, wholemeal (whole-wheat), through to various whole grain, sweet and crusty French-style breads. This is achieved by varying the kneading, rising and baking periods. The baking time is increased to give a crusty French loaf, while the baking temperature is reduced to minimize over-browning of the dough with higher sugar contents. The machine is programmed to operate these variations for you. All you have to do is select the programme.

One very useful benefit of a bread machine is the delay timer. This lets you pre-programme the machine 13–15 hours in advance, so the machine can be filled with ingredients before you go to bed and set to finish baking just before breakfast.

Preparing and Baking a Loaf
The following sequence shows how to make a basic loaf of walnut bread using a bread machine.

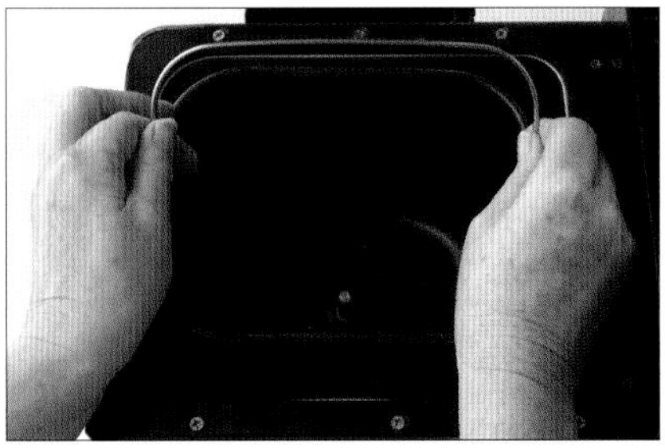

1 Stand the bread machine on a firm, level, heat-resistant surface. Place away from any heat source, such as a stove or direct sunlight, and also in a draught-free area, as these factors can affect the temperature inside the machine. Do not plug the bread machine into the power socket at this stage. Open the lid. Remove the bread pan by holding both sides of the handle and pulling upwards or twisting slightly, depending on the design of your particular model.

2 Make sure the kneading blade and shaft are free of any breadcrumbs. Fit the kneading blade on the shaft in the base of the bread pan. The blade will only fit in one position, as the hole in the blade and the outside of the shaft are D-shaped. Some machines are fixed-blade only.

3 Pour the water, milk and/or other liquids into the bread pan, unless the instructions for your particular machine require you to add the dry ingredients first. If so, reverse the order in which you add the liquid and dry ingredients, putting the yeast in the bread pan first.

4 Sprinkle over the flour, ensuring that it covers the liquid completely. Add any other dry ingredients specified in the recipe, such as dried milk powder. Add the salt, sugar or honey and butter or oil, placing them in separate corners so they do not come into contact with each other.

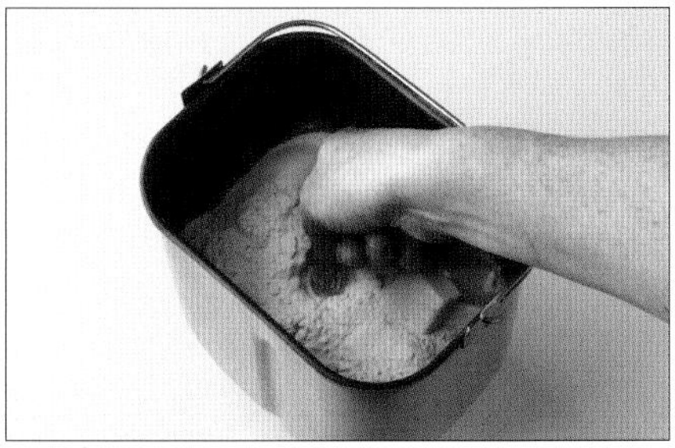

5 Make a small indent in the centre of the flour (but not down as far as the liquid) with the tip of your finger and add the yeast. If your indent reached the liquid below the dry ingredients, then the yeast would become wet and would be activated too quickly. Wipe away any spillages from the outside of the bread pan.

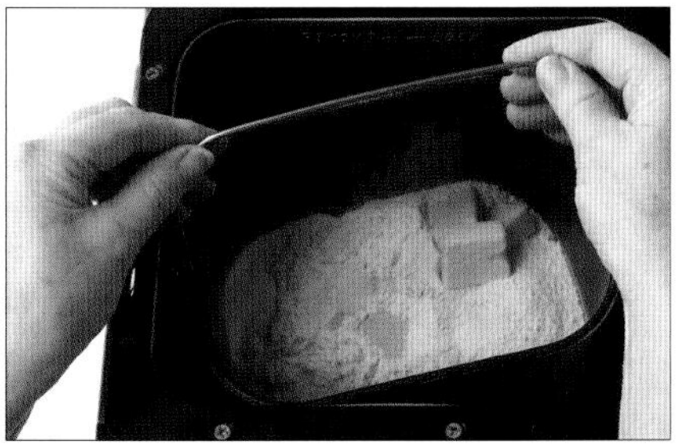

6 Place the pan inside the machine, fitting it firmly in place. Depending on the model of your machine, the pan may have a designated front and back, or clips on the outer edge which need to engage in the machine to hold the bread pan in position. Fold the handle down and close the lid. Plug into the socket and switch on the power.

7 Select the programme you require, followed by crust colour and size. Press Start.

8 Towards the end of the kneading process, the machine will beep to alert you to add any additional ingredients. Open the lid, add the ingredients, and close the lid. If you have an automatic dispenser, add ingredients to this before starting the machine; it will add them at the correct time. Ingredients that may melt or stick should be added manually as described above. Check your instructions.

9 At the end of the cycle, the machine will beep once more to let you know that either the dough is ready or the bread is cooked. Press Stop. Open the lid of the machine. Use oven gloves to lift out the bread pan, as it will be extremely hot. Avoid leaning over and looking into the bread machine when you open the lid, as the air escaping from the machine will be very hot and could cause you discomfort.

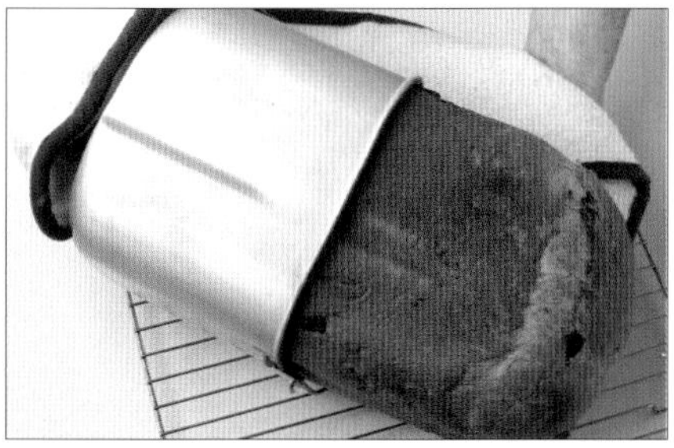

10 Still using oven gloves, turn the pan upside down and shake it several times to release the bread. If necessary, tap the base of the pan on a heatproof board.

11 If the kneading blade for your bread machine is not of the fixed type, and comes out inside the bread, use a heat-resistant utensil to remove it, such as a wooden spatula. It will come out easily.

12 Place the bread on a wire rack to cool. Unplug the bread machine and leave to cool before using it again. A machine which is too hot will not make a successful loaf, and many will not operate if they are too hot for this reason. Refer to the manufacturer's manual for guidance. Wash the pan and kneading blade and wipe down the machine. All parts of the machine must be cool and dry before you store it.

Cook's Tips

- *Some machines start all programmes with a warming phase, either prior to mixing or during the kneading phase. This feature can prove useful on colder days or when you are using larger quantities of ingredients, such as milk, straight from the refrigerator, as you do not have to wait for them to come to room temperature before making the bread.*
- *To serve bread warm, wrap it in foil and place in an oven preheated to 180°C/350°F/Gas 4 for 10–15 minutes. This is also a method that can be used to freshen bread.*

Basic Controls

Most bread machines come with informative and comprehensive manuals, which are the best starting point to familiarize yourself with your machine. Below are listed some of the common features and functions on bread machines.

Start and Stop Buttons

The Start button initiates the process. Press it once all the ingredients are in the pan and you have selected the appropriate settings. The Stop button may be the same button as the Start button, or a separate one. Press to cancel during the programme, or at the end to turn off the machine.

Time and Status Display

The time remaining, and often the programme selected, are electronically displayed on the machine. It can indicate what stage the process is at, such as kneading, resting, rising, baking or warming.

Programme Indicators or Menu

This function allows you to choose the appropriate programme for your recipe, indicating the chosen setting.

Delay Timer

This button allows you to pre-set the bread machine to switch on automatically at a specified time. It allows you, for example, to set the timer to start in the middle of the night so that you have fresh bread ready for breakfast.

Crust Colour Control

Most bread machines default to a medium crust setting. However, many machines will give you the option of a lighter or darker crust colour.

Warming Indicator

It is best to remove bread as soon as it is baked. If this is not possible, the warming facility will switch on to help prevent condensation of the steam which would otherwise result in a soggy loaf.

White Bread

This is the classic white loaf, the daily bread for many a home baker. It makes a good all-rounder for the family.

Makes 2

50ml/2fl oz/¼ cup lukewarm water
15ml/1 tbsp active dried yeast
30ml/2 tbsp caster (superfine) sugar
475ml/16fl oz/2 cups lukewarm milk
25g/1oz/2 tbsp butter or margarine, at room temperature
10ml/2 tsp salt
about 900g/2lb/8 cups strong white bread flour

1 Combine the water, yeast and 15ml/1 tbsp of the sugar in a measuring jug (cup) and leave for 15 minutes, or until frothy.

2 Pour the milk into a large bowl. Add the remaining sugar, the butter or margarine, and salt.

3 Stir in the yeast mixture, then stir in the flour, 150g/5oz/1¼ cups at a time, until a stiff dough is obtained.

4 Transfer the dough to a floured surface. Knead the dough until it is smooth and elastic, then place it in a large greased bowl, cover with clear film (plastic wrap), and leave to rise in a warm place until doubled in volume, about 2–3 hours.

5 Grease two 23 × 13cm/9 × 5in loaf tins (pans). Knock back (punch down) the dough and divide in half.

6 Form into loaf shapes and place in the tins, seam down. Cover and leave to rise again until almost doubled in volume, about 45 minutes. Meanwhile, preheat the oven to 190°C/375°F/Gas 5.

7 Bake the loaves until firm and brown, about 45–50 minutes. Turn out and tap the base of a loaf: if it sounds hollow the loaf is done. If necessary, return to the oven and bake for a few minutes longer. (Turn the loaf upside down in the tin if the top is done but the base is not.) Turn out the cooked loaf and cool on a wire rack.

Split Tin Loaf

The deep centre split down this loaf gives it its name and characteristic appearance. The split tin loaf slices well for making thick-cut sandwiches, or for serving hearty chunks of bread to accompany robust cheese and relish.

Makes 1

500g/1¼lb/5 cups unbleached strong white bread flour, plus extra for dusting
10ml/2 tsp salt
15g/½oz fresh yeast
300ml/½ pint/1¼ cups lukewarm water
60ml/4 tbsp lukewarm milk

1 Grease a 900g/2lb loaf tin (pan). Sift the flour and salt into a bowl and make a well in the centre. Mix the yeast with half the lukewarm water in a bowl. Stir in the remaining lukewarm water. Pour the yeast mixture into the centre of the flour and using your fingers, mix in a little flour to form a smooth batter.

2 Sprinkle a little more flour from around the edge over the batter and leave in a warm place for about 20 minutes to 'sponge'. Add the milk and remaining flour; mix to a firm dough.

3 Lay the dough on a lightly floured surface and knead for about 10 minutes, until smooth and elastic. Place it in a lightly oiled bowl, cover with lightly oiled clear film (plastic wrap) and leave to rise in a warm place for 1–1¼ hours, or until nearly doubled in bulk.

4 Knock back (punch down) the dough and turn out on to a lightly floured surface. Shape it into a rectangle, the length of the prepared tin. Roll the dough up lengthways, tuck the ends under and place, seam side down, in the tin. Cover the loaf and leave to rise in a warm place for about 20–30 minutes.

5 Using a sharp knife, make one deep central slash. Dust the top of the loaf with a little sifted flour. Leave for 10–15 minutes. Meanwhile, preheat the oven to 230°C/450°F/Gas 8. Bake for 15 minutes, then reduce the oven temperature to 200°C/400°F/Gas 6. Bake for 20–25 minutes, until golden and it sounds hollow when tapped on the base. Cool on a wire rack.

White Bread per loaf Energy 1796kcal/7623kJ; Protein 50.6g; Carbohydrate 376.6g, of which sugars 33.7g; Fat 20.2g, of which saturates 10g; Cholesterol 41mg; Calcium 925mg; Fibre 14g; Sodium 193mg.

Split Tin Loaf per loaf Energy 1733kcal/7367kJ; Protein 49g; Carbohydrate 391.3g, of which sugars 10.3g; Fat 7.5g, of which saturates 1.6g; Cholesterol 4mg; Calcium 773mg; Fibre 15.5g; Sodium 3971mg.

Cottage Loaf

Always a good-looking loaf, this round bread makes a great centrepiece.

Makes 1

675g/1½lb/6 cups unbleached strong white bread flour
10ml/2 tsp salt
20g/¾oz fresh yeast
400ml/14fl oz/1⅔ cups lukewarm water

1 Lightly grease two baking sheets. Sift the flour and salt into a large bowl and make a well in the centre. Dissolve the yeast in 150ml/¼ pint/⅔ cup of the water. Add to the flour, with the remaining water, and mix to a firm dough.

2 Knead the dough on a lightly floured surface for 10 minutes. Place in a lightly oiled bowl, cover with lightly oiled clear film (plastic wrap) and leave in a warm place to rise for about 1 hour, or until doubled in bulk.

3 Knock back (punch down) the dough on a lightly floured surface. Knead for 2–3 minutes, then divide the dough into two-thirds and one-third and shape each to a ball.

4 Place the balls of dough on the prepared baking sheets. Cover with inverted bowls and leave in a warm place to rise, for about 30 minutes.

5 Gently flatten the top of the larger ball of dough and cut a cross in the centre, 5cm/2in across. Brush with a little water and place the smaller ball on top. Make small cuts around each ball.

6 Carefully press a hole through both balls, using the thumb and first two fingers of one hand. Cover with lightly oiled clear film and leave to rest in a warm place for about 10 minutes.

7 Heat the oven to 220°C/425°F/Gas 7 and place the baking sheet on the lower shelf. The loaf will finish expanding as the oven heats up. Bake for 35–40 minutes, or until golden brown and sounding hollow when tapped. Cool on a wire rack.

Italian Country Bread

This classic Italian open-textured bread is moistened and flavoured with fruity olive oil. Its floured top gives it a true country feel.

Makes 1

For the starter
175g/6oz/1½ cups unbleached white bread flour
7g/¼oz fresh yeast
90ml/6 tbsp lukewarm water

For the dough
225g/8oz/2 cups unbleached strong white bread flour, plus extra for dusting
225g/8oz/2 cups wholemeal (whole-wheat) bread flour
5ml/1 tsp caster (superfine) sugar
10ml/2 tsp salt
15g/½oz fresh yeast
275ml/9fl oz/generous 1 cup lukewarm water
75ml/5 tbsp extra virgin olive oil

1 Sift the flour for the starter into a large bowl. Make a well in the centre. Cream the yeast with the water and pour into the well. Gradually mix in the flour to form a firm dough. Turn out on to a lightly floured surface and knead for 5 minutes until smooth and elastic. Return to the bowl, cover with lightly oiled clear film (plastic wrap) and leave in a warm place for 8–10 hours, or until well risen and starting to collapse.

2 Lightly flour a baking sheet. Mix the flours, sugar and salt for the dough in a large bowl. Cream the yeast and the water in another large bowl, then stir in the starter. Stir in the flour mixture a little at a time, then add the olive oil in the same way, and mix to a soft dough. Turn out on to a lightly floured surface and knead for 8–10 minutes until smooth and elastic. Place in a lightly oiled bowl, cover with lightly oiled clear film and leave in a warm place for 1–1½ hours, or until doubled in size.

3 Turn out on to a floured surface and knock back (punch down). Gently pull out the edges and fold under to make a round. Transfer to the baking sheet, cover again and leave in a warm place for 1–1½ hours, or until almost doubled in size.

4 Preheat the oven to 230°C/450°F/Gas 8. Lightly dust the loaf with flour and bake for 15 minutes. Reduce the temperature to 200°C/400°F/Gas 6 and bake for a further 20 minutes.

Cottage Loaf per loaf Energy 2302kcal/9794kJ; Protein 77.6g; Carbohydrate 508.3g, of which sugars 9.4g; Fat 9.4g, of which saturates 1.4g; Cholesterol 0mg; Calcium 946mg; Fibre 20.9g; Sodium 3950mg.

Italian Country Bread per loaf Energy 2502kcal/10567kJ; Protein 71.9g; Carbohydrate 430.4g, of which sugars 11.8g; Fat 66.7g, of which saturates 9.5g; Cholesterol 0mg; Calcium 468mg; Fibre 43g; Sodium 3949mg.

Bakestone Bread

A loaf of bread that is cooked on the hob is useful for when an oven isn't available. It's also a fun method because you can watch it rise. The finished article has a distinctive appearance with a soft texture and scorched crust. Make sure to use ordinary plain flour and not strong bread flour.

Makes 1

500g/1lb 2oz/4¼ cups plain (all-purpose) flour
5ml/1 tsp fine sea salt
5ml/1 tsp sugar
7.5ml/1½ tsp easy-blend (rapid-rise) yeast
150ml/¼ pint milk
15g/½ oz/1 tbsp butter, cut into small pieces
5ml/1 tsp oil

1 Put the flour into a large bowl and add the salt, sugar and yeast. Combine the milk with 150ml/¼ pint/⅔ cup water and add the butter. Heat gently until the liquid is lukewarm. Stir the liquid into the flour, then gather together to make a dough ball.

2 Transfer the dough on to a lightly floured surface and knead it until smooth, firm and elastic. Then put the oil in a large bowl and turn the dough in it until it is lightly coated. Cover the dough with clear film (plastic wrap) or a damp dish towel and leave to rise for about 1½ hours, or until just about doubled in size.

3 Turn out the dough on to a lightly floured surface and knead (gently this time) just until the dough becomes soft and stretchy. Using your hands, press the dough into a rough circle measuring about 20cm/8in in diameter and 2cm/¾ in thick. Leave to stand for 15 minutes to allow the dough to relax.

4 Meanwhile, heat a bakestone or heavy frying pan over medium heat. Using a wide spatula and your hands, lift the dough on to the warm surface and cook gently for 20 minutes.

5 Turn the bread over – it may sink, but will soon start rising again. Gently cook the second side for about 20 minutes. The top and bottom should be firm and browned while the sides remain pale. Leave to cool on a wire rack.

Tuscany Bread

This Tuscan bread is made without salt and probably originates from the days when salt was heavily taxed in Italy. To compensate for the lack of salt, serve it with salty foods, such as olives, feta cheese, anchovies or salami.

Makes 1

500g/1¼ lb/4½ cups unbleached strong white bread flour, plus extra for dusting
350ml/12fl oz/1½ cups boiling water
15g/½ oz fresh yeast

1 Sift 175g/6oz/1½ cups of the flour into a large bowl. Pour over the boiling water, leave for a couple of minutes, then mix well. Cover the bowl with a damp dish towel. Leave to stand for 10 hours or overnight.

2 Lightly flour a baking sheet and set aside. In a bowl, cream the yeast with 60ml/4 tbsp lukewarm water. Mix well into the flour mixture. Gradually add the remaining flour and mix to form a dough. Turn out on to a lightly floured surface and knead for 5–8 minutes, until smooth and elastic.

3 Place in a lightly oiled bowl, cover with lightly oiled clear film (plastic wrap) and leave to rise in a warm place for 1–1½ hours, or until doubled in bulk.

4 Turn the dough out on to a lightly floured surface, knock back (punch down) and shape into a round. Fold the sides of the round into the centre and seal. Place seam side up on the prepared baking sheet. Cover with oiled clear film and leave to rise in a warm place for 30–45 minutes, or until doubled in bulk.

5 Flatten the loaf to about half its risen height and flip over. Cover with a large upturned bowl and leave to rise again in a warm place for 30 minutes.

6 Meanwhile, preheat the oven to 220°C/425°F/Gas 7. Slash the top of the loaf, using a sharp knife, if you wish. Bake for 30–35 minutes, or until golden. Transfer to a wire rack to cool.

Bakestone Bread per loaf Energy 1928kcal/8179kJ; Protein 52.2g; Carbohydrate 399.8g, of which sugars 18.8g; Fat 24.4g, of which saturates 10.8g; Cholesterol 41mg; Calcium 885mg; Fibre 15.5g; Sodium 2136mg.

Tuscany Bread per loaf Energy 1713kcal/7286kJ; Protein 48.8g; Carbohydrate 388.7g, of which sugars 7.5g; Fat 6.6g, of which saturates 1g; Cholesterol 0mg; Calcium 704mg; Fibre 15.5g; Sodium 17mg.

Sicilian Scroll

A wonderful pale yellow, crusty loaf, enhanced with a nutty flavour from the sesame seeds. It's perfect for serving with cheese.

Makes 1

450g/1lb/4 cups finely ground semolina
115g/4oz/1 cup unbleached strong white bread flour
10ml/2 tsp salt
20g/¾oz fresh yeast
360ml/12½fl oz/generous 1½ cups lukewarm water
30ml/2 tbsp extra virgin olive oil
sesame seeds, for sprinkling

1 Lightly grease a baking sheet. Mix the semolina, white bread flour and salt in a large bowl and make a well in the centre.

2 Cream the yeast with half the water, then stir in the remainder. Add the creamed yeast to the centre of the semolina mixture with the olive oil and gradually incorporate the semolina and flour to form a firm dough.

3 Turn out the dough on to a lightly floured surface and knead for 8–10 minutes until smooth and elastic. Place in a lightly oiled bowl, cover with lightly oiled clear film and leave to rise, in a warm place, for 1–1½ hours, or until doubled in size.

4 Turn out on to a lightly floured surface and knock back (punch down). Knead gently, then shape into a fat roll about 50cm/20in long. Form into an 'S' shape.

5 Carefully transfer the dough to the prepared baking sheet, cover with lightly oiled clear film and leave to rise, in a warm place, for 30–45 minutes, or until doubled in size.

6 Meanwhile, preheat the oven to 220°C/425°F/Gas 7. Brush the top of the scroll with water and sprinkle with sesame seeds. Bake for 10 minutes. Spray the inside of the oven with water twice during this time.

7 Reduce the temperature to 200°C/400°F/Gas 6 and bake for a further 25–30 minutes, or until golden. Cool on a wire rack.

Pain Polka

This attractive, deeply cut crusty bread is as tasty as it looks.

Makes 1

For the starter
7g/¼oz fresh yeast
120ml/4fl oz/½ cup lukewarm water
115g/4oz/1 cup unbleached plain (all-purpose) flour

For the dough
7g/¼oz fresh yeast
280ml/scant ½ pint/scant 1¼ cups lukewarm water
450g/1lb/4 cups unbleached strong white bread flour, plus extra for dusting
15ml/1 tbsp salt

1 Lightly flour a baking sheet. Make the starter. Mix the yeast with the water, then gradually stir in sufficient flour to form a batter. Beat vigorously, then gradually add the remaining flour and mix to a soft dough. Knead for 5 minutes. Place in a bowl; cover with oiled clear film (plastic wrap). Leave for 4–5 hours.

2 In a bowl, mix the yeast for the dough with half of the water, then stir in the remainder. Add the starter and knead. Gradually add the flour and salt and mix to a dough. Turn out on to a floured surface and knead for 10 minutes until smooth.

3 Place the dough in a lightly oiled bowl, cover with lightly oiled clear film and leave to rise, in a warm place, for about 1½ hours, or until doubled in size.

4 Turn out on to a floured surface, knock back (punch down) and shape into a ball. Flatten slightly and place on the baking sheet. Cover with oiled clear film and leave to rise for 1 hour.

5 Dust the top of the loaf with flour and, using a sharp knife, cut the top fairly deeply in a criss-cross pattern. Leave to rest for 10 minutes. Preheat the oven to 230°C/450°F/Gas 8.

6 Bake for 25–30 minutes, until browned. Spray the inside of the oven with water when the bread goes in, and three times during the first 10 minutes of baking. Cool on a wire rack.

Sicilian Scroll per loaf Energy 2344kcal/9922kJ; Protein 64.4g; Carbohydrate 438.4g, of which sugars 1.8g; Fat 49g, of which saturates 5.9g; Cholesterol 0mg; Calcium 443mg; Fibre 15.4g; Sodium 63mg.

Pain Polka per loaf Energy 2387kcal/10150kJ; Protein 65.8g; Carbohydrate 543.9g, of which sugars 10.5g; Fat 9.1g, of which saturates 1.4g; Cholesterol 0mg; Calcium 982mg; Fibre 21.7g; Sodium 5916mg.

Oatmeal Bread

A healthy, rustic-looking bread made with rolled oats as well as flour.

Makes 2

475ml/16fl oz/2 cups milk
25g/1oz/2 tbsp butter
50g/2oz/¼ cup cup soft dark brown sugar
10ml/2 tsp salt
15ml/1 tbsp active dried yeast
50ml/2fl oz/¼ cup lukewarm water
400g/14oz/4 cups rolled oats
675–900g/1½–2lb/6–8 cups strong white bread flour

1 Put the milk in a small pan and bring to boiling point. Quickly remove from the heat and stir in the butter, brown sugar and salt. Leave the mixture to cool until lukewarm.

2 Combine the yeast and warm water in a large bowl and leave for about 15 minutes until frothy.

3 Stir the milk mixture into the bowl with the yeast. Add 275g/10oz/3 cups of the rolled oats and add enough flour to obtain a soft dough.

4 Transfer the dough to a floured surface and knead until smooth and elastic. Place in a greased bowl, cover with clear film (plastic wrap) and leave until doubled in volume, about 2–3 hours.

5 Grease a large baking sheet. Transfer the dough to a lightly floured surface and divide in half, then shape into rounds. Place the rounds on the baking sheet, cover with a clean dish towel or oiled clear film and leave to rise until doubled in volume, which will take about 1 hour.

6 Preheat the oven to 200°C/400°F/Gas 6. Score the tops of the loaves and sprinkle with the remaining oats.

7 Bake the loaves in the oven for about 45–50 minutes, until the base of each one sounds hollow when tapped. Turn out on to wire racks to cool.

Country Bread

A filling bread made with a mixture of wholemeal and white flour.

Makes 2

350g/12oz/3 cups strong wholemeal (whole-wheat) bread flour
350g/12oz/3 cups plain (all-purpose) flour
150g/5oz/1¼ cups strong white bread flour
20ml/4 tsp salt
50g/2oz/¼ cup butter, at room temperature
475ml/16fl oz/2 cups lukewarm milk

For the starter
15ml/1 tbsp active dried yeast
250ml/8fl oz/1 cup lukewarm water
150g/5oz/1¼ cups plain (all-purpose) flour
1.5ml/¼ tsp caster (superfine) sugar

1 To make the starter, mix the yeast, water, plain flour and sugar in a bowl. Cover and leave in a warm place for 2–3 hours.

2 Place the flours, salt and butter in bowl or food processor and mix or process until just blended, about 1–2 minutes.

3 Combine the milk and starter, then pour into the bowl, or processor with the motor running. Mix until a dough is formed. Turn the dough out onto a floured surface and knead until smooth.

4 Place in an ungreased bowl, cover with clear film (plastic wrap), and leave to rise in a warm place until doubled in size, about 1½ hours. Knock back (punch down) and then return to the bowl and leave until tripled in size, about 1½ hours.

5 Grease a baking sheet. Divide the dough in half. Cut off one-third of the dough from each half and shape all the pieces into balls. Top each large ball with a small ball and press the centre with the handle of a wooden spoon to secure. Cover with oiled clear film, slash the top, and leave the dough to rise once again.

6 Preheat the oven to 200°C/400°F/Gas 6. Dust the loaves with flour and bake until browned and the bases sound hollow when tapped, 45–50 minutes. Cool on a wire rack.

Oatmeal Bread per loaf Energy 2254kcal/9556kJ; Protein 64.8g; Carbohydrate 445.2g, of which sugars 42.4g; Fat 36.1g, of which saturates 9.8g; Cholesterol 41mg; Calcium 883mg; Fibre 24.1g; Sodium 256mg.

Country Bread per loaf Energy 1760kcal/7482kJ; Protein 60.9g; Carbohydrate 375.5g, of which sugars 19.7g; Fat 12.1g, of which saturates 3.7g; Cholesterol 14mg; Calcium 807mg; Fibre 25.8g; Sodium 2082mg.

Pain de Campagne Rustique

This country bread is made using a French chef starter to produce a rustic flavour.

Makes 1

For the chef
50g/2oz/½ cup wholemeal (whole-wheat) bread flour
45ml/3 tbsp warm water

For the 1st refreshment
60ml/4 tbsp warm water
75g/3oz/¾ cup wholemeal (whole-wheat) bread flour

For the 2nd refreshment
120ml/4fl oz/½ cup lukewarm water
115g/4oz/1 cup unbleached strong white bread flour
25g/1oz/¼ cup wholemeal (whole-wheat) bread flour

For the dough
150–175ml/5–6fl oz/⅔–¾ cup lukewarm water
350g/12oz/3 cups unbleached strong white bread flour
10ml/2 tsp salt

1 To make the chef, place the flour in a bowl, add the water and knead for 3–4 minutes to form a dough. Cover and leave for 2 days. Pull off the hardened crust and discard, then remove 30ml/2 tbsp of the moist centre. Place in a bowl and mix in the water for the 1st refreshment. Mix in the flour and knead for 3–4 minutes to form a dough then cover and leave for 1 day.

2 Discard the crust from the dough and mix in the water for the 2nd refreshment. Mix in the flours a little at a time, mixing well after each addition to form a firm dough. Cover and leave to rise for about 10 hours. For the final dough stage, mix the water into the dough, then mix in the flour, then the salt. Turn out on to a floured surface and knead for 5 minutes. Place the dough in an oiled bowl, cover and leave to rise for 1½–2 hours.

3 Knock back (punch down) the dough and shape into a ball. Line a large bowl with a dish towel and dust with flour. Place the dough ball in the bowl. Cover and leave to rise for 2–3 hours.

4 Invert the loaf on to a floured baking sheet and sprinkle with flour. Slash the top of the loaf to form a square pattern. Bake for 30–35 minutes at 230°C/450°F/Gas 8, until browned and sounds hollow when tapped on the base. Cool on a wire rack.

Grant Loaves

This quick and easy recipe was created by a baker called Doris Grant, and was published in the 1940s. It is a dream for busy cooks as the dough requires no kneading and takes only a minute to mix. Nowadays we can make the recipe even quicker by using easy-blend yeast, which is added directly to the dry ingredients.

Makes 3
1.3kg/3lb/12 cups wholemeal (whole-wheat) bread flour
15ml/1 tbsp salt
15ml/1 tbsp easy-blend (rapid-rise) dried yeast
15ml/1 tbsp muscovado (molasses) sugar
30ml/2 tbsp vegetable oil

1 Thoroughly grease three loaf tins (pans), each 21 × 11 × 6cm/8½ × 4½ × 2½in and set aside in a warm place.

2 Sift the flour and salt together in a large bowl and warm slightly to take off the chill.

3 Sprinkle the dried yeast over 150ml/¼ pint/⅔ cup lukewarm water. After a couple of minutes, stir in the muscovado sugar. Leave the mixture for 10 minutes.

4 Make a well in the centre of the flour. Pour in the yeast mixture and add a further 900ml/1½ pints/3¾ cups lukewarm water. Stir to form a slippery dough. Mix for about 1 minute, working the dry ingredients from the sides into the middle.

5 Divide among the prepared tins, cover with oiled clear film (plastic wrap) and leave to rise in a warm place for 30 minutes, or until the dough has risen by about one-third to within 1cm/½in of the top of the tins.

6 Meanwhile, preheat the oven to 200°C/400°F/Gas 6. Bake for 40 minutes, or until the loaves are crisp and sound hollow when tapped on the base. Turn out the cooked loaf on to a wire rack to cool.

Pain de Campagne Rustique per loaf Energy 2051kcal/8720kJ; Protein 62.8g; Carbohydrate 457.2g, of which sugars 10.1g; Fat 9.3g, of which saturates 1.4g; Cholesterol 0mg; Calcium 709mg; Fibre 27.9g; Sodium 3948mg.
Grant Loaves per loaf Energy 1363kcal/5795kJ; Protein 55.1g; Carbohydrate 282.1g, of which sugars 14.3g; Fat 9.5g, of which saturates 1.3g; Cholesterol 0mg; Calcium 168mg; Fibre 39g; Sodium 1978mg.

Wholemeal Bread

A simple wholesome bread to be enjoyed by the entire family at any time.

Makes 1

525g/1lb 5oz/5¼ cups strong wholemeal (whole-wheat) bread flour
10ml/2 tsp salt
20ml/4 tsp active dried yeast
450ml/¾ pint/scant 2 cups lukewarm water
30ml/2 tbsp honey
30ml/2 tbsp oil
40g/1½oz wheatgerm
milk, to glaze

1 Warm the flour and salt in a bowl in the oven at its lowest setting for 10 minutes.

2 Meanwhile, combine the yeast with half of the water in a bowl and leave to dissolve and for the yeast to become frothy.

3 Make a central well in the flour. Pour in the yeast mixture, the remaining water, honey, oil and wheatgerm. Stir in the flour from the centre, incorporating it as you go, until smooth.

4 Grease a 23 × 13cm/9 × 5in loaf tin (pan). Knead the dough just enough to shape into a loaf. Put it in the tin and cover with clear film (plastic wrap). Leave in a warm place until the dough is about 2.5cm/1in higher than the tin rim, about 1 hour.

5 Preheat the oven to 200°C/400°F/Gas 6. Brush the loaf with milk, and bake until the base sounds hollow when tapped, about 35–40 minutes. Cool on a wire rack.

Cook's Tip

Strong bread flours have a high gluten content, which allows yeast to rise well, and breads made with strong flours are light and have an airy crumb. Most yeast recipes use strong bread flour rather than plain (all-purpose) or self-raising (self-rising) flours. Soda breads or any other breads not made with yeast do not use strong flours, however.

Granary Cob

Serve this delicious Granary cob warm, so the house is infused with its welcoming fresh-baked aroma.

Makes 1

450g/1lb/4 cups Granary (whole-wheat) or malthouse flour, plus extra for dusting
10ml/2 tsp salt
15g/½oz fresh yeast
300ml/½ pint/1¼ cups lukewarm water, or milk and water mixed

For the topping
30ml/2 tbsp water
2.5ml/½ tsp salt
wheat flakes or cracked wheat, to sprinkle

1 Lightly flour a baking sheet. Sift the flour and salt into a large bowl. Place in a very low oven for 5 minutes to warm.

2 Crumble the yeast into a small bowl and add a little of the water or milk mixture. Mash with a fork, then blend in the remaining liquid. Add the yeast mixture to the flour and mix to form a dough.

3 Knead on a floured surface for about 10 minutes. Place in a lightly oiled bowl, cover with oiled clear film (plastic wrap) and leave in a warm place for 1¼ hours, or until doubled in bulk.

4 Knock back (punch down) the dough, knead for 2–3 minutes, then roll it into a ball. Flatten it slightly so that it resembles a plump round cushion in appearance. Place on the prepared baking sheet, cover with an inverted bowl and leave in a warm place to rise for 30–45 minutes.

5 Preheat the oven to 230°C/450°F/Gas 8. Mix the water and salt for the topping and brush over the bread. Sprinkle with wheat flakes or cracked wheat.

6 Bake for 15 minutes, then reduce the oven temperature to 200°C/400°F/Gas 6 and bake for 20 minutes more, or until the loaf is firm to the touch and sounds hollow when tapped on the base. Cool on a wire rack.

Wholemeal Bread per loaf Energy 1997kcal/8459kJ; Protein 77.4g; Carbohydrate 361g, of which sugars 25.1g; Fat 37.2g, of which saturates 4.7g; Cholesterol 0mg; Calcium 222mg; Fibre 53.5g; Sodium 19mg.

Granary Cob per loaf Energy 1395kcal/5931kJ; Protein 57.1g; Carbohydrate 287.6g, of which sugars 9.4g; Fat 9.9g, of which saturates 1.4g; Cholesterol 0mg; Calcium 172mg; Fibre 40.5g; Sodium 4926mg.

Multigrain Bread

You could also try different flours, such as rye, cornmeal, buckwheat or barley to replace the wheatgerm and the soya flour used here.

Makes 2

15ml/1 tbsp active dried yeast
50ml/2fl oz/¼ cup lukewarm water
65g/2½oz/¾ cup rolled oats
475ml/16fl oz/2 cups milk
10ml/2 tsp salt
50ml/2fl oz/¼ cup oil
50g/2oz/¼ cup soft light brown sugar
30ml/2 tbsp honey
2 eggs, lightly beaten
25g/1oz wheatgerm
175g/6oz/1½ cups soya flour
350g/12oz/3 cups strong wholemeal (whole-wheat) flour
about 450g/1lb/4 cups strong white bread flour

1 Mix the yeast and water in a bowl, stir, and leave for about 15 minutes to dissolve and for the yeast to become frothy. Place the oats in a bowl. Boil the milk, then pour over the oats. Stir in the salt, oil, sugar and honey. Leave until lukewarm.

2 Stir in the yeast mixture, eggs, wheatgerm, soya and wholemeal flours. Gradually stir in enough strong white bread flour to obtain a rough dough.

3 Transfer the dough to a floured surface and knead, adding flour if necessary, until smooth and elastic. This will take about 10 minutes. Return to a clean bowl, cover with clear film (plastic wrap) and leave to rise in a warm place until doubled in volume, about 2½ hours.

4 Grease two 21 × 12cm/8½ × 4½in loaf tins (pans). Knock back (punch down) the risen dough and knead briefly. Then divide the dough into quarters. Roll each quarter into a cylinder 4cm/1½in thick. Twist together two cylinders and place in a tin; repeat for the remaining cylinders. Cover with clear film and leave to rise until doubled in volume again, about 1 hour.

5 Meanwhile, preheat the oven to 190°C/375°F/Gas 5. Bake for about 45–50 minutes. Cool on a wire rack.

Simple White Sourdough Loaf

Sourdough makes fantastic bread with good flavour and texture. It not only keeps well, but is also excellent for toasting.

Makes 1

250g/9oz/2¼ cups strong white bread flour
5ml/1 tsp salt
warm water

For the starter

10g/⅓oz active dried yeast
450ml/¾ pint/scant 2 cups water
375g/13oz/3¼ cups strong white bread flour

1 At least three days before baking, make your starter. Mix the yeast, water and flour together and put in a bowl, covered with a dish towel, leaving it at room temperature for 3–5 days, until bubbles start to form on the surface and it smells vinegary. During the fermentation process you need to stir the mixture with a wooden spoon 2–3 times per day.

2 When you are ready to bake your loaf, put the flour and the salt in a large bowl. Measure 500g/1¼lb of your starter and add it to the flour, mix together with your hand, adding enough warm water, a little at a time, to make a soft dough.

3 Knead until the dough is smooth. Put in a clean bowl and cover with clear film (plastic wrap). Leave in a warm place to rise until doubled in size – this can take 2–3 hours.

4 Turn the dough back on to the surface and knock back (punch down). Rest the dough for 10 minutes, then shape into a round. Put in a well-floured basket to rise. This should take about 1½ hours, but may take longer.

5 Preheat the oven to 230°C/450°F/Gas 8. Turn the dough gently out of the basket on to a well-floured baking sheet. Slash the top of the loaf with a sharp knife. Bake for 30–40 minutes.

6 Bring the loaf out of the oven and tap the base to make sure it sounds hollow. Cool on a wire rack and wait for 30 minutes before serving.

Multigrain Bread per loaf Energy 2266kcal/9595kJ; Protein 104.9g; Carbohydrate 389.3g, of which sugars 69.5g; Fat 43.1g, of which saturates 8g; Cholesterol 204mg; Calcium 944mg; Fibre 38.7g; Sodium 211mg.

Simple White Sourdough Loaf per loaf Energy 1284kcal/5464kJ; Protein 44g; Carbohydrate 282g, of which sugars 5g; Fat 5g, of which saturates 1g; Cholesterol 0mg; Calcium 529mg; Fibre 14.5g; Sodium 3943mg.

German Sourdough Bread

This bread includes rye, wholemeal and plain flours for a superb depth of flavour. Serve it cut in thick slices, with creamy butter.

Makes 1

For the starter

75g/3oz/¾ cup rye flour
80ml/3fl oz/⅓ cup warm water
a pinch of caraway seeds

For the dough

15g/½oz fresh yeast
315ml/11fl oz/1⅓ cups lukewarm water
275g/10oz/2½ cups rye flour
150g/5oz/1¼ cups wholemeal (whole-wheat) bread flour
150g/5oz/1¼ cups unbleached white bread flour
10ml/2 tsp salt

1 Mix the rye flour, warm water and caraway for the starter together in a large bowl with your fingertips, to make a soft paste. Cover with a damp dish towel and leave in a warm place for about 36 hours. Stir after 24 hours.

2 In a measuring jug (cup), blend the yeast for the dough with the lukewarm water. Add to the starter and mix thoroughly.

3 Mix the rye flour, wholemeal bread flour and unbleached white bread flour for the dough with the salt in a large bowl; make a well in the centre. Pour in the yeast liquid and gradually incorporate the surrounding flour to make a smooth dough.

4 Turn out the dough on to a lightly floured surface and knead for 8–10 minutes until smooth. Place in an oiled bowl, cover with lightly oiled clear film (plastic wrap) and leave to rise, in a warm place, for 1½ hours, or until nearly doubled in bulk.

5 Turn out on to a lightly floured surface, knock back (punch down) and knead gently. Shape into a round and place in a floured basket, with the seam up. Cover with lightly oiled clear film and leave to rise, in a warm place, for 2–3 hours.

6 Meanwhile, preheat the oven to 200°C/400°F/Gas 6. Turn out the loaf on to a greased baking sheet and bake for 35–40 minutes. Cool on a wire rack.

Rye Bread

This bread is popular in Northern Europe, and makes an excellent base for open sandwiches.

Makes 2

350g/12oz/3 cups strong wholemeal (whole-wheat) flour
225g/8oz/2 cups rye flour
115g/4oz/1 cup strong white bread flour
7.5ml/1½ tsp salt
7g/¼oz easy-blend (rapid-rise) dried yeast
30ml/2 tbsp caraway seeds
475ml/16fl oz/2 cups lukewarm water
30ml/2 tbsp molasses
30ml/2 tbsp sunflower oil

1 Grease a baking sheet. Put the flours in a bowl with the salt and yeast. Set aside 5ml/1 tsp of the caraway seeds and add the remainder to the bowl. Mix well, then make a well in the centre.

2 Add the water to the bowl with the molasses and oil. Stir from the centre outwards, gradually incorporating the flour and mixing to a soft dough, adding a little extra water if needed.

3 Turn the dough on to a floured surface and knead for 5 minutes until smooth and elastic. Divide the dough in half and shape into two 23cm/9in long oval loaves.

4 Flatten the loaves slightly and place them on the prepared baking sheet. Brush them with water and sprinkle with the remaining caraway seeds. Cover and leave in a warm place until doubled in size, about 1½ hours. Meanwhile, preheat the oven to 220°C/425°F/Gas 7.

5 Bake the loaves for 30 minutes until golden, or when they sound hollow when tapped underneath. Cool on a wire rack.

Cook's Tip

Using warm rather than cold liquid helps the yeast to start working, as it is a living organism that thrives in warm and moist conditions.

German Sourdough Bread per loaf Energy 2065kcal/8793kJ; Protein 59.8g; Carbohydrate 459.1g, of which sugars 5.4g; Fat 11.7g, of which saturates 1.7g; Cholesterol 0mg; Calcium 372mg; Fibre 56.2g; Sodium 3942mg.

Rye Bread per loaf Energy 4323kcal/18332kJ; Protein 98.1g; Carbohydrate 893.3g, of which sugars 93.3g; Fat 64.4g, of which saturates 33.6g; Cholesterol 128mg; Calcium 1926mg; Fibre 49.8g; Sodium 6502mg.

Sour Rye Bread

You need to plan ahead to make this loaf, as the starter takes a day or two.

Makes 2

450g/1lb/4 cups rye flour
450g/1lb/4 cups strong white bread flour, plus extra for dusting
15ml/1 tbsp salt
7g/¼oz easy-blend (rapid-rise) dried yeast
25g/1oz/2 tbsp butter, softened
600ml/1 pint/2½ cups warm water
15ml/1 tbsp caraway seeds, for sprinkling

For the starter
60ml/4 tbsp rye flour
45ml/3 tbsp warm milk

1 For the starter, mix the rye flour and milk in a small bowl. Cover with clear film (plastic wrap) and leave in a warm place for 1–2 days, or until it smells pleasantly sour.

2 Sift both types of flour and the salt into a large bowl and stir in the yeast. Make a well in the centre and add the butter, water and sourdough starter. Mix to a soft dough.

3 Knead the dough on a floured surface for 10 minutes. Put it in a clean bowl, cover with lightly oiled clear film and leave in a warm place to rise for 1 hour, or until doubled in size.

4 Knead for 1 minute. Divide the dough in half. Shape each piece into a 15cm/6in round. Place on greased baking sheets. Cover with oiled clear film and leave to rise for 30 minutes.

5 Preheat the oven to 200°C/400°F/Gas 6. Brush the loaves with water, sprinkle with caraway seeds and bake them for 35–40 minutes. The loaves should have browned and sound hollow when tapped on the bottom. Cool on a wire rack.

Cook's Tip
Sour rye bread keeps fresh for up to a week. This recipe can also be made without yeast, but it will be much denser.

Scandinavian Sun Loaf

This Scandinavian bread is made with a blend of rye and white flours.

Makes 1

For the starter
60ml/4 tbsp lukewarm milk
60ml/4 tbsp lukewarm water
7g/¼oz fresh yeast
100g/3¾oz/scant 1 cup strong white bread flour

For the dough
15g/½oz fresh yeast
500ml/17fl oz/generous 2 cups lukewarm water
450g/1lb/4 cups rye flour
225g/8oz/2 cups strong white bread flour
15ml/1 tbsp salt
milk, for glazing
caraway seeds, for sprinkling

1 Pour the milk and water for the starter into a bowl. Mix in the yeast until dissolved. Gently stir in the flour. Cover with clear film (plastic wrap) and leave for 3–4 hours, or until risen.

2 Mix the yeast for the dough with 60ml/4 tbsp of the water until creamy, then stir in the remaining water. Gradually mix into the starter to dilute it. Gradually mix in the rye flour to form a smooth batter. Cover with lightly oiled clear film and leave in a warm place, for 3–4 hours, or until well risen.

3 Stir the bread flour and salt into the batter to form a dough. Turn on to a lightly floured surface and knead for 5 minutes until smooth. Place in a lightly oiled bowl, cover with lightly oiled clear film and leave to rise for about 1 hour.

4 Knock back (punch down) on a lightly floured surface. Cut the dough into five pieces. Roll one piece into a 50cm/20in 'sausage' and roll up into a spiral shape. Cut the remaining pieces of dough in half and shape each one into a 20cm/8in rope. Place in a circle on a large baking sheet, like rays of the sun, and curl the ends round. Place the spiral shape on top. Cover with oiled clear film and leave to rise for 30 minutes.

5 Preheat the oven to 230°C/450°F/Gas 8. Brush the bread with milk, sprinkle with caraway seeds and bake for 30 minutes, or until lightly browned. Transfer to a wire rack to cool.

Sour Rye Bread per loaf Energy 1731kcal/7355kJ; Protein 45.6g; Carbohydrate 369.7g, of which sugars 4.6g; Fat 19.8g, of which saturates 8g; Cholesterol 28mg; Calcium 499mg; Fibre 49.1g; Sodium 3047mg.
Scandinavian Sun Loaf per loaf Energy 2665kcal/11347kJ; Protein 77g; Carbohydrate 590g, of which sugars 8g; Fat 16g, of which saturates 4g; Cholesterol 11mg; Calcium 689mg; Fibre 12g; Sodium 5942mg.

Boston Brown Bread

Rich and moist, this bread is flavoured with molasses. In Boston it is often served with baked beans.

Makes 1–2

90g/3½oz/scant 1 cup cornmeal
90g/3½oz/scant 1 cup unbleached plain (all-purpose) white flour or wholemeal (whole-wheat) flour
90g/3½oz/scant 1 cup rye flour
2.5ml/½ tsp salt
5ml/1 tsp bicarbonate of soda (baking soda)
90g/3½oz/generous ½ cup raisins
120ml/4fl oz/½ cup milk
120ml/4fl oz/½ cup water
120ml/4fl oz/½ cup molasses

1 Line the base of one 1.2 litre/2 pint/5 cup cylindrical metal or glass container, such as a heatproof glass coffee jug (carafe), with greased baking parchment. Alternatively, remove the lids from two 450g/1lb coffee cans, wash and dry them thoroughly, then line with greased baking parchment.

2 Mix together the cornmeal, plain or wholemeal flour, rye flour, salt, bicarbonate of soda and raisins in a large bowl. Warm the milk and water in a small pan and stir in the molasses. Add the molasses mixture to the dry ingredients and mix together using a spoon until it just forms a moist dough. Be careful to avoid overmixing the dough.

3 Fill the jug or cans with the dough; they should be about two-thirds full. Cover neatly with foil or greased baking parchment and tie securely.

4 Bring water to a depth of 5cm/2in to the boil in a deep, pan large enough to accommodate the jug or cans. Place a trivet in the pan, stand the jug or cans on top, cover the pan and steam for 1½ hours, adding more boiling water to maintain the required level as necessary.

5 Cool the loaves for a few minutes, then turn them on their sides and the loaves should slip out. Serve warm.

Soda Bread

Finding the bread bin empty need never be a problem when your repertoire includes a recipe for soda bread. It takes only a few minutes to make and needs no rising or proving.

Makes 1

450g/1lb/4 cups plain (all-purpose) flour
5ml/1 tsp salt
5ml/1 tsp bicarbonate of soda (baking soda)
5ml/1 tsp cream of tartar
350ml/12fl oz/1½ cups buttermilk

1 Preheat the oven to 220°C/425°F/Gas 7 and lightly flour a baking sheet.

2 Sift the flour, salt, bicarbonate of soda and cream of tartar into a large mixing bowl, mix to combine and make a well in the centre.

3 Pour the buttermilk into the dry ingredients and mix quickly until a soft dough is formed. Turn the dough out on to a floured surface and knead lightly for a minute.

4 Shape the dough into a round, about 18cm/7in in diameter, and place on the prepared baking sheet.

5 Cut a deep cross on top of the loaf and sprinkle it with a little flour. Bake the soda bread for 25–30 minutes until golden-brown, then transfer to a wire rack and eat warm, or set it aside to cool.

Cook's Tips

- *Soda bread needs a light hand. The ingredients should be bound together quickly in the bowl and kneaded very briefly. The aim is just to get rid of the largest cracks, as the dough becomes tough if handled for too long.*
- *If possible, eat soda bread warm from the oven, as it does not keep well.*

Boston Brown Bread per loaf Energy 774kcal/3285kJ; Protein 15.8g; Carbohydrate 176.5g, of which sugars 75.2g; Fat 4.2g, of which saturates 0.8g; Cholesterol 4mg; Calcium 472mg; Fibre 8.6g; Sodium 611mg.

Soda Bread per loaf Energy 206kcal/875kJ; Protein 6.8g; Carbohydrate 45.6g, of which sugars 2.8g; Fat 0.9g, of which saturates 0.2g; Cholesterol 2mg; Calcium 132mg; Fibre 1.7g; Sodium 267mg.

Brown Soda Bread

Soda bread is best eaten on the day of baking, but it slices better if left to cool and 'set' for several hours. It is delicious with good butter, farmhouse cheese and some crisp sticks of celery or a bowl of home-made soup.

Makes 1

450g/1lb/4 cups wholemeal (whole-wheat) flour
175g/6oz/1½ cups plain (all-purpose) flour
5ml/1 tsp salt
7.5ml/1½ tsp bicarbonate of soda (baking soda)
about 450ml/¾ pint/scant 2 cups buttermilk

1 Preheat the oven to 200°C/400°F/Gas 6, and lightly grease a baking sheet. Combine the dry ingredients in a mixing bowl and stir in enough buttermilk to make a soft dough.

2 Turn on to a work surface dusted with wholemeal flour and knead until smooth.

3 Form the dough into a circle, about 4cm/1½in thick. Lay on the baking sheet and mark a deep cross in the top with a floured knife.

4 Bake for about 45 minutes, or until the bread is browned and sounds hollow when tapped on the base. Cool on a wire rack. If a soft crust is preferred, wrap the loaf in a clean dish towel while cooling.

Cook's Tip

Buttermilk can be cultured easily at home, using a 'buttermilk plant'. Cream 25g/1oz fresh yeast, 25g/1oz sugar and 950ml/2 pints/4 cups of tepid milk gradually. Pour the mixture into a well sterilized jug (pitcher). Cover and put in warm place to ferment. Leave until it smells like buttermilk, strain off the liquid and use. Pour tepid water over the lumps in the strainer to wash. Return to the jug and add more milk or milk and water to make more buttermilk.

Barley Bannock

Bannocks are flat loaves about the size of a dinner plate. They are traditionally baked on a griddle or 'girdle' (which is the preferred name in Scotland). Barley flour adds a wonderfully earthy flavour to the bread.

Makes 1

115g/4oz/1 cup barley flour
50g/2oz/½ cup unbleached plain (all-purpose) flour or wholemeal (whole-wheat) flour
2.5ml/½ tsp salt
2.5ml/½ tsp cream of tartar
25g/1oz/2 tbsp butter or margarine
175ml/6fl oz/¾ cup buttermilk
2.5ml/½ tsp bicarbonate of soda (baking soda)

1 Wipe the surface of a griddle with a little vegetable oil. Sift the flours, salt and cream of tartar together into a large bowl. Add the butter or margarine and rub into the flour until it resembles fine breadcrumbs.

2 Mix the buttermilk and bicarbonate of soda together. When the mixture starts to bubble add to the flour. Mix together to form a soft dough. Do not overmix the dough or it will toughen.

3 On a floured surface pat the dough out to form a round about 2cm/¾in thick. Mark the dough into four wedges, using a sharp knife, if you prefer.

4 Heat the griddle until hot. Cook the bannock on the griddle for about 8–10 minutes per side over a gentle heat. Do not cook too quickly or the outside will burn before the centre is cooked. Cool the bannock slightly on a wire rack and eat while still warm.

Cook's Tip

If you cannot locate buttermilk, then use soured milk instead. Stir 5ml/1 tsp lemon juice into 175ml/6fl oz/¾ cup milk and set aside for an hour to sour.

Brown Soda Bread per loaf Energy 2262kcal/9643kJ; Protein 88.5g; Carbohydrate 465.4g, of which sugars 31.4g; Fat 18.9g, of which saturates 6.5g; Cholesterol 27mg; Calcium 1.37g; Fibre 34.2g; Sodium 2.18g.

Barley Bannock per loaf Energy 827kcal/3493kJ; Protein 19.7g; Carbohydrate 143.7g, of which sugars 9.5g; Fat 23.6g, of which saturates 13.8g; Cholesterol 64mg; Calcium 307mg; Fibre 1.6g; Sodium 1269mg.

Simple Cornmeal Loaf

Serve this bread as an accompaniment to a meal or with soup, or alternatively you could take it on a picnic.

Makes 1

115g/4oz/1 cup plain (all-purpose) flour
65g/2½oz/generous ¼ cup caster (superfine) sugar
5ml/1 tsp salt
15ml/1 tbsp baking powder
175g/6oz/1½ cups cornmeal or polenta
350ml/12fl oz/1½ cups milk
2 eggs
75g/3oz/6 tbsp butter, melted
115g/4oz/½ cup margarine, melted

1 Preheat the oven to 200°C/400°F/Gas 6. Then line a 23 × 13cm/9 × 5in loaf tin (pan) with baking parchment and grease the paper.

2 Sift the flour, sugar, salt and baking powder into a mixing bowl. Add the cornmeal or polenta and stir to blend. Make a well in the centre. Whisk together the milk, eggs, melted butter and margarine. Pour the mixture into the well. Stir until just blended, taking care not to overmix.

3 Pour into the tin and bake until a skewer inserted in the centre comes out clean, about 45 minutes. Serve hot or at room temperature.

Cook's Tip

Often a loaf tin (pan) needs only to be greased and have a long strip of baking parchment placed along the base and up the short sides of the tin. At other times, however, it is best to line the whole tin. To do this cut another strip of baking parchment the length of the base of the tin and long enough to come up the long sides of the tin. Grease the paper you have already laid in the base of the tin and then lay the other sheet on top, smoothing both pieces up the sides of the tin. Finally, grease the paper.

Polenta Bread

Polenta is widely used in Italian cooking. Here it is combined with pine nuts to make a traditional bread with a fantastic flavour.

Makes 1

50g/2oz/½ cup polenta
300ml/½ pint/1¼ cups lukewarm water
15g/½oz fresh yeast
2.5ml/½ tsp clear honey
225g/8oz/2 cups unbleached white bread flour
25g/1oz/2 tbsp butter
45ml/3 tbsp pine nuts
7.5ml/1½ tsp salt

For the topping

1 egg yolk
15ml/1 tbsp water
pine nuts, for sprinkling

1 Lightly grease a baking sheet. Mix the polenta and 250ml/8fl oz/1 cup of the water in a pan and slowly bring to the boil, stirring continuously, then simmer for 2–3 minutes, stirring occasionally. Set aside to cool for 10 minutes, or until just warm.

2 Mix the yeast with the remaining water and honey until creamy. Sift 115g/4oz/1 cup of the flour and beat in the yeast mixture, then stir in the polenta mixture. Turn on to a floured surface and knead for 5 minutes until smooth and elastic. Put the dough in a lightly oiled polythene bag and leave in a warm place, for about 2 hours, or until it has doubled in size. Meanwhile, melt the butter, add the pine nuts and cook over medium heat, stirring, until pale golden. Set aside to cool.

3 Add the remaining flour and salt to the dough and mix to a soft dough. Knead in the pine nuts. Turn out on to a floured surface and knead for 5 minutes until smooth and elastic. Place in a lightly oiled bowl, cover and leave in a warm place, for 1 hour, or until doubled in bulk.

4 Knock back (punch down) the dough. Divide into two equal pieces and roll each piece into a sausage about 38cm/15in long. Plait together and place on the prepared baking sheet. Cover and leave for 45 minutes. Preheat the oven to 200°C/400°F/Gas 6. Mix the egg yolk and water and brush over the loaf. Sprinkle with pine nuts and bake for 30 minutes.

Simple Cornmeal Loaf per loaf Energy 3067kcal/12780kJ; Protein 55.6g; Carbohydrate 309.6g, of which sugars 88.4g; Fat 181.8g, of which saturates 46.9g; Cholesterol 646mg; Calcium 827mg; Fibre 9.9g; Sodium 5459mg.

Polenta Bread per loaf Energy 1994kcal/8427kJ; Protein 50.5g; Carbohydrate 366.8g, of which sugars 7.1g; Fat 44.7g, of which saturates 15g; Cholesterol 53mg; Calcium 1085mg; Fibre 14.9g; Sodium 2337mg.

Pan de Cebada

This Spanish cornmeal bread is perfect for serving with chilled soup, or it would also go well with a healthy dip.

Makes 1

For the starter

175g/6oz/1½ cups cornmeal
560ml/scant 1 pint/scant 2½ cups water
225g/8oz/2 cups wholemeal (whole-wheat) bread flour
75g/3oz/¾ cup barley flour

For the dough

20g/¾oz fresh yeast
45ml/3 tbsp lukewarm water
225g/8oz/2 cups wholemeal (whole-wheat) bread flour
15ml/1 tbsp salt
cornmeal, for dusting

1 In a pan, mix the cornmeal for the starter with half the water, then stir in the remainder. Stir over low heat until thickened. Transfer to a bowl and set aside to cool. Mix in the wholemeal and barley flours. Knead on a floured surface for 5 minutes, then return to the bowl, cover with lightly oiled clear film (plastic wrap) and leave in a warm place for about 36 hours.

2 Make the dough. Dust a baking sheet with cornmeal. In a small bowl, cream the yeast with the water, then add to the starter with the wholemeal flour and salt and work to a dough. Knead on a lightly floured surface for 4–5 minutes.

3 Put the dough in a lightly oiled bowl, cover with oiled clear film and leave in a warm place to rise for 1½–2 hours.

4 Knock back (punch down) the dough, shape it into a plump round and sprinkle with a cornmeal. Put it on the prepared baking sheet and cover with an upturned bowl. Leave in a warm place to rise, for about 1 hour, or until nearly doubled in size.

5 Place an empty roasting pan in the base of the oven. Preheat the oven to 220°C/425°F/Gas 7. Pour 300ml/½ pint/1¼ cups cold water into the pan. Lift the bowl off the loaf and place the baking sheet in the oven. Bake for 10 minutes. Remove the pan of water, reduce the oven temperature to 190°C/375°F/Gas 5 and bake the bread for 20 minutes more. Cool on a wire rack.

Harvest Festival Sheaf

Celebratory loaves, such as this centrepiece, often signal the start of harvest time.

Makes 1

900g/2lb/8 cups unbleached strong white bread flour
15ml/1 tbsp salt
15g/½oz fresh yeast
75ml/5 tbsp lukewarm milk
400ml/14fl oz/1⅔ cups cold water

For the glaze

1 egg
15ml/1 tbsp milk

1 Sift the flour and salt together into a bowl. Cream the yeast with the milk in a bowl. Add to the centre of the flour with the water and mix to a stiff dough. Knead on a floured surface for 10–15 minutes until smooth. Place in an oiled bowl, cover and leave for about 2 hours, or until doubled in size.

2 Turn the dough out on to a floured surface, knock back (punch down) and knead for 1 minute. Cover and leave for 10 minutes. Divide the dough in two. Roll out one piece to a large oblong. Fold loosely in half lengthways. Cut out a half mushroom shape. Place on a greased baking sheet and open out. Prick with a fork and brush with water. Reserve 75g/3oz of the trimmings for the tie. Cover and set aside.

3 Divide the remaining dough into two. Shape one piece on a floured surface into a rectangle and cut into 30 thin strips and place on the base. Beat the egg and milk for the glaze.

4 Preheat the oven to 220°C/425°F/Gas 7. Take the last piece of dough and divide into four, then divide each into 25 to make 100 wheat ears. Make each roll pointed at one end. Arrange the ears around the outer edge of the top of the mushroom shape. Repeat until they are all used. Brush all over with glaze.

5 Braid the trimmings for the tie. Place across the wheat stalks and brush with glaze. Prick using a sharp knife and bake for 15 minutes. Reduce to 180°C/350°F/Gas 4. Brush the bread with the remaining glaze and bake for a further 30–35 minutes, or until golden. Leave to cool on the baking sheet.

Pan de Cebada per loaf Energy 2365kcal/10014kJ; Protein 80g; Carbohydrate 498g, of which sugars 9g; Fat 15g, of which saturates 1g; Cholesterol 0mg; Calcium 512mg; Fibre 38g; Sodium 5911mg.

Harvest Festival Sheaf per loaf Energy 3104kcal/13196kJ; Protein 87.1g; Carbohydrate 703g, of which sugars 17.3g; Fat 13g, of which saturates 2.5g; Cholesterol 4mg; Calcium 1352mg; Fibre 27.9g; Sodium 5963mg.

Braided Honey Loaf

A touch of honey adds to the golden colour of this delicious braided loaf.

Makes 1

15ml/1 tbsp active dried yeast
5ml/1 tsp honey
250ml/8fl oz/1 cup lukewarm milk
50g/2oz/¼ cup butter, melted
425g/15oz/3⅔ cups strong white bread flour
5ml/1 tsp salt
1 egg, lightly beaten
1 egg yolk, beaten with 5ml/1 tsp milk, to glaze

1 Combine the yeast, honey, milk and butter in a small bowl. Stir and leave for 15 minutes to dissolve and for the yeast to become frothy.

2 In a large bowl, mix together the flour and salt. Make a central well in the flour, and add the yeast mixture and egg. With a wooden spoon, stir from the centre, gradually incorporating the flour into the liquid, to obtain a rough dough.

3 Transfer the dough to a floured surface and knead until smooth and elastic. This will take about 10 minutes.

4 Place in a clean bowl, cover with clear film (plastic wrap) and leave to rise in a warm place until doubled in volume, about 1½ hours.

5 Grease a baking sheet. Punch down (knock back) the dough and divide into three equal pieces.

6 Roll each piece into a long thin strip. Begin braiding with the centre strip, tucking in the ends neatly when you reach the end of the braid. Cover loosely with clear film and leave to rise in a warm place for 30 minutes.

7 Meanwhile, preheat the oven to 190°C/375°F/Gas 5. Brush the bread with the egg and milk glaze and bake until it is golden, about 40–45 minutes. Turn the loaf out on to a wire rack to cool.

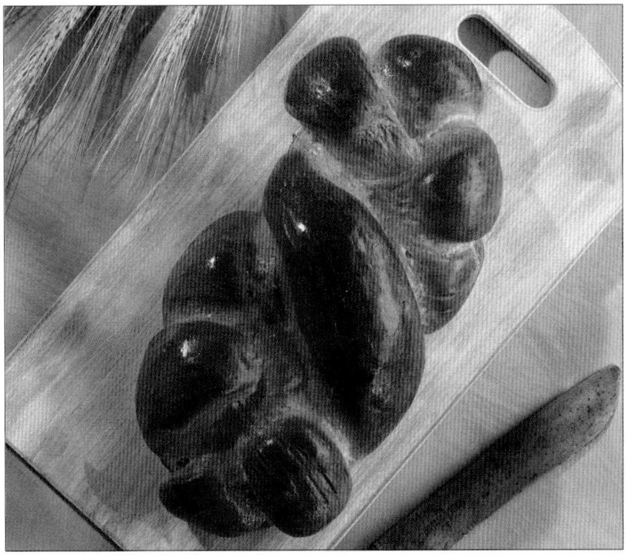

Swiss Braid

This braided loaf is known as *zupfe* in Switzerland. It has a glossy crust and a wonderfully light crumb.

Makes 1

350g/12oz/3 cups unbleached strong white bread flour
5ml/1 tsp salt
20g/¾oz fresh yeast
30ml/2 tbsp lukewarm water
150ml/¼ pint/⅔ cup sour cream
1 egg, lightly beaten
50g/2oz/¼ cup butter, softened

For the glaze
1 egg yolk
15ml/1 tbsp water

1 Sift the flour and salt together into a bowl and make a well in the centre. Mix the yeast with the water in a jug (pitcher).

2 Gently warm the sour cream in a small pan until it reaches blood heat (35–38°C). Add to the yeast mixture and mix. Then add the yeast mixture and egg to the centre of the flour and gradually mix to a dough. Beat in the softened butter.

3 Knead on a floured surface for 5 minutes until smooth. Place in a oiled bowl, cover with oiled clear film (plastic wrap) and leave in a warm place, for about 1½ hours until doubled in size.

4 Turn out on to a lightly floured surface and knock back (punch down). Cut in half and shape each piece of dough into a long rope about 35cm/14in in length.

5 To make the braid, place the two pieces of dough to form a cross. Fold the top end over and place between the two bottom ropes. Fold the remaining top rope over so that all four ropes are pointing downwards. Starting from the left, braid the first rope over the second, and the third rope over the fourth. Continue braiding in this way to form a tapered bread. Tuck the ends underneath and place on an oiled baking sheet. Cover and leave to rise, in a warm place, for about 40 minutes.

6 Meanwhile, preheat the oven to 190°C/375°F/Gas 5. Mix the egg yolk and water and brush over the loaf. Bake the bread for 30–35 minutes, or until golden. Cool on a wire rack.

Braided Honey Loaf per loaf Energy 2102kcal/8867kJ; Protein 58.9g; Carbohydrate 346.6g, of which sugars 22.7g; Fat 62.8g, of which saturates 33.1g; Cholesterol 557mg; Calcium 937mg; Fibre 17.6g; Sodium 2499mg.

Swiss Braid per loaf Energy 1870kcal/7858kJ; Protein 37.5g; Carbohydrate 277.6g, of which sugars 10.9g; Fat 75.3g, of which saturates 46.5g; Cholesterol 205mg; Calcium 638mg; Fibre 10.9g; Sodium 2412mg.

Challah

With its braided shape, light texture, rich flavour and a sprinkling of poppy seeds, this Jewish festival bread is a traditional favourite.

Makes 1

500g/1¼lb/5 cups unbleached white bread flour, plus extra
10ml/2 tsp salt
20g/¾oz fresh yeast
200ml/7fl oz/scant 1 cup lukewarm water
30ml/2 tbsp caster (superfine) sugar
2 eggs
75g/3oz/6 tbsp butter, melted

For the topping
1 egg yolk
15ml/1 tbsp water
10ml/2 tsp poppy seeds

1 Lightly grease a baking sheet. Sift the flour and salt into a bowl and make a well in the centre. Mix the yeast with the water and sugar; add to the well with the eggs and melted butter. Gradually mix in the flour to form a soft dough.

2 Knead on a lightly floured surface for 10 minutes. Place in a lightly oiled bowl, cover and leave in a warm place to rise for 1 hour, or until doubled in bulk.

3 Knock back, re-cover and leave to rise again in a warm place for about 1 hour. Knock back, turn out on to a lightly floured surface and knead gently. Divide into four equal pieces. Roll each piece into a rope about 45cm/18in long. Line them up next to each other. Pinch the ends together at one end.

4 Starting from the right, lift the first rope over the second and the third over the fourth. Place the fourth rope between the first and second ropes. Repeat, starting from the right, and continue until braided. Tuck the ends under and place the loaf on the baking sheet. Cover and leave in a warm place to rise for 30–45 minutes, or until doubled in size.

5 Preheat the oven to 200°C/400°F/Gas 6. Beat the egg yolk and water for the topping together. Gently brush the loaf with the mixture. Sprinkle with the poppy seeds and bake for 35–40 minutes, until deep golden brown. Cool on a wire rack.

Wheat Ear Loaf

This distinctively shaped loaf uses fermented French baguette dough as a starter.

Makes 2

7g/¼oz fresh yeast
275ml/9fl oz/generous 1 cup lukewarm water
115g/4oz/½ cup French baguette dough 6–10 hours old
225g/8oz/2 cups unbleached white bread flour
75g/3oz/¾ cup fine French plain (all-purpose) flour
5ml/1 tsp salt

1 Sprinkle a baking sheet with flour. Mix the yeast with the water. Place the French bread dough in a large bowl and break up. Add a little of the yeast water to soften the dough. Mix in a little of the bread flour, then yeast water and both flours alternately until fully incorporated. Sprinkle the salt over the dough and knead in. Turn the dough on to a lightly floured surface and knead for about 5 minutes until smooth and elastic.

2 Place in a lightly oiled bowl, cover with lightly oiled clear film (plastic wrap) and leave in a warm place for about 1 hour, or until the dough has doubled in bulk. Knock it back, then cover the bowl again and leave in a warm place, for about 1 hour.

3 Divide the dough into 2 equal pieces, place on a lightly floured surface and stretch each piece into a baguette. Let the dough rest between rolling for a few minutes if necessary to avoid tearing. Pleat a floured dish towel on a baking sheet to make 2 moulds for the loaves. Place them between the pleats of the towel, cover with lightly oiled clear film and leave in a warm place to rise for 30 minutes.

4 Meanwhile, preheat the oven to 230°C/450°F/Gas 8. Using scissors, make diagonal cuts halfway through the dough about 5cm/2in apart, alternating the cuts along the loaf. Gently pull the dough in the opposite direction.

5 Place on the baking sheet and bake for 20 minutes, or until golden. Spray the inside of the oven with water 2–3 times during the first 5 minutes. Transfer to a wire rack to cool.

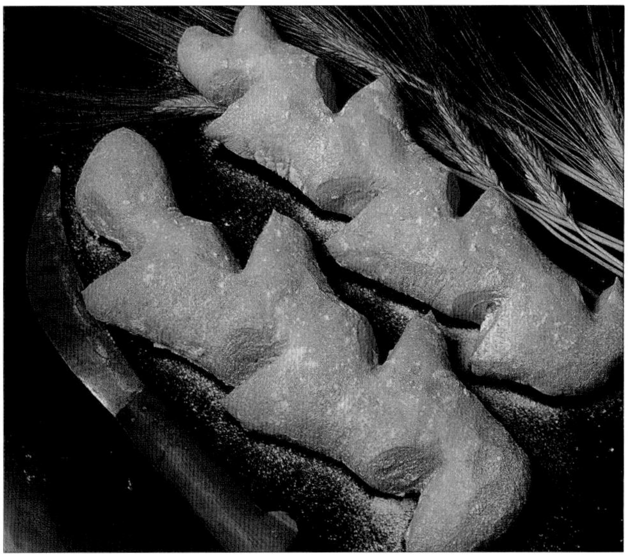

Challah per loaf Energy 1055kcal/4464kJ; Protein 29.8g; Carbohydrate 202.1g, of which sugars 11.6g; Fat 19.8g, of which saturates 3.4g; Cholesterol 190mg; Calcium 383mg; Fibre 7.8g; Sodium 78mg.

Wheat Ear Loaf per loaf Energy 705kcal/2996kJ; Protein 19.4g; Carbohydrate 160.5g, of which sugars 3.1g; Fat 2.7g, of which saturates 0.4g; Cholesterol 0mg; Calcium 290mg; Fibre 6.4g; Sodium 1351mg.

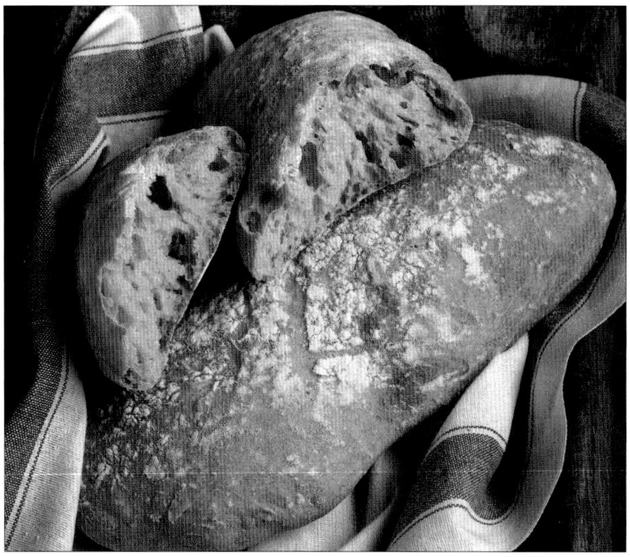

Ciabatta

This irregular-shaped Italian bread is so called because it looks like an old slipper.

Makes 3

For the starter

7g/¼oz fresh yeast
175–200ml/6–7fl oz/¾–scant 1 cup lukewarm water
350g/12oz/3 cups unbleached plain (all-purpose) flour
extra flour for dusting

For the dough

15g/½oz fresh yeast
400ml/14fl oz/1⅔ cups lukewarm water
60ml/4 tbsp lukewarm milk
500g/1¼lb/5 cups unbleached strong white bread flour
10ml/2 tsp salt
45ml/3 tbsp extra virgin olive oil

1 Cream the yeast for the starter with a little of the water. Sift the flour into a large bowl. Gradually mix in the yeast mixture and enough of the remaining water to form a firm dough. Turn out on to a floured surface and knead for about 5 minutes, or until smooth and elastic. Return the dough to the bowl, cover with lightly oiled clear film (plastic wrap) and leave in a warm place for 12–15 hours, until risen and starting to collapse.

2 Sprinkle three baking sheets with flour. Mix the yeast for the dough with a little of the water until creamy, then mix in the rest. Add to the starter and mix in. Mix in the milk, and, using your hand, gradually beat in the flour, lifting the dough as you mix. This will take about 15 minutes and form a very wet dough.

3 Mix in the salt and oil. Cover with oiled clear film and leave to rise in a warm place until doubled in size, about 1½–2 hours.

4 With a spoon, carefully tip one-third of the dough at a time on to the baking sheets without knocking it back (punching down) in the process. Using floured hands, shape into rough oblongs, about 2.5cm/1in thick, and flatten slightly. Sprinkle with flour and leave to rise in a warm place for 30 minutes.

5 Meanwhile, preheat the oven to 220°C/425°F/Gas 7. Bake for 25–30 minutes, or until golden and sounding hollow when tapped on the base. Transfer to a wire rack to cool.

Ciabatta with Polenta

As well as its mixture of strong and weak flours, this ciabatta has the addition of fine polenta.

Makes 6

For the starter

5g/⅙oz fresh yeast (or 1.5ml/¼ tsp dried yeast)
250ml/8fl oz/1 cup water
275g/10oz/2½ cups strong white bread flour

For the dough

10g/¼oz fresh yeast (or 5ml/1 tsp dried yeast)
400g/14oz/3½ cups strong white bread flour
100g/3¾oz/scant 1 cup fine polenta
5ml/1 tsp salt
15ml/1 tbsp olive oil
450ml/¾ pint/scant 2 cups warm water

1 Mix together the starter ingredients and beat with a wooden spoon for a minute or two until smooth, with no lumps. Cover with clear film (plastic wrap) and leave it to sit at room temperature for 12–24 hours, until slightly sour and bubbling.

2 In a bowl mix together the yeast, bread flour, polenta and salt then stir in all the starter. Add the olive oil and water and mix to make a batter.

3 Work the dough in the bowl by hand by pulling it up and letting it fall back for about 30 minutes, until it will clear the sides of the mixing bowl and feel elastic and strong.

4 Dampen your work surface with a wet cloth, and tip the dough on to it. Using a dough scraper or spatula, take each of the four edges of the dough, stretch out lightly, then fold it back over the top of the dough.

5 Flour a large board, the dough and your scraper and cut the dough carefully into six equal pieces and stretch lightly into an elongated ciabatta loaf shape. Rest the dough for 10 minutes.

6 Preheat oven to 230°C/450°F/Gas 8 and place the dough at the bottom of the oven. Bake the bread for barely 20 minutes, until risen and golden, then leave to cool on a wire rack.

Ciabatta per loaf Energy 985kcal/4176kJ; Protein 25g; Carbohydrate 202.8g, of which sugars 4.8g; Fat 13.8g, of which saturates 2.2g; Cholesterol 1mg; Calcium 386mg; Fibre 8.1g; Sodium 1217mg.

Ciabatta with Polenta per loaf Energy 405kcal/1718kJ; Protein 13g; Carbohydrate 84g, of which sugars 2g; Fat 4g, of which saturates 1g; Cholesterol 0mg; Calcium 157mg; Fibre 4.3g; Sodium 659mg.

French Baguettes

Baguettes made by an artisan baker are difficult to reproduce at home, but by using less yeast and triple fermentation you can produce bread far superior to mass-produced loaves.

Makes 3
500g/1¼lb/5 cups unbleached strong white bread flour
115g/4oz/1 cup fine French plain (all-purpose) flour
10ml/2 tsp salt
15g/½oz fresh yeast

1 Sift the flours and salt into a large bowl. Add the yeast to 550ml/18fl oz/2½ cups lukewarm water in a separate bowl and stir until combined. Gradually beat in half the flour mixture to form a batter. Cover with clear film (plastic wrap) and leave for about 3 hours, or until nearly trebled in size.

2 Add the remaining flour a little at a time, beating with your hand. Turn out on to a lightly floured surface and knead for 8–10 minutes to form a moist dough. Place the dough in a lightly oiled bowl, cover with lightly oiled clear film and leave to rise, in a warm place, for about 1 hour.

3 Knock back (punch down) the dough, turn out on to a floured surface and divide into three equal pieces. Shape each into a ball and then into a 15 × 7.5cm/6 × 3in rectangle. Fold the bottom third up lengthways and the top third down and press down. Seal the edges. Repeat two or three more times until each loaf is an oblong. Leave to rest for a few minutes between foldings.

4 Stretch each piece of dough into a 35cm/14in long loaf. Pleat a floured dish towel on a baking sheet to make three moulds for the loaves. Place the loaves between the pleats, cover with lightly oiled clear film and leave to rise for 45–60 minutes.

5 Preheat the oven to maximum. Roll the loaves on to a baking sheet, spaced apart. Slash the top of each diagonally several times. Place at the top of the oven, spray the inside of the oven with water and bake for 20–25 minutes. Spray the oven twice during the first 5 minutes of baking. Allow to cool.

Breadsticks

If you prefer, you could use other seeds, such as poppy seeds, in these sticks.

Makes 18–20
15ml/1 tbsp active dried yeast
300ml/½ pint/1¼ cups lukewarm water
425g/15oz/3⅔ cups strong white bread flour
10ml/2 tsp salt
5ml/1 tsp caster (superfine) sugar
30ml/2 tbsp olive oil
1 egg, beaten, to glaze
150g/5oz/10 tbsp sesame seeds, toasted
coarse salt, for sprinkling

1 Combine the yeast and water in a small bowl, stir and leave for about 15 minutes for the yeast to dissolve and become frothy.

2 Place the flour, salt, sugar and olive oil in a food processor. With the motor running, slowly pour in the yeast mixture and process until the dough forms a ball. Alternatively, use your hand to incorporate the liquid into the flour.

3 Knead until smooth. This will take about 10 minutes. Place in a bowl, cover with clear film (plastic wrap) and leave to rise in a warm place for 45 minutes. Grease two baking sheets.

4 Roll the dough into 18–20 30cm/12in sticks. Place on the baking sheets, brush with the egg glaze then sprinkle with toasted sesame seeds and coarse salt. Leave to rise, uncovered, for 20 minutes.

5 Preheat the oven to 200°C/400°F/Gas 6. Bake until golden, about 15 minutes. Turn off the heat but leave in the oven for a further 5 minutes. Serve warm or cool.

Variation
For Rye and Caraway Breadsticks, substitute 200g/7oz/scant 2 cups rye flour for 200g/7oz/scant 2 cups of the strong white bread flour. Sprinkle with caraway seeds instead of sesame seeds.

French Baguettes Energy 233kcal/991kJ; Protein 6.4g; Carbohydrate 53.1g, of which sugars 1g; Fat 0.9g, of which saturates 0.1g; Cholesterol 0mg; Calcium 96mg; Fibre 2.1g; Sodium 439mg.

Breadsticks Energy 128kcal/538kJ; Protein 3.4g; Carbohydrate 16.8g, of which sugars 0.6g; Fat 5.7g, of which saturates 0.8g; Cholesterol 0mg; Calcium 80mg; Fibre 1.3g; Sodium 199mg.

Multi-seed Loaf

This round multi-seeded loaf with a twisted top comes from Spain. The olive oil gives a soft crumb, and the millet and seeds provide an interesting mix of textures.

Makes 1

350g/12oz/3 cups unbleached strong white bread flour
115g/4oz/1 cup wholemeal (whole-wheat) bread flour
10ml/2 tsp salt
20g/¾oz fresh yeast
275ml/9fl oz/generous 1 cup lukewarm water
30ml/2 tbsp olive oil
30ml/2 tbsp pumpkin seeds
30ml/2 tbsp sunflower seeds
15ml/1 tbsp millet
cornmeal, for dusting

1 Sprinkle a baking sheet with cornmeal. Mix the flours and salt together in a large bowl and make a well in the centre.

2 Mix the yeast with the water and add to the well with the olive oil and mix to a firm dough. Turn out on to a lightly floured surface and knead for about 10 minutes until smooth and elastic. Place in a lightly oiled bowl, then cover with lightly oiled clear film (plastic wrap) and leave in a warm place, for about 1½–2 hours, or until doubled in bulk.

3 Knock back (punch down) the dough and turn out on to a floured surface. Gently knead in the seeds and millet. Re-cover and leave to rest for 5 minutes, then shape into a ball, twisting the centre to make a cap. Transfer to the prepared baking sheet and dust with cornmeal. Cover with an upturned bowl and leave in a warm place, for 45 minutes, or until doubled in bulk.

4 Meanwhile, place an empty roasting pan in the bottom of the oven. Preheat the oven to 220°C/425°F/Gas 7. Pour about 300ml/½ pint/1¼ cups water into the pan. Lift the bowl off the risen loaf and immediately place the baking sheet in the oven, above the roasting pan. Bake the bread for 10 minutes.

5 Remove the pan of water and bake the bread for a further 25–30 minutes, or until well browned and sounding hollow when tapped on the base. Transfer to a wire rack to cool.

Seeded Bloomer

This long, crusty loaf gets its fabulous flavour from the mixed seeds. Brushing with salted water before baking helps to give it a crisp finish. When cut into thick slices, it is perfect for mopping up the cooking juices of hearty stews, or for absorbing good dressing on summery salads.

Makes 1

675g/1½lb/6 cups unbleached strong white bread flour
12.5ml/2½ tsp salt
450ml/¾ pint/scant 2 cups lukewarm water
15g/½oz fresh yeast
45ml/3 tbsp seeds, for sprinkling (see Cook's Tip)
30ml/2 tbsp olive oil

1 Lightly grease a baking sheet. Sift the flour and 10ml/2 tsp salt into a large bowl and make a well in the centre.

2 Stir a third of the lukewarm water into the yeast. Add in the remaining water and pour into the flour well. Mix, gradually incorporating the flour, to a firm dough.

3 Turn out on to a lightly floured surface and knead the dough for at least 10 minutes, until smooth and elastic. Place in a lightly oiled bowl, cover with clear film (plastic wrap) and leave to rise, at cool room temperature (about 15–18°C/60–65°F), for 5–6 hours, or until doubled in bulk.

4 Knock back (punch down) the dough, turn out on to a lightly floured surface and knead it thoroughly for about 5 minutes. Return the dough to the bowl and re-cover. Leave to rise, at cool room temperature, for a further 2 hours or slightly longer.

5 Knock back again and repeat the kneading. Leave to rest for 5 minutes, then roll out on a lightly floured surface into a rectangle 2.5cm/1in thick. Roll the dough up from a long side. Shape it into a thick baton about 33 × 13cm/13 × 5in.

6 Place the loaf, seam side up, on a lightly floured baking sheet. Cover with lightly oiled clear film and leave to rest for 15 minutes. Turn the loaf over and place on the greased baking sheet. Plump the loaf up by tucking the dough under the sides and ends. Using a sharp knife, cut six diagonal slashes on the top.

7 Leave to rest, covered, in a warm place, for 10 minutes. Meanwhile, preheat the oven to 230°C/450°F/Gas 8.

8 Mix the remaining salt with 30ml/2 tbsp water and brush this glaze over the bread. Sprinkle with the seeds.

9 Spray the oven with water, bake the bread immediately for 20 minutes, then reduce the oven temperature to 200°C/400°F/Gas 6. Bake for 25 minutes more, or until golden and it sounds hollow when tapped on the base. Cool on a wire rack.

Cook's Tip
A variety of seeds can be used to add flavour, colour and texture to this loaf – sunflower, pumpkin, sesame and poppy seeds are all good to use in varying quantites.

Multi-seed Loaf per loaf Energy 1668kcal/7038kJ; Protein 47g; Carbohydrate 276.1g, of which sugars 6.9g; Fat 49.1g, of which saturates 6g; Cholesterol 0mg; Calcium 443mg; Fibre 20.8g; Sodium 12mg.
Seeded Bloomer per loaf Energy 2302kcal/9787kJ; Protein 63.5g; Carbohydrate 524.5g, of which sugars 10.1g; Fat 8.8g, of which saturates 1.3g; Cholesterol 0mg; Calcium 946mg; Fibre 20.9g; Sodium 3950mg.

Wholemeal Seed Loaf

This seeded loaf looks rustic and is great for picnics and other *al fresco* meals.

Makes 4

20g/ 3/4oz fresh yeast
300ml/1/2 pint/1 1/4 cups lukewarm milk
5ml/1 tsp caster (superfine) sugar
225g/8oz/2 cups wholemeal (whole-wheat) bread flour
225g/8oz/2 cups unbleached white bread flour, plus extra for dusting
5ml/1 tsp salt
50g/2oz/ 1/4 cup chilled butter, cubed
1 egg, lightly beaten
30ml/2 tbsp mixed seeds

1 Mash the yeast with a little of the milk and the sugar until it dissolves to make a paste. Sift both types of flour and the salt into a large warmed mixing bowl. Rub in the butter until the mixture resembles breadcrumbs.

2 Add the yeast mixture, remaining milk and egg and mix into a fairly soft dough. Knead on a floured surface for 15 minutes. Place in a lightly oiled bowl, cover with lightly oiled clear film (plastic wrap) and leave to rise in a warm place for at least 1 hour, until doubled in bulk.

3 Knock back the dough and knead it for 10 minutes. Divide the dough into four pieces and shape them into flattish rounds. Place them on a floured baking sheet and leave to rise for about 15 minutes more.

4 Preheat the oven to 200°C/400°F/Gas 6. Sprinkle the loaves with the mixed seeds. Bake for about 20 minutes, until golden and firm. Cool on wire racks.

Cook's Tip

15g/½oz fresh yeast is the equivalent of 15ml/1 tbsp dried. It must always be crumbled into a bowl and then mashed with a little lukewarm liquid before adding to the dry ingredients.

White Bloomer with Poppy Seeds

The slightly nutty flavour of the poppy seeds adds to the flavour of this versatile bread. It is a great slicer, excellent for making sandwiches or chunky toast. For a delicious snack, try ham, tomatoes and hot mustard between two thick slices.

Makes 1

10g/1/4oz fresh yeast
275ml/10fl oz/1 cup lukewarm water
450g/1lb/4 cups strong white bread flour
5ml/1 tsp salt
1 egg, beaten
45ml/3 tbsp poppy seeds

1 In a small bowl, dissolve the yeast in the lukewarm water. Sift the flour and salt into a large bowl, stir in the yeast and water mixture and mix to a soft dough. Turn the dough on to a clean work surface and knead it for about 10 minutes, until smooth, silky and elastic.

2 Place the dough back into the bowl, cover with clear film (plastic wrap) and leave in a warm place to rise for 60 minutes.

3 Turn the dough on to the work surface and shape tightly into a round-ended loaf shape. Cover, and leave it to prove in a warm place for another 30–45 minutes.

4 When the loaf has doubled in size, brush the surface with beaten egg, sprinkle over the poppy seeds and with a sharp knife make diagonal slashes about 2.5cm/1in apart.

5 Meanwhile preheat the over to 220°C/425°F/Gas 7.

6 Sprinkle plenty of flour on to a baking tin (pan), and transfer the loaf on to it. Place the loaf on the bottom of the oven. Bake with the door closed for 25–35 minutes, until golden brown, crusty and cooked through.

7 Use oven gloves to turn the loaf over and tap the base of the loaf; if cooked it should sound hollow. Leave to cool completely on a wire rack before slicing.

Wholemeal Seed Loaf per loaf Energy 563kcal/2371kJ; Protein 18.9g; Carbohydrate 84.9g, of which sugars 5.9g; Fat 18.7g, of which saturates 8.6g; Cholesterol 90mg; Calcium 203mg; Fibre 9.7g; Sodium 630mg.

White Bloomer with Poppy Seeds per loaf Energy 1629kcal/6925kJ; Protein 68g; Carbohydrate 339g, of which sugars 6g; Fat 30g, of which saturates 5g; Cholesterol 232mg; Calcium 1237mg; Fibre 17.3g; Sodium 4431mg.

Three-grain Bread

A mixture of grain flours and seed gives this bread a delightful nutty flavour.

Makes 1

225g/8oz/2 cups strong white bread flour
7.5ml/1 1/2 tsp salt
225g/8oz/2 cups malted brown flour
225g/8oz/2 cups rye flour
75g/3oz/ 1/2 cup medium oatmeal
7g/1/4oz easy-blend (rapid-rise) dried yeast
45ml/3 tbsp sunflower seeds
30ml/2 tbsp linseeds
475ml/16fl oz/2 cups lukewarm water
30ml/2 tbsp malt extract

1 Sift the strong white bread flour and salt into a mixing bowl and add the remaining flours, oatmeal, yeast and sunflower seeds. Set aside 5ml/1 tsp of the linseeds and add the rest to the flour mixture. Make a well in the centre.

2 Add the water to the bowl with the malt extract. Gradually incorporate the flour and mix to a soft dough, adding extra water if necessary.

3 Flour a baking sheet. Turn the dough on to a floured surface and knead for 5 minutes, or until smooth and elastic.

4 Divide the dough in half. Roll each half into a sausage about 30cm/12in in length. Twist the two pieces together, dampen each end and press together firmly.

5 Lift the loaf on to the prepared baking sheet. Brush with water, sprinkle with the remaining linseeds and cover loosely with clear film (plastic wrap), ballooning it to trap the air inside. Leave in a warm place until doubled in size, about 1½ hours. Meanwhile, preheat the oven to 220°C/425°F/Gas 7.

6 Bake the bread for 10 minutes, then lower the oven temperature to 200°C/400°F/Gas 6 and cook for 20 minutes more, or until the loaf sounds hollow when tapped underneath.

7 Transfer the cooked loaf to a wire rack to cool completely.

Multi-seeded Wholemeal & Spelt Loaf with Honey

Spelt makes the texture of this loaf cakier than regular bread, but it is more easily digested than wheat flour. Try serving it simply with butter and honey.

Makes 2

200g/7oz mixed seeds (pumpkin, sunflower, sesame and poppy)
450g/1lb/4 cups strong wholemeal (whole-wheat) bread flour
450g/1lb/4 cups strong spelt bread flour, brown or white
7.5ml/1½ tsp salt
15g/½oz fresh yeast
600ml/1 pint/2½ cups warm water
30ml/2 tbsp runny honey

1 Roughly break up the seeds with a mortar and pestle, or whizz briefly in a food processor or blender.

2 In a large bowl, mix together the flours and seeds with the salt and yeast. Add the water and the honey and mix to make a soft dough.

3 Transfer the dough to a floured board and knead for about 10 minutes, until smooth and shiny. Leave to rise covered with clear film (plastic wrap) in a clean bowl in a warm place for 2–3 hours, until roughly doubled in size.

4 Divide the dough in half and shape to fit into two 23cm/9in round loaf tins (pans). Leave to rise in a warm place covered with a dish towel for about 1 hour. When risen, slash the top of the loaves with a sharp knife.

5 Preheat the oven to 220°C/425°F/Gas 7. Place the loaf tins in the oven and bake for 30–40 minutes.

6 Take the loaf tins out of the oven and turn a loaf of bread out. If it sounds hollow when it is tapped, they are cooked. If not, put them back in the oven, close the door and bake until they do sound hollow. Cool on a wire rack and serve with butter and honey.

Three-grain Bread per loaf Energy 3098kcal/13139kJ; Protein 95.8g; Carbohydrate 586.8g, of which sugars 31.1g; Fat 57.3g, of which saturates 7.9g; Cholesterol 0mg; Calcium 978mg; Fibre 77.2g; Sodium 3001mg.

Multi-seeded Wholemeal and Spelt Loaf per loaf Energy 2081kcal/8792kJ; Protein 80g; Carbohydrate 340g, of which sugars 20g; Fat 54g, of which saturates 8g; Cholesterol 0mg; Calcium 442mg; Fibre 28.1g; Sodium 526mg.

Sesame Seed Bread

This delicious bread with a nutty flavour breaks into individual rolls, making it ideal for sharing.

Makes 1

10ml/2 tsp active dried yeast
300ml/½ pint/1¼ cups lukewarm water
200g/7oz/1¾ cups strong white bread flour
200g/7oz/scant 1¾ cups strong wholemeal (whole-wheat) bread flour
10ml/2 tsp salt
65g/2½oz/5 tbsp toasted sesame seeds
milk, to glaze
30ml/2 tbsp sesame seeds, for sprinkling

1 Combine the yeast and 75ml/5 tbsp of the water in a small bowl and leave to dissolve and for the yeast to become frothy.

2 Mix the flours and salt in a large bowl. Make a central well in the flour and pour in the yeast and water. Stir from the centre to obtain a rough dough.

3 Transfer to a floured surface and knead until smooth and elastic. This will take about 10 minutes. Return to the bowl and cover with clear film (plastic wrap). Leave in a warm place until the dough has doubled in size, about 1½–2 hours.

4 Grease a 23cm/9in round cake tin (pan). Knock back (punch down) the dough and knead in the sesame seeds.

5 Divide the dough into 16 balls and place in the tin. Cover with clear film (plastic wrap) and leave in a warm place until risen above the rim, about 1½ hours.

6 Preheat the oven to 220°C/425°F/Gas 7. Brush the loaf with milk and sprinkle with the sesame seeds. Bake for 15 minutes. Lower the heat to 190°C/375°F/Gas 5 and bake until the base sounds hollow when tapped, about 30 minutes. Turn the loaf out on a wire rack and leave to cool before breaking into individual rolls and serving.

Pain Bouillie

This is an old-fashioned style of rye bread. Rye flour is mixed with boiling water and left overnight to ferment.

Makes 2

For the porridge
225g/8oz/2 cups rye flour
450ml/¾ pint/1¾ cups boiling water
5ml/1 tsp clear honey

For the dough
7g/¼oz fresh yeast
30ml/2 tbsp lukewarm water
5ml/1 tsp caraway seeds, crushed
10ml/2 tsp salt
350g/12oz/3 cups unbleached strong white bread flour
olive oil, for brushing

1 Lightly grease a 23.5 × 13cm/9¼ × 5in loaf tin (pan). Place the rye flour for the porridge in a large bowl. Pour over the boiling water and leave to stand for 5 minutes. Stir in the honey. Cover with clear film (plastic wrap) and leave for 12 hours.

2 Make the dough. Put the yeast in a measuring jug (cup) and blend in the water. Stir the mixture into the porridge with the caraway seeds and salt. Add the flour a little at a time, until the mixture forms a firm dough. Turn out on to a lightly floured surface and knead for 6–8 minutes until smooth. Return to the bowl, cover with lightly oiled clear film (plastic wrap) and leave to rise, in a warm place, for 1½ hours, or until doubled in size.

3 Knock back (punch down) on a floured surface. Cut into two pieces and roll each piece into a rectangle 38 × 12cm/15 × 4½in. Fold the bottom third up and the top third down and seal the edges. Turn over. Brush one side of each piece of folded dough with olive oil and place side by side in the prepared tin, oiled edges next to each other. Cover and leave to rise for 1 hour, until the dough reaches the top of the tin.

4 Meanwhile, preheat the oven to 220°C/425°F/Gas 7. Brush the tops of the loaves with olive oil, and using a sharp knife, slash with one or two cuts. Bake for 30 minutes, then reduce the oven temperature to 190°C/375°F/Gas 5 and bake for a further 25–30 minutes. Turn out on to a wire rack to cool.

Sesame Seed Bread per loaf Energy 1691kcal/7142kJ; Protein 56g; Carbohydrate 283.8g, of which sugars 7.5g; Fat 44.7g, of which saturates 6.4g; Cholesterol 0mg; Calcium 793mg; Fibre 29.3g; Sodium 3955mg.

Pain Bouillie per loaf Energy 996kcal/4235kJ; Protein 26.4g; Carbohydrate 225g, of which sugars 4.6g; Fat 5.2g, of which saturates 0.8g; Cholesterol 0mg; Calcium 291mg; Fibre 18.6g; Sodium 1974mg.

Clay Pot Seeded Loaf

You can bake a bread dough in a clean, new flowerpot which gives the bread a distinctive thick crust.

Makes 2

225g/8oz/2 cups strong wholemeal (whole-wheat) bread flour
225g/8oz/2 cups strong white bread flour
5ml/1 tsp salt
10g/⅓oz fresh yeast
15ml/1 tbsp runny honey
270ml/9½fl oz/generous 1 cup warm water
50g/2oz mixed seeds (pumpkin, sunflower, sesame and poppy)

1 Put the flours and the salt into a large mixing bowl and crumble the yeast over the top. Stir the honey into the warm water, pour over the flour mixture and mix together. Turn the dough on to a clean work surface and knead vigorously for 10 minutes, until smooth, shiny and elastic.

2 Put the dough in a bowl, cover with clear film (plastic wrap) and leave to rise for 1–2 hours until doubled in size.

3 Sprinkle the seeds on to the work surface and turn the dough on top. Knead the seeds into the dough. Divide into two balls to fit into two seasoned clay plant pots (see Cook's Tip).

4 Cover the pots with a clean dish towel, and when the dough has reached the rim, sprinkle with a little more flour and mixed seeds. Make slashes in the top of the dough with a sharp knife.

5 Place the pots on the base of the oven and bake for 20–25 minutes at 220°C/425°F/Gas 7. Stand for 5 minutes before turning out and cooling completely on a wire rack.

Cook's Tip
To season the pots, brush with sunflower oil on the inside and around the rim. Put in the oven when it is cold and heat until the temperature reaches 200°C/400°F/Gas 6, then leave to cool down. Oil and heat the pots twice more.

Seeded Nutty Spelt Bread

A mixture of quinoa and spelt flour is used to make this rustic breakfast loaf. Serve buttered with your favourite jam or marmalade.

Makes 1

225g/8oz/2 cups quinoa flour
225g/8oz/2 cups spelt flour
10ml/2 tsp easy-blend (rapid-rise) dried yeast
10ml/2 tsp salt
60ml/4 tbsp sugar
25g/1oz/¼ cup mixed seeds (sunflower, pumpkin, flax and poppy), plus 15ml/1 tbsp extra, for sprinkling
25g/1oz/¼ cup nuts (such as walnuts or hazelnuts), roughly chopped
300ml/½ pint/1¼ cups lukewarm water
oil, for greasing
milk, to glaze

1 Sift the flours into a bowl, add the yeast, salt, sugar, mixed seeds and nuts, and stir to combine. Make a well in the centre. Pour the lukewarm water into the well, and stir to a dough.

2 Transfer the dough to a floured board, and knead for 6–8 minutes. Place the dough in a clean bowl, cover and leave in a warm place for 1–1½ hours, until doubled in size.

3 Knock back (punch down) the dough and knead for a couple of minutes. Cover with the damp cloth again and set aside to prove for another 30 minutes, until doubled in size. Preheat the oven to 220°C/425°F/Gas 7.

4 Oil a 450g/1lb loaf tin (pan), or a baking sheet. Shape the dough to neatly fill the tin, or if using the baking sheet, split it into three strands and braid it for a more decorative loaf.

5 Score the top of the loaf with a sharp knife lengthways and across, to help the dough rise. Brush the top with milk and sprinkle the top with seeds.

6 Bake for 35–40 minutes, until the loaf is risen and golden, and sounds hollow on the base when tapped.

7 Remove from the tin or baking tray, and cool on a wire rack.

Clay Pot Seeded Loaf per loaf Energy 933kcal/3951kJ; Protein 36g; Carbohydrate 167g, of which sugars 10g; Fat 18g, of which saturates 3g; Cholesterol 0mg; Calcium 217mg; Fibre 14.8g; Sodium 998mg.

Seeded Nutty Spelt Bread Energy 277kcal/1173kJ; Protein 21g; Carbohydrate 42g, of which sugars 8g; Fat 5g, of which saturates 2g; Cholesterol 0mg; Calcium 82mg; Fibre 3g; Sodium 3mg.

Caraway Rye Bread

To bring out the flavour of the caraway seeds, toast them lightly in the oven first, if you like.

Makes 1

200g/7oz/scant 1¾ cups rye flour
475ml/16fl oz/2 cups boiling water
120ml/4fl oz/½ cup black treacle (molasses)
65g/2½oz/5 tbsp butter, cut into pieces
15ml/1 tbsp salt
30ml/2 tbsp caraway seeds
15ml/1 tbsp active dried yeast
120ml/4fl oz/½ cup lukewarm water
about 850g/1lb 14oz/7½ cups strong white bread flour
semolina or flour, for dusting

1 Mix the rye flour, boiling water, treacle, butter, salt and caraway seeds in a large bowl. Leave to cool.

2 In another bowl, mix the yeast and lukewarm water and leave to dissolve and for the yeast to become frothy.

3 Stir into the rye flour mixture. Stir in just enough strong white bread flour to obtain a stiff dough. If it becomes too stiff to mix with the spoon, stir with your hands. Transfer to a floured surface and knead until the dough is no longer sticky and is smooth and shiny. This will take about 10 minutes.

4 Place in a greased bowl, cover with clear film (plastic wrap), and leave in a warm place until doubled in volume, about 1½ hours.

5 Knock back (punch down) the dough, cover, and leave to rise again for 30 minutes.

6 Preheat the oven to 180°C/350°F/Gas 4. Dust a baking sheet with semolina or flour.

7 Shape the dough into a ball. Place on the sheet and score several times across the top. Bake until the base sounds hollow when tapped, about 40 minutes. Cool on a wire rack.

Walnut Bread

This rich bread could be served at a dinner party with soup or the cheese course, or with a rustic ploughman's lunch.

Makes 1

420g/15oz/3⅔ cups strong wholemeal (whole-wheat) bread flour
150g/5oz/1¼ cups strong white bread flour
12.5ml/2½ tsp salt
550ml/18fl oz/2¼ cups lukewarm water
15ml/1 tbsp clear honey
15ml/1 tbsp active dried yeast
150g/5oz/1 cup walnut pieces, plus more to decorate
1 beaten egg, to glaze

1 Combine the wholemeal and white flours and salt in a large bowl. Make a well in the centre and add 250ml/8fl oz/1 cup of the water, the honey and the yeast. Set aside until the yeast dissolves and becomes frothy.

2 Add the remaining water. With a wooden spoon, stir from the centre, incorporating flour with each turn, to obtain a smooth dough. Add more flour if the dough is too sticky and use your hands if the dough becomes too stiff to stir.

3 Transfer to a floured board and knead, adding flour if necessary, until the dough is smooth and elastic. This will take about 10 minutes. Place in a greased bowl and roll the dough around in the bowl to coat thoroughly on all sides. Cover with clear film (plastic wrap) and leave in a warm place until doubled in size, about 1½ hours. Knock back (punch down) the dough and knead in the walnuts evenly.

4 Grease a baking sheet. Shape the dough into a round loaf and place on the baking sheet. Press in walnut pieces to decorate the top. Cover loosely with a damp cloth or clear film and leave to rise in a warm place until doubled in size, 25–30 minutes.

5 Preheat the oven to 220°C/425°F/Gas 7. With a sharp knife, score the top of the loaf. Brush with the egg glaze. Bake for 15 minutes. Lower the heat to 190°C/375°F/Gas 5 and bake until the base sounds hollow when tapped, about 40 minutes.

Caraway Rye Bread per loaf Energy 4386kcal/18592kJ; Protein 109.4g; Carbohydrate 893.8g, of which sugars 93.3g; Fat 73.1g, of which saturates 36.3g; Cholesterol 139mg; Calcium 2224mg; Fibre 66.3g; Sodium 6545mg.

Walnut Bread per loaf Energy 2786kcal/11722kJ; Protein 87.1g; Carbohydrate 393.2g, of which sugars 26g; Fat 107g, of which saturates 9.4g; Cholesterol 0mg; Calcium 489mg; Fibre 47g; Sodium 4941mg.

Pecan Nut Rye Bread

This is a tasty homespun loaf that recalls the old folk-cooking traditions of the United States.

Makes 2

25ml/1½ tbsp active dried yeast
700ml/22fl oz/2¾ cups lukewarm water
675g/1½lb/6 cups strong white bread flour
500g/1¼lb/5 cups rye flour
30ml/2 tbsp salt
15ml/1 tbsp clear honey
10ml/2 tsp caraway seeds, (optional)
115g/4oz/½ cup butter, at room temperature
225g/8oz pecan nuts, chopped

1 Combine the yeast and 120ml/4fl oz/½ cup of the water. Stir and leave for 15 minutes for the yeast to dissolve entirely and become frothy.

2 In the bowl of an electric mixer, combine the white and rye flours, salt, honey, caraway seeds and butter. With the dough hook, mix on low speed until well blended. Alternatively, use your hands to incorporate the liquid into the flour.

3 Add the yeast mixture and the remaining water and mix on medium speed, or use your hands, until the dough forms a ball. Transfer to a floured surface and knead in the chopped pecan nuts.

4 Return the dough to the bowl, cover with clear film (plastic wrap) and leave in a warm place until doubled, about 2 hours.

5 Grease two 21 × 11cm/8½ × 4½in loaf tins (pans). Knock back (punch down) the risen dough.

6 Divide the dough in half and form into two loaves. Place in the tins, seam sides down. Dust the tops with flour. Cover with oiled clear film and leave to rise in a warm place until doubled in volume, about 1 hour.

7 Preheat the oven to 190°C/375°F/Gas 5. Bake until the bases sound hollow when tapped, 45–50 minutes. Transfer to wire racks to cool completely.

Pain aux Noix

This delicious wholemeal bread is filled with walnuts.

Makes 2

50g/2oz/¼ cup butter
350g/12oz/3 cups wholemeal (whole-wheat) bread flour
115g/4oz/1 cup unbleached strong white bread flour
15ml/1 tbsp light muscovado (brown) sugar
7.5ml/1½ tsp salt
20g/¾oz fresh yeast
275ml/9fl oz/generous 1 cup lukewarm milk
175g/6oz/1½ cups walnut pieces

1 Lightly grease two baking sheets. Place the butter in a small pan and heat until melted and starting to turn brown, then set aside to cool. Mix the flours, sugar and salt in a large bowl and make a well in the centre. Cream the yeast with half the milk. Add to the centre of the flour with the remaining milk.

2 Pour the cool melted butter through a fine strainer into the centre of the flour so that it joins the liquids already there. Using your hand, mix the liquids together in the bowl and gradually mix in small quantities of the flour to make a batter. Continue until the mixture forms a moist dough.

3 Knead on a lightly floured surface for 6–8 minutes. Place in a lightly oiled bowl, cover with lightly oiled clear film (plastic wrap) and leave in a warm place, for 1 hour, or until doubled in size.

4 Turn out the dough on to a lightly floured surface and gently knock back (punch down). Roll out to flatten and then sprinkle over the nuts. Press the nuts into the dough, then roll it up. Return to the bowl, cover and leave for 30 minutes.

5 Turn out on to a lightly floured surface, divide in half and shape each piece into a ball. Place on the baking sheets, cover and leave to rise for 45 minutes, or until doubled in size.

6 Using a sharp knife, slash the top of each loaf three times. Bake for 35 minutes at 220°C/425°F/Gas 7, until the loaves sound hollow when tapped on the base. Cool on a wire rack.

Pecan Nut Rye Bread per loaf Energy 3213kcal/13513kJ; Protein 63g; Carbohydrate 464.6g, of which sugars 16g; Fat 135.5g, of which saturates 37.8g; Cholesterol 123mg; Calcium 633mg; Fibre 45g; Sodium 4293mg.

Pain aux Noix per loaf Energy 1618kcal/6775kJ; Protein 45.2g; Carbohydrate 174.1g, of which sugars 21.5g; Fat 87.3g, of which saturates 20.4g; Cholesterol 66mg; Calcium 403mg; Fibre 20.6g; Sodium 1751mg.

Norwegian Birthday Bread

This bread is presented fresh from the oven in the morning.

Makes 1

300ml/½ pint/1¼ cups milk
7g/¼oz active dried yeast
1 egg plus 1 egg yolk
30ml/2 tbsp sugar
450g/1lb/4 cups plain (all purpose) flour
225g/8oz/1 cup butter

For the filling

115g/4oz/1 cup ground almonds
115g/4oz/1 cup icing (confectioners') sugar
2 egg whites, lightly beaten

To glaze

1 egg yolk
15ml/1 tbsp milk
coarse sugar

1 Line a baking sheet with baking parchment. To make the filling, put the ground almonds and the icing sugar in a bowl, then add enough egg white to make a soft marzipan.

2 In a pan, bring the milk to just below boiling point then pour into a bowl and leave until lukewarm. Add the yeast and leave for 15 minutes until frothy. Add the egg and egg yolk, sugar and flour and mix to make a stiff dough.

3 Roll out the dough into a rectangle, three times as long as it is wide. Cut the cold butter into thin slices and cover the bottom two-thirds of the dough. Fold the top third over the middle and then fold on to the bottom third. Turn and roll out again to the same size rectangle. Fold again into three and roll out into a rectangle measuring 20 × 75cm/8 × 30in.

4 Spread the filling down the centre of the length of the dough, then fold each side over making a tube. Place on the baking sheet and bend the dough into a wreath. Cover loosely with clear film (plastic wrap) and put in the refrigerator overnight.

5 Preheat the oven to 230°C/450°F/Gas 8. Meanwhile, take the wreath out of the refrigerator. Beat together the egg yolk and milk and brush over the wreath. Sprinkle coarse sugar over the top. Lower the oven temperature to 220°C/425°F/Gas 7 and bake for 20 minutes until golden brown. Cool on a wire rack.

Polenta & Pepper Bread

Full of Mediterranean flavours, this satisfying sunshine-coloured bread is best eaten while it is still warm, drizzled with a little virgin olive oil.

Makes 2

175g/6oz/scant 1½ cups polenta
5ml/1 tsp salt
350g/12oz/3 cups unbleached white bread flour, plus extra for dusting
5ml/1 tsp sugar
7g/¼ oz easy-blend (rapid-rise) dried yeast
1 red (bell) pepper, roasted, peeled and diced
300ml/½ pint/1¼ cups lukewarm water
15ml/1 tbsp olive oil

1 Mix the polenta, salt, flour, sugar and yeast in a large bowl. Stir in the diced red pepper until it is evenly distributed, then make a well in the centre of the mixture. Grease two loaf tins (pans).

2 Add the warm water and the oil to the well in the dry ingredients and mix to a soft dough. Knead for 10 minutes. Place in an oiled bowl, cover and leave in a warm place to rise for 1 hour, until doubled in bulk.

3 Knock back the dough, knead it lightly, then divide it in half. Shape each piece into an oblong and place in a tin. Cover with oiled clear film (plastic wrap) and leave to rise for 45 minutes. Preheat the oven to 220°C/425°F/Gas 7.

4 Bake for 30 minutes, until golden and the loaves sound hollow when tapped underneath. Leave in the tins for about 5 minutes, then cool on a wire rack.

Cook's Tip

Grill the (bell) pepper until blistered and beginning to char, then place in a bowl, cover with kitchen paper and set aside until cool enough to peel.

Norwegian Birthday Bread Per loaf Energy 4779kcal/20001kJ; Protein 93.7g; Carbohydrate 524.6g, of which sugars 178.6g; Fat 271.1g, of which saturates 129.5g; Cholesterol 889mg; Calcium 1438mg; Fibre 22.5g; Sodium 1731mg.

Polenta and Pepper Bread per loaf Energy 1994kcal/8427kJ; Protein 50.5g; Carbohydrate 366.9g, of which sugars 7.1g; Fat 44.7g, of which saturates 15.1g; Cholesterol 53mg; Calcium 1085mg; Fibre 14.9g; Sodium 2337mg.

Spicy Buttermilk Corn Bread

An interesting variation on basic corn bread; adjust the number of chillies used according to taste.

Makes 1

3 or 4 whole canned chillies, drained
2 eggs
475ml/16fl oz/2 cups buttermilk
50g/2oz/¼ cup butter, melted
50g/2oz/½ cup plain (all-purpose) flour
5ml/1 tsp bicarbonate of soda (baking soda)
10ml/2 tsp salt
175g/6oz/scant 1½ cups cornmeal or polenta
350g/12oz/2½ cups canned corn or frozen corn, thawed

1 Preheat the oven to 200°C/400°F/Gas 6. Line the base and sides of a 23cm/9in square cake tin (pan) with baking parchment and lightly grease the paper.

2 With a sharp knife, finely chop the canned chillies and set aside until needed.

3 In a large bowl, whisk the eggs until frothy, then whisk in the buttermilk. Add the melted butter.

4 Sift the flour, bicarbonate of soda and salt together into another large bowl. Fold the dry ingredients into the buttermilk mixture in three batches, then fold in the cornmeal or polenta in three batches. Finally, fold in the chillies and corn and gently mix to combine thoroughly.

5 Pour the mixture into the tin and bake until a skewer inserted in the centre comes out clean; about 25–30 minutes. Leave in the tin for 2–3 minutes before unmoulding. Cut into squares and serve warm.

Cook's Tip

Bicarbonate of soda (baking soda) is used with buttermilk in this and many other recipes because the two together produce carbon dioxide to make the dough rise.

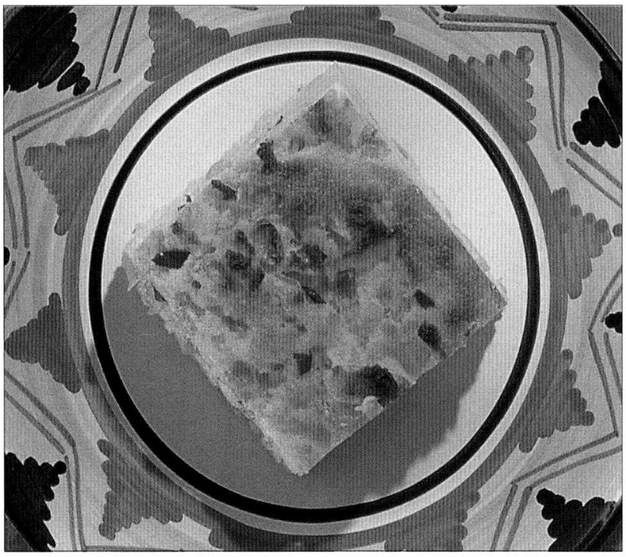

Double Corn Bread

In the American South, corn bread is made with white corn meal and is fairly flat, while in the North it is thicker and made with yellow cornmeal. Whatever the version, it's delicious, and this recipe combines yellow cornmeal with canned corn. It is marvellous served warm, cut into wedges and buttered.

Makes 1

75g/3oz/¾ cup unbleached white bread flour
150g/6oz/1½ cups yellow cornmeal
5ml/1 tsp salt
25ml/1½ tbsp baking powder
15ml/1 tbsp caster (superfine) sugar
50g/2oz/4 tbsp butter, melted
250ml/8fl oz/1 cup milk
3 eggs
200g/7oz/scant 1¼ cups canned corn, drained

1 Preheat the oven to 200°C/400°F/Gas 6. Grease and base line a 22cm/8½in round cake tin (pan). Sift the flour, corn meal, salt and baking powder together into a large bowl. Stir in the sugar and make a well in the centre.

2 Mix the melted butter, milk and eggs together. Add to the centre of the flour mixture and beat until just combined.

3 Using a wooden spoon, stir the canned corn quickly into the mixture. Pour into the prepared tin and bake for 20–25 minutes, or until a metal skewer inserted into the centre comes out clean.

4 Invert the bread on to a wire rack and lift off the lining paper. Cool slightly. Serve warm, cut into wedges.

Variations

• Bake this corn bread in a 20cm/8in square cake tin (pan) instead of a round one if you wish to cut it into squares.
• If you would prefer a more rustic corn bread, replace some or all of the white bread flour with wholemeal (whole-wheat) bread flour.

Spicy Buttermilk Corn Bread per loaf Energy 1888kcal/7915kJ; Protein 65.9g; Carbohydrate 253.5g, of which sugars 35g; Fat 69.9g, of which saturates 32.1g; Cholesterol 578mg; Calcium 745mg; Fibre 14.2g; Sodium 2120mg.

Double Corn Bread per loaf Energy 1818kcal/7623kJ; Protein 54.6g; Carbohydrate 248.9g, of which sugars 48.1g; Fat 70.3g, of which saturates 33.9g; Cholesterol 692mg; Calcium 520mg; Fibre 8.4g; Sodium 1164mg.

Cheese Corn Bread

This corn bread has the delicious addition of cheese.

Makes 1

2 eggs, lightly beaten
250ml/8fl oz/1 cup buttermilk
115g/4oz/1 cup plain (all-purpose) flour
115g/4oz/scant 1 cup cornmeal
10ml/2 tsp baking powder
2.5ml/½ tsp salt
15ml/1 tbsp caster (superfine) sugar
115g/4oz/1 cup grated Cheddar cheese
225g/8oz/1¼ cups corn, fresh or frozen and thawed

1 Preheat the oven to 200°C/400°F/Gas 6. Grease a 23cm/9in square baking tin (pan).

2 Combine the eggs and buttermilk in a small bowl and whisk until well mixed. Set aside.

3 In another bowl, stir together the flour, cornmeal, baking powder, salt and sugar.

4 Add the egg mixture to the dry ingredients and stir with a wooden spoon to combine thoroughly. Stir in the cheese and corn and combine.

5 Pour the mixture into the baking tin. Bake until a skewer inserted in the centre comes out clean, about 25 minutes.

6 Unmould the bread on to a wire rack and leave to cool. Cut into squares before serving.

Cook's Tip

Buttermilk is made from the skimmed milk which is left over after the fat from full cream (whole) milk has been skimmed off to be used for making butter. This skimmed milk is then soured by bacteria to produce buttermilk. Although the results are not quite the same, yogurt is sometimes mixed with sweet (fresh) milk, and works in a similar way to buttermilk.

Cornmeal, Parmesan & Olive Bread

This bread is great served warm with olive oil.

Makes 1–2

350g/12oz/3 cups unbleached strong bread flour
115g/4oz/1 cup yellow cornmeal, plus a little extra
rounded 5ml/1 tsp salt
15g/½oz fresh yeast or 10ml/2 tsp active dried yeast
5ml/1 tsp muscovado (molasses) sugar
270ml/9fl oz/1 cup warm water
5ml/1 tsp chopped fresh thyme
30ml/2 tbsp olive oil
1 onion, finely chopped
75g/3oz/1 cup freshly grated Parmesan cheese
90g/3½oz/scant 1 cup pitted black olives

1 If using fresh yeast, cream it with the sugar and stir in 120ml/4fl oz/½ cup of the warm water. If using dried yeast, stir the sugar into the water, then sprinkle the dried yeast on the surface. Leave in a warm place for 10 minutes, until frothy.

2 Mix the flour, cornmeal and salt, in a warmed bowl. Make a well in the centre and add the yeast liquid and 150ml/¼ pint/⅔ cup of the remaining warm water. Add the thyme and 15ml/1 tbsp of olive oil and mix thoroughly. Add a dash more warm water, if necessary, to make a soft, but not sticky, dough.

3 Knead the dough on a lightly floured work surface for 5 minutes, until smooth and elastic. Place in a lightly oiled bowl and cover with oiled clear film. Set aside to rise in a warm, not hot place for 1–2 hours or until well risen.

4 Fry the onion until soft, not browned. Once they have cooled, knead them, the Parmesan and olives into the dough. Shape the dough into one or two loaves. Sprinkle cornmeal on the work surface and roll the bread in it, then place on an oiled baking sheet. Make slits across the top. Cover with oiled clear film and leave in a warm place for 1 hour, or until risen.

5 Preheat the oven to 200°C/400°F/Gas 6. Bake for 30–35 minutes, or until the bread sounds hollow when tapped on the base. Cool on a wire rack.

Cheese Corn Bread per loaf Energy 1852kcal/7780kJ; Protein 82.6g; Carbohydrate 243.7g, of which sugars 34.5g; Fat 64.2g, of which saturates 30.1g; Cholesterol 579mg; Calcium 1507mg; Fibre 12.6g; Sodium 3308mg.

Cornmeal, Parmesan and Olive Bread Energy 571kcal/2402kJ; Protein 18.7g; Carbohydrate 91.3g, of which sugars 3.2g; Fat 16.2g, of which saturates 5.2g; Cholesterol 19mg; Calcium 367mg; Fibre 4.2g; Sodium 714mg.

Chilli Corn Bread

This golden yellow corn bread spiked with chilli makes an excellent accompaniment to soups and salads.

Makes 1

2 eggs
450ml/¾ pint/1⅞ cups buttermilk
50g/2oz/¼ cup butter, melted
65g/2½oz/½ cup plain (all-purpose) flour
2.5ml/½ tsp ground mace
5ml/1 tsp bicarbonate of soda (baking soda)
10ml/2 tsp salt
250g/9oz/2¼ cups fine cornmeal
2 fresh red chillies, seeded and finely chopped
shredded red chillies and sea salt, to serve

1 Preheat the oven to 200°C/400°F/Gas 6. Grease and line a 23 × 7.5 cm/9 × 3 in loaf tin (pan).

2 In a large bowl, whisk the eggs until frothy, then whisk in the buttermilk and melted butter.

3 Sift the flour, mace, bicarbonate of soda and salt together and gradually stir into the egg mixture. Fold in the cornmeal a little at a time, then stir in the fresh chillies. Pour the mixture into the prepared tin and bake for 25–30 minutes until the top is firm to the touch.

4 Leave the loaf to cool in the tin for a few minutes before turning out. Sprinkle over the red chillies and sea salt.

Variation
For a loaf with a more rustic appearance, use medium or coarse cornmeal.

Cook's Tip
This corn bread is flavoured with ground mace, a spice that comes from the same plant as nutmeg. It has a similar but more delicate flavour and also adds a bright orange colour.

Portuguese Corn Bread

The Portuguese make corn bread with a mixture of cornmeal and white flour. It has a hard crust with a moist crumb.

Makes 1

20g/¾oz fresh yeast
250ml/8fl oz/1 cup lukewarm water
225g/8oz/2 cups cornmeal
450g/1lb/4 cups unbleached white bread flour
150ml/¼ pint/⅔ cup lukewarm milk
30ml/2 tbsp olive oil
7.5ml/1½ tsp salt
polenta, for dusting

1 Dust a baking sheet with a little cornmeal. Put the yeast in a large bowl and gradually mix in the lukewarm water until smooth. Stir in half the cornmeal and 50g/2oz/½ cup of the flour and mix to a batter. Cover the bowl with lightly oiled clear film (plastic wrap) and leave in a warm place for about 30 minutes, or until bubbles appear on the surface.

2 Stir the milk into the batter, then stir in the olive oil. Gradually mix in the remaining cornmeal, flour and salt to form a pliable dough. Turn out on to a lightly floured surface and knead for about 10 minutes until smooth and elastic.

3 Place the dough in a lightly oiled bowl, cover and leave to rise, in a warm place, for 1½–2 hours, or until doubled in size.

4 Turn out the dough on to a lightly floured surface and knock back (punch down). Shape into a round ball, flatten slightly and place on the prepared baking sheet. Dust with polenta, cover with a large upturned bowl and leave in a warm place for about 1 hour, or until doubled in size. Meanwhile, preheat the oven to 230°C/450°F/Gas 8.

5 Bake for 10 minutes, spraying the inside of the oven with water 2–3 times. Reduce the oven temperature to 190°C/375°F/Gas 5 and bake for a further 20–25 minutes, or until golden and hollow sounding when tapped on the base. Transfer to a wire rack to cool.

Chilli Corn Bread Energy 229kcal/959kJ; Protein 6.9g; Carbohydrate 32.8g, of which sugars 4.9g; Fat 8.2g, of which saturates 1.4g; Cholesterol 48mg; Calcium 98mg; Fibre 1g; Sodium 514mg.

Portuguese Corn Bread per loaf Energy 3008kcal/12539kJ; Protein 52.7g; Carbohydrate 303.3g, of which sugars 87.7g; Fat 179.8g, of which saturates 46.1g; Cholesterol 561mg; Calcium 696mg; Fibre 7.4g; Sodium 1672mg.

Spicy Corn Bread with Chives

This hearth bread became popular among settlers in the southern United States because it was so quick to rustle up, and could be cooked on an open fire. Corn bread is often eaten with chilli con carne or Boston baked beans, but you can also serve it for breakfast with crispy bacon, butter and maple syrup.

Makes 1

300g/11oz/2¾ cups plain (all-purpose) flour
240g/8½oz/1¾ cups fine cornmeal
5ml/1 tsp ground cumin
5ml/1 tsp salt
5ml/1 tsp baking powder
450ml/¾ pint/2 cups milk
3 eggs, beaten
115g/4oz/½ cup melted butter, cooled but still liquid
1 fresh red chilli, seeded and very finely chopped
30ml/2 tbsp chopped fresh chives
90g/3½oz grated Gruyère cheese
butter and maple syrup, to serve

1 Preheat the oven to 200°C/400°F/Gas 6. Oil a 23cm/9in ovenproof frying pan or line a round 23cm/9in cake tin (pan) with baking parchment.

2 Sift the flour, cornmeal, cumin, salt and baking powder into a large bowl. Stir in the milk, eggs, butter, chilli and chives. Pour the mixture into the tin or frying pan and sprinkle the cheese on top.

3 Bake in the oven for 20–25 minutes, until golden brown. Take the corn bread out of the oven and test by inserting a skewer, which should come out clean.

4 Put the cake tin or frying pan on a wire rack to cool for a few minutes, then turn out the corn bread. Peel off the baking parchment and serve warm with butter and maple syrup.

Cook's Tip

Any corn bread leftovers can be crumbled and used as a stuffing for a roast chicken.

Moroccan Holiday Bread

The addition of cornmeal and seeds gives this superb loaf an interesting flavour and texture. Serve it with cooked lean sliced meats.

Makes 1

275g/10oz/2½ cups unbleached strong white bread flour
50g/2oz/½ cup cornmeal
5ml/1 tsp salt
20g/¾oz fresh yeast
120ml/4fl oz/½ cup lukewarm water
120ml/4fl oz/½ cup lukewarm semi-skimmed (low-fat) milk
15ml/1 tbsp pumpkin seeds
15ml/1 tbsp sesame seeds
30ml/2 tbsp sunflower seeds

1 Grease a baking sheet and set aside. Mix the flour, cornmeal and salt together in a large bowl and make a well in the centre.

2 Cream the yeast with a little of the water, then stir in the remaining water and the milk. Pour into the well in the flour and mix to form a fairly soft dough.

3 Turn the dough out on to a lightly floured surface and knead for about 5 minutes, or until smooth and elastic. Place the dough in a lightly oiled bowl, cover with lightly oiled clear film (plastic wrap) and leave in a warm place for about 1 hour, or until doubled in bulk.

4 Turn out the dough on to a lightly floured surface and knock back (punch down). Gently knead the pumpkin and sesame seeds into the dough. Shape the dough into a round ball and flatten slightly.

5 Place on the prepared baking sheet, cover with lightly oiled clear film and leave to rise in a warm place for 45 minutes, or until doubled in bulk.

6 Meanwhile, preheat the oven to 200°C/400°F/Gas 6. Brush the top of the loaf with water and sprinkle it evenly with the sunflower seeds. Bake the loaf in the oven for 30–35 minutes, or until it is golden and sounds hollow when tapped on the base. Transfer the loaf to a wire rack to cool. Serve in slices.

Spicy Corn Bread with Chives per loaf Energy 3179kcal/13297kJ; Protein 5g; Carbohydrate 404g, of which sugars 5g; Fat 141g, of which saturates 82g; Cholesterol 346mg; Calcium 1388mg; Fibre 21.7g; Sodium 3899mg.

Moroccan Holiday Bread Energy 241kcal/1017kJ; Protein 7.1g; Carbohydrate 42.7g, of which sugars 1.7g; Fat 5.6g, of which saturates 0.9g; Cholesterol 1mg; Calcium 139mg; Fibre 2.2g; Sodium 339mg.

American-style Corn Sticks

These traditional corn sticks are quick and simple to make, and can be enjoyed simply spread with butter or with jam.

Makes 6

1 egg
120ml/4fl oz/½ cup milk
15ml/1 tbsp vegetable oil
115g/4oz/scant 1 cup cornmeal or polenta
50g/2oz/½ cup plain (all-purpose) flour
10ml/2 tsp baking powder
45ml/3 tbsp caster (superfine) sugar

1 Preheat the oven to 190°C/375°F/Gas 5. Grease a cast-iron corn-stick mould and heat in the oven.

2 Beat the egg in a small bowl. Stir in the milk and vegetable oil, and set aside.

3 In a mixing bowl, stir together the cornmeal or polenta, flour, baking powder and sugar. Pour in the egg mixture and stir with a wooden spoon to combine.

4 Spoon the mixture into the prepared mould. Bake until a skewer inserted in the centre of a corn stick comes out clean, about 25 minutes.

5 Cool the corn sticks in the mould on a wire rack for 10 minutes before unmoulding.

Cook's Tips

- *The traditional way to make corn sticks is in a cast-iron corn-stick mould, which is heated in the oven before the mixture is added. A new mould needs to be seasoned before use. Grease it well with white vegetable fat (shortening) and then heat it in a hot oven for about 20 minutes. After use, wash in warm soapy water and then grease before storing.*
- *If you do not have a corn-stick mould, use éclair tins (pans) instead and reduce the cooking time by 10 minutes.*

Onion Bread

This hearty loaf makes a good accompaniment for grilled fish or meat, and is great as a base for a sandwich. If you want an even more flavourful variation, you can add garlic or fresh chopped herbs.

Makes 1

45ml/3 tbsp oil for frying
2 onions, finely chopped
800g/1¾lb strong white bread flour, plus extra for dusting
5ml/1 tsp sugar
40g/1½oz fresh yeast
500ml/17fl oz/generous 2 cups lukewarm water
salt and ground white pepper

1 Heat the oil in a frying pan over medium heat and fry the onions for 3 minutes until transparent, then remove the pan from the heat and leave to cool.

2 Mix the white bread flour with the sugar in a small bowl. Dissolve the fresh yeast in the water and stir into the flour.

3 Knead the dough for 5 minutes, then cover it and let it rest in a warm place for 20 minutes. Line a baking sheet with baking parchment and preheat the oven to 200°C/400°F/Gas 6.

4 On a floured surface, knead the cooked onion with its oil, salt and pepper into the dough. Shape into a round loaf and put it on the prepared baking sheet. Let it rest for 20–30 minutes until the dough has doubled in size.

5 Put the dough in the oven and bake for about 1 hour, until golden in colour. The bread should feel and sound firm when tapped on the base. Leave the loaf to cool on a wire rack before cutting it.

Cook's Tip

When you are ready to bake the bread, fill a metal container with water and place it in the oven with the bread. The steam that this produces gives the bread a better crust.

American-style Corn Sticks per stick Energy 167kcal/700kJ; Protein 4.4g; Carbohydrate 29.3g, of which sugars 8.9g; Fat 3.8g, of which saturates 0.7g; Cholesterol 33mg; Calcium 45mg; Fibre 0.7g; Sodium 21mg.

Onion Bread per loaf Energy 3184kcal/13487kJ; Protein 80g; Carbohydrate 657.4g, of which sugars 38.6g; Fat 44.2g, of which saturates 5g; Cholesterol 0mg; Calcium 1222mg; Fibre 30.4g; Sodium 36mg

Sun-dried Tomato Braid

This makes a marvellous centrepiece for a summer buffet. If you only have dried tomatoes, soak them in a little boiling water for 15 minutes and add 15ml/1 tbsp oil to the mixture.

Makes 1

225g/8oz/2 cups strong wholemeal (whole-wheat) flour
225g/8oz/2 cups strong white bread flour
5ml/1 tsp salt
1.5ml/¼ tsp ground black pepper
10ml/2 tsp easy-blend (rapid-rise) dried yeast
a pinch of sugar
300ml/½ pint/1¼ cups hand-hot water
115g/4oz/2 cups drained sun-dried tomatoes in oil, chopped, plus 15ml/1 tbsp oil from the jar
25g/1oz/⅓ cup freshly grated Parmesan cheese
30ml/2 tbsp red pesto
2.5ml/½ tsp coarse sea salt

1 Oil a baking sheet. Put the wholemeal flour in a large bowl. Sift in the white flour, salt and pepper. Add the yeast and sugar.

2 Make a well in the centre and add the water, the sun-dried tomatoes, oil, Parmesan cheese and pesto. Gradually incorporate the flour and mix to a soft dough, adding a little extra water if necessary.

3 Turn the dough on to a floured surface and knead for 5 minutes until smooth and elastic. Shape into three 33cm/13in long sausages.

4 Dampen the ends of the three sausages. Press them together at one end, braid them loosely, then press them together at the other end. Transfer to the baking sheet, and cover and leave in a warm place until doubled in size, about 1½ hours. Meanwhile, preheat the oven to 220°C/425°F/Gas 7.

5 Sprinkle the braid with coarse sea salt. Bake for 10 minutes, then lower the oven temperature to 200°C/400°F/Gas 6 and bake for a further 15–20 minutes, or until the loaf sounds hollow when tapped underneath. Leave on a wire rack to cool completely.

Sun-dried Tomato Bread

This is one bread that absolutely everyone seems to love. Onion and tomatoes give it an excellent flavour.

Makes 4

675g/1½ lb/6 cups strong plain (all-purpose) flour, plus extra for dusting
10ml/2 tsp salt
25g/1oz/2 tbsp caster (superfine) sugar
25g/1oz fresh yeast
400–475ml/14–16fl oz/1⅔–2 cups lukewarm milk
15ml/1 tbsp tomato purée (paste)
75g/3oz/¾ cup sun-dried tomatoes in oil, drained and chopped, plus 75ml/5 tbsp oil from the jar
75ml/5 tbsp extra virgin olive oil, plus extra for greasing
1 large onion, chopped

1 Sift the flour, salt and sugar into a bowl and make a well in the centre. Crumble the yeast into a jug or pitcher, mix with 150ml/¼ pint/⅔ cup of the milk and pour into the well.

2 Stir the tomato purée into the remaining milk, then add to the well in the flour, with the tomato oil and olive oil.

3 Mix the liquid ingredients, and gradually incorporate the surrounding flour to make a dough. Knead for about 10 minutes, then return the dough to the clean bowl, cover and leave to rise in a warm place for about 2 hours.

4 Knock back the dough, and add the tomatoes and onion. Knead until evenly distributed. Shape into four rounds and place on two greased baking sheets. Cover each pair with a dish towel and leave to rise again for about 45 minutes.

5 Preheat the oven to 190°C/375°F/Gas 5. Bake the bread for 45 minutes, or until the loaves sound hollow when you tap them underneath. Cool on a wire rack.

Cook's Tip
Use a pair of sharp kitchen scissors to cut up the tomatoes.

Sun-dried Tomato Braid Energy 190kcal/804kJ; Protein 7.7g; Carbohydrate 33.5g, of which sugars 2.4g; Fat 3.7g, of which saturates 1.4g; Cholesterol 6mg; Calcium 110mg; Fibre 3g; Sodium 89mg.

Sun-dried Tomato Bread per loaf Energy 1469kcal/6185kJ; Protein 31.2g; Carbohydrate 228.1g, of which sugars 23.6g; Fat 54.3g, of which saturates 9.1g; Cholesterol 9mg; Calcium 576mg; Fibre 8.8g; Sodium 1656mg.

Potato Bread

Vegetables incorporated into loaves make a moist crumb and help to keep the bread longer. Try this recipe with mashed carrot instead.

Makes 2

20ml/4 tsp active dried yeast
250ml/8fl oz/1 cup lukewarm milk
225g/8oz potatoes, boiled (reserve 250ml/8fl oz/1 cup of the cooking liquid)
30ml/2 tbsp oil
20ml/4 tsp salt
850–900g/1lb 4oz–2lb/ 7½–8 cups strong white bread flour

1 Combine the yeast and milk in a large bowl and leave to dissolve and for the yeast to become frothy, about 15 minutes. Meanwhile, mash the potatoes.

2 Add the potatoes, the oil and the salt to the yeast mixture and mix to combine thoroughly.

3 Stir in the reserved cooking water, then stir in the flour, in six separate batches, to form a stiff dough.

4 Knead on a lightly floured surface until smooth. This will take about 10 minutes. Return to the bowl, cover with clear film (plastic wrap), and leave in a warm place until doubled in size, about 1–1½ hours.

5 Knock back (punch down), then leave to rise again for 40 minutes, or until almost doubled in size.

6 Grease two 23 × 13cm/9 × 5in loaf tins (pans). Roll the dough into 20 small balls. Place two rows of balls in each tin. Leave until the dough has risen above the rims of the tins, about 1½ hours.

7 Meanwhile, preheat the oven to 200°C/400°F/Gas 6. Bake the dough for 10 minutes, then lower the heat to 190°C/375°F/Gas 5. Bake until the bases of the loaves sound hollow when tapped, about 40 minutes. Cool on a wire rack.

German Potato Bread

This is an adaptation of the classic German-style bread. This version is made with strong white flour and floury potatoes.

Makes 1

175g/6oz potatoes, peeled and cut into chunks
225g/8oz/2 cups strong white bread flour
10ml/2 tsp baking powder
5ml/1 tsp salt
15ml/1 tbsp vegetable oil
paprika, for dusting
mustard-flavoured butter, to serve

1 Put the potatoes in a large pan. Add water to cover and bring to the boil, then simmer for about 15 minutes, or until the potatoes are tender, but do not let them get too soft.

2 Drain the potatoes thoroughly in a colander and then return to the pan. Mash with a potato masher or pass through a potato ricer or food mill into the pan and set aside.

3 Preheat the oven to 230°C/450°F/Gas 8. Grease and line a 450g/1lb loaf tin (pan).

4 Sift the flour into a large bowl and mix together with baking powder and the salt. Rub the mashed potato into the dry ingredients making sure you achieve an even mixture.

5 Add the oil and 200ml/7fl oz/scant 1 cup lukewarm water to the dough, and mix to combine. Turn the dough into the tin and dust with the paprika.

6 Bake in the oven for 25 minutes. Turn out on to a wire rack to cool. Cut the bread into thick chunks and serve with mustard-flavoured butter.

Cook's Tip
This bread is best eaten while still warm, with lashings of the mustard-flavoured butter.

Potato Bread per loaf Energy 1693kcal/7186kJ; Protein 46.4g; Carbohydrate 356.3g, of which sugars 13.9g; Fat 19g, of which saturates 3.6g; Cholesterol 7mg; Calcium 754mg; Fibre 14.5g; Sodium 4011mg.

German Potato Bread per loaf Energy 989kcal/4191kJ; Protein 24.1g; Carbohydrate 203g, of which sugars 5.7g; Fat 14.4g, of which saturates 1.8g; Cholesterol 0mg; Calcium 326mg; Fibre 8.7g; Sodium 1991mg.

Russian Potato Bread

This lovely moist potato loaf is delicious when simply served with butter.

Makes 1

225g/8oz floury potatoes, diced
7g/¼oz easy-blend (rapid-rise) dried yeast
350g/12oz/3 cups unbleached white bread flour
115g/4oz/1 cup wholemeal (whole-wheat) bread flour, plus extra for sprinkling
2.5ml/½ tsp caraway seeds, crushed
10ml/2 tsp salt
25g/1oz/2 tbsp butter, diced

1 Lightly grease a baking sheet. Cook the potatoes in boiling water until tender. Drain well, reserving 150ml/¼ pint/⅔ cup of the cooking water. Mash the potatoes and leave to cool.

2 Mix together the yeast, white bread flour, wholemeal bread flour, caraway seeds and salt in a large bowl. Add the butter, cut into small pieces and rub in to form a breadcrumb consistency.

3 Mix together the reserved potato water and sieved potatoes. Gradually work this mixture into the flour mixture to form a soft dough. Turn out on to a lightly floured surface and knead for 8–10 minutes until smooth and elastic.

4 Place the dough in a large, lightly oiled bowl, cover with lightly oiled clear film (plastic wrap) and leave to rise, in a warm place, for about 1 hour, or until it has doubled in size.

5 Turn out on to a floured surface and knead gently. Shape into a plump oval loaf about 18cm/7in long. Place on the prepared baking sheet and sprinkle with a little wholemeal flour. Cover with lightly oiled clear film and leave to rise, in a warm place, for 30 minutes, or until doubled in size.

6 Preheat the oven to 200°C/400°F/Gas 6. Using a sharp knife, slash the top with 3–4 diagonal cuts to make a criss-cross effect. Bake for 30–35 minutes until golden and hollow sounding when tapped on the base. Cool on a wire rack.

Potato & Cheese Bread

This loaf uses baking powder as a raising agent. You can also try the recipe with mashed sweet potato, which gives a beautiful golden colour, and hard goat's cheese. The potato keeps the bread moist, while the oven crisps up the golden brown crust, with the cheese melting on top.

Makes 1

240g/8½oz/2 cups plain (all-purpose) flour
5ml/1 tsp baking powder
5ml/1 tsp salt
5ml/1 tsp chilli powder
15ml/1 tbsp chopped fresh rosemary
15ml/1 tbsp chopped fresh parsley
1 small red onion, very finely chopped
200g/7oz cooked, mashed potatoes, cooled
2 eggs, beaten
115g/4oz mature (sharp) or Cheddar cheese, diced

1 Sift the flour, baking powder, salt and chilli powder into a large bowl. Stir in the herbs. Mix in the onion, mashed potato, eggs and half the cheese. with your hands, bringing the ingredients together to form a soft dough.

2 Transfer the dough on to a lightly floured surface and knead quickly into a smooth round, approximately 20cm/8in in diameter. Preheat the oven to 190°C/375°F/Gas 5.

3 Sprinkle the remaining cubes of cheese on to the top of the dough, pushing them into the dough slightly.

4 Put the dough on a well-floured oven sheet. Close the door and bake in the oven for 20–25 minutes, until the bread is golden in colour and risen, and it sounds hollow when you tap it on its base.

5 Take the bread out of the oven and put it on a wire rack to cool. This bread is best enjoyed on the day you make it, once it has cooled, although it does make deliciously crunchy croûtons for soup the next day.

Russian Potato Bread per loaf Energy 1893kcal/8026kJ; Protein 51.5g; Carbohydrate 381.8g, of which sugars 10.7g; Fat 28.3g, of which saturates 14.3g; Cholesterol 53mg; Calcium 553mg; Fibre 23.4g; Sodium 4120mg.

Potato and Cheese Bread per loaf Energy 1737kcal/7311kJ; Protein 78g; Carbohydrate 219g, of which sugars 9g; Fat 68g, of which saturates 32g; Cholesterol 592mg; Calcium 1423mg; Fibre 13.1g; Sodium 3613mg.

Sweet Potato Bread with Cinnamon & Walnuts

Spicy and sweet, this tastes great both with savoury dishes and as a teabread, with cream cheese.

Makes 1

1 medium sweet potato
450g/1lb/4 cups strong white bread flour, plus extra for dusting
5ml/1 tsp ground cinnamon
5ml/1 tsp easy-blend (rapid-rise) dried yeast
50g/2oz/⅔ cup walnut pieces
300ml/½ pint/1¼ cups warmed milk
salt and ground black pepper

1 Bring a pan of water to the boil and cook the sweet potato whole, without peeling, for 45 minutes, or until tender. Meanwhile, sift the flour and cinnamon into a large bowl. Stir in the dried yeast.

2 Drain the sweet potato, cool it in cold water, then peel it. Mash the flesh with a fork, then mix it into the dry ingredients with the nuts and some salt and pepper.

3 Make a well in the centre of the mixture and pour in the milk. Mix with a round-bladed knife to a rough dough, then knead on a floured surface for 5 minutes.

4 Return the dough to a bowl and cover with oiled clear film (plastic wrap). Leave in a warm place to rise for 1 hour, or until doubled in bulk. Turn the dough out and knock it back to remove any air bubbles. Knead again for a few minutes.

5 Grease a 900g/2lb loaf tin (pan) lightly with oil and line the base with baking parchment. Shape the dough to fit the tin. Cover with lightly oiled clear film and leave in a warm place for 1 hour, or until doubled in size.

6 Preheat the oven to 200°C/400°F/Gas 6. Bake the loaf for 25 minutes. Turn it out and tap the base; if it sounds hollow the bread is cooked. Cool on a wire rack.

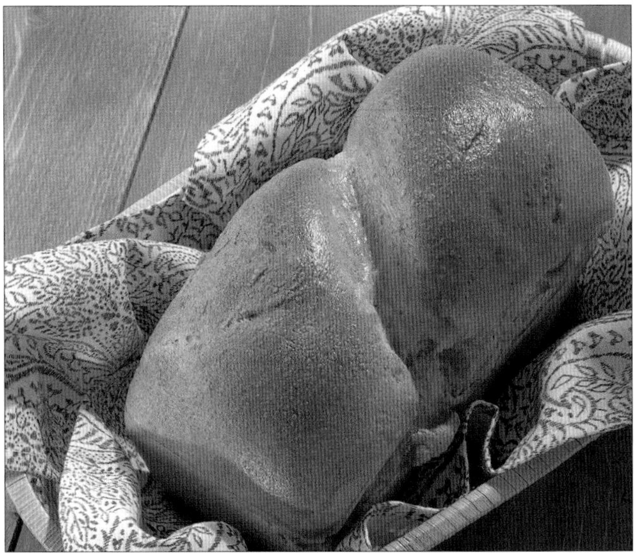

Cheese Bread

This flavoured bread is ideal to serve with hot soup for a hearty snack lunch.

Makes 1

15ml/1 tbsp active dried yeast
250ml/8fl oz/1 cup lukewarm milk
25g/1oz/2 tbsp butter
425g/15oz/3⅔ cups strong white bread flour
10ml/2 tsp salt
90g/3½oz/scant 1 cup grated mature (sharp) Cheddar cheese

1 Combine the yeast and milk in a small bowl. Stir and leave for 15 minutes to dissolve and for the yeast to become frothy.

2 Meanwhile, melt the butter, leave to cool, then add it to the yeast mixture.

3 Mix the flour and salt together in a large bowl. Make a central well in the flour and pour in the yeast mixture. With a wooden spoon, stir from the centre to obtain a rough dough. If the dough seems too dry, add 30–45ml/2–3 tbsp water.

4 Transfer to a floured surface and knead until smooth and elastic. This will take about 10 minutes.

5 Return to the bowl, cover and leave to rise in a warm place until doubled in volume, about 2–3 hours.

6 Grease a 23 × 13cm/9 × 5in loaf tin (pan). Knock back (punch down) the dough and knead in the cheese to distribute it evenly.

7 Twist the dough, form into a loaf shape and place in the tin, tucking the ends underneath. Leave in a warm place until the dough rises above the rim of the tin, about 1½ hours.

8 Meanwhile, preheat the oven to 200°C/400°F/Gas 6. Bake the bread for 15 minutes, then lower the heat to 190°C/375°F/Gas 5 and bake until the base sounds hollow when tapped, about a further 30 minutes.

Sweet Potato Bread per loaf Energy 2199kcal/9305kJ; Protein 63.8g; Carbohydrate 408.8g, of which sugars 34.1g; Fat 45.7g, of which saturates 8.2g; Cholesterol 21mg; Calcium 1096mg; Fibre 27.3g; Sodium 250mg.

Cheese Bread per loaf Energy 2125kcal/8967kJ; Protein 71.5g; Carbohydrate 342.2g, of which sugars 18.4g; Fat 59.8g, of which saturates 36.1g; Cholesterol 155mg; Calcium 1565mg; Fibre 13.2g; Sodium 2887mg.

Cheese Danish Crown

Filled with onions and Parmesan cheese, this bread ring is quite irresistible.

Makes 1

350g/12oz/3 cups unbleached white bread flour
5ml/1 tsp salt
185g/6½oz/generous ¾ cup butter, softened
20g/¾oz fresh yeast
200ml/7fl oz/scant 1 cup mixed lukewarm milk and water
1 egg, lightly beaten

For the filling
30ml/2 tbsp sunflower oil
2 onions, finely chopped
40g/1½oz/¾ cup breadcrumbs
25g/1oz/¼ cup ground almonds
50g/2oz/½ cup freshly grated Parmesan cheese
1 egg, lightly beaten
salt and ground black pepper

For the topping
15ml/1 tbsp sesame seeds
15ml/1 tbsp freshly grated Parmesan cheese

1 Sift the flour and salt into a bowl. Rub in 40g/1½ oz/3 tbsp of the butter. Mix the yeast with the milk and water. Add to the flour with the egg and mix to a soft dough. Knead for 10 minutes. Place in an oiled bowl, cover and leave for 1 hour.

2 Knock back (punch down) and turn out on to a floured surface. Roll into an oblong about 1cm/½in thick. Dot half the remaining butter over the top two-thirds of the dough. Fold the bottom third up and the top third down. Turn by 90 degrees and repeat. Cover and leave for 15 minutes. Rotate and roll and fold again without any butter. Repeat. Wrap in oiled clear film and chill for 30 minutes.

3 Meanwhile, cook the onions in the oil for 10 minutes. Remove from the heat and stir in the breadcrumbs, almonds, Parmesan and seasoning. Add half the beaten egg and bind together. Roll into a large rectangle. Spread the filling on top, then roll up. Cut in half lengthways. Braid together and shape into a ring. Place on an oiled baking sheet, cover and leave for 30 minutes.

4 Preheat the oven to 200°C/400°F/Gas 6. Brush the remaining egg over. Sprinkle with sesame seeds and Parmesan cheese and bake for 40–50 minutes, or until golden.

Cheese & Onion Loaf

Almost a meal in itself, this hearty bread tastes delicious as an accompaniment to salads and cold meats, or with soup.

Makes 1

1 onion, finely chopped
45g/1¾oz/3½ tbsp butter
450g/1lb/4 cups unbleached white bread flour
7g/¼oz easy-blend (rapid-rise) dried yeast
5ml/1 tsp mustard powder
175g/6oz/1½ cups grated mature (sharp) Cheddar cheese
150ml/¼ pint/⅔ cup lukewarm milk
150ml/¼ pint/⅔ cup lukewarm water
salt and ground black pepper

1 Lightly grease a 25 × 10cm/10 × 4in loaf tin (pan). Melt 25g/1oz/2 tbsp of the butter in a heavy frying pan and fry the onion until it is soft and light golden. Set aside to cool.

2 Sift the flour into a large bowl and stir in the yeast, mustard, salt and pepper. Stir in three-quarters of the grated cheese and the onion. Make a well in the centre. Add the milk and water; blend to a soft dough. Turn out on to a lightly floured surface and knead for 10 minutes until smooth and elastic.

3 Place the dough in a lightly oiled bowl, cover with oiled clear film (plastic wrap) and leave in a warm place, for about 45–60 minutes, until doubled in size.

4 Turn the dough out on to a lightly floured surface, knock back (punch down), and knead gently. Divide into 20 equal pieces and shape into small rounds. Place half in the prepared tin and brush with some melted butter. Top with the remaining rounds of dough and brush with the remaining butter.

5 Cover with oiled clear film and leave to rise for 45 minutes, until the dough reaches the top of the tin. Meanwhile, preheat the oven to 190°C/375°F/Gas 5.

6 Sprinkle the remaining cheese over the top. Bake for 40–45 minutes or until risen and golden. Cool on a wire rack.

Cheese Danish Crown per loaf Energy 3660kcal/15276kJ; Protein 85.2g; Carbohydrate 333.5g, of which sugars 29.2g; Fat 230.2g, of which saturates 121.5g; Cholesterol 687mg; Calcium 1734mg; Fibre 19g; Sodium 2551mg.

Cheese and Onion Loaf per loaf Energy 2707kcal/11384kJ; Protein 94.1g; Carbohydrate 363.1g, of which sugars 17.8g; Fat 104.8g, of which saturates 64.7g; Cholesterol 282mg; Calcium 2142mg; Fibre 14.8g; Sodium 1701mg.

Spring Onion & Ricotta Bread

Ricotta cheese makes a moist, well-flavoured loaf that is excellent for sandwiches. Shape the dough into rolls or one large loaf.

Makes 1 loaf or 16 rolls

5ml/1 tsp caster (superfine) sugar
270ml/9fl oz/generous 1 cup lukewarm water
10ml/2 tsp active dried yeast
450g/1lb unbleached white bread flour, plus a little extra
7.5ml/1 ½ tsp salt
1 large egg, beaten
115g/4oz/½ cup ricotta cheese
1 bunch spring onions (scallions), thinly sliced
30ml/2 tbsp extra virgin olive oil
45ml/3 tbsp chopped fresh chives
15ml/1 tbsp milk
10ml/2 tsp poppy seeds
coarse sea salt

1 Stir the sugar into 120ml/4fl oz/½ cup of the water, then sprinkle the dried yeast over the surface. Leave in a warm place for 10 minutes. Sift the flour and salt into a bowl. Make a well in the centre and pour in the yeast liquid and the remaining water. Reserve a little beaten egg, then put the rest in the bowl. Add the ricotta and mix to a dough. Add more flour if it is sticky.

2 Knead the dough on a floured work surface until smooth and elastic. Put an oiled bowl covered with lightly oiled clear film (plastic wrap) and leave in a warm place for 1–2 hours, until doubled in size. Meanwhile, cook the spring onions in the oil for 3–4 minutes, until soft. Set aside to cool.

3 Punch down the dough and knead in the onions, with their oil from cooking, and the chives. Shape into rolls or a loaf.

4 Grease a baking sheet or loaf tin (pan) and place the rolls or bread on it. Cover with oiled film and leave in a warm place to rise for about 1 hour. Preheat the oven to 200°C/400°F/Gas 6.

5 Beat the milk into the reserved beaten egg and use to glaze the rolls or loaf. Sprinkle with poppy seeds and a little sea salt, then bake rolls for about 15 minutes or a loaf for 30–40 minutes, or until golden. When tapped firmly on the base, the bread should feel and sound firm. Cool on a wire rack.

Cheese, Olive & Onion Potato Braid

A braided potato and olive loaf with a crisp cheese and onion topping.

Makes 1

225g/8oz floury potatoes
350g/12oz/3 cups strong white bread flour
7.5ml/1 ½ tsp easy-blend (rapid-rise) dried yeast
25g/1oz/2 tbsp butter, diced
50g/2oz/½ cup pitted green or black olives

For the topping

30ml/2 tbsp olive oil
1 onion, sliced into rings
50g/2oz/½ cup mature (sharp) Cheddar cheese, grated
salt and ground black pepper

1 Chop the potatoes and cook in a large pan with plenty of salted boiling water for 15–20 minutes or until tender.

2 Meanwhile, sift the flour into a bowl, add the yeast and a little salt. Rub in the butter to form fine crumbs. Drain the potatoes and mash well. Add to the dry ingredients with 300ml/½ pint/1 ¼ cups lukewarm water.

3 Bring the mixture together with a knife and then turn out on to a floured surface. Knead for about 5 minutes. Return to the bowl and cover with a damp cloth. Leave to rise for 1 hour or until doubled in size. Turn the dough out on to a floured surface and knock back (punch down) to remove any air bubbles. Knead in the olives. Cut the dough into three even pieces.

4 Roll each piece out to a long thick sausage. Twist the sausages over each other to form a plait. Lift on to a greased baking sheet. Cover with a damp cloth and leave to rise for 30 minutes or until doubled in size.

5 Preheat the oven to 220°C/425°F/Gas 7. Heat the oil in a pan and fry the onions for 10 minutes, stirring occasionally, until golden. Remove the onions from the pan and drain well on kitchen paper.

6 Sprinkle the onions and grated cheese over the bread and bake for 20 minutes until golden. Serve warm or cold.

Spring Onion and Ricotta Bread per loaf Energy 2042kcal/8626kJ; Protein 61.6g; Carbohydrate 356.9g, of which sugars 13.8g; Fat 50.8g, of which saturates 16.3g; Cholesterol 239mg; Calcium 716mg; Fibre 15.4g; Sodium 97mg.

Cheese, Olive and Onion Potato Braid Energy 231kcal/971kJ; Protein 8.7g; Carbohydrate 26.4g, of which sugars 0.8g; Fat 10.4g, of which saturates 5.2g; Cholesterol 21mg; Calcium 203mg; Fibre 1.2g; Sodium 162mg.

Cheese & Courgette Bread

This unusual bread owes its moist texture to grated courgettes, and its depth of flavour to freshly grated Parmesan cheese.

Makes 1

4 courgettes (zucchini), coarsely grated
675g/1½lb/6 cups strong white bread flour
15g/½oz easy-blend (rapid-rise) dried yeast
50g/2oz/⅔ cup freshly grated Parmesan cheese
30ml/2 tbsp olive oil, plus extra for greasing
milk, to glaze
poppy seeds or sesame seeds, to sprinkle
salt and ground black pepper

1 Put the grated courgettes into a colander and sprinkle with salt. Stand the colander in a sink for about 20 minutes to drain the juices, then rinse the courgettes thoroughly, drain again and pat dry with kitchen paper.

2 Sift the flour into a bowl. Add the yeast, cheese, 2.5ml/½ tsp salt and pepper to taste. Stir in the oil and courgettes, then add enough lukewarm water to make a firm but still soft dough.

3 Knead the dough for about 10 minutes, then return it to the bowl, cover with lightly oiled clear film and leave in a warm place for about 1 hour, or until doubled in size.

4 Lightly grease a deep 23cm/9in cake tin (pan). Knock back (punch down) the dough and knead it again. Divide it into eight pieces and roll into smooth balls. Fit these into the tin, placing one in the centre and the remainder around the outside.

5 Glaze the loaf with a little milk and sprinkle over the seeds. Cover lightly with oiled clear film and leave to rise in a warm place until the balls of dough have doubled in size.

6 Meanwhile, preheat the oven to 200°C/400°F/Gas 6. Bake the loaf for 35–45 minutes, until it is golden brown and sounds hollow when tapped on the base. Cool on a wire rack and eat as soon as possible.

Courgette Teabread

Like carrots, courgettes are a vegetable that works well in baking, adding a combination of moistness and lightness to the bread.

Makes 1

50g/2oz/¼ cup butter
3 eggs
250ml/8fl oz/1 cup vegetable oil
285g/10½oz/1½ cups caster (superfine) sugar
2 unpeeled courgettes (zucchini), grated
275g/10oz/2½ cups plain (all-purpose) flour
10ml/2 tsp bicarbonate of soda (baking soda)
5ml/1 tsp baking powder
5ml/1 tsp salt
5ml/1 tsp ground cinnamon
5ml/1 tsp freshly grated nutmeg
1.5ml/¼ tsp ground cloves
115g/4oz/1 cup chopped walnuts

1 Preheat the oven to 180°C/350°F/Gas 4. Line the base and sides of a 23 × 13cm/9 × 5in loaf tin (pan) with baking parchment and grease the paper.

2 In a pan, melt the butter over a low heat. Set aside.

3 With an electric mixer, beat the eggs and oil together until thick. Beat in the sugar, then stir in the melted butter and the grated courgettes. Set aside.

4 In another bowl, sift the flour with the bicarbonate of soda, baking powder, salt, ground cinnamon, grated nutmeg and ground cloves. Sift twice more and then carefully fold them into the courgette mixture. Fold in the chopped walnuts.

5 Pour into the tin and bake until a skewer inserted in the centre comes out clean, about 60–70 minutes. Leave to stand for 10 minutes before turning out on to a wire rack to cool.

Cook's Tip
Sifting the flour and dry ingredients three times helps to make the teabread mixture light. Be careful to fold in the other ingredients gently so that the air that was incorporated is not lost.

Cheese and Courgette Bread per loaf Energy 2876kcal/12165kJ; Protein 101.3g; Carbohydrate 539.9g, of which sugars 24.2g; Fat 49g, of which saturates 14.9g; Cholesterol 47mg; Calcium 1670mg; Fibre 37.5g; Sodium 414mg.

Courgette Teabread per loaf Energy 5135kcal/21437kJ; Protein 70.4g; Carbohydrate 522.8g, of which sugars 312g; Fat 321.5g, of which saturates 59.1g; Cholesterol 677mg; Calcium 839mg; Fibre 16.1g; Sodium 2515mg.

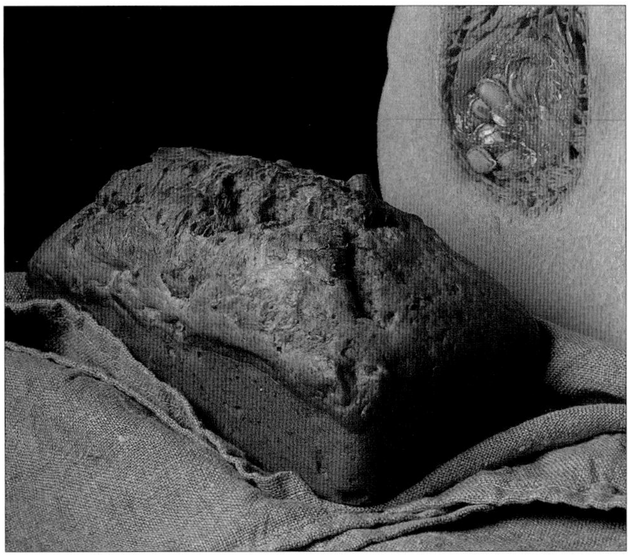

Pumpkin & Walnut Bread

Pumpkin, nutmeg and walnuts combine to yield a moist, tangy and slightly sweet bread with an indescribably good flavour. Serve partnered with meats or cheese, or simply lightly buttered.

Makes 1

500g/1¼lb pumpkin, peeled, seeded and cut into chunks
75g/3oz/6 tbsp caster (superfine) sugar
5ml/1 tsp grated nutmeg
50g/2oz/¼ cup butter, melted
3 eggs, lightly beaten
350g/12oz/3 cups unbleached white bread flour
10ml/2 tsp baking powder
2.5ml/½ tsp salt
75g/3oz/¾ cup walnuts, chopped

1 Grease and neatly base line a loaf tin (pan) measuring 21.5 × 11cm/8½ × 4½in. Place the pumpkin in a pan, add water to cover by about 5cm/2in, then bring to the boil. Cover, lower the heat and simmer for 20 minutes, or until the pumpkin is tender.

2 Drain the pumpkin, then purée in a food processor or blender. Leave to cool. Preheat the oven to 180°C/350°F/Gas 4.

3 Place 275g/10oz/1¼ cups of the purée in a large bowl. Add the sugar, nutmeg, melted butter and eggs to the purée and mix together. Sift the flour, baking powder and salt together into a large bowl and make a well in the centre.

4 Add the pumpkin mixture to the centre of the flour and stir until smooth. Mix in the walnuts.

5 Transfer to the prepared tin and bake for 1 hour, or until golden and starting to shrink from the sides of the tin. Turn out on to a wire rack to cool.

Cook's Tip
You may have slightly more pumpkin purée than you actually need – you could use the remainder in a soup.

Blue Cheese & Walnut Bread

This lattice-shaped loaf from the South of France can be plain or flavoured with cheese, herbs, nuts or olives.

Makes 2

450g/1lb/4 cups unbleached white bread flour
5ml/1 tsp salt
20g/¾oz fresh yeast
280ml/9fl oz/generous 1 cup lukewarm water
15ml/1 tbsp extra virgin olive oil

For the filling
50g/2oz/⅓ cup Roquefort cheese, crumbled
40g/1½oz/⅓ cup walnut pieces, chopped
25g/1oz/2 tbsp drained, canned anchovy fillets, soaked in milk and drained again, chopped
olive oil, for brushing

1 Lightly grease two baking sheets. Sift the flour and salt and make a well in the centre. Cream the yeast with 60ml/4 tbsp of the water and pour into well with the remaining water and the olive oil. Mix to a soft dough, turn out on to a floured surface and knead for 8–10 minutes until smooth and elastic.

2 Place the dough in a lightly oiled bowl, cover with lightly oiled clear film (plastic wrap) and leave to rise, in a warm place, for about 1 hour, or until doubled in bulk.

3 Knock back (punch down) the dough and divide in half. Flatten one piece, sprinkle with cheese and walnuts and fold over two to three times. Repeat with the other piece, using the anchovies. Shape each piece into a ball, flatten and fold the bottom third up and the top third down. Roll the cheese dough into a rectangle and make four diagonal cuts almost to the edge. Pull and stretch the dough evenly, so that it resembles a ladder.

4 Shape the anchovy dough into an oval and make three diagonal slits on each side. Transfer to the prepared baking sheets, cover and leave in a warm place for about 30–45 minutes.

5 Meanwhile, preheat the oven to 220°C/425°F/Gas 7. Brush both loaves with a little olive oil and bake for 25 minutes, or until golden. Transfer to a wire rack to cool.

Pumpkin and Walnut Bread per loaf Energy 2663kcal/11186kJ; Protein 66.8g; Carbohydrate 364.1g, of which sugars 94.4g; Fat 114.7g, of which saturates 36.1g; Cholesterol 677mg; Calcium 840mg; Fibre 18.5g; Sodium 1516mg.

Blue Cheese and Walnut Bread per loaf Energy 1014kcal/4284kJ; Protein 32.4g; Carbohydrate 175.5g, of which sugars 3.9g; Fat 25.1g, of which saturates 6.6g; Cholesterol 27mg; Calcium 494mg; Fibre 7.7g; Sodium 1787mg.

Virginia Spoon Bread

Spoon bread is a traditional dish from the southern states of North America that, according to legend, originated when too much water was added to a corn bread batter and the baked loaf had to be spooned out of the tin. Served hot from the oven, this ethereally light offering – enhanced with Cheddar cheese and a hint of garlic – is a popular favourite.

Makes 1

450ml/¾ pint/1¾ cups milk
75g/3oz/⅔ cup cornmeal
15g/½ oz/1 tbsp butter
75g/3oz/¾ cup grated mature (sharp) Cheddar cheese
1 garlic clove
3 eggs, separated
75g/3oz/½ cup corn kernels (optional)
salt and ground black pepper

1 Preheat the oven to 180°C/350°F/Gas 4. Grease a 1.5 litre/2½ pint/6 cup soufflé dish.

2 Place the milk in a large heavy pan. Heat gently, then gradually add the cornmeal, stirring. Add salt and slowly bring to the boil, stirring all the time. Cook for 5–10 minutes, stirring frequently, until thick and smooth.

3 Remove from the heat and stir in the butter, Cheddar cheese, garlic and egg yolks. Season to taste.

4 In a bowl, whisk the egg whites until they form soft peaks. Stir one-quarter into the corn meal mixture and then gently fold in the remainder. Fold in the well-drained corn, if using.

5 Spoon the mixture into the prepared soufflé dish and bake for 45–50 minutes, or until puffed and beginning to brown.

Variation
Add 115g/4oz fried chopped bacon or 5–10ml/1–2 tsp finely chopped green chilli for different-flavoured spoon breads.

Prosciutto Loaf

This savoury Italian bread from Parma is spiked with the local dried ham. Just a small amount fills the loaf with marvellous flavour.

Makes 1

350g/12oz/3 cups unbleached white bread flour
7.5ml/1½ tsp salt
15g/½ oz fresh yeast
250ml/8fl oz/1 cup lukewarm water
40g/1½ oz prosciutto, torn into small pieces
5ml/1 tsp ground black pepper

1 Sift the flour and salt together into a bowl and make a well in the centre. Cream the yeast with 30ml/2 tbsp of the water, then gradually mix in the rest. Pour into the centre of the flour.

2 Gradually beat in most of the flour with a spoon to make a batter. After most of the flour has been incorporated, beat in the remainder to form a moist dough.

3 Turn out on to a lightly floured surface and knead for 5 minutes until smooth and elastic. Place in a lightly oiled bowl, cover with oiled clear film (plastic wrap) and leave in a warm place, for 1½ hours, or until doubled in bulk.

4 Turn out the dough on to a lightly floured surface, knock back (punch down) and then knead for 1 minute. Flatten to a round, then sprinkle with half the prosciutto and pepper. Fold the dough in half and repeat with the remaining ham and pepper. Roll up, tucking in the sides. Place on an oiled baking sheet, cover and leave to rise, in a warm place, for 30 minutes.

5 On a lightly floured surface, roll into an oval, fold in half. Flatten and fold again. Seal and fold again to make a long loaf. Roll into a stubby long loaf. Place on the baking sheet, cover and leave to rise, in a warm place, for 45 minutes. Meanwhile, preheat the oven to 200°C/400°F/Gas 6.

6 Slash the top of the loaf diagonally three or four times, and bake for 30 minutes, or until golden. Cool on a wire rack.

Virginia Spoon Bread per loaf Energy 1126kcal/4699kJ; Protein 59.8g; Carbohydrate 77.4g, of which sugars 22.6g; Fat 63.6g, of which saturates 33.5g; Cholesterol 705mg; Calcium 1184mg; Fibre 1.6g; Sodium 1112mg.

Prosciutto Loaf per loaf Energy 1236kcal/5255kJ; Protein 40.3g; Carbohydrate 272.3g, of which sugars 5.7g; Fat 5.9g, of which saturates 1.1g; Cholesterol 23mg; Calcium 493mg; Fibre 10.8g; Sodium 490mg.

Bacon, Cheese & Quinoa Bread

Rustic breads make great breakfasts, and this loaf, using cooked quinoa to add extra sustenance, is lovely when toasted for breakfast.

Makes 1

225g/8oz/2 cups strong white bread flour
175g/6oz/1½ cups wholemeal (whole-wheat) bread flour
300g/12oz/2 cups cooked pearl quinoa
10ml/2 tsp easy blend (rapid-rise) yeast
7.5ml/1½ tsp salt
60ml/4 tbsp sugar
300ml/½ pint/1¼ cups lukewarm water
15ml/1 tbsp vegetable oil
1 small onion, finely diced
4 rashers (strips) streaky (fatty) bacon
50g/2oz/½ cup mature (sharp) Cheddar cheese, grated
milk, to glaze

1 Sift the flours into a large bowl, add the cooked quinoa, yeast, salt and sugar and stir to mix. Make a well in the centre and gradually mix in enough lukewarm water to form a soft dough.

2 Knead for 6–8 minutes, on a floured board, by holding the dough with one hand and stretching it with the palm of the other hand. Place in a bowl and cover for 1–1½ hours.

3 In a frying pan, heat the oil and add the onion, frying for 4–5 minutes until soft. Add two of the bacon rashers to the pan and fry for a further 3–4 minutes, until crispy. Cut the cooked bacon rashers into small pieces. Set aside.

4 When the dough has risen, knock back (punch down) and knead for a further few minutes. Add the bacon, onion and three-quarters of the grated cheese, and fold in.

5 Heat the oven to 200°C/400°F/Gas 6. Oil a 450g/1lb loaf tin (pan). Shape the dough to neatly fill the tin. Leave for another 20–30 minutes in a warm place.

6 Brush the top of the loaf with milk and bake for 15 minutes. Remove from the oven and sprinkle with the remaining cheese and 2 bacon rashers. Bake for a further 15–20 minutes.

Spinach & Bacon Bread

This bread is so tasty that it is a good idea to make double the quantity and freeze some of the loaves, so that you can enjoy more of them later.

Makes 2

15ml/1 tbsp olive oil
1 onion, chopped
115g/4oz rindless smoked bacon rashers (strips), chopped
675g/1½lb/6 cups plain (all-purpose) flour
7.5ml/1½ tsp salt
2.5ml/½ tsp freshly grated nutmeg
7g/¼oz easy-blend (rapid-rise) dried yeast
475ml/16fl oz/2 cups hand-hot water
225g/8oz chopped spinach, thawed if frozen
25g/1oz/¼ cup grated Cheddar cheese

1 Lightly oil two 23cm/9in cake tins (pans). Heat the oil in a frying pan and fry the onion and bacon for 10 minutes, or until golden brown.

2 Sift the flour, salt and grated nutmeg into a mixing bowl, add the yeast and make a well in the centre. Add the water.

3 Add the fried bacon and onion, with the oil it was cooked in, to the mixing bowl. Then add the well-drained thawed spinach. Stir from the centre outwards, gradually incorporating the flour, and mix to a soft dough.

4 Turn the dough on to a floured surface and knead for 5 minutes until smooth and elastic. Divide the mixture in half.

5 Shape each half into a ball, flatten slightly and place in a prepared tin, pressing the dough so that it extends to the edges.

6 Mark each loaf into six wedges and sprinkle with the cheese. Cover loosely with oiled clear film (plastic wrap) and leave in a warm place until each loaf has doubled in size, about 1½ hours. Meanwhile, preheat the oven to 200°C/400°F/Gas 6.

7 Bake the loaves for 25–30 minutes, or until they sound hollow when tapped underneath. Leave on a wire rack to cool completely.

Bacon, Cheese and Quinoa Bread Energy 314kcal/1325kJ; Protein 12g; Carbohydrate 51g, of which sugars 10g; Fat 8g, of which saturates 3g; Cholesterol 14mg; Calcium 103mg; Fibre 3g; Sodium 585mg.

Spinach and Bacon Bread Energy 160kcal/680kJ; Protein 5.8g; Carbohydrate 32.6g, of which sugars 1.2g; Fat 1.6g, of which saturates 0.3g; Cholesterol 1mg; Calcium 98mg; Fibre 1.7g; Sodium 216mg.

Prosciutto & Parmesan Bread

This nourishing bread can be made very quickly, and makes a delicious meal when served with a tomato and feta cheese salad.

Makes 1

225g/8oz/2 cups self-raising (self-rising) wholemeal (whole-wheat) flour
225g/8oz/2 cups self-raising (self-rising) flour
5ml/1 tsp salt
5ml/1 tsp ground black pepper
75g/3oz prosciutto, chopped
30ml/2 tbsp chopped fresh parsley
25g/1oz/2 tbsp freshly grated Parmesan cheese
45ml/3 tbsp Meaux mustard
350ml/12fl oz/1½ cups buttermilk
skimmed milk, to glaze

1 Preheat the oven to 200°C/400°F/Gas 6 and lightly flour a baking sheet.

2 Put the wholemeal flour in a bowl and sift in the plain flour, salt and pepper. Stir in the ham and parsley. Set aside about half of the grated Parmesan cheese and add the rest to the flour mixture. Make a well in the centre.

3 Mix the mustard and buttermilk in a jug or pitcher, pour into the bowl and quickly mix to a soft dough.

4 Turn on to a well-floured surface and knead very briefly. Shape into an oval loaf and place on the baking sheet.

5 Brush the loaf with milk, sprinkle with the reserved Parmesan cheese and bake for 25–30 minutes, or until golden brown. Cool on a wire rack.

Cook's Tip

When chopping the prosciutto, sprinkle it with flour so that it does not stick together. Do not knead the mixture as for a yeast dough, or it will become tough. It should be mixed quickly and kneaded very briefly before shaping.

Warm Herb & Tomato Bread

This mouthwatering Italian-style bread, flavoured with basil, rosemary, olive oil and sun-dried tomatoes, is ideal when served warm to accompany fresh salads.

Makes 3

1.3kg/3lb/12 cups white bread flour, plus extra for dusting
15ml/1 tbsp salt
5ml/1 tsp caster (superfine) sugar
7g/¼oz easy-blend (rapid-rise) dried yeast
about 900ml/1½ pints/3¾ cups lukewarm water
75g/3oz/1½ cups sun-dried tomatoes in oil, drained and roughly chopped
150ml/¼ pint/⅔ cup virgin olive oil, plus extra for greasing
75ml/5 tbsp chopped mixed fresh basil and rosemary

To finish

extra virgin olive oil
rosemary leaves
sea salt flakes

1 Sift the flour and salt into a bowl. Stir in the sugar and yeast. Make a well in the centre and add the water, tomatoes, oil and herbs. Beat well, gradually incorporating the surrounding flour.

2 As the mixture becomes stiffer, bring it together with your hands. Mix to a soft but not sticky dough, adding a little extra water if needed.

3 Knead the dough on a lightly floured surface for about 10 minutes, then return it to the bowl, cover loosely with oiled clear film (plastic wrap) and put in a warm place for 30–40 minutes, or until doubled in bulk.

4 Knead the dough again until smooth and elastic, then cut it into three pieces. Shape each into an oval loaf about 18cm/7in long and place each on an oiled baking sheet. Slash the top of each loaf in a criss-cross pattern. Cover loosely and leave in a warm place for 15–20 minutes, until well risen.

5 Preheat the oven to 220°C/425°F/Gas 7. Brush the loaves with a little olive oil and sprinkle with the rosemary leaves and salt flakes. Cook for about 25 minutes, until golden brown. The bases should sound hollow when tapped.

Prosciutto and Parmesan Bread per loaf Energy 1746kcal/7416kJ; Protein 74.2g; Carbohydrate 336.8g, of which sugars 29.6g; Fat 21.1g, of which saturates 7.2g; Cholesterol 30mg; Calcium 1663mg; Fibre 38.3g; Sodium 4506mg.

Warm Herb and Tomato Bread per loaf Energy 1952kcal/8236kJ; Protein 43.2g; Carbohydrate 341.1g, of which sugars 9g; Fat 55.3g, of which saturates 7.8g; Cholesterol 0mg; Calcium 680mg; Fibre 17.9g; Sodium 2231mg.

Rosemary Bread

Sliced thinly, this herb bread is delicious with cheese or as an accompaniment for soup for a light meal.

Makes 1

7g/¼oz easy-blend (rapid-rise) dried yeast
175g/6oz/1½ cups strong wholemeal (whole-wheat) bread flour
175g/6oz/1½ cups self-raising (self-rising) flour
25g/1oz/2 tbsp butter
50ml/2fl oz/¼ cup warm water
250ml/8fl oz/1 cup milk, at room temperature
15ml/1 tbsp sugar
5ml/1 tsp salt
15ml/1 tbsp sesame seeds
15ml/1 tbsp dried chopped onion
15ml/1 tbsp fresh rosemary leaves
115g/4oz/1 cup cubed Cheddar cheese
rosemary leaves and coarse salt, to decorate

1 Mix the yeast with the flours in a large mixing bowl. Melt the butter in a small pan, then stir with the warm water, milk, sugar, salt, sesame seeds, onion and rosemary into the flour.

2 Knead thoroughly until quite smooth. This will take about 10 minutes. Flatten the dough, then add the cheese cubes. Knead them in until they are well combined.

3 Place the dough in a large clean bowl. Cover the bowl with a dish towel or clear film (plastic wrap) and put it in a warm place for 1½ hours, or until the dough has doubled in size.

4 Grease a 23 × 13cm/9 × 5in loaf tin (pan) with butter. Knock back (punch down) the dough and shape it into a loaf.

5 Place in the tin, cover with the dish towel or oiled clear film and leave for about 1 hour, or until doubled in size. Preheat the oven to 190°C/375°F/Gas 5.

6 Bake for 30 minutes. Cover the loaf with foil for the last 5–10 minutes of baking. Turn the bread out on to a wire rack to cool. Garnish with some rosemary leaves and coarse salt sprinkled on top.

Sage Soda Bread

This wonderful loaf, quite unlike bread made with yeast, has a velvety texture and a powerful sage aroma.

Makes 1

225g/8oz/2cups plain (all-purpose) wholemeal (whole-wheat) flour
115g/4oz/1 cup plain (all-purpose) flour
2.5ml/½ tsp salt
5ml/1 tsp bicarbonate of soda (baking soda)
30ml/2 tbsp shredded fresh sage
300–450ml/½–¾ pint/1¼–scant 2 cups buttermilk

1 Preheat the oven to 220°C/425°F/Gas 7. Lightly grease a baking sheet and set aside.

2 Sift the wholemeal and white flours with the salt and bicarbonate of soda into a large bowl. Stir in the fresh sage and add enough buttermilk to make a soft dough. Do not overmix, or the bread will be heavy.

3 Shape the dough into a round loaf and place on the lightly greased baking sheet. Cut a cross in the top, cutting deep into the dough.

4 Bake in the oven for about 40 minutes, or until the loaf is well risen and sounds hollow when tapped on the base. Leave to cool on a wire rack.

Variations

- *Try this loaf made with all white flour rather than wholemeal (whole-wheat) and white flour for a finer and lighter texture.*
- *Fresh rosemary would also work well in place of the sage for this loaf.*
- *You could form the dough into two smaller loaves and bake them for 25–30 minutes.*
- *Fruit-flavoured soda bread tastes great too. In place of the sage, you could add 150g/5oz/1 cup raisins.*

Rosemary Bread per loaf Energy 1999kcal/8422kJ; Protein 77.3g; Carbohydrate 280.2g, of which sugars 37.4g; Fat 68.7g, of which saturates 41.5g; Cholesterol 180mg; Calcium 1489mg; Fibre 22g; Sodium 3069mg.

Sage Soda Bread per loaf Energy 1186kcal/5041kJ; Protein 49.6g; Carbohydrate 246.3g, of which sugars 19.6g; Fat 7.3g, of which saturates 1.3g; Cholesterol 11mg; Calcium 613mg; Fibre 23.8g; Sodium 1125mg.

Dill Bread

Tasty herb breads such as this are expensive to buy ready-made – and hard to find – and they never taste as good as home-made.

Makes 2

20ml/4 tsp active dried yeast
475ml/16fl oz/2 cups lukewarm water
30ml/2 tbsp caster (superfine) sugar
1.05kg/2lb 5½oz/scant 9½ cups strong white bread flour
½ onion, chopped
60ml/4 tbsp oil
a large bunch of dill, finely chopped
2 eggs, lightly beaten
150g/5oz/⅔ cup cottage cheese
20ml/4 tsp salt
milk, to glaze

1 Mix together the yeast, water and sugar in a large bowl and leave for 15 minutes to dissolve and for the yeast to become frothy. Stir in about half of the flour. Cover and leave to rise in a warm place for 45 minutes.

2 In a frying pan, cook the onion in 15ml/1 tbsp of the oil until soft, about 5 minutes. Set aside to cool, then stir into the yeast mixture.

3 Stir the dill, eggs, cottage cheese, salt and the remaining oil into the yeast. Gradually add the remaining flour until the dough is too stiff to stir.

4 Transfer to a floured surface and knead until smooth and elastic. This will take about 10 minutes. Place in a bowl, cover with clear film (plastic wrap) and leave to rise until doubled in volume, about 1–1½ hours.

5 Grease a large baking sheet. Cut the dough in half and shape into two rounds. Place on the sheet and leave to rise in a warm place for 30 minutes.

6 Preheat the oven to 190°C/375°F/Gas 5. Score the tops of the loaves, brush with the milk to glaze and bake until browned, about 50 minutes. Transfer to a wire rack to cool.

Spiral Herb Bread

When cut, this loaf looks very pretty with its swirls of garlic and herbs. It tastes pretty good too.

Makes 2

350g/12oz/3 cups strong white bread flour, plus extra for dusting
350g/12oz/3 cups wholemeal (whole-wheat) bread flour
2 x 7g/¼ oz easy-blend (rapid-rise) dried yeast
600ml/1 pint/2½ cups lukewarm water
25g/1oz/2 tbsp butter
1 bunch of spring onions (scallions), finely chopped
1 garlic clove, finely chopped
1 large bunch of fresh parsley, finely chopped
1 egg, lightly beaten
salt and ground black pepper
milk, for glazing

1 Mix the flours in a large bowl. Stir in 15ml/1 tbsp salt and the yeast. Make a well in the centre and pour in the water. Beat, gradually incorporating the flour to make a rough dough.

2 Knead the dough on a floured surface for 8–10 minutes. Return it to the bowl, cover with lightly oiled clear film and leave in a warm place to rise for 2 hours, until doubled in size.

3 Meanwhile, melt the butter in a pan and cook the spring onions and garlic over low heat, until softened. Season with salt and pepper, stir in the parsley and set aside.

4 Grease two 23 × 13cm/9 × 5in bread tins. When the dough has risen, cut it in half, then roll each half to a 35 × 23cm/14 × 9in rectangle. Brush with the beaten egg and divide the herb mixture between them, spreading it just to the edges.

5 Roll up each dough rectangle from a long side and pinch the short ends together to seal. Place in the tins, seam side down. Cover and leave in a warm place until the dough has risen above the rims of the tins.

6 Preheat the oven to 190°C/375°F/Gas 5. Brush the loaves with milk and bake for 55 minutes, until they are golden and sound hollow when tapped on the base. Cool on a wire rack.

Dill Bread per loaf Energy 2207kcal/9346kJ; Protein 65.5g; Carbohydrate 428.3g, of which sugars 27.6g; Fat 37.4g, of which saturates 6.9g; Cholesterol 202mg; Calcium 874mg; Fibre 16.7g; Sodium 313mg.

Spiral Herb Bread per loaf Energy 1726kcal/7323kJ; Protein 58.3g; Carbohydrate 345.9g, of which sugars 10.3g; Fat 21.9g, of which saturates 8.6g; Cholesterol 122mg; Calcium 465mg; Fibre 30.6g; Sodium 3077mg.

Welsh Clay Pot Loaves

These breads are flavoured with chives, sage, parsley and garlic. You can use any of your favourite herbs.

Makes 2

115g/4oz/1 cup wholemeal (whole-wheat) bread flour
350g/12oz/3 cups unbleached white bread flour
7.5ml/1½ tsp salt
15g/½oz fresh yeast
150ml/¼ pint/⅔ cup lukewarm milk
120ml/4fl oz/½ cup lukewarm water
50g/2oz/4 tbsp butter, melted
15ml/1 tbsp chopped fresh chives
15ml/1 tbsp chopped fresh parsley
5ml/1 tsp chopped fresh sage
1 garlic clove, crushed
beaten egg, for glazing
fennel seeds, for sprinkling (optional)

1 Grease two clean 14cm/5½in diameter, 11cm/4½in high clay flower pots. Sift the flours and salt into a bowl and make a well in the centre. Blend the yeast with a little of the milk until smooth, then stir in the remaining milk. Pour into the centre of the flour and sprinkle over a little of the flour from around the edge. Cover and leave in a warm place for 15 minutes.

2 Add the water, melted butter, herbs and garlic to the flour mixture and blend to a dough. Knead on a floured surface for about 10 minutes until the dough is smooth and elastic.

3 Place in a lightly oiled bowl, cover with lightly oiled clear film (plastic wrap) and leave for 1¼–1½ hours until doubled in size.

4 Turn out on to a lightly floured surface and knock back (punch down). Divide in two. Shape and fit into the prepared flower pots. They should about half fill the pots. Cover with oiled clear film and leave to rise for 30–45 minutes, in a warm place, or until the dough is 2.5cm/1in from the top of the pots.

5 Preheat the oven to 200°C/400°F/Gas 6. Brush the tops with beaten egg and sprinkle with fennel seeds, if using. Bake for 35–40 minutes or until golden. Cool on a wire rack.

Olive Bread

This wonderful country bread is made with olives combined with olive oil.

Makes 1

275g/10oz/2½ cups unbleached white bread flour, plus extra
50g/2oz/½ cup wholemeal (whole-wheat) bread flour
7g/¼oz easy-blend (rapid-rise) dried yeast
2.5ml/½ tsp salt
210ml/7½fl oz/scant 1 cup lukewarm water
15ml/1 tbsp extra virgin olive oil, plus extra for brushing
115g/4oz/1 cup pitted black and green olives, coarsely chopped

1 Lightly grease a baking sheet. Mix the flours, yeast and salt together in a large bowl and make a well in the centre.

2 Add the water and oil to the well in the flour and mix to a soft dough. Knead on a lightly floured surface until smooth and elastic, then place in a lightly oiled bowl, cover with lightly oiled clear film (plastic wrap) and leave in a warm place to rise for 1 hour, or until doubled in size.

3 Knock back (punch down) the dough on a lightly floured surface. Flatten it and sprinkle over the chopped olives. Fold up and knead to distribute the olives through the dough. Leave to rest for 5 minutes, then shape into an oval loaf. Place the loaf on the prepared baking sheet.

4 Make six deep cuts in the top of the loaf, and gently push the sections over. Cover with lightly oiled clear film and leave in a warm place to rise for 30–45 minutes, or until doubled in size.

5 Meanwhile, preheat the oven to 200°C/400°F/Gas 6. Brush the bread with olive oil and bake for 35–40 minutes. Cool on a wire rack.

Variation
You could increase the proportion of wholemeal (whole-wheat) flour to make this loaf more rustic.

Welsh Clay Pot Loaves per loaf Energy 1005kcal/4245kJ; Protein 27.3g; Carbohydrate 177.6g, of which sugars 8.2g; Fat 25.6g, of which saturates 14.8g; Cholesterol 62mg; Calcium 412mg; Fibre 12g; Sodium 1718mg.

Olive Bread per loaf Energy 1325kcal/5600kJ; Protein 31.6g; Carbohydrate 252.5g, of which sugars 4.9g; Fat 27.8g, of which saturates 4.2g; Cholesterol 0mg; Calcium 525mg; Fibre 13.4g; Sodium 3557mg.

Italian Olive & Herb Bread

Olive breads are popular all over Italy. This delicious version is enhanced with chopped fresh herbs and is perfect with pasta and salads.

Makes 2

2 red onions, thinly sliced
30ml/2 tbsp olive oil
225g/8oz/1½ cups pitted black or green olives
800g/1¾lb/7 cups strong white bread flour, plus extra for dusting
7.5ml/1½ tsp salt
20ml/4 tsp easy-blend (rapid-rise) dried yeast
45ml/3 tbsp roughly chopped fresh parsley, coriander (cilantro) or mint
475ml/16fl oz/2 cups lukewarm water

1 Fry the onions in the oil in a pan until soft. Remove the pan from the heat and set aside. Roughly chop the black or green olives and set aside.

2 Put the flour, salt, yeast and chopped fresh herbs in a large bowl with the olives and fried onions and pour in the water. Mix to a dough using a round-bladed knife, adding a little more water if the mixture feels dry.

3 Turn out on to a lightly floured surface and knead for about 10 minutes, until smooth and elastic. Put in a clean bowl, cover with clear film (plastic wrap) and leave in a warm place until doubled in bulk.

4 Preheat the oven to 220°C/425°F/Gas 7. Lightly grease two baking sheets.

5 Turn the dough out on to a lightly floured surface and cut in half. Shape into two rounds. Place on the prepared baking sheets, cover loosely with lightly oiled clear film and leave until doubled in bulk.

6 Slash the tops of the loaves with a sharp knife, then bake in the oven for about 40 minutes, or until they sound hollow when tapped underneath. Transfer to a wire rack to cool. Serve warm or cold, in slices.

Olive & Oregano Bread

Fresh herbs are fabulous in loaves. This is an excellent accompaniment to all salads and is very good with grilled goat's cheese.

Makes 1

15ml/1 tbsp olive oil
1 onion, chopped
450g/1lb/4 cups strong white bread flour
10ml/2 tsp easy-blend (rapid-rise) dried yeast
5ml/1 tsp salt
1.5ml/¼ tsp ground black pepper
50g/2oz/½ cup pitted black olives, roughly chopped
15ml/1 tbsp black olive paste
15ml/1 tbsp chopped fresh oregano
15ml/1 tbsp chopped fresh parsley
300ml/½ pint/1¼ cups lukewarm water

1 Lightly oil a baking sheet. Heat the olive oil in a frying pan and fry the onion until golden brown.

2 Sift the flour into a mixing bowl. Add the yeast, salt and pepper. Make a well in the centre.

3 Add the fried onion (with the oil from the pan) the olives, olive paste, chopped oregano and parsley, and the water to the well in the bowl. Stir from the centre outwards and gradually incorporate the flour. Mix until a soft dough forms, adding a little extra water if necessary.

4 Turn the dough on to a floured surface and knead for 5 minutes until smooth and elastic. Shape into a 20cm/8in round and place on the baking sheet.

5 Using a sharp knife, make criss-cross cuts over the top, cover and leave in a warm place until doubled in size, about 1½ hours. Preheat the oven to 220°C/425°F/Gas 7.

6 Bake the for 10 minutes, then lower the oven temperature to 200°C/400°F/Gas 6. Bake for a further 20 minutes, or until the loaf feels and sounds hollow when tapped underneath. Cool on a wire rack.

Italian Olive and Herb Bread Energy 1676kcal/7085kJ; Protein 45.3g; Carbohydrate 327.6g, of which sugars 17.7g; Fat 29.4g, of which saturates 4.3g; Cholesterol 0mg; Calcium 732mg; Fibre 26.1g; Sodium 4036mg.

Olive and Oregano Bread Energy 172kcal/727kJ; Protein 4.4g; Carbohydrate 35.4g, of which sugars 1g; Fat 2.3g, of which saturates 0.4g; Cholesterol 0mg; Calcium 68mg; Fibre 1.7g; Sodium 134mg.

Greek Olive & Herb Bread

The flavours of the Mediterranean simply ooze from this decorative bread, speckled with black olives, red onions and herbs.

Makes 2

675g/1½lb/6 cups unbleached white bread flour, plus extra for dusting
10ml/2 tsp salt
25g/1oz fresh yeast
350ml/12fl oz/1½ cups lukewarm water
75ml/5 tbsp olive oil
175g/6oz/1½ cups pitted black olives, roughly chopped
1 onion, finely chopped
30ml/2 tbsp chopped fresh coriander (cilantro) or mint

1 Sift the flour and salt together into a large bowl and make a well in the centre. In a jug (pitcher), blend the yeast with half of the water. Add to the centre of the flour with the remaining water and the olive oil; mix to a soft dough. Knead for 8–10 minutes until smooth. Place in a lightly oiled bowl, cover and leave to rise, in a warm place, for 1 hour.

2 Knock back (punch down). Cut off a quarter of the dough, cover with lightly oiled clear film and set aside.

3 Roll out the remaining, large piece of dough to a round. Sprinkle the olives, onion and herbs evenly over the surface, then bring up the sides of the circle and gently knead together. Cut the dough in half and shape each piece into a plump oval loaf, about 20cm/8in long. Place on greased baking sheets.

4 Divide the reserved dough into four equal pieces and roll each to a long strand 60cm/24in long. Twist together and cut in half. Brush the centre of each loaf with water and place two pieces of twisted dough on top of each, tucking the ends underneath the loaves.

5 Cover and leave to rise for about 45 minutes, or until the loaves are plump and nearly doubled in size. Meanwhile, preheat the oven to 220°C/425°F/Gas 7. Dust the loaves lightly with flour and bake for 35–40 minutes, or until the loaf sounds hollow when tapped underneath. Cool on a wire rack.

Garlic & Herb Bread

This irresistible garlic bread is quick to make using ready-prepared bread, whether home-made or from the store, and includes plenty of fresh herbs.

Makes 1

1 baguette or bloomer loaf for the garlic and herb butter
115g/4oz/½ cup unsalted (sweet) butter, softened
5–6 large garlic cloves, finely chopped or crushed
30–45ml/2–3 tbsp chopped fresh herbs (such as parsley, chervil and a little tarragon)
15ml/1 tbsp chopped fresh chives
salt and ground black pepper, to taste

1 Preheat the oven to 200°C/400°F/Gas 6. Beat the butter with the garlic, herbs, chives and seasoning.

2 Cut the bread into 1cm/½in thick diagonal slices, but be sure to leave them attached at the base so that the loaf stays intact.

3 Spread the garlic and herb butter between the slices evenly, being careful not to detach them, and then spread any remaining butter over the top of the loaf.

4 Wrap the loaf in foil, place in the preheated oven and bake for 20–25 minutes, until the butter is melted and the crust is golden and crisp. Cut the loaf into slices to serve.

Cook's Tip
This loaf makes an excellent addition to a barbecue. If space permits, place the foil-wrapped loaf on the top of the barbecue and cook for about the same length of time as for oven baking. Turn the foil parcel over several times to ensure it cooks evenly.

Variations
Flavour the butter with a little chopped fresh chilli, grated lime rind and chopped fresh coriander (cilantro).

Greek Olive and Herb Bread per loaf Energy 1527kcal/6440kJ; Protein 34g; Carbohydrate 270.4g, of which sugars 10.9g; Fat 41.8g, of which saturates 6g; Cholesterol 0mg; Calcium 567mg; Fibre 14.8g; Sodium 3950mg.

Garlic and Herb Bread Energy 920kcal/3877kJ; Protein 22.1g; Carbohydrate 135.1g, of which sugars 7.2g; Fat 36.2g, of which saturates 20.8g; Cholesterol 82mg; Calcium 317mg; Fibre 6.3g; Sodium 1714mg.

Spicy Millet Bread

This is a delicious spicy bread with a golden crust. Cut into wedges and serve warm with a thick soup.

Makes 1

90g/3½oz/½ cup millet
600g/1lb 6oz/5½ cups strong unbleached plain (all-purpose) flour, plus extra for dusting
10ml/2 tsp salt
7g/¼oz easy-blend (rapid-rise) dried yeast
5ml/1 tsp caster (superfine) sugar
5ml/1 tsp dried chilli flakes (optional)
25g/1oz/2 tbsp butter
1 onion, roughly chopped
15ml/1 tbsp cumin seeds
5ml/1 tsp ground turmeric

1 Bring 200ml/7fl oz/scant 1 cup water to the boil in a small pan. Add the millet, cover and simmer gently for 20 minutes, until the grains are soft and the water has been absorbed. Remove from the heat and leave to cool until just warm.

2 Mix the flour, salt, yeast, sugar and chilli flakes, if using, in a large bowl. Stir in the millet, then add 350ml/12fl oz/1½ cups warm water and mix to a soft dough.

3 Knead the dough on a floured surface for 10 minutes, then place it in an oiled bowl and cover with oiled clear film (plastic wrap). Leave in a warm place for 1 hour, or until doubled in size.

4 Meanwhile, melt the butter in a heavy frying pan, and fry the onion until softened. Add the cumin seeds and turmeric, and fry for 5–8 minutes more, stirring constantly, until the cumin seeds begin to pop. Set aside.

5 Knock back (punch down) the dough, knead it briefly again and shape it into a round. Place the onion mixture in the middle and bring the sides over to cover it. Seal well. Place the loaf on an oiled baking sheet, seam side down, cover with oiled clear film and leave in a warm place for 45 minutes, until doubled in size. Preheat the oven to 220°C/425°F/Gas 7.

6 Bake the bread for 30 minutes, until golden. It should sound hollow when tapped underneath. Cool on a wire rack.

Cornish Saffron Bread

This loaf is traditionally made at Easter, and is served sliced and buttered. Saffron, the precious spice from western Asia, may have been introduced to Cornwall by Phoenician traders 3,000 years ago.

Makes 1

a good pinch of saffron threads
450g/1lb/4 cups plain (all-purpose) flour
2.5ml/½ tsp salt
50g/2oz/4 tbsp butter, diced
50g/2oz/4 tbsp lard, diced
10ml/2 tsp easy-blend (rapid-rise) dried yeast
50g/2oz caster (superfine) sugar
115g/4oz/½ cup currants, raisins or sultanas (golden raisins), or a mixture
50g/2oz mixed chopped (candied) peel
150ml/¼ pint/⅔ cup milk
beaten egg, to glaze

1 Put the saffron in a bowl and add 150ml/¼ pint/⅔ cup boiling water. Cover and leave for several hours to allow the colour and flavour to develop.

2 Sift the flour and salt into a large bowl. Add the butter and lard and rub them into the flour until the mixture resembles fine breadcrumbs. Stir in the yeast granules, sugar, dried fruit and chopped mixed peel. Make a well in the centre.

3 Add the milk to the saffron water and warm to body heat. Pour the liquid into the flour and stir until it can be gathered into a ball. Cover with oiled clear film (plastic wrap) and leave in a warm place for about 1 hour, until doubled in size.

4 Grease and line a 900g/2lb loaf tin (pan) with baking parchment. Turn the dough on to a lightly floured surface and knead gently and briefly. Put the dough in the prepared tin, cover and leave in a warm place for 30 minutes until nearly doubled in size.

5 Preheat the oven to 200°C/400°F/Gas 6. Brush the top of the loaf with beaten egg and cook for 40 minutes or until risen and cooked through; cover with foil if it starts to brown too much. Leave for about 15 minutes before turning out to cool.

Spicy Millet Bread per loaf Energy 2464kcal/10426kJ; Protein 59.7g; Carbohydrate 509.5g, of which sugars 15.9g; Fat 31.5g, of which saturates 14.1g; Cholesterol 53mg; Calcium 957mg; Fibre 22.5g; Sodium 4209mg.

Cornish Saffron Bread per loaf Energy 3041kcal/12821kJ; Protein 50.7g; Carbohydrate 516.8g, of which sugars 173.9g; Fat 99.9g, of which saturates 48.7g; Cholesterol 162mg; Calcium 1018mg; Fibre 18.5g; Sodium 541mg.

Cardamom & Saffron Tea Loaf

An aromatic sweet bread ideal for afternoon tea, or lightly toasted for breakfast. The delicate spices of cardamom and saffron give it an unusual flavour.

Makes 1

a generous pinch of saffron threads
750ml/1¼ pints/3 cups lukewarm milk
25g/1oz/2 tbsp butter
1kg/2¼lb/9 cups strong white bread flour
15g/½oz easy-blend (rapid-rise) dried yeast
40g/1½oz/generous ¼ cup caster (superfine) sugar
6 cardamom pods, split open and seeds extracted
115g/4oz/scant ¾ cup raisins
30ml/2 tbsp clear honey, plus extra for glazing
1 egg, beaten

1 Crush the saffron straight into a cup containing a little of the warm milk and leave to infuse (steep) for 5 minutes.

2 Rub the butter into the flour using your fingertips or a pastry blender, then mix in the yeast, sugar, cardamom seeds and raisins.

3 Beat the remaining milk with the honey and egg, then mix this into the flour, along with the saffron milk and threads, until the mixture forms a firm dough. Turn out the dough and knead it on a lightly floured surface for 5 minutes.

4 Return the dough to the mixing bowl, cover with oiled clear film (plastic wrap) and leave in a warm place until doubled in size.

5 Preheat the oven to 200°C/400°F/Gas 6. Grease a 900g/2lb loaf tin (pan). Turn the dough out on to a floured surface, knock back (punch down) and knead for 3 minutes.

6 Shape the dough into a fat roll and fit into the tin. Cover with a sheet of lightly oiled clear film and leave to stand in a warm place until the dough begins to rise again.

7 Bake the loaf for 25 minutes, or until golden brown and firm on top. Turn out on to a wire rack and as it cools brush the top with clear honey.

Banana & Cardamom Bread

The combination of banana and fragrant cardamom is delicious in this soft-textured moist loaf.

Makes 1

10 cardamom pods
400g/14oz/3½ cups strong white bread flour
5ml/1 tsp salt
5ml/1 tsp easy-blend (rapid-rise) dried yeast
150ml/¼ pint/⅔ cup hand-hot water
30ml/2 tbsp malt extract
2 ripe bananas, mashed
5ml/1 tsp sesame seeds

1 Grease a 450g/1lb loaf tin (pan). Split the cardamom pods, and remove the seeds and then chop the pods finely.

2 Sift the flour and salt into a large bowl, add the yeast and make a well in the centre. Add the water with the malt extract, chopped cardamom pods and bananas. Stir from the centre outwards, gradually incorporating the flour and mixing to a soft dough, and adding a little extra water if necessary.

3 Turn the dough on to a floured surface and knead for 5 minutes until smooth and elastic. Shape into a braid and place in the prepared tin. Cover loosely with clear film (plastic wrap) (ballooning it to trap the air) and leave in a warm place until well risen, about 1½ hours. Meanwhile, preheat the oven to 220°C/425°F/Gas 7.

4 Brush the braid lightly with water and sprinkle with the sesame seeds. Bake for 10 minutes, then lower the oven to 200°C/400°F/Gas 6. Cook for 15 minutes more, or until the loaf sounds hollow when tapped underneath. Remove to a wire rack to cool.

Cook's Tip

Cardamom is a green or white seed pod containing tiny black seeds. It has a distinctive warm and pronounced scent that works really well in flavoured breads.

Cardamom and Saffron Tea Loaf per loaf Energy 4423kcal/18733kJ; Protein 139g; Carbohydrate 853g, of which sugars 188g; Fat 73g, of which saturates 38g; Cholesterol 401mg; Calcium 2242mg; Fibre 40g; Sodium 694mg.

Banana and Cardamom Bread Energy 279kcal/1185kJ; Protein 6.8g; Carbohydrate 63.5g, of which sugars 11.9g; Fat 1.5g, of which saturates 0.2g; Cholesterol 0mg; Calcium 102mg; Fibre 2.5g; Sodium 16mg.

Festive Swedish Bread

This bread is flavoured with warm spices and fresh orange. The beer and port soften the rye taste.

Makes 1

350g/12oz/3 cups rye flour
350g/12oz/3 cups unbleached white bread flour
2.5ml/½ tsp salt
25g/1oz/2 tbsp caster (superfine) sugar
5ml/1 tsp grated nutmeg
5ml/1 tsp ground cloves
5ml/1 tsp ground ginger
40g/1½oz fresh yeast
300ml/½ pint/1¼ cups light ale
120ml/4fl oz/½ cup port
15ml/1 tbsp molasses
25g/1oz/2 tbsp butter, melted
15ml/1 tbsp grated orange rind
75g/3oz/½ cup raisins
15ml/1 tbsp malt extract, for glazing

1 Grease a 30 × 10cm/12 × 4in loaf tin (pan). Mix the rye and white flours, salt, sugar, nutmeg, cloves and ginger in a bowl.

2 In another bowl, blend the yeast into the ale until dissolved, then stir in the port, molasses and melted butter.

3 Gradually add the flour mixture to the yeast liquid, beating to make a smooth batter. Continue adding the flour a little at a time and mixing until a soft dough forms. Transfer to a lightly floured surface and knead for 8–10 minutes until smooth. Place in a lightly oiled bowl, cover with oiled clear film (plastic wrap) and leave in a warm place, for 1 hour, or until doubled in size.

4 Turn out the dough on to a lightly floured surface and knock back (punch down). Gently knead in the orange rind and raisins. Roll into a 30cm/12in square.

5 Fold the bottom third of the dough up and the top third down, sealing the edges. Place in the prepared tin, cover with lightly oiled clear film and leave to rise, in a warm place, for 1 hour, or until the dough reaches the top of the tin.

6 Meanwhile, preheat the oven to 190°C/375°F/Gas 5. Bake for 35–40 minutes, or until browned. Turn out on to a wire rack, brush with malt extract and leave to cool.

Pumpernickel

This type of rye bread is from Germany, although no one knows how it got its name. This easy version of the traditional recipe uses cocoa powder to achieve the characteristic colour, and a combination of coffee and caraway seeds to add flavour.

Makes 2

65g/2½oz unsweetened cocoa powder
7g/¼oz easy-blend (rapid-rise) dried yeast
15ml/1 tbsp instant coffee powder
200g/7oz/1¾ cups rye flour
300–400g/11–14oz/2¾–3½ cups strong white bread flour
5ml/1 tsp salt
2.5ml/½ tsp sugar
15ml/1 tbsp caraway seeds
105ml/7 tbsp dark beer
15ml/1 tbsp vegetable oil
90ml/6 tbsp treacle (molasses)
cornmeal, for sprinkling

1 Mix the cocoa with 50ml/2fl oz/¼ cup boiling water, and set aside. In a large bowl, combine the yeast, coffee, flours, salt, sugar and caraway seeds.

2 Make a well in the flour mixture, then pour in the cocoa, 175ml/6fl oz/¾ cup water, the beer, oil and treacle. Mix well to form a dough. Turn out on to a lightly floured surface and knead for about 10 minutes, or until smooth.

3 Place the dough in a lightly oiled bowl and turn the dough to coat in oil. Cover with a dish towel and leave to rise for 1½ hours, or until doubled in size.

4 Oil a baking sheet and sprinkle with cornmeal. Turn the dough on to a lightly floured surface and punch down.

5 Knead for 3–4 minutes, then divide the dough and shape into two round or oval loaves. Place the loaves on the baking sheet, cover with a clean dish towel and leave to rise in a warm place for 45 minutes, or until doubled in size.

6 Preheat the oven to 185°C/360°F/Gas 4½. Bake the loaves for about 40 minutes, or until they sound hollow when tapped on the base. Leave to cool on a wire rack.

Festive Swedish Bread per loaf Energy 3362kcal/14252kJ; Protein 68.8g; Carbohydrate 666.2g, of which sugars 126.8g; Fat 34.9g, of which saturates 15.6g; Cholesterol 58mg; Calcium 812mg; Fibre 53.3g; Sodium 1302mg.

Pumpernickel per loaf Energy 1276kcal/5400kJ; Protein 27.3g; Carbohydrate 246.4g, of which sugars 42.4g; Fat 24.3g, of which saturates 8.6g; Cholesterol 5mg; Calcium 395mg; Fibre 9.1g; Sodium 187mg.

Kolach

This Bulgarian bread gets its name from its circular shape – *kolo*, which means circle. It has a golden crust sprinkled with poppy seeds and a moist crumb, which helps makes the loaf a good keeper.

Makes 1

675g/1½lb/6 cups unbleached white bread flour
10ml/2 tsp salt
25g/1oz fresh yeast
120ml/4fl oz/½ cup lukewarm milk
5ml/1 tsp clear honey
2 eggs
150ml/¼ pint/⅔ cup natural (plain) yogurt
50g/2oz/¼ cup butter, melted
beaten egg, for glazing
poppy seeds, for sprinkling

1 Grease a large baking sheet. Sift the flour and salt together into a large bowl and make a well in the centre.

2 Cream the yeast with the milk and honey. Add to the centre of the flour with the eggs, yogurt and melted butter. Gradually mix into the flour to form a firm dough.

3 Turn out on to a lightly floured surface and knead for 8–10 minutes until smooth and elastic. Place in a lightly oiled bowl, cover with lightly oiled clear film (plastic wrap). Leave in a warm place, for 1¼ hours, or until doubled in bulk.

4 Knock back (punch down) the dough and turn out on to a lightly floured surface. Knead lightly and shape into a ball. Place seam side down and make a hole in the centre with your fingers.

5 Gradually enlarge the cavity, turning the dough to make a 25cm/10in circle. Transfer to the baking sheet, cover with lightly oiled clear film (plastic wrap) and leave to rise, in a warm place, for 30–45 minutes, or until doubled in size.

6 Meanwhile, preheat the oven to 200°C/400°F/Gas 6. Brush the loaf with beaten egg and sprinkle with poppy seeds. Bake for 35 minutes, or until golden. Cool on a wire rack.

Two-tone Bread

A tasty, malty bread that reveals an attractive swirled interior when sliced.

Makes 2

25ml/1½ tbsp active dried yeast
120ml/4fl oz/½ cup warm water
55g/2¼oz/generous ¼ cup caster (superfine) sugar
675g/1½lb/6 cups strong white bread flour
7.5ml/1½ tsp salt
600ml/1 pint/2½ cups warm milk
65g/2½oz/5 tbsp butter or margarine, melted and cooled
45ml/3 tbsp black treacle (molasses)
275g/10oz/2½ cups strong wholemeal (whole-wheat) bread flour

1 In a small bowl, dissolve the yeast in the water with 5ml/1 tsp of the sugar. In a large bowl, sift 350g/12oz/3 cups of the white bread flour, the salt and remaining sugar. Make a well in the centre and add the yeast, milk and butter or margarine. Mix in gradually to form a smooth soft batter.

2 Divide the batter into two bowls. To one bowl, add 275g/10oz/2½ cups of the strong white flour and mix to a soft dough. Knead until smooth, about 10 minutes. Shape into a ball, put into a greased bowl and cover with clear film (plastic wrap).

3 Mix the treacle and wholemeal flour into the second bowl. Add enough white flour to make a soft dough, and knead until smooth. Shape into a ball, put in a greased bowl and cover with oiled clear film. Leave to rise in a warm place until doubled in size, about 1 hour.

4 Grease two 22 × 11cm/8½ × 4½in loaf tins (pans). Preheat the oven to 220°C/425°F/Gas 7. Knock back (punch down) the dough and divide each ball in half.

5 Roll out half of the light dough and half the dark dough to 30 × 20cm/12 × 8in rectangles. Set the dark dough rectangle on the light one, and roll up tightly from a short side. Set in a loaf tin. Repeat for the other loaf. Cover the tins and leave the dough to rise until doubled in size. Bake for 30–35 minutes.

Kolach per loaf Energy 2979kcal/12601kJ; Protein 87.8g; Carbohydrate 547.8g, of which sugars 33.5g; Fat 64.3g, of which saturates 33.4g; Cholesterol 505mg; Calcium 1440mg; Fibre 20.9g; Sodium 4657mg.

Two-tone Bread per loaf Energy 2123kcal/8994kJ; Protein 60g; Carbohydrate 408.3g, of which sugars 66g; Fat 39.3g, of which saturates 20.8g; Cholesterol 87mg; Calcium 1029mg; Fibre 22.9g; Sodium 383mg.

Black Bread

This bread's texture is similar to pumpernickel. It is slowly steamed rather than oven-baked. Empty fruit cans are perfect for producing bread in the traditional round shape.

Makes 2

50g/2oz/½ cup rye flour
40g/1½ oz/⅓ cup plain (all-purpose) flour
4ml/¾ tsp baking powder
2.5ml/½ tsp salt
1.5ml/¼ tsp cinnamon
1.5ml/¼ tsp nutmeg
50g/2oz/⅓ cup fine semolina
60ml/4 tbsp black treacle (molasses)
200ml/7fl oz/scant 1 cup cultured buttermilk
cherry jam, sour cream or crème fraîche, and a sprinkling of ground allspice, to serve

1 Grease and line 2 × 400g/14oz fruit cans. Sift the flours, baking powder, salt and spices into a large mixing bowl. Stir in the semolina. Add the black treacle and buttermilk and mix.

2 Divide the mixture evenly between the two cans, then cover each with a double layer of greased pleated foil.

3 Place the cans on a trivet in a large pan and pour in enough hot water to come halfway up the sides of the cans. Cover the pan tightly and steam for 2 hours, checking the water level occasionally, and topping up if necessary.

4 Carefully remove the cans from the steamer. Turn the bread out on to a wire rack and cool completely. Wrap in foil and use within 1 week.

5 Serve the bread in slices, spread with cherry jam, topped with a spoonful of soured cream or crème fraîche and a sprinkling of allspice.

Cook's Tip
If you cannot get buttermilk, use ordinary milk instead, first soured with 5ml/1 tsp lemon juice.

Anadama Bread

A traditional bread from Massachusetts, made with molasses, cornmeal, wholemeal and white flour.

Makes 2

40g/1½oz/3 tbsp butter
120ml/4fl oz/½ cup molasses
560ml/scant 1 pint/scant 2½ cups water
50g/2oz/½ cup cornmeal
10ml/2 tsp salt
25g/1oz fresh yeast
30ml/2 tbsp lukewarm water
275g/10oz/2½ cups wholemeal (whole-wheat) flour
450g/1lb/4 cups unbleached white bread flour

1 Grease two 1.5 litre/2½ pint/6 cup loaf tins (pans). Heat the butter, molasses and measured water in a pan until the butter has melted. Stir in the cornmeal and salt and stir over low heat until boiling. Cool until lukewarm.

2 In a small bowl, cream the yeast with the lukewarm water, then set aside for 5 minutes.

3 Mix the cornmeal mixture and yeast mixture together in a bowl. Fold in the wholemeal flour and then the unbleached white bread flour to form a sticky dough. Turn out on to a lightly floured surface and knead for 10–15 minutes until the dough is smooth and elastic. Add a little more flour if needed.

4 Place in a lightly oiled bowl, cover with lightly oiled clear film (plastic wrap) and leave in a warm place, for about 1 hour, or until doubled in bulk.

5 Knead the dough lightly on a floured surface, shape into two loaves and place in the tins. Cover with lightly oiled clear film and leave in a warm place until doubled in size, about 40 minutes.

6 Meanwhile, preheat the oven to 200°C/400°F/Gas 6. Using a sharp knife, slash the tops of the loaves three or four times. Bake for 15 minutes, then reduce the oven temperature to 180°C/350°F/Gas 4 and bake for a further 35–40 minutes, or until sounding hollow when tapped on the base. Serve warm.

Black Bread Energy 417kcal/1774kJ; Protein 12.3g; Carbohydrate 94g, of which sugars 25.1g; Fat 1.8g, of which saturates 0.3g; Cholesterol 4mg; Calcium 356mg; Fibre 4.7g; Sodium 103mg.

Anadama Bread per loaf Energy 1589kcal/6729kJ; Protein 41.8g; Carbohydrate 321.4g, of which sugars 46.5g; Fat 23.2g, of which saturates 11.3g; Cholesterol 43mg; Calcium 702mg; Fibre 19.9g; Sodium 240mg.

Cheese & Onion Herb Sticks

These tasty breads are very good with soup or salads. Use an extra-strong cheese to give plenty of flavour.

Makes 2

15ml/1 tbsp sunflower oil
1 red onion, chopped
450g/1lb/4 cups strong white flour, plus extra for dusting
5ml/1 tsp salt
5ml/1 tsp dry mustard powder
10ml/2 tsp easy-blend (rapid-rise) dried yeast
a pinch of sugar
45ml/3 tbsp chopped mixed fresh herbs
75g/3oz/¾ cup grated reduced-fat Cheddar cheese
about 300ml/½ pint/1¼ cups lukewarm water

1 Heat the oil in a frying pan and fry the onion until well coloured. Lightly grease two baking sheets.

2 Sift the flour, salt and mustard into a mixing bowl. Add the dried yeast, sugar and herbs. Set aside 30ml/2 tbsp of the cheese. Stir the rest into the flour mixture and make a well in the centre. Add the lukewarm water, with the fried onions and oil, then gradually incorporate the flour and mix to a soft dough, adding extra water if necessary.

3 Knead the dough on a floured surface for about 10 minutes. Return the dough to the clean bowl, cover with lightly oiled clear film (plastic wrap) and set aside in a warm place to rise for about 1 hour, until doubled in size.

4 Turn the dough on to a floured surface, knead it briefly, then divide the mixture in half and roll each piece into a 30cm/12in long stick. Place each stick on a baking sheet and make diagonal cuts along the top.

5 Sprinkle the sticks with the reserved cheese. Cover and leave for 30 minutes, until well risen.

6 Preheat the oven to 220°C/425°F/Gas 7. Bake the sticks for 25 minutes, or until they sound hollow when they are tapped underneath. Cool on a wire rack.

Tomato Breadsticks

Fresh, healthy and low in fat, these are delectable with dips. Make plenty, as they are very moreish.

Makes 16

225g/8oz/2 cups plain (all-purpose) flour, plus extra for dusting
2.5ml/½ tsp salt
7.5ml/1½ tsp easy-blend (rapid-rise) dried yeast
5ml/1 tsp clear honey
10ml/2 tsp olive oil, plus extra
about 150ml/¼ pint/⅔ cup lukewarm water
6 pieces of sun-dried tomatoes in olive oil, drained and chopped
15ml/1 tbsp skimmed milk
10ml/2 tsp poppy seeds

1 Place the flour, salt and yeast in a food processor. Add the honey and 5ml/1 tsp of the olive oil and, with the machine running, gradually pour in enough lukewarm water to make a dough. Process for 1 minute more.

2 Knead the dough on a lightly floured surface for 3–4 minutes. Knead in the chopped sun-dried tomatoes. Form the dough into a ball and place in a lightly oiled bowl. Set aside to rise for 5 minutes.

3 Preheat the oven to 150°C/300°F/Gas 2. Lightly brush a baking sheet with oil.

4 Divide the dough into 16 pieces and roll each piece into a stick about 28 × 1cm/11 × ½in long. Place the breadsticks on the prepared baking sheet and set aside in a warm place to rise for 15 minutes.

5 Brush the sticks with milk and sprinkle with poppy seeds. Bake for 30 minutes. Cool on a wire rack.

Cook's Tip

Flours vary in their absorbency, so you may not require all the water. Stop adding it as soon as soon as the dough starts to cling together.

Cheese and Onion Herb Sticks per stick Energy 154kcal/653kJ; Protein 5.6g; Carbohydrate 29.5g, of which sugars 0.8g; Fat 2.4g, of which saturates 0.8g; Cholesterol 3mg; Calcium 106mg; Fibre 1.2g; Sodium 43mg.

Tomato Breadsticks per stick Energy 53kcal/227kJ; Protein 1.5g; Carbohydrate 11.7g, of which sugars 1g; Fat 0.4g, of which saturates 0.1g; Cholesterol 0mg; Calcium 22mg; Fibre 0.5g; Sodium 68mg.

Sesame-studded Grissini

These crisp, pencil-like breadsticks are easy to make and far more delicious than commercially manufactured grissini. Once you start to nibble one, it will be difficult to stop eating them. Serve them with drinks and a variety of creamy dips.

Makes 20

225g/8oz/2 cups unbleached white bread flour
7.5ml/1½ tsp salt
15g/½oz fresh yeast
135ml/4½fl oz/scant ⅔ cup lukewarm water
30ml/2 tbsp extra virgin olive oil, plus extra for brushing
sesame seeds, for coating

1 Lightly oil two baking sheets. Sift the flour and salt together into a large bowl and make a well in the centre.

2 Cream the yeast with the water and pour into the well. Add the oil and mix to a soft dough. Turn out on to a lightly floured surface and knead for 8–10 minutes until smooth and elastic.

3 Roll the dough into a rectangle about 15 × 20cm/6 × 8in. Brush with olive oil, cover with lightly oiled clear film (plastic wrap) and leave in a warm place for 1 hour, or until doubled in size.

4 Preheat the oven to 200°C/400°F/Gas 6. Spread out the sesame seeds. Cut the dough into two 7.5 × 10cm/3 × 4in rectangles. Cut each piece into ten 7.5cm/3in strips. Stretch each strip gently until it is about 30cm/12in long.

5 Roll each grissini, as it is made, in the sesame seeds. Place on the prepared baking sheets, spaced well apart. Lightly brush with olive oil. Leave to rise in a warm place for 10 minutes, then bake for 15–20 minutes. Transfer to a wire rack to cool.

Cook's Tip
When baking the grissini, turn them over and change the position of the baking sheets halfway through the cooking time, so that they brown evenly.

Caraway Breadsticks

Ideal to nibble with drinks, these can be made in a wide variety of flavours, including cumin seed, poppy seed and celery seed, as well as the coriander and sesame variation suggested below.

Makes 20

225g/8oz/2 cups plain (all-purpose) flour
2.5ml/½ tsp salt
2.5ml/½ tsp easy-blend (rapid-rise) dried yeast
10ml/2 tsp caraway seeds
150ml/¼ pint/⅔ cup lukewarm water
a pinch of sugar

1 Grease two baking sheets. Sift the flour, salt, yeast and sugar into a large bowl, stir in the caraway seeds and make a well in the centre.

2 Add the water and stir from the centre outwards, gradually mixing the flour to make a soft dough, and adding a little extra water if necessary.

3 Turn the dough on to a lightly floured surface and knead for 5 minutes until smooth and elastic.

4 Divide the mixture into 20 pieces and roll each one into a 30cm/12in stick.

5 Arrange the breadsticks on the baking sheets, leaving room to allow for rising. Leave for 30 minutes, or until well risen. Meanwhile, preheat the oven to 220°C/425°F/Gas 7.

6 Bake the breadsticks for 10–12 minutes, or until golden brown. Cool on the baking sheets.

Variation
To make Coriander and Sesame Sticks, replace the caraway seeds with 15ml/1 tbsp crushed coriander seeds. Dampen the breadsticks lightly and sprinkle them with sesame seeds before baking.

Sesame-studded Grissini per stick Energy 53kcal/222kJ; Protein 1.2g; Carbohydrate 8.8g, of which sugars 0.2g; Fat 1.7g, of which saturates 0.2g; Cholesterol 0mg; Calcium 21mg; Fibre 0.4g; Sodium 148mg.

Caraway Breadsticks per stick Energy 41kcal/176kJ; Protein 1.2g; Carbohydrate 8.7g, of which sugars 0.2g; Fat 0.4g, of which saturates 0.1g; Cholesterol 0mg; Calcium 19mg; Fibre 0.4g; Sodium 50mg.

Pitta Bread

Soft, slightly bubbly pitta bread is a pleasure to make. It can be eaten in a variety of ways, such as filled with salad or little chunks of barbecued meat. Eat it with a main course or as part of a meze table.

Makes 12

500g/1¼lb/5 cups strong white bread flour, or half white and half wholemeal (whole-wheat)
12.5ml/2½ tsp easy-blend (rapid-rise) dried yeast
15ml/1 tbsp salt
15ml/1 tbsp olive oil

1 Combine the flour, yeast and salt. Combine the olive oil and 250ml/8fl oz/1 cup water, then add the flour mixture, stirring in the same direction, and then working with your hands until the dough is stiff. Place the dough in a clean bowl, cover with a clean damp dish towel and leave in a warm place for at least 30 minutes and up to 2 hours.

2 Knead the dough for 10 minutes, or until smooth. Lightly oil the bowl, place the dough in it, cover again and leave in a warm place for about 1 hour, or until doubled in size.

3 Divide the dough into 12 equal pieces. With lightly floured hands, flatten each piece, then roll out into a round measuring about 20cm/8in and about ½–1cm/¼–½in thick.

4 Heat a heavy frying pan over medium-high heat. When it is hot, lay one piece of flattened dough in the pan and cook for 15–20 seconds. Turn it over and cook the second side for about 1 minute.

5 When large bubbles start to form on the bread, which should be after about 1–2 minutes, turn it over again. It should puff up. Using a clean dish towel, gently press on the bread where the bubbles have formed. Cook for a total of 3 minutes, then remove from the pan. Repeat with the remaining dough.

6 Wrap the pitta breads in a clean dish towel, adding each one to the stack as it is cooked. Serve the pittas hot while they are soft and moist.

Thin & Crispy Flatbreads

These flatbreads are universally eaten throughout the Middle East. They are ideal for serving with soups and appetizers.

Makes 10

275g/10oz/2½ cups unbleached strong white bread flour
175g/6oz/1½ cups wholemeal (whole-wheat) flour
5ml/1 tsp salt
15g/½oz fresh yeast
250ml/8fl oz/1 cup lukewarm water
60ml/4 tbsp natural (plain) yogurt or milk

1 Sift the flours and salt together into a large bowl and make a well in the centre. Mix the yeast with half the lukewarm water until creamy, then stir in the remaining water.

2 Add the yeast mixture and yogurt or milk to the centre of the flour and mix to a soft dough. Turn out on to a lightly floured surface and knead for 8–10 minutes until smooth and elastic. Place in a lightly oiled bowl, cover with lightly oiled clear film (plastic wrap) and leave to rise, in a warm place, for about 1 hour, or until doubled in bulk. Knock back (punch down) the dough, re-cover and leave to rise for 30 minutes.

3 Turn the dough back out on to a lightly floured surface. Knock back gently and divide into ten equal pieces. Shape into balls, then flatten into discs with the palm of your hand. Cover and leave it to rest for 5 minutes.

4 Meanwhile, preheat the oven to the maximum temperature – it should be at least 230°C/450°F/Gas 8. Place three or four baking sheets in the oven to heat.

5 Roll the dough as thinly as possible, then lift it over the backs of your hands and stretch and turn the dough.

6 Place four on the baking sheets and bake for 6–8 minutes, or until starting to brown. Stack the remaining rolled dough, layered between clear film to keep moist. Transfer to a wire rack to cool and cook the remaining breads. Serve hot.

Pitta Bread Energy 150kcal/638kJ; Protein 3.9g; Carbohydrate 32.4g, of which sugars 0.6g; Fat 1.5g, of which saturates 0.2g; Cholesterol 0mg; Calcium 58mg; Fibre 1.3g; Sodium 493mg.

Thin and Crispy Flatbreads Energy 108kcal/456kJ; Protein 2.3g; Carbohydrate 19.2g, of which sugars 0.4g; Fat 3g, of which saturates 1.3g; Cholesterol 0mg; Calcium 35mg; Fibre 0.8g; Sodium 132mg.

West Indian Flatbreads

Eclectic Caribbean food is influenced by a wide range of international cultures. It is the Anglo-Indian connection that brought the Indian flatbread called *roti* to Trinidad in the West Indies. Serve these simple-to-make breads straight from the pan to accompany spicy seafood chowders or curries, or any other dish that has plenty of sauce for mopping up.

Makes 8

450g/1lb/4 cups atta or fine wholemeal (whole-wheat) flour
5ml/1 tsp baking powder
5ml/1 tsp salt
300ml/½ pint/1¼ cups water
30ml/2 tbsp vegetable oil
115–150g/4–5oz/8–10 tbsp clarified butter or ghee, melted

1 Mix the flour, baking powder and salt together in a large bowl and make a well in the centre. Gradually mix in enough water to make a firm dough.

2 Knead on a lightly floured surface until smooth. Place in a lightly oiled bowl, cover with lightly oiled clear film (plastic wrap). Leave to stand for 20 minutes.

3 Divide the dough into eight equal pieces and roll each one on a lightly floured surface into an 18cm/7in round. Brush the surface of each round with a little of the clarified butter or ghee, fold in half and half again. Cover the folded rounds with lightly oiled clear film and leave to rest for 10 minutes.

4 Take one flatbread and roll out on a lightly floured surface into a round about 20–23cm/8–9in in diameter. Brush both sides with some clarified butter or ghee.

5 Heat a griddle or heavy frying pan, add one flatbread at a time and cook for about 1 minute on the first side. Turn over and cook for 2 minutes, then turn over again and cook for 1 minute. Wrap the cooked flatbreads in a clean dish towel to keep warm while cooking the remaining ones. Serve warm with chowder or curry.

Yemeni Sponge Flatbreads

These flatbreads, known as *lahuhs*, are made from a batter, and are bubbly and soft. They are usually eaten with soups, but are also good accompaniments for salads, dips and cheese.

Makes 8

15ml/1 tbsp active dried yeast
500ml/17fl oz/generous 2 cups lukewarm water
350g/12oz/3 cups plain (all-purpose) flour
5ml/1 tsp salt
50g/2oz/¼ cup butter, melted, or 60ml/4 tbsp vegetable oil

1 In a bowl, dissolve the dried yeast in about 75ml/5 tbsp of the water. Leave in a warm place for about 10 minutes, or until frothy.

2 Stir the remaining water, the flour, salt and melted butter or vegetable oil into the yeast mixture and mix until it forms a smooth batter. Cover with a clean dish towel, then leave in a warm place for about 1 hour, until doubled in size.

3 Stir the thick, frothy batter and, if it seems too thick to ladle out, add a little extra water. Cover and leave the batter to stand in a warm place for about 1 hour.

4 Cook the flatbreads in a non-stick frying pan. Ladle 45–60ml/3–4 tbsp of batter into the pan and cook over low heat until the top is bubbling and the colour has changed. (Traditionally these breads are cooked on only one side, but the second side can be cooked for just a moment, if you like.)

5 Remove the cooked flatbread from the frying pan with a spatula and keep warm in a clean dish towel. Continue cooking until you have used up all the remaining batter.

Cook's Tip
Use several frying pans at the same time, so that the flatbreads are ready together and can be eaten piping hot.

West Indian Flatbreads Energy 303kcal/1270kJ; Protein 7.1g; Carbohydrate 36g, of which sugars 1.2g; Fat 15.5g, of which saturates 7.1g; Cholesterol 0mg; Calcium 21mg; Fibre 5.1g; Sodium 2mg.

Yemeni Sponge Flatbreads Energy 392kcal/1651kJ; Protein 8.3g; Carbohydrate 68.1g, of which sugars 1.4g; Fat 11.4g, of which saturates 6.7g; Cholesterol 27mg; Calcium 125mg; Fibre 2.7g; Sodium 570mg.

Spring Onion Flatbreads

Use these flatbreads to wrap around barbecue-cooked meat and chunky vegetable salads, or serve them with tasty dips such as hummus as part of a buffet or a meze table. They're at their best eaten as soon as they're cooked.

Makes 16

450g/1lb/4 cups strong white bread flour, plus extra for dusting
5ml/1 tsp salt
7g/¼oz easy-blend (rapid-rise) dried yeast
4 spring onions (scallions), finely chopped

1 Place the flour in a large bowl and stir in the salt, yeast and spring onions. Make a well in the centre and pour in 300ml/½ pint/1¼ cups lukewarm water. Mix to form a soft dough.

2 Turn out the dough on to a floured work surface and knead for about 5 minutes, until smooth and elastic.

3 Put the dough back in the bowl, cover with a clean, damp dish towel and leave in a warm place for about 1 hour, or until doubled in size.

4 Knock back (punch down) the dough, and turn it out on to a lightly floured work surface. Divide the dough into 16 equal pieces and roll each piece into a smooth ball. Roll out each ball to flatten it to a 13cm/5in round.

5 Heat a large frying pan or ridged griddle until hot. Dust off any excess flour from the first dough round and lay it in the pan. Cook for 1 minute, until the underside is slightly browned in parts, then flip over and cook for 30 seconds. Repeat with the remaining dough rounds. Wrap the completed flatbreads in a dish towel to keep them warm while you cook the rest.

Variation
To make Garlic Flatbreads, use 2 finely chopped garlic cloves in place of the spring onions (scallions).

Griddle-roasted Flatbreads

These Indian flatbreads, called *chapatis*, are dry-roasted on an iron griddle and are delicious spread with a little melted butter. Serve as part of an Indian meal, or with any kind of dips, appetizers or snacks. Freeze any leftovers.

Makes 16

400g/14oz/3½ cups chapati flour (atta) or fine wholemeal (whole-wheat) flour
5ml/1 tsp salt
250ml/9fl oz/1 cup water
a little extra flour, for dusting
melted butter, for brushing

1 Mix the flour and salt together in a mixing bowl. Gradually add the water, continuing to mix until a dough is formed.

2 Transfer the dough to a flat, lightly floured surface and knead it for 4–5 minutes. When all the excess moisture is absorbed by the flour, wrap the dough in clear film (plastic wrap) and let it rest for 30 minutes. Alternatively, make the dough in a food processor.

3 Divide the dough into two equal parts and pinch or cut eight equal portions from each. Form the portions into balls and flatten them into neat, round cakes.

4 Dust the cakes lightly in the flour and roll each one out to a 15cm/6in circle. Keep the rest covered with a damp cloth.

5 Pre-heat a heavy cast-iron griddle or frying pan over medium-high heat. Place a dough circle on it, cook for about 30 seconds and turn it over, using a thin metal spatula.

6 Cook until bubbles begin to appear on the surface and turn it over again. Press the edges down gently with a clean cloth to encourage the flatbread to puff up (they will not always puff up, but this does not affect the taste).

7 Cook until the underneath begins to brown. Keep cooked breads hot by wrapping them in foil lined with kitchen paper. Brush with a little melted butter, and serve warm and fresh.

Spring Onion Flatbreads Energy 97kcal/410kJ; Protein 2.7g; Carbohydrate 21.9g, of which sugars 0.5g; Fat 0.4g, of which saturates 0.1g; Cholesterol 0mg; Calcium 40mg; Fibre 0.9g; Sodium 124mg.

Griddle-roasted Flatbreads Energy 78kcal/330kJ; Protein 3.2g; Carbohydrate 16g, of which sugars 0.5g; Fat 0.6g, of which saturates 0.1g; Cholesterol 0mg; Calcium 10mg; Fibre 2.3g; Sodium 124mg.

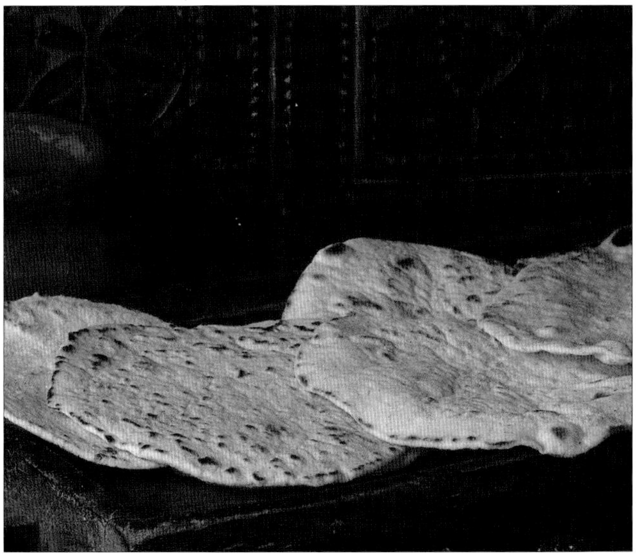

Wheat Tortillas

Tortillas are the staple flatbread in Mexico, where they are often made from masa harina, a flour milled from corn. These soft wheat tortillas are also popular in the south-western states of the USA.

Makes 12

225g/8oz/2 cups unbleached plain (all-purpose) flour
5ml/1 tsp salt
4ml/¾ tsp baking powder
40g/1½ oz/3 tbsp lard or white cooking fat
150ml/¼ pint/⅔ cup warm water

1 Put the plain flour, salt and baking powder in a large bowl. Mix together with a spoon.

2 Using your hands, rub in the lard or white cooking fat, stir in the warm water. Place the dough on to a lightly floured surface and gently knead to a soft, smooth dough.

3 Cover the bowl with lightly oiled clear film (plastic wrap) and leave to rest in a warm place for 15 minutes.

4 Divide the dough into 12 pieces and shape into round balls. Roll the balls out on a lightly floured surface into 15–18cm/6–7in rounds. Re-cover the flattened balls with the lightly oiled clear film to keep moist.

5 Heat a heavy frying pan or griddle, add one tortilla and cook for 1½–2 minutes, turning over as soon as the surface starts to bubble. It should stay flexible. Remove from the pan and wrap in a dish towel to keep warm while cooking the remaining tortillas in the same way.

Cook's Tips

- *Tortillas are delicious either as an accompaniment or filled with roast chicken or cooked minced (ground) meat, refried beans and/or salad to serve as a snack or light lunch.*
- *To reheat tortillas, wrap in foil and warm in a medium oven, 180°C/350°F/Gas 4, for about 5 minutes.*

Cheese & Chilli Tortillas

These cheese-filled tortillas are the Mexican equivalent of toasted sandwiches. Serve them as soon as they are cooked, or they will become chewy. If you are making them for a crowd, fill and fold the tortillas ahead of time, but only cook them to order.

Makes 8

200g/7oz mozzarella, Monterey Jack or mild Cheddar cheese
1 large fresh red chilli pepper (optional)
8 wheat flour tortillas, about 15cm/6in across
sliced onion and red chilli, to serve (optional)

1 If using mozzarella cheese, it must be drained thoroughly and then patted dry and sliced into thin strips. Monterey Jack and Cheddar should both be coarsely grated, as finely grated cheese will melt and ooze away when cooking. Set the cheese aside in a bowl.

2 If using the chilli, spear it on a long-handled metal skewer and roast it over the flame of a gas burner until the skin blisters and darkens. Do not let the flesh burn. Alternatively, dry-fry it in a griddle pan until the skin is scorched. Place the roasted chilli in a strong plastic bag and tie the top to keep the steam in. Set aside for 20 minutes.

3 Remove the chilli from the bag and peel off the skin. Cut off the stalk, then slit the chilli and scrape out the seeds. Cut the flesh into eight thin strips.

4 Warm a large frying pan. Place one tortilla on the pan at a time, sprinkle about an eighth of the cheese on to one half and add a strip of chilli, if using. Fold the tortilla over the cheese and press the edges together gently to seal. Cook the filled tortilla for about 1 minute until the cheese is beginning to melt, then carefully turn over and cook the other side for 1 minute.

5 Remove the filled tortilla from the pan or griddle, cut it into three triangles or four strips and serve immediately, with sliced onion and red chilli, if using.

Wheat Tortillas Energy 94kcal/394kJ; Protein 1.8g; Carbohydrate 14.6g, of which sugars 0.3g; Fat 3.5g, of which saturates 1.4g; Cholesterol 3mg; Calcium 26mg; Fibre 0.6g; Sodium 164mg.

Cheese and Chilli Tortillas Energy 418kcal/1764kJ; Protein 17g; Carbohydrate 66g, of which sugars 7g; Fat 11g, of which saturates 7g; Cholesterol 29mg; Calcium 303mg; Fibre 2.6g; Sodium 0.5mg.

Chilli & Herb Crackers

These spicy, crisp little crackers are very low in fat and ideal for serving as a nibble with drinks. They would also make an interesting alternative to bread or rolls served with a seafood appetizer.

Makes 12
50g/2oz/½ cup plain (all-purpose) flour
a pinch of salt
5ml/1 tsp curry powder
1.5ml/¼ tsp chilli powder
15ml/1 tbsp chopped fresh coriander (cilantro)
30ml/2 tbsp water

1 Preheat the oven to 180°C/350°F/Gas 4. Sift the plain flour and salt into a large mixing bowl, then add the curry powder and chilli powder and mix well.

2 Make a well in the centre of the flour mixture and add the chopped fresh coriander and the water. Gradually incorporate the flour and mix to a firm dough.

3 Turn the dough out on to a lightly floured surface, knead until smooth, then cover with lightly oiled clear film (plastic wrap) and leave to rest in a warm place for about 5 minutes.

4 Cut the dough into 12 even pieces and knead each one into a small ball. Roll each ball out very thinly to a 10cm/4in round, sprinkling flour over the dough if necessary to prevent sticking.

5 Arrange the dough rounds on two ungreased baking sheets, making sure there is plenty of space between them. Bake for 15 minutes, turning the crackers over once during cooking. Using a metal spatula, transfer the rounds to a wire rack and leave to cool.

Variation
Omit the curry and chilli powders and replace with 15ml/1 tbsp caraway, fennel or mustard seeds for an aromatic but less spicy alternative.

Knackerbröd

These traditional crispbreads are from Sweden, and are made with a hole in the centre so they can be hung over the oven to keep dry. They are ideal as a snack, or as an appetizer spread with pâté or soft cheese.

Makes 8
450g/1lb/4 cups rye flour
5ml/1 tsp salt
50g/2oz/¼ cup butter
20g/¾oz fresh yeast
275ml/9fl oz/generous 1 cup lukewarm water
75g/3oz/2 cups wheat bran

1 Lightly grease two baking sheets. Preheat the oven to 230°C/450°F/Gas 8. Mix the rye flour and salt in a large bowl. Rub in the butter, then make a well in the centre.

2 Cream the yeast with a little water, then stir in the remaining water. Pour the yeast mixture into the centre of the flour and mix to a dough, then mix in the bran.

3 Place the dough on to a lightly floured surface and knead for 5 minutes until the dough is smooth and elastic.

4 Divide the dough into eight equal pieces and roll each one out on a lightly floured surface, to a 20cm/8in round.

5 Place two rounds on the prepared baking sheets and prick all over with a fork. Cut a hole in the centre of each round, using a 4cm/1½in cutter.

6 Bake for 15–20 minutes, or until the crispbreads are golden. Transfer to a wire rack. Repeat with the remaining crispbreads.

Cook's Tip
The hole in the centre of these crispbreads is a reminder of the days when breads were strung on a pole, which was hung across the rafters over the oven to dry. Make smaller crispbreads, if you like, and tie them together with bright red ribbon for an unusual Christmas gift.

Chilli and Herb Crackers Energy 16kcal/69kJ; Protein 0.5g; Carbohydrate 3.5g, of which sugars 0.1g; Fat 0.1g, of which saturates 0g; Cholesterol 0mg; Calcium 9mg; Fibre 0.2g; Sodium 1mg.

Knackerbröd Energy 254kcal/1075kJ; Protein 6g; Carbohydrate 45.2g, of which sugars 0.4g; Fat 6.8g, of which saturates 3.6g; Cholesterol 14mg; Calcium 29mg; Fibre 10g; Sodium 296mg.

Crisp Rye Breads

These crispbreads are flavoured with caraway or cumin seeds to make them spicy and aromatic.

Makes 15

600ml/1 pint/2½ cups milk
50g/2oz fresh yeast
500g/1¼lb/5 cups rye flour, plus 225g/8oz/2 cups, for dusting
500g/1¼lb/5 cups strong white bread flour
10ml/2 tsp caraway or cumin seeds
5ml/1 tsp salt

1 Put the milk in a pan and heat gently until warm to the touch. Remove from the heat. In a bowl, blend the yeast with a little of the warmed milk. Add the remaining milk, then add the rye flour, bread flour, caraway or cumin seeds and salt and mix together to form a dough.

2 Using the rye flour for dusting, turn the dough out on to a lightly floured surface and knead the dough for about 2 minutes. Cut the dough into 15 equal pieces, then roll out each piece into a thin, flat round. Place on baking sheets and leave to rise in a warm place for 20 minutes.

3 Preheat the oven to 150°C/300°F/Gas 2. Using the rye flour, roll out the pieces of dough again into very thin, flat rounds. Return to the baking sheets. Make a pattern on the surface using a fork or knife.

4 Bake the breads in the oven for 8–10 minutes, turning after about 5 minutes, until hard and crispy. Transfer to a wire rack and leave to cool. Store the breads in an airtight container.

Cook's Tip
Swedes use a special rolling pin with a knobbly surface to create the distinctive texture. An ordinary rolling pin is a good substitute, with the texture created by the head of a fork.

Scottish Oatcakes

The crunchy texture of these tempting oatcakes makes them difficult to resist. Serve with butter and slices of a good cheese.

Makes 8

115g/4oz/1 cup medium or fine oatmeal
1.5ml/¼ tsp salt
a pinch of bicarbonate of soda (baking soda)
15ml/1 tbsp melted butter or lard or white cooking fat
45–60ml/3–4 tbsp hot water

1 Very lightly oil a griddle or heavy frying pan. Mix the oatmeal, salt and soda together in a bowl.

2 Add the melted butter, lard or white cooking fat and sufficient hot water to make a dough. Lightly knead on a surface dusted with oatmeal until it is smooth. Cut the dough in half.

3 Dust a surface with oatmeal and roll each piece of dough out into a round, about 15cm/6in across and 5mm/¼in thick.

4 Cut each round into four quarters or farls. Heat the griddle over medium heat until warm. Transfer four farls, using a spatula or fish slice, to the griddle and cook over low heat for about 4–5 minutes. The edges may start to curl.

5 Carefully turn the farls over and cook for about 1–2 minutes. If preferred, the second side can be cooked under a preheated grill (broiler) until crisp, but not brown. Transfer to a wire rack to cool. Repeat with the remaining farls.

Variations
- *Oatcakes are traditionally cooked on the griddle, but they can also be cooked in the oven at 180°C/350°F/Gas 4 for about 20 minutes, or until pale golden in colour.*
- *Small round oatcakes can be stamped out using a 7.5cm/3in plain cutter, if preferred.*

Crisp Rye Breads Energy 323kcal/1376kJ; Protein 9.2g; Carbohydrate 71.1g, of which sugars 2.4g; Fat 2.2g, of which saturates 0.7g; Cholesterol 2mg; Calcium 118mg; Fibre 7.3g; Sodium 19mg.
Scottish Oatcakes Energy 102kcal/430kJ; Protein 2.7g; Carbohydrate 16g, of which sugars 0g; Fat 3.5g, of which saturates 1g; Cholesterol 4mg; Calcium 12mg; Fibre 1.5g; Sodium 142mg.

Chapatis

A chapati is an unleavened bread made from chapati flour, a ground wholemeal flour known as *atta*, which is finer than the Western equivalent. An equal quantity of standard wholemeal flour and plain flour will also produce satisfactory results, although chapati flour is available from Indian grocers. This is the everyday bread of the Indian home.

Makes 8–10

225g/8oz/2 cups chapati flour or wholemeal (whole-wheat) flour
2.5ml/½ tsp salt
175ml/6fl oz/¾ cup water

1 Sift the flour and salt into a mixing bowl. Make a well in the centre and gradually stir in the water, mixing well with your fingers.

2 Form a supple dough and knead for 7–10 minutes. Ideally, cover with clear film (plastic wrap) and leave to one side for 15–20 minutes to rest.

3 Divide the dough into 8–10 equal portions. Roll out each piece to a circle on a well-floured surface.

4 Place a tava (chapati griddle) or heavy frying pan over high heat. When steam rises from it, lower the heat to medium and add the first chapati to the pan.

5 When the chapati begins to bubble, turn it over. Press down with a clean dish towel or a flat spoon and turn once again.

6 Remove the cooked chapati from the pan and keep warm in a piece of foil lined with kitchen paper while you cook the other chapatis.

7 Repeat the process until all the breads are cooked. Serve the chapatis hot.

Naan Bread

Probably the most popular bread enjoyed with an Indian curry is naan, which was introduced from Persia. In Persian, the word *naan* means bread. Traditionally, naan is not rolled, but patted and stretched until the teardrop shape is achieved. You can, of course, roll it out to a circle, then gently pull the lower end, which will give you the appropriate shape.

Makes 3

225g/8oz/2 cups unbleached strong white bread flour
2.5ml/½ tsp salt
15g/½oz fresh yeast
60ml/4 tbsp lukewarm milk
15ml/1 tbsp vegetable oil
30ml/2 tbsp natural (plain) yogurt
1 egg
30–45ml/2–3 tbsp melted ghee or butter, for brushing

1 Sift the flour and salt together into a large bowl. In a smaller bowl, cream the yeast with the milk. Set aside for 15 minutes. Add the yeast and milk mixture, vegetable oil, yogurt and egg to the flour. Combine the mixture using your hands until it forms a soft dough. Add a little more of the lukewarm water if the dough is too dry.

2 Turn the dough out on to a lightly floured surface and knead for about 10 minutes, or until it feels smooth. Return the dough to the bowl, cover and leave in a warm place for about 1 hour, or until it has doubled in size. Preheat the oven to its highest setting – it should not be any lower than 230°C/450°F/Gas 8.

3 Turn out the dough back on to the floured surface and knead for a further 2 minutes. Divide into three equal pieces, shape into balls and roll out into teardrop shapes 25cm/10in long, 13cm/5in wide and 5mm–8mm/¼–⅓in thick.

4 Preheat the grill (broiler) to its highest setting. Meanwhile, place the naan on preheated baking sheets and bake for 3–4 minutes, or until puffed up. Remove from the oven and place under the hot grill for a few seconds until the tops brown slightly. Brush with ghee or butter and serve warm.

Chapatis Energy 99kcal/421kJ; Protein 3.7g; Carbohydrate 19.9g, of which sugars 0.5g; Fat 1.1g, of which saturates 0.2g; Cholesterol 0mg; Calcium 38mg; Fibre 1.9g; Sodium 165mg.

Naan Bread Energy 353kcal/1490kJ; Protein 11g; Carbohydrate 61g, of which sugars 4g; Fat 9g, of which saturates 2g; Cholesterol 45mg; Calcium 191mg; Fibre 2.8g; Sodium 375mg.

Spiced Naan

Another excellent recipe for naan bread, this time with fennel seeds, onion seeds and cumin seeds.

Makes 6

450g/1lb/4 cups strong white bread flour
5ml/1 tsp baking powder
2.5ml/½ tsp salt
7g/¼oz easy-blend (rapid-rise) dried yeast
5ml/1 tsp caster (superfine) sugar
5ml/1 tsp fennel seeds
10ml/2 tsp onion seeds
5ml/1 tsp cumin seeds
150ml/¼ pint/⅔ cup lukewarm milk
30ml/2 tbsp oil, plus extra for brushing
150ml/¼ pint/⅔ cup natural (plain) yogurt
1 egg, beaten

1 Sift the flour, baking powder and salt into a mixing bowl. Stir in the yeast, sugar, fennel seeds, onion seeds and cumin seeds. Make a well in the centre. Stir the lukewarm milk into the flour mixture, then add the oil, yogurt and beaten egg. Mix to form a ball of dough.

2 Transfer the dough out on to a lightly floured surface and knead it for 10 minutes until smooth. Return to the clean, lightly oiled bowl and roll the dough to coat it with oil. Cover the bowl with clear film (plastic wrap) and set aside in a warm place until the dough has doubled in size.

3 Put a heavy baking sheet in the oven and preheat the oven to 240°C/475°F/Gas 9. Also preheat the grill (broiler). Knead the dough again lightly and divide it into six pieces. Keep five pieces covered while working with the sixth. Quickly roll the piece of dough out to a teardrop shape, brush lightly with oil and slap the naan on to the hot baking sheet. Repeat with the remaining dough.

4 Bake the naan in the oven for 3 minutes until puffed up, then place the baking sheets under the grill for about 30 seconds or until the naan are lightly browned. Serve hot or warm as an accompaniment to an Indian curry.

Garlic & Coriander Naan

Traditionally cooked in a very hot clay oven known as a *tandoor*, naan are usually eaten with dry meat or vegetable dishes.

Makes 3

275g/10oz/2½ cups unbleached strong white bread flour
5ml/1 tsp salt
5ml/1 tsp active dried yeast
60ml/4 tbsp natural (plain) yogurt
15ml/1 tbsp melted butter or ghee, plus 30–45ml/2–3 tbsp for brushing
1 garlic clove, finely chopped
5ml/1 tsp black onion seeds
15ml/1 tbsp fresh coriander (cilantro)
10ml/2 tsp clear honey

1 Sift the flour and salt together into a large bowl. In a smaller bowl, cream the yeast with the yogurt. Set aside for 15 minutes. Add the yeast mixture to the flour with the smaller quantity of melted butter or ghee, and add the chopped garlic, black onion seeds and chopped coriander, mixing to a soft dough.

2 Transfer the dough on to a lightly floured surface and knead for about 10 minutes until smooth and elastic. Place in a lightly oiled bowl, cover with lightly oiled clear film (plastic wrap) and leave to rise in a warm place for 45 minutes, or until the dough has doubled in size.

3 Preheat the oven to 230°C/450°F/Gas 8. Place three heavy baking sheets in the oven to heat. Turn the dough out on to a lightly floured surface and knock back (punch down). Divide into three equal pieces and shape each into a ball.

4 Cover two of the balls of dough with oiled clear film and roll out the third into a teardrop shape about 25cm/10in long, 13cm/5in wide and about 5mm–8mm/¼–⅓in thick. Preheat the grill (broiler) to its highest setting. Place the single naan on the hot baking sheets and bake for 3–4 minutes, or until puffy.

5 Remove the naan from the oven and place under the hot grill for a few seconds or until browned slightly. Wrap in a dish towel to keep warm while you roll out and cook the remaining naan. Brush with melted butter or ghee and serve warm.

Spiced Naan Energy 311kcal/1319kJ; Protein 11g; Carbohydrate 63.8g, of which sugars 4.9g; Fat 3.2g, of which saturates 0.9g; Cholesterol 34mg; Calcium 197mg; Fibre 2.3g; Sodium 211mg.

Garlic and Coriander Naan Energy 374kcal/1585kJ; Protein 10.4g; Carbohydrate 74.2g, of which sugars 2.9g; Fat 6.1g, of which saturates 3g; Cholesterol 11mg; Calcium 176mg; Fibre 2.8g; Sodium 706mg.

Paratha*s*

Making a paratha is similar to making flaky pastry. The difference lies in the handling of the dough; this can be handled freely, unlike that for a flaky pastry.

Makes 12–15

350g/12oz/3 cups chapati flour or an equal quantity of wholemeal (whole-wheat) flour and plain (all-purpose) flour, plus 50g/2oz/½ cup for dusting

50g/2oz/½ cup plain (all-purpose) flour

5ml/1 tsp salt

40g/1½oz/3 tbsp ghee or unsalted (sweet) butter

water, to mix

1 Sift the flours and salt into a bowl. Make a well in the centre and add 10ml/2 tsp melted ghee or butter. Fold it into the flour to make a crumbly texture.

2 Gradually add water to make a soft, pliable dough. Knead until smooth. Cover and leave to rest for 30 minutes.

3 Melt the remaining ghee or butter over low heat. Divide the dough into 12–15 equal portions and keep covered. Take one portion at a time and roll out on a lightly floured surface to about 10cm/4in in diameter.

4 Brush the dough with a little of the melted ghee or sweet butter and sprinkle with flour.

5 With a sharp knife, make a straight cut from the centre to the edge of the dough, then lift a cut edge and roll the dough into a cone shape. Lift it and flatten it again into a ball. Roll the dough out again on a lightly floured surface until it is 18cm/7in wide.

6 Heat a griddle and cook one paratha at a time, placing a little of the remaining ghee along the edges. Cook on each side until golden brown. Serve hot.

Missi Rotis

This is a speciality from the Punjab. Gram flour, also known as *besan*, is used instead of the usual chapati flour. In the Punjab, missi rotis are very popular with a glass of lassi, a refreshing yogurt drink.

Makes 4

115g/4oz/1 cup gram flour

115g/4oz/1 cup wholemeal (whole-wheat) flour

1 fresh green chilli, seeded and chopped

½ onion, finely chopped

15ml/1 tbsp chopped fresh coriander (cilantro)

2.5ml/½ tsp ground turmeric

2.5ml/½ tsp salt

15ml/1 tbsp vegetable oil

120–150ml/4–5fl oz/½–⅔ cup lukewarm water

30–45ml/2–3 tbsp melted unsalted (sweet) ghee or butter

1 Mix the two types of flour, the chilli, onion, coriander, turmeric and salt together in a large bowl. Stir in the oil.

2 Mix in sufficient water to make a pliable soft dough. Transfer the dough on to a lightly floured surface and knead until smooth and elastic.

3 Place the dough in a lightly oiled bowl, cover with lightly oiled clear film (plastic wrap) and leave to rest for 30 minutes.

4 Place the dough on to a lightly floured surface. Divide into four equal pieces and shape into balls in the palms of your hands. Roll out each ball into a thick round about 15–18cm/6–7in in diameter.

5 Heat a griddle or heavy frying pan over medium heat for a few minutes until hot. Brush both sides of one roti with a little melted ghee or butter.

6 Add the roti to the griddle or frying pan and cook for about 2 minutes, turning after 1 minute. Brush the cooked roti lightly with melted ghee or butter again, slide it on to a plate and keep warm in a low oven while cooking the remaining rotis in the same way. Serve the rotis warm.

Parathas Energy 190kcal/791kJ; Protein 2.1g; Carbohydrate 17.7g, of which sugars 0.3g; Fat 12.7g, of which saturates 7.8g; Cholesterol 28mg; Calcium 32mg; Fibre 0.7g; Sodium 122mg.

Missi Rotis Energy 298kcal/1267kJ; Protein 8.5g; Carbohydrate 65.8g, of which sugars 1.6g; Fat 2g, of which saturates 0.3g; Cholesterol 0mg; Calcium 114mg; Fibre 3.2g; Sodium 3mg.

Tandoori Rotis

Roti means bread, and is the most common food eaten in central and northern India. Tandoori roti is traditionally baked in a tandoor, or clay oven, but it can also be made successfully in an electric or gas oven at the highest setting.

Makes 6

350g/12oz/3 cups chapati flour or wholemeal (whole-wheat) flour
5ml/1 tsp salt
250ml/8fl oz/1 cup water
30–45ml/2–3 tbsp melted ghee or unsalted (sweet) butter

1 Sift the chapati or wholemeal flour and salt together into a large mixing bowl. Add the water and mix until a soft, pliable dough forms.

2 Gently knead on a lightly floured surface for 3–4 minutes until smooth and elastic.

3 Place the dough in a lightly oiled bowl, cover with lightly oiled clear film (plastic wrap) and leave to rest for about 1 hour.

4 Transfer the dough on to a lightly floured surface. Divide the dough into six equal pieces and shape each into a ball.

5 Press each ball out into a larger round with the palm of your hand, cover with lightly oiled clear film and leave to rest for about 10 minutes. Meanwhile, preheat the oven to 230°C/450°F/Gas 8. Place three baking sheets in the oven to heat.

6 On a lightly floured surface roll the rotis into 15cm/6in rounds. Place two on each baking sheet and bake in the oven for 8–10 minutes. Brush each roti with melted ghee or butter and serve warm.

Cook's Tip
Chapati flour, known as atta, *is a fine wholemeal flour used in Indian breads.*

Bhaturas

These leavened and deep-fried breads are from the Punjab, where the local people enjoy them with a bowl of spicy chickpea curry. The combination has become a classic over the years, and is known as *choley bhature*. Bhaturas must be eaten hot and cannot be reheated.

Makes 10

15g/½oz fresh yeast
5ml/1 tsp sugar
120ml/4fl oz/½ cup lukewarm water
200g/7oz/1¾ cups strong white bread flour
50g/2oz/⅓ cup semolina
2.5ml/½ tsp salt
15g/½oz/1 tbsp ghee or butter
30ml/2 tbsp natural (plain) yogurt
oil, for frying

1 Mix the yeast with the sugar and water in a jug (pitcher).

2 Sift the flour into a large bowl and stir in the semolina and salt. Rub in the butter or ghee.

3 Add the yeast mixture and yogurt, and mix to a dough. Turn out on to a lightly floured surface and knead for 10 minutes, or until smooth and elastic.

4 Place the dough in an oiled bowl, cover with oiled clear film (plastic wrap) and leave to rise in a warm place for about 1 hour, or until doubled in bulk.

5 Turn the dough out on to a lightly floured surface and knock back (punch down). Divide into ten equal pieces and shape each into a ball. Flatten into discs with the palm of your hand. Roll out on a lightly floured surface into 13cm/5in rounds.

6 Pour oil to a depth of 1cm/½in into a deep frying pan. Heat, and slide one bhatura into the oil. Fry for about 1 minute, turning over after 30 seconds.

7 Drain the bhatura well on kitchen paper. Keep each bhatura warm in a low oven while frying the remaining bhaturas. Serve immediately, while hot.

Tandoori Rotis Energy 226kcal/953kJ; Protein 7.4g; Carbohydrate 37.3g, of which sugars 1.2g; Fat 6.3g, of which saturates 2.6g; Cholesterol 0mg; Calcium 22mg; Fibre 5.3g; Sodium 329mg.

Bhaturas Energy 141kcal/590kJ; Protein 2.6g; Carbohydrate 19.7g, of which sugars 0.5g; Fat 6.3g, of which saturates 1.3g; Cholesterol 0mg; Calcium 35mg; Fibre 0.7g; Sodium 102mg.

Red Lentil Dosas

Dosas and *idlis* are the breads of southern India. They are very different from traditional north Indian breads, as they are made from lentils or beans and rice rather than flour. Dosas are more like pancakes; they are eaten freshly cooked, often at breakfast time, with chutney.

Makes 6

150g/5oz/¾ cup long grain rice
50g/2oz/¼ cup red lentils
250ml/8fl oz/1 cup warm water
5ml/1 tsp salt
2.5ml/½ tsp ground turmeric
2.5ml/½ tsp ground black pepper
30ml/2 tbsp chopped fresh coriander (cilantro)
oil, for frying and drizzling

1 Place the rice and lentils in a bowl, cover with the water and leave to soak for 8 hours.

2 Drain off the water and reserve. Place the long grain rice and red lentils in a food processor and blend until smooth. Blend in the reserved water.

3 Scrape the mixture into a large bowl, and cover with clear film (plastic wrap) and leave in a warm place to ferment for about 24 hours.

4 Stir the salt, turmeric, pepper and coriander in to the bowl. Heat a heavy frying pan over medium heat for a few minutes until hot but not smoking. Smear with oil and add about 30–45ml/2–3 tbsp batter.

5 Using the rounded bottom of a soup spoon, gently spread the batter out, using a circular motion, to make a 15cm/6in diameter dosa.

6 Cook for 1½–2 minutes, or until set. Drizzle a little oil over the dosa and around the edges. Turn over and cook for about 1 minute, or until golden.

7 Keep the cooked dosas warm in a low oven over simmering water while cooking the remaining dosas. Serve warm.

Pooris

These delicious little deep-fried breads, shaped into discs, make it temptingly easy to overindulge. In most areas, they are made of wholemeal flour, but in the east and north-east of India they are made from plain refined flour, and are known as *loochis*.

Makes 12

115g/4oz/1 cup unbleached plain (all-purpose) flour
115g/4oz/1 cup wholemeal (whole-wheat) flour
2.5ml/½ tsp salt
2.5ml/½ tsp chilli powder
30ml/2 tbsp vegetable oil
100–120ml/3½–4fl oz/7–8 tbsp water
oil, for frying

1 Sift the flours, salt and chilli powder, if using, into a large mixing bowl. Add the vegetable oil then add sufficient water to mix to a dough.

2 Transfer the dough on to a lightly floured surface and knead for 8–10 minutes until smooth.

3 Place in an oiled bowl and cover with oiled clear film (plastic wrap). Leave for 30 minutes.

4 Place the dough on the floured surface. Divide into 12 pieces. Keeping the rest of the dough covered, roll one piece into a 13cm/5in round. Repeat with the remaining dough. Stack the pooris, layered between clear film, to keep them moist.

5 Pour the oil for frying to a depth of 2.5cm/1in in a deep frying pan and heat it to 180°C/350°F. Using a metal spatula, lift one poori and slide it into the oil; it will sink but then return to the surface and begin to sizzle. Gently press the poori into the oil. It will puff up. Turn the poori over after a few seconds and allow it to cook for a further 20–30 seconds.

6 Remove the poori from the pan and pat dry with kitchen paper. Place the cooked poori on a large baking tray and keep warm in a low oven while you cook the remaining pooris. Serve warm.

Pooris Energy 120kcal/501kJ; Protein 2.1g; Carbohydrate 13.5g, of which sugars 0.3g; Fat 6.7g, of which saturates 0.8g; Cholesterol 0mg; Calcium 17mg; Fibre 1.2g; Sodium 164mg.

Red Lentil Dosas Energy 153kcal/641kJ; Protein 4.1g; Carbohydrate 25.1g, of which sugars 0.3g; Fat 4.1g, of which saturates 0.4g; Cholesterol 0mg; Calcium 21mg; Fibre 0.7g; Sodium 333mg.

Navajo Fried Bread

These bread rounds are great served with a salsa.

Makes 8
225g/8oz/2 cups plain (all-purpose) flour
10ml/2 tsp baking powder
2.5ml/½ tsp salt
250ml/8fl oz/1 cup lukewarm water
oil for frying

1 Sift the flour, baking powder and salt into a bowl. Pour in the lukewarm water and stir quickly with a fork until the dough gathers into a ball.

2 With floured hands, gently knead the dough by rolling it around the bowl. Be careful not to overknead; the dough should be very soft.

3 Divide the dough into eight pieces. With floured hands, pat each piece into a round about 13cm/5in in diameter. Place the rounds on a floured baking sheet.

4 Put a 2.5cm/1in layer of oil in a frying pan and heat until hot but not smoking. To test the temperature, drop in a small piece of dough; if the oil bubbles immediately, then it is ready.

5 Add the dough rounds to the hot oil and press down with a slotted spoon to submerge them. Release the dough and cook until puffed and golden on both sides, 3–5 minutes total, turning for even browning. Fry in batches, if necessary.

6 Drain the bread on kitchen paper and serve immediately. They are good as an accompaniment to a bowl of spicy chilli or with grated cheese and an assortment of home-made salsas and guacamole.

Cook's Tip
These fried bread rounds are best eaten on the day they are made, as they will not keep well.

Barbari

These small Iranian flatbreads can be made in a variety of sizes. For a change, make two large breads and break off pieces to scoop up dips.

Makes 6
225g/8oz/2 cups unbleached white bread flour
5ml/1 tsp salt
15g/½oz fresh yeast
140ml/scant ¼ pint/scant ⅔ cup lukewarm water
oil, for brushing

1 Lightly dust two baking sheets with flour. Sift the flour and salt together into a large bowl and make a well in the centre.

2 Mix the yeast with the water in a small bowl. Pour the mixture into the centre of the flour, and sprinkle a little flour over and leave in a warm place for 15 minutes.

3 Mix to a dough, then turn out on to a lightly floured surface and knead for 8–10 minutes until smooth and elastic. Place in a lightly oiled bowl, cover with oiled clear film (plastic wrap) and leave for 45–60 minutes, or until doubled in size.

4 Knock back (punch down) the dough and turn out on to a lightly floured surface. Divide into six equal pieces and shape into rectangles.

5 Roll each one out to about 10 × 5cm/4 × 2in and about 1cm/½in thick. Space well apart on the baking sheets, and make four slashes in the tops.

6 Cover the breads with lightly oiled clear film and leave to rise, in a warm place, for 20 minutes. Meanwhile, preheat the oven to 200°C/400°F/Gas 6. Brush the breads with oil and bake for 12–15 minutes, or until pale golden. Serve warm.

Variation
Sprinkle with sesame or caraway seeds before baking.

Navajo Fried Bread Energy 295kcal/1240kJ; Protein 5.4g; Carbohydrate 44.7g, of which sugars 0.9g; Fat 11.7g, of which saturates 1.3g; Cholesterol 0mg; Calcium 107mg; Fibre 1.8g; Sodium 542mg.

Barbari Energy 128kcal/544kJ; Protein 3.5g; Carbohydrate 29.1g, of which sugars 0.6g; Fat 0.5g, of which saturates 0.1g; Cholesterol 0mg; Calcium 53mg; Fibre 1.2g; Sodium 329mg.

Syrian Onion Bread

These unusual small breads come from Syria, and have a spicy topping spiked with chopped fresh mint.

Makes 8
450g/1lb/4 cups unbleached white bread flour, plus extra
5ml/1 tsp salt
20g/¾oz fresh yeast
280ml/9fl oz/scant 1¼ cups lukewarm water
oil, for greasing

For the topping
60ml/4 tbsp finely chopped onion
5ml/1 tsp ground cumin
10ml/2 tsp ground coriander
10ml/2 tsp chopped fresh mint
30ml/2 tbsp olive oil

1 Lightly flour two baking sheets. Sift the flour and salt together into a large bowl and make a well in the centre. Cream the yeast with a little of the water, then mix in the remainder.

2 Add the yeast mixture to the centre of the flour and mix to a firm dough. Knead on a lightly floured surface for 8–10 minutes, until smooth and elastic. Place in a lightly oiled bowl, cover with lightly oiled clear film (plastic wrap) and leave in a warm place for about 1 hour, until doubled in size.

3 Knock back (punch down) the dough and turn it out on to a lightly floured surface. Divide into eight pieces and roll each into a 13–15cm/5–6in round. Make the rounds slightly concave. Prick them all over and space well apart on the baking sheets. Cover with lightly oiled clear film and leave to rise for 15–20 minutes.

4 Meanwhile, preheat the oven to 200°C/400°F/Gas 6. Mix the chopped onion, ground cumin, ground coriander and chopped mint in a bowl.

5 Brush the breads with the oil, sprinkle them evenly with the onion mixture and bake for 15–20 minutes. Serve warm.

Cook's Tip
If you haven't any fresh mint, add 15ml/1 tbsp dried mint.

Finnish Barley Bread

In Northern Europe, breads are often made using cereals such as barley and rye, which produce very satisfying and tasty breads. This quick-to-prepare flatbread is delicious when served warm with lashings of butter.

Makes 1
225g/8oz/2 cups barley flour
5ml/1 tsp salt
10ml/2 tsp baking powder
25g/1oz/2 tbsp butter, melted
120ml/4fl oz/¼ cup single (light) cream
60ml/4 tbsp milk

1 Lightly grease a baking sheet. Preheat the oven to 200°C/400°F/Gas 6. Sift the barley flour, salt, and baking powder together into a large bowl.

2 Add the melted butter, single cream and milk to the bowl with the dry ingredients. Mix until the dough becomes smooth and elastic.

3 Turn out the dough on to a lightly floured surface and shape into a flat round about 1cm/½in thick.

4 Transfer the flat round to the prepared baking sheet and using a small sharp knife, lightly mark the surface into six equal sections.

5 Using a fork, gently prick the surface of the flat round evenly all over. Bake in the oven for about 15–18 minutes, or until pale golden in colour.

6 Cut the bread into even wedges and serve warm.

Cook's Tip
• *This flatbread tastes very good with cottage cheese, especially cottage cheese with chives.*
• *For a citrusy tang, add 10–15ml/2–3 tsp finely grated lemon, lime or orange rind to the flour mixture in step 1.*

Syrian Onion Bread Energy 220kcal/932kJ; Protein 5.5g; Carbohydrate 44.4g, of which sugars 1.3g; Fat 3.5g, of which saturates 0.5g; Cholesterol 0mg; Calcium 85mg; Fibre 1.9g; Sodium 248mg.

Finnish Barley Bread per loaf Energy 1259kcal/5309kJ; Protein 23g; Carbohydrate 196g, of which sugars 7.9g; Fat 48.2g, of which saturates 28.4g; Cholesterol 127mg; Calcium 230mg; Fibre 0g; Sodium 2251mg.

Langos

This recipe was originally Hungarian, made from bread dough leftovers, but it is so popular in the Czech and Slovak Republics that it has become part of their culture, too.

Makes 4

100ml/3½fl oz/scant ½ cup ketchup
3 garlic cloves, peeled and crushed
400g/14oz/3½ cups plain (all-purpose) flour
350ml/12fl oz/1½ cups milk
40g/1½oz fresh yeast or 15g/½oz active dried yeast
5ml/1 tsp salt
200ml/7fl oz/scant 1 cup oil
ketchup, garlic spread and 115g/4oz/1 cup grated Cheddar cheese, to serve
100ml/3½fl oz/scant ½ cup sour cream (optional)

1 Combine the ketchup and garlic. Sift the plain flour into a large bowl. Heat a 100ml/3½fl oz scant ½ cup of the milk until tepid. Crumble the fresh yeast into the milk and whisk for 1 minute, then add to the flour, or follow the instructions for the dry yeast. Add the remaining milk.

2 Add the salt and mix to form a soft dough; add more milk if the dough is too hard to work with. Take a quarter of the dough and stretch it out with your hands into a flat pancake. (Or divide it to make four little pancakes.)

3 Preheat the oil in a frying pan. The langos is supposed to 'swim' in the oil, so it needs to be about 2cm/¾in deep. Fry the dough for 4–5 minutes on each side, until golden, depending on the size of the pancakes. Take care, as it is easy to burn them.

4 Transfer the langos to kitchen paper to drain. Serve hot with 45ml/3 tbsp ketchup and garlic spread or 45ml/3 tbsp sour cream, and topped with grated cheese.

Cook's Tip
When working with the dough, put some oil on your fingers to prevent it from sticking to your hands.

Easy Rosemary Focaccia

This Italian flatbread is very quick and easy to make. Additions may include olives and sun-dried tomatoes.

Makes 2

450g/1lb packet white bread mix
60ml/4 tbsp extra virgin olive oil
10ml/2 tsp dried rosemary, crushed
8 sun-dried tomatoes, chopped
12 pitted black olives, chopped
200ml/7fl oz/scant 1 cup lukewarm water
sea salt flakes, for sprinkling

1 Following the instructions on the packet, combine the bread mix with half the oil, the rosemary, tomatoes, olives and enough water to form a firm dough.

2 Transfer the dough on to a lightly floured surface. Knead for about 5 minutes.

3 Return the dough to the mixing bowl and cover with a piece of oiled clear film (plastic wrap). Leave the dough to rise in a warm place until doubled in size, about 1 hour.

4 Meanwhile, lightly grease two baking sheets and preheat the oven to 220°C/425°F/Gas 7.

5 On a lightly floured surface, knock back (punch down) the dough and knead again. Divide in half and shape into flat rounds. Place on the baking sheet, and make indentations with your fingertips. Sprinkle with the remaining oil and the sea salt flakes.

6 Bake the focaccia for 12–15 minutes until golden brown and cooked. Turn out on to wire racks to cool. This bread is best eaten slightly warm.

Cook's Tip
A bread mix is quick, but you can also make focaccia dough by mixing 500g/1¼lb/5 cups strong white bread flour with 5ml/1 tsp salt and 5ml/1 tsp easy-blend (rapid-rise) yeast. Then follow the recipe as above.

Langos Energy 398kcal/2929kJ; Protein 21g; Carbohydrate 92g, of which sugars 15g; Fat 30g, of which saturates 13g; Cholesterol 55mg; Calcium 483mg; Fibre 3.6g; Sodium 866mg.

Easy Rosemary Focaccia Energy 1001kcal/4225kJ; Protein 22.4g; Carbohydrate 177.7g, of which sugars 6.2g; Fat 27.2g, of which saturates 4g; Cholesterol 0mg; Calcium 334mg; Fibre 8.1g; Sodium 505mg.

Focaccia with Olives & Tomatoes

This Italian flatbread makes a delicious snack with olives and feta cheese.

Makes 1

450g/1lb/4 cups strong white bread flour
5ml/1 tsp salt
1.5ml/¼ tsp ground black pepper
10ml/2 tsp easy-blend (rapid-rise) dried yeast
a pinch of sugar
300ml/½ pint/1¼ cups hand-hot water
15ml/1 tbsp pesto
115g/4oz/⅔ cup pitted black olives, chopped
25g/1oz/½ cup drained sun-dried tomatoes in oil, chopped, plus 15ml/1 tbsp oil from the jar
5ml/1 tsp coarse sea salt
5ml/1 tsp chopped fresh rosemary

1 Lightly oil a 30 × 20cm/12 × 8in Swiss roll tin (jelly roll pan). Sift the flour, salt and pepper into a bowl. Add the yeast and sugar, and make a well in the centre.

2 Add the water with the pesto, olives and sun-dried tomatoes to the dry ingredients, reserving the oil. Mix to a soft dough, adding a little extra water if necessary. Turn on to a floured surface and knead for 5 minutes until smooth and elastic.

3 Roll into a rectangle measuring 33 × 23cm/13 × 9in. Drape over the rolling pin and place in the prepared tin. Leave to rise until doubled in size, about 1½ hours. Meanwhile, preheat the oven to 220°C/425°F/Gas 7.

4 Using your fingertips, make indentations all over the dough. Brush with the oil from the sun-dried tomatoes, then sprinkle over the salt and chopped rosemary. Bake for 20–25 minutes, or until golden. Remove to a wire rack and serve warm.

Variation
Try adding 15ml/1 tbsp fresh chopped sage and half a chopped onion to the dough and the same again sprinkled over the top before baking.

Saffron Focaccia

A dazzling yellow bread that is both light in texture and distinctive in flavour. The olive oil drizzled over the top makes the bread moist, and it keeps well.

Makes 1

a pinch of saffron threads
150ml/¼ pint/⅔ cup boiling water
225g/8oz/2 cups strong white bread flour
2.5ml/½ tsp salt
5ml/1 tsp easy-blend (rapid-rise) dried yeast
15ml/1 tbsp olive oil

For the topping
2 garlic cloves, sliced
1 red onion, cut into thin wedges
rosemary sprigs
12 black olives, pitted and coarsely chopped
15ml/1 tbsp olive oil

1 Place the saffron in a heatproof jug or pitcher and pour in the boiling water. Leave to infuse (steep) until lukewarm.

2 Place the flour, salt, yeast and olive oil in a food processor. Turn on and gradually add the saffron and its liquid. Process until the dough forms a ball. Alternatively, use your hands to incorporate the liquid into the flour.

3 Turn out on to a floured surface and knead for 10–15 minutes. Place in a bowl, cover with clear film (plastic wrap) and leave to rise until doubled in size, about 30–40 minutes.

4 Knock back (punch down) the dough and roll into an oval shape about 1cm/½in thick. Place on a lightly greased baking sheet and leave to rise for 30 minutes.

5 Preheat the oven to 200°C/400°F/Gas 6. With your fingers, press indentations over the surface of the bread.

6 To make the topping, cover the dough with the sliced garlic, onion wedges, rosemary sprigs and chopped olives.

7 Brush lightly with olive oil and bake for 25 minutes, or until the loaf sounds hollow when tapped on the base. Leave to cool on a wire rack.

Focaccia with Olives and Tomatoes Energy 230kcal/973kJ; Protein 6.3g; Carbohydrate 44.2g, of which sugars 1.3g; Fat 4.3g, of which saturates 0.9g; Cholesterol 2mg; Calcium 111mg; Fibre 2.3g; Sodium 353mg.

Saffron Focaccia Energy 1135kcal/4779kJ; Protein 24g; Carbohydrate 188g, of which sugars 12g; Fat 37g, of which saturates 5g; Cholesterol 0mg; Calcium 376mg; Fibre 12g; Sodium 822mg.

Focaccia with Green Peppercorns & Rock Salt

There's something irresistible about this loaf of freshly baked focaccia with its fabulous flavour.

Makes 1

350g/12oz/3 cups white bread flour, plus extra for dusting
2.5ml/ ½ tsp salt
10ml/2 tsp easy-blend (rapid-rise) dried yeast
10ml/2 tsp drained green peppercorns in brine, lightly crushed
25ml/5 tsp fruity extra virgin olive oil
about 250ml/8fl oz/1 cup lukewarm water
20ml/4 tsp roughly crushed rock salt, for the topping
fresh basil leaves, to garnish

1 Sift the flour and salt into a mixing bowl. Stir in the yeast and peppercorns. Make a well in the centre and add 15ml/1 tbsp of the oil, with half the water. Mix, gradually incorporating the flour and adding more water to make a soft dough.

2 Knead the dough on a floured surface for 10 minutes. Return to the clean, lightly oiled bowl, cover with lightly oiled clear film (plastic wrap). Leave in a warm place until doubled in size.

3 Knock back (punch down) the dough and knead lightly for 2–3 minutes. Place on an oiled baking sheet and pat out to an oval. Cover with lightly oiled clear film and leave for 30 minutes.

4 Preheat the oven to 190°C/375°F/Gas 5. Make a few dimples in the surface of the dough with your fingers. Drizzle with the remaining oil and sprinkle with the salt. Bake for 25–30 minutes, until pale gold. Scatter with basil leaves and serve warm.

Cook's Tip
Kneading is a vital step in bread-making as it develops the gluten in the flour. Press and stretch the dough, using the heel of your hand and turning the dough frequently.

Red Onion Focaccia

This delicious pizza-like flatbread is topped with a combination of red onions and coarse sea salt.

Makes 2

675g/1½lb/6 cups strong plain (all-purpose) flour, plus extra for dusting
2.5ml/ ½ tsp salt
2.5ml/ ½ tsp caster (superfine) sugar
15ml/1 tbsp easy-blend (rapid-rise) dried yeast
60ml/4 tbsp extra virgin olive oil, plus extra for greasing
about 450ml/¾ pint/scant 2 cups lukewarm water

To finish
2 red onions, thinly sliced
45ml/3 tbsp extra virgin olive oil
15ml/1 tbsp coarse salt

1 Sift the flour, salt and sugar into a large bowl. Stir in the yeast, oil and water and mix to a dough using a round-bladed knife. Add a little extra water if the dough is dry.

2 Knead on a lightly floured surface for about 10 minutes, then put the dough in a clean, lightly oiled bowl and cover with lightly oiled clear film (plastic wrap). Leave in a warm place for about 1 hour, until doubled in size.

3 Preheat the oven to 200°C/400°F/Gas 6. Place two 25cm/10in plain metal flan rings on baking sheets. Oil the insides of the rings and the baking sheets.

4 Halve the dough and roll each piece to a 25cm/10in round. Press into the flan rings, cover each with a dampened dish towel and leave for 30 minutes to rise.

5 With your fingers, make dimples about 2.5cm/1in apart, in the dough. Cover and leave for 20 minutes more.

6 To finish, sprinkle the surface of the two loaves with the sliced onions and drizzle over the olive oil. Sprinkle with the coarse salt, then a little cold water, to stop a crust from forming. Bake for about 25 minutes, sprinkling with water once during cooking. Cool on a wire rack.

Focaccia with Green Peppercorns Energy 1345kcal/5701kJ; Protein 36.5g; Carbohydrate 272.3g, of which sugars 5.2g; Fat 19.7g, of which saturates 2.8g; Cholesterol 0mg; Calcium 500mg; Fibre 14.5g; Sodium 8858mg.

Red Onion Focaccia Energy 1582kcal/6671kJ; Protein 36.8g; Carbohydrate 278.3g, of which sugars 16.3g; Fat 43.4g, of which saturates 6.2g; Cholesterol 0mg; Calcium 530mg; Fibre 17.7g; Sodium 3459mg.

Mini Focaccia with Pine Nuts

Pine nuts add little bites of nutty texture and flavour to these simple mini focaccias. They can be eaten as an appetizer cut into cubes and dipped into some extra virgin olive oil.

Makes 4

350g/12oz/3 cups plain (all-purpose) flour
2.5ml/½ tsp salt
10ml/2tsp easy-blend (rapid-rise) dried yeast
about 250ml/8fl oz/1 cup lukewarm water
45ml/3 tbsp olive oil
45–60ml/3–4 tbsp pine nuts
10ml/2tsp coarse sea salt

1 Sift the flour and salt into a mixing bowl. Stir in the yeast, then make a well and pour in the water and 30ml/2 tbsp of the oil. Mix and add more water if the mixture is dry.

2 Turn on to a floured surface and knead for 10 minutes until smooth and elastic.

3 Place the dough in a greased bowl, cover and leave in a warm place for about 1 hour until doubled in size. Knock back (punch down) and knead the dough for 2–3 minutes.

4 Divide the dough into four pieces.

5 Using your hands, pat out each piece on greased baking sheets to a 10 x 7.5cm/4 x 3in oblong, which is rounded at the ends.

6 Scatter over the pine nuts and press them into the surface. Sprinkle with salt and brush with the remaining oil. Cover with greased clear film (plastic wrap) and leave to rise for about 30 minutes.

7 Meanwhile, preheat the oven to 220°C/425°F/Gas 7. Remove the clear film and bake the focaccias for 15–20 minutes until golden. Serve warm.

Thin Potato Bread

This traditional bread from Norway is known as *lefse*. The many types of lefse are all very thin, slightly soft potato breads. They can be eaten buttered and sprinkled with sugar or served with honey or cloudberry jam. Lefse can also be wrapped around a hotdog or filled with meat and a salad.

Makes 35

1kg/2¼lb potatoes
40g/1½oz/3 tbsp butter
120ml/4fl oz/½ cup single (light) cream
450–600g/1–1⅓lb/4–5 cups plain (all-purpose) flour
salt

1 Put the potatoes in a large pan. Add water to cover and bring to the boil, then simmer for about 15 minutes, or until the potatoes are tender, but do not let them get too soft.

2 Drain the potatoes thoroughly in a colander and then return to the pan. Mash with a potato masher or pass through a potato ricer or food mill into the pan and set aside. Add the butter, single cream and about 5ml/1 tsp of salt and beat together. Set aside to cool.

3 When the potatoes are cool enough to handle, add enough flour to form a firm dough. On a lightly floured surface, knead the dough until smooth.

4 Divide the dough into pieces about the size of a large egg, roll into balls and put on a baking tray. Chill in the refrigerator for 30 minutes.

5 On a floured surface, roll out each ball of dough until very thin. Heat a large ungreased frying pan or flat griddle until hot.

6 Cook the breads in batches over medium heat, one at a time, until brown spots appear on the upper surface. Turn them over with a metal spatula and cook the second side. Put the breads between two dish towels to prevent them from drying out. Serve immediately.

Mini Focaccia with Pine Nuts Energy 454kcal/1911kJ; Protein 10.7g; Carbohydrate 68.5g, of which sugars 1.8g; Fat 17.1g, of which saturates 1.9g; Cholesterol 0mg; Calcium 126mg; Fibre 3.9g; Sodium 1232mg.

Thin Potato Bread Energy 71kcal/301kJ; Protein 1.8g; Carbohydrate 14.7g, of which sugars 0.6g; Fat 1g, of which saturates 0.5g; Cholesterol 2mg; Calcium 23mg; Fibre 0.7g; Sodium 5mg.

Potato Bread with Onions

This potato bread is utterly delicious served warm with a simple vegetable soup.

Makes 1

450g/1lb/4 cups strong white bread flour
5ml/1 tsp easy-blend (rapid-rise) dried yeast
a pinch of salt, for the dough
15g/½oz/1 tbsp butter
325ml/11fl oz/1⅓ cups warmed milk
15ml/1 tbsp olive oil
2 medium onions, sliced into rings
115g/4oz maincrop potatoes, grated
1 sprig rosemary, chopped
2.5ml/½ tsp sea salt
oil, for greasing and to serve

1 Sift the flour into a bowl. Make a well in the centre and stir in the yeast and the salt. Rub in the butter until the mixture resembles breadcrumbs. Gradually pour in the milk. Incorporate the ingredients, then bring together with your fingers.

2 Turn the dough out and knead on a floured surface until it is smooth and elastic. Return the bread to a clean bowl and cover with a damp cloth. Leave to rise in a warm place for 45 minutes or until the dough has doubled in size.

3 Meanwhile, heat the oil in a pan and add the onions, stir over low heat and cook for about 20 minutes until the onions are golden brown and very soft. Set aside. Boil the grated potatoes in lightly salted water for 5 minutes or until just tender.

4 Turn the dough out of the bowl and knock back (punch down). Roll out on a lightly floured surface. Drain the potatoes and sprinkle half over the surface with a little rosemary and half the onions. Carefully roll the dough up into a sausage shape.

5 Lift the dough into an oiled 23 × 23cm/9 × 9in flan tin (pan). Using the palms of your hands, flatten the dough out. Sprinkle with the remaining potatoes, onions, salt and rosemary. Cover again with a damp cloth and leave to rise for 20 minutes.

6 Meanwhile, preheat the oven to 220°C/425°F/Gas 7. Bake for 15–20 minutes. Serve warm drizzled with a little oil.

Savoury Cranberry & Potato Bread Slice

This bread is an interesting combination of cranberries with bacon and potatoes.

Makes 1

450g/1lb/4 cups strong white bread flour
5ml/1 tsp easy-blend (rapid-rise) dried yeast
5ml/1 tsp salt
25g/1oz/2 tbsp butter, diced
325ml/11fl oz/1⅓ cups lukewarm water
75g/3oz/¾ cup fresh or frozen cranberries, thawed
oil, for greasing
225g/8oz floury potatoes, halved
6 rashers (strips) rindless streaky (fatty) bacon, chopped
30ml/2 tbsp runny honey
salt and ground black pepper

1 Sift the flour into a bowl, stir in the yeast and 5ml/1 tsp salt. Rub in the butter to form breadcrumbs. Make a well in the centre and stir in the water.

2 Bring the mixture together with a round-bladed knife and then turn out on to a floured surface. Knead for 5 minutes. Place the dough in a bowl and cover with a damp cloth. Leave to rise for 1 hour or until doubled in size.

3 Turn the dough out and knock back (punch down) to remove the air bubbles. Knead for a few minutes. Carefully knead the cranberries into the bread. Roll the dough out to a rectangle and place in an oiled 23 × 23cm/9 × 9in flan tin (pan). Push the dough into the corners and cover with a damp cloth. Leave to rise in a warm place for 30 minutes.

4 Preheat the oven to 220°C/425°F/Gas 7. Meanwhile, boil the potatoes in plenty of salted water for 15 minutes or until just tender. Drain and when cool enough to handle, slice thinly.

5 Sprinkle the potatoes and bacon over the risen bread dough, season, then drizzle with the honey and bake for 25 minutes, covering loosely with foil after 20 minutes to prevent burning. Remove from the oven, transfer to a wire rack to cool.

Potato Bread with Onions per loaf Energy 2154kcal/9113kJ; Protein 61.1g; Carbohydrate 423.9g, of which sugars 52.5g; Fat 36g, of which saturates 13.9g; Cholesterol 54mg; Calcium 1154mg; Fibre 22.1g; Sodium 332mg.

Savoury Cranberry and Potato Bread per loaf Energy 2196kcal/9292kJ; Protein 58.4g; Carbohydrate 415.5g, of which sugars 39.3g; Fat 44.7g, of which saturates 20.8g; Cholesterol 106mg; Calcium 657mg; Fibre 17.4g; Sodium 3141mg.

Basic Pizza Dough

Making your own pizza base is easy – and it tastes great.

Makes 1

175g/6oz/1½ cups strong white bread flour
1.25ml/¼ tsp salt
5ml/1 tsp easy-blend (rapid-rise) dried yeast
120–150ml/4–5fl oz/½–¾ cup lukewarm water
15ml/1 tbsp olive oil

1 Sift the flour and salt into a large mixing bowl and stir in the yeast. Make a well in the centre and pour in the water and oil. Mix to a soft dough. Knead the dough on a lightly floured board for 10 minutes until smooth and elastic.

2 Place in a greased bowl, cover with clear film (plastic wrap) and leave to double in size for about 1 hour. Turn out on to a floured surface; knead gently for 2–3 minutes. Use as required.

Onion & Gorgonzola Pizzas

These small pizzas are good for snacks or party food.

Makes 4

1 quantity Basic Pizza Dough (see above)
30ml/2 tbsp garlic oil
2 small red onions
150g/5oz Gorgonzola cheese, rind removed and diced
2 garlic cloves, cut into strips lengthways
10ml/2 tsp chopped fresh sage
a pinch of black pepper

1 Preheat the oven to 220°C/425°F/Gas 7. Divide the dough into eight pieces and roll out to small ovals about 5mm/¼in thick. Place well apart on two greased baking sheets and prick with a fork. Brush well with 15ml/1 tbsp of the garlic oil.

2 Halve, then slice the onions into thin wedges. Sprinkle over the pizza bases. Top with the cheese, then the garlic and sage. Drizzle the remaining oil on top and grind over plenty of pepper. Bake for 10–15 minutes until crisp and golden.

Classic Margherita Pizza with Mozzarella

A margherita pizza makes a lovely simple supper, but of course you can add any extra toppings you like. Prosciutto and rocket make a great addition – just add them to the pizza after it is cooked.

Makes 1

1 quantity Basic Pizza Dough (see above left)
15ml/1 tbsp herb-infused olive oil
45ml/3 tbsp ready-made tomato and basil sauce
150g/5oz mozzarella, sliced
salt and ground black pepper
basil leaves, to garnish

1 Make the pizza base according to the instructions for Basic Pizza Dough. Preheat the oven to 220°C/425°F/Gas 7.

2 Brush the pizza base with a little of the herb-infused olive oil Spread the tomato and basil sauce evenly over the base, using the back of a spoon, not quite to the edges.

3 Arrange the slices of mozzarella evenly on top of the pizza. Place on a baking sheet and bake in the preheated oven for about 20–25 minutes, or until the pizza dough is golden and the cheese is melted and bubbling.

4 Drizzle the remaining oil over the pizza, season to taste and serve immediately, garnished with fresh basil leaves.

Cook's Tip

You can make your own herb-infused oil, if you prefer. You will need a whole bunch of fresh herbs, such as rosemary, thyme, basil, coriander (cilantro) or parsley, and a bottle of olive oil, about 500ml/17fl oz/generous 2 cups. Simply bruise all the fresh herbs with a rolling pin to release their aromas, and stuff them into the bottle of oil. Leave the oil for a week or two before using.

Basic Pizza Dough per pizza Energy 696kcal/2944kJ; Protein 16.4g; Carbohydrate 136g, of which sugars 2.6g; Fat 13.3g, of which saturates 1.9g; Cholesterol 0mg; Calcium 245mg; Fibre 5.4g; Sodium 5mg.
Onion and Gorgonzola Pizzas per pizza Energy 371kcal/1550kJ; Protein 12.5g; Carbohydrate 38g, of which sugars 3.5g; Fat 19.8g, of which saturates 8.5g; Cholesterol 28mg; Calcium 263mg; Fibre 2.2g; Sodium 461mg.
Classic Margherita Pizza with Mozzarella Energy 420kcal/1761kJ; Protein 7.6g; Carbohydrate 49.8g, of which sugars 7.8g; Fat 22.6g, of which saturates 2.2g; Cholesterol 2mg; Calcium 133mg; Fibre 3.4g; Sodium 130mg.

Quattro Formaggi

Rich and cheesy, these individual pizzas are quick to make, and irresistible.

Makes 1

1 quantity Basic Pizza Dough (see page 84)
15ml/1 tbsp garlic oil
½ small red onion, very thinly sliced
50g/2oz Dolcelatte cheese
50g/2oz mozzarella cheese
50g/2oz/½ cup grated Gruyère cheese
30ml/2 tbsp freshly grated Parmesan cheese
15ml/1 tbsp chopped fresh thyme
ground black pepper

1 Preheat the oven to 220°C/425°F/Gas 7. Divide the dough into four pieces and roll out each one on a lightly floured surface into a 13cm/5in circle.

2 Place well apart on two greased baking sheets, then push up the dough edges to make a thin rim. Brush with garlic oil and top with the red onion.

3 Cut the Dolcelatte and mozzarella cheeses into dice and arrange over the bases. Mix together the Gruyère, Parmesan and thyme and sprinkle over the pizzas.

4 Grind plenty of pepper over the pizzas. Bake for about 15–20 minutes until the base is crisp and golden and the cheeses are bubbling. Serve immediately.

Cook's Tip
To make garlic oil, put 3–4 peeled garlic cloves in a jar and pour in 120ml/4fl oz/½ cup olive oil. Cover tightly and store in the refrigerator for up to 1 month.

Variation
Any variety of cheese that melts readily can be used, but a mixture of soft and hard cheeses gives the best result.

Rocket & Tomato Pizza

Peppery rocket leaves and aromatic basil add colour and flavour to this pizza.

Makes 1

10ml/2 tsp olive oil, plus extra for oiling and drizzling
1 garlic clove, crushed
150g/5oz/1 cup canned chopped tomatoes
2.5ml/½ tsp sugar
30ml/2 tbsp torn basil leaves
2 tomatoes, seeded and chopped
150g/5oz/⅔ cup mozzarella cheese, sliced
20g/¾oz/1 cup rocket (arugula) leaves
rock salt and ground black pepper

For the pizza base
225g/8oz/2 cups strong white bread flour, sifted
5ml/1 tsp salt
2.5ml/½ tsp easy-blend (rapid-rise) dried yeast
15ml/1 tbsp olive oil
150ml/¼ pint/⅔ cup warm water

1 To make the base, place the flour, salt and yeast in a bowl. Make a well in the centre, and mix in the oil and warm water.

2 Turn out the dough on to a lightly floured work surface and knead for 5 minutes. Cover with the upturned bowl and leave to rest for about 5 minutes, then knead for a further 5 minutes until the dough is smooth and elastic. Place in a lightly oiled bowl and cover with clear film (plastic wrap). Leave in a warm place for about 45 minutes until doubled in size.

3 Preheat the oven to 220°C/425°F/Gas 7. For the topping, heat the oil in a frying pan. Fry the garlic for 1 minute. Add the tomatoes and sugar and cook for 5–7 minutes until thickened. Stir in the basil and season to taste. Set aside.

4 Knead the risen dough lightly, then roll out to form a rough 30cm/12in round. Place on a lightly oiled baking sheet and push up the edges of the dough to form a shallow, even rim. Spoon the tomato mixture over the pizza base, then top with the fresh tomatoes and mozzarella. Adjust the seasoning and drizzle with a little olive oil. Bake for 10–12 minutes until crisp and golden. Arrange the rocket over the pizza just before serving.

Quattro Formaggi Energy 397kcal/1661kJ; Protein 14.6g; Carbohydrate 39.7g, of which sugars 3.9g; Fat 20.8g, of which saturates 9.3g; Cholesterol 37mg; Calcium 283mg; Fibre 2.3g; Sodium 405mg.

Rocket and Tomato Pizza Energy 735Kcal/3087kJ; Protein 26.1g; Carbohydrate 93g, of which sugars 7.3g; Fat 31.3g, of which saturates 12.7g; Cholesterol 44mg; Calcium 459mg; Fibre 5.5g; Sodium 330mg.

Bresaola & Rocket Pizza

Although the Armenians initiated the idea of topping flattened dough with savoury ingredients before baking it, it was the Italians who developed the pizza in the 1830s.

Makes 1

150g/5oz packet pizza base mix
120ml/4fl oz/½ cup lukewarm water
225g/8oz/3¼ cups mixed wild mushrooms
25g/1oz/2 tbsp butter
2 garlic cloves, coarsely chopped
60ml/4 tbsp pesto
8 slices bresaola
4 tomatoes, sliced
75g/3oz/⅓ cup full-fat (whole) cream cheese
25g/1oz rocket (arugula)

1 Preheat the oven to 200°C/400°F/Gas 6. Place the packet of pizza base mix into a large mixing bowl and pour in enough of the water to mix to a soft, not sticky, dough.

2 Turn out the dough on to a lightly floured surface and knead for about 5 minutes, or until smooth and elastic. Divide the dough into two equal pieces, knead lightly to form two balls, then pat out the balls of dough into flat rounds.

3 Roll out each piece of dough on a lightly floured surface to a 23cm/9in round and transfer to baking sheets.

4 Slice the wild mushrooms. Melt the butter in a frying pan and cook the garlic for 2 minutes. Add the mushrooms and cook over a high heat for about 5 minutes, or until the mushrooms have softened but are not overcooked.

5 Spread pesto on the pizza bases to within 2cm/¾in of the edge of each one. Arrange the bresaola and tomato slices around the rims of the pizzas, then spoon the cooked mushrooms into the middle.

6 Dot the cream cheese on top of the pizzas and bake for 15–18 minutes, or until the bases are crisp. Top each pizza with a handful of rocket leaves just before serving. Serve immediately.

Wild Mushroom Pizzas

With their delicate earthy flavour, wild mushrooms make a delicious topping for these little pizzas. Serve as an unusual starter, or for a stylish light meal.

Makes 4

45ml/3 tbsp olive oil
350g/12oz fresh mixed wild mushrooms, washed and sliced
2 shallots, chopped
2 garlic cloves, finely chopped
30ml/2 tbsp chopped fresh mixed thyme and flat leaf parsley
1 quantity Basic Pizza Dough (see page 84)
40g/1½oz/generous ¼ cup grated Gruyère cheese
30ml/2 tbsp freshly grated Parmesan cheese
salt and ground black pepper

1 Preheat the oven to 220°C/425°F/Gas 7. Heat 30ml/2 tbsp of the oil in a frying pan and fry the mushrooms, shallots and garlic over medium heat, stirring occasionally, until all the juices have evaporated.

2 Stir in half the herbs and season with salt and pepper, then set aside to cool.

3 Divide the dough into four pieces and roll out each one on a lightly floured surface to a 13cm/5in circle. Place well apart on two greased baking sheets, then push up the dough edges to form a thin rim around the dough circles.

4 Brush the pizza bases with the remaining oil and spoon the wild mushrooms on top. Mix together the Gruyère and Parmesan, then sprinkle over the mushroom mixture.

5 Bake the pizza for 15–20 minutes until crisp and golden. Remove from the oven and sprinkle over the remaining herbs.

Cook's Tip
Fresh wild mushrooms add a distinctive flavour to the topping, but if they are unavailable, a mixture of cultivated mushrooms, such as shiitake, oyster and chestnut, would do just as well.

Bresaola and Rocket Pizza Energy 448kcal/1873kJ; Protein 16.6g; Carbohydrate 34.7g, of which sugars 6g; Fat 28g, of which saturates 12.8g; Cholesterol 56mg; Calcium 179mg; Fibre 3.5g; Sodium 213mg.

Wild Mushroom Pizzas Energy 340kcal/1425kJ; Protein 11.4g; Carbohydrate 35.6g, of which sugars 1.7g; Fat 17.8g, of which saturates 5.5g; Cholesterol 17mg; Calcium 234mg; Fibre 2.5g; Sodium 160mg.

Mushroom & Pesto Pizza

Home-made Italian-style pizzas are a little time-consuming to make, but the results are worth the effort.

Makes 1

For the pizza base

350g/12oz/3 cups strong plain (all-purpose) flour
1.5ml/¼ tsp salt
15g/½oz easy-blend (rapid-rise) dried yeast
15ml/1 tbsp olive oil

For the topping

50g/2oz dried porcini mushrooms
25g/1oz/¾ cup fresh basil
25g/1oz/⅓ cup pine nuts
40g/1½oz Parmesan cheese, thinly sliced
105ml/7 tbsp olive oil
2 onions, thinly sliced
225g/8oz brown cap (cremini) mushrooms, sliced
salt and ground black pepper

1 To make the pizza base, put the flour in a bowl with the salt, dried yeast and olive oil. Add 250ml/8fl oz/1 cup lukewarm water and mix to a dough using a round-bladed knife.

2 Turn on to a work surface and knead for 5 minutes until smooth. Place in a clean bowl, cover with clear film (plastic wrap) and leave in a warm place until doubled in size.

3 Meanwhile, make the topping. Soak the dried mushrooms in hot water for 20 minutes. Place the basil, pine nuts, Parmesan and 75ml/5 tbsp of the olive oil in a blender or food processor, and process to make a smooth pesto paste. Set the pesto aside.

4 Fry the onions in the remaining olive oil for 3–4 minutes until just browning. Fry the brown cap mushrooms for 2 minutes. Stir in the drained porcini mushrooms and season lightly.

5 Preheat the oven to 220°C/425°F/Gas 7. Lightly grease a large baking sheet. Turn the pizza dough on to a floured surface and roll out to a 30cm/12in round. Place on the baking sheet.

6 Spread the pesto mixture to within 1cm/½in of the edges of the pizza base. Spread the mushroom mixture on top. Bake the pizza in the oven for 35–40 minutes until risen and golden.

Polenta Pan-pizza with Red Onions

This yeast-free pizza is cooked in a frying pan rather than the oven.

Makes 1

30ml/2 tbsp olive oil
1 large red onion, sliced
3 garlic cloves, crushed
115g/4oz/1½ cups brown cap (cremini) mushrooms, sliced
5ml/1 tsp dried oregano
115g/4oz mozzarella cheese
15ml/1 tbsp pine nuts (optional)

For the base

50g/2oz/½ cup unbleached plain (all-purpose) flour, sifted
2.5ml/½ tsp salt
115g/4oz/1 cup fine polenta
5ml/1 tsp baking powder
1 egg, beaten
150ml/¼ pint/⅔ cup milk
25g/1oz/⅓ cup freshly grated Parmesan cheese
2.5ml/½ tsp dried chilli flakes
15ml/1 tbsp olive oil

1 To make the topping, heat half the oil in a frying pan. Cook the onion for 10 minutes until tender. Remove the onion from the pan and set aside. Add the remaining oil to the pan. Fry the garlic for 1 minute, then add the sliced mushrooms and oregano and cook for 5 minutes more until the mushrooms are tender.

2 To make the pizza base, mix together the flour, salt, polenta and baking powder in a bowl. Make a well in the centre and add the egg. Gradually add the milk, and mix well to make into a thick, smooth batter. Stir in the Parmesan and chilli flakes.

3 Heat the olive oil in a 25cm/10in heavy flameproof frying pan until hot. Spread in the batter and cook over medium heat for about 3 minutes or until the base is set.

4 Remove from the heat and run a knife around the edge of the pizza base. Place a plate over the pan and flip over. Slide the base back into the pan on its uncooked side and cook for 2 minutes until golden.

5 Preheat the grill (broiler) to high. Spoon the onions over the base, then top with the mushroom mixture. Crumble the mozzarella cheese on top, then grill (broil) until the cheese has melted. Sprinkle over the pine nuts, if using, and grill until golden.

Mushroom and Pesto Pizza Energy 631kcal/2642kJ; Protein 15.6g; Carbohydrate 76.6g, of which sugars 7.4g; Fat 31.3g, of which saturates 5.7g; Cholesterol 10mg; Calcium 285mg; Fibre 5.3g; Sodium 120mg.

Polenta Pan-pizza with Red Onions Energy 782kcal/3262kJ; Protein 31.9g; Carbohydrate 77.1g, of which sugars 12.4g; Fat 39.1g, of which saturates 14.5g; Cholesterol 145mg; Calcium 540mg; Fibre 4.8g; Sodium 439mg.

Fiorentina Pizza

Fresh spinach is the star ingredient of this pizza. A grating of nutmeg heightens its flavour.

Makes 1

1 quantity Basic Pizza Dough (see page 84)
175g/6oz/1 ½ cups fresh spinach
45ml/3 tbsp olive oil
1 small red onion, thinly sliced
1 jar ready-made tomato sauce or pizza topping
a pinch of freshly grated nutmeg
150g/5oz mozzarella cheese
1 egg
25g/1oz/¼ cup grated Gruyère cheese

1 Preheat the oven to 220°C/425°F/Gas 7. Roll out the pizza dough to a 25–30cm/10–12in circle and place on a greased baking sheet. Push up the edge of the dough to form a thin rim.

2 Remove the stalks from the spinach and wash the leaves in plenty of cold water. Drain well and pat dry with kitchen paper.

3 Heat 15ml/1 tbsp of the oil in a large frying pan and fry the onion until softened. Add the spinach and continue to fry until just wilted. Drain off any excess liquid.

4 Brush the pizza base with half the remaining oil. Spread over the tomato sauce or pizza topping, then top with the spinach mixture. Grate over some nutmeg.

5 Thinly slice the mozzarella cheese and arrange over the spinach. Drizzle over the remaining oil. Bake for 10 minutes, then remove from the oven.

6 Make a small well in the centre of the pizza and drop the egg into the hole. Sprinkle over the Gruyère and return to the oven for a further 5–10 minutes until crisp and golden.

Cook's Tip
The egg adds the finishing touch to this spinach pizza. Try not to overcook it, as it is best when the yolk is still slightly soft.

Marinara Pizza

The combination of garlic, good-quality olive oil and oregano gives this pizza an unmistakably Italian flavour.

Makes 1

1 quantity Basic Pizza Dough (see page 84)
675g/1 ½lb ripe plum tomatoes
60ml/4 tbsp extra virgin olive oil
4 garlic cloves, cut into slivers
15ml/1 tbsp chopped fresh oregano
salt and ground black pepper

1 Roll out the pizza dough to a 25–30cm/10–12in circle and place on a greased baking sheet. Push up the edge of the dough to form a thin rim around the dough circle.

2 Make a slash in the skin of each tomato, then put them all in a heatproof bowl and pour over boiling water. Leave for 30 seconds, then plunge the tomatoes into cold water. Peel and seed, then roughly chop the flesh.

3 Preheat the oven to 220°C/425°F/Gas 7. Heat 30ml/2 tbsp of the oil in a pan. Add the tomatoes and cook, stirring frequently, for about 5 minutes until soft.

4 Place the tomatoes in a metal sieve (strainer) and leave them to drain for about 5 minutes. Transfer the tomatoes to a food processor or blender and purée until smooth.

5 Brush the pizza base with half the remaining oil. Spoon over the tomatoes and sprinkle with garlic and oregano. Drizzle over the remaining oil and season to taste.

6 Bake for 15–20 minutes until crisp. Serve immediately.

Cook's Tip
Ready-made pizza bases are handy if you are short of time. They are available from most supermarkets, and come in a range of sizes. It is always useful to keep a few in the freezer.

Fiorentina Pizza Energy 515kcal/2150kJ; Protein 20.9g; Carbohydrate 40.8g, of which sugars 5.2g; Fat 30.8g, of which saturates 11.4g; Cholesterol 104mg; Calcium 415mg; Fibre 3.2g; Sodium 634mg.

Marinara Pizza Energy 415kcal/1742kJ; Protein 8.1g; Carbohydrate 54.5g, of which sugars 8.1g; Fat 19.8g, of which saturates 3g; Cholesterol 0mg; Calcium 100mg; Fibre 4.6g; Sodium 23mg.

Feta & Roasted Garlic Pizzettes

These pizzettes are for garlic lovers. Mash down the cloves as you eat them – they should be meltingly soft and sweet-tasting.

Makes 4

1 garlic bulb, unpeeled
45ml/3 tbsp olive oil
1 red (bell) pepper, seeded and quartered
1 yellow (bell) pepper, seeded and quartered
2 plum tomatoes
1 quantity Basic Pizza Dough (see page 84)
175g/6oz/1½ cups crumbled feta cheese
a pinch of black pepper
15–30ml/1–2 tbsp chopped fresh oregano, to garnish

1 Preheat the oven to 220°C/425°F/Gas 7. Break the garlic into cloves, discarding the outer papery layers. Toss in 15ml/1 tbsp of the olive oil.

2 Place the peppers skin side up on a baking sheet and grill (broil), turning them until the skins are evenly charred. Place in a covered bowl for 10 minutes, then peel off the skins. Cut the flesh into strips.

3 Make a slash in the skin of each tomato, then put them in a bowl and pour over boiling water. Leave for 30 seconds, then plunge into cold water. Peel, seed and roughly chop the flesh.

4 Divide the pizza dough into four pieces and roll out each one on a lightly floured surface to equal circles of about 13cm/5in diameter. Place the dough circles well apart on two greased baking sheets, then push up the dough edges to form a thin rim around the dough circles.

5 Brush the dough circles with half the remaining oil and sprinkle over the chopped tomatoes. Top with the peppers, crumbled feta cheese and garlic cloves. Drizzle over the remaining oil and season to taste with pepper.

6 Bake in the oven for 15–20 minutes until crisp and golden. Garnish with chopped oregano and serve immediately.

Potato, Smoked Mozzarella & Garlic Pizza

New potatoes, smoked mozzarella and garlic make this pizza unique.

Makes 1

350g/12oz small new or salad potatoes
45ml/3 tbsp olive oil
2 garlic cloves, crushed
1 pizza base, about 25–30cm/10–12in diameter
1 red onion, thinly sliced
150g/5oz/1¼ cups smoked mozzarella cheese, grated
10ml/2 tsp chopped fresh rosemary or sage
salt and ground black pepper
30ml/2 tbsp freshly grated Parmesan cheese, to garnish

1 Preheat the oven to 220°C/425°F/Gas 7. Put the potatoes in a large pan. Add water to cover and bring to the boil. Add salt, then simmer for about 5 minutes, or until the potatoes are just becoming tender. Drain thoroughly and leave to cool.

2 When the potatoes are cool enough to handle, peel and slice them thinly.

3 Heat 30ml/2 tbsp of the oil in a frying pan. Add the sliced potatoes and garlic and fry for 5–8 minutes, turning frequently until tender.

4 Brush the pizza base with the remaining oil. Sprinkle the onion over, then arrange the potatoes on top. Sprinkle over the mozzarella and rosemary or sage and plenty of black pepper.

5 Bake for 15–20 minutes until golden. Remove from the oven, sprinkle with Parmesan and more ground black pepper.

Variation
For non-vegetarians, you can add sliced smoked pork sausage or pastrami to the pizza to make it even more substantial.

Feta and Roasted Garlic Pizzettes Energy 419kcal/1751kJ; Protein 14.1g; Carbohydrate 45.9g, of which sugars 8.6g; Fat 21.1g, of which saturates 7.8g; Cholesterol 31mg; Calcium 234mg; Fibre 4.3g; Sodium 640mg.

Potato, Smoked Mozzarella and Garlic Pizza Energy 413kcal/1727kJ; Protein 14.1g; Carbohydrate 39.5g, of which sugars 3.7g; Fat 23.1g, of which saturates 8.5g; Cholesterol 29mg; Calcium 222mg; Fibre 2.1g; Sodium 302mg.

Caramelized Onion, Salami & Black Olive Pizza

The flavour of the sweet caramelized onion is offset by the salty black olives and herbs in the pizza base and the sprinkling of Parmesan to finish.

Makes 1

675g/1½lb red onions, sliced
60ml/4 tbsp olive oil
1 quantity pizza dough (see Cook's Tip)
12 pitted black olives, chopped
5ml/1 tsp dried herbes de Provence
6–8 slices Italian salami, quartered
30–45ml/2–3tbsp freshly grated Parmesan
ground black pepper

1 Preheat the oven to 220°C/425°F/Gas 7. Heat 30 ml/2 tbsp of the oil in a pan and add the onions. Cover and cook gently for 15–20 minutes, stirring occasionally, until they are soft and lightly coloured. Leave to cool.

2 Knead the dough on a lightly floured surface, adding the black olives and dried herbs. Roll out and use to line a 30 × 18cm/12 × 7in shallow tin (pan). Push up the dough edges to make a thin rim and brush with half the remaining oil.

3 Spoon half the onions over the base, top with the salami and the remaining onions. Grind over plenty of black pepper and drizzle over the remaining oil.

4 Bake for 15–20 minutes, or until the dough is crisp and golden. Sprinkle over the Parmesan to serve.

Cook's Tip

To make a pizza this size, sift 200g/7oz/1¼ cups strong white bread flour with a pinch of salt into a bowl. Add 1.5ml/¼ tsp easy-blend (rapid-rise) dried yeast, 50ml/2fl oz/¼ cup olive oil and 75ml/5 tbsp water, and mix to a dough. Knead for 10 minutes and leave in a covered, oiled bowl for about 1 hour.

Four Seasons Pizza

The topping on this pizza is divided into four quarters, one for each 'season', creating a colourful effect.

Makes 1

450g/1lb peeled plum tomatoes, weighed whole (or canned without their juice)
75ml/5 tbsp olive oil
115g/4oz mushrooms, thinly sliced
1 garlic clove, finely chopped
1 quantity Basic Pizza Dough (see page 84)
350g/12oz/scant 2½ cups diced mozzarella cheese
4 thin slices of ham, cut into 5cm/2in squares
32 pitted black olives, halved
8 artichoke hearts, preserved in oil, drained and cut in half
5ml/1 tsp oregano leaves, fresh or dried
salt and ground black pepper

1 Preheat the oven to 240°C/475°F/Gas 9 for at least 20 minutes before baking the pizza. Strain the tomatoes through the medium holes of a food mill placed over a bowl, scraping in all the pulp.

2 Heat 30ml/2 tbsp of the oil in a pan and lightly fry the mushrooms. Stir in the garlic and set aside.

3 Roll out the pizza dough to a 25–30cm/10–12in circle and place on a greased baking sheet. Push up the edge of the dough to form a thin rim around the dough circle.

4 Spread the puréed tomatoes on the prepared pizza dough, up to the rim. Sprinkle evenly with the mozzarella cheese. Spread the mushrooms over one quarter of the pizza.

5 Arrange the ham on one quarter and the olives on another quarter. Arrange the artichoke hearts on the remaining quarter.

6 Sprinkle the whole of the pizza with oregano, and season with salt and pepper. Sprinkle over the remaining olive oil. Immediately place the pizza in the oven and bake for about 15–20 minutes, or until the crust is golden brown and the topping is bubbling.

Caramelized Onion, Salami and Black Olive Pizza Energy 462kcal/1928kJ; Protein 14.1g; Carbohydrate 49.8g, of which sugars 11.9g; Fat 24.3g, of which saturates 5.9g; Cholesterol 22mg; Calcium 242mg; Fibre 4.1g; Sodium 804mg.

Four Seasons Pizza Energy 586kcal/2442kJ; Protein 24.3g; Carbohydrate 37.9g, of which sugars 4.5g; Fat 38.5g, of which saturates 15.2g; Cholesterol 58mg; Calcium 410mg; Fibre 3.7g; Sodium 1080mg.

Farmhouse Pizza

This is the ultimate party pizza. Served cut into fingers, it is ideal for a large and hungry gathering.

Makes 1

90ml/6 tbsp olive oil
225g/8oz button (white) mushrooms, sliced
2 quantities Basic Pizza Dough (see page 84)
1 jar ready-made tomato sauce or pizza topping
300g/10oz mozzarella cheese, thinly sliced
115g/4oz wafer-thin smoked ham slices
6 bottled artichoke hearts in oil, drained and sliced
50g/2oz can anchovy fillets, drained and halved lengthways
10 pitted black olives, halved
30ml/2 tbsp chopped fresh oregano
15ml/3 tbsp freshly grated Parmesan cheese
ground black pepper

1 Preheat the oven to 220°C/425°F/Gas 7. In a large frying pan, heat 30ml/2 tbsp of the oil. Gently fry the mushrooms for 5 minutes until all the juices have evaporated. Remove from the heat and leave to cool.

2 Roll out the dough on a lightly floured surface to make a 30 × 25cm/12 × 10in rectangle. Transfer to a greased baking sheet, then push up the dough edges to form a thin rim. Brush with 30ml/2 tbsp of the oil.

3 Spread the tomato sauce or pizza topping over the dough, then arrange the sliced mozzarella over the sauce.

4 Scrunch up the ham and arrange on top with the artichoke hearts, mushrooms and anchovies.

5 Dot with the black olives, then sprinkle over the chopped oregano and grated Parmesan. Drizzle over the remaining oil, and season to taste with pepper.

6 Bake for about 25 minutes until the pizza crust is crisp and golden. Serve immediately.

Mushroom & Pancetta Pizzas

Try to use a mixture of wild and cultivated mushrooms to give these individual pizzas lots of earthy flavour.

Makes 4

1 quantity Basic Pizza Dough (see page 84)
60ml/4 tbsp olive oil
2 garlic cloves, crushed
225g/8oz fresh mixed ceps and chestnut mushrooms, roughly chopped
75g/3oz pancetta, roughly chopped
15ml/1 tbsp chopped fresh oregano
45ml/3 tbsp freshly grated Parmesan cheese
salt and ground black pepper

1 Preheat the oven to 220°C/425°F/Gas 7. Divide the dough into four pieces and roll out each one on a lightly floured surface to a 13cm/5in circle. Place well apart on two greased baking sheets.

2 Heat 30ml/2 tbsp of the olive oil in a frying pan and fry the garlic and mushrooms gently until the mushrooms are tender and the juices have evaporated. Season to taste with salt and pepper, then cool.

3 Brush the pizza bases with 15ml/1 tbsp oil, then spoon over the mushrooms. Sprinkle over the pancetta and oregano.

4 Sprinkle the toppings with grated Parmesan cheese and drizzle over the remaining oil. Bake for 10–15 minutes, until crisp. Serve immediately.

Cook's Tips

- *Pancetta is available in larger supermarkets and Italian delicatessens. If you have difficulty finding it, use chopped slices of streaky (fatty) bacon in its place.*
- *If fresh ceps are not available, you can add extra flavour to cultivated mushrooms by adding some dried porcini mushrooms, which are sold in larger supermarkets. Soak them in hot water for 20 minutes until soft, before adding to the pan in step 2.*

Farmhouse Pizza Energy 412kcal/1725kJ; Protein 17.2g; Carbohydrate 36.4g, of which sugars 2g; Fat 23g, of which saturates 8g; Cholesterol 38mg; Calcium 259mg; Fibre 2.4g; Sodium 822mg.

Mushroom and Pancetta Pizzas Energy 344kcal/1435kJ; Protein 12g; Carbohydrate 27g, of which sugars 1.7g; Fat 21.6g, of which saturates 5.5g; Cholesterol 23mg; Calcium 180mg; Fibre 1.6g; Sodium 488mg.

Pepperoni Pizza

This classic pizza is sure to go down well with family and friends alike. Who can resist a slice of home-made pizza, topped with a luscious combination of tangy pepperoni, sweet pepper and lashings of cheese?

Makes 1

For the sauce

30ml/2 tbsp olive oil
1 onion, finely chopped
1 garlic clove, crushed
400g/14oz can chopped tomatoes with herbs
15ml/1 tbsp tomato purée (paste)

For the pizza base

275g/10oz/2½ cups plain (all-purpose) flour
2.5ml/½ tsp salt
5ml/1 tsp easy-blend (rapid-rise) dried yeast
30ml/2 tbsp olive oil

For the topping

½ each red, yellow and green (bell) pepper, sliced into rings
150g/5oz mozzarella cheese, sliced
75g/3oz pepperoni sausage, thinly sliced
8 pitted black olives
3 sun-dried tomatoes, chopped
2.5ml/½ tsp dried oregano
olive oil, for drizzling

1 To make the sauce, heat the oil and fry the onions and garlic until softened. Add the tomatoes and tomato purée, then boil rapidly for 5 minutes until reduced slightly. Leave to cool.

2 To make the pizza base, sift the flour and salt into a bowl. Sprinkle over the yeast and make a well in the centre. Pour in 175ml/6fl oz/¾ cup warm water and the olive oil. Mix to a soft dough. Knead the dough on a lightly floured surface for about 5–10 minutes until smooth. Roll out to a 25cm/10in round, press up the edges slightly and place on a greased baking sheet.

3 Spread over the tomato sauce and top with the peppers, mozzarella, pepperoni, olives and sun-dried tomatoes. Sprinkle over the oregano and drizzle with olive oil. Cover loosely and leave in a warm place for 30 minutes.

4 Meanwhile, preheat the oven to 220°C/425°F/Gas 7. Bake the pizza for 25–30 minutes, then serve.

Hot Pepperoni Pizza with Chillies

This version of the classic pepperoni pizza includes dried red chillies to add extra heat.

Makes 1

225g/8oz/2 cups strong white bread flour
10ml/2 tsp easy-blend (rapid-rise) dried yeast
5ml/1 tsp sugar
5ml/½ tsp salt
15ml/1 tbsp olive oil, plus extra for greasing
175ml/6fl oz/¾ cup mixed hand-hot milk and water

For the topping

400g/14oz can chopped tomatoes, well drained
2 garlic cloves, crushed
1 tsp dried oregano, plus extra to garnish
225g/8oz mozzarella cheese, coarsely grated
2 dried red chillies, crumbled
225g/8oz pepperoni, sliced
30ml/2 tbsp drained capers

1 Sift the flour into a bowl. Stir in the yeast, sugar and salt. Make a well in the centre. Stir the olive oil into the milk and water, then stir the mixture into the flour. Mix to a soft dough.

2 Knead the dough on a lightly floured surface for 5-10 minutes until it is smooth and elastic. Return it to the clean, lightly oiled, bowl and cover with clear film (plastic wrap). Leave in a warm place until the dough has doubled in size.

3 Preheat the oven to 220°C/425°F/Gas 7. Turn the dough out on to a lightly floured surface and knead for 1 minute. Divide it in half and roll each piece out to a 25cm/10in circle. Place on oiled baking sheets.

4 To make the topping, mix the tomatoes, garlic and oregano in a bowl. Spread half the mixture over each base. Set half the mozzarella aside. Divide the rest between the pizzas. Bake for 7–10 minutes until the dough rim on each pizza is pale golden.

5 Sprinkle the crumbled chillies over the pizzas, then arrange the pepperoni slices and capers on top. Sprinkle the remaining mozzarella, then return the pizzas to the oven and bake for 7–10 minutes more. Sprinkle over the oregano and serve.

Pepperoni Pizza Energy 521kcal/2184kJ; Protein 17.5g; Carbohydrate 62.4g, of which sugars 8.6g; Fat 24g, of which saturates 8.2g; Cholesterol 43mg; Calcium 256mg; Fibre 4.7g; Sodium 484mg.

Hot Pepperoni Pizza with Chillies Energy 631kcal/2640kJ; Protein 28.8g; Carbohydrate 47.6g, of which sugars 4.7g; Fat 37.6g, of which saturates 16.8g; Cholesterol 80mg; Calcium 318mg; Fibre 2.7g; Sodium 1499mg.

Chilli Beef Pizza

Minced beef and red kidney beans combined with oregano, cumin and chillies turn this pizza into a Mexican extravaganza.

Makes 1

1 quantity Basic Pizza Dough (see page 84)
30ml/2 tbsp olive oil
1 red onion, finely chopped
1 garlic clove, crushed
½ red (bell) pepper, seeded and finely chopped
175g/6oz/¾ cup lean minced (ground) beef
2.5ml/½ tsp ground cumin
2 fresh red chillies, seeded and chopped
115g/4oz/scant ½ cup (drained weight) canned red kidney beans, rinsed
1 jar ready-made tomato sauce or pizza topping
15ml/1 tbsp chopped fresh oregano
50g/2oz/½ cup grated mozzarella cheese
75g/3oz/¾ cup grated oak-smoked Cheddar cheese
salt and ground black pepper

1 Preheat the oven to 220°C/425°F/Gas 7. Roll out the pizza dough to a 25–30cm/10–12in circle and place on a greased baking sheet. Push up the edge of the dough to form a thin rim.

2 Heat 15ml/1 tbsp of the oil in a frying pan and gently fry the onion, garlic and pepper until soft. Increase the heat, add the beef and brown well, stirring constantly.

3 Add the cumin and chillies and continue to cook, stirring, for about 5 minutes. Add the kidney beans and season with salt and pepper. Remove from the heat.

4 Spread the tomato sauce over the pizza base. Spoon the beef mixture over the top, then sprinkle with the oregano.

5 Arrange over the mozzarella and Cheddar cheeses on top, then sprinkle with the remaining olive oil.

6 Place the pizza in the oven and bake for about 15–20 minutes, or until the crust is golden brown and the topping is bubbling. Serve hot.

Salmon & Avocado Pizza

Smoked and fresh salmon make a delicious and luxurious pizza topping when mixed with avocado.

Makes 1

150g/5oz salmon fillet
120ml/4fl oz/½ cup dry white wine
1 quantity Basic Pizza Dough (see page 84)
15ml/1 tbsp olive oil
400g/14oz can chopped tomatoes, drained well
115g/4oz/scant 1 cup grated mozzarella
1 small avocado
10ml/2 tsp lemon juice
30ml/2 tbsp crème fraîche
75g/3oz smoked salmon, cut into strips
15ml/1 tbsp capers
30ml/2 tbsp chopped fresh chives, to garnish
ground black pepper

1 Place the salmon fillet in a frying pan, pour over the wine and season with pepper. Bring slowly to the boil over low heat, remove from the heat, cover with a tight-fitting lid and leave to cool. (The fish will cook in the cooling liquid.) Skin and flake the salmon into small pieces, removing any bones.

2 Preheat the oven to 220°C/425°F/Gas 7. Roll out the pizza dough to a 25–30cm/10–12in circle and place on a greased baking sheet. Push up the edge of the dough to form a thin rim.

3 Brush the pizza base with the oil and spread the drained tomatoes over the top. Sprinkle half the mozzarella. Bake for 10 minutes, then remove from the oven.

4 Meanwhile, halve, stone and peel the avocado. Cut the flesh into small dice and toss in the lemon juice.

5 Dot teaspoonfuls of the crème fraîche over the pizza base. Arrange the fresh and smoked salmon, avocado, capers and remaining mozzarella on top. Season to taste with pepper.

6 Bake for 5–10 minutes until crisp and golden. Sprinkle over the chives and serve immediately.

Chilli Beef Pizza Energy 494kcal/2067kJ; Protein 22.7g; Carbohydrate 43.9g, of which sugars 5g; Fat 26.1g, of which saturates 10.6g; Cholesterol 54mg; Calcium 280mg; Fibre 4.1g; Sodium 411mg.

Salmon and Avocado Pizza Energy 451kcal/1884kJ; Protein 22g; Carbohydrate 31g, of which sugars 5.3g; Fat 25.3g, of which saturates 8.6g; Cholesterol 53mg; Calcium 193mg; Fibre 3.3g; Sodium 282mg.

Tuna, Anchovy & Caper Pizza

Packed with Italian flavours, this substantial pizza is great for an informal gathering.

Makes 1

115g/4oz/1 cup self-raising (self-rising) flour
115g/4oz/1 cup self-raising wholemeal (self-rising whole-wheat) flour
a pinch of salt
50g/2oz/¼ cup butter, diced
about 150ml/¼ pint/⅔ cup milk

For the topping
30ml/2 tbsp olive oil
1 jar ready-made tomato sauce or pizza topping
1 small red onion
200g/7oz can tuna, drained
15ml/1 tbsp capers
12 black olives, pitted
45ml/3 tbsp freshly grated Parmesan cheese
50g/2oz can anchovy fillets, drained and halved lengthways
ground black pepper

1 Place the flours and salt in a bowl and rub in the butter until the mixture resembles fine breadcrumbs. Add the milk and mix to a soft dough with a wooden spoon. Knead on a lightly floured surface until smooth.

2 Preheat the oven to 220°C/425°F/Gas 7. Roll out the dough on a lightly floured surface to a 25cm/10in circle. Place on a greased baking sheet and brush with 15ml/1 tbsp of the oil. Spread the tomato sauce or pizza topping evenly over the dough, leaving the edge uncovered.

3 Cut the onion into thin wedges and arrange on top. Roughly flake the tuna with a fork and scatter over the onion. Sprinkle over the capers, black olives and Parmesan cheese.

4 Place the anchovy fillets over the top of the pizza in a criss-cross pattern. Drizzle over the remaining oil, then grind over plenty of pepper. Bake for 15–20 minutes until crisp and golden. Serve immediately.

Variation
If you have time, make your own herb-flavoured tomato sauce.

Pissaladière

This famous onion and anchovy dish is best eaten lukewarm rather than piping hot. Serve with a salad and fresh bread.

Makes 1

250g/9oz/2¼ cups strong plain (all-purpose) white flour, plus extra for dusting
50g/2oz/⅓ cup fine polenta or semolina
5ml/1 tsp salt
175ml/6fl oz/¾ cup lukewarm water
5ml/1 tsp active dried yeast
5ml/1 tsp sugar
30ml/2 tbsp extra virgin olive oil

For the topping
60–75ml/4–5 tbsp extra virgin olive oil
6 large sweet Spanish (Bermuda) onions, thinly sliced
2 large garlic cloves, thinly sliced
5ml/1 tsp chopped fresh thyme, plus several sprigs
1 fresh rosemary sprig
1–2 x 50g/2oz cans anchovies in olive oil, drained
50–75g/2–3oz small black olives
salt and ground black pepper

1 Mix the flour, polenta or semolina and salt in a large bowl. Pour half the water into a bowl. Add the yeast and sugar, then leave in a warm place for 10 minutes, until frothy. Pour into the flour mixture with the remaining water and the olive oil.

2 Mix all the ingredients together to form a dough, then turn out and knead until smooth and elastic. Return the dough to the clean, floured bowl and cover until doubled in size.

3 Meanwhile, prepare the topping. Heat 45ml/3 tbsp of the olive oil in a large pan and stir in the onions. Cover and cook over very low heat for 20–30 minutes. Add the garlic, chopped thyme and rosemary and a little salt. Cook for 15–25 minutes. Remove and discard the rosemary. Set the onions aside to cool.

4 Preheat the oven to 220°C/425°F/Gas 7. Roll out the dough and place on a baking sheet. Spread the onions over the top. Cut the anchovies in half lengthways and arrange in a lattice pattern over the onions. Sprinkle the olives and thyme sprigs over and drizzle with the remaining olive oil. Bake for about 20–25 minutes. Season with pepper and serve warm in slices.

Tuna, Anchovy and Caper Pizza Energy 713kcal/2985kJ; Protein 37.8g; Carbohydrate 58.5g, of which sugars 3.8g; Fat 38.1g, of which saturates 15g; Cholesterol 97mg; Calcium 328mg; Fibre 5.7g; Sodium 1518mg.
Pissaladière Energy 436kcal/1815kJ; Protein 5.9g; Carbohydrate 37.4g, of which sugars 5.8g; Fat 31.1g, of which saturates 1.5g; Cholesterol 0mg; Calcium 77mg; Fibre 1.5g; Sodium 542mg.

Spanish Pizza with Onion & Anchovy Topping

Called *cocas* in Spain, these have a similar tradition to pissaladière. Fresh bread dough is baked with savoury toppings, including salt fish.

Makes 1

400g/14oz/3½ cups strong white bread flour
2.5ml/½ tsp salt
15g/½oz easy-blend (rapid-rise) dried yeast
120ml/4fl oz/½ cup olive oil
150ml/¼ pint/⅔ cup milk and water, in equal quantities, mixed
3 large onions, thinly sliced
50g/2oz can anchovies, drained and roughly chopped
30ml/2 tbsp pine nuts
30ml/2 tbsp Muscatel raisins or sultanas (golden raisins), soaked
5ml/1 tsp dried chilli flakes or powder
salt and ground black pepper

1 Put the flour and salt into a food processor with the yeast. Process, gradually working in 60ml/4 tbsp oil and a little of the milk and water. Gradually add the remaining milk and water. Turn the dough into a bowl, cover with a dish towel, then leave in a warm place for about 1 hour to rise.

2 Preheat the oven to 240°C/475°F/Gas 9. Heat the remaining oil in a large pan, add the onions, and cook gently until soft.

3 Return the dough to the food processor and knead it. On a lightly floured surface, roll out the dough to a rectangle about 30 × 38cm/12 × 15in. Place on an oiled baking sheet.

4 Cover the dough with the onions. Scatter with the anchovies, pine nuts, raisins or sultanas and chilli flakes or powder and season. Bake for about 10 minutes, until puffed up and beginning to brown at the edges. Serve hot, cut into wedges.

Variation
You can eat cocas with a wide range of different toppings. Try spinach sautéed with garlic or sweet red (bell) peppers.

Mussel & Leek Pizzas

Serve these lovely little seafood pizzas with a crisp green salad for a light lunch.

Makes 1

450g/1lb live mussels in the shell
120ml/4fl oz/½ cup dry white wine
1 quantity Basic Pizza Dough (see page 84)
15ml/1 tbsp olive oil
50g/2oz Gruyère cheese
50g/2oz mozzarella cheese
2 small leeks, thinly sliced
salt and ground black pepper

1 Preheat the oven to 220°C/425°F/Gas 7. Place the mussels in a bowl of cold water to soak, then scrub well. Remove the beards, and discard any mussels that are open.

2 Place the mussels in a pan. Pour over the dry white wine, cover with a tight-fitting lid and cook over high heat, shaking the pan occasionally, for 5–10 minutes until the mussels open.

3 Drain off the cooking liquid. Remove the mussels from their shells, discarding any that remain closed. Leave to cool.

4 Divide the dough into four pieces and roll out each one on a lightly floured surface to a 13cm/5in circle. Place well apart on two greased baking sheets, then push up the dough edges to form a thin rim around the dough circles.

5 Brush the pizza bases with the oil. Grate the cheeses and sprinkle half evenly over the bases. Arrange the leeks over the cheese. Bake for 10 minutes, then remove from the oven.

6 Arrange the mussels on top. Season with salt and pepper and sprinkle over the remaining cheese. Bake for a further 5–10 minutes until crisp and golden. Serve immediately.

Cook's Tip
Frozen or canned mussels can also be used, but these will give a different flavour and texture to these pizzettes.

Spanish Pizza with Onion and Anchovy Topping Energy 335kcal/1407kJ; Protein 7.8g; Carbohydrate 47.5g, of which sugars 7.7g; Fat 14g, of which saturates 1.8g; Cholesterol 4mg; Calcium 110mg; Fibre 2.8g; Sodium 252mg.

Mussel and Leek Pizzas Energy 343kcal/1441kJ; Protein 16.3g; Carbohydrate 35.6g, of which sugars 2g; Fat 13.6g, of which saturates 5.5g; Cholesterol 33mg; Calcium 280mg; Fibre 2.5g; Sodium 214mg.

Ham & Mozzarella Calzone

A calzone is a kind of 'inside-out' pizza – the dough is on the outside and the filling on the inside. This is particularly good food for eating *al fresco.*

Makes 2

1 quantity Basic Pizza Dough (see page 84)
115g/4oz/½ cup ricotta cheese
30ml/2 tbsp freshly grated Parmesan cheese
1 egg yolk
30ml/2 tbsp chopped fresh basil
75g/3oz cooked ham, finely chopped
75g/3oz mozzarella cheese, cut into small dice
olive oil, for brushing
salt and ground black pepper

1 Preheat the oven to 220°C/425°F/Gas 7. Divide the dough in half and roll out each piece on a lightly floured surface to an 18cm/7in circle.

2 In a bowl, mix together the ricotta and Parmesan cheeses, then stir in the egg yolk and basil. Season with salt and pepper.

3 Spread the mixture over half of each circle, leaving a 2.5cm/1in border, then arrange the ham and mozzarella on top.

4 Dampen the edges with water, then fold over the dough to enclose the filling.

5 Press the edges firmly together to seal. Place on two greased baking sheets. Brush with oil and make a small hole in the top of each to allow the steam to escape.

6 Bake for 15–20 minutes until golden. Serve immediately.

Cook's Tips

- *For a vegetarian version, replace the ham with fried mushrooms or chopped cooked spinach.*
- *For a decorative finishing touch, seal the edges of the uncooked dough circles by pressing them with a fork.*

Calzone with Red Onion, Tomato & Chorizo

The traditional tomato and garlic can be enlivened with chunks of sweet, melting cheese, olives, crumbled grilled bacon, slices of pepperoni or chorizo or a few chopped anchovy fillets.

Makes 4

30ml/2 tbsp extra virgin olive oil
1 small red onion, thinly sliced
2 garlic cloves, crushed
400g/14oz can chopped tomatoes
50g/2oz sliced chorizo sausage
50g/2oz/½ cup pitted black olives
2 quantities Basic Pizza Dough (see page 84)
200g/7oz mozzarella or other semi-soft cheese, diced
5ml/1 tsp dried oregano
salt and ground black pepper
oregano sprigs, to garnish

1 Heat the oil in a frying pan and fry the onion and garlic for 5 minutes, until softened.

2 Add the tomatoes and cook for 5 minutes more or until slightly reduced. Add the chorizo and olives. Season well.

3 Knock back (punch down) the pizza dough and divide it into four portions. Roll out each portion to a 20cm/8in circle. Preheat the oven to 200°C/400°F/Gas 6. Lightly grease two baking sheets.

4 Spread the filling on half of each dough circle, leaving a margin around the edge. Sprinkle over the cheese.

5 Sprinkle the filling with the dried oregano. Dampen the edges of the dough with cold water. Fold the dough in half and press well to seal.

6 Place two calzones on each baking sheet. Bake for about 12–15 minutes until risen and golden in colour. Cool for 2 minutes, then loosen with a metal spatula and serve immediately garnished with the oregano.

Ham and Mozzarella Calzone Energy 686kcal/2877kJ; Protein 34.8g; Carbohydrate 70.2g, of which sugars 3.5g; Fat 31.5g, of which saturates 15.6g; Cholesterol 183mg; Calcium 453mg; Fibre 2.7g; Sodium 769mg.

Calzone with Red Onion, Tomato and Chorizo Energy 625kcal/2626kJ; Protein 22.5g; Carbohydrate 75g, of which sugars 7.3g; Fat 28.2g, of which saturates 9.8g; Cholesterol 39mg; Calcium 305mg; Fibre 4g; Sodium 1053mg.

Ham, Pepper & Mozzarella 'Pizzas'

Succulent roasted peppers, salty proscuitto and creamy mozzarella make the topping for these ciabatta 'pizzas'.

Makes 1

1 red (bell) pepper
1 yellow (bell) pepper
4 thick slices ciabatta bread
4 slices proscuitto, cut into thick strips
75g/3oz mozzarella cheese
ground black pepper
tiny fresh basil leaves, to garnish

1 Place the peppers skin side up on a baking sheet and grill (broil), turning them until the skins are evenly charred. Place in a bowl, cover with a cloth and leave for 10 minutes.

2 Peel the skins from the peppers and remove the seeds and cores. Cut the flesh into thick strips.

3 Lightly toast the slices of ciabatta bread on both sides until they are golden.

4 Arrange the strips of pepper on the toasted bread with the strips of proscuitto.

5 Thinly slice the mozzarella and arrange on top. Grind over plenty of pepper. Place under a hot grill (broiler) for about 2–3 minutes until the cheese is bubbling.

6 Garnish each 'pizza' with basil leaves and serve immediately.

Cook's Tip
For added flavour, cut a garlic clove in half and rub the cut side over the toasted bread before adding the topping.

Variation
Try using pieces of sun-dried tomato in oil instead of the peppers, and use Emmenthal cheese instead of mozzarella.

Fruity French Bread 'Pizzas'

Using a base of French bread, these pizza-style snacks are quick and easy to make. They are perfect for all the family.

Makes 4

2 small baguettes
1 jar ready-made tomato sauce or pizza topping
75g/3oz sliced cooked ham
4 rings canned pineapple, drained and chopped
½ small green (bell) pepper, seeded and cut into thin strips
75g/3oz mature (sharp) Cheddar cheese
salt and ground black pepper

1 Preheat the oven to 200°C/400°F/Gas 6. Cut the baguettes in half lengthways and toast the outsides under a grill (broiler) until crisp and golden.

2 Spread the tomato sauce or pizza topping over the toasted baguette halves.

3 Cut the ham into strips and arrange on the baguettes with the pineapple and pepper. Season with salt and pepper.

4 Grate the Cheddar and sprinkle over the top of the pineapple and pepper. Bake in the oven for 15–20 minutes until crisp and golden. Serve immediately.

Cook's Tip
These 'pizzas' may be grilled (broiled) instead of baked in the oven. Cook them for the same length of time under a medium grill (broiler), but check that they do not burn.

Variation
If you have time, make your own tomato sauce. Soften a sliced garlic clove and small onion in olive oil. Add a handful of herbs and 400g/14oz can tomatoes with 15ml/1 tbsp sun-dried tomato paste and a splash of wine. Simmer for 30 minutes.

Ham, Pepper and Mozzarella 'Pizzas' Energy 466kcal/1965kJ; Protein 26.3g; Carbohydrate 63.6g, of which sugars 14.2g; Fat 13.6g, of which saturates 6.4g; Cholesterol 45mg; Calcium 274mg; Fibre 5.1g; Sodium 1173mg.

Fruity French Bread 'Pizzas' Energy 420kcal/1779kJ; Protein 18.3g; Carbohydrate 67.4g, of which sugars 13g; Fat 10.1g, of which saturates 5.1g; Cholesterol 31mg; Calcium 281mg; Fibre 4g; Sodium 1056mg.

Egg Crostini with Rouille

Crostini are extremely quick to make, so they are perfect for brunch parties or as a speedy appetizer. The spicy rouille gives them a hint of a Mediterranean flavour, providing the perfect complement to the lightly fried eggs.

Makes 8

8 slices of ciabatta bread
extra virgin olive oil, for brushing
90ml/6 tbsp home-made mayonnaise
10ml/2 tsp harissa
8 eggs
8 small slices smoked ham
watercress, rocket (arugula) or salad leaves, to serve

1 Preheat the oven to 200°C/400°F/Gas 6. Use a pastry brush to brush each slice of ciabatta bread lightly with a little olive oil. Place the bread on a baking sheet and bake for 10 minutes, or until crisp and turning golden brown.

2 Meanwhile, make the rouille. Put the mayonnaise and harissa in a small bowl and mix well together.

3 Fry the eggs lightly in a little oil in a large non-stick frying pan until cooked.

4 Top the bread with the ham, eggs and a small spoonful of rouille. Serve immediately with watercress or salad leaves.

Cook's Tip

Harissa is a fiery North African chilli paste made from dried red chillies, cumin, garlic, coriander, caraway and olive oil.

Variation

You can use four small portions of smoked haddock instead of ham, and poach them for 5–7 minutes.

Italian Bread with Spicy Aromatic Tomatoes

This *al fresco* snack is a great way to keep hunger pangs at bay while you wait for the main course to come off the barbecue. As soon as the coals are hot enough, simply grill the sliced bread, heap on the sauce and drizzle over plenty of good-quality extra virgin olive oil. To accompany the breads, put out little bowls of lightly toasted pine nuts.

Makes 6

2 sfilatino (Italian bread sticks), sliced lengthways into 3 pieces
1 garlic clove, cut in half
leaves from 4 fresh oregano sprigs
18 kalamata olives, pitted and sliced
extra virgin olive oil, for drizzling
ground black pepper

For the tomatoes

800g/1¾lb ripe plum tomatoes
30ml/2 tbsp extra virgin olive oil
2 garlic cloves, crushed to a paste with a pinch of salt
1 small piece of dried chilli, seeds removed, finely chopped

1 Prepare the barbecue. Plunge the tomatoes into boiling water for 30 seconds, then refresh in cold water. Peel away the skins, remove the seeds and core and roughly chop the flesh. Mix the oil and crushed garlic in a large frying pan. Place on the stove over high heat. When the garlic sizzles, add the tomatoes and the chilli. Cook for 2 minutes. The aim is to evaporate the liquid not to pulp the tomatoes, which should keep their shape.

2 Once the flames have died down, position a lightly oiled grill rack over the hot coals. When the coals are medium-hot, or with a moderate coating of ash, toast the bread on both sides. Generously rub each slice with the cut side of a piece of garlic.

3 Roughly chop all but a few of the oregano leaves and mix them into the tomato sauce. Pile the mixture on to the toasted sfilatino. Sprinkle over the whole oregano leaves and the olive slices. Sprinkle with plenty of pepper, drizzle with lots of extra virgin olive oil and serve immediately.

Egg Crostini with Rouille Energy 259kcal/1083kJ; Protein 15.8g; Carbohydrate 13.6g, of which sugars 1.3g; Fat 16.3g, of which saturates 3.4g; Cholesterol 220mg; Calcium 62mg; Fibre 0.6g; Sodium 705mg.

Italian Bread with Spicy Aromatic Tomatoes Energy 473kcal/2000kJ; Protein 13.7g; Carbohydrate 80.3g, of which sugars 8g; Fat 13.1g, of which saturates 2.1g; Cholesterol 0mg; Calcium 177mg; Fibre 5.1g; Sodium 1021mg.

Cannellini Bean & Rosemary Bruschetta

This delicious variation on the theme of everyday beans on toast makes a sophisticated appetizer.

Makes 12

150g/5oz/⅔ cup dried cannellini beans
5 tomatoes
45ml/3 tbsp olive oil, plus extra for drizzling
2 sun-dried tomatoes in oil, drained and finely chopped
1 garlic clove, crushed
30ml/2 tbsp chopped fresh rosemary
12 slices Italian-style bread, such as ciabatta
1 large garlic clove
salt and ground black pepper
handful of fresh basil leaves, to garnish

1 Place the dried beans in a bowl, cover with cold water and leave to soak overnight.

2 Drain and rinse the beans, then place in a pan and cover with fresh water. Bring to the boil and boil rapidly for about 10 minutes, then simmer for 50–60 minutes or until tender. Drain, return to the pan and keep warm.

3 Meanwhile, place the tomatoes in a bowl, cover with boiling water, leave for 30 seconds, then peel, seed and chop the flesh.

4 Heat the oil in a frying pan, add the fresh and sun-dried tomatoes, garlic and rosemary. Cook for 2 minutes until the tomatoes begin to break down and soften.

5 Add the tomato mixture to the cannellini beans and season to taste. Mix together well. Keep the bean mixture warm.

6 Rub the cut sides of the bread slices with the garlic clove, then toast them lightly.

7 Spoon the cannellini bean mixture on top of the toast. Sprinkle with basil leaves and drizzle each bruschetta with a little extra olive oil before serving.

Crostini with Tomato, Red Pepper, Anchovy & Mozzarella Toppings

This Italian appetizer was originally a way of using up an over-abundance of tomatoes at harvest time.

Makes 16

1 ciabatta loaf

For the tomato, red pepper and anchovy topping

400g/14oz can or bottle Italian roasted red (bell) peppers and tomatoes, in vinegar or brine
50g/2oz can anchovy fillets
15ml/1 tbsp extra virgin olive oil
15–30ml/1–2 tbsp balsamic vinegar
1 garlic clove
25ml/1½ tbsp red pesto
30ml/2 tbsp chopped fresh chives, oregano or sage, to garnish
15ml/1 tbsp capers, to garnish

For the mozzarella and tomato topping

25ml/1½ tbsp green pesto
120ml/4fl oz/½ cup thick home-made or bottled tomato sauce
75g/3oz mozzarella cheese, cut into 8 thin slices
2–3 ripe plum tomatoes, seeded and cut into strips
fresh basil leaves, to garnish

1 Preheat the grill (broiler) to high. Cut the ciabatta into 16 slices. Toast until golden on both sides. Cool on a wire rack.

2 For the tomato, pepper and anchovy topping, drain the tomatoes and peppers and wipe dry with kitchen paper. Cut into 1cm/½in strips and place in a shallow dish. Rinse and dry the anchovy fillets and add to the peppers and tomatoes. Drizzle with the olive oil and sprinkle with the balsamic vinegar.

3 Peel and halve the garlic clove. Rub eight toasts with the cut edge of the clove and lightly brush the toasts with a little red pesto. Arrange the tomatoes, peppers and anchovies on the toasts and sprinkle with chopped herbs and capers.

4 For the mozzarella and tomato topping, lightly brush the remaining toasts with the green pesto and spoon on some tomato sauce. Arrange a slice of mozzarella on each and cover with the tomato strips. Garnish with basil leaves.

Cannellini Bean and Rosemary Bruschetta Energy 499kcal/2111kJ; Protein 20.2g; Carbohydrate 84.3g, of which sugars 8.5g; Fat 11.3g, of which saturates 1.7g; Cholesterol 0mg; Calcium 195mg; Fibre 8.1g; Sodium 749mg.

Crostini with Tomato, Red Pepper, Anchovy and Mozzarella Energy 116kcal/488kJ; Protein 4.8g; Carbohydrate 15.9g, of which sugars 3.2g; Fat 4.1g, of which saturates 1g; Cholesterol 5mg; Calcium 60mg; Fibre 1.3g; Sodium 301mg.

Soft Morning Rolls

These rolls are best served warm, as soon as they are baked. They are perfect for breakfast with bacon or jam.

Makes 10

450g/1lb/4 cups plain (all-purpose) white flour, plus extra for dusting
10ml/2 tsp salt
20g/¾oz fresh yeast
150ml/¼ pint/⅔ cup lukewarm milk
150ml/¼ pint/⅔ cup lukewarm water
30ml/2 tbsp milk, for glazing

1 Grease two baking sheets. Sift the flour and salt together into a large bowl and make a well in the centre. Mix the yeast with the milk, then mix in the water. Add to the centre of the flour and mix together to form a soft dough.

2 Knead the dough lightly in the bowl, then cover with lightly oiled clear film (plastic wrap) and leave to rise, in a warm place, for 1 hour, or until doubled in size. Turn the dough out on to a lightly floured surface and knock back (punch down).

3 Divide the dough into ten equal pieces. Knead lightly and, using a rolling pin, shape each piece to a flat oval 10 × 7.5cm/ 4 × 3in or a flat round 9cm/3½in.

4 Transfer to the prepared baking sheets, spaced well apart, and cover with oiled clear film. Leave to rise, in a warm place, for about 30 minutes.

5 Preheat the oven to 200°C/400°F/Gas 6. Press each roll with the three fingers to equalize the air bubbles and help prevent blistering. Brush with milk and dust with flour. Bake in the preheated oven for about 15–20 minutes or until lightly and evenly browned. Dust with more flour and cool slightly on a wire rack. Serve warm.

Cook's Tip
These rolls are ideal for serving with home-made beef burgers.

Wholemeal Rolls

To add interest, make these individual rolls into different shapes if you wish.

Makes 12

15ml/2 tbsp active dried yeast
50ml/2fl oz/¼ cup lukewarm water
5ml/1 tsp caster (superfine) sugar
175ml/6fl oz/¾ cup lukewarm buttermilk
1.5ml/¼ tsp bicarbonate of soda (baking soda)
5ml/1 tsp salt
40g/1½oz/3 tbsp butter, at room temperature
200g/7oz/scant 1¾ cups strong wholemeal (whole-wheat) bread flour
150g/5oz/1¼ cups plain (all-purpose) flour
1 beaten egg, to glaze

1 In a bowl, combine the yeast, water and sugar. Stir, and leave for 15 minutes to dissolve and for the yeast to become frothy.

2 Add the buttermilk, bicarbonate of soda, salt and butter, and stir to blend. Stir in the strong wholemeal bread flour. Add just enough of the plain flour to obtain a rough dough.

3 Knead on a floured surface until smooth. This will take about 10 minutes. Divide into three equal parts. Roll each into a cylinder, then cut into four pieces.

4 Grease a baking sheet. Form the pieces into torpedo shapes, place on the baking sheet, cover with a clean dish towel and leave in a warm place until doubled in size, about 1 hour.

5 Preheat the oven to 200°C/400°F/Gas 6. Brush the rolls with egg. Bake until firm, about 15–20 minutes. Cool on a wire rack.

Cook's Tip
Kneading is the most important part of bread-making, as it develops the dough and helps it to rise. You can be as rough as you like: make the dough into a ball and then press down and push it away from you with one hand, so that it stretches. Repeat until the dough is elastic.

Soft Morning Rolls Energy 160kcal/682kJ; Protein 4.7g; Carbohydrate 35.7g, of which sugars 1.4g; Fat 0.8g, of which saturates 0.3g; Cholesterol 1mg; Calcium 81mg; Fibre 1.4g; Sodium 401mg.

Wholemeal Rolls Energy 127kcal/538kJ; Protein 3.8g; Carbohydrate 21.5g, of which sugars 1.7g; Fat 3.5g, of which saturates 2g; Cholesterol 8mg; Calcium 42mg; Fibre 1.9g; Sodium 27mg.

Mini Bread Rolls with Garlic Sauce

These little Russian rolls are small, sweet and fluffy, and are delicious served warm, dipped into an aromatic garlic sauce.

Makes 60

25g/1oz/2 tbsp butter
250ml/8fl oz/1 cup milk
420–480g/14½–1lb 1oz/ generous 1⅔–2 cups plain white (all-purpose) flour
5g/⅛oz easy-blend (rapid-rise) dried yeast
2.5ml/½ tsp salt
5ml/1 tsp sugar
1 egg

For the garlic sauce
3 garlic cloves
a pinch of salt
30ml/2 tbsp rapeseed (canola) oil
75ml/5 tbsp lukewarm water

1 Melt the butter in a small pan. Pour in the milk and warm until it reaches blood temperature. Remove from heat.

2 Put 420g/14½oz/generous 1⅔ cups of the flour, yeast, salt and sugar in a large bowl. Add the warmed milk mixture and mix well together, then knead for about 5 minutes, until the dough is smooth, adding more flour if necessary. Cover the bowl with a clean dish towel and leave in a warm place for about 40 minutes, until doubled in size.

3 Preheat the oven to 230°C/450°F/Gas 8. Line a large baking tray with baking parchment. Transfer the dough to a lightly floured surface and knead lightly. Divide the dough into four pieces then roll out each piece into a long thin roll.

4 Cut each roll into 15 small pieces and form each piece into a small ball. Put the rolls on the prepared baking tray. Brush the tops with beaten egg. Bake in the oven for 10–15 minutes until golden brown. Transfer to a wire rack, cover with a clean dish towel and leave to cool.

5 To make the garlic sauce, crush the garlic into a bowl and mix with the salt, oil and water.

6 Serve the warm rolls with the garlic sauce as a dip.

Poppy Seed Rolls

Serve these soft rolls in a for breakfast or with dinner.

Makes 12

450g/1lb/4 cups strong white bread flour
5ml/1 tsp salt
5ml/1 tsp easy-blend (rapid-rise) dried yeast
300ml/½ pint/1¼ cups lukewarm skimmed milk
1 egg, beaten

For the topping
1 egg, beaten
poppy seeds

1 Lightly grease two baking sheets with oil. Sift the flour and salt into a mixing bowl.

2 Add the yeast. Make a well in the centre and pour in the milk and the egg. Stir from the centre outwards, gradually incorporating the flour and mixing to a soft dough.

3 Turn the dough on to a floured surface and knead for 5 minutes, or until smooth and elastic. Cut into 12 pieces and shape into rolls (make a variety of shapes or just simple round rolls, if you prefer).

4 Place the rolls on the prepared baking sheets, cover loosely with clear film (plastic wrap), ballooning it to trap the air inside, and leave in a warm place until the rolls have doubled in size, which will take about 1½ hours. Meanwhile, preheat the oven to 220°C/425°F/Gas 7.

5 Glaze the rolls with beaten egg, sprinkle with poppy seeds and bake for 12–15 minutes, or until golden brown. Transfer to a wire rack to cool completely.

Variation
You can vary the toppings. Linseed, sesame and caraway seeds all look good; try adding caraway seeds to the dough, too, for extra crunch and flavour.

Mini Bread Rolls with Garlic Sauce Energy 34kcal/143kJ; Protein 0.9g; Carbohydrate 5.8g, of which sugars 0.4g; Fat 1g, of which saturates 0.4g; Cholesterol 4mg; Calcium 15mg; Fibre 0.2g; Sodium 7mg.

Poppy Seed Rolls Energy 142kcal/603kJ; Protein 4.9g; Carbohydrate 30.2g, of which sugars 1.7g; Fat 1g, of which saturates 0.2g; Cholesterol 17mg; Calcium 85mg; Fibre 1.2g; Sodium 18mg.

Shaped Dinner Rolls

These rolls are the perfect choice for entertaining.

Makes 12

450g/1lb/4 cups unbleached white bread flour, plus extra
10ml/2 tsp salt
2.5ml/½ tsp caster (superfine) sugar
7g/¼oz easy-blend (rapid-rise) dried yeast
50g/2oz/¼ cup butter
250ml/8fl oz/1 cup lukewarm milk
1 egg, beaten

For the topping
1 egg yolk
15ml/1 tbsp water
sesame seeds and poppy seeds, for sprinkling

1 Grease two baking sheets. Sift the flour and salt into a bowl. Stir in the sugar and yeast. Rub in the butter. Add the milk and egg and mix to a dough. Knead for 10 minutes. Place in a lightly oiled bowl, cover and leave for 1 hour, until doubled in size.

2 Knock back (punch down) the dough and knead for about 2–3 minutes. Divide into 12 equal pieces and make shapes.

3 Braid: Divide a piece of dough into three sausages. Pinch together at one end, braid, then pinch the ends and tuck under.
Trefoil: Make three balls from a piece of dough and fit them together in a triangular shape.
Baton: Shape a piece of dough into an oblong. Slash the surface.
Cottage roll: Divide a piece of dough into two-thirds and one-third and shape into two rounds. Place the small one on top of the large one and make a hole through the centre.
Knot: Shape a piece of dough into a rope and tie a single knot.

4 Place the rolls on the baking sheets, cover and leave in a warm place for 30 minutes, until doubled in bulk. Meanwhile, preheat the oven to 220°C/425°F/Gas 7.

5 Mix the egg yolk and water and brush the rolls. Sprinkle some with sesame seeds and some with poppy seeds. Bake for 15–18 minutes or until golden. Cool on a wire rack.

Caraway Seed Rolls

It is very common, especially in the southern part of Germany, to add whole or ground caraway seeds to bread dough, whether to dark rye bread made with sourdough or white bread. This recipe comes from the area around Lake Constance in the far south. It is very simple, but so delicious! Try these rolls filled with sausages, cheese or ham.

Makes 10

1kg/2¼lb/9 cups strong white bread flour, plus extra to dust
20g/¾oz/1 tbsp salt
5ml/1 tsp caraway seeds, or 2.5ml/½ tsp ground caraway seeds
40g/1½oz fresh yeast
coarse sea salt

1 Mix the flour with the salt and caraway seeds. Dissolve the yeast in 600ml/1 pint/2½ cups lukewarm water and stir it into the flour. Knead the dough for 5 minutes, then cover it and leave it to rest in a warm place for 1 hour.

2 Preheat the oven to 240°C/475°F/Gas 9. Knead the dough again and leave it to rest for another 20 minutes. Then turn it out on to a floured work surface and shape it into a sausage about 30cm/12in long.

3 Cut off pieces of the dough about 5cm/2in thick and roll each piece with your hands until it forms a roll about 15–20cm/6–8in long.

4 Line a baking sheet with baking parchment. Arrange the rolls on the sheet and leave them to rest for 20–30 minutes. Then brush them with water and sprinkle some coarse sea salt on top.

5 Put the tray in the preheated oven. Bake for 10 minutes, then reduce the oven temperature to 160°C/325°F/Gas 3 and continue to bake the rolls for another 10–15 minutes, until they are golden brown all over and sound hollow when tapped on the base.

Shaped Dinner Rolls Energy 195kcal/822kJ; Protein 5.5g; Carbohydrate 30.4g, of which sugars 1.8g; Fat 6.6g, of which saturates 3g; Cholesterol 43mg; Calcium 99mg; Fibre 1.4g; Sodium 378mg.

Caraway Seed Rolls Energy 342kcal/1456kJ; Protein 9.5g; Carbohydrate 77.9g, of which sugars 1.5g; Fat 1.4g, of which saturates 0.2g; Cholesterol 0mg; Calcium 141mg; Fibre 3.1g; Sodium 1575mg

Granary Baps

These baps make excellent picnic fare, and are also good buns for hamburgers.

Makes 8

450g/1lb/4 cups malted brown flour
5ml/1 tsp salt
10ml/2 tsp easy-blend (rapid-rise) dried yeast
15ml/1 tbsp malt extract
300ml/½ pint/1¼ cups lukewarm water
15ml/1 tbsp rolled oats

1 Lightly oil a large baking sheet. Put the malted flour, salt and yeast in a large bowl and make a well in the centre. Dissolve the malt extract in the water and add it to the well.

2 Stir from the centre outwards, gradually incorporating the flour and mixing to a soft dough.

3 Turn the dough on to a floured surface and knead for 5 minutes, or until smooth and elastic. Divide the dough into eight equal pieces.

4 Shape into balls and flatten with the palm of your hand to make 10cm/4in rounds.

5 Place the rounds on the prepared baking sheet, cover loosely with oiled clear film (plastic wrap), ballooning it to trap the air inside, and leave in a warm place until the baps have doubled in size. Preheat the oven to 220°C/425°F/Gas 7.

6 Brush the baps with water, sprinkle with the oats and bake for 20–25 minutes, or until they sound hollow when tapped underneath. Cool on a wire rack.

Variation
To make a large loaf, shape the dough into a round, flatten it slightly and bake for 30–40 minutes. Test by tapping the base of the loaf – if it sounds hollow, it is cooked.

French Dimpled Rolls

A French speciality, these attractive white rolls are distinguished by the split down the centre. They have a crusty finish while remaining soft and light inside, thanks to the steaming technique used to bake them – they taste lovely, too.

Makes 10

400g/14oz/3½ cups unbleached white bread flour
7.5ml/1½ tsp salt
5ml/1 tsp caster (superfine) sugar
15g/½oz fresh yeast
120ml/4fl oz/½ cup lukewarm milk
175ml/6fl oz/¾ cup lukewarm water

1 Lightly grease two baking sheets. Sift the flour and salt into a large bowl. Stir in the sugar and make a well in the centre.

2 Cream the yeast with the milk until dissolved, then pour into the centre of the flour mixture. Sprinkle over a little of the flour from around the edge. Leave at room temperature for 15–20 minutes, or until the mixture starts to bubble.

3 Add the water and gradually mix in the flour to form a fairly moist, soft dough. Turn out on to a lightly floured surface and knead for 8–10 minutes until smooth and elastic. Place in a lightly oiled bowl, cover with lightly oiled clear film (plastic wrap) and leave at room temperature for about 1½ hours, or until doubled in size.

4 Knock back (punch down) the dough. Re-cover and leave to rest for 5 minutes. Divide the dough into 10 pieces. Shape into balls, then roll into ovals. Lightly flour the tops. Space well apart on the baking sheets, cover with lightly oiled clear film and leave to rise for about 30 minutes, or until almost doubled in size.

5 Lightly oil the side of your hand and press the centre of each roll to make a deep split. Re-cover and leave to rest for 15 minutes. Meanwhile, place a roasting pan in the bottom of the oven and preheat the oven to 230°C/450°F/Gas 8. Pour 250ml/8fl oz/1 cup water into the pan and bake the rolls for 15 minutes, or until golden. Cool on a wire rack.

Granary Baps Energy 195kcal/834kJ; Protein 7.3g; Carbohydrate 41.4g, of which sugars 2.4g; Fat 1.3g, of which saturates 0.2g; Cholesterol 0mg; Calcium 75mg; Fibre 3.7g; Sodium 254mg.

French Dimpled Rolls Energy 145kcal/614kJ; Protein 4.4g; Carbohydrate 31.9g, of which sugars 1.4g; Fat 0.8g, of which saturates 0.3g; Cholesterol 1mg; Calcium 77mg; Fibre 1.2g; Sodium 9mg.

Panini All'olio

The Italians adore these elaborately shaped rolls.

Makes 16

60ml/4 tbsp extra virgin olive oil, plus extra for greasing and brushing
450g/1lb/4 cups unbleached white bread flour, plus extra for dusting
10ml/2 tsp salt
15g/½oz fresh yeast
250ml/8fl oz/1 cup lukewarm water

1 Lightly oil three baking sheets. Sift the flour and salt into a bowl. Cream the yeast with half of the water, then stir in the remainder. Add to the flour with the oil and mix to a dough.

2 Knead the dough on a floured surface for 8–10 minutes. Place in a lightly oiled bowl, cover with lightly oiled clear film (plastic wrap) and leave in a warm place for about 1 hour, or until the dough has nearly doubled in bulk.

3 Knock back (punch down) on a lightly floured surface. Divide into 12 equal pieces and shape into rolls as described below.

4 Tavalli (twisted spirals): Roll each piece of dough into a strip about 30cm/12in long and 4cm/1½in wide. Twist each strip into a loose spiral and join the ends of dough in a circle.
Filoncini (finger-shaped rolls): Flatten each piece of dough into an oval and roll to about 23cm/9in long. Make it 5cm/2in wide at one end and 10cm/4in wide at the other. Roll up from the wider end, then stretch to 20–23cm/8–9in long. Cut in half.
Carciofi (artichoke-shaped rolls): Shape each piece of dough into a ball.

5 Place the rolls on the baking sheets. Brush with olive oil, cover with oiled clear film and leave in a warm place for 30 minutes. Meanwhile, preheat the oven to 200°C/400°F/Gas 6.

6 To finish the carciofi, snip four or five 5mm/¼in deep cuts in a circle on the top of each ball, then make five larger horizontal cuts around the sides. Bake the rolls for about 15 minutes. Cool on a wire rack.

Rohlíky

This bread is central to Czech and Slovak cuisines, accompanying soups and main courses. It is also served as a street food with mustard, ketchup and a frankfurter.

Makes 16

20g/¾oz fresh yeast, or 7g/¼oz active dried yeast
5ml/1 tsp caster (superfine) sugar
300ml/½ pint/1¼ cups whole milk, tepid
500g/1¼lb/5 cups strong white bread flour
75g/3oz/6 tbsp lard or white cooking fat, softened, or butter
10ml/2 tsp salt
1 egg, beaten
butter, for greasing

1 Crumble the yeast in a bowl with the sugar. Gradually add 100ml/3½fl oz/scant ½ cup tepid milk. Cover and leave in a warm place for 10 minutes until frothy.

2 Put the remaining ingredients, except the egg, into a large bowl and add the yeast mixture. Mix the ingredients with an electric mixer with dough hook or knead for 5 minutes. Cover and leave in a warm place to rise for 30 minutes. Preheat the oven to 180°C/350°F/Gas 4 and grease a baking sheet.

3 Divide the dough into two. Roll out each piece into a square 3cm/1¼in thick. Cut each into eight equal squares and roll each from corner to corner into a roll. Cover and leave to stand for 15 minutes. Put on to the baking sheet, brush with egg and bake for 15 minutes, or until very light golden brown and crisp. Cool on a wire rack.

Cook's Tips

- *Serve the bread to accompany soups and main courses, as a delicious breakfast with butter or jam, or as a fried bread with garlic or pâté.*
- *The breads make a good accompaniment to soups, main courses, mayonnaise-based salads, or as a breakfast roll with yogurt, butter or ham.*

Panini All'olio Energy 121kcal/509kJ; Protein 2.6g; Carbohydrate 21.9g, of which sugars 0.4g; Fat 3.1g, of which saturates 0.5g; Cholesterol 0mg; Calcium 39mg; Fibre 0.9g; Sodium 246mg.

Rohlíky Energy 168kcal/705kj; Protein 5g; Carbohydrate 25g, of which sugars 2g; Fat 6g, of which saturates 3g; Cholesterol 21mg; Calcium 68mg; Fibre 1.2g; Sodium 260mg.

Wholemeal Herb Triangles

These make a good lunchtime snack when stuffed with ham and salad, and also taste good when served with soup.

Makes 8

225g/8oz/2 cups strong wholemeal (whole-wheat) bread flour
115g/4oz/1 cup strong white bread flour
5ml/1 tsp salt
2.5ml/½ tsp bicarbonate of soda (baking soda)
5ml/1 tsp cream of tartar
2.5ml/½ tsp chilli powder
50g/2oz/¼ cup soft margarine
250ml/8fl oz/1 cup skimmed milk
60ml/4 tbsp chopped mixed fresh herbs
15ml/1 tbsp sesame seeds

1 Preheat the oven to 220°C/425°F/Gas 7. Lightly flour a large baking sheet.

2 Put the wholemeal flour in a large bowl. Sift in the strong white bread flour, the salt, bicarbonate of soda, cream of tartar and the chilli powder, then rub in the margarine.

3 Add the milk and herbs and mix quickly to a soft dough. Turn on to a lightly floured surface. Knead only very briefly or the dough will become tough.

4 Roll out to a 23cm/9in circle and place on the prepared baking sheet. Brush lightly with water and sprinkle with the sesame seeds.

5 Cut the dough round into eight wedges, separate slightly and bake for 15–20 minutes. Transfer the triangles to a wire rack to cool. Serve warm or cold.

Variation

To make Sun-dried Tomato Triangles, replace the mixed herbs with 30ml/2 tbsp chopped, drained sun-dried tomatoes in oil, and add 15ml/1 tbsp mild paprika, 15ml/1 tbsp chopped fresh parsley and 15ml/1 tbsp chopped fresh marjoram.

Bagels

These are great fun to make and taste wonderful with cream cheese, either on its own or with grilled vegetables and fresh herbs.

Makes 10

350g/12oz/3 cups unbleached white bread flour, plus extra
10ml/2 tsp salt
7g/¼oz easy-blend (rapid-rise) dried yeast
5ml/1 tsp malt extract
210ml/7½fl oz/scant 1 cup lukewarm water

For poaching

2.5 litres/4¼ pints/10⅔ cups water
15ml/1 tbsp malt extract

For the topping

1 egg white
10ml/2 tsp cold water
30ml/2 tbsp poppy, sesame or caraway seeds, or a mixture

1 Grease two baking sheets. Sift the flour and salt into a bowl. Stir in the yeast. Mix the malt extract and water, add to the flour and mix to a dough. Knead on a floured surface for 10 minutes. Place in a lightly oiled bowl, cover with lightly oiled clear film (plastic wrap) and leave in a warm place for about 1 hour, or until doubled in size.

2 Knock back (punch down), knead for 1 minute, then divide into ten equal pieces. Shape into balls, cover with clear film and leave to rest for 5 minutes. Gently flatten each ball and make a hole through the centre. Place on a floured tray; re-cover and leave in a warm place, for 10–20 minutes, or until the rings begin to rise.

3 Meanwhile, preheat the oven to 220°C/425°F/Gas 7. Place the water and malt extract for poaching in a large pan, bring to the boil, then reduce to a simmer. Poach two or three bagels at a time for about 1 minute. They will sink and then rise again when first added to the pan. Turn them over and poach the other side for 30 seconds. Remove and drain on a dish towel.

4 Place five bagels on each baking sheet. Beat the egg white with the water and brush over the bagels. Sprinkle with the seeds. Bake for 25 minutes, until golden. Cool on a wire rack.

Wholemeal Herb Triangles Energy 204kcal/858kJ; Protein 6.3g; Carbohydrate 30.6g, of which sugars 2.3g; Fat 7.1g, of which saturates 0.3g; Cholesterol 1mg; Calcium 82mg; Fibre 3.1g; Sodium 65mg.

Bagels Energy 157kcal/668kJ; Protein 4.2g; Carbohydrate 35g, of which sugars 3.2g; Fat 1g, of which saturates 0.2g; Cholesterol 17mg; Calcium 62mg; Fibre 1.3g; Sodium 822mg.

Pretzels

These pretty breads are ideal for a buffet or picnic.

Makes 12

For the yeast sponge

10g/⅓oz fresh yeast
75ml/5 tbsp water
15ml/1 tbsp unbleached plain (all-purpose) white flour

For the dough

10g/⅓oz fresh yeast
150ml/¼ pint/⅔ cup lukewarm water
75ml/5 tbsp lukewarm milk
400g/14oz/3½ cups unbleached strong white bread flour
7.5ml/1½ tsp salt
25g/1oz/2 tbsp butter, melted

For the topping

1 egg yolk
15ml/1 tbsp milk
salt or caraway seeds, to sprinkle

1 Flour two baking sheets and grease two baking sheets. Cream the yeast for the yeast sponge with the water. Add the flour, cover and stand at room temperature for 2 hours.

2 Mix the yeast for the dough with the water, then stir in the milk. Sift 350g/12oz/3 cups of the flour and the salt into a bowl. Add the yeast sponge and the butter and mix for 3–4 minutes. Turn out on to a floured surface and knead in the remaining flour. Place in an oiled bowl, cover with lightly oiled clear film (plastic wrap) and leave to rise in a warm place for 30 minutes.

3 Knock back (punch down) the dough. Return to the bowl, cover and leave for 30 minutes.

4 Divide into 12 balls. Roll each ball into a stick 46cm/18in long and about 1cm/½in thick in the middle and thinner at the ends. Bend each end into a horseshoe. Cross over and place the ends on top of the thick part.

5 Place on the floured baking sheets to rest for 10 minutes. Preheat the oven to 190°C/375°F/Gas 5. Bring a large pan of water to the boil, then simmer the pretzels, in batches, for about 1 minute. Drain and place on the greased baking sheets. Mix the egg yolk and milk and brush over the pretzels. Sprinkle with salt or seeds and bake the pretzels for 25 minutes.

Potato Buns

Fill one of these with a couple of slices of good ham and some plain cheese, and you will be instantly transported to a farmhouse in the country with chickens in the front yard.

Makes 24

15g/½oz easy-blend (rapid-rise) dried yeast
15ml/1 tbsp caster (superfine) sugar
15ml/1 tbsp salt
150ml/¼ pint/⅔ cup warm milk
30ml/2 tbsp vegetable oil
350g/12oz/1 cup mashed potato, cooled and pushed through a ricer
1 egg, beaten
about 400g/14oz/4 cups plain (all-purpose) flour

1 Put the yeast, sugar, salt, milk and vegetable oil in a large bowl and whisk together well. Add the potato and the beaten egg to the bowl, and stir well with a sturdy spoon or spatula to mix all the ingredients.

2 Gradually sift the flour over the mixture and work it in with your hand. Stop adding flour when the mixture stops sticking to your hand; the less you add, the lighter the buns will be.

3 Transfer the dough to a floured surface and knead for 5–8 minutes, until smooth.

4 Add a few more dustings of flour if needed, but do not exceed the quantity given in the recipe. Form the dough into a sausage shape and cut into about 24 pieces.

5 Grease and flour two baking sheets. Using the palms of your hand, roll the pieces of dough into balls and place them on the baking sheets. Cover with a slightly damp cloth and set aside in a warm draught-free place to rest and rise for 1 hour.

6 Preheat the oven to 190°C/375°F/Gas 5. Bake the buns for 20–30 minutes, until the tops are golden and the buns are cooked. Remove from the oven and leave them to cool on the trays for 5–10 minutes, before serving with some good butter or creamy cheese.

Pretzels Energy 281kcal/1190kJ; Protein 7.5g; Carbohydrate 53.9g, of which sugars 1.8g; Fat 5.4g, of which saturates 2.7g; Cholesterol 43mg; Calcium 119mg; Fibre 2.1g; Sodium 521mg.

Potato Buns Energy 83kcal/352kJ; Protein 2.6g; Carbohydrate 16.4g, of which sugars 1.3g; Fat 1.2g, of which saturates 0.3g; Cholesterol 10mg; Calcium 34mg; Fibre 0.9g; Sodium 90mg.

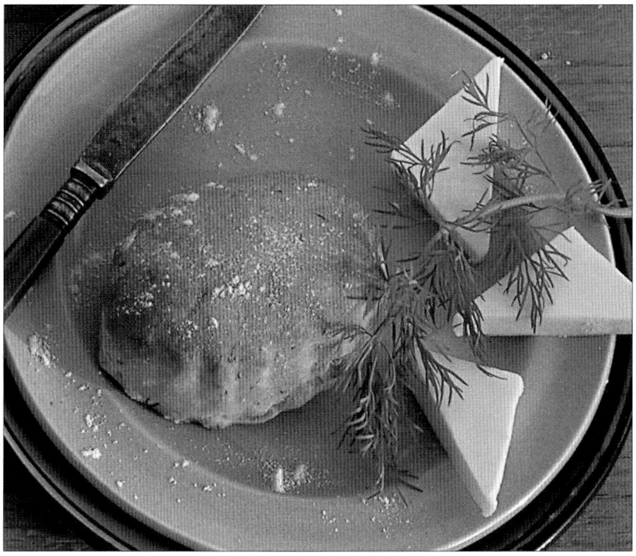

Dill & Potato Cakes

Adding dill to these potato cakes makes them irresistible.

Makes 10

225g/8oz/2 cups self-raising (self-rising) flour
40g/1½oz/3 tbsp butter, softened
a pinch of salt
15ml/1 tbsp chopped fresh dill
175g/6oz/2 cups mashed potato, freshly made
30–45ml/2–3 tbsp milk

1 Preheat the oven to 230°C/450°F/Gas 8. Grease a baking sheet. Sift the flour into a bowl and add the butter, salt and dill. Mix in the mashed potato and enough milk to make a soft, pliable dough.

2 Roll out the dough on a well-floured surface until fairly thin. Cut into circles with a 7.5cm/3in cookie cutter. Place the potato cakes on the baking sheet and bake them for 20–25 minutes, or until risen and golden.

Savoury Cheese Whirls

Makes 20

250g/9oz frozen puff pastry, thawed
15ml/1 tbsp vegetable extract
1 egg, beaten
50g/2oz/½ cup grated Cheddar cheese

1 Preheat the oven to 220°C/425°F/Gas 7. Grease a large baking sheet. Roll out the pastry on a lightly floured surface to a large rectangle, measuring about 35 × 25cm/14 × 10in.

2 Spread the pastry with vegetable extract, leaving a 1cm/½in border. Brush the edges of the pastry with egg and sprinkle over the cheese. Roll the pastry up quite tightly, starting from a long edge. Brush the outside with beaten egg. Cut the pastry roll into slices 4cm/1½in thick and place on the baking sheet.

3 Bake for 12–15 minutes, until the pastry is well risen and golden. Arrange on a serving plate, and serve warm or cold.

Sweet Potato & Honey Bread Rolls

These sweet potato rolls taste delicious served with jams or a savoury soup.

Makes 12

1 large sweet potato
225g/8oz/2 cups strong white bread flour
5ml/1 tsp easy-blend (rapid-rise) dried yeast
a pinch of ground nutmeg
a pinch of cumin seeds
5ml/1 tsp runny honey
200ml/7fl oz/scant 1 cup lukewarm milk
oil, for greasing

1 Cook the potato in plenty of boiling water for 45 minutes or until very tender. Preheat the oven to 220°C/425°F/Gas 7.

2 Meanwhile, sift the flour into a large bowl, add the yeast, ground nutmeg and cumin seeds. Give the ingredients a good stir.

3 Mix the honey and milk together. Drain the potato and peel the skin. Mash the flesh and mix into the flour with the liquid.

4 Bring the mixture together and knead for 5 minutes on a floured surface. Place the dough in a bowl and cover with a damp cloth. Leave to rise for 30 minutes.

5 Turn the dough out and knock back (punch down) to remove any air bubbles. Divide the dough into 12 pieces and shape each one into a round.

6 Place the rolls on a greased baking sheet. Cover with a damp cloth and leave to rise in a warm place for 30 minutes or until doubled in size.

7 Bake for 10 minutes. Remove from the oven and drizzle with more honey and cumin seeds before serving.

Cook's Tip
This dough is quite sticky, so use plenty of flour on the surface when you are kneading and rolling it.

Dill and Potato Cakes Energy 121kcal/508kJ; Protein 2.6g; Carbohydrate 20.6g, of which sugars 0.6g; Fat 3.7g, of which saturates 2.2g; Cholesterol 9mg; Calcium 37mg; Fibre 0.9g; Sodium 27mg.
Savoury Cheese Whirls Energy 63kcal/262kJ; Protein 2g; Carbohydrate 4.7g, of which sugars 0.2g; Fat 4.2g, of which saturates 2g; Cholesterol 21mg; Calcium 28mg; Fibre 0g; Sodium 93mg.
Sweet Potato and Honey Bread Rolls Energy 87kcal/372kJ; Protein 2.5g; Carbohydrate 19.3g, of which sugars 2.4g; Fat 0.6g, of which saturates 0.2g; Cholesterol 1mg; Calcium 50mg; Fibre 1g; Sodium 16mg.

Herb Popovers

Popovers can be served as a snack, and they are especially delicious when flavoured with mixed herbs.

Makes 12

3 eggs
250ml/8fl oz/1 cup milk
25g/1oz/2 tbsp butter, melted
75g/3oz/⅔ cup plain (all-purpose) flour
1.5ml/¼ tsp salt
1 small sprig each mixed fresh herbs, such as chives, tarragon, dill and parsley

1 Preheat the oven to 220°C/425°F/Gas 7. Grease 12 small ramekins or individual baking cups.

2 With an electric mixer, beat the eggs until blended. Beat in the milk and melted butter.

3 Sift together the flour and salt, then beat into the egg mixture to combine thoroughly.

4 Strip the herb leaves from the stems and chop finely. Mix together and measure out 30ml/2 tbsp. Stir the measured herbs into the batter.

5 Half-fill the prepared ramekins or baking cups. Bake until golden, 25–30 minutes. Do not open the oven door during baking time or the popovers may collapse.

6 For drier popovers, pierce each one with a knife after 30 minutes' baking time and then bake for a further 5 minutes. Serve the herb popovers piping hot.

Variation

For basic plain popovers, simply omit the herbs. To make a traditional popover, heat a knob (pat) of dripping or lard (white cooking fat) in each cup of a patty tin (muffin pan). Heat the tin in the preheated oven and then pour in the batter until the cups are two-thirds full. Bake at the top of the oven as before.

Cheese Popovers

Serve these popovers simply as an accompaniment to a meal, or make a filling and serve them as an appetizer.

Makes 12

3 eggs
250ml/8fl oz/1 cup milk
25g/1oz/2 tbsp butter, melted
75g/3oz/⅔ cup plain (all-purpose) flour
1.5ml/¼ tsp salt
1.5ml/¼ tsp paprika
25g/1oz/⅓ cup freshly grated Parmesan cheese

1 Preheat the oven to 220°C/425°F/Gas 7. Grease 12 small ramekins or individual baking cups.

2 With an electric mixer, beat the eggs until blended. Beat in the milk and melted butter.

3 Sift together the flour, salt and paprika, then beat into the egg mixture. Add the Parmesan cheese and stir in.

4 Half-fill the prepared cups and bake until golden, about 25–30 minutes. Do not open the oven door or the popovers may collapse.

5 For drier popovers, pierce each one with a knife after about 30 minutes' baking time and then bake for another 5 minutes. Serve hot.

Cook's Tips

- *Although some believe that batters for pancakes and popovers will be improved by resting for a while before cooking, this is not absolutely necessary. However, if you wish to prepare the batter in advance, it can be left to stand for up to 4 hours, or 24 hours in a refrigerator.*
- *Always cook popovers on the top shelf of the oven.*
- *This recipe can be cooked in a well-greased, small baking tin (pan), if you prefer. It will take 35–40 minutes. Cut into wedges and serve warm.*

Herb Popovers Energy 65kcal/272kJ; Protein 2.9g; Carbohydrate 5.9g, of which sugars 1.1g; Fat 3.5g, of which saturates 1.7g; Cholesterol 53mg; Calcium 41mg; Fibre 0.2g; Sodium 39mg.

Cheese Popovers Energy 74kcal/311kJ; Protein 3.7g; Carbohydrate 5.9g, of which sugars 1.1g; Fat 4.2g, of which saturates 2.1g; Cholesterol 55mg; Calcium 66mg; Fibre 0.2g; Sodium 62mg.

Bitesize Cheese Brioches

These mouthfuls of golden, buttery dough have melting cheese in the middle, so are best enjoyed warm.

Makes 40

450g/1lb/4 cups plain (all-purpose) or strong white bread flour, plus extra for kneading
5ml/1 tsp salt
5ml/1 tsp ground turmeric
7g/¼oz easy-blend (rapid-rise) dried yeast
150ml/¼ pint/⅔ cup warm milk
2 eggs, plus 2 egg yolks
75g/3oz/6 tbsp butter, melted and slightly cooled
50g/2oz mature (sharp) Cheddar cheese, grated
50g/2oz cheese, such as Gouda, Cheshire or Port Salut, cut into cubes

1 Sift the dry ingredients with the yeast and make a hollow. Mix the milk, eggs and 1 yolk with the butter and Cheddar.

2 Pour the liquid into the dry ingredients and blend with a fork. Continue blending until it is evenly mixed. Turn out the mixture on to a lightly floured surface and knead, working in as little flour as possible, until the surface is smooth and dry.

3 Place the dough in a lightly greased mixing bowl. Lightly grease the top of the dough, cover with a cloth and leave in a warm place for at least 1 hour, until the dough doubles in size.

4 Turn out on to a floured surface and knead the dough until it becomes firm and elastic again. Divide the dough into four batches, then divide each batch into eight to ten pieces. Knead each piece until smooth.

5 Press a cube of cheese into the middle of each piece of dough, shape into a round and place in a paper sweet case. Place the cases in mini muffin trays, or put the dough in doubled paper cases. Set aside until they are well risen.

6 Preheat the oven to 200°C/400°F/Gas 6. Mix the remaining yolk with 15ml/1 tbsp water and glaze the brioches with the mixture, using a pastry brush. Bake for about 15 minutes until golden brown, well risen and firm underneath if tapped.

Cheesy Cassava Dough Balls

These little golden dough balls, known as *pão de queijo* in Brazil, are a great example of the versatility of cassava as a cooking ingredient. *Pão de queijo* can be found in the majority of Brazilian bakeries, snack bars, grill houses and restaurants.

Makes 24

500g/1¼lb/5 cups sour cassava starch (polvilho azedo)
20ml/4 tsp salt
450ml/¾ pint/2 cups milk
250ml/8fl oz/1 cup vegetable oil
225g/8oz/1 cup feta cheese, finely crumbled
100g/4oz/1 cup Parmesan cheese, grated
4 eggs
cream cheese or butter, to serve

1 Preheat the oven to 200°C/400°F/Gas 6. Carefully put the sour starch into a bowl; it is very fine and easily blows away. Add the salt.

2 Heat the milk and oil in a pan until it reaches boiling point. Just as the boiling liquid starts to rise, remove from the heat and pour it over the sour starch, mixing well with a wooden spoon. Keep mixing until the starch and liquid clump together in a texture similar to scrambled eggs. Set aside to cool.

3 Once the starch mixture has cooled down completely, add the feta and Parmesan cheeses and eggs. Use a mixer with a bread hook, or use your hands to mix. Mix or squeeze the dough until all the ingredients have come together; the dough will get firmer as you mix it.

4 Grease the palm of your hands with a dab of oil. Take a small piece of dough, and roll it in your your palms to form a ball. Repeat until all the mixture is used up. Place the balls on an ungreased baking sheet as you go.

5 Bake on the top shelf of the oven for 15 minutes. Reduce the temperature to 150°C/300°F/Gas 2 and bake for a further 10–15 minutes or until lightly browned and cooked. Serve warm, accompanied with some cream cheese or good butter.

Bitesize Cheese Brioches Energy 64kcal/270kJ; Protein 2.1g; Carbohydrate 9g, of which sugars 0.4g; Fat 2.5g, of which saturates 1.3g; Cholesterol 25mg; Calcium 27mg; Fibre 0.4g; Sodium 75mg.

Cheesy Cassava Dough Balls Energy 232kcal/967kJ; Protein 5g; Carbohydrate 20.2g, of which sugars 1.1g; Fat 15.1g, of which saturates 3.8g; Cholesterol 50mg; Calcium 108mg; Fibre 0g; Sodium 527mg.

English Muffins

Perfect served warm, split open and buttered for breakfast or afternoon tea, these muffins are the ultimate comfort food, especially with a large spoonful of strawberry jam. Try these all-time favourites toasted, split and topped with ham and eggs for lunch.

Makes 9

450g/1lb/4 cups unbleached strong white bread flour, plus extra for dusting
7.5ml/1½ tsp salt
350–375ml/12–13fl oz/1½–1⅔ cups lukewarm milk
2.5ml/½ tsp caster (superfine) sugar
15g/½oz fresh yeast
15ml/1 tbsp melted butter or olive oil

1 Flour a baking sheet. Lightly grease a griddle or heavy frying pan. Sift the flour and salt together into a large bowl and make a well in the centre. Blend 150ml/¼ pint/⅔ cup of the milk, sugar and yeast together. Stir in the remaining milk and butter or oil.

2 Add the yeast mixture to the centre of the flour and beat for 4–5 minutes, until smooth and elastic. The dough will be soft but just hold its shape.

3 Cover with lightly oiled clear film (plastic wrap) and leave to rise, in a warm place, for 45–60 minutes, or until it has doubled in bulk.

4 Turn out the dough on a well floured surface and knock back. Roll out to about 1cm/½ in thick. Using a floured 7.5cm/3in plain cutter, cut out nine rounds.

5 Dust with rice flour or semolina and place on the prepared baking sheet. Cover and leave to rise, in a warm place, for about 20–30 minutes.

6 Warm the griddle over a medium heat. Carefully transfer the muffins in batches to the griddle. Cook slowly for about 7 minutes on each side, or until golden brown. Transfer to a wire rack to cool.

Cheese & Chive Scones

Feta cheese is used instead of butter in these delicious savoury scones, which make a tasty alternative to traditional scones.

Makes 9

115g/4oz/1 cup self-raising (self-rising) flour
150g/5oz/1 cup self-raising (self-rising) wholemeal (whole-wheat) flour
2.5ml/½ tsp salt
75g/3oz feta cheese
15ml/1 tbsp chopped fresh chives
150ml/¼ pint/⅔ cup milk, plus extra to glaze
1.5ml/¼ tsp cayenne pepper

1 Preheat the oven to 200°C/400°F/Gas 6. Sift the flours and salt into a large mixing bowl. Add any bran left in the sifter.

2 Crumble the feta cheese and rub it into the dry ingredients until the mixture resembles breadcrumbs. Stir in the chives, then add the milk and mix to a soft dough.

3 Turn the dough out on to a floured surface and lightly knead until smooth. Roll out to a 2cm/¾in thickness and stamp out scones with a 6cm/2½in cookie cutter.

4 Transfer the scones to a non-stick baking sheet. Brush with milk, then sprinkle with the cayenne pepper. Bake for 15 minutes, or until risen and golden. Cool slightly on a wire rack before serving.

Variation

For Cheddar Cheese and Mustard Scones, add 2.5ml/½ tsp mustard powder to the flours. Dice 50g/2oz/½ cup cold butter, and rub it into the dry ingredients until the mixture resembles breadcrumbs. Stir 50g/2oz/½ cup grated mature (sharp) Cheddar cheese into the mixture, then pour in the milk. Stir gently to make a soft dough. Roll out on a lightly floured surface and cut into triangles. Place on a baking sheet, brush with milk, and sprinkle with 25g/1oz/¼ cup cheese. Bake for 15 minutes, or until well risen.

English Muffins Energy 60kcal/254kJ; Protein 1.5g; Carbohydrate 12.8g, of which sugars 6g; Fat 0.6g, of which saturates 0.2g; Cholesterol 14mg; Calcium 25mg; Fibre 0.3g; Sodium 8mg.

Cheese and Chive Scones Energy 124kcal/524kJ; Protein 5.2g; Carbohydrate 21.5g, of which sugars 1.5g; Fat 2.5g, of which saturates 1.4g; Cholesterol 7mg; Calcium 74mg; Fibre 1.9g; Sodium 128mg.

Crumpets

These yeast pancakes can be served hot and buttered, or with sweet or savoury accompaniments. Try them for breakfast, American-style, with crispy bacon and a thin drizzle of clear honey or maple syrup. The best results come from using strong bread flour, although ordinary plain flour works well, too.

Makes 8–10

225g/8oz/2 cups strong white bread flour or plain (all-purpose) flour
2.5ml/½ tsp fine sea salt
6.25ml/1¼ tsp easy-blend (rapid-rise) dried yeast
150ml/¼ pint/⅔ cup milk
15g/½oz/1 tbsp butter
1 egg
melted butter, for brushing

1 Sift the flour and salt into a large bowl and stir in the yeast. Combine the milk with 150ml/¼ pint/⅔ cup water and add the butter. Warm gently on the stove until the liquid is lukewarm when tested with your little finger. With a whisk, beat in the egg.

2 Whisk the liquid into the flour to make a thick smooth batter. Cover and leave to stand at room temperature for about 1 hour to allow the yeast to start working.

3 Preheat a bakestone or heavy frying pan over medium to medium-low heat. Brush melted butter on the inside of three or four metal rings (each measuring about 9cm/3½in) and lightly butter the hot bakestone or pan.

4 Place the metal rings on the hot surface. Pour a large spoonful of batter into each one. Alternatively, drop generous spoonfuls of batter on to the hot buttered surface to make pancakes about 9cm/3½in in diameter, allowing some space between each one for the spreading of the batter.

5 Cook for a minute or two until the underside is golden brown, bubbles have burst on the surface and the top is just set. Carefully remove the metal rings and gently turn the crumpets over. Cook the second side until light golden brown. Lift off and keep warm. Repeat with the remaining batter.

Blinis

These are the celebrated leavened Russian pancakes. Traditionally served with sour cream and caviar, they have a very distinctive flavour and a wonderfully fluffy, light texture.

Makes 10

50g/2oz/½ cup buckwheat flour
50g/2oz/½ cup unbleached plain (all-purpose) flour
2.5ml/½ tsp ground black pepper
5ml/1 tsp salt
15g/½oz fresh yeast
200ml/7fl oz/scant 1 cup lukewarm milk
1 egg, separated

1 Mix the buckwheat flour, plain flour, pepper and salt together in a large bowl.

2 In a small bowl, cream the yeast with 60ml/4 tbsp of the milk, then mix in the remaining milk.

3 Add the egg yolk to the flour mixture and gradually whisk in the yeast mixture to form a smooth batter. Cover with lightly oiled clear film (plastic wrap) and leave to stand in a warm place for 1 hour.

4 Whisk the egg white until it forms soft peaks and fold into the batter. Lightly oil a heavy frying pan and heat it.

5 Add about 45ml/3 tbsp of the batter to the hot pan to make a 10cm/4in round pancake. Cook until the surface begins to dry out, then turn the pancake over using a metal spatula and cook for 1–2 minutes. Repeat with the remaining batter. Serve the blinis warm.

Variation
You can use all buckwheat flour, if you prefer, which will give the blinis a stronger flavour.

Crumpets Energy 102kcal/432kJ; Protein 3.3g; Carbohydrate 18.2g, of which sugars 1.1g; Fat 2.3g, of which saturates 1.1g; Cholesterol 23mg; Calcium 53mg; Fibre 0.7g; Sodium 23mg.

Blinis Energy 113kcal/471kJ; Protein 2.7g; Carbohydrate 8g, of which sugars 1.4g; Fat 8g, of which saturates 4.9g; Cholesterol 45mg; Calcium 21mg; Fibre 1g; Sodium 143mg.

Slovak Easter Bread

This is eaten in Slovakia on Easter Sunday. A similar bread is made in the Czech Republic, decorated with raisins and almonds.

Makes 1

200ml/7fl oz/scant 1 cup lukewarm full-fat (whole) milk
75g/3oz/6 tbsp caster (superfine) sugar
20g/¾oz fresh yeast or 7g/¼oz active dried yeast
400g/14oz/3½ cups polohruba flour, or 300g/11oz/2¾ cups strong white bread flour and 115g/4oz/⅔ cup semolina, sifted, plus extra for dusting
20g/¾oz/1½ tbsp vanilla sugar
a pinch of salt
115g/4oz/½ cup butter, diced, plus extra for greasing
3 egg yolks
1 egg, beaten

1 Grease a 20cm/8in round cake tin (pan) or a round baking dish. Mix 100ml/3½fl oz/scant ½ cup lukewarm milk with 15ml/1 tbsp caster sugar in a bowl. Crumble in the fresh yeast and gradually stir in 15ml/1 tbsp flour. Mix well. Cover with a dish towel and put in a warm place for 10-15 minutes.

2 In a large bowl mix together the remaining flour, or flour mixture, caster sugar, vanilla sugar, salt and butter, then add the yeast mixture.

3 Beat the egg yolks, individually, into the remaining milk, then add this to the flour mixture.

4 Stir the dough and transfer to a floured work surface, knead for 5 minutes and form into a large round ball.

5 Return the dough to the bowl, dust with flour and cover with a dish towel. Put in a warm place for 1–2 hours, or until the dough rises. Preheat the oven to 180°C/350°F/Gas 4.

6 Put the dough into the prepared cake tin and leave to rest for 15 minutes. Cut a cross on top, brush with the beaten egg and bake for 35–40 minutes. The bread is cooked when a skewer comes out clean, or it sounds hollow if you tap the base.

Sally Lunn

This loaf is traditionally served warm, sliced into three layers horizontally, spread with clotted cream or butter and re-assembled.

Makes 1

25g/1oz/2 tbsp butter
150ml/¼ pint/⅔ cup milk or double (heavy) cream
15ml/1 tbsp caster (superfine) sugar
15g/½oz fresh yeast
275g/10oz/2½ cups unbleached white bread flour
2.5ml/½ tsp salt
finely grated rind of ½ lemon

For the glaze

15ml/1 tbsp milk
15ml/1 tbsp caster (superfine) sugar

1 Lightly butter a 15cm/6in round cake tin (pan), 7.5cm/3in deep. Dust lightly with flour, if the tin lacks a non-stick finish. Melt the butter in a small pan and then stir in the milk or cream and sugar. The mixture should be tepid. Remove from the heat, add the yeast and blend thoroughly until the yeast has dissolved. Leave for 10 minutes, until the yeast starts to work.

2 Sift the flour and salt together into a large bowl. Stir in the lemon rind and make a well in the centre. Add the yeast mixture to the centre of the flour and mix together to make a soft dough just stiff enough to form a shape.

3 Knead for about 10 minutes until smooth and elastic. Shape into a ball and place in the prepared tin. Cover with lightly oiled clear film (plastic wrap) and leave in a warm place, for 1¼–1½ hours. When the dough has risen almost to the top of the tin, remove the clear film.

4 Preheat the oven to 220°C/425°F/Gas 7. Bake for about 15–20 minutes or until golden. While the loaf is baking, heat the milk and sugar for the glaze in a small pan until the sugar has dissolved, then bring to the boil. Brush the glaze over the bread

5 Leave to cool in the tin for 10 minutes, then cool slightly on a wire rack before slicing and filling.

Slovak Easter Bread Energy 765kcal/3214kJ; Protein 16g; Carbohydrate 108g, of which sugars 28g; Fat 33g, of which saturates 18g; Cholesterol 277mg; Calcium 203mg; Fibre 3.7g; Sodium 240mg.

Sally Lunn per loaf Energy 1250kcal/5290kJ; Protein 31g; Carbohydrate 236.9g, of which sugars 27.3g; Fat 26.6g, of which saturates 15.6g; Cholesterol 66mg; Calcium 577mg; Fibre 8.5g; Sodium 1262mg.

Peanut Butter Teabread

Crunchy peanut butter gives this teabread a richness as well as a distinctive flavour and texture. The topping of salted peanuts contrasts with the sweetness of the bread. This loaf will keep for two days in an airtight container.

Makes 1

225g/8oz/2 cups plain (all-purpose) flour
7.5ml/1 ½ tsp baking powder
2.5ml/½ tsp bicarbonate of soda (baking soda)
50g/2oz/¼ cup butter, softened
175g/6oz/½ cup crunchy peanut butter
50g/2oz/¼ cup caster (superfine) sugar
2 eggs, beaten
250ml/8fl oz/1 cup milk
25g/1oz/¼ cup roasted salted peanuts

1 Preheat the oven to 180°C/350°F/Gas 4. Grease and line a 900g/2lb loaf tin (pan) with baking parchment.

2 Sift the flour, baking powder and bicarbonate of soda together into a large bowl.

3 Put the butter and peanut butter into a large mixing bowl and beat together with a wooden spoon to soften. Beat in the caster sugar until the mixture is light and fluffy and the sugar grains have disintegrated.

4 Gradually whisk in the eggs a little at a time, then beat in the milk with the sifted flour and mix until smooth.

5 Pour into the prepared tin and sprinkle the peanuts on top. Bake for 1 hour or until a skewer inserted into the centre comes out clean. Cool in the tin for 5 minutes, then turn out on to a wire rack. Remove the lining paper, serve warm, cut in thick slices.

Cook's Tip
This teabread is tasty with soup or cold meats.

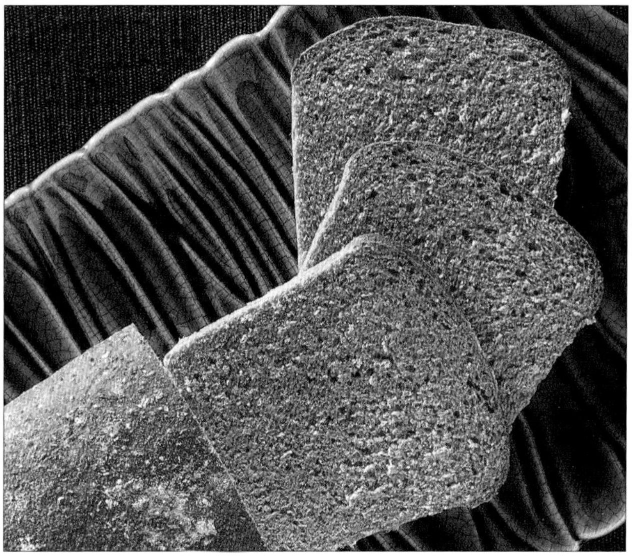

Orange Wheatloaf

This loaf is perfect just with butter as a breakfast teabread, or for making delicious banana sandwiches.

Makes 1

275g/10oz/2½ cups plain (all-purpose) wholemeal (whole-wheat) flour
2.5ml/½ tsp salt
25g/1oz/2 tbsp butter
25g/1oz/2 tbsp soft light brown sugar
3.5g/⅛oz easy-blend (rapid-rise) dried yeast
grated rind and juice of ½ orange

1 Lightly grease a 450g/1lb loaf tin (pan). Sift the flour into a large bowl and add any wheat flakes from the sieve (strainer) to the flour. Add the salt and rub in the butter lightly with your fingertips or a pastry blender.

2 Stir in the sugar, yeast and orange rind. Pour the orange juice into a measuring jug (pitcher) and use lukewarm water to make up to 200ml/7fl oz/scant 1 cup.

3 Stir the liquid into the flour mixture and mix to a soft ball of dough. Knead gently on a lightly floured surface until quite smooth and elastic.

4 Place the dough in the tin and leave it in a warm place until nearly doubled in size. Preheat the oven to 220°C/425°F/Gas 7.

5 Bake the bread for 30–35 minutes, or until it sounds hollow when removed from the tin and tapped underneath. Turn out of the tin and cool on a wire rack.

Cook's Tip
Easy-blend (rapid-rise) yeast is mixed directly with the dry ingredients, and is the easiest yeast to use. Don't confuse this with active dried yeast, which needs to be mixed with liquid first and left to become frothy before it is blended in with the dry ingredients.

Peanut Butter Teabread per loaf Energy 1527kcal/6439kJ; Protein 45.8g; Carbohydrate 238.4g, of which sugars 81.2g; Fat 48.8g, of which saturates 11.8g; Cholesterol 196mg; Calcium 497mg; Fibre 10.3g; Sodium 400mg.

Orange Wheatloaf per loaf Energy 1146kcal/4848kJ; Protein 35.3g; Carbohydrate 204.2g, of which sugars 34.3g; Fat 26.6g, of which saturates 13.8g; Cholesterol 53mg; Calcium 125mg; Fibre 24.8g; Sodium 164mg.

Orange & Honey Teabread

Honey gives a special flavour to this teabread. Serve just with a scraping of butter.

Makes 1

385g/13½oz/scant 3½ cups plain (all-purpose) flour
12.5ml/2½ tsp baking powder
2.5ml/½ tsp bicarbonate of soda (baking soda)
2.5ml/½ tsp salt
25g/1oz/2 tbsp margarine
250ml/8fl oz/1 cup clear honey
1 egg, at room temperature, lightly beaten
25ml/1½ tbsp grated orange rind
175ml/6fl oz/¾ cup freshly squeezed orange juice
115g/4oz/1 cup chopped walnuts

1 Preheat the oven to 160°C/325°F/Gas 3. Line the base and sides of a 23 x 13cm/9 x 5in loaf tin (pan) with baking parchment and grease the paper.

2 Sift the flour, baking powder, bicarbonate of soda and salt together in a bowl.

3 Cream the margarine until soft. Stir in the honey until blended, then stir in the egg. Add the orange rind and combine well.

4 Fold the flour mixture into the honey mixture in three batches, alternating with the orange juice. Stir in the walnuts.

5 Pour into the prepared tin and bake in the oven until a skewer inserted in the centre comes out clean, about 60–70 minutes. Leave for 10 minutes before turning out on to a wire rack to cool completely.

Cook's Tip

Although you can buy beautifully scented honey with the fragrance of wild flowers and herbs, the scents are usually destroyed in cooking, so for recipes such as this, a less expensive honey will do perfectly well. Clear honey gradually becomes cloudy, but this can be rectified simply by gently heating it.

Mexican 'Bread of the Dead'

A celebratory loaf made for All Souls' Day. Even though the name of the bread may suggest otherwise, it is a very happy day when both Mexicans and Spanish people pay their respects to the souls of their dead.

Makes 1

3 star anise
90ml/6 tbsp cold water
675g/1½lb/6 cups unbleached white bread flour
5ml/1 tsp salt
115g/4oz/½ cup caster (superfine) sugar
25g/1oz fresh yeast
175ml/6fl oz/¾ cup lukewarm water
3 eggs
60ml/4 tbsp orange liqueur
115g/4oz/½ cup butter, melted
grated rind of 1 orange
icing (confectioners') sugar, for dusting

1 Grease a 26cm/10½in fluted round cake tin (pan). Place the star anise in a pan with the water. Boil for 3–4 minutes, or until the liquid has reduced to 45ml/3 tbsp. Discard the star anise and leave the liquid to cool. Sift the flour and salt together into a large bowl. Stir in the sugar and make a well in the centre.

2 In a jug (pitcher), dissolve the yeast in the lukewarm water. Pour into the centre of the flour and mix in a little flour until a smooth, thick batter forms. Sprinkle over a little of the remaining flour, cover and leave the batter in a warm place for 30 minutes, or until the mixture starts to bubble.

3 Beat the eggs, the reserved liquid flavoured with star anise, orange liqueur and melted butter together. Gradually incorporate into the flour mixture to form a smooth dough.

4 Gently knead in the orange rind. Knead for 5–6 minutes until smooth and elastic. Shape into a 26cm/10½in round and place in the prepared tin. Cover and leave to rise, in a warm place, for 2–3 hours, or until almost at the top of the tin.

5 Preheat the oven to 190°C/375°F/Gas 5. Bake for about 45–50 minutes. Cool on a wire rack to cool. Dust with icing sugar.

Orange and Honey Teabread per loaf Energy 3145kcal/13251kJ; Protein 61.3g; Carbohydrate 509.6g, of which sugars 215.4g; Fat 109.9g, of which saturates 8.8g; Cholesterol 190mg; Calcium 707mg; Fibre 16.1g; Sodium 335mg.

Mexican 'Bread of the Dead' per loaf Energy 3617kcal/15231kJ; Protein 82.8g; Carbohydrate 554.8g, of which sugars 40.4g; Fat 119.4g, of which saturates 68.1g; Cholesterol 835mg; Calcium 1056mg; Fibre 20.9g; Sodium 3062mg.

Marmalade Teabread

Chunky orange marmalade adds a touch of citrus zest to this spicy teabread. It is very quick and easy to make, and perfect for serving with a hot cup of tea. Keep for up to three days in an airtight container, or freeze for up to two months wrapped in foil.

Makes 1

200g/7oz/1¾ cups plain (all-purpose) flour
5ml/1 tsp baking powder
6.25ml/1¼ tsp ground cinnamon
100g/3¾oz/7 tbsp butter, diced
50g/2oz/¼ cup soft light brown sugar
1 egg, lightly beaten
60ml/4 tbsp chunky orange marmalade
about 45ml/3 tbsp milk
60ml/4 tbsp glacé icing, to decorate
shreds of orange and lemon rind, to decorate

1 Preheat the oven to 160°C/325°F/Gas 3. Grease and line a 450g/1lb loaf tin (pan) with baking parchment.

2 Sift the flour, baking powder and cinnamon into a large mixing bowl. Add the diced butter and rub in with your fingertips until the mixture resembles fine breadcrumbs. Stir in the brown sugar.

3 In a small bowl, mix the beaten egg with the marmalade and most of the milk.

4 Mix the milk mixture into the flour mixture, adding more milk if necessary to give a soft, dropping consistency.

5 Spoon the mixture into the prepared tin and smooth the top level. Bake for 1¼ hours, or until the cake is firm to the touch and cooked through.

6 Cool in the tin for 5 minutes, then turn out to cool on a wire rack. Peel off the lining paper.

7 Drizzle the glacé icing over the top of the cake and decorate with shreds of orange and lemon rind.

Lemon & Walnut Teabread

The beaten egg whites give this citrus-flavoured nutty loaf a lovely light and crumbly texture.

Makes 1

115g/4oz/½ cup butter or margarine, at room temperature
90g/3½oz/½ cup caster (superfine) sugar
2 eggs, at room temperature, separated
grated rind of 2 lemons
30ml/2 tbsp lemon juice
215g/7½oz/scant 2 cups plain (all-purpose) flour
10ml/2 tsp baking powder
120ml/4fl oz/½ cup milk
50g/2oz/½ cup chopped walnuts
1.5ml/¼ tsp salt

1 Preheat the oven to 180°C/350°F/Gas 4. Line a 23 × 13cm/9 × 5in loaf tin (pan) with baking parchment and grease the paper.

2 Cream the butter or margarine with the sugar until light and fluffy. Beat in the egg yolks. Add the lemon rind and juice, and stir until blended. Set aside.

3 In another bowl, sift together the plain flour and baking powder three times. Gently fold into the butter mixture in three batches, alternating with the milk. Fold in the chopped walnuts. Set aside.

4 Beat the egg whites and salt until stiff peaks form. Fold a large spoonful of the egg whites into the walnut mixture. Fold in the remaining egg whites carefully until the mixture is just blended.

5 Pour the batter into the prepared loaf tin and bake until a skewer inserted in the centre of the loaf comes out clean, for about 45–50 minutes. Leave to cool in the tin for 5 minutes before turning out on to a wire rack to cool completely.

Cook's Tip
Make sure that there is no egg yolk in the white, or it will stop it from whisking up properly.

Marmalade Teabread Energy 287kcal/1206kJ; Protein 8.3g; Carbohydrate 34.8g, of which sugars 9.3g; Fat 13.7g, of which saturates 8.1g; Cholesterol 63mg; Calcium 68mg; Fibre 1g; Sodium 554mg.

Lemon and Walnut Teabread per loaf Energy 2490kcal/10413kJ; Protein 45.3g; Carbohydrate 269.1g, of which sugars 104.9g; Fat 144.7g, of which saturates 67.5g; Cholesterol 633mg; Calcium 617mg; Fibre 8.4g; Sodium 904mg.

Sweet Sesame Loaf

Lemon and sesame seeds make a great partnership in this light teabread.

Makes 1

75g/3oz/6 tbsp sesame seeds
275g/10oz/2½ cups plain (all-purpose) flour
12.5ml/2½ tsp baking powder
5ml/1 tsp salt
50g/2oz/¼ cup butter or margarine, at room temperature
130g/4½oz/scant ¾ cup caster (superfine) sugar
2 eggs, at room temperature
grated rind of 1 lemon
350ml/12fl oz/1½ cups milk

1 Preheat the oven to 180°C/350°F/Gas 4. Carefully line a 23 × 13cm/9 × 5in loaf tin (pan) with baking parchment and then grease the paper.

2 Reserve 25g/1oz/2 tbsp of the sesame seeds. Spread the rest on a baking sheet and bake in the oven until lightly toasted, about 10 minutes.

3 Sift the flour, baking powder and salt into a bowl. Stir in the toasted sesame seeds and set aside.

4 Cream the butter or margarine and sugar together until light and fluffy. Beat in the eggs, then stir in the lemon rind and milk. Pour the milk mixture over the dry ingredients and fold in with a large metal spoon until just blended.

5 Pour into the tin and sprinkle over the reserved sesame seeds. Bake until a skewer inserted in the centre comes out clean, about 1 hour. Cool in the tin for 10 minutes. Turn out on to a wire rack to cool completely.

Cook's Tip
Sesame seeds are nutty-flavoured and slightly sweet. Their taste is enhanced by light toasting in a dry pan. However, because of their high oil content they do not store well, so you should always buy them in small quantities.

Apple Loaf

The apple sauce in this loaf makes it beautifully moist. Serve spread with butter.

Makes 1

1 egg
250ml/8fl oz/1 cup bottled or home-made apple sauce
50g/2oz/¼ cup butter or margarine, melted
100g/3¾oz/scant ½ cup soft dark brown sugar
45g/1¾oz/scant ¼ cup caster (superfine) sugar
275g/10oz/2½ cups plain (all-purpose) flour
10ml/2 tsp baking powder
2.5ml/½ tsp bicarbonate of soda (baking soda)
2.5ml/½ tsp salt
5ml/1 tsp ground cinnamon
2.5ml/½ tsp freshly grated nutmeg
65g/2½oz/½ cup currants or raisins
50g/2oz/½ cup pecan nuts or walnuts, chopped

1 Preheat the oven to 180°C/350°F/Gas 4. Line the base and sides of a 23 × 13cm/9 × 5in loaf tin (pan) with baking parchment and grease the paper.

2 Break the egg into a bowl and beat lightly. Stir in the apple sauce, butter or margarine, and both sugars. Set aside.

3 In another bowl, sift together the flour, baking powder, bicarbonate of soda, salt, cinnamon and nutmeg. Fold the dry ingredients, including the currants or raisins and the nuts, into the apple sauce mixture in three batches.

4 Pour into the prepared tin and bake in the oven until a skewer inserted in the centre of the loaf comes out clean, about 1 hour. Leave to stand in the tin for 10 minutes, then turn out on to a wire rack to cool completely.

Variation
Ring the changes with this moist loaf by using different nuts and dried fruit. You could try ready-to-eat dried apricots with hazelnuts, for example.

Sweet Sesame Loaf per loaf Energy 2578kcal/10849kJ; Protein 64.8g; Carbohydrate 367g, of which sugars 157g; Fat 105.2g, of which saturates 39.7g; Cholesterol 508mg; Calcium 1443mg; Fibre 14.4g; Sodium 2590mg.

Apple Loaf per loaf Energy 2558kcal/10777kJ; Protein 42.6g; Carbohydrate 432.4g, of which sugars 222.5g; Fat 85g, of which saturates 30.9g; Cholesterol 297mg; Calcium 586mg; Fibre 15.3g; Sodium 442mg.

Mango Teabread

This delicious teabread is baked with juicy ripe mango.

Makes 2

275g/10oz/2½ cups plain (all-purpose) flour
10ml/2 tsp bicarbonate of soda (baking soda)
10ml/2 tsp ground cinnamon
2.5ml/½ tsp salt
115g/4oz/½ cup margarine
3 eggs, at room temperature
285g/10½oz/1½ cups caster (superfine) sugar
120ml/4fl oz/½ cup vegetable oil
1 large ripe mango, peeled and chopped
85g/3¼oz/generous 1 cup desiccated (dry unsweetened shredded) coconut
65g/2½oz/½ cup raisins

1 Preheat the oven to 180°C/350°F/Gas 4. Line the base and sides of two 23 × 13cm/9 × 5in loaf tins (pans) with baking parchment and grease the paper.

2 Sift together the flour, bicarbonate of soda, cinnamon and salt into a large mixing bowl.

3 In a separate bowl, cream the margarine until soft. Beat in the eggs and sugar until light and fluffy. Beat in the oil.

4 Fold the dry ingredients into the creamed ingredients in three batches, then fold in the mango, two-thirds of the coconut and the raisins.

5 Spoon the batter into the tins. Sprinkle over the remaining coconut. Bake until a skewer inserted in the centre comes out clean, about 50–60 minutes. Leave to stand for 10 minutes before turning out on to a wire rack to cool completely.

Cook's Tip

To dice a mango, take two thick slices from either side of the large flat stone without peeling the fruit. Make criss-cross cuts in the flesh on each slice and then turn inside out. The cubes of flesh will stand proud of the skin and can be easily cut off.

Coconut Bread

This bread is delicious served with a cup of hot chocolate or a glass of fruit punch.

Makes 1

175g/6oz/¾ cup butter
115g/4oz/½ cup demerara (raw) sugar
225g/8oz/2 cups self-raising (self-rising) flour
200g/7oz/1¾ cups plain (all-purpose) flour
115g/4oz/1⅓ cups desiccated (dry unsweetened shredded) coconut
5ml/1 tsp mixed (apple pie) spice
10ml/2 tsp vanilla extract
15ml/1 tbsp rum
2 eggs
about 150ml/¼ pint/⅔ cup milk
15ml/1 tbsp caster (superfine) sugar, blended with 30ml/2 tbsp water, to glaze

1 Preheat the oven to 180°C/350°F/Gas 4. Grease two 450g/1lb loaf tins (pans).

2 Place the butter and sugar in a large bowl and sift in the flour. Rub the ingredients together using your fingertips or a pastry cutter until the mixture resembles fine breadcrumbs.

3 Add the coconut, mixed spice, vanilla extract, rum, eggs and milk to the butter and sugar mixture, and mix together well with your hands. If you think that the mixture is too dry, moisten with milk. Turn out on to a floured board and knead until firm and pliable.

4 Halve the mixture and place in the prepared loaf tins. Glaze with sugared water and bake for 1 hour, or until the loaves are cooked. Test with a skewer; the loaves are ready when the skewer comes out clean.

Cook's Tips

This coconut bread is a cross between a teabread and a yeast bread. It is quick to make and needs no rising time. It is delicious when spread with butter or a fruit preserve.

Mango Teabread per loaf Energy 1777kcal/7404kJ; Protein 28.1g; Carbohydrate 143.3g, of which sugars 38.3g; Fat 125.6g, of which saturates 30.6g; Cholesterol 347mg; Calcium 342mg; Fibre 16.9g; Sodium 2485mg.

Coconut Bread per loaf Energy 4148kcal/17357kJ; Protein 65.6g; Carbohydrate 465.9g, of which sugars 142g; Fat 234.3g, of which saturates 158.1g; Cholesterol 763mg; Calcium 951mg; Fibre 28.9g; Sodium 1317mg.

Banana Bread

For a change, add 50–75g/2–3oz/½–¾ cup chopped walnuts or pecan nuts to the dry ingredients of this moist banana bread.

Makes 1

200g/7oz/1⅔ cups plain (all-purpose) flour
11.5ml/2¼ tsp baking powder
2.5ml/½ tsp salt
4ml/¾ tsp ground cinnamon (optional)
60ml/4 tbsp wheatgerm
65g/2½oz/5 tbsp butter, at room temperature
115g/4oz/generous ½ cup caster (superfine) sugar
4ml/¾ tsp grated lemon rind
3 ripe bananas, mashed
2 eggs, beaten

1 Preheat the oven to 180°C/350°F/Gas 4. Grease and flour a 21 × 12cm/8½ × 4½in loaf tin (pan).

2 Sift the flour, baking powder, salt and cinnamon, if using, into a bowl. Stir in the wheatgerm.

3 In another bowl, combine the butter with the caster sugar and grated lemon rind. Beat thoroughly until the mixture is light and fluffy.

4 Add the mashed bananas and eggs, and mix well. Add the dry ingredients and blend quickly and evenly.

5 Spoon into the loaf tin. Bake for 50–60 minutes, or until a skewer inserted in the centre comes out clean.

6 Cool the bread in the tin for 5 minutes, then turn out on to a wire rack to cool completely.

Cook's Tip
Wheatgerm is the heart of the wheat grain, and contains many nutrients and important vitamins. It must be used fresh, and should be stored in an airtight container. Do not store for long periods, as it will become bitter.

Wholemeal Banana Nut Loaf

With its tasty combination of banana and chopped walnuts, this hearty and filling loaf makes an ideal winter teatime treat.

Makes 1

115g/4oz/½ cup butter, at room temperature
115g/4oz/generous ½ cup caster (superfine) sugar
2 eggs, at room temperature
115g/4oz/1 cup plain (all-purpose) flour
5ml/1 tsp bicarbonate of soda (baking soda)
1.5ml/¼ tsp salt
5ml/1 tsp ground cinnamon
50g/2oz/½ cup wholemeal (whole-wheat) flour
3 large ripe bananas
5ml/1 tsp vanilla extract
50g/2oz/½ cup chopped walnuts

1 Preheat the oven to 180°C/350°F/Gas 4. Line the base and sides of a 23 × 13cm/9 × 5in loaf tin (pan) with baking parchment and grease the paper.

2 With an electric mixer, or by hand, cream the butter and sugar together until light and fluffy. Add the eggs, one at a time, beating well after each addition.

3 Sift the plain flour, bicarbonate of soda, salt and cinnamon over the butter mixture, and stir to blend. Stir in the wholemeal flour.

4 With a fork, mash the bananas to a purée, then stir into the mixture. Stir in the vanilla and nuts.

5 Pour the mixture into the prepared tin and spread level. Bake until a skewer inserted in the centre comes out clean, about 50–60 minutes. Leave to stand for 10 minutes before transferring to a wire rack to cool completely.

Cook's Tip
Wholemeal (whole-wheat) flour contains the wheat germ and bran, giving it a higher fibre, fat and nutritional content than white flour. Because of its fat content, it is best stored in a cool pantry.

Banana Bread per loaf Energy 2265kcal/9548kJ; Protein 51.9g; Carbohydrate 372.4g, of which sugars 195.9g; Fat 73.6g, of which saturates 38.4g; Cholesterol 519mg; Calcium 461mg; Fibre 18.9g; Sodium 553mg.
Wholemeal Banana Nut Loaf per loaf Energy 2632kcal/11017kJ; Protein 41.9g; Carbohydrate 313.4g, of which sugars 187.6g; Fat 143.4g, of which saturates 66.5g; Cholesterol 626mg; Calcium 384mg; Fibre 13.1g; Sodium 855mg.

Glazed Banana Spiced Loaf

The lemony glaze perfectly sets off the warm flavours of nutmeg and cloves in this deliciously moist and light banana teabread.

Makes 1

115g/4oz/½ cup butter, at room temperature
165g/5½oz/¾ cup caster (superfine) sugar
2 eggs, at room temperature
215g/7½oz/scant 2 cups plain (all-purpose) flour
5ml/1 tsp salt
5ml/1 tsp bicarbonate of soda (baking soda)
2.5ml/½ tsp freshly grated nutmeg
1.5ml/¼ tsp mixed spice
1.5ml/¼ tsp ground cloves
175ml/6fl oz/¾ cup sour cream
1 large ripe banana, mashed
5ml/1 tsp vanilla extract

For the glaze

115g/4oz/1 cup icing (confectioners') sugar
15–30ml/1–2 tbsp lemon juice

1 Preheat the oven to 180°C/350°F/Gas 4. Line a 23 × 13cm/ 9 × 5in loaf tin (pan) with baking parchment and grease the paper.

2 Cream the butter and sugar until light and fluffy. Add the eggs, one at a time, beating well after each addition.

3 Sift together the flour, salt, bicarbonate of soda, nutmeg, mixed spice and cloves. Add to the butter mixture and stir to combine well.

4 Add the sour cream, banana and vanilla extract, and mix to just blend. Pour this mixture into the prepared tin.

5 Bake until the top springs back when touched lightly, about 45–50 minutes. Cool in the tin for 10 minutes. Turn out on to a wire rack.

6 To make the glaze, combine the icing sugar and lemon juice until smooth, then stir until smooth. Place the cooled loaf on a rack set over a baking sheet. Pour the glaze over the loaf and allow to set.

Banana Orange Loaf

For the best banana flavour and a really good moist texture, make sure that the bananas are perfectly ripe for this delicious loaf. The sugar-sprinkled orange slices make a pretty decoration.

Makes 1

90g/3½oz/¾ cup plain (all-purpose) wholemeal (whole-wheat) flour
90g/3½oz/¾ cup plain (all-purpose) flour
5ml/1 tsp baking powder
5ml/1 tsp mixed (apple pie) spice
45ml/3 tbsp flaked (sliced) hazelnuts, toasted
2 large ripe bananas
1 egg
30ml/2 tbsp sunflower oil
30ml/2 tbsp clear honey
finely grated rind and juice of 1 small orange
4 orange slices, halved
10ml/2 tsp icing (confectioners') sugar

1 Preheat the oven to 180°C/350°F/Gas 4. Brush a 23 x 13cm/ 9 x 5in loaf tin (pan) with sunflower oil and line the base with baking parchment.

2 Sift the flours with the baking powder and spice into a large bowl, adding any bran that is caught in the sieve (strainer). Stir the hazelnuts into the dry ingredients.

3 Peel and mash the bananas in a large bowl. Add the egg, sunflower oil, honey, and the orange rind and juice to the mashed bananas and beat together. Add the banana mixture to the dry ingredients and mix to combine thoroughly.

4 Spoon the mixture into the prepared tin and smooth the top. Bake in the oven for 40–45 minutes, or until the cake is firm and golden brown. Remove from the oven and turn out on to a wire rack to cool.

5 Meanwhile, sprinkle the orange slices with the icing sugar and place on a grill (broiling) rack. Grill (broil) until the orange slices are lightly golden. Arrange the glazed orange slices on the top of the loaf.

Glazed Banana Spiced Loaf per loaf Energy 3293kcal/13836kJ; Protein 41.1g; Carbohydrate 490.2g, of which sugars 324.1g; Fat 143.6g, of which saturates 85.4g; Cholesterol 731mg; Calcium 696mg; Fibre 7.8g; Sodium 933mg.

Banana Orange Loaf per loaf Energy 1483kcal/6238kJ; Protein 35.3g; Carbohydrate 214.3g, of which sugars 84.6g; Fat 59.9g, of which saturates 7g; Cholesterol 190mg; Calcium 276mg; Fibre 16.1g; Sodium 89mg.

Banana & Ginger Teabread

The creaminess of the banana is given a delightful lift with chunks of stem ginger in this tasty teabread. If you like a strong ginger flavour, add 5ml/1 tsp ground ginger with the flour.

Makes 1

175g/6oz/1½ cups self-raising (self-rising) flour
5ml/1 tsp baking powder
40g/1½oz/3 tbsp soft margarine
50g/2oz/¼ cup soft light brown sugar
50g/2oz/⅓ cup drained preserved stem ginger, chopped
60ml/4 tbsp skimmed milk
2 ripe bananas

1 Preheat the oven to 180°C/350°F/Gas 4. Line and grease a 450g/1lb loaf tin (pan). Sift the flour and baking powder into a large bowl.

2 Using your fingertips or a pastry blender rub the margarine into the dry ingredients until the mixture resembles breadcrumbs, then stir in the sugar.

3 Peel and mash the bananas in a separate bowl. Add the preserved stem ginger, milk and mashed bananas to the mixture and mix to a soft dough.

4 Spoon the dough into the prepared tin and bake in the oven for about 40–45 minutes.

5 Run a metal spatula around the edges, then turn the teabread on to a wire rack and leave to cool completely.

Variation
To make Banana and Walnut Teabread, add 5ml/1 tsp mixed (apple pie) spice and omit the chopped stem ginger. Stir in 50g/2oz/½ cup chopped walnuts and add 50g/2oz/⅓ cup sultanas (golden raisins).

Banana Gingerbread Slices

Bananas make this spicy bake delightfully moist. The flavour develops on keeping, so store the gingerbread for a few days before cutting into slices, if possible.

Makes 1

275g/10oz/2½ cups plain (all-purpose) flour
5ml/1 tsp bicarbonate of soda (baking soda)
20ml/4 tsp ground ginger
10ml/2 tsp mixed (apple pie) spice
115g/4oz/⅔ cup soft light brown sugar
60ml/4 tbsp sunflower oil
30ml/2 tbsp black treacle (molasses)
30ml/2 tbsp malt extract
2 eggs
60ml/4 tbsp orange juice
3 ripe bananas
115g/4oz/⅔ cup raisins or sultanas (golden raisins)

1 Preheat the oven to 180°C/350°F/Gas 4. Lightly grease and line a 28 × 18cm/11 × 7in shallow baking tin (pan).

2 Sift the flour, bicarbonate of soda and spices into a mixing bowl. Place the sugar in the sieve (strainer) over the bowl, add some of the flour mixture and rub through with a spoon.

3 Make a well in the centre of the dry ingredients. Add the oil, treacle, malt extract, eggs and juice. Mix thoroughly.

4 Mash the bananas on a plate. Add the raisins or sultanas to the gingerbread mixture, then mix in the mashed bananas.

5 Scrape the mixture into the prepared baking tin. Bake for about 35–40 minutes, or until the centre of the gingerbread springs back when lightly pressed. Leave to cool for 5 minutes, then turn out on to a wire rack to cool completely. Cut into 20 slices to serve.

Cook's Tip
If your brown sugar is lumpy, mix it with a little flour and it will then be easier to sift.

Banana and Ginger Teabread Energy 162kcal/685kJ; Protein 2.7g; Carbohydrate 29.7g, of which sugars 12.5g; Fat 4.5g, of which saturates 0.1g; Cholesterol 0mg; Calcium 45mg; Fibre 1g; Sodium 45mg.

Banana Gingerbread Slices Energy 133kcal/563kJ; Protein 2.3g; Carbohydrate 25.9g, of which sugars 15.2g; Fat 3g, of which saturates 0.5g; Cholesterol 19mg; Calcium 37mg; Fibre 0.7g; Sodium 18mg.

Gingerbread

Cinnamon as well as ginger gives gingerbread its familiar warm flavouring, which wouldn't be achieved by using ginger alone. Treacle and golden syrup are the essential ingredients to ensure the finished loaf is soft and sticky. Store, foil-wrapped, for five days in an airtight container.

Makes 1

115g/4oz/½ cup soft light brown sugar
75g/3oz/6 tbsp butter
75g/3oz/¼ cup golden (light corn) syrup
75g/3oz/¼ cup treacle (molasses)
105ml/7 tbsp milk
1 egg, beaten
175g/6oz/1½ cups plain (all-purpose) flour
50g/2oz/½ cup gram flour
a pinch of salt
10ml/2 tsp ground ginger
5ml/1 tsp ground cinnamon
7.5ml/1½ tsp baking powder

1 Preheat the oven to 160°C/325°F/Gas 3. Grease and line a 900g/2lb loaf tin (pan) with baking parchment.

2 Put the brown sugar, butter, golden syrup and treacle in a pan and heat gently until melted, stirring occasionally.

3 Remove the pan from the heat and leave to cool slightly. Then pour in the milk and beaten egg and mix.

4 Sift the plain flour, gram flour, salt, spices and baking powder together into a large bowl. Make a small well in the centre and pour the liquid mixture into the well. Beat well until a smooth batter forms.

5 Pour the batter into the prepared tin. Bake in the oven for 1–1¼ hours, or until firm.

6 Turn out on to a wire rack and leave to cool. Peel off the lining. Serve in slices.

Sticky Gingerbread

This dark rich gingerbread cries out to be smothered in cool butter or swirls of cream cheese as a contrast to the loaf's taste and texture. It tastes better when kept for a few days, so prepare ahead before serving with afternoon tea on a chilly winter's day.

Makes 1

225g/8oz/2 cups plain (all-purpose) flour
10ml/2 tsp ground ginger
5ml/1 tsp mixed (apple pie) spice
a pinch of salt
2 pieces preserved stem ginger, drained and chopped
115g/4oz/½ cup butter, softened
115g/4oz/½ cup dark muscovado (molasses) sugar, sifted
275g/10oz/scant 1 cup black treacle (molasses)
2 eggs, beaten
2.5ml/½ tsp bicarbonate of soda (baking soda)
30ml/2 tbsp milk, warmed
butter or cream cheese, to serve

1 Preheat the oven to 160°C/325°F/Gas 3. Grease and line an 18cm/7in square cake tin (pan), that measures about 7.5cm/3in deep.

2 Sift the flour, ground ginger, mixed spice and salt together into a bowl. Add the stem ginger and toss it in the flour to coat.

3 In a separate bowl, cream the butter and sugar together until fluffy, then gradually beat in the treacle. Add the eggs and the flour mixture.

4 Dissolve the bicarbonate of soda in the milk and gradually beat into the batter. Pour into the prepared tin and bake for about 45 minutes. Reduce the oven temperature to 150°C/300°F/Gas 2 and bake for a further 30 minutes. To test whether the loaf is cooked, insert a metal skewer into the middle; it should come out clean.

5 Cool for 5 minutes in the tin and then turn out on to a wire rack to cool completely. Keep for two to three days in an airtight container so that the gingerbread becomes sticky and moist. Cut into pieces and serve with butter or cream cheese.

Gingerbread Energy 191kcal/802kJ; Protein 1.6g; Carbohydrate 24.7g, of which sugars 24.6g; Fat 10.3g, of which saturates 6.3g; Cholesterol 45mg; Calcium 128mg; Fibre 0g; Sodium 116mg.

Sticky Gingerbread Energy 373kcal/1572kJ; Protein 5.2g; Carbohydrate 60.9g, of which sugars 38.7g; Fat 13.9g, of which saturates 8.1g; Cholesterol 78.5mg; Calcium 253.6mg; Fibre 0.9g; Sodium 170.5mg.

Cardamom Loaf

A favourite spice for Scandinavians, cardamom's warm flavour is used in a variety of cakes, buns and other dishes. This loaf is a traditional tea or coffee-time treat in Norway, and is delicious without being elaborate or too rich.

Makes 1

250g/9oz/1 cup and 2 tbsp butter, softened, plus extra for greasing
375g/13oz/3¼ cups plain (all-purpose) flour
45ml/3 tbsp baking powder
10 cardamom pods, seeds removed and finely crushed
250g/9oz/1¼ cups caster (superfine) sugar
3 large (US extra large) eggs, lightly beaten
150ml/¼ pint/⅔ cup milk
45ml/3 tbsp raisins
45ml/3 tbsp candied peel
15ml/1 tbsp flaked (sliced) almonds

1 Preheat the oven to 190°C/375°F/Gas 5. Grease a 1kg/2lb loaf tin (pan) with the extra butter and line the bottom with baking parchment.

2 In a large mixing bowl, sift together the flour, baking powder and cardamom.

3 In a separate bowl, cream together the butter and caster sugar with a wooden spoon until light and fluffy. Beat in the eggs, a little at a time, then fold in the sifted flour.

4 Add the milk to the mixture, a little at a time, folding in well with a metal spoon after each addition, until all the ingredients are well combined. Add the raisins, candied peel and almonds to the mixture and fold in.

5 Transfer the mixture to the prepared loaf tin and bake in the preheated oven for about 50 minutes, or until risen and firm to the touch. Turn out the loaf on to a wire rack and leave to cool before serving.

Swedish Spice Bread

Another traditional Scandinavian loaf, this Swedish version uses a combination of cardamom and caraway seeds.

Makes 1

25g/1oz/2 tbsp butter
45ml/3 tbsp clear honey
225g/8oz/2 cups strong white bread flour
225g/8oz/2 cups rye flour
2.5ml/½ tsp salt
7g/¼oz easy-blend (rapid-rise) dried yeast
5ml/1 tsp ground cardamom
5ml/1 tsp ground caraway seeds
2.5ml/½ tsp ground star anise
30ml/2 tbsp caster (superfine) sugar
grated rind and juice of 1 orange
175ml/6fl oz/¾ cup lager
1 egg, beaten

For the glaze
60ml/4 tbsp boiling water
15ml/1 tbsp clear honey

1 Melt the butter with the honey in a small pan, then leave to cool. Sift the flours and salt into a bowl and stir in the yeast, cardamom, caraway, star anise, caster sugar and orange rind.

2 Mix the lager with the boiling water. Stir the orange juice and beaten egg into the butter and honey, then stir this mixture into the flour. Add enough lager and water to make a soft and slightly sticky, but manageable dough. Place the dough on a lightly floured surface and knead for 5 minutes until smooth and elastic. Place in an oiled bowl, cover and leave to rise until doubled in size. Knead briefly, then divide the dough in two. Roll out each piece into a long snake.

3 Grease a 23cm/9in round cake tin (pan). Starting at the edge of the tin, coil the dough round and round to the centre, joining the second piece to the first with a little water. Cover with oiled clear film (plastic wrap) and leave until doubled in size. Preheat the oven to 190°C/375°F/Gas 5. Bake the bread for 10 minutes, then turn the oven down to 160°C/325°F/Gas 3 and bake for 40–50 minutes more, until the bread is lightly browned and sounds hollow when rapped underneath.

4 To make the glaze, mix the honey with 15ml/1 tbsp hot water, then brush it over the loaf. Leave on a wire rack to cool.

Cardamom Loaf per portion Energy 786kcal/3295kJ; Protein 11g; Carbohydrate 103.2g, of which sugars 55.5g; Fat 39.6g, of which saturates 23.8g; Cholesterol 192mg; Calcium 179mg; Fibre 2.6g; Sodium 392mg.

Swedish Spice Bread per loaf Energy 2195kcal/9299kJ; Protein 52.8g; Carbohydrate 425.4g, of which sugars 69.3g; Fat 38.7g, of which saturates 16.5g; Cholesterol 244mg; Calcium 519mg; Fibre 33.3g; Sodium 263mg.

Apricot Nut Loaf

Raisins and walnuts combine with apricots to make a lovely light teabread. Full of flavour, this is also ideal for a morning snack or children's lunchboxes.

Makes 1

115g/4oz/½ cup ready-to-eat dried apricots
1 large orange
75g/3oz/generous ½ cup raisins
150g/5oz/¾ cup caster (superfine) sugar
85ml/5½ tbsp/⅓ cup oil
2 eggs, lightly beaten
250g/9oz/2¼ cups plain (all-purpose) flour
10ml/2 tsp baking powder
2.5ml/½ tsp salt
5ml/1 tsp bicarbonate of soda (baking soda)
50g/2oz/½ cup chopped walnuts

1 Place the apricots in a bowl, cover with lukewarm water and leave to stand for 30 minutes. Preheat the oven to 180°C/350°F/Gas 4. Line a 23 × 13cm/9 × 5in loaf tin (pan) with baking parchment and grease the paper.

2 With a vegetable peeler, remove the orange rind, leaving the pith. Chop the strips finely.

3 Drain the softened apricots and chop them coarsely. Place in a bowl with the orange rind and raisins. Squeeze the peeled orange over a bowl. Measure the orange juice and add enough hot water to obtain 175ml/6fl oz/¾ cup liquid.

4 Add the orange juice mixture to the apricot mixture. Stir in the sugar, oil and eggs. Set aside.

5 In another bowl, sift together the flour, baking powder, salt and bicarbonate of soda. Fold the flour mixture into the apricot mixture in three batches, then stir in the walnuts.

6 Spoon the mixture into the prepared tin and bake until a skewer inserted in the centre of the loaf comes out clean, about 55–60 minutes. If the loaf browns too quickly, protect the top with a sheet of foil. Cool in the tin for 10 minutes, then transfer to a wire rack to cool completely.

Date & Walnut Loaf

This fruit loaf is lower in sugar than many cakes, but the dates and bananas add sweetness as well as a depth of flavour. As these also make the loaf very moist, it's great for keeping for an unexpected tea party. Keep for one week in an airtight container, or freeze for up to two months.

Makes 1

150g/5oz/scant 1 cup stoned (pitted), chopped, dried dates
finely grated rind and juice of 1 lemon
5ml/1 tsp bicarbonate of soda (baking soda)
75g/3oz/6 tbsp butter, softened
50g/2oz/¼ cup soft light brown sugar
150g/5oz/½ cup sweetened condensed milk
2 eggs, beaten
150g/5oz ripe bananas, peeled and mashed
225g/8oz/2 cups self-raising (self-rising) flour
5ml/1 tsp baking powder
75g/3oz/¾ cup walnuts, chopped
butter, to serve

1 Preheat the oven to 160°C/325°F/Gas 3. Grease and line a 900g/2lb loaf tin (pan) with baking parchment.

2 Put the dates in a heatproof bowl with the lemon rind and juice, and 30ml/2 tbsp boiling water. Stir in the bicarbonate of soda. Leave to cool.

3 Put the butter, sugar and condensed milk in a bowl and whisk by hand or with an electric mixer until smooth. Gradually whisk in the eggs. Stir in the bananas and the date mixture.

4 Sift the flour and baking powder into the bowl, then add the chopped nuts and stir together until smooth.

5 Spoon the mixture into the tin and smooth the top level. Bake for about 1 hour 10–15 minutes, or until a skewer inserted into the middle comes out clean.

6 Leave to set for 10 minutes, then turn out on to a wire rack to go cold. Remove the lining paper. Serve sliced and buttered.

Apricot Nut Loaf per loaf Energy 2904kcal/12229kJ; Protein 51.6g; Carbohydrate 456.8g, of which sugars 265.9g; Fat 109.6g, of which saturates 13.6g; Cholesterol 381mg; Calcium 708mg; Fibre 20.3g; Sodium 227mg.

Date and Walnut Loaf Energy 266kcal/1124kJ; Protein 6.1g; Carbohydrate 42.9g, of which sugars 24.3g; Fat 9g, of which saturates 1.2g; Cholesterol 1.8mg; Calcium 64mg; Fibre 3.4g; Sodium 16mg.

Date & Pecan Loaf

Walnuts may be used instead of pecan nuts to make this luxurious fruity teabread.

Makes 1

175g/6oz/1 cup chopped stoned (pitted) dates
175ml/6fl oz/¾ cup boiling water
50g/2oz/¼ cup unsalted (sweet) butter, at room temperature
50g/2oz/¼ cup soft dark brown sugar
50g/2oz/¼ cup caster (superfine) sugar
1 egg, at room temperature
30ml/2 tbsp brandy
165g/5½oz/generous 1¼ cups plain (all-purpose) flour
10ml/2 tsp baking powder
2.5ml/½ tsp salt
4ml/¾ tsp freshly grated nutmeg
75g/3oz/¾ cup coarsely chopped pecan nuts

1 Place the dates in a bowl and pour over the boiling water. Set aside to cool. Preheat the oven to 180°C/350°F/Gas 4. Line a 23 × 13cm/9 × 5in loaf tin (pan) with baking parchment and then grease the paper.

2 With an electric mixer, cream the butter and sugars until light and fluffy. Beat in the egg and brandy, then set aside.

3 Sift the flour, baking powder, salt and nutmeg together, at least three times. Fold the dry ingredients into the sugar mixture in three batches, alternating with the dates and water. Fold in the chopped pecan nuts.

4 Pour the mixture into the prepared tin and bake until a skewer inserted in the centre comes out clean, about 45–50 minutes. Leave the loaf to cool in the tin for 10 minutes before transferring it to a wire rack to cool completely.

Cook's Tip
Nutmeg is a particularly useful spice for sweet loaves, but it is only ever used in small quantities, because the spice is actually poisonous in larger quantities.

Date & Nut Maltloaf

Choose any type of nut you like to include in this deliciously rich and fruit-packed teabread.

Makes 2

300g/11oz/2⅔ cups strong plain (all-purpose) flour
275g/10oz/2½ cups wholemeal (whole-wheat) bread flour
5ml/1 tsp salt
75g/3oz/⅓ cup soft light brown sugar
7g/¼oz easy-blend (rapid-rise) dried yeast
50g/2oz/¼ cup butter or margarine
15ml/1 tbsp black treacle (molasses)
60ml/4 tbsp malt extract
scant 250ml/8fl oz/1 cup lukewarm milk
115g/4oz/⅔ cup chopped dates
75g/3oz/½ cup sultanas (golden raisins)
50g/2oz/½ cup chopped nuts
75g/3oz/generous ½ cup raisins
30ml/2 tbsp clear honey, to glaze

1 Sift the flours and salt into a large bowl, then tip in the wheat flakes from the sieve (strainer). Stir in the sugar and yeast.

2 Put the butter or margarine in a small pan with the treacle and malt extract. Stir over low heat until melted. Leave to cool, then combine with the milk.

3 Stir the milk mixture into the dry ingredients and knead thoroughly for 15 minutes, or until the dough is elastic.

4 Knead in the chopped dates, sultanas and chopped nuts. Transfer the dough to an oiled bowl, cover and leave in a for about 1½ hours, or until the dough has doubled in size.

5 Grease two 450g/1lb loaf tins (pans). Knock back (punch down) the dough and knead lightly. Divide the dough in half, form into loaves and place in the tins. Cover and leave in a warm place for 30 minutes, or until risen. Meanwhile, preheat the oven to 190°C/375°F/Gas 5.

6 Bake for 35–40 minutes, or until well risen. Cool on a wire rack. Brush with honey while warm.

Date and Pecan Loaf per loaf Energy 2458kcal/10331kJ; Protein 35.2g; Carbohydrate 356.4g, of which sugars 229.5g; Fat 101.7g, of which saturates 32.4g; Cholesterol 297mg; Calcium 446mg; Fibre 15.6g; Sodium 402mg.

Date and Nut Maltloaf per loaf Energy 1939kcal/8200kJ; Protein 43.9g; Carbohydrate 361.7g, of which sugars 162.2g; Fat 45.2g, of which saturates 16.6g; Cholesterol 61mg; Calcium 693mg; Fibre 21.7g; Sodium 308mg.

Dried Fruit Loaf

Use any combination of dried fruit you like in this delicious teabread. The fruit is soaked in a bowl of cold tea first, making the loaf superbly moist.

Makes 1

450g/1lb/2¾ cups mixed dried fruit, such as currants, raisins, chopped ready-to-eat dried apricots and dried cherries
300ml/½ pint/1¼ cups cold strong tea
200g/7oz/scant 1 cup soft dark brown sugar
grated rind and juice of 1 small orange
grated rind and juice of 1 lemon
1 egg, lightly beaten
200g/7oz/1¾ cups plain (all-purpose) flour
15ml/1 tbsp baking powder
1.5ml/¼ tsp salt

1 In a large bowl, mix the dried fruit with the cold tea and leave to soak overnight.

2 Preheat the oven to 180°C/350°F/Gas 4. Line the base and sides of a 23 x 13cm/9 x 5in loaf tin (pan) with baking parchment and grease the paper.

3 Strain the soaked fruit, reserving the liquid. In a bowl, combine the sugar, orange and lemon rind, and strained fruit.

4 Pour the orange and lemon juice into a measuring jug (cup); if the quantity is less than 250ml/8fl oz/1 cup, then top up with the soaking liquid.

5 Stir the citrus juices and lightly beaten egg into the dried fruit mixture until combined.

6 Sift the flour, baking powder and salt together into another bowl. Stir the dry ingredients into the fruit mixture until well blended.

7 Transfer to the tin and bake until a skewer inserted in the centre comes out clean: about 1¼ hours. Leave in the tin for 10 minutes before unmoulding, and place on a wire rack to cool completely.

Quick & Easy Teabread

This succulent, fruity teabread can be served just as it is, or spread with a little butter. The loaf can be stored, tightly wrapped in foil or in an airtight container for up to five days. A great way to get children to eat some fruit, this teabread is ideal for packed lunches, picnics, or simply served with a cup of tea for afternoon tea.

Makes 1

350g/12oz/2 cups luxury mixed dried fruit
75g/3oz/scant ⅓ cup demerara (raw) sugar, plus 15ml/1 tbsp
1 large (US extra large) egg
175g/6oz/1½ cups self-raising (self-rising) flour

1 Put the fruit in a bowl. Add 150ml/¼ pint/⅔ cup boiling water and leave to stand for 30 minutes.

2 Preheat the oven to 180°C/350°F/Gas 4. Grease and line the base and long sides of a 450g/1lb loaf tin (pan).

3 Beat the main quantity of sugar and the egg into the fruit. Sift the flour into the bowl and stir until combined.

4 Turn into the prepared tin and level the surface. Sprinkle with the remaining sugar.

5 Bake the teabread for about 50 minutes, until risen and firm to the touch. When the bread is cooked, a skewer inserted into the centre will come out without any sticky mixture on it. Leave the loaf in the tin for 10 minutes before turning out on to a wire rack to cool.

Variation

You can make a moist version of this simple teabread by adding 5ml/1 tsp mixed (apple pie) spice and a cup of 225ml/8fl oz/1 cup hot strong tea to the ingredients.

Dried Fruit Loaf per loaf Energy 2763kcal/11770kJ; Protein 36.6g; Carbohydrate 673.9g, of which sugars 521.5g; Fat 10g, of which saturates 2g; Cholesterol 190mg; Calcium 838mg; Fibre 14.8g; Sodium 156mg.

Quick and Easy Teabread Energy 236kcal/1004kJ; Protein 3.8g; Carbohydrate 56.1g, of which sugars 39.9g; Fat 1.1g, of which saturates 0.2g; Cholesterol 24mg; Calcium 117mg; Fibre 1.6g; Sodium 109mg.

Monkey Bread

This American favourite is also called bubble bread, because of the 'bubbles' of dough. The pieces of dough are tossed in a coating of butter, nuts, cinnamon and rum-soaked fruit.

Makes 1

7g/¼oz easy-blend (rapid-rise) dried yeast
450g/1lb/4 cups unbleached white bread flour
2.5ml/½ tsp salt
15ml/1 tbsp caster (superfine) sugar
120ml/4fl oz/½ cup lukewarm milk
120ml/4fl oz/½ cup lukewarm water
1 egg, lightly beaten

For the coating
75g/3oz/½ cup sultanas (golden raisins)
45ml/3 tbsp rum or brandy
115g/4oz/1 cup walnuts, finely chopped
10ml/2 tsp ground cinnamon
115g/4oz/⅔ cup soft light brown sugar
50g/2oz/¼ cup butter, melted

1 Lightly grease a 23cm/9in springform ring cake tin (pan). Mix the dried yeast, flour, salt and sugar in a large bowl and make a well in the centre. Add the milk, water and egg to the well and mix to a soft dough and knead for 10 minutes until smooth. Place in a lightly oiled bowl, cover for 45–60 minutes.

2 Place the sultanas in a small pan, pour over the rum or brandy and heat for 1–2 minutes, or until warm. Take care not to overheat. Remove from the heat and set aside. Mix the walnuts, cinnamon and sugar in a small bowl.

3 Knead the dough gently and divide into 30 small balls. Dip the balls into the melted butter, then roll them in the walnut mixture. Place half in the prepared tin, spaced slightly apart. Sprinkle over all the soaked sultanas. Top with the remaining dough balls, dipping and coating as before. Sprinkle over any remaining walnut mixture and melted butter. Cover and leave for 45 minutes, or until the dough reaches the top of the tin.

4 Preheat the oven to 190°C/375°F/Gas 5. Bake for about 35–40 minutes, until well risen and golden. Cool on a wire rack.

Panettone

This Italian cake is perfect for Christmas festivities.

Makes 1

150ml/¼ pint/⅔ cup lukewarm milk
7g/¼oz easy-blend (rapid-rise) dried yeast
about 400g/14oz/3½ cups plain (all-purpose) flour
60g/2½oz/⅓ cup sugar
10ml/2 tsp salt
2 eggs
5 egg yolks
175g/6oz/¾ cup unsalted (sweet) butter, at room temperature
115g/4oz/¾ cup raisins
grated rind of 1 lemon
75g/3oz/½ cup candied citrus peel, chopped

1 Combine the milk and yeast in a large, warmed mixing bowl and leave for 10 minutes to dissolve the yeast. Sift in 115g/4oz/1 cup of the flour, stir in and cover loosely, and leave in a warm place for 30 minutes.

2 Sift over the remaining flour. Make a well in the centre and add the sugar, salt, eggs and egg yolks. Stir the dough mixture with a wooden spoon until it becomes too stiff, then continue to stir the mixture with your hands to obtain a very elastic and sticky dough. Add a little more flour, if necessary, blending it in well, to keep the dough as soft as possible.

3 Smear the butter into the dough, then work it in with your hands. When evenly distributed, cover and leave to rise in a warm place until doubled in size, about 3–4 hours.

4 Line the bottom of a 2 litre/3½ pint/8 cup Charlotte mould with baking parchment, then grease the bottom and sides.

5 Knock back (punch down) the dough and transfer to a floured surface. Knead in the raisins, lemon rind and citrus peel. Transfer the dough to the mould. Cover and leave to rise until the dough is above the top of the mould, about 2 hours.

6 Preheat the oven to 200°C/400°F/Gas 6. Bake for 15 minutes, cover with foil, and lower the heat to 180°C/350°F/Gas 4. Bake for 30 minutes. Cool in the mould.

Monkey Bread per loaf Energy 3579kcal/15056kJ; Protein 67.9g; Carbohydrate 541.3g, of which sugars 197.6g; Fat 131.3g, of which saturates 35.9g; Cholesterol 305mg; Calcium 878mg; Fibre 19.5g; Sodium 2484mg.

Panettone per loaf Energy 2453kcal/10412kJ; Protein 62.2g; Carbohydrate 515.1g, of which sugars 210.3g; Fat 30.7g, of which saturates 8.2g; Cholesterol 791mg; Calcium 1032mg; Fibre 19.4g; Sodium 1590mg.

Eggy Bread Panettone

The light texture and deliciously spiced flavour of this Italian speciality bread transforms an old favourite into a memorable treat. Serve with a selection of summer fruits for a great finale to a meal.

Makes 4

2 large (US extra large) eggs
50g/2oz/¼ cup butter or 30ml/2 tbsp sunflower oil
4 large panettone slices
30ml/2 tbsp caster (superfine) sugar
450g/1lb/4 cups mixed fresh summer fruit, such as strawberries, raspberries and blackcurrants

1 Break the eggs into a bowl and beat with a fork, then transfer to a shallow dish. Dip the panettone slices into the beaten egg, turning them to coat evenly.

2 Heat the butter or oil in a large non-stick frying pan and add the panettone slices: you will probably have to do this in batches, depending on the size of the pan. Fry the panettone slices over medium heat for 2–3 minutes on each side, until golden brown.

3 Remove the panettone slices from the pan and drain on kitchen paper. Cut the slices in half diagonally and dust with the sugar. Serve immediately with the mixed summer fruit.

Cook's Tip

Panettone, which literally translates as 'big bread', is a light-textured, spiced yeast bread containing sultanas (golden raisins) and candied fruit. Originally a speciality of Milan, it is now sold all over Italy as a Christmas delicacy, and is traditionally given as a gift. Panettoni are widely exported these days, and you can usually buy them from specialist food shops and delicatessens. Packed attractively in pastel-coloured dome-shaped boxes, they can vary in size from small to enormous. Panettone is usually served sliced into wedges and eaten like cake.

Swedish Sultana Bread

A lightly sweetened sultana bread that goes very well with a selection of cheeses, and also tastes excellent when toasted at teatime.

Makes 1

225g/8oz/2 cups strong wholemeal (whole-wheat) bread flour
225g/8oz/2 cups strong white bread flour
5ml/1 tsp easy-blend (rapid-rise) dried yeast
5ml/1 tsp salt
115g/4oz/⅔ cup sultanas (golden raisins)
50g/2oz/½ cup walnuts, chopped
15ml/1 tbsp clear honey
150ml/¼ pint/⅔ cup lukewarm water
175ml/6fl oz/¾ cup lukewarm skimmed milk, plus extra for glazing

1 Grease a baking sheet. Put the flours in a bowl with the yeast, salt and sultanas.

2 Set aside 15ml/1 tbsp of the walnuts and add the remainder to the bowl. Mix the ingredients lightly and make a well in the centre.

3 Dissolve the honey in the water and add the mixture to the bowl with the milk. Stir from the centre outwards, gradually incorporating the flour, and mixing to a soft dough, and adding a little extra water if necessary.

4 Turn the dough on to a floured surface and knead for 5 minutes, or until smooth and elastic. Shape into a 28cm/11in long sausage shape. Place on the prepared baking sheet.

5 Make diagonal cuts down the length of the loaf. Brush the top with milk, sprinkle with the remaining walnuts and leave in a warm place until doubled in size, about 1½ hours. Meanwhile, preheat the oven to 220°C/425°F/Gas 7.

6 Bake the loaf in the oven for 10 minutes, then lower the temperature to 200°C/400°F/Gas 6 and bake for 20 minutes more or until the loaf sounds hollow when tapped underneath. Remove to a wire rack to cool.

Eggy Bread Panettone Energy 344kcal/1442kJ; Protein 8.4g; Carbohydrate 39.5g, of which sugars 17g; Fat 18.1g, of which saturates 7.5g; Cholesterol 151mg; Calcium 89mg; Fibre 0g; Sodium 256mg.

Swedish Sultana Bread Energy 225kcal/953kJ; Protein 5.9g; Carbohydrate 43.9g, of which sugars 9.6g; Fat 4.1g, of which saturates 0.4g; Cholesterol 1mg; Calcium 96mg; Fibre 1.8g; Sodium 12mg.

Fruit Malt Loaf

Malt extract gives this traditional fruity loaf its wonderful chewy consistency, and wholemeal flour adds depth of flavour. When cut in slices and spread with butter, it's just right for giving to hungry guests with afternoon tea. It will keep for up to five days in an airtight container.

Makes 1

250g/9oz/2¼ cups wholemeal (whole-wheat) self-raising (self-rising) flour
a pinch of salt
2.5ml/½ tsp bicarbonate of soda (baking soda)
175g/6oz/1 cup mixed dried fruit
15ml/1 tbsp malt extract
250ml/8fl oz/1 cup milk

1 Preheat the oven to 160°C/325°F/Gas 3. Grease a 900g/2lb loaf tin (pan) with butter and line with baking parchment.

2 Sift the wholemeal flour, salt, bicarbonate of soda into a large bowl. Add the mixed dried fruit and mix well.

3 Heat the malt extract and milk in a small pan, stirring until the malt extract has dissolved. Pour into the bowl with the flour and dried fruit. Mix together well until combined.

4 Using a wooden spoon, pour the mixture into the prepared loaf tin, scraping the all mixture from the sides of the bowl.

5 Bake for 45 minutes until golden, or until a skewer inserted into the loaf comes out clean.

6 Leave to stand for a few minutes, then turn out on to a wire rack to go cold. Remove the lining paper.

Variations

- *For a nutty version, substitute broken pieces of pecans and walnuts in place of half the dried fruit.*
- *For a Rum and Raisin Loaf, replace the mixed dried fruit with raisins, and add a spoonful of rum to the milk.*

Stollen

This is a fruity yeast bread that is traditionally served at Christmas time.

Makes 1

150ml/¼ pint/⅔ cup lukewarm milk
40g/1½oz/3 tbsp caster (superfine) sugar
10ml/2 tsp easy-blend (rapid-rise) dried yeast
350g/12oz/3 cups plain (all-purpose) flour, plus extra for dusting
1.5ml/¼ tsp salt
115g/4oz/½ cup butter, softened
1 egg, beaten
50g/2oz seedless raisins
25g/1oz cup sultanas (golden raisins)
40g/1½oz/⅓ cup candied orange peel, chopped
25g/1oz/¼ cup blanched almonds, chopped
5ml/1 tbsp rum
40g/1½oz/3 tbsp butter, melted
50g/2oz/½ cup icing (confectioners') sugar

1 Mix together the warm milk, sugar and yeast and leave it in a warm place until it is frothy.

2 Sift together the flour and salt, make a well in the centre and pour on the yeast mixture. Add the softened butter and egg and mix to form a soft dough. Mix in the raisins, sultanas, peel and almonds and sprinkle on the rum. Knead the dough on a lightly floured board until it is pliable.

3 Place the dough in a large, greased mixing bowl, cover it with baking parchment and set it aside in a warm place for about 2 hours, until it has doubled in size.

4 Turn the dough out on to a floured board and knead it lightly until it is smooth and elastic again. Shape the dough to a rectangle about 25 × 20cm/10 × 8in. Fold the dough over along one of the long sides and press the two layers together. Cover the loaf and leave it to stand for 20 minutes.

5 Heat the oven to 200°C/400°F/Gas 6. Bake the loaf in the oven for 25–30 minutes, until it is well risen. Allow it to cool slightly on the baking sheet, then brush it with melted butter. Sift the sugar over the top and cool on a wire rack.

Fruit Malt Loaf Energy 260kcal/1103kJ; Protein 5.3g; Carbohydrate 58.6g, of which sugars 25.3g; Fat 2.1g, of which saturates 0.3g; Cholesterol 1mg; Calcium 97mg; Fibre 1.8g; Sodium 38mg.

Stollen per loaf Energy 3828kcal/16064kJ; Protein 55.8g; Carbohydrate 511.7g, of which sugars 256.5g; Fat 178.8g, of which saturates 95.2g; Cholesterol 393mg; Calcium 1064mg; Fibre 21.5g; Sodium 1590mg.

Poppy Seed Roll

Popular in both Poland and Hungary, this loaf has a delicious and unusual filling.

Makes 1

350g/12oz/3 cups unbleached white bread flour, sifted
2.5ml/½ tsp salt
25g/1oz/2 tbsp caster (superfine) sugar
1 egg, lightly beaten
50g/2oz/¼ cup butter, melted
20g/¾ oz fresh yeast
120ml/4fl oz/½ cup lukewarm milk
15ml/1 tbsp toasted flaked (sliced) almonds

For the filling

115g/4oz/⅔ cup poppy seeds
50g/2oz/¼ cup butter
75g/3oz/6 tbsp caster (superfine) sugar
75g/3oz/½ cup raisins
50g/2oz/½ cup ground almonds
50g/2oz/⅓ cup mixed (candied) peel, finely chopped
2.5ml/½ tsp ground cinnamon

For the icing

115g/4oz/1 cup icing (confectioners') sugar
15ml/1 tbsp lemon juice
10–15ml/2–3 tsp water

1 In a bowl stir the flour, salt and sugar together and add the egg and melted butter. Cream the yeast with the milk and add to the mixture and mix to a dough. Turn out on to a floured surface and knead until smooth. Place in a lightly oiled bowl, cover and leave to rise for 1–1½ hours, or until doubled in size.

2 In a pan, pour boiling water over the poppy seeds for the filling. Cool and drain. Melt the butter, add the poppy seeds, stirring, for 1 minute then stir in the rest of the filling ingredients.

3 Turn the dough out on to a floured surface, knock back (punch down) and knead. Roll out into a rectangle and spread the filling to within 2cm/¾in of the edges then roll up the dough. Place on a floured baking sheet. Cover and leave for 30 minutes.

4 Meanwhile, preheat the oven to 190°C/375°F/Gas 5. Bake for 30 minutes, or until golden brown. Cool on a wire rack.

5 To make a stiff icing, mix the icing sugar, lemon juice and water together in a pan and gently heat until warm. Drizzle over the loaf and sprinkle with the flaked almonds. Cool, then serve sliced.

Raisin Bread

Enjoy this loaf with either savoury or sweet dishes.

Makes 2

15ml/1 tbsp active dried yeast
450ml/¾ pint/1¾ cups lukewarm milk
150g/5oz/1 cup raisins
65g/2½oz/½ cup currants
15ml/1 tbsp sherry or brandy
2.5ml/½ tsp freshly grated nutmeg
grated rind of 1 large orange
60g/2¼oz/generous ¼ cup caster (superfine) sugar
15ml/1 tbsp salt
115g/4oz/½ cup butter, melted
700–850g/1lb 8oz–1lb 14oz/6–7½ cups strong white bread flour
1 egg beaten with 15ml/1 tbsp single (light) cream, to glaze

1 Stir the yeast with 120ml/4fl oz/½ cup of the milk and leave to stand for 15 minutes to dissolve. Mix the raisins, currants, sherry or brandy, nutmeg and orange rind together.

2 In another bowl, mix the remaining milk, sugar, salt and half the butter. Add the yeast mixture. With a wooden spoon, stir in half the flour, 150g/5oz at a time, until blended. Add the remaining flour as needed to form a stiff dough. Transfer to a floured surface and knead until smooth and elastic. This will take about 10 minutes. Place in a greased bowl, cover and leave to rise in a warm place until doubled in volume, about 2½ hours.

3 Knock back (punch down) the dough, return to the bowl, cover and leave to rise in a warm place for 30 minutes. Grease two 21 × 11cm/8½ × 4½in loaf tins (pans). Divide the dough in half and roll each half into a 50 × 18cm/20 × 7in rectangle.

4 Brush the rectangles with the remaining melted butter. Sprinkle over the raisin mixture, then roll up tightly, tucking in the ends slightly as you roll. Place in the prepared tins, cover, and leave to rise until almost doubled in volume, about 1 hour. Preheat the oven to 200°C/400°F/Gas 6. Brush the loaves with the egg glaze. Bake for 20 minutes. Lower the oven to 180°C/350°F/Gas 4 and bake until golden, 25–30 minutes more. Cool on wire racks.

Poppy Seed Roll per loaf Energy 4341kcal/18218kJ; Protein 91.1g; Carbohydrate 557g, of which sugars 211.5g; Fat 206.1g, of which saturates 69.5g; Cholesterol 426mg; Calcium 1982mg; Fibre 32.8g; Sodium 986mg.

Raisin Bread per loaf Energy 2187kcal/9239kJ; Protein 46.5g; Carbohydrate 388.3g, of which sugars 121.6g; Fat 58.9g, of which saturates 33.9g; Cholesterol 231mg; Calcium 866mg; Fibre 13g; Sodium 3490mg.

Welsh Bara Brith

This rich, fruity bread – the name literally means 'speckled bread' – is a speciality from Wales.

Makes 1

20g/¾oz fresh yeast
210ml/7fl oz/scant 1 cup lukewarm milk
450g/1lb/4 cups unbleached strong white bread flour
75g/3oz/6 tbsp butter or lard
5ml/1 tsp mixed (apple pie) spice
2.5ml/½ tsp salt
50g/2oz/⅓ cup light brown sugar
1 egg, lightly beaten
115g/4oz/⅔ cup seedless raisins, slightly warmed
75g/3oz/scant ½ cup currants, slightly warmed
40g/1½oz/¼ cup mixed chopped (candied) peel
15–30ml/1–2 tbsp clear honey, for glazing

1 Grease a baking sheet. Blend the yeast with a little of the milk, then stir in the remainder. Set aside for 10 minutes.

2 Sift the flour into a large bowl and rub in the butter or lard until the mixture resembles breadcrumbs. Stir in the mixed spice, salt and sugar and make a well in the centre. Add the yeast mixture and beaten egg to the centre of the flour and mix to a rough dough.

3 Turn out the dough on to a lightly floured surface and knead for about 10 minutes until smooth. Place in a lightly oiled bowl, cover with lightly oiled clear film (plastic wrap) and leave to rise, in a warm place, for 1½ hours, or until doubled in size.

4 Turn out on to a lightly floured surface, knock back (punch down), and knead in the dried fruits and peel. Shape into a round and place on the baking sheet. Cover with oiled clear film and leave to rise for 1 hour, or until the dough doubles in size.

5 Meanwhile, preheat the oven to 200°C/400°F/Gas 6. Bake for 30 minutes or until the bread sounds hollow when tapped on the base. If the bread starts to over-brown, cover it loosely with foil for the last 10 minutes. Transfer the bread to a wire rack, brush with honey and leave to cool.

Bara Brith Teabread

This variation of Welsh bara brith is easy to make – first, the fruit is plumped up by soaking it in tea; and second, the recipe uses self-raising flour. Serve the teabread sliced, with a little butter, if you like.

Makes 1

225g/8oz/1⅓ cups mixed dried fruit and chopped mixed (candied) peel
225ml/8fl oz/1 cup hot strong tea, strained
225g/8oz/2 cups self-raising (self-rising) flour
5ml/1 tsp mixed (apple pie) spice
25g/1oz/2 tbsp butter
100g/3¾oz/scant ½ cup soft light brown sugar
1 egg, lightly beaten

1 Put the fruit into a heatproof bowl and pour the hot tea over it. Cover and leave to stand at room temperature for several hours or overnight.

2 Preheat the oven to 180°C/350°F/Gas 4. Grease a 900g/2lb loaf tin (pan) and line it with baking parchment.

3 Sift the flour and the mixed spice into a large mixing bowl. Add the butter and, with your fingertips, rub it into the flour until the mixture starts to resemble fine breadcrumbs.

4 Stir in the sugar, then add the soaked fruit and its liquid along with the egg. Stir well to make a mixture with a soft consistency.

5 Transfer the mixture to the prepared loaf tin and level the surface. Put into the hot oven and cook for about 1 hour or until a skewer inserted in the centre comes out clean. Turn out on a wire rack and leave to cool completely.

Cook's Tip
The flavour of the loaf can be varied subtly by using a variety of teas – try the distinctive perfume of Earl Grey.

Welsh Bara Brith per loaf Energy 2729kcal/11566kJ; Protein 49.7g; Carbohydrate 557.8g, of which sugars 214.9g; Fat 48.7g, of which saturates 27.5g; Cholesterol 110mg; Calcium 890mg; Fibre 18.9g; Sodium 2414mg.
Bara Brith Teabread per loaf Energy 2024kcal/8588kJ; Protein 33.2g; Carbohydrate 432.7g, of which sugars 261.3g; Fat 29.9g, of which saturates 15g; Cholesterol 244mg; Calcium 565mg; Fibre 11.9g; Sodium 342mg.

Pear & Sultana Teabread

This is an ideal teabread to make when pears are plentiful. There's no better use for autumn windfalls.

Makes 1

25g/1oz/3 cups rolled oats
50g/2oz/¼ cup soft light brown sugar
30ml/2 tbsp pear or apple juice
30ml/2 tbsp sunflower oil
1 large or 2 small ripe pears
115g/4oz/1 cup self-raising (self-rising) flour
115g/4oz/¾ cup sultanas (golden raisins)
2.5ml/½ tsp baking powder
10ml/2 tsp mixed (apple pie) spice
1 egg

1 Preheat the oven to 180°C/350°F/Gas 4. Line a 450g/1lb loaf tin (pan) with baking parchment.

2 Put the oats in a bowl with the sugar, and pour over the pear or apple juice and oil.

3 Mix the ingredients together well using a wooden spoon or electric whisk. Leave to stand for 15 minutes.

4 Quarter, core and grate the pear(s). Add to the bowl with the flour, sultanas, baking powder, spice and egg. Using a wooden spoon, mix thoroughly.

5 Spoon the teabread mixture into the prepared loaf tin. Bake for 55–60 minutes, or until a skewer inserted into the centre comes out clean.

6 Invert the teabread on a wire rack and remove the lining paper. Leave to cool.

Cook's Tips

Health-food stores sell concentrated pear juice, ready for diluting as required. You will also find some good-quality sultanas (golden raisins) there, and organic oats if you want to make a really healthy treat.

Fruity Walnut Teabread

Serve this orange and berry bread either thinly sliced, toasted or plain, with butter or cream cheese and home-made jam.

Makes 1

225g/8oz/2 cups plain (all-purpose) flour
115g/4oz/generous ½ cup caster (superfine) sugar
15ml/1 tbsp baking powder
2.5ml/½ tsp salt
grated rind of 1 large orange
160ml/5½fl oz/generous ⅔ cup fresh orange juice
2 eggs, lightly beaten
75g/3oz/6 tbsp butter or margarine, melted
115g/4oz/1 cup fresh cranberries or bilberries
50g/2oz/½ cup chopped walnuts

1 Preheat the oven to 180°C/350°F/Gas 4. Line a 23 × 13cm/9 × 5in loaf tin (pan) with baking parchment and grease the paper.

2 Sift the flour, sugar, baking powder and salt into a mixing bowl. Then stir in the orange rind. Make a well in the centre and add the fresh orange juice, eggs and melted butter or margarine. Stir from the centre until the ingredients are blended; do not overmix. Add the berries and walnuts, and stir until blended.

3 Transfer the mixture to the prepared tin and bake until a skewer inserted in the centre of the loaf comes out clean, about 45–50 minutes. Leave to cool in the tin for 10 minutes before transferring to a wire rack to cool completely.

Cook's Tip

Margarine can be used instead of butter for most recipes except those with a high fat content, such as shortbread. Margarine will not, however, produce the same flavour as butter, but it is usually less expensive, so can be useful. Block margarines are better than soft margarines for teabreads, buns and muffins.

Pear and Sultana Teabread Energy 184kcal/780kJ; Protein 3.1g; Carbohydrate 36.3g, of which sugars 23.1g; Fat 4g, of which saturates 0.6g; Cholesterol 24mg; Calcium 43mg; Fibre 1.8g; Sodium 16mg.

Fruity Walnut Teabread per loaf Energy 2356kcal/9885kJ; Protein 43.9g; Carbohydrate 317g, of which sugars 145.2g; Fat 110.3g, of which saturates 45.4g; Cholesterol 540mg; Calcium 557mg; Fibre 12.4g; Sodium 630mg.

Barm Brack

The traditional yeasted Hallowe'en barm brack contains all kinds of symbolic tokens, of which the best known is a ring. Serve this version sliced and buttered while still warm.

Makes 2

450g/1lb/4 cups plain (all-purpose) flour
5ml/1 tsp mixed (apple pie) spice
2.5ml/½ tsp salt
15g/½oz easy-blend (rapid-rise) dried yeast
75g/3oz/6 tbsp soft dark brown sugar
115g/4oz/½ cup butter, melted
300ml/½ pint/1¼ cups lukewarm milk
1 egg, lightly beaten
375g/13oz/generous 2 cups dried mixed fruit
25g/1oz/⅓ cup chopped mixed (candied) peel
15ml/1 tbsp caster (superfine) sugar

1 Butter two 450g/1lb loaf tins (pans). Mix the flour, spice, salt, yeast and sugar in a large bowl and make a well in the centre.

2 Mix the melted butter with the tepid milk and lightly beaten egg and add to the bowl. Add the mixed fruit and peel to the bowl and mix well.

3 Turn the mixture into the loaf tins. Leave in a warm place for about 30 minutes to rise. Meanwhile, preheat the oven to 200°C/400°F/Gas 6.

4 When the dough has doubled in size, bake in the hot oven for about 45 minutes, or until the loaves begin to shrink slightly from the sides of the tins; when turned out and rapped underneath they should sound hollow.

5 Make a glaze by mixing the caster sugar with 30ml/2 tbsp boiling water. Remove the loaves from the oven and brush over with the glaze.

6 Return the loaves to the oven for about 3 minutes, or until the tops have turned a rich shiny brown. Turn on to a wire rack to cool slightly for 5–10 minutes before serving.

Banana, Fig & Brazil Nut Teabread

Mashed bananas are a classic ingredient in teabreads, and help to create a moist texture as well as adding a full fruity flavour.

Makes 1

225g/8oz/2 cups plain (all-purpose) flour
10ml/2 tsp baking powder
5ml/1 tsp mixed (apple pie) spice
115g/4oz/½ cup butter, diced
115g/4oz/½ cup light soft brown sugar
2 eggs, lightly beaten
30ml/2 tbsp milk
30ml/2 tbsp dark rum
2 bananas
115g/4oz/⅔ cup dried figs, chopped
50g/2oz/⅓ cup brazil nuts, chopped

For the decoration

8 whole brazil nuts
4 whole dried figs, halved
30ml/2 tbsp apricot jam
5ml/1 tsp dark rum

1 Preheat the oven to 180°C/350°F/Gas 4. Grease and base-line a 23 × 13cm/9 × 5in loaf tin (pan). Sift the flour, baking powder and mixed spice into a bowl.

2 Rub in the butter using your fingertips or a pastry blender until the mixture resembles fine breadcrumbs. Stir in the sugar.

3 Make a well in the centre and work in the eggs, milk and rum until combined. Peel and mash the bananas. Stir in the mashed bananas, chopped figs and brazil nuts and transfer to the prepared loaf tin.

4 To decorate the teabread press the whole brazil nuts and halved figs gently into the mixture, to form an attractive pattern. Bake for 1¼ hours, or until a skewer inserted in the centre comes out clean. Cool in the tin for 10 minutes, then transfer to a wire rack.

5 Heat the jam and rum together in a small pan. Increase the heat and boil for 1 minute. Remove from the heat and pass through a fine sieve (strainer). Cool the glaze slightly, brush over the warm loaf, and leave to cool completely.

Barm Brack per loaf Energy 2019kcal/8524kJ; Protein 34.9g; Carbohydrate 364.6g, of which sugars 193.2g; Fat 57g, of which saturates 32.8g; Cholesterol 246mg; Calcium 704mg; Fibre 11.7g; Sodium 590mg.

Banana, Fig and Brazil Nut Teabread per loaf Energy 3095kcal/12984kJ; Protein 49.5g; Carbohydrate 405.9g, of which sugars 229.5g; Fat 145.6g, of which saturates 72.2g; Cholesterol 628mg; Calcium 874mg; Fibre 19.9g; Sodium 938mg.

Bilberry Teabread

A lovely crumbly topping with a hint of cinnamon makes this teabread extra special.

Makes 1

50g/2oz/¼ cup butter or margarine, at room temperature
175g/6oz/scant 1 cup caster (superfine) sugar
1 egg, at room temperature
120ml/4fl oz/½ cup milk
225g/8oz/2 cups plain (all-purpose) flour
10ml/2 tsp baking powder
2.5ml/½ tsp salt
275g/10oz/2½ cups fresh bilberries or blueberries

For the topping
115g/4oz/generous ½ cup caster (superfine) sugar
40g/1½oz/⅓ cup plain (all-purpose) flour
2.5ml/½ tsp ground cinnamon
50g/2oz/¼ cup butter, cut into pieces

1 Preheat the oven to 190°C/375°F/Gas 5. Grease a 23cm/9in baking dish.

2 With an electric mixer, or by hand, cream the butter or margarine with the sugar until light and fluffy. Add the egg and beat to combine, then mix in the milk until well blended.

3 Sift over the flour, baking powder and salt, and stir the mixture just enough to blend the ingredients. Add the bilberries and stir gently. Transfer the teabread mixture to the prepared baking dish.

4 To make the topping, place the caster sugar, flour, ground cinnamon and butter in a mixing bowl. Cut the butter into the dry ingredients using a pastry blender until the mixture resembles coarse breadcrumbs. Sprinkle the topping over the mixture in the baking dish. Bake until a skewer inserted in the centre comes out clean, about 45 minutes. Serve warm or cold.

Variation
In late summer and early autumn, when blackberries are plentiful, try to gather some to use instead of bilberries for this delicious teabread.

Raspberry & Almond Teabread

Fresh raspberries and almonds combine perfectly to flavour this mouthwatering loaf, with its crunchy, toasted flaked-almond topping. Serve warm with a spoonful of crème fraîche as part of a tea table buffet. Eat this cake on the day of making.

Makes 1

175g/6oz/1½ cups self-raising (self-rising) flour
90g/3½oz/7 tbsp butter
90g/3½oz/½ cup caster (superfine) sugar
40g/1½oz/scant ½ cup ground almonds
2 eggs, beaten
30ml/2 tbsp milk
115g/4oz/1 cup fresh raspberries or partly thawed frozen raspberries
30ml/2 tbsp toasted flaked (sliced) almonds

1 Preheat the oven to 180°C/350°F/Gas 4.

2 Grease a 450g/1lb loaf tin (pan) and then line it with a sheet of baking parchment.

3 Sift the self-raising flour into a large mixing bowl or the bowl of a food processor. Add the butter and rub into the flour with your hands, or process, until the mixture resembles fine breadcrumbs.

4 Stir in the sugar and ground almonds, then gradually mix in the eggs and milk, and beat until smooth.

5 Gently fold the raspberries into the mixture, being careful not to crush them.

6 Spoon the mixture into the prepared tin and sprinkle over the flaked almonds.

7 Bake for about 55 minutes, or until a skewer inserted into the centre comes out clean. Cool in the tin for 5 minutes, then turn out on to a wire rack to go cold. Remove the lining paper.

Bilberry Teabread Energy 374kcal/1575kJ; Protein 5g; Carbohydrate 66.2g, of which sugars 40.9g; Fat 11.7g, of which saturates 6.9g; Cholesterol 51mg; Calcium 104mg; Fibre 2.1g; Sodium 95mg.

Raspberry and Almond Teabread Energy 215kcal/902kJ; Protein 4.3g; Carbohydrate 24.1g, of which sugars 10.5g; Fat 12g, of which saturates 5.3g; Cholesterol 44mg; Calcium 59mg; Fibre 1.4g; Sodium 79mg.

Twelfth Night Bread

This special cake is baked in Spain for Epiphany on January 6. Traditionally, it contains a bean, coin or tiny china doll, and whoever finds it is king of the party.

Makes 1

450g/1lb/4 cups unbleached strong white bread flour
2.5ml/½ tsp salt
25g/1oz fresh yeast
140ml/scant ¼ pint/scant ⅔ cup mixed warm milk and water
75g/3oz/6 tbsp butter
75g/3oz/6 tbsp caster (superfine) sugar
10ml/2 tsp grated lemon rind
10ml/2 tsp grated orange rind
2 eggs
15ml/1 tbsp brandy
15ml/1 tbsp orange flower water
silver coin or dried bean (optional)
1 egg white, lightly beaten

For the decoration
mixed candied fruit slices
flaked (sliced) almonds

1 Lightly grease a large baking sheet. Sift together the flour and salt into a large bowl. Make a well in the centre. Mix the yeast with the milk and water until dissolved. Pour into the well and stir in enough of the flour to make a thick batter. Sprinkle a little of the remaining flour over the top and leave in a warm place, for about 15 minutes or until frothy.

2 Beat the butter and sugar until soft and creamy. Add the citrus rinds, eggs, brandy and orange flower water to the flour mixture and mix to a sticky dough. Gradually add the butter mixture and beat until smooth and elastic. Cover with lightly oiled clear film (plastic wrap) and leave for about 1½ hours

3 Knock back (punch down) the dough and turn on to a floured surface. Knead gently for 2 or 3 minutes, adding the coin or bean, if using, then roll out into a long strip measuring about 65 × 13cm/26 × 5in. Roll up from one long side, join the ends and place seam side down on the baking sheet. Cover and leave in a warm place for 1–1½ hours until doubled in size.

4 Preheat the oven to 180°C/350°F/Gas 4. Brush the ring with lightly beaten egg white and decorate with glacé fruit slices. Sprinkle with flaked almonds and bake for 30–35 minutes.

Danish Julekage

This exotic bread is enriched with butter and a selection of glacé and dried fruits.

Makes 1

25g/1oz fresh yeast
75ml/5 tbsp lukewarm milk
450g/1lb/4 cups unbleached white bread flour
10ml/2 tsp salt
75g/3oz/6 tbsp butter
15 cardamom pods
2.5ml/½ tsp vanilla extract
50g/2oz/⅓ cup soft light brown sugar
grated rind of ½ lemon
2 eggs, lightly beaten
50g/2oz/¼ cup ready-to-eat dried apricots, chopped
50g/2oz/¼ cup glacé (candied) pineapple pieces, chopped
50g/2oz/¼ cup red and green glacé (candied) cherries, chopped
25g/1oz/3 tbsp dried dates, chopped
25g/1oz/2 tbsp crystallized stem ginger, chopped

For the glaze
1 egg white
10ml/2 tsp water

For the decoration
15ml/1 tbsp caster (superfine) sugar
2.5ml/½ tsp ground cinnamon
8 pecan nuts or whole blanched almonds

1 Lightly grease a 23 × 13cm/9 × 5in loaf tin (pan). In a measuring jug (cup), cream the yeast with the milk. Sift the flour and salt into a large bowl. Add the butter and rub in. Make a well in the centre and add the yeast mixture. Stir in sufficient flour to form a thick batter. Set aside for 15 minutes.

2 Remove the seeds from the cardamom pods. Put them in a mortar and crush with a pestle. Add them to the flour with the vanilla extract, sugar, lemon rind, eggs and sufficient lukewarm water to mix to a soft dough. Knead for 8–10 minutes until smooth and elastic. Place in a lightly oiled bowl, cover and leave in a warm place, for 1–1½ hours.

3 Knock back (punch down) the dough and turn it out on to a lightly floured surface. Flatten into a rectangle and sprinkle over half of the apricots, pineapple, cherries, dates and ginger. Fold the sides into the centre and then fold in half to contain the fruit. Flatten into a rectangle again and sprinkle over the remaining fruit. Fold and knead gently to distribute the fruit. Cover the and leave to rest for 10 minutes.

4 Roll the fruited dough into a rectangle 38 × 25cm/15 × 10in. With a short side facing you, fold the bottom third up lengthways and the top third down, tucking in the sides, to form a 23 × 13cm/9 × 5in loaf. Place in the prepared tin, seam side down. Cover and leave to rise, in a warm place, for 1 hour, or until the dough has reached the top of the tin.

5 Meanwhile, preheat the oven to 180°C/350°F/Gas 4. Using a sharp knife, slash the top of the loaf lengthways and then make diagonal slits on either side.

6 Mix together the egg white and water for the glaze, and brush over the top. Mix the sugar and cinnamon in a bowl, then sprinkle over the top. Decorate with pecan nuts or almonds. Bake for 45–50 minutes, or until risen and browned. Transfer to a wire rack to cool.

Twelfth Night Bread Energy 217kcal/914kJ; Protein 4.8g; Carbohydrate 36g, of which sugars 7.4g; Fat 6.7g, of which saturates 3.7g; Cholesterol 45mg; Calcium 69mg; Fibre 1.2g; Sodium 54mg.

Danish Julekage per loaf Energy 2703kcal/11407kJ; Protein 59.2g; Carbohydrate 468.3g, of which sugars 125.4g; Fat 78.6g, of which saturates 44.6g; Cholesterol 553mg; Calcium 814mg; Fibre 20g; Sodium 4685mg.

Chocolate Bread

In Italy it is the custom to serve this bread as a snack with mascarpone or Gorgonzola cheese and a glass of red wine. Although this combination may sound unusual, it is really delicious. Chocolate bread tastes good spread with butter at teatime, and is also excellent when toasted the next day for breakfast, served with butter and jam.

Makes 2

450g/1lb/4 cups strong plain (all-purpose) flour
2.5ml/½ tsp salt
30ml/2 tbsp butter
30ml/2 tbsp caster (superfine) sugar
10ml/2 tsp easy-blend (rapid-rise) dried yeast
30ml/2 tbsp unsweetened cocoa powder
75g/3oz/½ cup plain (semisweet) chocolate chips
melted butter, for brushing

1 Sift the flour and salt into a bowl, cut in the butter with a knife, then stir in the sugar, yeast and cocoa powder.

2 Gradually add 300 ml/½ pint/1¼ cups of tepid water to the flour mixture, stirring with a spoon at first, then gathering the dough together with your hands.

3 Turn the dough out on to a floured surface and knead for about 10 minutes until smooth and elastic.

4 Cut the dough in half and knead half the chocolate chips into each piece of dough until they are evenly distributed.

5 Shape into rounds, place on lightly oiled baking sheets and cover with oiled clear film. Leave to rise in a warm place for 1–2 hours until the dough has doubled in size.

6 Preheat the oven to 220°C/425°F/Gas 7. Uncover the loaves and bake for 10 minutes, then reduce the oven temperature to 190°C/375°F/Gas 5 and bake for a further 15–20 minutes.

7 Place the loaves on a wire rack and brush liberally with butter. Cover with a dish towel and leave to cool.

Chocolate Chip Walnut Loaf

This is a nutty, chocolate loaf that is the perfect treat to accompany an afternoon cup of tea or coffee.

Makes 1

115g/4oz/generous ½ cup caster (superfine) sugar
115g/4oz/1 cup plain (all-purpose) flour
5ml/1 tsp baking powder
60ml/4 tbsp cornflour (cornstarch)
115g/4oz/½ cup butter, softened
2 eggs, beaten
5ml/1 tsp vanilla extract
30ml/2 tbsp currants or raisins
25g/1oz/¼ cup walnuts, finely chopped
grated rind of ½ lemon
45ml/3 tbsp plain (semisweet) chocolate chips
icing (confectioners') sugar, for dusting

1 Preheat the oven to 180°C/350°F/Gas 4. Grease and line a 22 × 12cm/8½ × 4½in loaf tin (pan). Sprinkle 25ml/1½ tbsp of the caster sugar into the tin and tilt to distribute the sugar in an even layer over the bottom and sides. Shake out any excess sugar from the tin.

2 Sift the flour, baking powder and cornflour into a mixing bowl. Repeat this twice more. Set aside.

3 With an electric mixer, cream the butter until soft. Add the remaining sugar and continue beating until light and fluffy. Add the eggs, one at a time, beating after each addition.

4 Gently fold the dry ingredients into the butter mixture, in three batches; do not overmix.

5 Fold in the vanilla extract, currants or raisins, walnuts, lemon rind and chocolate chips until just blended.

6 Pour the mixture into the prepared tin and bake for 45–50 minutes. Leave to cool in the tin for 5 minutes before transferring to a wire rack to cool completely. Place on a serving plate and dust with an even layer of icing sugar before serving. Alternatively, top with glacé icing and decorate with walnut halves.

Chocolate Bread per loaf Energy 1148kcal/4855kJ; Protein 29g; Carbohydrate 210g, of which sugars 42g; Fat 27g, of which saturates 15g; Cholesterol 34mg; Calcium 340mg; Fibre 8g; Sodium 649mg.

Chocolate Chip Walnut Loaf per loaf Energy 3759kcal/15650kJ; Protein 60.1g; Carbohydrate 294g, of which sugars 149.5g; Fat 268.6g, of which saturates 76.5g; Cholesterol 626mg; Calcium 543mg; Fibre 12.5g; Sodium 913mg.

Chocolate Chip Marzipan Loaf

This is the perfect sweet loaf for chocolate lovers who enjoy the rich, nutty taste of marzipan.

Makes 1

115g/4oz/½ cup unsalted (sweet) butter, softened
150g/5oz/¾ cup light muscovado (brown) sugar
2 eggs, beaten
45ml/3 tbsp unsweetened cocoa powder
150g/5oz/1¼ cups self-raising (self-rising) flour
130g/4½oz marzipan
60ml/4 tbsp plain (semisweet) chocolate chips

1 Preheat the oven to 180°C/350°F/Gas 4. Lightly grease a 900g/2lb loaf tin (pan) and line the base of it with a sheet of baking parchment.

2 Cream the butter and sugar together in a large mixing bowl, beating with a wooden spoon until the mixture becomes light and fluffy.

3 Add the eggs to the creamed mixture one at a time, beating well after each addition until well combined.

4 Sift the cocoa powder and flour over the mixture and fold in evenly with a metal spoon until blended.

5 Chop the marzipan into small pieces with a sharp knife. Transfer to a bowl and mix with the chocolate chips. Set aside about 60ml/4 tbsp and gently fold the rest of the mixture evenly into the cake batter.

6 Scrape the mixture into the prepared tin and level the top with a knife. Sprinkle the top with the reserved marzipan and chocolate chips.

7 Bake the loaf in the oven for 45–50 minutes or until the loaf is risen and firm. Leave to cool for a few minutes in the tin to firm up, then it turn out on to a wire rack to cool completely, before slicing and serving.

Bitter Marmalade Chocolate Loaf

Zesty marmalade provides this loaf with the delicious combination of chocolate and orange.

Makes 1

115g/4oz plain (semisweet) chocolate, chopped into pieces
3 eggs
200g/7oz/1 cup caster (superfine) sugar
175ml/6fl oz/¾ cup sour cream
200g/7oz/1¾ cups self-raising (self-rising) flour

For the filling and glaze
175g/6oz/⅔ cup bitter orange marmalade
115g/4oz plain (semisweet) chocolate, chopped into pieces
60ml/4 tbsp sour cream
shredded orange rind, to decorate

1 Preheat the oven to 180°C/350°F/Gas 4. Lightly grease a 900g/2lb loaf tin (pan), then line it with baking parchment. Melt the chocolate in a double boiler or a heatproof bowl over a pan of hot water, stirring occasionally, until smooth.

2 Combine the eggs and sugar in a mixing bowl. Using a hand-held electric mixer, whisk the mixture until it is thick and creamy, then stir in the sour cream and the melted chocolate. Fold in the self-raising flour evenly.

3 Scrape the mixture into the prepared tin and bake for about 1 hour or until well risen and firm to the touch. Cool for a few minutes in the tin, then turn out on to a wire rack and leave the loaf to cool completely.

4 Make the filling. Spoon two-thirds of the marmalade into a small pan and melt over a gentle heat, stirring constantly. Melt the chocolate and stir it into the marmalade. Add the sour cream and mix until thoroughly combined.

5 Slice the cake across into three layers and sandwich the layers back together with about half the marmalade filling. Spread the rest of the filling mixture over the top of the cake and set aside until set. Spoon the remaining marmalade over the cake as a glaze. To finish, sprinkle the shredded orange rind on top, to decorate.

Chocolate Chip Marzipan Loaf per loaf Energy 2919kcal/12240kJ; Protein 46.1g; Carbohydrate 368.6g, of which sugars 248.6g; Fat 150.7g, of which saturates 80.5g; Cholesterol 629mg; Calcium 513mg; Fibre 14.1g; Sodium 1305mg.
Bitter Marmalade Chocolate Loaf Energy 475kcal/2004kJ; Protein 7.1g; Carbohydrate 80.1g, of which sugars 60.8g; Fat 16.3g, of which saturates 9.1g; Cholesterol 91mg; Calcium 101mg; Fibre 1.6g; Sodium 56mg.

Pane al Cioccolato

This slightly sweet chocolate bread from Italy is often served with creamy mascarpone cheese as a dessert or snack. The dark chocolate pieces add texture to the light loaf.

Makes 1

350g/12oz/3 cups unbleached white bread flour
25ml/1½ tbsp unsweetened cocoa powder
2.5ml/½ tsp salt
25g/1oz/2 tbsp caster (superfine) sugar
15g/½oz fresh yeast
250ml/8fl oz/1 cup lukewarm water
25g/1oz/2 tbsp butter, softened
75g/3oz plain (semisweet) continental chocolate, coarsely chopped
melted butter, for brushing

1 Lightly grease a 15cm/6in round deep cake tin (pan). Sift the flour, cocoa powder and salt together into a large bowl. Stir in the sugar. Make a well in the centre.

2 Cream the yeast with 60ml/4 tbsp of the water, then stir in the rest. Add to the centre of the flour and mix to a dough.

3 Knead in the softened butter, then knead on a floured surface until smooth and elastic. Place in a lightly oiled bowl, cover with lightly oiled clear film (plastic wrap) and leave to rise, in a warm place, for about 1 hour, or until doubled in size.

4 Turn out on to a lightly floured surface and knock back (punch down). Gently knead in the chocolate, then cover with lightly oiled clear film; leave to rest for 5 minutes.

5 Shape the dough into a round and place in the tin. Cover with lightly oiled clear film and leave to rise, in a warm place, for 45 minutes, or until doubled; the dough should reach the top of the tin. Preheat the oven to 220°C/425°F/Gas 7.

6 Bake for 10 minutes, then reduce to 190°C/375°F/Gas 5 and bake for a further 25–30 minutes. Brush with melted butter and cool on a wire rack.

Cappuccino Chocolate Panettone

This light Italian bread is traditionally a tall loaf with a dome on the top, formed by the rich yeasted dough as it rises. The chocolate chips give a lovely texture.

Makes 1

450g/1lb/4 cups strong plain (all-purpose) flour
2.5ml/½ tsp salt
75g/3oz/scant ½ cup caster (superfine) sugar
7g/¼oz easy-blend (rapid-rise) dried yeast
115g/4oz/½ cup butter
100ml/3½fl oz/scant ½ cup very hot strong brewed espresso coffee
100ml/3½fl oz/scant ½ cup milk
4 egg yolks
115g/4oz/⅔ cup plain (semisweet) chocolate chips
beaten egg, to glaze

1 Preheat the oven to 190°C/375°F/Gas 5. Lightly grease and line a deep 14–15cm/5½–6in cake tin (pan) with baking parchment. Sift the flour and salt into a large bowl. Stir in the sugar and yeast.

2 Add the butter to the coffee and stir until melted. Stir in the milk, then add to the dry ingredients with the egg yolks. Mix together to make a dough.

3 Turn the dough out on to a floured surface and knead for 10 minutes, until smooth. Gently knead in the chocolate chips.

4 Shape into a ball, place in the tin and cover with oiled clear film (plastic wrap). Leave to rise in a warm place for 1 hour or until the dough reaches the top of the tin. Lightly brush with beaten egg and bake for 35 minutes.

5 Turn down the oven to 180°C/350°F/Gas 4 and cover the panettone with foil if it has browned enough. Cook for a further 10–15 minutes, or until done.

6 Allow the panettone to cool in the tin for 10 minutes, then transfer to a wire rack. Remove the lining paper just before slicing and serving.

Pane al Cioccolato per loaf Energy 1939kcal/8188kJ; Protein 41.5g; Carbohydrate 348.7g, of which sugars 78.5g; Fat 51.5g, of which saturates 29.5g; Cholesterol 58mg; Calcium 565mg; Fibre 15.8g; Sodium 406mg.

Cappuccino Chocolate Panettone Energy 445kcal/1871kJ; Protein 8g; Carbohydrate 63.3g, of which sugars 20.3g; Fat 19.5g, of which saturates 10.9g; Cholesterol 133mg; Calcium 118mg; Fibre 2.1g; Sodium 100mg.

Ensaimadas

These sweet bread rolls are a popular snack in the Philippines, and come with various fillings.

Makes 10–12

30ml/2 tbsp caster (superfine) sugar, plus extra for sprinkling
150ml/¼ pint/⅔ cup warm water
15ml/1 tbsp active dried yeast
450g/1lb/4 cups strong white bread flour
5ml/1 tsp salt
115g/4oz/½ cup butter, softened, plus 30ml/2 tbsp melted butter for the filling
4 egg yolks
90–120ml/6–8 tbsp warm milk
115g/4oz/1 cup grated Cheddar cheese, or similar well-flavoured hard cheese

1 Dissolve 5ml/1 tsp of the sugar in the warm water, then sprinkle in the dried yeast. Stir, then set aside for 10 minutes or until frothy. Sift the flour and salt into a large bowl.

2 Cream the softened butter with the remaining sugar in a large bowl. When it is fluffy, beat in the egg yolks and a little of the sifted flour. Gradually stir in the remaining flour with the yeast mixture and enough milk to form a soft but not sticky dough. Transfer to an oiled plastic bag. Close the bag loosely, leaving plenty of room for the dough to rise. Leave in a warm place for about 1 hour, until the dough doubles in size.

3 On a lightly floured surface, knock back (punch down) the dough, then roll it out into a large rectangle. Brush the surface with half the melted butter, sprinkle with the cheese, then roll up from a long side like a Swiss (jelly) roll. Knead the dough thoroughly, then divide into 10–12 pieces.

4 Roll each piece of dough into a thin rope, 38cm/15in long. On greased baking sheets, coil each rope into a loose spiral. Leave to rise for about 45 minutes or until doubled in size. Preheat the oven to 220°C/425°F/Gas 7. Bake the ensaimadas for 15–20 minutes, until golden. Remove from the oven, then brush with the remaining melted butter and sprinkle with caster sugar. Serve warm.

Mallorcan Sweet Rolls

These spiral- or snail-shaped rolls are a popular Spanish treat enjoyed at breakfast time. Traditionally, lard, or *saim*, was used to brush over the sweetened dough.

Makes 16

225g/8oz/2 cups unbleached white bread flour
2.5ml/½ tsp salt
50g/2oz/¼ cup caster (superfine) sugar
15g/½oz fresh yeast
75ml/5 tbsp lukewarm milk
1 egg
30ml/2 tbsp sunflower oil
50g/2oz/¼ cup butter, melted
icing (confectioner's) sugar, for dusting

1 Grease two baking sheets. Sift the flour and salt into a large mixing bowl. Stir in the sugar and make a well in the centre.

2 Cream the yeast with the milk, pour into the well, then sprinkle a little of the flour mixture evenly over the top of the liquid. Leave in a warm place for 15 minutes, or until frothy.

3 Beat the egg and oil together. Add to the flour mixture and mix to a smooth dough. Turn out on to a lightly floured surface and knead for 8–10 minutes until smooth and elastic. Place in a lightly oiled bowl, cover with oiled clear film (plastic wrap) and leave in a warm place for 1 hour, or until doubled in bulk.

4 Turn out the dough on to a lightly floured surface. Knock back (punch down) and divide into 16 equal pieces. Shape each piece into a thin rope about 38cm/15in long. Pour the melted butter on to a plate and dip the ropes into the butter to coat.

5 On the baking sheets, curl each rope into a loose spiral, spacing well apart. Tuck the ends under to seal. Cover with lightly oiled clear film and leave in a warm place for about 45 minutes, or until doubled in size.

6 Meanwhile, preheat the oven to 190°C/375°F/Gas 5. Brush the rolls with water and dust with icing sugar. Bake for 10 minutes, or until light golden brown. Cool on a wire rack. Dust again with icing sugar and serve warm.

Ensaimadas Energy 293kcal/1228kJ; Protein 7.7g; Carbohydrate 32.2g, of which sugars 3.6g; Fat 15.7g, of which saturates 9.1g; Cholesterol 103mg; Calcium 144mg; Fibre 1.6g; Sodium 314mg.

Mallorcan Sweet Rolls Energy 327kcal/1371kJ; Protein 8.7g; Carbohydrate 38.6g, of which sugars 4.3g; Fat 16.1g, of which saturates 9.3g; Cholesterol 117mg; Calcium 172mg; Fibre 1.4g; Sodium 162mg.

New England Fantans

These fantail rolls look stylish, and are so versatile that they are equally suitable for a simple snack or a gourmet dinner party.

Makes 9

15g/½oz fresh yeast
75ml/5 tbsp buttermilk, at room temperature
10ml/2 tsp caster (superfine) sugar
75ml/5 tbsp milk
65g/2½oz/5 tbsp butter
375g/13oz/3¼ cups unbleached white bread flour
5ml/1 tsp salt
1 egg, lightly beaten

1 Grease a muffin sheet with 9 × 7.5cm/3in cups or foil cases. Mix the yeast with the buttermilk and sugar and then leave to stand for 15 minutes.

2 In a pan, heat the milk with 40g/1½oz/3 tbsp of the butter until the butter has melted. Cool until lukewarm.

3 Sift the flour and salt together into a large bowl. Add the yeast mixture, milk mixture and egg and mix to a soft dough. Turn out on to a lightly floured surface and knead for about 5–8 minutes until smooth and elastic. Place in a lightly oiled bowl, cover with oiled clear film (plastic wrap) and leave in a warm place, for about 1 hour, until doubled in size.

4 Turn out on to a lightly floured surface, knock back (punch down) and knead until smooth and elastic. Roll into an oblong measuring 45 × 30cm/18 × 12in and about 5mm/¼in thick. Melt the remaining butter, brush over the dough and cut it lengthways into five equal strips. Stack on top of each other and cut across into nine equal 5cm/2in strips.

5 Pinch one side of each layered strip together, then place pinched side down into a prepared muffin cup or foil case. Cover with lightly oiled clear film and leave to rise, in a warm place, for 30–40 minutes, or until the fantans have almost doubled in size. Preheat the oven to 200°C/400°F/Gas 6. Bake for 20 minutes, or until golden. Cool on a wire rack.

Buchty

Popular in both Poland and Germany as breakfast treats, these rolls are also excellent split and toasted, and served with cured meats.

Makes 16

450g/1lb/4 cups unbleached white bread flour
5ml/1 tsp salt
50g/2oz/¼ cup caster (superfine) sugar
90g/3½oz/scant ½ cup butter
120ml/4fl oz/½ cup milk
20g/¾oz fresh yeast
3 eggs, lightly beaten
40g/1½oz/3 tbsp butter, melted
icing (confectioners') sugar, for dusting

1 Grease a 20cm/8in square loose-bottomed cake tin (pan). Sift the flour and salt into a large bowl, then stir in the sugar. Make a well in the centre.

2 Melt 50g/2oz/¼ cup of the butter in a small pan, then remove from the heat and stir in the milk. Leave to cool until lukewarm. Stir the yeast into the milk mixture until it has dissolved.

3 Pour into the centre of the flour and stir in sufficient flour to form a thick batter. Sprinkle with a little of the surrounding flour, cover and leave in a warm place for 30 minutes.

4 Gradually beat in the eggs and remaining flour to form a soft, smooth dough. This will take about 10 minutes. Cover with oiled clear film (plastic wrap) and leave in a warm place, for about 1½ hours, or until doubled in size.

5 Turn out the dough on to a floured surface and knock back (punch down). Divide into 16 equal pieces and shape into rounds. Melt the remaining butter, roll the rounds in it to coat, then place, slightly apart, in the tin. Cover with oiled clear film and leave to rise for about 1 hour, or until doubled in size.

6 Preheat the oven to 190°C/375°F/Gas 5. Spoon any remaining melted butter evenly over the rolls and bake for 25 minutes, or until golden brown. Cool on a wire rack. If serving as a breakfast bread, dust with icing sugar.

New England Fantans per roll Energy 215kcal/905kJ; Protein 5.2g; Carbohydrate 34.4g, of which sugars 2.6g; Fat 7.2g, of which saturates 4.3g; Cholesterol 39mg; Calcium 83mg; Fibre 1.3g; Sodium 291mg.

Buchty per roll Energy 185kcal/779kJ; Protein 4.1g; Carbohydrate 25.5g, of which sugars 4.1g; Fat 8.2g, of which saturates 4.8g; Cholesterol 55mg; Calcium 57mg; Fibre 0.9g; Sodium 79mg.

Oat & Cinnamon Breakfast Rolls

The combination of sugar and cinnamon is perfect at breakfast, especially with a cup of aromatic coffee.

Makes 12

350g/12oz/3 cups strong white bread flour
115g/4oz/1 cup quinoa flakes
50g/2oz/scant ½ cup rolled oats
10ml/2 tsp easy-blend (rapid-rise) dried yeast
7.5ml/1½ tsp salt
30ml/2 tbsp soft light brown sugar
10ml/2 tsp ground cinnamon
175ml/6fl oz/¾ cup boiled water
175ml/6fl oz/¾ cup milk
a little milk and 10ml/2 tsp soft light brown sugar, to glaze
butter and clear honey or fresh fruit, to serve

1 Sift the flour into a large bowl, then stir in the quinoa flakes, oats and dried yeast. Make a well in the centre.

2 Mix the boiled water with the milk to make a lukewarm liquid, then add this to the dry ingredients, stirring to a dough.

3 Transfer the dough to a floured board and knead for 5–8 minutes until the dough is smooth and elastic. Place in a lightly oiled bowl, cover and leave in a warm place for 1–1½ hours, until nearly doubled in size.

4 Knock back (punch down) the dough and knead on a lightly floured surface for a further few minutes.

5 Divide the dough into 12 rolls, braiding or shaping them as desired. Place on greased baking sheets.

6 Glaze the rolls with milk, sprinkle with light brown sugar and leave for a further 20 minutes in a warm place. Preheat the oven to 220°C/425°F/Gas 7.

7 Bake for 12–15 minutes, until the rolls are risen and golden and sound hollow when tapped. Allow to cool on a wire rack for 15 minutes. They are delicious served warm with clear honey and a platter of fresh fruit.

Sweet Buns

These round sweet buns are a traditional Czech recipe.

Makes 12–16

250ml/7fl oz/scant 1 cup milk
80g/3oz caster (superfine) sugar
30g/1¼oz fresh yeast
500g/1¼lb plain (all-purpose) flour, plus extra for dusting
50g/2oz butter, melted but cooled
2 egg yolks, whisked
a pinch of salt
1 egg for glazing, whisked

For the cheese topping
250g/9oz Tvaroh (or substitute Quark or other curd cheese)
45ml/3 tbsp vanilla sugar
50g/2oz icing (confectioners') sugar
1 egg yolk
20g/¾oz butter
a pinch of lemon rind
dried raisins

For the jam topping
50g/2oz butter
100g/3¾oz icing (confectioners') sugar
50g/2oz plain (all-purpose) flour or dried breadcrumbs
150g/5oz Povidla (or substitute plum jam)

For the poppy seed topping
300g/11oz ground poppy seeds
50g/2oz icing (confectioner's) sugar
50ml/3½ tbsp milk

For the breadcrumb topping
25g/1oz/2 tbsp butter
65g/2½oz/generous ½ cup icing (confectioners') sugar
50g/2oz/½ cup plain (all-purpose) flour

1 Warm 100ml/3¾oz of the milk in a small pan. Then add a tablespoon of caster sugar and crumble in the yeast. Whisk together, cover and leave to activate and rise for 10 minutes.

2 Sift the flour into a bowl, add the butter, egg yolks, salt, the remaining milk and caster sugar and the activated yeast. Mix for 5 minutes. Dust with flour, cover with a dish towel and leave to rise for 2 hours – until it has doubled in size.

3 In the meantime prepare the toppings – for the cheese topping mix all of the ingredients together; for the jam topping, heat the butter in a pan, add the sugar and breadcrumbs (or flour) and mix until you get a crumble texture; for the poppy seed topping bring the milk to the boil, add sugar and poppy seeds and cook for 3 minutes and leave to cool, this is sprinkled on top of the Povidla or plum jam.

4 When the dough is ready, use a tablespoon to cut out large pieces and place them on a floured surface. Roll each one in a ball about 4–5cm/1½–2in diameter and pat it down to make a pancake roughly 2cm/¾in thick. Make an indent in the middle of each one where the topping will sit.

5 Spoon roughly a tablespoon of each topping on the indents on each pancake. Use all of the toppings you have, providing generous servings. When using the Povidla or plum jam, top this with the breadcrumb topping. Preheat the oven to 180°C/350°F/Gas 4.

6 Glaze each with the beaten egg. Bake in the oven for about 20–25 minutes until golden. Transfer to a wire rack and leave to cool and serve.

Oat and Cinnamon Breakfast Rolls per 2 rolls Energy 330kcal/1397kJ; Protein 12g; Carbohydrate 65g, of which sugars 8g; Fat 4g, of which saturates 1g; Cholesterol 4mg; Calcium 162mg; Fibre 2g; Sodium 462mg

Sweet Buns Energy 1313kcal/5540kJ; Protein 30g; Carbohydrate 230g, of which sugars 30g; Fat 36g, of which saturates 20g; Cholesterol 287mg; Calcium 412mg; Fibre 6.1g; Sodium 489mg.

Sweet Buns with Vanilla Cream

These plump yeasty buns have a smooth cream filling.

Makes 24

50ml/2fl oz/¼ cup tepid water
40g/1½oz fresh yeast
175g/6oz/¾ cup butter, softened
50g/2oz/¼ cup caster (superfine) sugar
2 eggs, plus 1 extra yolk
175ml/6fl oz/¾ cup milk
2.5ml/½ tsp salt
5ml/1 tsp ground cardamom
400g/14oz/3½ cups strong white bread flour

For the filling

3 egg yolks
45ml/3 tbsp caster (superfine) sugar
10ml/2 tsp vanilla sugar
15ml/1 tbsp potato flour or cornflour (cornstarch)
475ml/16fl oz/2 cups milk
a pinch of salt

For the icing

1 egg white
150g/5oz/1¼ cups icing (confectioners') sugar, sifted
25g/1oz/¼ cup unsweetened cocoa powder, sifted
a pinch of salt
5ml/1 tsp double (heavy) cream
30ml/2 tbsp pearl sugar, to decorate

1 Stir the yeast into the tepid water. Cream the butter and sugar in a mixing bowl. Beat in one whole egg and the extra yolk. Warm the milk in a pan, add the yeast mixture and stir into the butter mixture. Add the salt and cardamom. Stir in the flour and mix to a dough. Knead for 5–7 minutes. Cover for 1 hour.

2 To make the filling, whisk together the egg yolks and sugar in a pan. Whisk in the vanilla sugar, potato flour or cornflour and milk. Add the salt. Cook over low heat, stirring, for 6 minutes, until thickened. Remove from the heat and leave to cool.

3 Divide the dough into 24 balls. Place them on greased baking sheets. Make a well in each ball and fill with a spoonful of filling. Cover for 1½–2 hours. Preheat the oven to 220°C/425°F/Gas 7.

4 Beat the remaining egg and brush over the buns. Bake for 12–15 minutes. To make the icing, beat the egg white until stiff. Stir in the icing sugar, cocoa and salt. Stir in the cream. Spread over the tops of the buns and sprinkle with pearl sugar.

Chinese Bean Paste Buns

There are scores of different buns in Chinese cuisine to sample. Many of them use the same pastry base, and vary only in the fillings they contain.

Makes 12

200g/7oz/1¾ cups bun flour or self-raising (self-rising) flour
5ml/1 tsp sugar
a pinch of salt
15g/½oz easy-blend (rapid-rise) dried yeast
120ml/4fl oz/½ cup warm water
1 can sweet bean paste (about 300g/11oz depending on the brand)

1 Put the flour, sugar and salt in a large mixing bowl and sprinkle in the yeast. Make a well in the centre and pour in the warm water. Mix to a dough.

2 Place the dough on a floured board and knead for 10 minutes. Return it to the bowl, cover and set aside in a warm place to rise for 20 minutes or until it has doubled in bulk.

3 Knock back (punch down) the dough, knead it again, return it to the bowl and set aside in a warm place for 15 minutes.

4 Roll out the dough on a floured board and shape it into a 30cm/12in long roll about 5cm/2in in diameter.

5 Cut the roll into 2.5cm/1in slices and flatten each of these with a rolling pin to a thin round, about 10cm/4in across.

6 Holding a pastry round on the palm of one hand, spoon a tablespoon of the filling into the centre. Cup your hand so that the dough enfolds the filling, pleating and pinching it where necessary. Pinch off the excess dough at the top and seal with a twisting action. Sealing is important or the buns will gape when steamed. Fill the remaining dumplings in the same way.

7 Cut 5cm/2in squares of baking parchment. Stand a dumpling on each piece of paper in a steamer. Steam for 15 minutes. Serve immediately.

Sweet Buns with Vanilla Cream per bun Energy 186kcal/782kJ; Protein 3.9g; Carbohydrate 25.6g, of which sugars 12.2g; Fat 8.3g, of which saturates 4.6g; Cholesterol 67mg; Calcium 70mg; Fibre 0.6g; Sodium 77mg.

Chinese Bean Paste Buns per portion Energy 112kcal/477kJ; Protein 4.5g; Carbohydrate 24.1g, of which sugars 5g; Fat 0.4g, of which saturates 0.1g; Cholesterol 0mg; Calcium 36mg; Fibre 1.5g; Sodium 3mg.

Scones

Traditionally, scones should be served warm from the oven, with butter, clotted or whipped cream, and jam.

Makes 10–12

225g/8oz/2 cups plain (all-purpose) flour
15ml/1 tbsp baking powder
50g/2oz/4 tbsp cold butter, diced
1 egg, beaten
75ml/5 tbsp milk
1 beaten egg, to glaze

1 Preheat the oven to 220°C/425°F/Gas 7. Lightly butter a baking sheet. Sift the flour and baking powder together, then rub in the butter using your fingertips.

2 Make a well in the centre of the flour mixture, add the egg and milk and mix to a soft dough using a round-bladed knife.

3 Turn out the scone dough on to a floured surface, and knead very lightly until smooth.

4 Roll out the dough to about a 2cm/¾in thickness and cut into ten or twelve circles using a 5cm/2in plain or fluted (cookie) cutter dipped in flour.

5 Transfer to the baking sheet, brush with egg, then bake for about 8 minutes, or until risen and golden. Cool slightly on a wire rack before serving.

Cook's Tips

- *For perfectly delicate scones every time, handle the dough as little as possible.*
- *Always have the oven preheated, so that once the dough is made and cut into rounds the scones can go straight into the oven.*
- *As well as served warm from the oven, scones taste delicious when cool, and are even tasty the next day split and toasted under a preheated grill (broiler). Butter them while they are still hot.*

Wholemeal Scones

Split these wholesome scones in two with a fork while still warm, and spread with butter and home-made jam, if you wish.

Makes 16

175g/6oz/¾ cup cold butter
350g/12oz/3 cups plain (all-purpose) wholemeal (whole-wheat) flour
150g/5oz/1¼ cups plain (all-purpose) flour
30ml/2 tbsp caster (superfine) sugar
2.5ml/½ tsp salt
12.5ml/2½ tsp bicarbonate of soda (baking soda)
2 eggs
175ml/6fl oz/¾ cup buttermilk
35g/1¼oz/¼ cup raisins

1 Preheat the oven to 200°C/400°F/Gas 6. Grease and flour a large baking sheet.

2 Cut the butter into small pieces. Combine the wholemeal and plain flours with the sugar, salt and bicarbonate of soda in a bowl. Add the butter and rub in using your fingertips or a pastry cutter until the mixture resembles coarse breadcrumbs. Set aside.

3 In another bowl, whisk together the eggs and buttermilk. Set aside 30ml/2 tbsp for glazing, then stir the remaining egg mixture into the dry ingredients until it just holds together. Stir in the raisins.

4 Roll out the dough to about 2cm/¾in thickness. Stamp out circles with a cookie cutter. Place on the baking sheet and brush with the reserved egg and buttermilk glaze.

5 Bake until golden, about 12–15 minutes. Allow to cool slightly before serving.

Cook's Tip

These scones also go particularly well with cheese, so serve them for tea with a mature (sharp) Cheddar, a full-flavoured blue cheese or a creamy soft cheese such as Camembert or Brie.

Scones Energy 104kcal/437kJ; Protein 2.5g; Carbohydrate 14.9g, of which sugars 0.6g; Fat 4.2g, of which saturates 2.4g; Cholesterol 25mg; Calcium 37mg; Fibre 0.6g; Sodium 34mg.

Wholemeal Scones Energy 207kcal/869kJ; Protein 4.9g; Carbohydrate 25.3g, of which sugars 4.6g; Fat 10.3g, of which saturates 6g; Cholesterol 48mg; Calcium 42mg; Fibre 2.3g; Sodium 82mg.

Buttermilk Scones

If time is short, drop heaped tablespoonfuls of the mixture on to the baking sheet.

Makes 10

225g/8oz/2 cups plain (all-purpose) flour
5ml/1 tsp baking powder
2.5ml/½ tsp bicarbonate of soda (baking soda)
5ml/1 tsp salt
50g/2oz/¼ cup butter or margarine, chilled
175ml/6fl oz/¾ cup buttermilk

1 Preheat the oven to 220°C/425°F/Gas 7. Sift the dry ingredients into a mixing bowl. Rub in the butter or margarine until the mixture resembles coarse breadcrumbs.

2 Add the buttermilk and combine well to form a soft dough. Turn on to a lightly floured surface and knead for 30 seconds.

3 Roll out to a 1cm/½in thickness. Cut rounds with a floured 6cm/2½in cookie cutter. Transfer to a baking sheet and bake for 10–12 minutes. Serve with butter and honey.

Lavender Scones

Makes 12

225g/8oz/2 cups plain (all-purpose) flour
15ml/1 tbsp baking powder
50g/2oz/¼ cup butter
40g/1½oz/3 tbsp caster (superfine) sugar
10ml/2 tsp fresh lavender florets, chopped
about 175ml/6fl oz/¾ cup milk

1 Preheat the oven to 220°C/425°F/Gas 7. Grease a baking sheet. Sift the flour and baking powder into a bowl. Rub in the butter until the mixture resembles breadcrumbs.

2 Stir in the sugar and most of the lavender, reserving a little to decorate. Add enough milk to make a soft dough. Turn on to a floured surface and roll out to 2.5cm/1in thick. Cut 12 rounds with a floured cutter and place on the baking sheet. Brush the tops with milk and sprinkle with lavender. Bake for 10–12 minutes.

Orange & Raisin Scones

As well as being served warm from the oven, these scones are also superb split when cool and toasted under a preheated grill. Butter them while still hot.

Makes 16

275g/10oz/2½ cups plain (all-purpose) flour
25ml/1½ tbsp baking powder
60g/2¼oz/generous ¼ cup caster (superfine) sugar
2.5ml/½ tsp salt
65g/2½oz/5 tbsp butter, diced
65g/2½oz/5 tbsp margarine, diced
grated rind of 1 large orange
50g/2oz/scant ½ cup raisins
120ml/4fl oz/½ cup buttermilk
milk, to glaze

1 Preheat the oven to 220°C/425°F/Gas 7. Grease and flour a large baking sheet.

2 Combine the flour with the baking powder, sugar and salt in a large bowl. Add the butter and margarine, and rub in using your fingertips or a pastry cutter until the mixture resembles coarse breadcrumbs.

3 Add the orange rind and raisins. Gradually stir in the buttermilk to form a soft dough.

4 Roll out the dough to about a 2cm/¾in thickness. Stamp out circles with a cookie cutter. Place on the baking sheet and brush the tops with milk.

5 Bake until golden, about 12–15 minutes. Serve hot or warm, with butter, or whipped or clotted cream and jam.

Cook's Tip

Try these scones the Cornish way (usually reserved for plain scones): split them and spread each half with a little home-made raspberry or strawberry jam (no butter); now add a dollop of real Cornish or Devon clotted cream. Enjoy with a cup of tea, and preferably choose a summer's afternoon so that you can eat them outdoors for the authentic experience.

Buttermilk Scones Energy 120kcal/503kJ; Protein 2.7g; Carbohydrate 18.3g, of which sugars 1.1g; Fat 4.5g, of which saturates 2.7g; Cholesterol 11mg; Calcium 54mg; Fibre 0.7g; Sodium 235mg.
Lavender Scones Energy 115kcal/484kJ; Protein 2.3g; Carbohydrate 18.8g, of which sugars 4.5g; Fat 3.9g, of which saturates 2.4g; Cholesterol 10mg; Calcium 46mg; Fibre 0.6g; Sodium 32mg.
Orange and Raisin Scones Energy 145kcal/606kJ; Protein 2g; Carbohydrate 19.8g, of which sugars 6.7g; Fat 6.9g, of which saturates 2.2g; Cholesterol 9mg; Calcium 38mg; Fibre 0.6g; Sodium 63mg.

Sunflower Sultana Scones

Sunflower seeds give these fruit scones an interesting flavour and texture.

Makes 10–12

225g/8oz/2 cups self-raising (self-rising) flour
5ml/1 tsp baking powder
25g/1oz/2 tbsp soft sunflower margarine
30ml/2 tbsp golden caster (superfine) sugar
50g/2oz/⅓ cup sultanas (golden raisins)
30ml/2 tbsp sunflower seeds
150g/5oz/scant ⅔ cup natural (plain) yogurt
about 30–45ml/2–3 tbsp skimmed milk

1 Preheat the oven to 230°C/450°F/Gas 8. Lightly oil a baking sheet. Sift the flour and baking powder into a bowl and rub in the margarine evenly.

2 Stir in the sugar, sultanas and half the sunflower seeds, then mix in the yogurt, with just enough milk to make a fairly soft, but not sticky, dough.

3 Roll out on a lightly floured surface to about a 2cm/¾in thickness. Cut into 6cm/2½in flower shapes or rounds with a cookie cutter and lift on to the baking sheet.

4 Brush with milk and sprinkle with the reserved sunflower seeds, then bake for 10–12 minutes, or until well risen and golden brown. Cool the scones on a wire rack. Serve split, spread with jam or low-fat spread.

Cook's Tip

Sunflower seeds are a wonder food, and a good and tasty way to add nutrients to the diet, especially selenium, which is often lacking. Don't buy too many at one time, and source them from a store where they have a quick turnover so that the ones you buy are fresh. As sunflower seeds have a high fat content, they don't store well for long periods. Buy small quantities at a time and put them in a sealed container in a cool place – even a refrigerator.

Lusse Bröd

Saint Lucia Day, on December 12, marks the beginning of Christmas in Sweden, when these buns are offered to the townspeople.

Makes 12

120ml/4fl oz/½ cup milk
a pinch of saffron threads
400g/14oz/3½ cups unbleached white bread flour
50g/2oz/½ cup ground almonds
2.5ml/½ tsp salt
75g/3oz/6 tbsp caster (superfine) sugar
25g/1oz fresh yeast
120ml/4fl oz/½ cup lukewarm water
few drops of almond extract
50g/2oz/¼ cup butter, softened

For the glaze
1 egg
15ml/1 tbsp water

1 Lightly grease two baking sheets. Place the milk in a small pan and bring to the boil. Add the saffron, remove from the heat and leave to infuse (steep) for about 15 minutes. Mix the flour, ground almonds, salt and sugar together in a bowl.

2 Cream the yeast with the water. Add the saffron liquid, yeast mixture and almond extract to the flour mixture and mix to a dough. Gradually beat in the softened butter. Knead for 5 minutes until smooth and elastic. Place in a lightly oiled bowl, cover with lightly oiled clear film (plastic wrap) and leave for about 1 hour, or until doubled in bulk.

3 Knock back (punch down). Divide into 12 equal pieces and make into different shapes: roll into a long rope and shape into an 'S' shape; to make a star, cut a dough piece in half and roll into two ropes, cross one over the other and coil the ends; make an upturned 'U' shape and coil the ends; divide a dough piece in half, roll into two thin ropes and twist together.

4 Place on the prepared baking sheets, spaced well apart, cover and leave to rise, in a warm place, for about 30 minutes. Preheat the oven to 200°C/400°F/Gas 6. Beat the egg with the water for the glaze, and brush over the rolls. Bake for 15 minutes, or until golden. Transfer to a wire rack to cool slightly.

Sunflower Sultana Scones Energy 121kcal/513kJ; Protein 3g; Carbohydrate 21.2g, of which sugars 6.9g; Fat 3.3g, of which saturates 0.6g; Cholesterol 0mg; Calcium 99mg; Fibre 0.8g; Sodium 97mg.

Lusse Bröd Energy 199kcal/840kJ; Protein 4.4g; Carbohydrate 33.2g, of which sugars 7.7g; Fat 6.3g, of which saturates 2.6g; Cholesterol 10mg; Calcium 73mg; Fibre 1.3g; Sodium 121mg.

Individual Brioches

These buttery rolls, with their distinctive topknots, are delicious served with jam at coffee time.

Makes 8

15ml/1 tbsp active dried yeast
15ml/1 tbsp caster (superfine) sugar
30ml/2 tbsp warm milk
2 eggs
about 200g/7oz/1¾ cups strong white bread flour
2.5ml/½ tsp salt
75g/3oz/6 tbsp butter, cut into six pieces, at room temperature
1 egg yolk, beaten with 10ml/2 tsp water, to glaze

1 Butter eight individual brioche tins (pans) or muffin cups. Put the yeast and sugar in a small bowl, add the milk and stir until dissolved. Leave the yeast mixture to stand for 5 minutes so that the yeast begins to work, then beat in the eggs.

2 Put the flour and salt into a food processor, then, with the machine running, slowly pour in the yeast mixture. Scrape down the sides and process until the dough forms a ball.

3 Add the butter and pulse to blend. Alternatively, use your hand to incorporate the flour into the liquid.

4 Transfer the dough to a lightly buttered bowl and cover with a clean dish towel or clear film (plastic wrap). Leave to rise in a warm place for about 1 hour, then knock back (punch down) the dough.

5 Shape three-quarters of the dough into eight balls and place them into the prepared tins. Shape the last quarter into eight small balls, make a depression in the top of each large ball and set a small ball into it.

6 Leave the brioches to rise in a warm place for 30 minutes. Preheat the oven to 200°C/400°F/Gas 6.

7 Brush the brioches with the egg glaze. Bake for about 15–18 minutes, or until golden brown. Transfer to a wire rack and leave to cool completely.

Orange & Coriander Brioches

The warm and spicy flavour of coriander seeds combines really well with orange.

Makes 12

225g/8oz/2 cups strong white bread flour
10ml/2 tsp easy-blend (rapid-rise) dried yeast
2.5ml/½ tsp salt
15ml/1 tbsp caster (superfine) sugar
10ml/2 tsp coriander seeds, coarsely ground
grated rind of 1 orange
2 eggs, beaten
50g/2oz/¼ cup butter, melted
1 small egg, beaten, to glaze

1 Grease 12 individual brioche tins (pans). Sift the flour into a bowl and stir in the yeast, salt, sugar, coriander seeds and orange rind. Make a well in the centre, pour in 30ml/2 tbsp of lukewarm water, the eggs and the melted butter and beat to make a soft dough. Turn on to a lightly floured surface and knead for 5 minutes until smooth and elastic. Return to the clean, lightly oiled bowl, cover with clear film (plastic wrap) and leave in a warm place for 1 hour until doubled in size.

2 Turn on to a floured surface, knead briefly and roll into a sausage. Cut into 12 pieces. Break off a quarter of each piece. Shape the larger pieces into balls and place in the prepared tins.

3 With a floured wooden spoon, press a hole in each dough ball. Shape each small piece of dough into a little plug and press into the holes. Place the brioche tins on a baking sheet. Cover with lightly oiled clear film and leave in a warm place until the dough rises almost to the top of the tins.

4 Preheat the oven to 220°C/425°F/Gas 7. Brush the brioches with beaten egg and bake for 15 minutes until golden brown. Sprinkle over shreds of orange rind, and serve warm with butter.

Cook's Tip

These brioches look particularly attractive if they are made in special brioche tins, but they can also be made in muffin tins.

Individual Brioches per brioche Energy 183kcal/765kJ; Protein 4.1g; Carbohydrate 21.6g, of which sugars 2.6g; Fat 9.5g, of which saturates 5.4g; Cholesterol 68mg; Calcium 49mg; Fibre 0.8g; Sodium 77mg.

Orange and Coriander Brioches per brioche Energy 112kcal/471kJ; Protein 2.8g; Carbohydrate 15.9g, of which sugars 1.6g; Fat 4.6g, of which saturates 2.5g; Cholesterol 41mg; Calcium 32mg; Fibre 0.6g; Sodium 119mg.

Chocolate & Apricot Brioche

The lovely soft texture of brioche comes from the egg and milk in the dough. Rich and substantial, it is delicious with frothy hot chocolate.

Makes 1

115g/4oz/1 cup strong white bread flour
115g/4oz/1 cup quinoa flour
50g/2oz/½ cup unsweetened cocoa powder
10ml/2 tsp easy-blend (rapid-rise) dried yeast
60ml/4 tbsp soft light brown sugar
5ml/1 tsp salt
50g/2oz/¼ cup butter, melted
3 eggs, beaten
45ml/3 tbsp milk
45ml/3 tbsp warm water
5ml/1 tsp vanilla extract
50g/2oz plain (semisweet) chocolate, chopped into chunks
50g/2oz/¼ cup dried apricots, finely chopped
30ml/2 tbsp milk and 15ml/1 tbsp soft light brown sugar, to glaze

1 Place all of the ingredients, except the chocolate and apricots, in a large bowl or in a food mixer if using a dough hook, and mix together to create a soft dough.

2 Transfer to a floured board and knead for about 10 minutes by hand, until the dough is smooth and elastic. Set aside in a bowl covered with a damp cloth and leave to rise in a warm place for about 1½ hours.

3 Knock back (punch down) the dough and stretch it out to form a rough rectangle. Sprinkle the chocolate chunks and apricots on top and fold in the sides to envelop them. Fold and knead again until the chocolate and apricots are evenly distributed. Divide the dough into two manageable balls and then shape as desired; you can divide it into 12 smaller brioche rolls, braid it or form it into a more traditional round shape. Leave for 30 minutes until risen again.

4 Preheat the oven to 190°C/375°F/Gas 5. Place the shaped dough on to a greased baking sheet, brush with the milk and sprinkle with soft light brown sugar. Bake in the centre of the oven until the brioche has a crispy top. This will take about 30 minutes for a larger loaf, and 10–15 minutes for smaller rolls.

Blueberry Muffins

Light and fruity, these well-known American muffins are delicious at any time of day. Serve them warm for breakfast or brunch, or as a special teatime treat.

Makes 12

2 eggs
50g/2oz/4 tbsp butter, melted
175ml/6fl oz/¾ cup milk
5ml/1 tsp vanilla extract
5ml/1 tsp grated lemon rind
180g/6¼oz/generous 1½ cups plain (all-purpose) flour
60g/2¼oz/generous ¼ cup sugar
10ml/2 tsp baking powder
a pinch of salt
175g/6oz/1½ cups fresh blueberries

1 Preheat the oven to 200°C/400°F/Gas 6. Arrange 12 paper cases in a muffin tin (pan) or grease the tin.

2 In a bowl, whisk the eggs until blended. Add the melted butter, milk, vanilla and lemon rind, and stir to combine.

3 Sift the flour, sugar, baking powder and salt into a large bowl. Make a well in the centre and pour in the egg mixture. With a metal spoon, stir until the flour is just moistened.

4 Add the blueberries to the muffin mixture and gently fold in.

5 Spoon the batter into the muffin tin or paper cases, leaving enough room for the muffins to rise.

6 Bake for 20–25 minutes, until the tops spring back when touched lightly. Leave the muffins in the tin, if using, for 5 minutes before turning out on to a wire rack to cool.

Variation
Muffins are delicious with all kinds of different fruits. Try out some variations using this basic muffin recipe – replace the blueberries with the same weight of bilberries, blackcurrants, pitted cherries or raspberries.

Chocolate and Apricot Brioche Energy 335kcal/1410kJ; Protein 9g; Carbohydrate 46g, of which sugars 18g; Fat 14g, of which saturates 8g; Cholesterol 82mg; Calcium 105mg; Fibre 2g; Sodium 471mg.

Blueberry Muffins Energy 236kcal/992kJ; Protein 4.9g; Carbohydrate 34.7g, of which sugars 12.4g; Fat 9.6g, of which saturates 5.6g; Cholesterol 54mg; Calcium 88mg; Fibre 1.4g; Sodium 82mg.

Banana Muffins

Use really ripe bananas for these muffins, not just because those are the sweetest, but also because they are easy to mash to the proper smooth consistency.

Makes 12

225g/8oz/2 cups plain (all-purpose) flour
5ml/1 tsp baking powder
5ml/1 tsp bicarbonate of soda (baking soda)
a pinch of salt
2.5ml/½ tsp ground cinnamon
1.5ml/¼ tsp grated nutmeg
3 large ripe bananas
1 egg
50g/2oz/¼ cup soft dark brown sugar
50ml/2fl oz/¼ cup vegetable oil
40g/1½oz/⅓ cup raisins

1 Preheat the oven to 190°C/375°F/Gas 5. Arrange 12 paper cases in a muffin tin (pan).

2 Sift together the flour, baking powder, bicarbonate of soda, salt, cinnamon and nutmeg. Set aside.

3 Using a fork, mash the peeled bananas to a smooth consistency in a large bowl.

4 Beat the egg, sugar and oil into the mashed bananas until fully combined.

5 Add the dry ingredients and beat in gradually, using an electric whisk set at low speed. Mix until just blended. With a wooden spoon, stir in the raisins until just combined. Spoon the mixture into the muffin tins, filling them two-thirds full.

6 Bake for 20–25 minutes, until the tops spring back when touched lightly with your finger. Transfer the muffins to a wire rack to cool completely before serving.

Variation
For Banana and Chocolate Muffins, substitute 50g/2oz/⅓ cup plain (semisweet) chocolate chips for the raisins.

Wholemeal Banana Muffins

This is a wholemeal version of banana muffins. You can slice the tops off and fill with a teaspoon of jam or marmalade, then replace the tops before serving.

Makes 12

75g/3oz/¾ cup plain (all-purpose) wholemeal (whole-wheat) flour
50g/2oz/½ cup plain (all-purpose) white flour
10ml/2 tsp baking powder
a pinch of salt
5ml/1 tsp mixed (apple pie) spice
40g/1½oz/scant ¼ cup soft light brown sugar
50g/2oz/¼ cup butter
1 egg, beaten
150ml/¼ pint/⅔ cup semi-skimmed (low-fat) milk
grated rind of 1 orange
1 ripe banana
20g/¾oz/¼ cup rolled oats
20g/¾oz/scant ¼ cup chopped hazelnuts

1 Preheat the oven to 200°C/400°F/Gas 6. Arrange 12 paper cases in a muffin tin (pan).

2 Sift together both flours, the baking powder, salt and mixed spice into a bowl, then tip the bran remaining in the sieve (strainer) into the bowl. Stir in the sugar.

3 Melt the butter in a pan over a very low heat. Remove from the heat and leave to cool slightly, then beat in the egg, milk and grated orange rind. Make a well in the centre of the flour mixture, pour in the butter mixture and beat well to incorporate the dry ingredients.

4 Mash the banana with a fork, then stir it gently into the mixture, being careful not to overmix. Spoon the mixture into the paper cases.

5 Combine the oats and hazelnuts and sprinkle a little of the mixture over each muffin.

6 Bake for 20 minutes until the muffins are well risen and golden, and a skewer inserted in the centre comes out clean. Transfer to a wire rack and serve warm or cold.

Banana Muffins Energy 152kcal/642kJ; Protein 2.8g; Carbohydrate 29g, of which sugars 13.9g; Fat 3.6g, of which saturates 0.5g; Cholesterol 16mg; Calcium 34mg; Fibre 1g; Sodium 9mg.

Wholemeal Banana Muffins Energy 116kcal/489kJ; Protein 3g; Carbohydrate 15g, of which sugars 6g; Fat 6g, of which saturates 3g; Cholesterol 29mg; Calcium 42mg; Fibre 1.2g; Sodium 151mg.

Apricot & Orange Muffins

Serve these fruity muffins freshly baked and warm.

Makes 12

115g/4oz/1 cup cornmeal
75g/3oz/¾ cup rice flour
15ml/1 tbsp baking powder
a pinch of salt
50g/2oz/4 tbsp butter, melted
50g/2oz/¼ cup light soft brown sugar
1 egg, beaten
200ml/7fl oz/scant 1 cup semi-skimmed (low-fat) milk
finely grated rind of 1 orange
115g/4oz/½ cup ready-to-eat dried apricots, chopped

1 Preheat the oven to 200°C/400°F/Gas 6. Arrange 12 paper cases in a muffin tin (pan).

2 Place the cornmeal, rice flour, baking powder and salt in a bowl and mix together.

3 Stir together the melted butter, sugar, egg, milk and orange rind, then pour the mixture over the dry ingredients. Fold the ingredients gently together. The mixture will look quite lumpy, which is correct, as over-mixing will result in heavy muffins.

4 Fold in the chopped dried apricots, then spoon the mixture into the prepared paper cases, dividing it equally among them.

5 Bake for 15–20 minutes, until the muffins have risen and are golden brown and springy to the touch. Turn them out on to a wire rack to cool.

6 Serve the muffins warm or cold, on their own or cut in half and spread with a little butter or low-fat spread. Store in an airtight container for up to 1 week, or seal in plastic bags and freeze for up to 3 months.

Variation
Try substituting grapefruit rind for the orange, and the same quantity of chopped dried mango for the apricots.

Lemon Meringue Muffins

This recipe is a delightful variation on the classic fairy cake – soft lemon sponge cake is topped with crisp meringue.

Makes 18

115g/4oz/½ cup butter
200g/7oz/scant 1 cup caster (superfine) sugar
2 eggs
115g/4oz/1 cup self-raising (self-rising) flour
5ml/1 tsp baking powder
grated rind of 2 lemons
30ml/2 tbsp lemon juice
2 egg whites

1 Preheat the oven to 190°C/375°F/Gas 5. Arrange 18 paper cases in a muffin tin (pan).

2 Put the butter in a bowl and beat until soft. Add 115g/4oz/generous ½ cup of the caster sugar and continue to beat until the mixture is smooth and creamy.

3 Beat in the eggs. Sift together the flour and baking powder over the mixture, add half the lemon rind and all the lemon juice and beat well until thoroughly combined.

4 Divide the the mixture among the paper cases.

5 To make the meringue, whisk the egg whites in a clean grease-free bowl until they stand in soft peaks. Stir in the remaining caster sugar and lemon rind. Put a spoonful of the meringue mixture on each cake.

6 Cook for 20–25 minutes, until the meringue is crisp and brown. Serve hot or cold.

Cook's Tip
Make sure that you whisk the egg whites enough before adding the sugar. When you lift out the whisk, they should stand in peaks that just flop over slightly at the top.

Apricot and Orange Muffins Energy136kcals/572kJ; Fat, total 4.6g; saturated fat 1g; Protein2.9g; Carbohydrate 21g; sugar, total 8.5g; Fibre 0.9g; Sodium 195mg.

Lemon Meringue Muffins Energy 123kcal/514kJ; Protein 1.7g; Carbohydrate 16.6g, of which sugars 11.7g; Fat 6g, of which saturates 3.5g; Cholesterol 35mg; Calcium 19mg; Fibre 0.2g; Sodium 54mg.

Raspberry Buttermilk Muffins

Buttermilk gives these muffins a light and spongy texture. Make them in the summer, when fresh raspberries are at their seasonal best.

Makes 10–12

300g/11oz/2¾ cups plain (all-purpose) flour
15ml/1 tbsp baking powder
115g/4oz/generous ½ cup caster (superfine) sugar
1 egg
250ml/8fl oz/1 cup buttermilk
60ml/4 tbsp sunflower oil
150g/5oz/1 cup raspberries

1 Preheat the oven to 200°C/400°F/Gas 6. Arrange 10–12 paper cases in a muffin tin (pan).

2 Sift the flour and baking powder into a mixing bowl. Stir in the sugar, then make a well in the centre.

3 Mix the egg, buttermilk and sunflower oil together in a bowl, pour into the flour mixture and mix quickly until just combined.

4 Add the raspberries and lightly fold them into the mixture with a metal spoon until just combined. Spoon the mixture into the prepared paper cases, filling them about two-thirds full.

5 Bake for 20–25 minutes, until golden brown and firm in the centre. Transfer to a wire rack and serve warm or cold.

Cook's Tips

• As with other soft fruits – which can also be used in these delicious muffins – don't buy more raspberries than you require, as they deteriorate quickly, although they do freeze well. If they're sold in packs, make sure that there are no squashed ones underneath. Avoid soaking them in water when washing them; just wipe with damp kitchen paper.

• Raspberry muffins make a fabulous breakfast treat with butter and honey, and are great at teatime when served warm with raspberry jam and thickly whipped cream.

Raspberry Crumble Buns

For total luxury, serve these tangy buns like scones, with raspberry jam and cream.

Makes 12

175g/6oz/1½ cups plain (all-purpose) flour
10ml/2 tsp baking powder
a pinch of salt
5ml/1 tsp ground cinnamon
50g/2oz/¼ cup sugar
50g/2oz/¼ cup soft light brown sugar
115g/4oz/½ cup butter, melted
1 egg
120ml/4fl oz/½ cup milk
225g/8oz/1⅓ cups fresh raspberries
grated rind of 1 lemon

For the topping

50g/2oz/½ cup pecan nuts, finely chopped
50g/2oz/¼ cup soft dark brown sugar
45ml/3 tbsp plain (all-purpose) flour
5ml/1 tsp ground cinnamon
40g/1½oz/3 tbsp butter, melted

1 Preheat the oven to 180°C/350°F/Gas 4. Arrange 12 paper cases in a muffin tin (pan).

2 Sift the flour, baking powder, salt and cinnamon into a bowl. Stir in the sugars. Make a well in the centre.

3 Beat together the butter, egg and milk in a large bowl until light. Add the flour mixture to it and stir until just combined. Stir in the raspberries and lemon rind.

4 Spoon the batter into the muffin tins, filling them almost to the top.

5 To make the topping, mix the pecans, sugar, flour and cinnamon in a bowl. Stir in the melted butter.

6 Spoon a little of the crumble topping over the top of each muffin. Bake for about 25 minutes.

7 Transfer to a wire rack to cool slightly. Serve the muffins warm.

Raspberry Buttermilk Muffins Energy 132kcal/555kJ; Protein 4g; Carbohydrate 19g, of which sugars 5.7g; Fat 5g, of which saturates 2.7g; Cholesterol 42mg; Calcium 48mg; Fibre 1.5g; Sodium 45mg.

Raspberry Crumble Buns Energy 225kcal/940kJ; Protein 2.7g; Carbohydrate 25.2g, of which sugars 14.1g; Fat 13.3g, of which saturates 7.3g; Cholesterol 45mg; Calcium 48mg; Fibre 0.9g; Sodium 93mg.

Date & Apple Muffins

These muffins are very filling. If possible, use fresh Medjool dates from Egypt, as they have sweet, dense flesh and an opulent flavour.

Makes 12

150g/5oz/1¼ cups self-raising (self-rising) wholemeal (whole-wheat) flour
150g/5oz/1¼ cups self-raising (self-rising) flour
5ml/1 tsp ground cinnamon
5ml/1 tsp baking powder
25g/1oz/2 tbsp butter
75g/3oz/⅓ cup light muscovado (brown) sugar
250ml/8fl oz/1 cup apple juice
30ml/2 tbsp pear and apple jam
1 egg, lightly beaten
1 eating apple
75g/3oz/½ cup chopped dates
15ml/1 tbsp chopped pecan nuts

1 Preheat the oven to 200°C/400°F/Gas 6. Arrange 12 paper cases in a muffin tin (pan).

2 Sift together both flours, the cinnamon and baking powder into a large bowl. Add the butter and rub it in with your fingertips until the mixture resembles fine breadcrumbs. Add the sugar and stir well to mix.

3 In a mixing bowl, stir a little of the apple juice with the pear and apple jam until smooth. Mix in the remaining apple juice, then add to the rubbed-in mixture with the beaten egg.

4 Quarter and core the apple, and peel it if you like, then chop the flesh finely. Add to the batter and stir in the dates. Divide the mixture among the muffin cases.

5 Sprinkle the chopped pecans on top. Bake for 20–25 minutes, until golden brown and firm in the middle. Transfer to a wire rack and serve while still warm.

Cook's Tip
If self-raising (self-rising) wholemeal (whole-wheat) flour is not available, use more self-raising (self-rising) white flour instead.

Apple & Cinnamon Muffins

These fruity, spicy muffins are quick and easy to make, and are perfect for serving for breakfast or teatime. The appetizing aroma as they bake is out of this world.

Makes 6

1 egg, beaten
40g/1½oz/3 tbsp caster (superfine) sugar
120ml/4fl oz/½ cup milk
50g/2oz/¼ cup butter, melted
150g/5oz/1¼ cups plain (all-purpose) flour
7.5ml/1½ tsp baking powder
a pinch of salt
2.5ml/½ tsp ground cinnamon
2 small eating apples, peeled, cored and finely chopped

For the topping
12 brown sugar cubes, coarsely crushed
5ml/1 tsp ground cinnamon

1 Preheat the oven to 200°C/400°F/Gas 6. Arrange 6 paper cases in a muffin tin (pan).

2 Mix the egg, sugar, milk and melted butter in a large bowl. Sift in the flour, baking powder, salt and cinnamon. Add the chopped apple and mix roughly.

3 Spoon the mixture into the prepared muffin cases. To make the topping, mix the crushed sugar cubes with the cinnamon. Sprinkle over the uncooked muffins.

4 Bake for 30–35 minutes, until well risen and golden brown on top. Transfer the muffins to a wire rack to cool. Serve them warm or at room temperature.

Cook's Tip
Do not overmix the muffin mixture – it should still be slightly lumpy when spooned into the cases.

Date and Apple Muffins Energy 158kcal/670kJ; Protein 3.2g; Carbohydrate 30.7g, of which sugars 11.7g; Fat 3.4g, of which saturates 0.3g; Cholesterol 16mg; Calcium 45mg; Fibre 1g; Sodium 25mg.

Apple and Cinnamon Muffins Energy 236kcal/995kJ; Protein 4.3g; Carbohydrate 38.2g, of which sugars 19.1g; Fat 8.5g, of which saturates 4.9g; Cholesterol 51mg; Calcium 74mg; Fibre 1.2g; Sodium 73mg.

Apple & Cranberry Muffins

A really sweet variety of apple will provide a lovely contrast with the sharp flavour of the cranberries.

Makes 12

50g/2oz/¼ cup butter
1 egg
90g/3½oz/½ cup caster (superfine) sugar
grated rind of 1 large orange
120ml/4fl oz/½ cup freshly squeezed orange juice
150g/5oz/1¼ cups plain (all-purpose) flour
5ml/1 tsp baking powder
2.5ml/½ tsp bicarbonate of soda (baking soda)
5ml/1 tsp ground cinnamon
2.5ml/½ tsp freshly grated nutmeg
2.5ml/½ tsp ground allspice
1.5ml/¼ tsp ground ginger
a pinch of salt
1–2 eating apples
150g/6oz/1½ cups cranberries
50g/2oz/¼ cup walnuts, chopped
icing (confectioners') sugar, for dusting (optional)

1 Preheat the oven to 180°C/350°F/Gas 4. Arrange 12 paper cases in a muffin tin (pan).

2 Melt the butter over a gentle heat. Set aside to cool.

3 In a large bowl, whisk the egg lightly. Add the melted butter and whisk to combine. Add the sugar, orange rind and juice. Whisk to blend, then set aside.

4 In a mixing bowl, sift together the flour, baking powder, bicarbonate of soda, cinnamon, nutmeg, allspice, ginger and salt. Set aside.

5 Make a well in the dry ingredients and pour in the egg mixture. With a spoon, stir until just blended.

6 Quarter, core and peel the apples. Chop coarsely. Add the apples, cranberries and walnuts, and stir to blend.

7 Fill the cases three-quarters full and bake for 25–30 minutes, until the tops spring back when touched lightly. Transfer to a rack to cool. Dust with icing sugar.

Cranberry & Orange Muffins

These delicious muffins are perfect to eat at any time of day, and are a real energy boost for breakfast or as a lunchbox treat. You can use fresh or frozen cranberries.

Makes 10–12

350g/12oz/3 cups plain (all-purpose) flour, sifted
15ml/1 tsp baking powder
a pinch of salt
115g/4oz/generous ½ cup caster (superfine) sugar
2 eggs
150ml/¼ pint/⅔ cup milk
50ml/2fl oz/¼ cup corn oil
finely grated rind of 1 orange
150g/5oz/1¼ cups cranberries, thawed if frozen

1 Preheat the oven to 190°C/375°F/Gas 5. Arrange 10–12 paper cases in a muffin tin (pan).

2 Sift together the flour, baking powder and salt into a large bowl. Add the sugar and stir well to mix.

3 Lightly beat the eggs with the milk and corn oil in another bowl until thoroughly combined.

4 Make a well in the centre of the dry ingredients and pour in the egg mixture. Stir with a wooden spoon until blended to a smooth batter. Gently fold in the grated orange rind and cranberries with a metal spoon.

5 Divide the mixture among the paper cases and bake for about 25 minutes, until risen and golden. Transfer to a wire rack to cool, and serve warm or cold.

Cook's Tip

The flared sides of a proper muffin tin (pan) increase the surface area, encouraging the dough to rise.

Apple and Cranberry Muffins Energy 149kcal/624kJ; Protein 2.5g; Carbohydrate 20.4g, of which sugars 10.8g; Fat 6.9g, of which saturates 2.6g; Cholesterol 25mg; Calcium 30mg; Fibre 0.9g; Sodium 34mg.

Cranberry and Orange Muffins Energy 184kcal/780kJ; Protein 4.3g; Carbohydrate 34.4g, of which sugars 12.2g; Fat 4.3g, of which saturates 0.9g; Cholesterol 32mg; Calcium 66mg; Fibre 1.1g; Sodium 19mg.

Dried Cherry Muffins

Cherries are always a great favourite, so why not spoil the family and serve these scrumptious muffins freshly baked and still warm from the oven, smothered with butter and cherry jam. Dried cherries are full of antioxidants, and are a healthy food to eat.

Makes 16

250ml/8fl oz/1 cup natural (plain) yogurt
225g/8oz/1 cup dried cherries
115g/4oz/½ cup butter, softened
175g/6oz/scant 1 cup caster (superfine) sugar
2 eggs
5ml/1 tsp vanilla extract
200g/7oz/1¾ cups plain (all-purpose) flour
10ml/2 tsp baking powder
5ml/1 tsp bicarbonate of soda (baking soda)
a pinch of salt

1 In a mixing bowl, combine the yogurt and dried cherries. Cover with clear film (plastic wrap) and leave to stand for about 30 minutes.

2 Preheat the oven to 180°C/350°F/Gas 4. Arrange 12 paper cases in a muffin tin (pan).

3 Beat together the butter and caster sugar in a bowl until light and fluffy. Add the eggs, one at a time, beating well after each addition until fully incorporated.

4 Add the vanilla extract and yogurt and cherry mixture and stir well until thoroughly mixed.

5 Sift the flour, baking powder, bicarbonate of soda and salt over the batter in batches. Gently fold in using a metal spoon after each addition.

6 Spoon the mixture into the prepared muffin tins, filling them about two-thirds full. Bake for 20 minutes, or until risen and golden and the tops spring back when touched lightly. Transfer to a wire rack to cool completely before serving or storing in an airtight container.

Oat & Raisin Muffins

Often the simplest things are the nicest – and that is certainly the case with these flavour-packed oaty muffins.

Makes 12

75g/3oz/scant 1 cup rolled oats
250ml/8fl oz/1 cup buttermilk
115g/4oz/½ cup butter, at room temperature
90g/3½oz/generous ⅓ cup soft dark brown sugar
1 egg, at room temperature
115g/4oz/1 cup plain (all-purpose) flour
5ml/1 tsp baking powder
2.5ml/½ tsp bicarbonate of soda (baking soda)
a pinch of salt
25g/1oz/2 tbsp raisins

1 In a bowl, combine the oats and buttermilk, and leave to soak for 1 hour.

2 Preheat the oven to 200°C/400°F/Gas 6. Arrange 12 paper cases in a muffin tin (pan).

3 In a bowl, cream the butter and sugar until light and fluffy. Beat in the egg.

4 Sift the flour, baking powder, bicarbonate of soda and salt into the butter mixture in batches. Alternate with batches of the oat mixture. Stir to combine after each addition. Fold in the raisins. Do not overmix.

5 Fill the prepared cups two-thirds full. Bake for about 20–25 minutes, until a skewer inserted in the centre comes out clean. Transfer to a rack to cool.

Cook's Tip

Buttermilk is made from skimmed milk fermented with a special culture under controlled conditions, resulting in an acidic product that helps dough to rise. If it is not available, add 5ml/1 tsp lemon juice or vinegar to milk, and leave to stand for a few minutes until curdled.

Dried Cherry Muffins Energy 196kcal/825kJ; Protein 3.2g; Carbohydrate 32.1g, of which sugars 22.6g; Fat 7g, of which saturates 4g; Cholesterol 39mg; Calcium 67mg; Fibre 0.7g; Sodium 69mg.

Oat and Raisin Muffins Energy 177kcal/742kJ; Protein 3g; Carbohydrate 22.3g, of which sugars 10.4g; Fat 9.1g, of which saturates 5.2g; Cholesterol 37mg; Calcium 51mg; Fibre 0.8g; Sodium 77mg.

Pear & Sultana Bran Muffins

These tasty muffins are best eaten freshly baked and served warm or cold, on their own or spread with butter, jam or honey.

Makes 12

75g/3oz/¾ cup plain (all-purpose) wholemeal (whole-wheat) flour, sifted
50g/2oz/½ cup plain (all-purpose) white flour, sifted
50g/2oz/3 cups bran
15ml/1 tbsp baking powder
a pinch of salt
50g/2oz/4 tbsp butter
50g/2oz/¼ cup soft light brown sugar
1 egg
200ml/7fl oz/scant 1 cup skimmed milk
50g/2oz/½ cup ready-to-eat dried pears, chopped
50g/2oz/⅓ cup sultanas (golden raisins)

1 Preheat the oven to 200°C/400°F/Gas 6. Arrange 12 paper cases in a muffin tin (pan).

2 Mix together the flours, bran, baking powder and salt in a bowl. Set aside.

3 Gently heat the butter in a small pan until melted.

4 Mix together the melted butter, sugar, egg and milk.

5 Pour the butter mixture over the dry ingredients. Gently fold the ingredients together, only enough to combine. The mixture should look quite lumpy.

6 Fold in the pears and sultanas.

7 Spoon the mixture into the prepared muffin tins. Bake for 15–20 minutes, until well risen and golden brown. Turn out on to a wire rack to cool.

Cook's Tip
For a quick and easy way to chop dried fruit, chop with kitchen scissors.

Carrot Buns

Carrots have a natural moistness that makes them an ideal ingredient for cakes and muffins. If you haven't used them before when baking, you are likely to be pleasantly surprised.

Makes 12

175g/6oz/¾ cup butter, at room temperature, diced
75g/3oz/⅓ cup soft dark brown sugar
1 egg
15ml/1 tbsp water
275g/10oz/2 cups grated carrots
150g/5oz/1¼ cups plain (all-purpose) flour
5ml/1 tsp baking powder
2.5ml/½ tsp bicarbonate of soda (baking soda)
5ml/1 tsp ground cinnamon
1.5ml/¼ tsp grated nutmeg
a pinch of salt

1 Preheat the oven to 180°C/350°F/Gas 4. Arrange 12 paper cases in a muffin tin (pan).

2 In a large bowl, beat the butter and sugar until light and fluffy. Beat in the egg and water.

3 Stir the grated carrots into the butter mixture until evenly combined. Sift over the flour, baking powder, bicarbonate of soda, cinnamon, nutmeg and salt. Stir to blend evenly.

4 Spoon the batter into the prepared muffin tins, filling them almost to the top.

5 Bake for about 35 minutes, until the tops spring back when touched lightly with your fingers. Leave to stand for 10 minutes before transferring to a wire rack to cool completely.

Cook's Tip
Unless the carrots are very old and coarse – in which case, they are probably not suitable for this recipe – you do not need to peel them before grating. Simply trim and wash first. Use the fine side of the grater.

Pear and Sultana Bran Muffins Energy 121kcal/510kJ; Protein 3g; Carbohydrate 18.7g, of which sugars 9.8g; Fat 4.3g, of which saturates 2.4g; Cholesterol 25mg; Calcium 51mg; Fibre 2.2g; Sodium 42mg.

Carrot Buns Energy 190kcal/791kJ; Protein 2g; Carbohydrate 18.1g, of which sugars 8.5g; Fat 12.7g, of which saturates 7.8g; Cholesterol 47mg; Calcium 32mg; Fibre 0.9g; Sodium 101mg.

Prune Muffins

Sticky and full of flavour, the humble prune is low in fat, full of fibre and contains antioxidants and minerals in abundance, making it a healthy choice of dried fruit. French Agen prunes are considered the best for flavour, and here they are flavoured with grated nutmeg.

Makes 12

1 egg
250ml/8fl oz/1 cup milk
120ml/4fl oz/½ cup vegetable oil
50g/2oz/4 tbsp caster (superfine) sugar
25g/1oz/2 tbsp soft dark brown sugar
285g/10oz/2½ cups plain (all-purpose) flour
10ml/2 tsp baking powder
a pinch of grated nutmeg
115g/4oz cooked pitted prunes, chopped

1 Preheat the oven to 200°C/400°F/Gas 6. Lightly grease the cups of a muffin tin (pan) or line them with paper cases.

2 Break the egg into a bowl and beat with a fork. Beat in the milk and oil.

3 Stir in the sugars. Set aside.

4 Sift the flour, baking powder and nutmeg into a mixing bowl. Make a well in the centre, pour in the egg mixture and stir until moistened. Do not overmix; the batter should be slightly lumpy.

5 Fold in the prunes. Fill the prepared cups two-thirds full. Bake until golden brown, about 20 minutes. Let stand for 10 minutes before turning out on to a wire rack. Serve warm or at room temperature.

Cook's Tips

- *Prunes are full of fibre, and are a well-known natural laxative.*
- *Store in an airtight container for up to 3 days.*

Yogurt & Honey Muffins

Yogurt and honey are known to boost energy levels, so these muffins go really well in lunchboxes.

Makes 12

50g/2oz/4 tbsp butter
75ml/5 tbsp clear honey
250ml/8fl oz/1 cup natural (plain) yogurt
1 egg
grated rind of 1 lemon
50ml/2fl oz/¼ cup lemon juice
115g/4oz/1 cup plain (all-purpose) flour
115g/4oz/1 cup wholemeal (whole-wheat) flour
7.5ml/1½ tsp bicarbonate of soda (baking soda)
a pinch of grated nutmeg

1 Preheat the oven to 190°C/375°F/Gas 5. Arrange 12 paper cases in a muffin tin (pan).

2 Put the butter and honey into a small pan and heat gently, stirring frequently, until melted and smooth. Remove the pan from the heat and leave to cool slightly.

3 In a large bowl, whisk together the yogurt, egg, lemon rind and juice. Add the butter and honey mixture and whisk well until thoroughly combined.

4 In another bowl, sift together the flours, bicarbonate of soda and nutmeg. Fold the dry ingredients into the yogurt mixture just enough to blend them.

5 Fill the prepared muffin tins two-thirds full. Bake for 20–25 minutes, then leave to cool in the tins for about 5 minutes before transferring to a wire rack.

Variation

For Yogurt, Honey and Walnut Muffins, add 50g/2oz/½ cup chopped walnuts, folded in with the flour, and substitute ground cinnamon for the nutmeg.

Prune Muffins Energy 190kcal/801kJ; Protein 3.7g; Carbohydrate 28.1g, of which sugars 10.7g; Fat 7.8g, of which saturates 1.2g; Cholesterol 17mg; Calcium 66mg; Fibre 1.3g; Sodium 17mg.

Yogurt and Honey Muffins Energy 155kcal/652kJ; Protein 4.7g; Carbohydrate 25.4g, of which sugars 6.9g; Fat 4.6g, of which saturates 2.5g; Cholesterol 25mg; Calcium 66mg; Fibre 1.7g; Sodium 50mg.

Raisin & Bran Muffins

Low in fat and sugar, these dense and filling muffins are made with a combination of wholemeal flour and bran, and are flavoured with spicy cinnamon and juicy raisins. The brown sugar adds caramel notes.

Makes 5
40g/1½oz/⅓ cup plain (all-purpose) flour
55g/2oz/½ cup wholemeal (whole-wheat) flour
7.5ml/1½ tsp bicarbonate of soda (baking soda)
5ml/1 tsp ground cinnamon
30g/1oz/⅓ cup bran
85g/3oz raisins
65g/2½oz/⅓ cup soft dark brown sugar
50g/2oz/¼ cup caster (superfine) sugar
1 egg, beaten
250ml/8fl oz/1 cup buttermilk
juice of ½ lemon
50g/2oz/¼ cup butter, melted

1 Preheat the oven to 200°C/400°F/Gas 6.

2 Grease the cups of a muffin tin (pan) or line them with paper cases.

3 In a mixing bowl, sift together the flours, bicarbonate of soda and cinnamon.

4 Add the bran, raisins and sugars and stir until blended.

5 In another bowl, mix together the egg, buttermilk, lemon juice and melted butter.

6 Add the buttermilk mixture to the dry ingredients and whisk lightly until just moistened. Do not overmix the batter.

7 Spoon the mixture into the prepared paper cases, filling the cups almost to the top. Half-fill any empty cups with water so that the muffins bake evenly.

8 Bake for 15–20 minutes. Let stand for 5 minutes, before turning out on to a wire rack to cool. Serve warm or at room temperature. Store in an airtight container for up to 3 days.

Spiced Sultana Muffins

Sunday breakfasts will never be the same again, once you have tried these delicious muffins! They are easy to prepare and take only a short time to bake.

Makes 6
75g/3oz/6 tbsp butter
1 small (US medium) egg
120ml/4fl oz/½ cup unsweetened coconut milk
150g/5oz/1¼ cups wholemeal (whole-wheat) flour
7.5ml/1½ tsp baking powder
5ml/1 tsp ground cinnamon
a generous pinch of salt
115g/4oz/⅔ cup sultanas (golden raisins)

1 Preheat the oven to 190°C/375°F/Gas 5. Arrange 6 paper cases in a muffin tin (pan).

2 Beat the butter, egg and coconut milk in a bowl until well combined.

3 Sift the wholemeal flour, baking powder, ground cinnamon and salt over the beaten mixture. Fold in carefully, then beat well. Fold in the sultanas. Divide the mixture among the paper cases.

4 Bake for 20 minutes, or until the muffins have risen well and are firm to the touch. Cool slightly on a wire rack before serving warm.

Variation
The heath-conscious or those following a slimming plan can substitute the same quantity of low-fat spread for the butter. The muffins will still be utterly delicious, although not quite so rich in flavour.

Raisin and Bran Muffins Energy 89kcal/374kJ; Protein 2g; Carbohydrate 13.4g, of which sugars 8.9g; Fat 3.4g, of which saturates 1.9g; Cholesterol 20mg; Calcium 34mg; Fibre 1.1g; Sodium 36mg.

Spiced Sultana Muffins Energy 240kcal/1006kJ; Protein 4.9g; Carbohydrate 30.3g, of which sugars 14.9g; Fat 11.9g, of which saturates 6.9g; Cholesterol 58mg; Calcium 35mg; Fibre 2.6g; Sodium 114mg.

Swedish Deep-fried Cakes

These small deep-fried cakes, similar to doughnuts, are an essential part of the Christmas celebrations in Sweden. The characteristic shape is created by cutting a hole in each strip and threading one end through the hole in the middle.

Makes 6–8

15g/½oz/1 tbsp unsalted (sweet) butter
350g/12oz/3 cups plain (all-purpose) flour
5ml/1 tsp baking powder
120ml/4fl oz/½ cup double (heavy) cream
5 egg yolks, beaten
vegetable oil, for deep-frying
200g/7oz/1 cup caster (superfine) sugar

1 Melt the butter and then leave to cool but not set. Sift the flour and baking powder into a large bowl. Add the cream, egg yolks and melted butter and beat together to form a smooth dough. Leave the dough to rest for about 2 hours.

2 On a lightly floured work surface, thinly roll out the dough into a rectangle. Cut the rectangle into 1cm/½in strips, and then cut each strip into 5cm/2in pieces.

3 Cut a slit in the centre of each piece of dough, fold each piece in half and then put one end through the hole and press down to flatten the cake.

4 Heat the vegetable oil in a large pan or deep-fryer to 180°C/350°F or until a cube of bread, dropped into the oil, turns brown in 1 minute. Put the caster sugar on a large plate and set it aside.

5 Drop the cakes, in batches so that the pan is not overcrowded, into the hot oil and cook them, turning once with a slotted spoon, until they are golden brown and crispy. Remove the cakes and drain on kitchen paper.

6 Transfer the cakes to the sugar and turn them coating them on both sides. Serve them warm or cold.

Sugar-dusted Ring Doughnuts

These are the ultimate classic doughnuts – light, fluffy, delicious and sweet.

Makes 12

225g/8oz/2 cups strong white bread flour, plus extra for dusting
7g/¼oz/1½ tsp easy-blend (rapid-rise) dried yeast
15ml/1 tbsp caster (superfine) sugar
a pinch of salt
65g/2½oz/5 tbsp butter, cubed and chilled
1 egg, beaten
120ml/4fl oz/½ cup full-fat (whole) milk, lukewarm
about 1 litre/1¾ pints/4 cups sunflower oil, for frying

For the coating

115g/4oz/generous ½ cup caster (superfine) sugar

1 Sift the flour together with the yeast, sugar and salt into a bowl. Add the butter and rub into the flour mixture. Add the egg and milk, and knead the mixture until it all comes together.

2 Turn out the dough on to a lightly floured work surface and knead for 10 minutes, or until silky smooth. Roll into a ball and place in a clean, lightly greased bowl. Cover with clear film (plastic wrap) and leave to rest in a warm place for about 1 hour, or until doubled in size.

3 Roll out the dough on a lightly floured work surface until it is roughly 1cm/½in thick. Using a doughnut cookie cutter, cut out 12 rings and place each of these on to a baking parchment square. Cover loosely with clear film and leave to stand in a warm place for 30 minutes, until slightly risen.

4 Heat the oil for deep-frying in a large, deep pan to 170°C/340°F. Gently lift the doughnuts and slide each one (minus the baking parchment) into the hot oil in batches of three. Cook them for 30–60 seconds on each side, or until golden brown all over. Remove the doughnuts from the oil with a slotted spoon, and drain on kitchen paper.

5 Place the sugar for sprinkling on a plate. While the doughnuts are still warm, toss them in the sugar, coating them all over.

Swedish Deep-fried Cakes Energy 436kcal/1830kJ; Protein 6.3g; Carbohydrate 60.4g, of which sugars 27.1g; Fat 20.5g, of which saturates 7.9g; Cholesterol 151mg; Calcium 97mg; Fibre 1.4g; Sodium 23mg.

Sugar-dusted Ring Doughnuts Energy 203kcal/853kJ; Protein 2.6g; Carbohydrate 29.4g, of which sugars 16.3g; Fat 9.2g, of which saturates 2.4g; Cholesterol 10mg; Calcium 34mg; Fibre 0g; Sodium 95mg.

Cinnamon Doughnuts

These doughnuts are made to an Eastern European recipe and are, of course, best eaten on the day they are made. They are dusted with sugar and cinnamon, and are also an ideal showcase for your finest home-made jam. In the Balkans they are usually filled with a thick fruity jam such as cherry, plum or apricot.

Makes 10–12

225g/8oz/2 cups strong white bread flour
2.5ml/½ tsp salt
7g/¼oz easy-blend (rapid-rise) dried yeast
1 egg, beaten
60–90ml/4–6 tbsp milk
15ml/1 tbsp sugar
about 60ml/4 tbsp cherry jam
oil, for deep-fat frying
50g/2oz/¼ cup caster (superfine) sugar
2.5ml/½ tsp cinnamon

1 Sift the flour into a bowl with the salt. Stir in the yeast. Make a well in the dry ingredients and add the egg, milk and sugar. Mix together thoroughly, adding a little more milk if necessary, to make a smooth, but not sticky, dough. Beat well, then cover with clear film (plastic wrap) and leave for about 1–1½ hours in a warm place until the dough has doubled in size.

2 Grease a baking sheet. Knead the dough on a lightly floured surface and divide it into 10–12 pieces. Shape each into a round and put 5ml/1 tsp of jam in the centre.

3 Dampen the edges of the dough with water, then draw up to form a ball, closing firmly so the jam will not escape during cooking. Place on the baking sheet and leave for 15 minutes.

4 Heat the oil in a large pan or deep fryer to 180°C/350°F, or until a 2.5cm/1in cube of bread dropped into the oil turns golden in about 60 seconds. Fry the doughnuts fairly gently for 5–10 minutes, until golden brown. Drain well on kitchen paper.

5 Mix the caster sugar and ground cinnamon together on a plate or in a large plastic bag and use to liberally coat the doughnuts while still warm.

Baked Coffee Ring Doughnuts

A soft, velvety coffee glaze covers these delicious cakey doughnuts.

Makes 12

non-stick baking oil or melted butter, for greasing
100g/33⁄4oz/scant ½ cup butter, softened
150g/5oz/¾ cup caster (superfine) sugar
5ml/1 tsp vanilla extract
2 eggs
275g/10oz/2½ cups plain (all-purpose) flour
10ml/2 tsp baking powder
15ml/1 tbsp instant coffee
a pinch of salt
150ml/¼ pint/⅔ cup full-fat (whole) milk

For the topping

300g/11oz/3¾ cups icing (confectioners') sugar
10ml/2 tsp instant coffee
50ml/2fl oz/¼ cup water

1 Preheat the oven to 180°C/350°F/Gas 4. Spray a 12-cup doughnut baking tin (pan) with non-stick baking oil, or brush with melted butter.

2 Place the softened butter, caster sugar and vanilla extract in a bowl, and whisk together until light and creamy. Add the eggs, one at a time, whisking to make sure the first one is fully incorporated before adding the second.

3 Sift the flour, baking powder, coffee and salt into the mixture and fold in. Add the milk and mix just until it all comes together.

4 Transfer the mixture to a piping (pastry) bag fitted with a round nozzle, then pipe the mixture into the prepared baking tin, dividing it evenly between the cups.

5 Place the tin in the middle of the oven and bake for 15 minutes, or until golden brown. Remove from the oven and leave to stand for 5 minutes before removing the doughnuts from the tin.

6 For the topping, mix the icing sugar with the coffee and water in a small bowl to make a smooth paste, then spoon over the tops of the doughnuts while they are still slightly warm.

Cinnamon Doughnuts per doughnut Energy 192kcal/803kJ; Protein 2.5g; Carbohydrate 22.6g, of which sugars 8.3g; Fat 10.8g, of which saturates 1.4g; Cholesterol 16mg; Calcium 37mg; Fibre 0.6g; Sodium 11mg.

Baked Coffee Ring Doughnuts Energy 311kcal/1314kJ; Protein 3.9g; Carbohydrate 57.7g, of which sugars 40g; Fat 8.8g, of which saturates 5g; Cholesterol 58mg; Calcium 58mg; Fibre 1g; Sodium 74mg.

Double Chocolate Ring Doughnuts

These doughnuts are dark, indulgent and chocolatey through and through.

Makes 12

225g/8oz/2 cups plain (all-purpose) flour
25g/1oz/¼ cup unsweetened cocoa powder
25g/1oz/2 tbsp caster (superfine) sugar
7g/¼oz/1½ tsp easy-blend (rapid-rise) dried yeast
a pinch of salt
65g/2½oz/5 tbsp butter, cubed and chilled
1 egg
120ml/4fl oz/½ cup full-fat (whole) milk, lukewarm
about 1 litre/1¾ pints/4 cups sunflower oil, for frying

For the glaze

100g/3¾oz dark (bittersweet) chocolate, broken into pieces
100ml/3½fl oz/scant ½ cup golden (light corn) syrup
50g/2oz/¼ cup butter

1 Sift the flour together with the cocoa powder, sugar, yeast and salt into a bowl. Add the butter and rub into the flour mixture. Add the egg and milk, and knead the mixture.

2 Turn out the dough on to a lightly floured work surface and knead for 10 minutes. Roll into a ball and place in a clean, lightly greased bowl. Cover with clear film (plastic wrap) and leave to rest in a warm place for about 1 hour, or until doubled in size.

3 Cut the dough into 12 pieces and roll into balls, placing each one on to a baking parchment square. Cover the balls with clear film, then leave to stand in a warm place for 30 minutes.

4 Heat the oil in a large, deep pan to 170°C/340°F. Lift the doughnuts and slide each one (minus the baking parchment) into the hot oil in batches of three. Cook them for 30–60 seconds on each side. Remove the doughnuts from the oil with a slotted spoon and drain on kitchen paper.

5 To make the glaze, melt the chocolate, golden syrup and butter together in a non-stick pan over a low heat, stirring until smooth and glossy. Pour the glaze into a bowl and dip each doughnut into it, while still slightly warm. Allow to set.

Caramel-filled Doughnuts

These rich doughnuts are filled with thick caramel.

Makes 12

225g/8oz/2 cups strong white bread flour, plus extra for dusting
7g/¼oz/1½ tsp easy-blend (rapid-rise) dried yeast
15ml/1 tbsp caster (superfine) sugar
a pinch of salt
65g/2½oz/5 tbsp butter, cubed and chilled
1 egg, beaten
120ml/4fl oz/½ cup full-fat (whole) milk, lukewarm
about 1 litre/1¾ pints/4 cups sunflower oil, for frying
handful of strawberries, to serve

For the filling

150ml/¼ pint/⅔ cup caramel sauce

1 Sift the flour together with the yeast, sugar and salt into a bowl. Add the butter and rub into the flour mixture. Add the egg and milk, and knead the mixture until it all comes together.

2 Turn out the dough on to a lightly floured work surface and knead for 10 minutes. Roll into a ball and place back into the bowl, cover with clear film (plastic wrap) and leave to rest in a warm place for about 1 hour, or until doubled in size.

3 Cut the dough into 12 even pieces, and roll into balls. Place each one on to a baking parchment square. Cover loosely with clear film and leave to stand in a warm place for 30 minutes.

4 Heat the oil in a large, deep pan to 170°C/340°F. Lift the doughnuts and slide each one (minus the baking parchment) into the hot oil in batches of three. Cook them for 30–60 seconds on each side, or until golden brown. Remove the doughnuts from the oil with a slotted spoon, and drain on kitchen paper.

5 Poke the handle of a teaspoon into the side of each doughnut, moving the handle around in a circular motion to make room for the filling. Fill a piping (pastry) bag with the caramel, then pipe a small amount into each doughnut, while they are still slightly warm. Serve with strawberries and any leftover caramel.

Double Chocolate Ring Doughnuts Energy 270kcal/1131kJ; Protein 3.4g; Carbohydrate 31.5g, of which sugars 18.1g; Fat 15.4g, of which saturates 6.2g; Cholesterol 19mg; Calcium 39mg; Fibre 0.6g; Sodium 162mg.
Caramel-filled Doughnuts Energy 220kcal/923kJ; Protein 2.9g; Carbohydrate 29.4g, of which sugars 16.3g; Fat 10.9g, of which saturates 3.5g; Cholesterol 15mg; Calcium 46mg; Fibre 0g; Sodium 112mg.

Wholemeal Ring Doughnuts

These doughnuts offer a wholesome alternative to plain doughnuts.

Makes 12

225g/8oz/2 cups strong wholemeal (whole-wheat) bread flour, plus extra for dusting
7g/¼oz/1½ tsp easy-blend (rapid-rise) dried yeast
15ml/1 tbsp caster (superfine) sugar
a pinch of salt
65g/2½oz/5 tbsp butter, cubed and chilled
1 egg, beaten
120ml/4fl oz/½ cup full-fat (whole) milk, lukewarm
about 1 litre/1¾ pints/4 cups sunflower oil, for frying

For the coating

115g/4oz/generous ½ cup demerara (raw) sugar

1 Sift the flour together with the yeast, sugar and salt into a bowl. Add the butter and rub into the flour mixture. Add the egg and milk, and knead the mixture until it all comes together.

2 Turn out the dough on to a lightly floured work surface and knead for 10 minutes. Roll into a ball and place in a clean, lightly greased bowl. Cover with clear film (plastic wrap) and leave to rest in a warm place for about 1 hour, or until doubled in size.

3 Roll out the dough on a lightly floured work surface until it is roughly 1cm/½in thick. Using a doughnut cookie cutter, cut out 12 rings and place each of these on to a baking parchment square. Cover loosely with clear film and leave to stand in a warm place for 30 minutes, until slightly risen.

4 Heat the oil in a large, deep pan to 170°C/340°F. Gently lift the doughnuts using the edges of the baking parchment, without disturbing the doughnuts, and slide each one (minus the baking parchment) into the hot oil in batches of three. Cook them for 30–60 seconds on each side or until golden brown all over. Remove the doughnuts from the oil with a slotted spoon, and drain on kitchen paper.

5 Place the demerara sugar on a plate, and toss the doughnuts in the sugar, while they are still slightly warm.

Baked Banana Bread Doughnuts

This is a good way of using up any overripe bananas, as they impart sweet and fruity flavours to these light and fluffy baked doughnuts.

Makes 12

non-stick baking oil or melted butter, for greasing
100g/3¾oz/scant ½ cup butter, softened
150g/5oz/¾ cup caster (superfine) sugar
5ml/1 tsp vanilla extract
2 eggs
275g/10oz/2½ cups plain (all-purpose) flour
10ml/2 tsp baking powder
a pinch of salt
50ml/2fl oz/¼ cup full-fat (whole) milk
3 ripe bananas
icing (confectioners') sugar, for sprinkling

1 Preheat the oven to 180°C/350°F/Gas 4. Spray a 12-cup doughnut baking tin (pan) with non-stick baking oil, or brush with melted butter.

2 Place the softened butter, caster sugar and vanilla extract in a bowl, and whisk together until light and creamy. Add the eggs, one at a time, whisking to make sure the first one is fully incorporated before adding the second.

3 Sift the flour, baking powder and salt into the mixture, and fold in. Add the milk, and mix just until it all comes together. Peel and mash the bananas with a fork and then fold into the batter until fully incorporated.

4 Transfer the mixture to a piping (pastry) bag fitted with a round nozzle, then pipe the mixture into the prepared baking tin, dividing it evenly between the cups. Piping the mixture makes it easier to create neat circles, but you can spoon the mixture into the tin, if you prefer.

5 Place the tin in the middle of the oven. Bake for 15 minutes, or until golden brown. Leave to stand for 5 minutes before removing them from the tin. Lightly sprinkle with icing sugar, while they are still slightly warm.

Wholemeal Ring Doughnuts Energy 203kcal/853kJ; Protein 2.6g; Carbohydrate 29.4g, of which sugars 16.3g; Fat 9.2g, of which saturates 2.4g; Cholesterol 10mg; Calcium 34mg; Fibre 3.5g; Sodium 95mg.

Baked Banana Bread Doughnuts per doughnut 153kcal/640kJ; Protein 1.8g; Carbohydrate 19.1g, of which sugars 18.5g; Fat 8.2g, of which saturates 4.8g; Cholesterol 57mg; Calcium 17mg; Fibre 0.4g; Sodium 67mg.

Fruit & Honey Pancakes

The batter for these delightfully fluffy pancakes uses yeast to make them extra light. For the topping, you can use a mixture of any berries that are in season. When dusted with white icing sugar, the finished dish is both attractive and irresistible.

Makes 12

165g/5½oz/generous 1¼ cups plain (all-purpose) flour
150ml/¼ pint/⅔ cup warm milk
10ml/2 tsp sugar
5ml/1 tsp salt
2 eggs, separated
10g/¼oz fresh yeast, crumbled
15ml/1 tbsp sour cream
10ml/2 tsp clarified butter

For the topping

60ml/4 tbsp clear honey
115g/4oz/1 cup fresh berries, such as raspberries, blueberries or strawberries
icing (confectioners') sugar, for dusting

1 Put the flour in a large bowl and make a well in the centre. Add the warm milk, sugar and salt, and combine. Stir in the egg yolks and add the yeast. Mix well until you have a smooth batter.

2 Cover and leave in a warm place for 1 hour, or until the batter has doubled in size.

3 Put the egg whites into a clean, grease-free bowl and whisk until they form soft peaks. Fold them into the pancake batter. Stir in the sour cream.

4 Put a heavy, non-stick frying pan, about 18cm/7in in diameter, on medium-high heat. Brush the surface of the pan with a little clarified butter.

5 Pour a ladleful of the pancake mixture into the pan and cook for about 40 seconds, or until golden brown on the underside and the top is set. Flip over and cook the other side until golden.

6 Serve the pancakes hot with a drizzle of honey and some berries, gently dusted with a sprinkling of icing sugar.

Blueberry Pancakes

These are rather like the thick American breakfast pancakes – although they can, of course, be eaten at any time of the day.

Makes 6–8

115g/4oz/1 cup self-raising (self-rising) flour
a pinch of salt
45–60ml/3–4 tbsp caster (superfine) sugar
2 eggs
120ml/4fl oz/½ cup milk
15–30ml/1–2 tbsp oil
115g/4oz/1 cup fresh or frozen blueberries, plus extra to decorate
maple syrup, to serve
lemon wedges, to decorate

1 Sift the flour into a bowl with the salt and sugar. Beat together the eggs thoroughly. Make a well in the middle of the flour and stir in the eggs.

2 Gradually blend in a little of the milk to make a smooth batter. Then whisk in the rest of the milk and whisk for 1–2 minutes. Allow to rest for 20–30 minutes.

3 Heat a few drops of oil in a pancake pan or heavy frying pan until just hazy. Pour about 30ml/2 tbsp of the batter and swirl the batter around until it makes an even shape.

4 Cook for 2–3 minutes and when almost set on top, sprinkle over 15–30ml/1–2 tbsp blueberries. As soon as the base is loose and golden brown, turn the pancake over.

5 Cook on the second side for only about 1 minute, until golden and crisp. Slide the pancake on to a plate and serve drizzled with maple syrup. Continue with the rest of the batter. Serve decorated with lemon wedges and a few extra blueberries.

Cook's Tip
Instead of blueberries, you could use blackberries or raspberries. If you use canned fruit, make sure it is very well drained.

Fruit and Honey Pancakes Energy 85kcal/361kJ; Protein 2.9g; Carbohydrate 16g, of which sugars 5.5g; Fat 1.6g, of which saturates 0.6g; Cholesterol 33mg; Calcium 42mg; Fibre 0.5g; Sodium 21mg.

Blueberry Pancakes Energy 111Kcal/468kJ; Protein 3.5g; Carbohydrate 18.2g, of which sugars 7.5g; Fat 3.2g, of which saturates 0.8g; Cholesterol 48mg; Calcium 84mg; Fibre 0.9g; Sodium 76mg.

Cherry Pancakes

These pancakes are virtually fat-free, and they are lower in calories and higher in fibre than traditional ones. They also freeze well, which is handy – layer them, separated by waxed paper, before freezing.

Serves 4

50g/2oz/½ cup plain (all-purpose) flour
50g/2oz/½ cup wholemeal (whole-wheat) flour
a pinch of salt
1 egg white
150ml/¼ pint/⅔ cup skimmed milk
150ml/¼ pint/⅔ cup water
a little oil, for frying

For the filling

425g/15oz can black cherries in juice
7.5ml/1½ tsp arrowroot

1 Sift the flours and salt into a bowl, adding any bran left in the sieve (strainer) to the bowl at the end.

2 Make a well in the centre of the flour and add the egg white. Gradually beat in the milk and the water, whisking hard until all the liquid is incorporated and the batter is smooth and bubbly.

3 Heat a non-stick pan with a small amount of oil until the pan is very hot. Pour in just enough batter to cover the base of the pan, swirling the pan to cover the base evenly.

4 Cook until the pancake is set and golden, and then turn to cook the other side. Remove to a sheet of kitchen paper and then cook the remaining batter to make about eight pancakes.

5 Drain the cherries, reserving the juice. Blend about 30ml/2 tbsp of the juice from the can of cherries with the arrowroot in a pan. Stir in the rest of the juice. Heat gently, stirring, until boiling. Stir over a moderate heat for about 2 minutes, until thickened and clear.

6 Add the cherries and stir until thoroughly heated. Spoon the cherries into the pancakes and fold them into quarters.

Pineapple & Cinnamon Drop Scones

Making the batter with pineapple juice instead of milk cuts down on the fat and adds a fruity piquancy to the flavour of these delicious drop scones.

Makes 24

115g/4oz/1 cup self-raising (self-rising) wholemeal (whole-wheat) flour
115g/4oz/1 cup self-raising (self-rising) white flour
5ml/1 tsp ground cinnamon
15ml/1 tbsp caster (superfine) sugar
1 egg
300ml/½ pint/1¼ cups pineapple juice
75g/3oz/½ cup semi-dried pineapple, chopped

1 Put the wholemeal flour in a mixing bowl. Sift in the white flour, add the cinnamon and caster sugar and mix together. Make a well in the centre. Add the egg with half of the pineapple juice to the well.

2 Gradually incorporate the flour to make a smooth batter, then beat in the remaining pineapple juice and stir in the chopped pineapple.

3 Heat a griddle, then lightly grease it. Drop tablespoons of the batter on to the surface, spacing them apart, and leave them until they bubble and the bubbles begin to burst.

4 Turn over the drop scones with a metal spatula and cook until the underside is golden brown. Continue to cook in successive batches.

Cook's Tips
- *Drop scones do not keep well, and are best eaten freshly cooked. In any case, they are especially delicious served hot.*
- *If self-raising (self-rising) wholemeal (whole-wheat) flour is not readily available, use white self-raising flour instead.*

Cherry Pancakes Energy 200Kcal/852kJ; Protein 4.9g; Carbohydrate 40.7g, of which sugars 21.7g; Fat 3.2g, of which saturates 0.4g; Cholesterol 1mg; Calcium 97mg; Fibre 1.4g; Sodium 41mg.

Pineapple and Cinnamon Drop Scones Energy48kcal/202kJ; Protein 1g; Carbohydrate 10g, of which sugars 3g; Fat 0g, of which saturates 0g; Cholesterol 10mg; Calcium 27mg; Fibre 0.9g; Sodium 32mg.

Coconut Pancakes

These light and sweet pancakes are often served in the streets of Bangkok, and they make a delightful tasty dessert.

Makes 8

75g/3oz/⅔ cup plain (all-purpose) flour, sifted
50g/2oz/¼ cup rice flour
40g/1½oz caster (superfine) sugar
50g/2oz/⅔ cup desiccated (dry unsweetened shredded) coconut
1 egg
275ml/9fl oz/generous 1 cup coconut milk
vegetable oil, for frying
lime wedges and maple syrup, to serve

1 Place the plain flour, rice flour, sugar and coconut in a bowl, stir to mix and then make a small well in the centre. Break the egg into the well and pour in the coconut milk.

2 With a whisk or fork, beat the egg into the coconut milk and then gradually incorporate the surrounding dry ingredients, whisking constantly until the mixture forms a batter. The mixture will not be entirely smooth, because of the coconut, but there shouldn't be any large lumps.

3 Heat a little oil in a 13cm/5in non-stick frying pan. Pour in about 45ml/3 tbsp of the mixture and quickly spread to a thin layer with the back of a spoon. Cook over a high heat for about 30–60 seconds, until bubbles appear on the surface of the pancake, then turn it over with a spatula and cook the other side until golden.

4 Slide the pancake on to a plate and keep warm in a very low oven. Make more pancakes in the same way. Serve warm with lime wedges for squeezing and maple syrup for drizzling.

Cook's Tip
Maple syrup is an international favourite for serving with pancakes, and tastes very good with these ones. It is best to buy the pure syrup to ensure the best flavour.

Chocolate Chip Banana Pancakes

These tasty little morsels will go down well with both adults and children alike.

Makes 16

2 ripe bananas
2 eggs
200ml/7fl oz/scant 1 cup milk
150g/5oz/1¼ cups self-raising (self-rising) flour, sifted
25g/1oz/⅓ cup ground almonds
15g/½oz/1 tbsp caster (superfine) sugar
a pinch of salt
15ml/1 tbsp plain (semisweet) chocolate chips
butter, for frying
50g/2oz/½ cup toasted flaked (sliced) almonds

For the topping

150ml/¼ pint/⅔ cup double (heavy) cream
15g/½oz/1 tbsp icing (confectioners') sugar

1 Mash the bananas in a bowl. Beat in the eggs and half the milk. Mix in the flour, ground almonds, sugar and salt. Add the remaining milk and the chocolate chips.

2 Stir the mixture well until it makes a thick batter. Heat a little butter in a non-stick frying pan. Spoon the pancake mixture into the pan in heaps, allowing room for them to spread. When the pancakes are lightly browned underneath and bubbling on top, flip them over to cook the other side. Slide on to a plate and keep hot. Make more pancakes in the same way.

3 Make the topping. Pour the cream into a bowl. Add the icing sugar to sweeten it slightly, and whip to soft peaks. Spoon the cream on to the pancakes and decorate with flaked almonds. Serve immediately.

Cook's Tips
• *To toast flaked (sliced) almonds, simply put under the grill (broiler) for a few minutes, shaking the pan, until lightly golden.*
• *You could add sliced banana, tossed in lemon juice, to the topping to enhance the banana flavour of the pancakes. If you prefer, use yogurt as a low-fat alternative to cream.*

Coconut Pancakes Energy 136Kcal/572kJ; Protein 2.6g; Carbohydrate 21.3g, of which sugars 8.1g; Fat 4.9g, of which saturates 3.6g; Cholesterol 24mg; Calcium 33mg; Fibre 1.3g; Sodium 49mg.

Chocolate Chip Banana Pancakes Energy 192Kcal/798kJ; Protein 3.4g; Carbohydrate 13.7g, of which sugars 6.3g; Fat 14.1g, of which saturates 7.1g; Cholesterol 51mg; Calcium 70mg; Fibre 0.8g; Sodium 89mg.

Chocolate & Orange Scotch Pancakes

Fabulous mini pancakes in a rich orange liqueur sauce.

Serves 4

115g/4oz/1 cup self-raising (self-rising) flour
30ml/2 tbsp cocoa powder (unsweetened)
2 eggs
50g/2oz plain (semisweet) chocolate, broken into squares
200ml/7fl oz/scant 1 cup milk
finely grated rind of 1 orange
30ml/2 tbsp orange juice
butter or oil, for frying
60ml/4 tbsp chocolate curls, to decorate

For the sauce

2 large oranges
25g/1oz/2 tbsp unsalted (sweet) butter
40g/1½oz/3 tbsp light muscovado (brown) sugar
250ml/8fl oz/1 cup crème fraîche
30ml/2 tbsp orange liqueur

1 Sift the flour and cocoa into a bowl and make a well in the centre. Add the eggs and beat well, gradually incorporating the surrounding dry ingredients to make a smooth batter.

2 Mix the chocolate and milk in a heavy pan. Heat gently until the chocolate has melted, then beat into the batter until smooth and bubbly. Stir in the grated orange rind and juice.

3 Heat a large heavy frying pan or griddle. Grease with a little butter or oil. Drop large spoonfuls of batter on to the hot surface. Cook over a moderate heat. When the pancakes are lightly browned underneath and bubbling on top, flip them over to cook the other side. Slide on to a plate and keep hot, then make more in the same way.

4 Make the sauce. Grate the rind of 1 of the oranges into a bowl and set aside. Peel both oranges, taking care to remove all the pith, then slice the flesh fairly thinly. Heat the butter and sugar in a wide, shallow pan over a low heat, stirring until the sugar dissolves. Stir in the crème fraîche and heat gently.

5 Add the pancakes and orange slices to the sauce, heat gently for 1–2 minutes, then spoon on the liqueur. Sprinkle with the reserved orange rind. Scatter over chocolate curls and serve.

Chocolate Crêpes with Plums & Port

The crêpes, filling and sauce can be made in advance and assembled at the last minute.

Serves 6

50g/2oz plain (semisweet) chocolate, broken into squares
200ml/7fl oz/scant 1 cup milk
120ml/4fl oz/½ cup single (light) cream
30ml/2 tbsp cocoa powder (unsweetened)
115g/4oz/1 cup plain (all-purpose) flour
2 eggs

For the filling

500g/1¼lb red or golden plums
50g/2oz/¼ cup caster (superfine) sugar
30ml/2 tbsp water
30ml/2 tbsp port
oil, for frying
175g/6oz/¾ cup crème fraîche

For the sauce

150g/5oz plain (semisweet) chocolate, broken into squares
175ml/6fl oz/¾ cup double (heavy) cream
30ml/2 tbsp port

1 Place the chocolate and milk in a heavy pan. Heat gently until the chocolate dissolves. Pour into a blender or food processor and add the cream, cocoa, flour and eggs. Process until smooth. Pour into a jug (pitcher) and chill for 30 minutes.

2 Meanwhile, make the filling. Halve and stone (pit) the plums. Place in a pan with the sugar and water. Bring to the boil, then lower the heat, cover and simmer for about 10 minutes or until the plums are tender. Stir in the port and simmer for a further 30 seconds. Remove from the heat and keep warm.

3 Have ready a sheet of baking parchment. Heat a crêpe pan, grease lightly with a little oil, then pour in just enough batter to cover the base of the pan, swirling to coat it evenly. Cook until the crêpe has set, then flip it over to cook the other side. Slide on to the paper, then cook 9–11 more crêpes in the same way.

4 Make the sauce. Put the chocolate and cream in a pan. Heat gently, stirring until smooth. Add the port and stir for 1 minute.

5 Divide the plums between the crêpes, add a dollop of crème fraîche to each and roll up. Serve with the sauce spooned over.

Chocolate and Orange Scotch Pancakes Energy 752Kcal/3131kJ; Protein 12.1g; Carbohydrate 58.1g, of which sugars 35.5g; Fat 53.2g, of which saturates 27g; Cholesterol 185mg; Calcium 282mg; Fibre 3.9g; Sodium 304mg.

Chocolate Crêpes with Plums and Port Energy 867Kcal/3604kJ; Protein 10.6g; Carbohydrate 57.4g, of which sugars 41.7g; Fat 67g, of which saturates 36.7g; Cholesterol 184mg; Calcium 175mg; Fibre 3.4g; Sodium 115mg.

Croissants

Enjoy breakfast Continental-style with these melt-in-the-mouth croissants.

Makes 18

15ml/1 tbsp active dried yeast
325ml/11fl oz/1 1/3 cups lukewarm milk
10ml/2 tsp caster (superfine) sugar
12.5ml/1 1/2 tsp salt
450g/1lb/4 cups strong white bread flour
225g/8oz/1 cup cold unsalted (sweet) butter
1 egg, beaten with 10ml/2 tsp water, to glaze

1 In a large bowl, stir together the yeast and milk. Leave for about 15 minutes for the yeast to become frothy. Stir in the sugar and salt, and about 150g/5oz/1 1/4 cups of the flour.

2 Slowly add the remaining flour. Mix well until the dough pulls away from the sides of the bowl. Cover and leave to rise in a warm place until doubled in size, about 1 1/2 hours.

3 Turn out on to a lightly floured surface and knead until smooth. Wrap in baking parchment and chill for 15 minutes.

4 Roll out the butter between two sheets of baking parchment to make two 15 x 10cm/6 x 4in rectangles. Roll out the dough to a 30 x 20cm/12 x 8in rectangle.

5 Interleave the butter with the dough. With a short side facing you, roll it out again to 30 x 20cm/12 x 8in. Fold in thirds again, wrap and chill for 30 minutes. Repeat this procedure twice, then chill for 2 hours.

6 Roll out the dough to a rectangle about 3mm/1/8in thick. Trim the sides, and then cut into 18 equal triangles. Roll up from the base to the point. Place point down on baking sheets and curve to form crescents. Cover and leave to rise in a warm place until more than doubled in size, about 1–1 1/2 hours.

7 Preheat the oven to 240°C/475°F/Gas 9. Brush with egg glaze. Bake for 2 minutes. Lower the heat to 190°C/375°F/Gas 5 and bake until golden, about 10–12 minutes. Serve warm.

Apricot Triangles

These quite substantial pastries have a luscious filling of dried apricots poached with cinnamon, but a variety of other fillings are also popular. If serving them as snacks, you can make the pastry cases smaller and more delicate.

Makes 24

115g/4oz/1/2 cup unsalted (sweet) butter, softened
250g/9oz/generous 1 cup sugar
30ml/2 tbsp milk
1 egg, beaten
5ml/1 tsp vanilla extract
a pinch of salt
200–250g/7–9oz/1 1/4–2 1/4 cups plain (all-purpose) flour, plus extra for dusting
icing (confectioners') sugar, for dusting (optional)

For the filling

250g/9oz/generous 1 cup dried apricots
1 cinnamon stick
45ml/3 tbsp sugar

1 Beat the butter and sugar until pale and fluffy. In another bowl, mix together the milk, egg, vanilla extract and salt.

2 Add one-third of the flour, stir, then add the rest in batches, alternating with the milk mixture. Cover and chill for 1 hour.

3 To make the filling, put the ingredients in a pan and add enough water to cover. Heat gently, then simmer for 15 minutes, until the apricots are tender and most of the liquid has evaporated. Remove the cinnamon stick, then purée the apricots in a food processor or blender with a little of the cooking liquid until they form a consistency like thick jam.

4 Preheat the oven to 180°C/350°F/Gas 4. On a lightly floured surface, roll out the dough to 5mm/1/4in thick, then cut into 7.5cm/3in rounds using a cookie cutter.

5 Place 15–30ml/1–2 tbsp of filling in the centre of each round, then pinch the pastry together to form three corners.

6 Place on a baking sheet and bake for 15 minutes, or until pale golden. Serve warm or cold, dusted with icing sugar.

Croissants Energy 189kcal/789kJ; Protein 3g; Carbohydrate 20.9g, of which sugars 1.9g; Fat 10.9g, of which saturates 6.8g; Cholesterol 28mg; Calcium 59mg; Fibre 0.8g; Sodium 357mg.

Apricot Triangles Energy 125kcal/528kJ; Protein 1.6g; Carbohydrate 21.3g, of which sugars 14.9g; Fat 4.4g, of which saturates 2.6g; Cholesterol 18mg; Calcium 28mg; Fibre 0.9g; Sodium 35mg.

Fruit-filled Empanadas

Imagine biting through crisp buttery pastry to discover a rich fruity filling flavoured with oranges and cinnamon. These are the stuff that dreams are made of.

Makes 12

275g/10oz/2½ cups plain (all-purpose) flour
30ml/2 tbsp sugar
75g/3oz/6 tbsp chilled butter, cubed
1 egg yolk
iced water
milk, to glaze
sugar, for sprinkling
whole almonds and orange wedges, to serve

For the filling

30ml/2 tbsp butter
3 ripe plantains, peeled and mashed
2.5ml/½ tsp ground cloves
5ml/1 tsp ground cinnamon
200g/7oz/1⅓ cups raisins
grated rind and juice of 2 oranges

1 Make the pastry. Combine the flour and sugar in a mixing bowl. Rub in the chilled cubes of butter until the mixture resembles fine breadcrumbs.

2 Beat the egg yolk and add to the flour mixture. Add enough iced water to make a smooth dough, then shape into a ball.

3 Make the filling. Melt the butter in a pan. Add the plantains, cloves and cinnamon and cook over medium heat for 2–3 minutes. Stir in the raisins with the orange rind and juice. Lower the heat so that the mixture barely simmers. Cook for about 15 minutes, until the raisins are plump and the juice has evaporated. Set the mixture aside to cool.

4 Preheat the oven to 200°C/400°F/Gas 6. Roll out the pastry on a lightly floured surface. Cut it into 10cm/4in rounds. Place the rounds on a baking sheet and spoon on a little of the filling. Dampen the rim of the pastry rounds with water, fold the pastry over the filling and crimp the edges to seal.

5 Brush the empanadas with milk. Bake in batches for about 15 minutes or until golden. Allow to cool a little, sprinkle with sugar and serve warm, with almonds and orange wedges.

Baked Sweet Ravioli

These sweet pastries have a wonderful ricotta filling.

Serves 4

175g/6oz/¾ cup ricotta cheese
50g/2oz/¼ cup caster (superfine) sugar
4ml/¾ tsp vanilla extract
small egg, beaten, plus 1 egg yolk
15ml/1 tbsp mixed glacé (candied) fruits
25g/1oz dark (bittersweet) chocolate, finely chopped

For the pastry

225g/8oz/2 cups plain (all-purpose) flour
65g/2½oz/5 tbsp caster (superfine) sugar
90g/3½oz/scant ½ cup butter, diced
1 egg
5ml/1 tsp finely grated lemon rind

1 Make the pastry. Place the flour and sugar in a food processor and gradually process in the butter. Keep the motor running while you add the egg and lemon rind to make a dough.

2 Transfer the dough to a sheet of clear film (plastic wrap), cover with another sheet of film and flatten into a round. Chill.

3 Press the ricotta through a sieve (strainer) into a bowl. Stir in the sugar, vanilla, egg yolk, glacé fruits and dark chocolate.

4 Bring the pastry back to room temperature. Divide in half and roll each between clear film to make rectangles measuring 15 x 56cm/6 x 22in. Preheat the oven to 180°C/350°F/Gas 4.

5 Arrange heaped tablespoonfuls of the filling in two rows along one of the pastry strips, leaving a 2.5cm/1in margin around each. Brush the pastry between the mounds of filling with beaten egg. Place the second strip of pastry on top and press down between each mound of filling to seal.

6 Use a 6cm/2½in plain pastry (cookie) cutter to cut around each mound of filling to make small circular ravioli. Gently pinch each ravioli with your fingertips to seal the edges. Place on a greased baking sheet and bake for 15 minutes until golden brown. Serve warm, sprinkled with lemon rind, if you wish.

Fruit-filled Empanadas Energy 235Kcal/990kJ; Protein 3.2g; Carbohydrate 39.7g, of which sugars 21.6g; Fat 8.1g, of which saturates 4.8g; Cholesterol 35mg; Calcium 47mg; Fibre 1.4g; Sodium 66mg.

Baked Sweet Ravioli Energy 628Kcal/2636kJ; Protein 13.1g; Carbohydrate 81.4g, of which sugars 38.5g; Fat 30.1g, of which saturates 17.7g; Cholesterol 162mg; Calcium 119mg; Fibre 2.1g; Sodium 186mg.

Greek Fruit & Nut Pastries

Aromatic pastries are packed with citrus peel and walnuts, soaked in a coffee syrup.

Makes 16

450g/1lb/4 cups plain (all-purpose) flour, plus extra for dusting
2.5ml/½ tsp ground cinnamon
2.5ml/½ tsp baking powder
a pinch of salt
150g/5oz/10 tbsp unsalted (sweet) butter
30ml/2 tbsp caster (superfine) sugar
1 egg
120ml/4fl oz/½ cup milk, chilled

For the filling

60ml/4 tbsp clear honey
60ml/4 tbsp strong freshly brewed coffee
75g/3oz/½ cup mixed candied citrus peel, finely chopped
175g/6oz/1½ cups walnuts, chopped
1.5ml/¼ tsp freshly grated nutmeg
milk, to glaze
caster (superfine) sugar, for sprinkling

1 Preheat the oven to 180°C/350°F/Gas 4. To make the dough, sift the flour, ground cinnamon, baking powder and salt into a bowl. Rub in the butter until the mixture resembles fine breadcrumbs. Stir in the sugar. Make a well in the middle.

2 Beat the egg and milk together and add to the well in the dry ingredients. Mix to a soft dough. Divide the dough into two and wrap in clear film (plastic wrap). Chill for 30 minutes.

3 To make the filling, mix the honey and coffee. Add the peel, walnuts and nutmeg. Stir well and leave to soak for 20 minutes.

4 Roll out a portion of dough on a lightly floured surface to about 3mm/⅛in thick. Stamp out 10cm/4in rounds.

5 Place a heaped teaspoonful of filling on one side of each round. Brush the edges with milk, then fold over and press the edges together to seal. Repeat until all the filling is used.

6 Put the pastries on non-stick baking sheets, brush with milk and sprinkle with caster sugar. Prick each with a fork and bake for 35 minutes. Cool on a wire rack.

Gazelles' Horns

Originating from Morocco, these horn-shaped pastries are filled with fragrant sweet almond paste – an unusual and lovely treat.

Makes 16

200g/7oz/1¾ cups plain (all-purpose) flour, plus extra for dusting
a pinch of salt
25g/1oz/2 tbsp butter, melted
about 30ml/2 tbsp orange flower water
1 egg yolk, beaten
60–90ml/4–6 tbsp chilled water

For the filling

200g/7oz/scant 2 cups ground almonds
115g/4oz/1 cup icing (confectioners') sugar, plus extra for dusting
30ml/2 tbsp orange flower water
25g/1oz/2 tbsp butter, melted
2 egg yolks, beaten
2.5ml/½ tsp ground cinnamon

1 Mix the almonds, icing sugar, orange flower water, butter, egg yolks and cinnamon in a bowl to make a smooth paste.

2 To make the dough, sift the flour and salt into a large bowl, then stir in the melted butter, orange flower water and about three-quarters of the egg yolk. Stir in enough chilled water to make a fairly soft dough.

3 Knead the dough until it is smooth, then place it on a floured surface and roll it out thinly. Cut it into long strips 7.5cm/3in wide. Preheat the oven to 180°C/350°F/Gas 4. Grease a baking sheet.

4 Roll small pieces of the almond paste into thin sausages about 7.5cm/3in long with tapering ends. Place these in a line along one side of the strips of dough, about 3cm/1¼in apart. Dampen the dough edges with water, then fold the other half of the strip over the filling and press the edges together firmly.

5 Cut around each dough sausage to make a crescent shape. Make sure that the edges are firmly pinched together. Prick the crescents with a fork and place on the baking sheet. Brush with the remaining egg yolk and bake for 12–16 minutes until lightly coloured. Leave to cool, then dust with icing sugar.

Greek Fruit and Nut Pastries Energy 278kcal/1162kJ; Protein 5g; Carbohydrate 30.2g, of which sugars 8.7g; Fat 16.1g, of which saturates 5.7g; Cholesterol 32mg; Calcium 69mg; Fibre 1.5g; Sodium 80mg.

Gazelles' Horns Energy 182kcal/762kJ; Protein 4.4g; Carbohydrate 18.1g, of which sugars 8.2g; Fat 10.7g, of which saturates 2.5g; Cholesterol 44mg; Calcium 56mg; Fibre 1.3g; Sodium 23mg.

Chocolate Eclairs

These crisp pastry fingers are filled with fresh cream, sweetened with vanilla.

Makes 12

65g/2½oz/9 tbsp plain (all-purpose) flour
a pinch of salt
50g/2oz/¼ cup butter, diced
150ml/¼ pint/⅔ cup water
2 eggs, lightly beaten

For the filling

300ml/½ pint/1¼ cups double (heavy) cream
10ml/2 tsp icing (confectioners') sugar, sifted
1.5ml/¼ tsp vanilla extract

For the glaze

115g/4oz plain (semisweet) chocolate
25g/1oz/2 tbsp butter

1 Preheat the oven to 200°C/400°F/Gas 6. Grease and line a baking sheet. For the pastry, sift the flour and salt on to a sheet of baking parchment.

2 Melt the butter with the water in a pan, then bring to a rolling boil. Remove from the heat, add all the flour and beat until combined. Return to a low heat, beating until the mixture leaves the side of the pan and forms a ball. Leave to cool for 2–3 minutes. Beat in the eggs to make a smooth, shiny paste.

3 Spoon the pastry into a piping (pastry) bag fitted with a 2.5cm/1in plain nozzle. Pipe 10cm/4in lengths on to the baking sheet. Use a wet knife to cut off the pastry at the nozzle. Bake for 25–30 minutes, until risen and golden.

4 Make a slit along the side of each éclair to release the steam, lower the oven temperature to 180°C/350°F/Gas 4 and bake for 5 minutes more. Cool on a wire rack.

5 For the filling, whip the cream with the sugar and vanilla. Spoon into a piping bag and use to fill the éclairs.

6 Melt the chocolate with 30ml/2 tbsp water in a heatproof bowl over a pan of simmering water. Remove from the heat and gradually stir in the butter. Dip the top of each éclair in the chocolate. Leave to cool until set.

Coffee Cream Profiteroles

Crisp-textured coffee choux pastry puffs are filled with cream and drizzled with a white chocolate sauce.

Serves 6

65g/2½oz/9 tbsp plain (all-purpose) flour
a pinch of salt
50g/2oz/¼ cup butter, diced
150ml/¼ pint/⅔ cup freshly brewed coffee
2 eggs, lightly beaten

For the filling and sauce

50g/2oz/¼ cup sugar
100ml/3½fl oz/scant ½ cup water
150g/5oz good-quality white chocolate, broken up
25g/1oz/2 tbsp butter
300ml/½ pint/1¼ cups double (heavy) cream
30ml/2 tbsp coffee liqueur, such as Tia Maria or Kahlúa

1 Preheat the oven to 220°C/425°F/Gas 7. To make the pastry, sift the flour and salt on to a sheet of baking parchment and set aside. Put the butter into a pan with the coffee. Bring to a rolling boil, then remove from the heat and add all the flour. Beat vigorously with a wooden spoon until the mixture forms a ball and comes away from the side. Let stand for 2 minutes.

2 Gradually add the beaten eggs to the flour mixture, beating thoroughly after each addition. Spoon into a piping (pastry) bag fitted with a 1cm/½in plain nozzle.

3 Pipe 24 buns on to a damp baking sheet and bake for about 20 minutes. Transfer to a wire rack. Pierce each one to let out the steam. Leave to cool.

4 To make the sauce, put the sugar and water in a pan and heat until the sugar has dissolved. Bring to the boil, then simmer for 3 minutes. Remove from the heat and add the chocolate and butter, stirring until smooth. Stir in 45ml/3 tbsp of the cream and the coffee liqueur.

5 To assemble, whip the remaining cream in a small bowl until soft peaks form. Spoon into a piping bag and use to fill the buns through the slits in the sides. Pour a little sauce over.

Chocolate Eclairs Energy 253kcal/1050kJ; Protein 2.5g; Carbohydrate 11.6g, of which sugars 7.4g; Fat 22.2g, of which saturates 13.5g; Cholesterol 80mg; Calcium 29mg; Fibre 0.4g; Sodium 56mg.

Coffee Cream Profiteroles Energy 579kcal/2401kJ; Protein 6g; Carbohydrate 32.6g, of which sugars 24.4g; Fat 46.8g, of which saturates 28.4g; Cholesterol 159mg; Calcium 123mg; Fibre 0.3g; Sodium 138mg.

Spiced Apple Cake

As grated apple and dates give this cake a natural sweetness, it may not be necessary to add all the sugar.

Makes 1

225g/8oz/2 cups self-raising (self-rising) wholemeal (whole-wheat) flour
5ml/1 tsp baking powder
10ml/2 tsp ground cinnamon
175g/6oz/1 cup chopped dates
75g/3oz/scant ½ cup soft light brown sugar
15ml/1 tbsp pear and apple spread
120ml/4fl oz/½ cup apple juice
2 eggs, beaten
90ml/6 tbsp sunflower oil
2 eating apples, cored and grated
15ml/1 tbsp chopped walnuts

1 Preheat the oven to 180°C/350°F/Gas 4. Line and grease a 20cm/8in deep round cake tin (pan).

2 Sift the flour, baking powder and cinnamon into a mixing bowl, then mix in the dates and make a well in the centre.

3 Mix some of the sugar with the pear and apple spread in a small bowl. Gradually stir in the apple juice.

4 Add to the dry ingredients with the eggs, oil and apples. Mix thoroughly. Taste and add the rest of the sugar if necessary.

5 Spoon into the prepared cake tin, sprinkle with the walnuts and bake for 60–65 minutes, or until a skewer inserted into the centre of the cake comes out clean.

6 Invert on a wire rack, remove the lining paper and leave to cool.

Cook's Tip
It is not necessary to peel the apples – the skin adds extra fibre and softens on cooking.

Lemon & Apricot Cake

This cake is soaked in a tangy lemon syrup to keep it moist.

Makes 1

175g/6oz/¾ cup butter, softened
175g/6oz/1½ cups self-raising (self-rising) flour
2.5ml/½ tsp baking powder
175g/6oz/generous ¾ cup caster (superfine) sugar
3 eggs, lightly beaten
finely grated rind of 1 lemon
175g/6oz/1½ cups ready-to-eat dried apricots, finely chopped
75g/3oz/¾ cup ground almonds
40g/1½oz/6 tbsp pistachio nuts, chopped
50g/2oz/½ cup flaked (sliced) almonds
15g/½oz/2 tbsp whole pistachio nuts

For the syrup
45ml/3 tbsp caster (superfine) sugar
freshly squeezed juice of 1 lemon

1 Preheat the oven to 180°C/350°F/Gas 4. Grease and line a 23 × 13cm/9 × 5in loaf tin (pan) with baking parchment and grease the paper.

2 Place the butter in a large bowl. Sift over the flour and baking powder, then add the sugar, eggs and lemon rind.

3 Using an electric whisk or a wooden spoon, beat for 1–2 minutes, or until smooth and glossy, then stir in the apricots, ground almonds and chopped pistachio nuts.

4 Spoon the mixture into the loaf tin and smooth the surface. Sprinkle with the flaked almonds and the whole pistachio nuts.

5 Bake for 1¼ hours, or until a skewer inserted into the centre of the cake comes out clean. Check the cake after 45 minutes and cover with a piece of foil when the top is nicely browned. Leave the cake to cool in the tin.

6 To make the lemon syrup, gently dissolve the sugar in the lemon juice in a small pan over low heat. Spoon the syrup over the cake. When the cake is completely cooled, turn it carefully out of the tin and peel off the lining paper.

Spiced Apple Cake Energy 282kcal/1186kJ; Protein 4.9g; Carbohydrate 42.8g, of which sugars 21.3g; Fat 11.3g, of which saturates 1.5g; Cholesterol 48mg; Calcium 60mg; Fibre 1.6g; Sodium 22mg.

Lemon and Apricot Cake per cake Energy 4358kcal/18221kJ; Protein 80.6g; Carbohydrate 443.9g, of which sugars 305.8g; Fat 264g, of which saturates 105.8g; Cholesterol 944mg; Calcium 967mg; Fibre 29.1g; Sodium 1622mg.

Black Welsh Cake

A group of settlers from Wales came to the Chubut river region in Patagonia in the late 18th century. The area retains many Welsh traditions such as 'afternoon tea', and this cake is served in quaint tea houses. It is traditional to have a black Welsh cake as the bottom tier of a wedding cake.

Makes 1

200g/7oz/scant cup soft dark brown sugar
30ml/2 tbsp clear honey
200g/7oz/generous cup raisins
250ml/8fl oz/1 cup water
225g/8oz/1 cup butter
300g/11oz/2¾ cups plain (all-purpose) flour
10ml/2 tsp bicarbonate of soda (baking soda)
5ml/1 tsp ground cinnamon
75g/3oz/¾ cup walnut halves
50g/2oz/½ cup blanched almonds
100g/3½ oz/½ cup candied fruit, roughly chopped
100g/3½oz/generous ½ cup prunes, roughly chopped
100ml/7 tbsp brandy

1 Put the sugar, honey, raisins and water in a pan and slowly bring to the boil. Cover and simmer over low heat for 5 minutes.

2 Cut the butter into chunks, add to the pan, re-cover and let it stand for about 5 minutes until the butter has melted and the mixture cooled a little.

3 Preheat the oven to 150°C/300°F/Gas 2. Line the base of a deep 20cm/8in round cake tin (pan) with baking parchment.

4 Pour the warm raisin mixture into a large bowl. Sift over the flour, bicarbonate of soda and cinnamon and gently mix and fold together until almost combined. Add the nuts, fruit and brandy and fold into the mixture until well mixed. Spoon and scrape the mixture into the tin and level the top with a spoon. Make a very slight dip in the middle, so that the cake rises evenly.

5 Bake for 1 hour, or until a skewer inserted into the middle of the cake comes out clean. Leave to cool in the tin for 15 minutes, then turn out onto a wire rack and leave to cool completely before slicing and serving with tea.

Irish Whiskey Cake

This moist rich fruit cake is drizzled with whiskey as soon as it comes out of the oven. It is high in fibre and full of flavour.

Makes 1

115g/4oz/¾ cup sultanas (golden raisins)
115g/4oz/scant 1 cup raisins
115g/4oz/½ cup currants
115g/4oz/½ cup glacé (candied) cherries
175g/6oz/1¼ cups soft light brown sugar
300ml/½ pint/1¼ cups cold tea
1 egg, beaten
300g/11oz/2⅔ cups self-raising (self-rising) flour, sifted
45ml/3 tbsp Irish whiskey

1 Mix the sultanas, raisins, currants, cherries, sugar and tea in a large bowl. Leave to soak overnight until the tea has been absorbed.

2 Preheat the oven to 180°C/350°F/Gas 4. Line and grease a 1kg/2¼lb loaf tin (pan).

3 Add the egg and flour to the fruit mixture and beat thoroughly until well mixed.

4 Pour into the prepared tin and bake for 1½ hours or until a skewer inserted into the centre comes out clean.

5 Prick over the top of the cake with a skewer and drizzle over the whiskey while the cake is still hot.

6 Allow to stand for 5 minutes, then remove from the tin and cool completely on a wire rack.

Variation
For a tangy finish, drizzle with lemon icing. Mix the juice of 1 lemon with 225g/8oz/2 cup icing (confectioners') sugar and enough warm water for the icing to have a thin consistency. Drizzle the icing over the cooled cake and decorate with crystallized lemon slices, if you like.

Black Welsh Cake Energy 437kcal/1833kJ; Protein 5g; Carbohydrate 58g, of which sugars 39g; Fat 23g, of which saturates 10g; Cholesterol 40mg; Calcium 88mg; Fibre 4g; Sodium 338mg.

Irish Whiskey Cake per cake Energy 311kcal/1323kJ; Protein 4.4g; Carbohydrate 73g, of which sugars 50.1g; Fat 1.1g, of which saturates 0.2g; Cholesterol 19mg; Calcium 84mg; Fibre 1.7g; Sodium 23mg.

Jewel Cake

This pretty cake is excellent served as a teatime treat.

Makes 1

115g/4oz/½ cup mixed glacé (candied) cherries, halved, washed and dried
50g/2oz/4 tbsp preserved stem ginger in syrup, chopped, washed and dried
50g/2oz/⅓ cup chopped mixed (candied) peel
115g/4oz/1 cup self-raising (self-rising) flour
75g/3oz/⅔ cup plain (all-purpose) flour
25g/1oz/¼ cup cornflour (cornstarch)
175g/6oz/¾ cup butter
175g/6oz/scant 1 cup caster (superfine) sugar
3 eggs
grated rind of 1 orange

To decorate

175g/6oz/1½ cups icing (confectioners') sugar, sifted
30–45ml/2–3 tbsp freshly squeezed orange juice
50g/2oz/¼ cup mixed glacé (candied) cherries, chopped
25g/1oz/2½ tbsp mixed (candied) peel, chopped

1 Preheat the oven to 180°C/350°F/Gas 4. Grease and line a 23 × 13cm/9 × 5in loaf tin (pan) and grease the paper.

2 Place the glacé cherries, stem ginger and mixed peel in a plastic bag with 25g/1oz/¼ cup of the self-raising flour and shake to coat evenly. Sift together the remaining flours and cornflour.

3 In a large bowl, beat together the butter and sugar until light and fluffy. Beat in the eggs, one at a time. Fold in the sifted flours with the orange rind, then stir in the dried fruit.

4 Transfer the mixture to the cake tin and bake for 1¼ hours, or until a skewer inserted into the centre comes out clean. Leave in the tin for 5 minutes, then cool on a wire rack.

5 For the decoration, mix the icing sugar with the orange juice until smooth. Drizzle the icing over the cake.

6 Mix together the glacé cherries and mixed peel, then use to decorate the cake. Allow the icing to set before serving.

Pineapple & Carrot Cake

Universally loved, this is one of the most irresistible cakes there is. The poppy seeds and walnut pieces add crunch, and the pineapple and carrot give moisture. A tangy citrus mascarpone icing makes a tasty topping.

Makes 1

250g/9oz/2¼ cups plain (all-purpose) flour
10ml/2 tsp baking powder
5ml/1 tsp bicarbonate of soda (baking soda)
a pinch of salt
5ml/1 tsp ground cinnamon
45ml/3 tbsp poppy seeds
225g/8oz/1 cup soft light brown sugar
3 eggs, beaten
finely grated rind of 1 orange
225g/8oz raw carrots, grated
75g/3oz fresh or canned pineapple, drained and finely chopped
75g/3oz/¾ cup walnut pieces
115g/4oz/½ cup butter, melted and cooled

For the icing

150g/5oz/scant ¾ cup mascarpone
30ml/2 tbsp icing (confectioners') sugar, sifted
finely grated rind of 1 orange

1 Preheat the oven to 180°C/350°F/Gas 4. Grease and line a 900g/2lb loaf tin (pan) with baking parchment.

2 Sift the flour, baking powder, bicarbonate of soda, salt and cinnamon into a bowl. Stir in the poppy seeds. In another large bowl, put the sugar, eggs and orange rind. Beat together until smooth and frothy.

3 Squeeze the excess moisture from the carrots and stir into the egg mixture with the pineapple and walnut pieces.

4 Stir the flour into the egg mixture, then gently fold in the butter. Spoon the batter into the prepared tin and smooth the top level. Bake for 1–1¼ hours, or until risen and golden. Leave to cool for 10 minutes, then turn out on a wire rack. Remove the paper when cold.

5 To make the icing, beat the mascarpone with the icing sugar and orange rind. Spread thickly over the cake top.

Jewel Cake per cake Energy 4369kcal/18404kJ; Protein 41.5g; Carbohydrate 726.1g, of which sugars 560.5g; Fat 164.9g, of which saturates 96.5g; Cholesterol 982mg; Calcium 1042mg; Fibre 11.5g; Sodium 2007mg.

Pineapple and Carrot Cake Energy 400kcal/1668kJ; Protein 4.2g; Carbohydrate 39.1g, of which sugars 29.9g; Fat 26.3g, of which saturates 7.2g; Cholesterol 55mg; Calcium 62mg; Fibre 1g; Sodium 67mg.

Plum Cake

This appetizing cake is sweetened with fresh plums.

Makes 1

450g/1lb stoned (pitted) plums, chopped, plus 9 extra plums, stoned and halved, to decorate
300ml/½pint/1¼ cups water
115g/4oz/½ cup unsalted butter, softened
200g/7oz/1 cup caster (superfine) sugar
3 eggs
90g/3½oz/¾ cup toasted, finely chopped almonds
5ml/1 tsp bicarbonate of soda (baking soda)
7.5ml/1½ tsp baking powder
5ml/1 tsp ground cardamom
1.5ml/¼ tsp salt
250g/9oz/2¼ cups plain (all-purpose) flour
15ml/1 tbsp pearl sugar, to decorate
250ml/8fl oz/1 cup double (heavy) cream
10ml/2 tsp vanilla sugar
10ml/2 tsp icing (confectioners') sugar

1 Place the plums in a pan and add the water. Bring to the boil over medium heat and cook for 10–15 minutes, until soft. Set aside to cool. You will need 350ml/12fl oz/1½ cups stewed plums for the cake. Preheat the oven to 180°C/350°F/Gas 4. Grease and flour a 24cm/9½in springform cake tin (pan).

2 Cream the butter with the caster sugar in a large mixing bowl until light and fluffy, then beat in the eggs, one at a time. Stir in the stewed plums and the finely chopped almonds.

3 Add the bicarbonate of soda, baking powder, cardamom and salt and stir well. Gradually stir in the flour until well blended.

4 Pour the mixture into the prepared tin. Place plum halves around the circumference of the cake and place the remaining halves in the centre, cut sides down. Sprinkle the pearl sugar over the cake. Bake for 1 hour, or until the top springs back when lightly touched. Cool in the tin for 15 minutes.

5 Beat the double cream until soft peaks form. Stir in the vanilla sugar and the icing sugar and beat the cream until thick. Serve the cake while it is still slightly warm with whipped cream.

Cherry Batter Cake

This colourful tray bake looks pretty cut into neat squares or fingers. Its unusual topping makes it especially tasty.

Makes 1

225g/8oz/2 cups self-raising (self-rising) flour
5ml/1 tsp baking powder
75g/3oz/6 tbsp butter, softened
150g/5oz/scant 1 cup soft light brown sugar
1 egg, lightly beaten
150ml/¼ pint/⅔ cup milk
icing (confectioners') sugar, for dusting
whipped cream, to serve (optional)

For the topping

675g/1½lb jar black cherries or blackcurrants, drained
175g/6oz/¾ cup soft light brown sugar
50g/2oz/½ cup self-raising (self-rising) flour
50g/2oz/¼ cup butter, melted

1 Preheat the oven to 190°C/375°F/Gas 5. Grease and line a 33 × 23cm/13 × 9in Swiss roll tin (jelly roll pan) with baking parchment, and grease the paper.

2 To make the base, sift the flour and baking powder into a large bowl. Add the butter, sugar, egg and milk.

3 Beat until the mixture becomes smooth, then turn into the prepared tin and smooth the surface.

4 To make the topping, sprinkle the drained cherries or blackcurrants evenly over the batter mixture.

5 Mix together the brown sugar, flour and melted butter, and spoon evenly over the fruit.

6 Bake for 40 minutes, or until the top is golden brown and the centre is firm to the touch.

7 Leave to cool for 15 minutes in the tin, then turn out and leave on a wire rack to cool completely. Dust with icing sugar. Serve with whipped cream, if you like.

Plum Cake Energy 311kcal/1308kJ; Protein 6.4g; Carbohydrate 44.5g, of which sugars 15.9g; Fat 13.2g, of which saturates 7.4g; Cholesterol 89mg; Calcium 86mg; Fibre 2.4g; Sodium 102mg.

Cherry Batter Cake per cake Energy 3770kcal/15932kJ; Protein 43g; Carbohydrate 686g, of which sugars 476.4g; Fat 114.4g, of which saturates 68.8g; Cholesterol 466mg; Calcium 890mg; Fibre 12.6g; Sodium 974mg.

Cassava Cake

This cake's rich flavour and fluffy texture is made even lighter with the addition of whisked egg whites, and it contains little fat. It is popular at carnivals held in June in the north of Brazil. The ubiquitous cassava root gives the cake a lovely moist texture.

Makes 1

20g/¾oz/1½ tbsp butter, softened
450g/1lb/2 cups caster (superfine) sugar
4 eggs, separated
100g/4oz/1 cup grated fresh coconut
300g/11oz cassava root, finely grated
250ml/8fl oz/1 cup milk
175g/6oz/1½ cups self-raising (self-rising) flour

1 Preheat the oven to 190°C/375°F/Gas 5. Grease the base of a 23cm/9in square cake tin (pan) with butter, then line with baking parchment.

2 In a large mixing bowl, beat the butter and sugar together until the mixture resembles breadcrumbs.

3 Add the egg yolks one at a time, ensuring each yolk is well incorporated before adding the next one.

4 Beat the egg mixture for about 3–4 minutes, then add in the grated coconut, cassava and milk. Mix thoroughly until all the ingredients are combined.

5 Sift the flour into the bowl, and with a metal spoon, gently fold it in to the egg mixture.

6 In a separate bowl, whisk the egg whites into stiff peaks, then add to the egg yolk and cassava mixture and carefully fold in.

7 Spoon the cake mixture into the prepared tin and bake for 40 minutes, or until golden-brown and firm.

8 Remove from the oven and leave in the tin for 10 minutes before turning out and cooling on a wire rack.

Kulich

This rich Russian yeast cake is traditionally made at Easter time.

Makes 2

15ml/1 tbsp active dried yeast
90ml/6 tbsp lukewarm milk
75g/3oz/6 tbsp caster (superfine) sugar
500g/1¼lb/5 cups plain (all-purpose) flour
a pinch of saffron threads
30ml/2 tbsp dark rum
2.5ml/½ tsp ground cardamom seeds
2.5ml/½ tsp ground cumin
50g/2oz/¼ cup unsalted (sweet) butter
2 eggs plus 2 egg yolks
½ vanilla pod (bean), finely chopped
25g/1oz/2 tbsp each crystallized ginger, mixed (candied) peel, almonds and currants, chopped

For the decoration

75g/3oz/¾ cup icing (confectioners') sugar, sifted
7.5–10ml/1½–2 tsp warm water
a drop of almond extract
blanched almonds
mixed (candied) peel

1 Blend together the yeast, milk, 25g/1oz/¼ cup sugar and 50g/2oz/½ cup flour. Leave in a warm place for 15 minutes, or until frothy. Soak the saffron in the rum for 15 minutes.

2 Sift together the remaining flour and spices and rub in the butter. Stir in the rest of the sugar. Add the yeast mixture, saffron liquid and remaining ingredients. Knead the dough until smooth. Put in an oiled bowl, cover with clear film (plastic wrap) and leave until doubled in size.

3 Preheat the oven to 190°C/375°F/Gas 5. Grease, line and flour two 500g/1¼lb coffee tins or 15cm/6in clay flowerpots.

4 Knock back (punch down) the dough and form into two rounds. Press into the tins or pots, cover and leave to rise for 30 minutes. Bake for 35 minutes for the pots or 50 minutes for the tins. Remove from the tins or pots and cool.

5 To decorate, mix together the icing sugar, water and almond extract. Pour over the cakes. Decorate with nuts and peel.

Cassava Cake Energy 357kcal/1523kJ; Protein 4.5g; Carbohydrate 73.9g, of which sugars 40.1g; Fat 6.8g, of which saturates 4.1g; Cholesterol 81mg; Calcium 77mg; Fibre 2.3g; Sodium 94mg

Kulich per cake Energy 1521kcal/6432kJ; Protein 33.3g; Carbohydrate 282.3g, of which sugars 91.8g; Fat 33g, of which saturates 16.4g; Cholesterol 347mg; Calcium 505mg; Fibre 8.4g; Sodium 293mg.

Panforte

This rich, spicy nougat-type cake is a Christmas speciality of Siena in Italy. Choose the best-quality exotic peel you can find, as it really makes a difference to the flavour.

Makes 1

275g/10oz/1⅔ cups mixed chopped exotic (candied) peel, including lemon, orange, citron, papaya and pineapple
115g/4oz/⅔ cup unblanched almonds
50g/2oz/½ cup walnut halves
50g/2oz/½ cup plain (all-purpose) flour
5ml/1 tsp ground cinnamon
1.5ml/¼ tsp each freshly grated nutmeg, ground cloves and ground coriander
175g/6oz/scant 1 cup caster (superfine) sugar
60ml/4 tbsp water
icing (confectioners') sugar, for dusting

1 Preheat the oven to 180°C/350°F/Gas 4. Grease and base-line a 20cm/8in round loose-based cake tin (pan) with rice paper.

2 Put the mixed peel and nuts in a bowl. Sift in the flour and spices, and mix well.

3 Dissolve the caster (superfine) sugar and water in a small pan, then boil until the mixture reaches thread stage (107°C/225°F on a sugar thermometer). Pour on to the fruit mixture, stirring to coat well.

4 Transfer the cake mixture to the cake tin, pressing into the sides with a metal spoon.

5 Bake for 25–30 minutes, or until the mixture is bubbling. Cool in the tin for 5 minutes.

6 Use a lightly oiled metal spatula to work around the edges of the cake to loosen it. Remove the cake from the tin, leaving the base in place.

7 Leave to cool completely, then remove the base and dust the cake generously with icing sugar.

Courgette & Double Ginger Cake

Both fresh and preserved ginger are used to flavour this unusual cake, which is made with oil rather than butter. Courgettes, like several other vegetables, bring moisture to a cake mix, making it soft and tasty. Keep for up to five days in an airtight container, or freeze for two months.

Makes 1

3 eggs
225g/8oz/generous 1 cup caster (superfine) sugar
250ml/8fl oz/1 cup sunflower oil
5ml/1 tsp vanilla extract
15ml/1 tbsp syrup from a jar of preserved stem ginger
225g/8oz courgettes (zucchini), grated, drained
2.5cm/1in piece fresh root ginger, peeled and grated
350g/12oz/3 cups plain (all-purpose) flour
5ml/1 tsp baking powder
5ml/1 tsp ground cinnamon
a pinch of salt
2 pieces preserved stem ginger, chopped
15ml/1 tbsp demerara (raw) sugar

1 Preheat the oven to 190°C/325°F/Gas 5. Grease and line a 900g/2lb loaf tin (pan) with baking parchment.

2 In a large bowl, beat together the eggs and caster sugar until light and fluffy.

3 Slowly beat in the sunflower oil until a batter forms. Mix in the vanilla extract and ginger syrup, then stir in the courgettes and fresh ginger.

4 Sift the flour, baking powder, cinnamon and salt over the batter and stir in to combine.

5 Pour the mixture into the prepared tin and smooth the top with a palette knife or metal spatula until level. Sprinkle the chopped ginger and demerara sugar on top.

6 Bake for 1 hour, or until a skewer inserted into the centre comes out clean. Leave to cool in the tin for 20 minutes, then cool on a wire rack.

Panforte per cake Energy 3233kcal/13647kJ; Protein 38.9g; Carbohydrate 576.7g, of which sugars 535.2g; Fat 101.5g, of which saturates 8g; Cholesterol 0mg; Calcium 936mg; Fibre 25g; Sodium 812mg.

Courgette and Double Ginger Cake per cake Energy 252kcal/1060kJ; Protein 5.6g; Carbohydrate 35.6g, of which sugars 8.8g; Fat 10.7g, of which saturates 1.6g; Cholesterol 57mg; Calcium 73mg; Fibre 1.3g; Sodium 82mg.

Traditional Bread Pudding

This special pudding made with stale bread can be served either as a cake or alternatively as a dessert served with cream.

Makes 1

225g/8oz/4 cups stale bread, weighed after removing crusts
300ml/½ pint/1¼ cups milk
50g/1¾oz/4 tbsp dark muscovado (molasses) sugar
85g/3oz/½ cup shredded suet (US chilled, grated shortening) or chilled, grated butter
225g/8oz/1⅓ cups mixed dried fruit, including currants, sultanas (golden raisins) and chopped citrus peel
15ml/1 tbsp mixed (apple pie) spice
2.5ml/½ tsp freshly grated nutmeg
finely grated rind of 1 small orange and 1 small lemon, plus a little orange or lemon juice
1 egg, lightly beaten
caster (superfine) sugar, for sprinkling

1 Break the bread into small pieces. Place the bread in a large mixing bowl, pour the milk over and leave for about 30 minutes. Preheat the oven to 180°C/350°F/Gas 4. Butter an 18cm/7in square and 5cm/2in deep ovenproof dish. Using a fork, break up the bread in the milk.

2 Stir the sugar, suet, dried fruit, spices and citrus rinds into the bread and milk mixture. Beat in the egg, adding some orange or lemon juice to make a soft mixture.

3 Spread the pudding mixture into the prepared dish and level the surface. Put into the hot oven and cook for about 1¼ hours or until the top is brown and firm to the touch.

4 Sprinkle caster sugar over the surface while still warm, then cool before cutting into squares and removing from the dish.

Cook's Tip
Although suet is the traditional ingredient in this recipe, you may prefer to use grated chilled butter.

Bread Pudding with Cherry Syrup

Bakeries in Peru prepare large trays of this pudding ready for the afternoon when children get home from school. It has long been considered especially suitable for the young, because it is very gentle on the stomach.

Makes 1

1 small loaf of white bread (12 slices) or 6 bread rolls, reduced to crumbs
2 x 350ml/12fl oz cans evaporated milk
60ml/4 tbsp caster (superfine) sugar
3 eggs, lightly beaten
15ml/1 tbsp butter, melted, plus extra for greasing
5ml/1 tsp ground cinnamon
30ml/2 tbsp port
a pinch of salt
150g/5oz/1 cup raisins, tossed in flour

For the cherry syrup
250g/9oz/1¼ cups dried cherries
250g/9oz/1¼ cups caster (superfine) sugar
500ml/17fl oz/generous 2 cups water

1 Preheat the oven to 160°C/325°F/Gas 3 and grease a 25cm/10in diameter cake tin (pan). Put the breadcrumbs in a mixing bowl with the milk and soak for 5–10 minutes.

2 Add the sugar, eggs, butter, cinnamon, port and salt. Mix everything together thoroughly, then lightly stir in the raisins.

3 Pour the mixture into the prepared tin and bake for about 40 minutes, or until a skewer pushed into the middle comes out clean. Leave to cool.

4 To make the syrup, place the cherries in a small pan with the sugar and water. Heat gently, stirring, until the sugar has dissolved, then bring to the boil and simmer for 15 minutes until syrupy. Leave to cool.

5 When the pudding is cold, run a knife or spatula around the sides and turn it out on to a plate, removing the tin slowly. Serve in slices with the syrup poured over.

Traditional Bread Pudding Energy 254kcal/1072kJ; Protein 4.3g; Carbohydrate 39.7g, of which sugars 27g; Fat 10.2g, of which saturates 5.3g; Cholesterol 31mg; Calcium 103mg; Fibre 1.4g; Sodium 147mg.

Bread Pudding with Cherry Syrup Energy 300kcal/1269kJ; Protein 11.3g; Carbohydrate 51.4g, of which sugars 32.7g; Fat 6.6g, of which saturates 3.2g; Cholesterol 72mg; Calcium 251mg; Fibre 1.1g; Sodium 333mg.

Apple & Cinnamon Bread Pudding

This classic recipe is comfort food at its very best, and is perfect when accompanied by a scoop of ice cream.

Makes 1

200g/7oz white bread slices, crusts removed
150ml/¼ pint/⅔ cup single (light) cream
50g/2oz/¼ cup butter, melted
4 eggs, separated
45ml/3 tbsp caster (superfine) sugar
200g/7oz sliced dried apples, chopped
50g/2oz/scant ½ cup raisins
2 teaspoons of cinnamon
75g/2oz/¼ cup flaked (sliced) almonds

1 Preheat the oven to 180°C/350°F/Gas 4 and grease a 15 × 20cm/6 × 8in ovenproof dish.

2 Process the bread in a food processor or blender until you have breadcrumbs. Transfer into a bowl and add the cream and butter, mixing well.

3 In another bowl, whisk the egg yolks and sugar until light and creamy. Fold the apples, raisins and cinnamon into the egg and sugar mix. Add this to the breadcrumb mix, and combine well.

4 Put the egg whites into a clean, grease-free bowl and whisk until they form stiff peaks. Stir a spoonful of the whites into the breadcrumb mixture to lighten it, then fold in the remaining whites. Pour into the prepared dish.

5 Sprinkle with the almonds and bake for 25–30 minutes, or until it is golden and firm.

Variation
The addition of a grated apple to the dry apple and raisin mixture will make this pudding even more moist.

Argentinian Bread Pudding

Every culture seems to have a bread pudding recipe, originally a way to use up leftover stale bread. The Argentinian version is now a glorious dessert in its own right, flavoured with caramel and tangy citrus rind, and enriched with cream.

Makes 1

100g/3¾oz/scant 1 cup caster (superfine) sugar
200ml/7fl oz/scant 1 cup full-fat (whole) milk
75g/3oz/¾ cup caster (superfine) sugar
200g/7oz white bread, at least one-day old, crusts removed, processed to coarse crumbs
50ml/2fl oz/¼ cup double (heavy) cream
5ml/1 tsp vanilla extract
2 eggs, lightly beaten
finely grated rind of 1 lemon
finely grated rind of 1 orange
a handful of raisins
a handful of chopped walnuts
whipped cream and dulce de leche, to serve

1 To make the caramel, put the sugar in a heavy pan and heat gently, without stirring, until it is dissolved. Increase the heat and boil rapidly for a few minutes until the syrup turns to a rich golden brown.

2 Pour into a non-stick loaf tin (pan), measuring about 25 × 12 × 6cm/10 × 4½ × 2½in, and tilt to partly coat the sides of the tin. Preheat the oven to 180°C/350°F/Gas 4.

3 Pour the milk into the pan used to make caramel. Add the sugar and heat until warm, stirring occasionally to dissolve the sugar. Remove the pan from the heat and stir in the breadcrumbs, cream, vanilla, and beaten eggs. Mix the lemon and orange rind, raisins and walnuts in a bowl. Pour over the bread and milk mixture and stir together. Pour and scrape into the caramel-coated tin.

4 Put the tin in a deep roasting pan and pour in enough hot water to come 5–7.5cm/2–3in up the sides of the tin. Bake for 1 hour or until lightly set. Remove from the hot water and leave to cool. Chill for 8 hours, at least, or overnight. Turn out of the tin and slice. Serve with whipped cream and dulce de leche.

Apple and Cinnamon Bread Pudding Energy 379kcal/1585kJ; Protein 10.6g; Carbohydrate 34.9g, of which sugars 19g; Fat 23g, of which saturates 9.2g; Cholesterol 160mg; Calcium 119mg; Fibre 2.1g; Sodium 303mg.

Argentinian Bread Pudding Energy 548kcal/2296kJ; Protein 14g; Carbohydrate 68g, of which sugars 53g; Fat 26g, of which saturates 11g; Cholesterol 124mg; Calcium 313mg; Fibre 3g; Sodium 303mg.

Fresh Currant Bread & Butter Pudding

Delicious mixed currants add a tart touch to this scrumptious hot pudding.

Serves 6

8 medium-thick slices day-old bread, crusts removed
50g/2oz/¼ cup butter, softened
115g/4oz/1 cup redcurrants
115g/4oz/1 cup blackcurrants
4 eggs, beaten
75g/3oz/6 tbsp caster (superfine) sugar
475ml/16fl oz/2 cups creamy milk
5ml/1 tsp pure vanilla extract
freshly grated nutmeg
30ml/2 tbsp demerara (raw) sugar
single (light) cream, to serve

1 Preheat the oven to 160°C/325°F/Gas 3. Generously butter a 1.2 litre/2 pint/5 cup oval baking dish.

2 Spread the slices of bread generously with the butter, then cut them in half diagonally. Layer the slices in the dish, buttered side up, sprinkling the currants between the layers.

3 Beat the eggs and caster sugar lightly together in a large mixing bowl, then gradually whisk in the milk, vanilla extract and a large pinch of freshly grated nutmeg. Pour the milk mixture over the bread, pushing the slices down. Sprinkle the demerara sugar and a little nutmeg over the top.

4 Place the dish in a roasting pan and then add hot water so that the water reaches halfway up the sides of the dish. Bake for 40 minutes, then increase the oven temperature to 180°C/350°F/Gas 4 and bake for 20–25 minutes until golden. Serve with single cream.

Variation
A mixture of blueberries and raspberries would work very successfully instead of the currants.

Peach Cobbler

A satisfying pudding in which fresh peaches are topped with a hearty almond-flavoured pastry.

Serves 6

about 1.5kg/3lb peaches, peeled and sliced
45ml/3 tbsp caster (superfine) sugar
30ml/2 tbsp peach brandy
15ml/1 tbsp freshly squeezed lemon juice
15ml/1 tbsp cornflour (cornstarch)
ice cream or crème fraîche, to serve

For the topping
115g/4oz/1 cup plain (all-purpose) flour
7.5ml/1½ tsp baking powder
1.5ml/¼ tsp salt
40g/1½oz/¼ cup finely ground almonds
50g/2oz/¼ cup caster (superfine) sugar
50g/2oz/¼ cup butter or margarine
85ml/3fl oz/⅓ cup milk
1.5ml/¼ tsp almond extract

1 Preheat the oven to 220°C/425°F/Gas 7. Place the peaches in a bowl and add the sugar, peach brandy, lemon juice and cornflour. Toss together, then spoon the peach mixture into a 2 litre/3½ pint/8 cup baking dish.

2 Now make the topping. Sift the flour, baking powder and salt into a mixing bowl. Stir in the ground almonds and all but 15ml/1 tbsp of the sugar. With two knives, or a pastry blender, cut in the butter or margarine until the mixture resembles coarse breadcrumbs.

3 Add the milk and almond extract and stir until the topping mixture is just combined.

4 Carefully drop the topping in spoonfuls on to the peaches in the baking dish. Sprinkle the top with the remaining tablespoon of caster sugar.

5 Bake for 30–35 minutes until the cobbler topping is browned. Serve hot with ice cream or crème fraîche, if you prefer.

Fresh Currant Bread and Butter Pudding Energy 328Kcal/1377kJ; Protein 10.3g; Carbohydrate 42.2g, of which sugars 25.4g; Fat 14.3g, of which saturates 7.4g; Cholesterol 156mg; Calcium 186mg; Fibre 1.9g; Sodium 321mg.

Peach Cobbler Energy 299Kcal/1265kJ; Protein 4.9g; Carbohydrate 53.5g, of which sugars 36.6g; Fat 7.6g, of which saturates 4.5g; Cholesterol 19mg; Calcium 72mg; Fibre 4.4g; Sodium 62mg.

Rhubarb Spiral Cobbler

Orange in the fruit filling and in the topping gives this pudding added zest.

Serves 4

675g/1½lb rhubarb, sliced
50g/2oz/¼ cup caster (superfine) sugar
45ml/3 tbsp orange juice

For the topping

200g/7oz/1¾ cups self-raising (self-rising) flour
30ml/2 tbsp caster (superfine) sugar
about 200g/7oz/scant 1 cup natural (plain) yogurt
grated rind of 1 medium orange
30ml/2 tbsp demerara (raw) sugar
5ml/1 tsp ground ginger
yogurt or fresh ready-made custard, to serve

1 Preheat the oven to 200°C/400°F/Gas 6. Cook the rhubarb, sugar and orange juice in a covered pan until tender. Transfer to an ovenproof dish.

2 Make the topping. Put the flour in a mixing bowl, add the caster sugar and mix together. Stir in enough of the yogurt to bind to a soft dough.

3 Roll out on a floured surface to a 25cm/10in square. Mix together the orange rind, demerara sugar and ginger in a bowl, then sprinkle the mixture evenly over the surface of the dough.

4 Roll up quite tightly, then cut into about ten slices, using a sharp knife. Arrange the slices over the rhubarb.

5 Bake in the oven for 15–20 minutes, or until the spirals are well risen and golden brown. Serve warm, with yogurt or fresh custard.

Variation

For a cinnamon cobbler topping, leave out the orange rind and replace the ginger with ground cinnamon.

Maple & Pecan Croissant Pudding

This variation of the classic English bread and butter pudding uses rich, flaky croissants topped with a delicious mixture of fruit and nuts. Custard flavoured with maple syrup completes this mouthwatering dessert.

Serves 4

75g/3oz/scant ½ cup sultanas (golden raisins)
45ml/3 tbsp brandy
4 large croissants
50g/2oz/¼ cup butter or margarine, plus extra for greasing
40g/1½oz/⅓ cup pecan nuts, roughly chopped
3 eggs, lightly beaten
300ml/½ pint/1¼ cups milk
150ml/¼ pint/⅔ cup single (light) cream
120ml/4fl oz/½ cup maple syrup
25g/1oz/2 tbsp demerara (raw) sugar
maple syrup and pouring (half-and-half) cream, to serve

1 Lightly grease the base and sides of a small, shallow ovenproof dish. Place the sultanas and brandy in a small pan and heat gently, until warm. Leave to stand for 1 hour.

2 Cut the croissants into thick slices and spread with butter on one side. Arrange the slices, buttered side uppermost and slightly overlapping, in the greased dish. Sprinkle the brandy-soaked sultanas and the pecan nuts evenly over the croissant slices.

3 In a large bowl, beat the eggs and milk together, then gradually beat in the single cream and maple syrup. Pour the egg custard through a sieve (strainer), over the croissants, fruit and nuts in the dish. Leave the pudding to stand for 30 minutes so that some of the custard is absorbed by the croissants. Meanwhile, preheat the oven to 180°F/350°C/Gas 4.

4 Sprinkle the demerara sugar evenly over the top, then cover the dish with foil. Bake the pudding for 30 minutes, then remove the foil and continue to cook for about 20 minutes, or until the custard is set and the top is golden brown.

5 Leave the pudding to cool for about 15 minutes before serving warm with extra maple syrup and pouring cream.

Rhubarb Spiral Cobbler Energy 317Kcal/1355kJ; Protein 8.7g; Carbohydrate 72.6g, of which sugars 35.5g; Fat 1.3g, of which saturates 0.4g; Cholesterol 1mg; Calcium 443mg; Fibre 3.9g; Sodium 229mg.

Maple and Pecan Croissant Pudding Energy 738Kcal/3088kJ; Protein 15.1g; Carbohydrate 74.2g, of which sugars 51.3g; Fat 45.6g, of which saturates 19.5g; Cholesterol 226mg; Calcium 218mg; Fibre 1.8g; Sodium 508mg.

Steamed Chocolate & Fruit Puddings

Some things always turn out well, just like these wonderful little puddings. Dark, fluffy chocolate sponge with tangy cranberries and apple is served with a honeyed chocolate syrup.

Serves 4

butter or oil, for greasing
115g/4oz/½ cup muscovado (molasses) sugar
1 eating apple, peeled and cored
75g/3oz/¾ cup cranberries, thawed if frozen
115g/4oz/½ cup soft margarine
2 eggs
75g/3oz/⅔ cup plain (all-purpose) flour
2.5ml/½ tsp baking powder
45ml/3 tbsp cocoa powder (unsweetened)

For the chocolate syrup

115g/4oz plain (semisweet) chocolate, broken into squares
30ml/2 tbsp clear honey
15ml/1 tbsp unsalted (sweet) butter
2.5ml/½ tsp vanilla extract

1 Prepare a steamer or half fill a pan with water and bring it to the boil. Grease four individual heatproof bowls and sprinkle each one with a little of the muscovado sugar to coat all over.

2 Dice the apple into a bowl. Add the cranberries and mix well. Divide the mixture equally among the prepared bowls.

3 Put the remaining sugar in a mixing bowl. Add the margarine, eggs, flour, baking powder and cocoa. Beat well until smooth.

4 Spoon the mixture into the bowls, on top of the fruit, and cover each with a double thickness of foil. Steam for about 45 minutes, topping up the boiling water as required, until the puddings are well risen and firm.

5 Make the syrup. Mix together the chocolate, honey, butter and vanilla in a small pan. Heat gently, stirring, until smooth.

6 Run a knife around the edge of each pudding to loosen it, then turn out on to individual plates. Serve immediately, with the chocolate syrup poured over the top.

Chocolate Chip & Banana Pudding

Hot and steamy, this superb light pudding tastes extra special when served with ready-made fresh chocolate sauce or custard.

Serves 4

200g/7oz/1¾ cups self-raising (self-rising) flour
75g/3oz/6 tbsp unsalted (sweet) butter or margarine
2 ripe bananas
75g/3oz/6 tbsp caster (superfine) sugar
60ml/4 tbsp milk
1 egg, beaten
60ml/4 tbsp plain (bittersweet) chocolate chips or chopped chocolate
whipped cream, to serve

1 Prepare a steamer or half fill a pan with water and bring to the boil. Grease a 1 litre/1¾ pint/4 cup ovenproof bowl.

2 Sift the flour into a mixing bowl and rub in the butter or margarine until the mixture resembles breadcrumbs. Mash the bananas in a bowl. Stir them into the creamed mixture, with the caster sugar.

3 Whisk the milk with the egg in a bowl, then beat into the pudding mixture. Stir in the chocolate.

4 Spoon the mixture into the prepared bowl, cover closely with a double thickness of foil, and steam for 2 hours, topping up the water as required during cooking.

5 Run a knife around the top edge of the pudding to loosen it, then turn it out on to a warm serving dish. Serve hot, with a spoonful of whipped cream.

Cook's Tip

If you have a food processor, make a quick-mix version by processing all the ingredients, except the chocolate, until smooth. Then stir in the chocolate, spoon into the prepared bowl and finish as described in the recipe.

Steamed Chocolate and Fruit Puddings Energy 672Kcal/2811kJ; Protein 8.7g; Carbohydrate 73.1g, of which sugars 57.3g; Fat 40.4g, of which saturates 13.9g; Cholesterol 105mg; Calcium 84mg; Fibre 3.2g; Sodium 366mg.

Chocolate Chip and Banana Pudding Energy 528Kcal/2220kJ; Protein 8.1g; Carbohydrate 79.3g, of which sugars 40.9g; Fat 22g, of which saturates 13g; Cholesterol 89mg; Calcium 222mg; Fibre 2.5g; Sodium 320mg.

Chocolate, Date & Walnut Pudding

This tempting pudding is not steamed in the traditional way, but baked in the oven. The result is completely irresistible.

Serves 4

25g/1oz/¼ cup chopped walnuts
25g/1oz/2 tbsp chopped dates
2 eggs, separated
5ml/1 tsp vanilla extract
30ml/2 tbsp golden caster (superfine) sugar
45ml/3 tbsp plain wholemeal (all-purpose whole-wheat) flour
15ml/1 tbsp cocoa powder (unsweetened)
30ml/2 tbsp skimmed milk

1 Preheat the oven to 180°C/350°F/Gas 4. Grease and base-line with baking parchment a 1.2 litre/2 pint/5 cup ovenproof bowl. Spoon in the walnuts and dates.

2 Combine the egg yolks, vanilla extract and sugar in a heatproof bowl. Place over a pan of hot water.

3 Whisk the egg whites to soft peaks. Whisk the egg yolk mixture until it is thick and pale, then remove the bowl from the heat. Sift the flour and cocoa over the mixture and fold them in with a metal spoon. Stir in the milk, to soften the mixture, then fold in the egg whites.

4 Spoon the mixture over the walnuts and dates in the prepared bowl and bake for 40–45 minutes or until the pudding is well risen and firm to the touch. Run a knife around the pudding to loosen it from the bowl, and then turn it out on to a plate and serve immediately.

Cook's Tips

- *Pudding fans won't be satisfied without custard to accompany this dessert. Why not serve a real custard, Crème Anglaise, made using cream, egg yolks, caster (superfine) sugar and a few drops of vanilla extract?*
- *If you wish, the cocoa can be omitted, and the sponge mix flavoured with grated orange rind instead.*

Rich Chocolate Brioche Bake

This brioche dessert is amazingly easy to make and doesn't require many ingredients. Richly flavoured and quite delicious, it's the perfect dish for mid-week entertaining, when you are pushed for time. Serve with a platter of sliced tropical fruit as a foil to the richness of the dish.

Serves 4

40g/1½oz/3 tbsp unsalted (sweet) butter, plus extra for greasing
200g/7oz plain (semisweet) chocolate, chopped into small pieces
60ml/4 tbsp bitter marmalade
4 individual brioches, cut into halves, or 1 large brioche loaf, cut into thick slices
3 eggs
300ml/½ pint/1¼ cups milk
300ml/½ pint/1¼ cups single (light) cream
30ml/2 tbsp demerara (raw) sugar
crème fraîche, to serve

1 Preheat the oven to 180°C/350°F/Gas 4. Using the extra butter, lightly grease a shallow ovenproof dish.

2 Melt the chocolate with the marmalade and butter in a heatproof bowl over just simmering water, stirring the mixture occasionally, until smooth.

3 Spread the melted chocolate mixture over the brioche slices, then carefully arrange them in the dish so that the slices overlap in neat rows.

4 Beat the eggs in a large bowl, then add the milk and cream and mix well. Transfer to a jug (pitcher) and pour evenly over the slices.

5 Sprinkle the mixture with the demerara sugar and bake for 40–50 minutes, until the custard has set lightly and the brioche slices are golden brown. Serve immediately, topped with dollops of crème fraîche.

Chocolate, Date and Walnut Pudding Energy 171Kcal/716kJ; Protein 6.2g; Carbohydrate 19.5g, of which sugars 10.5g; Fat 8.2g, of which saturates 1.7g; Cholesterol 96mg; Calcium 55mg; Fibre 1.1g; Sodium 76mg.

Rich Chocolate Brioche Bake Energy 987Kcal/4143kJ; Protein 25.9g; Carbohydrate 127.8g, of which sugars 59.1g; Fat 45g, of which saturates 25.4g; Cholesterol 213mg; Calcium 460mg; Fibre 4.4g; Sodium 1060mg.

Magic Chocolate Mud Cake

Guaranteed to be a big hit, this scrumptious dessert can be put together in no time at all.

Serves 4

50g/2oz/¼ cup butter, plus extra for greasing
90g/3½oz/¾ cup self-raising (self-rising) flour
5ml/1 tsp ground cinnamon
75ml/5 tbsp cocoa powder (unsweetened)
200g/7oz/1 cup light muscovado (brown) or demerara (raw) sugar
475ml/16fl oz/2 cups milk
crème fraîche, Greek (US strained plain) yogurt or vanilla ice cream, to serve

1 Preheat the oven to 180°C/350°F/Gas 4. Grease a 1.5 litre/2½ pint/6¼ cup ovenproof dish with butter. Place the dish on a baking sheet and set aside.

2 Sift the flour and ground cinnamon into a bowl. Sift in 15ml/1 tbsp of the cocoa and mix well.

3 Place the butter in a pan. Add 115g/4oz/½ cup of the sugar and 150ml/¼ pint/⅔ cup of the milk. Heat gently without boiling, stirring from time to time, until the butter has melted and all the sugar has dissolved. Remove the pan from the heat.

4 Stir in the flour mixture, mixing evenly. Pour the mixture into the prepared dish and level the surface.

5 Mix the remaining sugar and cocoa in a bowl, then sprinkle over the pudding mixture. Pour the remaining milk evenly over the pudding.

6 Bake for 45–50 minutes or until the sponge has risen to the top and is firm to the touch. Serve hot, with the crème fraîche, yogurt or ice cream.

Cook's Tip
A delicious sauce 'magically' appears beneath the sponge.

Dutch Apple Cake

The apple topping makes this cake really moist. It is just as good hot as it is cold.

Serves 8–10

250g/9oz/2¼ cups self-raising (self-rising) flour
10ml/2 tsp baking powder
5ml/1 tsp ground cinnamon
130g/4½oz/generous ½ cup caster (superfine) sugar
50g/2oz/¼ cup butter, melted
2 eggs, beaten
150ml/¼ pint/⅔ cup milk

For the topping
2 eating apples
15g/½oz/1 tbsp butter, melted
60ml/4 tbsp demerara (raw) sugar
1.5ml/¼ tsp ground cinnamon

1 Preheat the oven to 200°C/400°F/Gas 6. Grease and line a 20cm/8in round cake tin (pan). Sift the flour, baking powder and cinnamon into a large mixing bowl. Stir in the caster sugar. In a separate bowl, whisk the melted butter, eggs and milk together, then stir the mixture into the dry ingredients.

2 Pour the cake mixture into the prepared tin, smooth the surface, then make a shallow hollow in a ring around the edge of the mixture.

3 Make the topping. Peel and core the apples, slice them into wedges and slice the wedges thinly. Arrange the slices around the edge of the cake mixture, in the hollowed ring. Brush with the melted butter, then scatter the demerara sugar and ground cinnamon over the top.

4 Bake for 45–50 minutes or until the cake has risen well, is golden and a skewer inserted into the centre comes out clean.

5 Serve immediately, or remove from the tin, peel off the lining paper and cool on a wire rack before serving cold with cream.

Variation
Add a few seedless raisins to the sliced apples, if you like.

Magic Chocolate Mud Cake Energy 480Kcal/2025kJ; Protein 10g; Carbohydrate 77.6g, of which sugars 58.3g; Fat 16.7g, of which saturates 10.2g; Cholesterol 34mg; Calcium 227mg; Fibre 3g; Sodium 309mg.

Dutch Apple Cake Energy 225Kcal/951kJ; Protein 3.7g; Carbohydrate 40g, of which sugars 21.4g; Fat 6.8g, of which saturates 3.8g; Cholesterol 52mg; Calcium 105mg; Fibre 1g; Sodium 145mg.

Bread & Apple Bake

Bread has always been the basic staple food of Russian cuisine. It is treated with great respect, bought fresh each day and used to the last crumb. This recipe makes a new dish out of old bread – it is frugal and simple, but also very good. Sweet dessert apples are best for this recipe.

Makes 1

a loaf of white bread, about 2–3 days old
60g/2¼oz/4½ tbsp cold butter
1 egg
150ml/¼ pint/⅔ cup milk
6–8 apples
130g/4½oz/⅔ cup caster (superfine) sugar

1 Preheat the oven to 200°C/400°F/Gas 6. Use 10g/¼oz/1½ tsp of the butter to grease a 20cm/8in flan tin (pan).

2 Slice the loaf fairly thickly; you will need around 10 slices. Cut off the crusts.

3 Break the egg into a bowl and beat lightly. Add the milk to the bowl and whisk together. Cut five of the bread slices in half.

4 Dip the halved slices of bread, one at a time, into the egg and milk mixture and place the bread slices in the flan tin so that they cover the edges.

5 Dip the remaining uncut bread slices in the milk mixture and place tightly in the bottom of the tin.

6 Cut the remaining 50g/2oz/4 tbsp butter into small cubes. Peel and core the apples and cut the flesh into small pieces.

7 Put half of the apples on top of the bread, sprinkle with half of the sugar and half of the butter cubes. Top with the remaining apples, sugar and butter.

8 Bake in the oven for 15 minutes. Lower the temperature to 180°C/350°F/Gas 4 and bake for a further 35 minutes, until golden brown. Serve warm, straight from the tin.

Sticky Toffee Pudding

Filling and warming, this tasty variation on a classic pudding will soon become a firm family favourite.

Serves 6

115g/4oz/1 cup toasted walnuts, chopped
175g/6oz/¾ cup butter
175g/6oz/scant 1 cup soft brown sugar
60ml/4 tbsp single (light) cream
30ml/2 tbsp freshly squeezed lemon juice
2 eggs, beaten
115g/4oz/1 cup self-raising (self-rising) flour

1 Prepare a steamer or half fill a pan with water and bring it to the boil. Grease a 900ml/1½ pint/3¾ cup heatproof bowl and add half the walnuts.

2 Heat 50g/2oz/4 tbsp of the butter with 50g/2oz/4 tbsp of the sugar, the cream and 15ml/1 tbsp of the lemon juice in a small pan, stirring until smooth. Pour half the sauce into the greased bowl, then swirl to coat it a little way up the sides. Reserve the remaining sauce.

3 Beat the remaining butter and sugar until light and fluffy, then gradually beat in the eggs. Fold in the flour and the remaining nuts and lemon juice and spoon into the bowl.

4 Cover the bowl with baking parchment with a pleat folded in the centre, then tie securely with string. Steam the pudding for about 1¼ hours, topping up the boiling water as required, until it is set in the centre.

5 Just before serving, gently warm the remaining sauce. To serve, run a knife around the edge of the pudding to loosen it, then turn out on to a warm plate and pour over the sauce.

Cook's Tip
Putting a pleat in the paper cover allows room for the pudding to rise. Secure tightly to prevent water or steam from entering.

Bread and Apple Bake Energy 245kcal/1038kJ; Protein 4.6g; Carbohydrate 41.8g, of which sugars 26.1g; Fat 7.9g, of which saturates 4.3g; Cholesterol 41mg; Calcium 77mg; Fibre 1.6g; Sodium 240mg.
Sticky Toffee Pudding Energy 571Kcal/2378kJ; Protein 7.3g; Carbohydrate 46g, of which sugars 31.6g; Fat 41.1g, of which saturates 18g; Cholesterol 131mg; Calcium 124mg; Fibre 1.3g; Sodium 275mg.

Gingerbread Upside-down Pudding

A proper pudding goes down well on a cold winter's day. This one is quite quick and easy to make, and yet looks very impressive.

Serves 4–6

sunflower oil, for brushing
15ml/1 tbsp soft brown sugar
4 medium peaches, halved and stoned (pitted), or canned peach halves
8 walnut halves

For the base

130g/4½oz/generous 1 cup wholemeal (whole-wheat) flour
2.5ml/½ tsp bicarbonate of soda (baking soda)
7.5ml/1½ tsp ground ginger
5ml/1 tsp ground cinnamon
115g/4oz/scant ½ cup muscovado (molasses) sugar
1 egg
120ml/4fl oz/½ cup skimmed milk
50ml/2fl oz/¼ cup sunflower oil

1 Preheat the oven to 180°C/350°F/Gas 4. For the topping, brush the base and sides of a 23cm/9in round springform cake tin (pan) with oil. Sprinkle the sugar over the base.

2 Arrange the peaches, cut side down, in the tin, placing a walnut half in each.

3 Sift together the flour, bicarbonate of soda, ginger and cinnamon, then stir in the sugar. Beat together the egg, milk and oil, then mix into the dry ingredients.

4 Pour the mixture evenly over the peaches and bake for 35–40 minutes, until firm to the touch. Turn out and serve hot.

Cook's Tips

- *To turn out successfully, run the point of a sharp knife around the edge of the pudding, then place a serving plate upside down on top. Holding the plate and tin (pan) firmly, invert. Release the sides of the tin and remove.*
- *To accentuate the ginger flavour, finely chop 15ml/1 tbsp drained stem ginger in syrup, and add at the end of step 3.*

Glazed Apricot Sponge

Proper puddings can be extremely high in saturated fat, but this particular version uses the minimum of oil and no eggs. Fat-free natural or apricot yogurt would make a suitably healthy and tasty accompaniment to this delicious dessert.

Serves 4

10ml/2 tsp golden (light corn) syrup
411g/14½oz can apricot halves in fruit juice
150g/5oz/1¼ cups self-raising (self-rising) flour
75g/3oz/1½ cups fresh breadcrumbs
90g/3½oz/½ cup light muscovado (brown) sugar
5ml/1 tsp ground cinnamon
30ml/2 tbsp sunflower oil
175ml/6fl oz/¾ cup skimmed milk

1 Preheat the oven to 180°C/350°F/Gas 4. Lightly oil a 900ml/1½ pint/3¾ cup ovenproof bowl. Carefully spoon in the golden syrup.

2 Drain the apricots and reserve the juice. Arrange about 8 halves, rounded side up, in the bowl. Purée the rest of the apricots with the juice and set aside.

3 Mix together the flour, breadcrumbs, sugar and cinnamon in a mixing bowl, then beat in the oil and milk. Spoon into the ovenproof bowl on top of the apricots.

4 Bake the mixture for 50–55 minutes, or until firm to the touch and golden on top. Run a knife around the pudding to loosen it from the bowl, then turn it out on to a plate. Serve with the puréed fruit as an accompaniment.

Cook's tips

To make fresh breadcrumbs, use bread that is a couple of days old and process in a blender or food processor, or use a grater.

Gingerbread Upside-down Pudding Energy 272Kcal/1145kJ; Protein 4.8g; Carbohydrate 44.1g, of which sugars 27.5g; Fat 9.7g, of which saturates 1.4g; Cholesterol 33mg; Calcium 77mg; Fibre 1.5g; Sodium 23mg.

Glazed Apricot Sponge Energy 348Kcal/1485kJ; Protein 7.6g; Carbohydrate 79.1g, of which sugars 37.2g; Fat 2.4g, of which saturates 0.6g; Cholesterol 3mg; Calcium 242mg; Fibre 2.5g; Sodium 310mg.

Lemon Surprise Pudding

This is a much-loved dessert that many of us remember from childhood. The surprise is the unexpected sauce concealed beneath the delectable sponge.

Serves 4

50g/2oz/¼ cup butter, plus extra for greasing
grated rind and juice of 2 lemons
115g/4oz/generous ½ cup caster (superfine) sugar
2 eggs, separated
50g/2oz/½ cup self-raising (self-rising) flour
300ml/½ pint/1¼ cups milk

1 Preheat the oven to 190°C/375°F/Gas 5. Use a little butter to grease a 1.2 litre/2 pint/5 cup baking dish.

2 Beat the lemon rind, remaining butter and caster sugar in a bowl until pale and fluffy. Add the egg yolks and flour and beat together well. Gradually whisk in the lemon juice and milk (do not be alarmed if the mixture curdles).

3 In a grease-free bowl, whisk the egg whites until they form stiff peaks. Fold the egg whites lightly into the lemon mixture, then pour into the prepared baking dish.

4 Place the dish in a roasting tin (pan) and pour in hot water to come halfway up the side of the dish. Bake for about 45 minutes until golden. Serve immediately.

Cook's Tips

- *The uncooked mixture may look like a curdled disaster, but as the dessert cooks it separates into a top layer of firm sponge, with a luscious lemony sauce beneath.*
- *Standing the dish in a layer of water in the pan creates a gentle method of cooking – this 'bain-marie' method is often used for custards and other delicate egg dishes.*
- *For a slightly different accompaniment, whip thick cream with a little vanilla extract and icing (confectioners') sugar.*

Hot Plum Batter Pudding

Other fruits can be used in place of plums, depending on the season. Canned black cherries are a convenient substitute to keep in the store cupboard.

Serves 4

450g/1lb ripe red plums, quartered and stoned (pitted)
200ml/7fl oz/scant 1 cup skimmed milk
60ml/4 tbsp skimmed milk powder
15ml/1 tbsp light muscovado (brown) sugar
5ml/1 tsp vanilla extract
75g/3oz/⅔ cup self-raising (self-rising) flour
2 egg whites
icing (confectioners') sugar, to sprinkle
natural (plain) yogurt or crème fraîche, to serve

1 Preheat the oven to 220°C/425°F/Gas 7. Lightly oil a wide, shallow ovenproof dish and add the plums.

2 Pour the milk, milk powder, sugar, vanilla extract, flour and egg whites into a blender or food processor. Process the mixture to form a smooth batter.

3 Pour the batter over the plums in the dish. Bake for 25–30 minutes, or until the top is puffed and golden. Sprinkle with icing sugar and serve immediately with yogurt or crème fraîche.

Cook's Tips

- *If you don't have a food processor, place the dry ingredients for the batter in a large bowl and gradually whisk in the milk and egg whites.*
- *Flavoured cream would be delicious served with this dessert. Lightly whip double (heavy) cream, stir in a spoonful or two of your favourite liqueur, and sweeten to taste.*

Variation

Halved fresh or canned apricots are tasty instead of the plums, or try cherries, pre-soaked in a little kirsch for an added kick.

Lemon Surprise Pudding Energy 319Kcal/1341kJ; Protein 7g; Carbohydrate 43.1g, of which sugars 33.8g; Fat 14.5g, of which saturates 8.1g; Cholesterol 126mg; Calcium 166mg; Fibre 0.4g; Sodium 190mg.

Hot Plum Batter Pudding Energy 139Kcal/594kJ; Protein 5.5g; Carbohydrate 30.2g, of which sugars 16.3g; Fat 0.5g, of which saturates 0.1g; Cholesterol 2mg; Calcium 144mg; Fibre 2.4g; Sodium 123mg.

White Bread

This simple recipe makes the perfect basis for experimenting. Be prepared to make minor alterations to quantities, to find the right recipe for your bread machine.

Makes 1

Small

250ml/8fl oz/1 cup water
375g/13oz/3¼ cups unbleached white bread flour
7.5ml/1½ tsp salt
7.5ml/1½ tsp sugar
25g/1oz/2 tbsp butter
5ml/1 tsp easy-blend (rapid-rise) dried yeast

Medium

330ml/scant 12fl oz/1¼ cups plus 2 tbsp water
500g/1lb 2oz/4½ cups unbleached white bread flour
7.5ml/1½ tsp salt
10ml/2 tsp sugar
25g/1oz/2 tbsp butter
5ml/1 tsp easy-blend (rapid-rise) dried yeast

Large

370ml/13fl oz/1½ cups plus 1 tbsp water
600g/1lb 5oz/5¼ cups unbleached white bread flour
7.5ml/1½ tsp salt
15ml/1 tbsp sugar
40g/1½oz/3 tbsp butter
7.5ml/1½ tsp easy-blend (rapid-rise) dried yeast

1 Pour the water into the bread machine pan. However, if the instructions for your machine specify that the yeast is to be placed in the pan first, reverse the order in which you add the liquid and dry ingredients.

2 Sprinkle over the flour, ensuring that it covers the water. Add the salt, sugar and butter in separate corners of the bread pan. Make a small indent in the centre of the flour (but not down as far as the liquid) and add the yeast.

3 Set the bread machine to the basic/normal setting, medium crust. Press Start.

4 Remove the bread at the end of the baking cycle and turn out on to a wire rack to cool.

Rapid White Bread

A delicious basic white loaf cooked on the fastest setting.

Makes 1

Small

210ml/7½fl oz/scant 1 cup lukewarm water
25ml/1½ tbsp sunflower oil
375g/13oz/3¼ cups unbleached white bread flour
15ml/1 tbsp skimmed milk powder (non fat dry milk)
7.5ml/1½ tsp salt
15ml/1 tbsp sugar
5ml/1 tsp easy-blend (rapid-rise) dried yeast

Medium

315ml/11fl oz/1⅓ cups lukewarm water
30ml/2 tbsp sunflower oil
500g/1lb 2oz/4½ cups unbleached white bread flour
25ml/1½ tbsp skimmed milk powder (non fat dry milk)
7.5ml/1½ tsp salt
15ml/1 tbsp sugar
5ml/1 tsp easy-blend (rapid-rise) dried yeast

Large

385ml/13½fl oz/1⅝ cups lukewarm water
45ml/3 tbsp sunflower oil
625g/1lb 6oz/5½ cups unbleached white bread flour
30ml/2 tbsp skimmed milk powder (non fat dry milk)
10ml/2 tsp salt
25ml/1½ tbsp sugar
10ml/2 tsp easy-blend (rapid-rise) dried yeast

1 Pour the water and the sunflower oil into the bread machine pan. However, if the instructions for your machine specify that the yeast is to be placed in the pan first, reverse the order in which you add the liquid and dry ingredients.

2 Sprinkle over the flour, covering the water. Add the milk powder. Place the salt and sugar in separate corners of the bread pan. Make a shallow indent in the centre of the flour (but not down as far as the liquid) and add the yeast.

3 Set the machine to the white rapid/basic rapid/fastbake setting, medium crust. Size: 500g for small, large/750g for medium, or 1kg/2lb for large. Press Start.

4 Remove the bread at the end of the baking cycle. Turn out on to a wire rack.

White Bread per loaf Energy 1493kcal/6321kJ; Protein 35.4g; Carbohydrate 299.2g, of which sugars 13.5g; Fat 25.3g, of which saturates 14.3g; Cholesterol 58mg; Calcium 533mg; Fibre 11.6g; Sodium 3147mg.

Rapid White Bread per loaf Energy 1528kcal/6476kJ; Protein 38.6g; Carbohydrate 312.1g, of which sugars 26.3g; Fat 22.6g, of which saturates 3.7g; Cholesterol 6mg; Calcium 653mg; Fibre 11.6g; Sodium 67mg.

Egg-enriched White Loaf

Adding egg to a basic white loaf gives a richer flavour and creamier crumb, as well as a wonderfully golden finish to the crust.

Makes 1

Small

1 egg
water
375g/13oz/3¼ cups unbleached white bread flour
7.5ml/1½ tsp sugar
7.5ml/1½ tsp salt
20g/¾oz/1½ tbsp butter
4ml/¾ tsp easy-blend (rapid-rise) dried yeast

Medium

1 egg plus 1 egg yolk
water
500g/1lb 2oz/4½ cups unbleached white bread flour
10ml/2 tsp sugar
7.5ml/1½ tsp salt
25g/1oz/2 tbsp butter
5ml/1 tsp easy-blend (rapid-rise) dried yeast

Large

2 eggs
water
600g/1lb 5oz/5¼ cups unbleached white bread flour
10ml/2 tsp sugar
7.5ml/1½ tsp salt
25g/1oz/2 tbsp butter
7.5ml/1½ tsp easy-blend (rapid-rise) dried yeast

1 Put the egg(s) in a measuring jug (cup) and add sufficient water to give 240ml/8½fl oz/generous 1 cup, 300ml/½ pint/1¼ cups or 385ml/13½fl oz/1⅝ cups, according to the size of loaf selected.

2 Mix lightly and pour into the bread pan. If your instructions specify that the yeast is to be placed in the pan first, reverse the order in which you add the liquid and the dry ingredients.

3 Sprinkle over the flour, covering the water. In separate corners of the pan, add the sugar, salt and butter. Make an indent in the centre of the flour. Add the yeast.

4 Set the bread machine to the white/basic setting, medium crust. Size: 500g for small, large/750g for medium, or 1kg/2lb for large. Press Start. At the end of the cycle, cool on a wire rack.

Farmhouse Loaf

The flour-dusted split top gives a charmingly rustic look.

Makes 1

Medium

320ml/11¼fl oz/generous 1⅓ cups water
425g/15oz/3¾ cups unbleached white bread flour, plus extra for dusting
75g/3oz/¾ cup wholemeal (whole-wheat) bread flour
25ml/1½ tbsp skimmed milk powder (non fat dry milk)
7.5ml/1½ tsp salt
7.5ml/1½ tsp sugar
25g/1oz/2 tbsp butter
5ml/1 tsp easy-blend (rapid-rise) dried yeast
water, for glazing

Large

375ml/13½fl oz/1½ cups plus 1 tbsp water
525g/1lb 3oz/4¾ cups unbleached white bread flour, plus extra for dusting
75g/3oz/⅔ cup wholemeal (whole-wheat) bread flour
30ml/2 tbsp skimmed milk powder (non fat dry milk)
10ml/2 tsp salt
10ml/2 tsp sugar
25g/1oz/2 tbsp butter
7.5ml/1½ tsp easy-blend (rapid-rise) dried yeast
water, for glazing

1 Pour the water into the bread pan. If the instructions for your machine specify that the yeast is to be placed first, reverse the order in which you add the liquid and dry ingredients.

2 Sprinkle over both the flours, covering the water completely. Add the milk powder. Add the salt, sugar and butter in separate corners. Make a small indent in the centre of the flour (but not down as far as the liquid) and add the yeast.

3 Set the bread machine to the white/basic setting, medium crust. Size: 750g for medium, or 1kg/2lb for large. Press Start.

4 Ten minutes before baking, brush the loaf with water, and dust with white bread flour. Slash the top with a sharp knife.

5 Remove the bread at the end of the baking cycle. Turn out on to a wire rack and leave to cool.

Egg-enriched White Loaf per loaf Loaf Energy 1529kcal/6476kJ; Protein 41.6g; Carbohydrate 299.2g, of which sugars 13.5g; Fat 26.8g, of which saturates 13.1g; Cholesterol 236mg; Calcium 561mg; Fibre 11.6g; Sodium 3179mg.

Farmhouse Loaf per loaf Energy 1457kcal/6180kJ; Protein 39.5g; Carbohydrate 300.8g, of which sugars 18.6g; Fat 19.1g, of which saturates 9.9g; Cholesterol 40mg; Calcium 626mg; Fibre 13.1g; Sodium 3127mg.

Milk Loaf

Adding milk to the dough results in a soft, velvety grained loaf with a beautifully browned crust. Milk also helps to improve the keeping quality of the bread.

Makes 1

Small

180ml/6½fl oz/generous ¾ cup milk
60ml/2fl oz/¼ cup water
375g/13oz/3¼ cups unbleached white bread flour
7.5ml/1½ tsp salt
10ml/2 tsp sugar
20g/¾oz/1½ tbsp butter
2.5ml/½ tsp easy-blend (rapid-rise) dried yeast

Medium

230ml/8fl oz/1 cup milk
100ml/3½fl oz/7 tbsp water
500g/1lb 2oz/4½ cups unbleached white bread flour
7.5ml/1½ tsp salt
10ml/2 tsp sugar
25g/1oz/2 tbsp butter
5ml/1 tsp easy-blend (rapid-rise) dried yeast

Large

250ml/9fl oz/generous 1 cup milk
115ml/4fl oz/½ cup water
600g/1lb 5oz/5¼ cups unbleached strong white bread flour
10ml/2 tsp salt
10ml/2 tsp sugar
25g/1oz/2 tbsp butter
7.5ml/1½ tsp easy-blend (rapid-rise) dried yeast

1 Pour the milk and water into the bread machine pan. If the instructions for your machine specify that the yeast is to be placed in the pan first, reverse the order in which you add the liquid and dry ingredients.

2 Sprinkle over the flour, ensuring that it covers the water. Add the salt, sugar and butter in separate corners of the bread pan. Make a small indent in the centre of the flour (but not down as far as the liquid) and add the yeast.

3 Set the bread machine to the white/basic setting, medium crust. Size: 500g for small, large/750g for medium, or 1kg/2lb for large. Press Start.

4 Remove the bread at the end of the baking cycle and turn out on to a wire rack to cool.

French Couronne

This crown-shaped loaf is made with a chef starter, which is fermented for at least two days before baking the dough.

Makes 1

For the chef

0.75ml/⅛ tsp easy-blend (rapid-rise) dried yeast
50g/2oz/½ cup white bread flour
45ml/3 tbsp water

For the 1st refreshment

65ml/4½ tbsp water
115g/4oz/1 cup white bread flour

For the levain

115ml/4fl oz/½ cup water
115g/4oz/1 cup unbleached white bread flour

For the couronne dough

240ml/8½fl oz/generous 1 cup cold water
325g/11½oz/scant 3 cups unbleached white bread flour, plus extra for dusting
7.5ml/1½ tsp salt
5ml/1 tsp sugar
2.5ml/½ tsp easy-blend (rapid-rise) dried yeast

1 Mix the yeast and white bread flour for the chef in a bowl. Add the water and mix to a stiff dough. Cover and set aside in a warm place for 2–3 days.

2 Break open the crust on the chef. Mix in the water and flour for the first refreshment, stirring to form a fairly stiff dough. Cover and set aside for a further 2 days in a warm place.

3 Transfer the chef to the machine pan. Add the water for the levain. Sprinkle over the flour, ensuring that it covers the water. Set the bread machine to the basic dough setting. Press Start.

4 When finished, transfer the levain to a bowl, cover it with a damp dish towel and leave for 8 hours.

5 Put 200g/7oz/scant 1 cup of the levain back in the bread machine pan. Reserve the spare levain to use for your next loaf. Meanwhile pour the water for the dough into the bread pan. Sprinkle over the flour. Add the salt and sugar, placing them in separate corners of the bread pan. Make a small indent in the centre of the flour and add the yeast.

6 Set the bread machine to the dough setting; use basic dough setting (if available). Press Start.

7 When the dough cycle has finished, remove the dough from the machine, place it on a lightly floured surface and knock back (punch down) gently, then shape it into a ball and make a hole in the centre. Gradually enlarge this cavity, using your fingertips and turning the dough, then use both hands to stretch the dough gently into a large doughnut shape. The cavity should measure 13–15cm/5–6in across.

8 Lightly oil a baking sheet and place the shaped dough on to the sheet. Fit a small bowl into the centre to prevent the dough from filling in the hole when it rises. Cover and leave for an hour.

9 Preheat the oven to 230°C/450°F/Gas 8. Dust the loaf with flour and make four slashes at equal intervals around the couronne. Bake for 35–40 minutes. Cool on a wire rack.

Milk Loaf per loaf Energy 1548kcal/6563kJ; Protein 41.3g; Carbohydrate 310.8g, of which sugars 25.1g; Fat 24.3g, of which saturates 13.4g; Cholesterol 57mg; Calcium 750mg; Fibre 11.6g; Sodium 3208mg.

French Couronne per loaf Energy 1465kcal/6230kJ; Protein 40g; Carbohydrate 334.4g, of which sugars 10.6g; Fat 5.5g, of which saturates 0.8g; Cholesterol 0mg; Calcium 598mg; Fibre 13.2g; Sodium 2960mg.

Crispy French Bread

This is an easy way to make a delicious crispy bread. The French bread setting on the machine will produce a light-textured bread with the extra-crispy crust that is commonly associated with French bread.

Makes 1

Small

300ml/10½fl oz/1¼ cups water
400g/14oz/3½ cups unbleached white bread flour
15g/½oz/1 tbsp butter
5ml/1 tsp salt
5ml/1 tsp easy-blend (rapid-rise) dried yeast

Medium

350ml/12fl oz/1½ cups water
500g/1lb 2oz/4½ cups unbleached white bread flour
15g/½oz/1 tbsp butter
7.5ml/1½ tsp salt
7ml/1⅖ tsp easy-blend (rapid-rise) dried yeast

Large

420ml/15fl oz/1¾ cups water
600g/1lb 5oz/5¼ cups unbleached white bread flour
25g/1oz/2 tbsp butter
10ml/2 tsp salt
7.5ml/1½ tsp easy-blend (rapid-rise) dried yeast

1 Pour the water into the bread machine pan. If the manufacturer's instructions for your particular machine specify that the yeast is to be placed in the pan first, reverse the order in which you add the liquid and the dry ingredients.

2 Sprinkle the flour into the bread pan, ensuring that it covers the water. Add the butter and salt in two separate corners of the bread pan.

3 Make a small indent in the centre of the flour (but not down as far as the liquid) and add the yeast into the indent.

4 Set the bread machine to the French setting, medium crust. Size: 500g for small, large/750g for medium, or 1kg/2lb for large. Press Start.

5 Remove the bread from the pan at the end of the baking cycle. Turn out the cooked loaf on to a wire rack and leave to cool.

Pane All'olio

This bread uses an unsalted yeast starter known as 'biga'. This is a traditional Italian way of making bread that has a light texture with holes.

Makes 1

For the biga

105ml/7 tbsp water
175g/6oz/1½ cups white bread flour
5ml/1 tsp easy-blend (rapid-rise) dried yeast

For the dough

90ml/6 tbsp water
60ml/4 tbsp extra virgin olive oil
225g/8oz/2 cups unbleached white bread flour, plus extra for dusting
10ml/2 tsp salt
5ml/1 tsp sugar

1 Pour the water for the biga into the bread machine pan. Sprinkle over the flour, covering the water. Make a shallow indent in the centre of the flour and add the yeast. Set the machine to the basic dough setting. Press Start. When finished, leave the biga inside, with the lid closed, for 8 hours.

2 Remove the bread pan from the machine. Break the biga into three or four pieces. Pour in the water and olive oil for the dough. Sprinkle over the flour, covering the liquid. Add the salt and sugar in separate corners of the bread pan.

3 Set the bread machine to the basic dough setting. Press Start. When finished, place the dough on a floured surface. Knock it back (punch it down) gently, then shape it into a plump round.

4 Gently roll the dough, until it forms a torpedo-shaped loaf about 30cm/12in long. Place the loaf on a floured baking sheet and cover and leave to rise for 45–60 minutes. Place a baking stone in the oven. Preheat the oven to 230°C/450°F/Gas 8.

5 Dust the top of the bread with flour and slash it along its length. Transfer to the hot baking stone. Mist the inside of the oven with water. Bake the loaf for 15 minutes, misting the oven again after 2 minutes and then after 4 minutes. Reduce the oven temperature to 190°C/375°F/Gas 5 and bake the loaf for 20–25 minutes more. Turn out on to a wire rack to cool.

Crispy French Bread per loaf Energy 1475kcal/6255kJ; Protein 37.7g; Carbohydrate 310.8g, of which sugars 6g; Fat 17.5g, of which saturates 8.9g; Cholesterol 35mg; Calcium 563mg; Fibre 12.4g; Sodium 2090mg.

Pane All'olio per loaf Energy 1775kcal/7493kJ; Protein 37.6g; Carbohydrate 315g, of which sugars 10.2g; Fat 49.2g, of which saturates 7g; Cholesterol 0mg; Calcium 563mg; Fibre 12.4g; Sodium 1977mg.

Challah

This Jewish festival bread is often braided, but can also be shaped into a coil.

Makes 1

For the sponge

200ml/7fl oz/scant 1 cup water
225g/8oz/2 cups unbleached white bread flour
15ml/1 tbsp sugar
5ml/1 tsp salt
7.5ml/1½ tsp easy-blend (rapid-rise) dried yeast

For the dough

2 eggs
225g/8oz/2 cups unbleached white bread flour
15ml/1 tbsp sugar
5ml/1 tsp salt
50g/2oz/¼ cup butter, melted

For the topping

1 egg yolk
15ml/1 tbsp water
poppy seeds

1 Pour the water for the sponge into the bread machine pan. Sprinkle over the flour covering the water. Add the sugar and salt in separate corners. Make an indent in the flour and add the yeast. Set to the basic dough setting. Press Start.

2 When the dough cycle has finished, switch the machine off, leaving the sponge inside. Leave the sponge for 8 hours.

3 Add the eggs for the dough to the sponge. Sprinkle over the flour. Place the sugar, salt and melted butter in separate corners of the bread pan. Set to the basic dough setting. Press Start.

4 When the dough cycle has finished, remove the dough from the machine and place it on a lightly floured surface. Knock back (punch down) the dough gently, then flatten until it is 2.5cm/1in thick. Fold both sides to the centre and press to seal.

5 Roll the dough into a rope about 50cm/20in long. Coil into a spiral shape, tucking the end under the loaf. Place on an oiled baking sheet. Cover and leave for 45–60 minutes.

6 Preheat the oven to 190°C/375°F/Gas 5. Beat the egg yolk with the water and brush over the challah. Sprinkle with the poppy seeds and bake for 35–40 minutes. Cool on a wire rack.

Fresh Yeast Bread

Bread machine manufacturers do not recommend using fresh yeast, but the machine can be used to prepare the dough stage.

Makes 1

15g/½oz fresh yeast
5ml/1 tsp sugar
260ml/9fl oz/1⅛ cups water
30ml/2 tbsp sunflower oil
450g/1lb/4 cups unbleached white bread flour
30ml/2 tbsp skimmed milk powder (non fat dry milk)
10ml/2 tsp salt
75ml/5 tbsp sunflower seeds, for coating

1 In a small bowl, cream the fresh yeast with the sugar and 30ml/2 tbsp of the water. Leave to stand for 5 minutes, then scrape the mixture into the bread machine pan. Add the remaining water and the sunflower oil. However, if the instructions for your bread machine specify that the dry ingredients are to be placed in the pan first, simply reverse the order in which you add the wet and dry ingredients to the pan.

2 Sprinkle over the flour, ensuring that it covers the water. Add the skimmed milk powder and salt to the bread pan. Set the bread machine to the basic dough setting. Press Start.

3 When the dough cycle has finished, remove the dough from the machine and place it on a lightly floured surface. Knock it back (punch down) gently, and then knead for 2–3 minutes. Roll the dough into a ball and pat it into a plump round shape.

4 Sprinkle the sunflower seeds on a clean area of work surface and roll the bread in them until evenly coated. Place on an oiled baking sheet. Cover with lightly oiled clear film (plastic wrap) or a large inverted bowl and leave to rise in a warm place for 30–45 minutes, or until doubled in size.

5 Meanwhile, preheat the oven to 230°C/450°F/Gas 8. Cut four slashes at right angles to make a square. Bake the loaf for 15 minutes, then reduce the oven temperature to 200°C/400°F/Gas 6. Bake for 20 minutes more, or until the bread sounds hollow when tapped on the base. Cool on a wire rack.

Challah per loaf Energy 2235kcal/9460kJ; Protein 63.1g; Carbohydrate 428.3g, of which sugars 24.6g; Fat 41.9g, of which saturates 7.1g; Cholesterol 403mg; Calcium 811mg; Fibre 16.4g; Sodium 165mg.

Fresh Yeast Bread per loaf Energy 1757kcal/7444kJ; Protein 43g; Carbohydrate 354.8g, of which sugars 11.9g; Fat 28.2g, of which saturates 3.7g; Cholesterol 1mg; Calcium 657mg; Fibre 13.9g; Sodium 3955mg.

Buttermilk Bread

Buttermilk adds a pleasant, slightly sour note to this bread. It also gives a light texture and a golden crust.

Makes 1

Small

250ml/8fl oz/1 cup buttermilk
30ml/2 tbsp water
15ml/1 tbsp clear honey
15ml/1 tbsp sunflower oil
250g/9oz/2¼ cups unbleached white bread flour
125g/4¼oz/generous 1 cup wholemeal (whole-wheat) bread flour
7.5ml/1½ tsp salt
5ml/1 tsp easy-blend (rapid-rise) dried yeast

Medium

285ml/10fl oz/1¼ cups buttermilk
65ml/4½ tbsp water
25ml/1½ tbsp clear honey
25ml/1½ tbsp sunflower oil
350g/12oz/3 cups unbleached white bread flour
150g/5oz/1⅓ cups wholemeal bread flour
7.5ml/1½ tsp salt
7.5ml/1½ tsp easy-blend (rapid-rise) dried yeast

Large

330ml/scant 12fl oz/1¼ cups plus 2 tbsp buttermilk
70ml/2½fl oz/⅓ cup water
25ml/1½ tbsp clear honey
30ml/2 tbsp sunflower oil
425g/15oz/3¾ cups unbleached white bread flour
175g/6oz/generous 1½ cups wholemeal (whole-wheat) bread flour
7.5ml/1½ tsp salt
7.5ml/1½ tsp easy-blend (rapid-rise) dried yeast

1 Pour the buttermilk, water, honey and oil into the bread machine pan. If your instructions specify that the yeast is to be placed in the pan first, reverse the order of the liquid and dry ingredients.

2 Sprinkle over both the white and wholemeal flours, ensuring that the water is completely covered. Add the salt in one corner of the pan. Make a small indent in the centre of the flour (but not down as far as the liquid) and add the yeast.

3 Set the bread machine to the white/basic setting, medium crust. Size: 500g for small, large/750g for medium, or 1kg/2lb for large. Press Start. When finished, cool on a wire rack.

Pain de Campagne

This rustic-style French bread is made using a 'poolish' or sponge. The fermentation period is fairly short, which makes for a loaf that is not as sour as some breads of this type.

Makes 1

For the poolish

200ml/7fl oz/scant 1 cup water
175g/6oz/1½ cups unbleached white bread flour
50g/2oz/½ cup wholemeal (whole-wheat) bread flour
1.5ml/¼ tsp easy-blend (rapid-rise) dried yeast

For the dough

120ml/4fl oz/½ cup water
225g/8oz/2 cups unbleached white bread flour, plus extra for dusting
50g/2oz/½ cup wholemeal (whole-wheat) bread flour
25g/1oz/¼ cup rye flour
7.5ml/1½ tsp salt
2.5ml/½ tsp sugar
2.5ml/½ tsp easy-blend (rapid-rise) dried yeast

1 Pour the water for the poolish into the bread machine pan. Sprinkle over both types of flour, covering the water. Make a small indent in the centre of the flour; add the yeast. Set the bread machine to the basic dough setting. Press Start.

2 When finished, leave the poolish inside, with the lid closed, for 2–8 hours, depending on how sour you like your bread to taste.

3 Pour in the water for the dough. Sprinkle over each type of flour, then add the salt and sugar in separate corners. Make a small indent in the centre of the flour; add the yeast. Set the bread machine to the basic dough setting. Press Start.

4 When finished, knock back (punch it down) the dough, and shape into a ball. Place on an oiled baking sheet. Cover with a glass bowl and leave for 30–45 minutes. Preheat the oven to 220°C/425°F/Gas 7.

5 Dust the top of the loaf with flour. Cut three parallel slashes across the loaf, then cut three more slashes at right angles. Transfer the baking sheet and bake the bread for 40 minutes, or until it is golden. Turn out on to a wire rack.

Buttermilk Bread per loaf Energy 1458kcal/6185kJ; Protein 47g; Carbohydrate 297.1g, of which sugars 29.3g; Fat 17.7g, of which saturates 2.4g; Cholesterol 9mg; Calcium 745mg; Fibre 19g; Sodium 2702mg.

Pain de Campagne per loaf Energy 2051kcal/8719kJ; Protein 62.8g; Carbohydrate 457.2g, of which sugars 10.1g; Fat 9.3g, of which saturates 1.4g; Cholesterol 0mg; Calcium 709mg; Fibre 27.9g; Sodium 3948mg.

Wholemeal Bread

This is a hearty bread with a full nutty flavour and coarse texture that comes from the wheatgerm and bran found in the wholemeal flour.

Makes 1

Small

280ml/10fl oz/1 cup plus 3 tbsp water
10ml/2 tsp lemon juice
385g/13½ oz/3⅜ cups wholemeal (whole-wheat) bread flour
20g/¾oz/1½ tbsp butter
7.5ml/1½ tsp salt
7.5ml/1½ tsp sugar
5ml/1 tsp easy-blend (rapid-rise) dried yeast

Medium

350ml/12fl oz/1½ cups water
10ml/2 tsp lemon juice
500g/1lb 2oz/4½ cups wholemeal (whole-wheat) bread flour
25g/1oz/2 tbsp butter
10ml/2 tsp salt
10ml/2 tsp sugar
5ml/1 tsp easy-blend (rapid-rise) dried yeast

Large

380ml/13½fl oz/1⅝ cups water
15ml/1 tbsp lemon juice
600g/1lb 5oz/5¼ cups wholemeal (whole-wheat) bread flour
25g/1oz/2 tbsp butter
10ml/2 tsp salt
15ml/1 tbsp sugar
6.5ml/1⅓ tsp easy-blend (rapid-rise) dried yeast

1 Pour the water into the bread machine pan. Add the lemon juice. If the instructions for your machine specify that the yeast is to be placed in the pan first, reverse the order in which you add the liquid and the dry ingredients.

2 Sprinkle over the flour, ensuring that it covers the water. Add the butter, salt and sugar in separate corners of the bread pan. Make a small indent in the centre of the flour (but not down as far as the liquid) and add the yeast.

3 Set the bread machine to the whole-wheat setting, medium crust, if available. Size: 500g for small, large/750g for medium, or 1kg/2lb for large. Press Start.

4 Remove the bread from the bread pan at the end of the baking cycle, then turn it out on to a wire rack to cool.

Light Wholemeal Bread

This is a lighter wholemeal loaf that can be cooked on the quicker basic or normal setting of your bread machine.

Makes 1

Medium

350ml/12fl oz/1½ cups water
350g/12oz/3 cups wholemeal (whole-wheat) bread flour
150g/5oz/1⅓ cups white bread flour
30ml/2 tbsp skimmed milk powder (non fat dry milk)
7.5ml/1½ tsp salt
10ml/2 tsp sugar
25g/1oz/2 tbsp butter
7.5ml/1½ tsp easy-blend (rapid-rise) dried yeast

Large

400ml/14fl oz/scant 1¾ cups water
425g/15oz/3¾ cups wholemeal (whole-wheat) bread flour
175g/6oz/generous 1½ cups white bread flour
30ml/2 tbsp skimmed milk powder (non fat dry milk)
10ml/2 tsp salt
15ml/1 tbsp sugar
25g/1oz/2 tbsp butter
7.5ml/1½ tsp easy-blend (rapid-rise) dried yeast

1 Pour the water into the bread machine pan. If the instructions for your bread machine specify that the yeast is to be placed in the pan first, reverse the order in which you add the liquid and dry ingredients to the pan.

2 Sprinkle over both flours ensuring that the water is completely covered. Add the skimmed milk powder. Add the salt, sugar and butter in separate corners of the bread pan. Make a small indent in the centre of the flour and add the yeast to the centre.

3 Set the bread machine to the white/basic setting, medium or light crust. Size: 750g for medium, or 1kg/2lb for large. Press Start.

4 Remove the bread at the end of the baking cycle. Turn out on to a wire rack.

Wholemeal Bread per loaf Energy 1370kcal/5807kJ; Protein 49g; Carbohydrate 253.9g, of which sugars 15.9g; Fat 24.8g, of which saturates 12g; Cholesterol 46mg; Calcium 154mg; Fibre 34.6g; Sodium 3110mg.

Light Wholemeal Bread per loaf Energy 1277kcal/5429kJ; Protein 46.8g; Carbohydrate 269.7g, of which sugars 20g; Fat 8.8g, of which saturates 2g; Cholesterol 6mg; Calcium 395mg; Fibre 26.4g; Sodium 3014mg.

Bran & Yogurt Bread

This soft-textured yogurt bread is enriched with bran. It is high in fibre, and makes wonderful toast.

Makes 1

Small

150ml/5fl oz/⅔ cup water
125ml/4¼fl oz/generous ½ cup natural (plain) yogurt
15ml/1 tbsp sunflower oil
15ml/1 tbsp molasses
200g/7oz/1¾ cups unbleached white bread flour
150g/5oz/1⅓ cups wholemeal (whole-wheat) bread flour
25g/1oz/⅓ cup wheat bran
5ml/1 tsp salt
4ml/¾ tsp easy-blend (rapid-rise) dried yeast

Large

200ml/7fl oz/⅞ cup water
190ml/6¾fl oz/scant ⅞ cup natural (plain) yogurt
30ml/2 tbsp sunflower oil
30ml/2 tbsp molasses
350g/12oz/3 cups unbleached white bread flour
225g/8oz/2 cups wholemeal (whole-wheat) bread flour
40g/½oz/⅔ cup wheat bran
10ml/2 tsp salt
7.5ml/1½ tsp easy-blend (rapid-rise) dried yeast

1 Pour the water, yogurt, oil and molasses into the bread machine pan. If the instructions for your machine specify that the yeast is to be placed in the pan first, reverse the order in which you add the liquid and dry ingredients.

2 Sprinkle over both the white and the wholemeal flours, ensuring that the liquid mixture is completely covered.

3 Add the wheat bran and salt, then make a small indent in the centre of the dry ingredients (but not down as far as the liquid) and add the easy bake dried yeast.

4 Set the bread machine to the white/basic setting, medium crust. Size: 500g for small, or 1kg/2lb for large. Press Start.

5 Remove the bread from the pan at the end of the baking cycle and turn out on to a wire rack to cool.

6 Serve when still just warm, if you like.

Granary Bread

Granary flour – like Malthouse flour – is a blend, and contains malted wheat grain which gives a crunchy texture to this loaf.

Makes 1

Small

240ml/8½fl oz/generous 1 cup water
375g/13oz/3¼ cups Granary (whole-wheat) bread flour
5ml/1 tsp salt
10ml/2 tsp sugar
20g/¾oz/1½ tbsp butter
5ml/1 tsp easy-blend (rapid-rise) dried yeast

Medium

325ml/11½fl oz/generous 1⅓ cups water
500g/1lb 2oz/4½ cups Granary (whole-wheat) bread flour
7.5ml/1½ tsp salt
15ml/1 tbsp sugar
25g/1oz/2 tbsp butter
7.5ml/1½ tsp easy-blend (rapid-rise) dried yeast

Large

375ml/13½fl oz/1½ cups plus 1 tbsp water
625g/1lb 6oz/5½ cups Granary (whole-wheat) bread flour
10ml/2 tsp salt
15ml/1 tbsp sugar
25g/1oz/2 tbsp butter
7.5ml/1½ tsp easy-blend (rapid-rise) dried yeast

1 Add the water to the bread machine pan. If the instructions for your particular machine specify that the yeast is to be placed in the pan first, simply reverse the order in which you add the liquid and dry ingredients to the bread machine pan.

2 Sprinkle over the flour, ensuring that it covers the water, then add the salt, sugar and butter in separate corners of the bread pan. Make a small indent in the centre of the flour (but not down as far as the liquid) and add the yeast to the indent.

3 Set the machine to the whole-wheat setting, medium crust. Size: 500g for small, large/750g for medium, or 1kg/2lb for large. Press Start.

4 Remove the bread at the end of the baking cycle. Turn out on to a wire rack.

Bran and Yogurt Bread per loaf Energy 1406kcal/5961kJ; Protein 47.9g; Carbohydrate 277.4g, of which sugars 26.6g; Fat 19.5g, of which saturates 3g; Cholesterol 2mg; Calcium 678mg; Fibre 28.8g; Sodium 2101mg.

Granary Bread per loaf Energy 1349kcal/5717kJ; Protein 47.8g; Carbohydrate 250.1g, of which sugars 18.3g; Fat 24.6g, of which saturates 11.9g; Cholesterol 46mg; Calcium 151mg; Fibre 33.8g; Sodium 2127mg.

Multigrain Bread

This healthy mixed-grain bread owes its rich flavour to honey and malt extract.

Makes 1
300ml/½ pint/1¼ cups water
30ml/2 tbsp clear honey
15ml/1 tbsp malt extract
150g/5oz/1⅓ cups Granary (whole-wheat) flour
75g/3oz/¾ cup rye flour
75g/3oz/¾ cup unbleached white bread flour
200g/7oz/1¾ cups wholemeal (whole-wheat) bread flour
30ml/2 tbsp jumbo oats
30ml/2 tbsp skimmed milk powder (non fat dry milk)
7.5ml/1½ tsp salt
25g/1oz/2 tbsp butter
5ml/1 tsp easy-blend (rapid-rise) dried yeast

1 Add the water, honey and malt extract to the pan. If your machine's instructions specify that the yeast is to be placed in the pan first, reverse the order in which you add the liquid and dry ingredients.

2 Sprinkle over the Granary flour, rye flour, white bread flour and wholemeal flour, ensuring that the liquid is completely covered. Add the jumbo oats and skimmed milk powder.

3 Place the salt and butter in separate corners of the bread pan. Make a small indent in the centre of the flour (but not down as far as the liquid). Add the yeast.

4 Set the machine to white/basic. Use light crust, 750g for medium; or medium crust. Press Start.

5 Remove the bread at the end of the baking cycle. Turn out on to a wire rack to cool.

Cook's Tip
Depending on your machine, this bread may rise more if cooked on the whole-wheat setting, but you should experiment to get the best results. You may need to add 1 × 100mg vitamin C tablet, crushed, to strengthen the dough.

Sourdough Bread

The sour flavour of this traditional sourdough bread develops during the process of several fermentations. By using a live natural yogurt, you can produce a light bread baked in your machine.

Makes 1
Small
175ml/6fl oz/¾ cup water
125g/4¼oz/generous ½ cup natural (plain) live yogurt
10ml/2 tsp lemon juice
325g/11½oz/scant 3 cups unbleached white bread flour
75g/3oz/⅔ cup wholemeal (whole-wheat) bread flour
15g/½oz/1 tbsp butter
5ml/1 tsp salt
2.5ml/½ tsp sugar
5ml/1 tsp easy-blend (rapid-rise) dried yeast

Large
250ml/8fl oz/1 cup water
175g/6oz/¾ cup natural (plain) live yogurt
15ml/1 tbsp lemon juice
475g/1lb 1oz/4¼ cups unbleached white bread flour
125g/4¼oz/generous 1 cup wholemeal (whole-wheat) bread flour
25g/1oz/2 tbsp butter
7.5ml/1½ tsp salt
2.5ml/½ tsp sugar
7.5ml/1½ tsp easy-blend (rapid-rise) dried yeast

1 Pour the water into the bread machine pan. Add the yogurt and lemon juice. If the instructions for your machine specify that the yeast is to be placed in the pan first, reverse the order in which you add the liquid and the dry ingredients.

2 Sprinkle over the flours, ensuring they cover the water. Add the butter, salt and sugar in separate corners of the bread pan.

3 Make a small indent in the centre of the flour (but not down as far as the liquid) and add the yeast.

4 Set the bread machine to the French setting, medium crust. You may need to use light crust on smaller machines. Size: 750g for small, or 1kg/2lb for large. Press Start.

5 Remove the bread at the end of the baking cycle. Turn out on to a wire rack to cool.

Multigrain Bread per loaf Energy 1511kcal/6403kJ; Protein 48.9g; Carbohydrate 286.5g, of which sugars 22.9g; Fat 26.9g, of which saturates 12.9g; Cholesterol 52mg; Calcium 350mg; Fibre 32.1g; Sodium 2187mg.

Sourdough Bread per loaf Energy 1702kcal/7218kJ; Protein 51.2g; Carbohydrate 351.3g, of which sugars 19.2g; Fat 20g, of which saturates 9.7g; Cholesterol 36mg; Calcium 795mg; Fibre 18.4g; Sodium 2195mg.

Cornmeal Bread

This scrumptious bread has a sweet flavour and crumbly texture. Use a finely ground cornmeal (also known as maize meal), usually available from a health-food store. The coarsely ground meal used for polenta makes a good topping.

Makes 1

Medium

210ml/7½fl oz/scant 1 cup warm water
90ml/3fl oz/6 tbsp lukewarm milk
25ml/1½ tbsp corn oil
350g/12½oz/3 cups unbleached white bread flour
150g/5oz/1¼ cups cornmeal
5ml/1 tsp salt
10ml/2 tsp light muscovado (brown) sugar
5ml/1 tsp easy-blend (rapid-rise) dried yeast
water, for glazing
polenta, for sprinkling

Large

225ml/8fl oz/scant 1 cup warm water
140ml/5fl oz/⅝ cup lukewarm milk
30ml/2 tbsp corn oil
400g/14oz/3½ cups unbleached white bread flour
200g/7oz/1¾ cups cornmeal
7.5ml/1½ tsp salt
10ml/2 tsp light muscovado (brown) sugar
7.5ml/1½ tsp easy-blend (rapid-rise) dried yeast
water, for glazing
polenta, for sprinkling

1 Pour the water, milk and corn oil into the pan. Reverse the order in which you add the wet and dry ingredients if the instructions to your machine specify this.

2 Add the flour and the cornmeal, covering the water. Place the salt and sugar in separate corners. Make a shallow indent in the flour; add the yeast.

3 Set the bread machine to the white rapid/basic rapid/fastbake setting, medium crust. Size: 750g for medium, or 1kg/2lb for large. Press Start. Just before the baking cycle starts, brush the top of the loaf with water and sprinkle with polenta.

4 Remove the bread at the end of the baking cycle. Turn out on to a wire rack.

Spelt & Bulgur Wheat Bread

Two unusual grains are used here. The bulgur wheat contributes crunch, while the spelt flour adds a nutty flavour.

Makes 1

Small

110ml/scant 4fl oz/scant ½ cup water
100ml/3½fl oz/7 tbsp buttermilk
5ml/1 tsp lemon juice
250g/9oz/2¼ cups unbleached white bread flour
100g/3¾oz/scant 1 cup spelt flour
30ml/2 tbsp bulgur wheat
5ml/1 tsp salt
10ml/2 tsp sugar
5ml/1 tsp easy-blend (rapid-rise) dried yeast

Large

250ml/9fl oz/generous 1 cup water
125ml/4¼fl oz/generous ½ cup buttermilk
10ml/2 tsp lemon juice
375g/13oz/3¼ cups unbleached white bread flour
175g/6oz/generous 1½ cups spelt flour
60ml/4 tbsp bulgur wheat
10ml/2 tsp salt
15ml/1 tbsp sugar
7.5ml/1½ tsp easy-blend (rapid-rise) dried yeast

1 Pour the water, buttermilk and lemon juice into the bread machine pan. If the instructions for your machine specify that the yeast is to be placed in the pan first, reverse the order in which you add the liquid and dry ingredients.

2 Sprinkle over both types of flour, then the bulgur wheat, so that the liquid is completely covered. Add the salt and sugar into separate corners of the bread pan. Make a small indent in the centre of the flour (but not down as far as the liquid) and add the yeast. Set the machine to the white/basic setting, medium crust. Size: 500g for small, or 1kg/2lb for large. Press Start.

3 Remove the bread from the bread machine pan at the end of the cycle and turn out on to a wire rack to cool.

Variation
You can replace the buttermilk with low-fat natural (plain) yogurt or semi-skimmed (low-fat) milk, for a less tangy flavour.

Cornmeal Bread per loaf Energy 1473kcal/6226kJ; Protein 38.1g; Carbohydrate 298.9g, of which sugars 16.2g; Fat 19.3g, of which saturates 2.5g; Cholesterol 5mg; Calcium 494mg; Fibre 10.7g; Sodium 2020mg.

Spelt and Bulgur Wheat Bread per loaf Energy 1341kcal/5695kJ; Protein 42.5g; Carbohydrate 296.5g, of which sugars 21.3g; Fat 6.3g, of which saturates 0.9g; Cholesterol 4mg; Calcium 527mg; Fibre 16.8g; Sodium 2032mg.

Potato Flour Bread

If gluten- and wheat-free bread is part of your dietary requirements, this bread is a perfect loaf to bake.

Makes 1
2 eggs
45ml/3 tbsp sunflower oil
5ml/1 tsp cider vinegar
300g/11oz/2½ cups brown rice flour
100g/3¾oz/generous ½ cup potato flour
15ml/1 tbsp xanthum gum
75ml/5 tbsp skimmed milk powder (non fat dry milk)
5ml/1 tsp salt
15ml/1 tbsp sugar
5ml/1 tsp easy-blend (rapid-rise) dried yeast

1 Put the eggs in a measuring jug (cup) and add sufficient tepid water to give 560ml/19fl oz/2½ cups.

2 Mix the eggs and water lightly and pour into the bread machine pan. Add the sunflower oil and cider vinegar. If the instructions for your machine specify that the yeast is to be placed in the pan first, reverse the order in which you add the liquid and the dry ingredients. Check your manufacturer's instructions as you may need to add the water first for the gluten-free programme.

3 Sprinkle over the flours, ensuring they cover the water. Add the xanthum gum and skimmed milk powder. Add the salt and sugar in separate corners of the bread pan. Make a small indent in the centre of the flour (but not down as far as the liquid) and add the yeast.

4 Set the bread machine to the gluten-free setting, dark crust, if available, or white/basic setting, medium crust. Size: 750g for medium. Weight settings are not available on some gluten-free cycles. You may need to scrape down the mixture after 5 minutes, if it is stuck around the pan. Use a plastic spatula, as metal may damage the surface.

5 Remove the bread at the end of the baking cycle. Turn out on to a wire rack.

Ciabatta

This flat loaf is irregularly shaped and typically has large air holes in the crumb.

Makes 2
For the biga
200ml/7fl oz/scant 1 cup water
175g/6oz/1½ cups unbleached white bread flour
2.5ml/½ tsp easy-blend (rapid-rise) dried yeast

For the ciabatta dough
200ml/7fl oz/scant 1 cup water
30ml/2 tbsp milk
30ml/2 tbsp extra virgin olive oil
325g/11½oz/scant 3 cups unbleached white bread flour, plus extra for dusting
7.5ml/1½ tsp salt
2.5ml/½ tsp sugar
1.5ml/¼ tsp easy-blend (rapid-rise) dried yeast

1 Pour the water for the biga into the bread pan. Sprinkle over the bread flour, covering the water. Make an indent in the centre of the flour and add the yeast into the indent.

2 Set the bread machine to the basic dough setting. Press Start. Mix for 5 minutes, then switch off the machine. Leave the biga in the machine overnight or for at least 12 hours.

3 Add the water, milk and oil for the ciabatta dough. Sprinkle over the flour. Add the salt and sugar in separate corners. Make a small indent in the centre of the flour and add the yeast. Set the bread machine to the basic dough setting. Press Start. When finished, transfer the dough to a bowl. Cover and leave to rise for about 1 hour, until the dough has tripled in size.

4 Divide the dough into two portions. Carefully transfer one portion of the dough on to a floured baking sheet, trying to avoid knocking the air out of the dough. Using well-floured hands shape the dough into a rectangular loaf about 2.5cm/1in thick. Repeat with the remaining piece of dough.

5 Sprinkle both loaves with flour. Leave uncovered for about 20–30 minutes. Preheat the oven to 220°C/425°F/Gas 7.

6 Bake for 25–30 minutes, or until both loaves have risen and are light golden in colour. Transfer them to a wire rack to cool.

Potato Flour Bread per loaf Energy 1641kcal/6856kJ; Protein 33.6g; Carbohydrate 298.3g, of which sugars 17.9g; Fat 30.8g, of which saturates 4.3g; Cholesterol 196mg; Calcium 298mg; Fibre 7g; Sodium 2134mg.
Ciabatta per loaf Energy 986kcal/4179kJ; Protein 25.1g; Carbohydrate 202.9g, of which sugars 4.8g; Fat 13.8g, of which saturates 2.2g; Cholesterol 1mg; Calcium 387mg; Fibre 8.1g; Sodium 1218mg.

French Baguettes

French bread traditionally has a crisp crust and light, chewy crumb. Use the special French bread setting on your bread machine to help to achieve this unique texture.

Makes 2–3

315ml/11fl oz/1 1/3 cups water
450g/1lb/4 cups unbleached white bread flour
7.5ml/1 1/2 tsp salt
7.5ml/1 1/2 tsp easy-blend (rapid-rise) dried yeast

1 Add the water to the bread machine pan. If the instructions for your machine specify that the yeast is to be placed in the pan first, reverse the order in which you add the liquid and dry ingredients.

2 Sprinkle the flour over the water. Add the salt in a corner. Make an indent in the centre of the flour and add the yeast. Use the French dough/Artisan dough setting. Press Start.

3 When the dough cycle has finished, remove the dough from the machine, place it on a floured surface and knock it back (punch it down). Divide it into two or three equal portions.

4 On a floured surface shape each piece of dough into a ball, then roll out to a rectangle measuring 18–20 × 7.5cm/7–8 × 3in. Fold one-third up lengthways and one-third down, then press. Repeat twice more, leaving the dough to rest between foldings to avoid tearing.

5 Gently roll and stretch each piece to a 28–33cm/11–13in loaf. Place each loaf in a floured banneton or between the folds of a floured and pleated dish towel, so that the French bread shape is maintained during rising. Cover with lighly oiled clear film (plastic wrap) and leave in a warm place for 30–45 minutes. Preheat the oven to 230°C/450°F/Gas 8.

6 Roll the loaf or loaves on to a baking sheet, spaced well part. Slash the tops with a knife. Place at the top of the oven, spray the inside of the oven with water and bake for 15–20 minutes, or until golden. Transfer to a wire rack.

Italian Breadsticks

The dough for these crisp breadsticks can be made in any size of bread machine. The sticks will keep for a couple of days if stored in an airtight container. If you like, you can refresh them in a hot oven for a few minutes before serving.

Makes 30

200ml/7fl oz/7/8 cup water
45ml/3 tbsp olive oil, plus extra
350g/12oz/3 cups unbleached white bread flour
7.5ml/1 1/2 tsp salt
7.5ml/1 1/2 tsp easy-blend (rapid-rise) dried yeast
poppy seeds and coarse sea salt, for coating (optional)

1 Pour the water and olive oil into the bread machine pan. If the instructions for your machine specify that the yeast is to be placed in the pan first, reverse the order in which you add the liquid and dry ingredients.

2 Sprinkle over the flour, ensuring that it covers the water completely. Add the salt in one corner of the pan. Make a small indent in the centre of the flour (but not down as far as the liquid) and add the easy bake dried yeast.

3 Set the bread machine to the dough setting; use basic dough setting (if available). Press Start.

4 When the dough cycle has finished, remove the dough from the machine, place it on a lightly floured surface and knock it back (punch it down). Roll it out to a rectangle measuring 23 × 20cm/9 × 8in. Preheat the oven to 200°C/400°F/Gas 6.

5 Cut into three 20cm/8in long strips. Cut each strip widthways into ten. Roll and stretch each piece to 30cm/12in.

6 Roll in poppy seeds or sea salt if you like. Space well apart on oiled baking sheets. Brush lightly with olive oil, cover with clear film (plastic wrap) and leave for 10–15 minutes.

7 Bake for 15–20 minutes, or until golden, turning once. Transfer to a wire rack to cool.

French Baguettes per loaf Energy 767kcal/3263kJ; Protein 21.1g; Carbohydrate 174.8g, of which sugars 3.4g; Fat 2.9g, of which saturates 0.5g; Cholesterol 0mg; Calcium 316mg; Fibre 7g; Sodium 1972mg.

Italian Breadsticks per stick Energy 50kcal/210kJ; Protein 1.1g; Carbohydrate 9.1g, of which sugars 0.2g; Fat 1.3g, of which saturates 0.2g; Cholesterol 0mg; Calcium 16mg; Fibre 0.4g; Sodium 99mg.

Four-seed Bread

The four seeds in this light loaf are pumpkin, sunflower, linseed and sesame.

Makes 1

280ml/10fl oz/1 $\frac{1}{4}$ cups water
30ml/2 tbsp extra virgin olive oil
400g/14oz/3 $\frac{1}{2}$ cups unbleached white bread flour
50g/2oz/$\frac{1}{2}$ cup millet flour
50g/2oz/$\frac{1}{2}$ cup wholemeal (whole-wheat) bread flour
15ml/1 tbsp sugar
10ml/2 tsp salt
5ml/1 tsp easy-blend (rapid-rise) dried yeast
30ml/2 tbsp pumpkin seeds
30ml/2 tbsp sunflower seeds
25ml/1 $\frac{1}{2}$ tbsp linseeds
25ml/1 $\frac{1}{2}$ tbsp sesame seeds, lightly toasted
15ml/1 tbsp milk
30ml/2 tbsp golden linseeds

1 Pour the water and oil into the bread pan. Reverse the order in which you add the wet and dry ingredients if your machine specifies this. Sprinkle over all three types of flour, ensuring that the water is completely covered. Add the sugar and salt in separate corners of the bread pan.

2 Make a shallow indent in the centre of the flour and add the yeast. Set the bread machine to the dough setting; use basic raisin dough setting (if available). Press Start. Add the seeds, except the golden linseeds, when the machine beeps to add extra ingredients or during the last 5 minutes of kneading.

3 When the dough cycle has finished, place the dough on a lightly floured surface and knock back (punch down) gently. Shape the dough into a round flat loaf. Make a hole in the centre with your finger. Gradually enlarge the cavity, turning the dough, until you have a ring. Place on an oiled baking sheet. Cover it with and leave in a warm place for 30–45 minutes, or until the dough has doubled in size.

4 Meanwhile, preheat the oven to 200°C/400°F/Gas 6. Brush the top of the bread with milk and sprinkle it with the golden linseeds. Make slashes around the loaf, radiating outwards.

5 Bake for 30–35 minutes, or until golden. Cool on a wire rack.

Gluten-free Seed Bread

Gluten-free breads do not keep as long as wheat-based breads, so consume this within two days. Alternatively, slice part of the loaf after cooling, and freeze.

Makes 1

Small
300ml/10 $\frac{1}{2}$fl oz/1 $\frac{1}{4}$ cups water
15ml/1 tbsp sunflower oil
350g/12 $\frac{1}{2}$oz/3 cups gluten-free flour
15ml/1 tbsp pumpkin seeds
15ml/1 tbsp sunflower seeds
15ml/1 tbsp poppy seeds
2.5ml/$\frac{1}{2}$ tsp salt
5ml/1 tsp easy-blend (rapid-rise) dried yeast

Medium and large
400ml/14fl oz/scant 1 $\frac{3}{4}$ cups water
25ml/1 $\frac{1}{2}$ tbsp sunflower oil
500g/1lb 2oz/4 $\frac{1}{2}$ cups gluten-free flour
25ml/1 $\frac{1}{2}$ tbsp pumpkin seeds
30ml/2 tbsp sunflower seeds
15ml/1 tbsp poppy seeds
2.5ml/$\frac{1}{2}$ tsp salt
7.5ml/1 $\frac{1}{2}$ tsp easy-blend (rapid-rise) dried yeast

1 Pour the water into the bread machine pan. Add the sunflower oil. If the instructions for your machine specify that the yeast is to be placed in the pan first, reverse the order in which you add the liquid and the dry ingredients.

2 Sprinkle over the gluten-free mix, covering the water. Add the pumpkin seeds, sunflower seeds and poppy seeds. Add the salt in one corner of the bread pan. Make a small indent in the centre of the flour (but not down as far as the liquid) and add the yeast.

3 Set the bread machine to the gluten-free setting if available, if not the white/basic setting. Use dark crust on the gluten-free setting, if available, and medium on white/basic setting. Size: 500g for small, 750g for medium, or 1kg/2lb for large. The weight setting is not available on some gluten-free cycles. Press Start. You may need to scrape down the mixture after 5 minutes, if it is stuck around the pan.

4 Remove the bread at the end of the baking cycle and turn out on to a wire rack to cool.

Four-seed Bread per loaf Energy 2657kcal/11186kJ; Protein 71.2g; Carbohydrate 419.2g, of which sugars 25.5g; Fat 86.4g, of which saturates 9.6g; Cholesterol 1mg; Calcium 758mg; Fibre 24.1g; Sodium 3967mg.

Gluten-free Seed Bread per loaf Energy 1554kcal/6566kJ; Protein 41.8g; Carbohydrate 280.3g, of which sugars 6g; Fat 36.9g, of which saturates 4g; Cholesterol 0mg; Calcium 540mg; Fibre 13.6g; Sodium 994mg.

Poppy Seed Loaf

Poppy seeds are popular in Eastern European breads. They have a mild, sweet and slightly nutty flavour, and make an interesting addition to this loaf.

Makes 1

Small

180ml/6½fl oz/generous ¾ cup milk
60ml/2fl oz/¼ cup water
375g/13oz/3¼ cups unbleached white bread flour
45ml/3 tbsp poppy seeds
7.5ml/1½ tsp salt
10ml/2 tsp sugar
20g/¾oz/1½ tbsp butter
5ml/1 tsp easy-blend (rapid-rise) dried yeast

Medium

200ml/7fl oz/scant 1 cup milk
100ml/3½fl oz/7 tbsp water
450g/1lb/4 cups unbleached white bread flour
60ml/4 tbsp poppy seeds
7.5ml/1½ tsp salt
10ml/2 tsp sugar
25g/1oz/2 tbsp butter
5ml/1 tsp easy-blend (rapid-rise) dried yeast

For the glaze (optional)

½ egg white
5ml/1 tsp water

1 Pour the milk and water into the bread machine pan. If the instructions for your machine specify that the yeast is to be placed in the pan first, reverse the order in which you add the liquid and dry ingredients.

2 Sprinkle over the flour, ensuring that it covers the water. Then add the poppy seeds.

3 Add the salt, sugar and butter in separate corners of the bread pan.

4 Make a small indent in the centre of the flour (but not down as far as the liquid) and add the yeast.

5 Set the machine to white/basic, medium crust. Size: 500g for small, or 750g for medium. Press Start.

6 If glazing, mix the egg white and water and brush over the loaf just before the baking cycle starts.

Apple & Cider Seeded Bread

This bread is perfect served with a selection of cold meats, pâté or cheese for a delicious lunchtime spread.

Makes 1

Medium

260ml/9fl oz/1⅛ cups medium sweet cider, left to become flat
30ml/2 tbsp sunflower oil
125g/4¼oz/1 cup finely chopped green eating apple
525g/1lb 3oz/4¾ cups seeded white bread flour
25ml/1½ tbsp skimmed milk powder (non fat dry milk)
7.5ml/1½ tsp salt
7.5ml/1½ tsp sugar
5ml/1 tsp easy-blend (rapid-rise) dried yeast

Large

320ml/11½fl oz/1⅓ cups medium sweet cider, left to become flat
30ml/2 tbsp sunflower oil
150g/5oz/generous 1 cup finely chopped green eating apple
625g/1lb 5oz/5½ cups seeded white bread flour
30ml/2 tbsp skimmed milk powder (non fat dry milk)
7.5ml/1½ tsp salt
10ml/2 tsp sugar
7.5ml/1½ tsp easy-blend (rapid-rise) dried yeast

1 Pour the cider into the bread machine pan. Add the sunflower oil and chopped apple. If the instructions for your machine specify that the yeast is to be placed in the pan first, reverse the order in which you add the liquid and the dry ingredients.

2 Sprinkle over the white bread flour, ensuring that it completely covers the water.

3 Add the skimmed milk powder, salt and sugar in separate corners of the bread pan. Make a small indent in the centre of the flour (but not down as far as the liquid) and add the yeast.

4 Set the bread machine to the white/basic setting, light crust. Size: 750g for medium, or 1kg/2lb for large. Press Start.

5 Remove the bread from the pan at the end of the baking cycle. Turn out on to a wire rack to cool.

Poppy Seed Loaf per loaf Energy 1817kcal/7674kJ; Protein 49.5g; Carbohydrate 311.2g, of which sugars 25.3g; Fat 50.4g, of which saturates 17.1g; Cholesterol 57mg; Calcium 1052mg; Fibre 15.2g; Sodium 3217mg.

Apple and Cider Seeded Bread per loaf Energy 1663kcal/7053kJ; Protein 41.3g; Carbohydrate 342.5g, of which sugars 37.7g; Fat 18g, of which saturates 3.1g; Cholesterol 6mg; Calcium 705mg; Fibre 14.2g; Sodium 2049mg.

Light Rye & Caraway Bread

Rye breads can be dense, so the flour is usually mixed with wheat flour to lighten the texture.

Makes 1

Medium

300ml/10½fl oz/1¼ cups water
10ml/2 tsp lemon juice
25ml/1½ tbsp sunflower oil
125g/4¼oz/generous 1 cup rye flour
375g/13oz/3¼ cups unbleached white bread flour
25ml/1½ tbsp skimmed milk powder (non fat dry milk)
7.5ml/1½ tsp caraway seeds
7.5ml/1½ tsp salt
15ml/1 tbsp light muscovado (brown) sugar
5ml/1 tsp easy-blend (rapid-rise) dried yeast

Large

330ml/scant 12fl oz/1¼ cups plus 2 tbsp water
10ml/2 tsp lemon juice
30ml/2 tbsp sunflower oil
165g/5½oz/1⅓ cups rye flour
450g/1lb/4 cups unbleached white bread flour
30ml/2 tbsp skimmed milk powder (non fat dry milk)
10ml/2 tsp caraway seeds
10ml/2 tsp salt
15ml/1 tbsp light muscovado (brown) sugar
7.5ml/1½ tsp easy-blend (rapid-rise) dried yeast

1 Add the water, lemon juice and oil to the bread pan. If your instructions specify that the yeast is to be placed in the pan first, reverse the order in which you add the liquid and dry ingredients.

2 Sprinkle over the rye flour and the white bread flour, covering the water. Add the milk powder and caraway seeds. Add the salt and sugar in separate corners of the bread pan.

3 Make a small indent in the centre of the flour, but not down as far as the liquid, and add the yeast to the well.

4 Set the bread machine to the white/basic setting, medium crust. Size: 750g for medium, or 1kg/2lb for large. Press Start.

5 Remove the bread from the pan at the end of the cycle and transfer to a wire rack to cool.

Russian Black Bread

European rye breads often include cocoa and coffee to add colour to this dark, traditionally dense, chewy bread. Try it as the basis of an open sandwich.

Makes 1

360ml/12½fl oz/generous 1½ cups water
30ml/2 tbsp sunflower oil
40ml/2½ tbsp molasses
155g/5½oz/1⅓ cups rye flour
90g/3¼oz/¾ cup wholemeal (whole-wheat) bread flour
250g/9oz/2¼ cups unbleached white bread flour
40g/1½oz/3 tbsp oat bran
75g/3oz/¾ cup dried breadcrumbs
25ml/1½ tbsp unsweetened cocoa powder
30ml/2 tbsp instant coffee granules
7.5ml/1½ tsp caraway seeds
7.5ml/1½ tsp salt
7.5ml/1½ tsp easy-blend (rapid-rise) dried yeast

1 Pour the water, sunflower oil and molasses into the bread machine pan. If the instructions for your machine specify that the yeast is to be placed in the bread machine pan first, then simply reverse the order in which you add the liquid and dry ingredients.

2 Sprinkle over the rye, wholemeal and white flours, then the oat bran and breadcrumbs, ensuring that the water is completely covered.

3 Add the cocoa powder, coffee granules, caraway seeds and salt. Make a small indent in the centre of the flour (but not down as far as the liquid) and add the yeast.

4 Set the bread machine to the whole-wheat setting, medium crust. Size: 750g for medium. Press Start.

5 Remove the bread at the end of the baking cycle from the bread pan. Turn out on to a wire rack to cool. Serve sliced with lemon wedges and smoked salmon if you wish.

Light Rye and Caraway Bread per loaf Energy 1441kcal/6116kJ; Protein 37.1g; Carbohydrate 301.4g, of which sugars 19.7g; Fat 18.1g, of which saturates 3.1g; Cholesterol 6mg; Calcium 552mg; Fibre 18.8g; Sodium 2030mg.
Russian Black Bread per loaf Energy 1746kcal/7397kJ; Protein 44.7g; Carbohydrate 335.6g, of which sugars 21.2g; Fat 34.4g, of which saturates 5.4g; Cholesterol 0mg; Calcium 503mg; Fibre 27.8g; Sodium 2345mg.

Toasted Millet & Rye Bread

The dough is made in the bread machine, but it is shaped by hand before being baked in the oven.

Makes 1

300ml/10½fl oz/1¼ cups water
50g/2oz/½ cup rye flour
450g/1lb/4 cups unbleached white bread flour
25g/1oz/¼ cup millet flakes
15ml/1 tbsp light muscovado (brown) sugar
5ml/1 tsp salt
25g/1oz/2 tbsp butter
5ml/1 tsp easy-blend (rapid-rise) dried yeast
50g/2oz/⅓ cup millet seeds
millet flour, for dusting

1 Pour the water into the bread pan. If the instructions for your bread machine specify that the yeast is to be placed in the pan first, reverse the order in which you add the ingredients.

2 Sprinkle over both types of flour, then add the millet flakes, covering the water completely. Add the sugar, salt and butter, placing them in separate corners. Make an indent in the centre of the flour (not down as far as the liquid) and add the yeast.

3 Set the bread machine to the dough setting; use white/basic, raisin setting (if available). Press Start. Add the millet seeds when the machine beeps or during the last 5 minutes of kneading. Lightly flour a baking sheet.

4 When the dough cycle has finished, knock the dough back (punch it down) gently on a lightly floured surface. Shape the dough into a rectangle. Roll it up lengthways, then shape it into a thick baton with square ends. Place it on the prepared baking sheet, with the seam is underneath. Cover it with lightly oiled clear film (plastic wrap) and leave in a warm place for 30–45 minutes, or until almost doubled in size.

5 Dust the top of the loaf with the millet flour. Using a sharp knife, make slanting cuts in alternate directions along the top of the loaf. Leave it to stand for 10 minutes. Meanwhile, preheat the oven to 220°C/425°F/Gas 7. Bake the loaf for 25–30 minutes. Turn out on to a wire rack to cool.

Barley-enriched Farmhouse Loaf

Barley adds a very distinctive earthy, slightly nutty flavour to this crusty white loaf.

Makes 1

260ml/9fl oz/1⅛ cups water
45ml/3 tbsp double (heavy) cream
400g/14oz/3½ cups unbleached white bread flour
115g/4oz/1 cup barley flour
10ml/2 tsp sugar
10ml/2 tsp salt
7.5ml/1½ tsp easy-blend (rapid-rise) dried yeast
25g/1oz/2 tbsp pumpkin seeds
flour, for dusting

1 Pour the water and cream into the pan. Sprinkle over both types of flour, covering the water completely. Add the sugar and salt, placing them in separate corners of the pan. Make a shallow indent in the centre of the flour and add the yeast.

2 Set the bread machine to the dough setting; use basic raisin dough setting (if available). Press Start. Add the pumpkin seeds when the machine beeps or during the last 5 minutes of kneading. Lightly oil a 900g/2lb loaf tin (pan) measuring 18.5 × 12cm/7¼ × 4½in.

3 When the dough cycle has finished, remove the dough and place on a floured surface. Knock back (punch down) gently. Shape the dough into a rectangle the same length as the tin.

4 Roll the dough up lengthways, and tuck the ends under. Place it in the prepared tin, with the seam underneath. Cover with oiled clear film (plastic wrap) and leave for 30–45 minutes, or until the dough reaches the top of the tin.

5 Dust the loaf with flour then make a deep lengthways cut along the top. Leave to rest for 10 minutes. Preheat the oven to 220°C/425°F/Gas 7.

6 Bake the loaf for 15 minutes, then reduce the oven to 200°C/400°F/Gas 6 and bake for 20–25 minutes more, or until the bread is golden and sounds hollow when tapped on the base. Transfer it to a wire rack to cool.

Toasted Millet and Rye Bread per loaf Energy 2211kcal/9360kJ; Protein 50.9g; Carbohydrate 459.8g, of which sugars 22.4g; Fat 28.6g, of which saturates 14.6g; Cholesterol 58mg; Calcium 688mg; Fibre 19.8g; Sodium 2183mg.

Barley-enriched Farmhouse Loaf per loaf Energy 2143kcal/9070kJ; Protein 54.2g; Carbohydrate 416.5g, of which sugars 19.8g; Fat 42.7g, of which saturates 15.7g; Cholesterol 59mg; Calcium 777mg; Fibre 17.5g; Sodium 3963mg.

Mixed Herb Cottage Loaf

This loaf makes a perfect centrepiece for the table.

Makes 1

300ml/½ pint/1¼ cups water
450g/1lb/4 cups unbleached white bread flour, plus extra for dusting
7.5ml/1½ tsp sugar
7.5ml/1½ tsp salt
7.5ml/1½ tsp easy-blend (rapid-rise) dried yeast
15ml/1 tbsp chopped fresh chives
10ml/2 tsp chopped fresh thyme
15ml/1 tbsp chopped fresh tarragon
30ml/2 tbsp chopped fresh parsley
5ml/1 tsp salt, to glaze
15ml/1 tbsp water, to glaze

1 Pour the water into the bread machine pan. Sprinkle over the flour, ensuring that it covers the water completely. Add the sugar and the salt, placing them in separate corners of the bread machine pan. Make a small indent in the centre of the flour and add the dried yeast.

2 Set the bread machine to the basic raisin dough setting (if available). Press Start. Add the chives, thyme, tarragon and parsley when the machine beeps to add extra ingredients, or during the final 5 minutes of kneading. Lightly flour two baking sheets.

3 When the dough cycle has finished, knock the dough back (punch it down) gently and then divide it into two pieces, making one piece twice as large as the other and shape it into a ball. Place the on the baking sheets and cover each with an oiled mixing bowl. Leave for 20–30 minutes, until doubled.

4 Cut a cross, about 4cm/1½in across, in the top of the larger dough. Brush with water and place the smaller round on top. Press the handle of a wooden spoon through the centre of both pieces of dough. Cover and leave for 10 minutes.

5 Preheat the oven to 220°C/425°F/Gas 7. Mix the salt and water for the glaze in a bowl, then brush over the bread. Make eight slashes around the top of the bread and 12 small slashes around the base. Dust lightly with white bread flour. Bake for 30–35 minutes, or until golden. Cool on a wire rack.

Dill, Onion & Rye Bread

These crusty loaves are perfect partners for your favourite sandwich filling.

Makes 2

280ml/10fl oz/1¼ cups water
30ml/2 tbsp extra virgin olive oil
100g/3½oz/scant 1 cup rye flour
350g/12½oz/generous 3 cups unbleached white bread flour, plus extra for dusting
30ml/2 tbsp skimmed milk powder (non fat dry milk)
10ml/2 tsp light muscovado (brown) sugar
5ml/1 tsp salt
5ml/1 tsp easy-blend (rapid-rise) dried yeast
15ml/1 tbsp dried dill
15ml/1 tbsp dill seeds
30ml/2 tbsp dried onion slices

1 Pour the water and oil into the bread pan. Sprinkle both types of flour over the water. Add the milk powder. Place the sugar and salt in separate corners. Make a shallow indent in the centre of the flour; add the yeast. Set the machine to the basic raisin dough setting (if available). Press Start. Add the dried dill, dill seeds and dried onion as the machine beeps or during the last 5 minutes of kneading.

2 When the dough cycle has finished, remove the dough from the machine and place it on a lightly floured surface. Knock it back (punch it down) gently and divide the dough into two equal pieces.

3 Roll out each piece to a disc, about 2.5cm/1in thick. Fold one side to the centre and press gently with the rolling pin to seal. Repeat with the other side, then fold again along the centre line. Press gently along the seam to seal it, then roll backwards and forwards to make a loaf about 30cm/12in in length. Make a second loaf with the remaining dough. Place the loaves on an oiled baking sheet. Cover and leave in a warm place for 30–45 minutes, or until doubled in size.

4 Dust the loaves with flour. Make slashes along the top of both of them. Leave to stand for 10 minutes. Meanwhile, preheat the oven to 220°C/425°F/Gas 7. Bake the loaves for 20 minutes. Transfer to a wire rack to cool.

Mixed Herb Cottage Loaf per loaf Energy 1581kcal/6722kJ; Protein 43.8g; Carbohydrate 358.8g, of which sugars 15.7g; Fat 6.5g, of which saturates 0.9g; Cholesterol 0mg; Calcium 734mg; Fibre 16.4g; Sodium 1995mg.
Dill, Onion and Rye Bread per loaf Energy 928kcal/3931kJ; Protein 23.4g; Carbohydrate 184.3g, of which sugars 10.4g; Fat 16.1g, of which saturates 2.7g; Cholesterol 3mg; Calcium 338mg; Fibre 11.3g; Sodium 1019mg.

Garlic & Herb Walnut Bread

Walnut bread is very popular in France. This variation includes garlic and basil for additional flavour.

Makes 1

Small

150ml/¼ pint/⅔ cup milk
60ml/2fl oz/4 tbsp water
30ml/2 tbsp extra virgin olive oil
325g/11½oz/scant 3 cups unbleached white bread flour
40g/1½oz/scant ⅓ cup rolled oats
40g/1½oz/⅓ cup chopped walnuts
1 garlic clove, finely chopped
5ml/1 tsp dried oregano
5ml/1 tsp chopped fresh basil
5ml/1 tsp salt
7.5ml/1½ tsp sugar
2.5ml/½ tsp easy-blend (rapid-rise) dried yeast

Medium

180ml/6½fl oz/generous ¾ cup milk
105ml/7 tbsp water
45ml/3 tbsp extra virgin olive oil
450g/1lb/4 cups unbleached white bread flour
50g/2oz/½ cup rolled oats
50g/2oz/½ cup chopped walnuts
1 1/2 garlic cloves, finely chopped
7.5ml/1½ tsp dried oregano
10ml/2 tsp chopped fresh basil
7.5ml/1½ tsp salt
10ml/2 tsp sugar
5ml/1 tsp easy-blend (rapid-rise) dried yeast

1 Pour the milk, water and olive oil into the bread machine pan. If the instructions for your machine specify that the yeast is to be placed in the pan first, reverse the order in which you add the liquid and dry ingredients.

2 Sprinkle over the flour and rolled oats, ensuring that they completely cover the liquid mixture. Add the chopped walnuts, garlic, oregano and basil.

3 Place the salt and sugar in separate corners of the bread machine pan. Make a small indent in the centre of the flour (but do not go down as far as the liquid) and add the dried yeast.

4 Set the machine to white/basic, medium crust. Size: 500g for small, or 750g for medium. Press Start.

5 Remove the bread at the end of the baking cycle and turn out on to a wire rack to cool.

Buckwheat & Walnut Bread

Buckwheat flour has a distinctive earthy taste, perfectly mellowed when blended with white flour and walnuts in this compact bread, flavoured with molasses.

Makes 1

Small

210ml/7½fl oz/scant 1 cup water
10ml/2 tsp molasses
30ml/2 tbsp walnut or olive oil
325g/11½oz/scant 3 cups unbleached white bread flour
50g/2oz/½ cup buckwheat flour
15ml/1 tbsp skimmed milk powder (non fat dry milk)
5ml/1 tsp salt
2.5ml/½ tsp sugar
5ml/1 tsp easy-blend (rapid-rise) dried yeast
40g/1½oz/⅓ cup walnut pieces

Large

360ml/12¾fl oz/generous 1½ cups water
20ml/4 tsp molasses
45ml/3 tbsp walnut or olive oil
500g/1lb 2oz/4½ cups unbleached white bread flour
100g/3¾oz/scant 1 cup buckwheat flour
30ml/2 tbsp skimmed milk powder (non fat dry milk)
10ml/2 tsp salt
5ml/1 tsp sugar
7.5ml/1½ tsp easy-blend (rapid-rise) dried yeast
65g/2½oz/⅝ cup walnut pieces

1 Pour the water, molasses and walnut or olive oil into the bread pan. If the instructions for your machine specify that the yeast is to be placed in the pan first, reverse the order in which you add the liquid and dry ingredients.

2 Sprinkle over the flours, covering the liquid. Add the milk powder. Place the salt and sugar in separate corners. Make a small indent in the centre of the flour (but not down as far as the liquid) and add the yeast.

3 Set the machine to white/basic, raisin setting (if available), medium crust. Size: 500g for small, or 1kg/2lb for large. Add the walnuts to the automatic dispenser, if available. Press Start. If adding manually, do so when the machine beeps during the kneading cycle, or after the first kneading.

4 Remove the bread and turn out on to a wire rack to cool.

Garlic and Herb Walnut Bread per loaf Energy 1836kcal/7739kJ; Protein 46g; Carbohydrate 297.8g, of which sugars 20.8g; Fat 59.5g, of which saturates 7.4g; Cholesterol 8mg; Calcium 687mg; Fibre 14.2g; Sodium 2068mg.

Buckwheat and Walnut Bread per loaf Energy 1825kcal/7690kJ; Protein 45.2g; Carbohydrate 310.3g, of which sugars 22.4g; Fat 53.5g, of which saturates 6.6g; Cholesterol 6mg; Calcium 488mg; Fibre 2.5g; Sodium 2082mg.

Grainy Mustard & Beer Loaf

For a superior ploughman's lunch, serve chunks of this wonderful bread with cheese and pickles.

Makes 1

Small

210ml/7½fl oz/scant 1 cup flat beer
15ml/1 tbsp vegetable oil
30ml/2 tbsp wholegrain mustard
250g/9oz/2¼ cups unbleached white bread flour
125g/4¼oz/generous 1 cup wholemeal (whole-wheat) bread flour
15ml/1 tbsp skimmed milk powder (non fat dry milk)
5ml/1 tsp salt
7.5ml/1½ tsp sugar
5ml/1 tsp easy-blend (rapid-rise) dried yeast

Medium

280ml/10fl oz/1¼ cups flat beer
15ml/1 tbsp vegetable oil
45ml/3 tbsp wholegrain mustard
350g/12oz/3 cups unbleached white bread flour
150g/5oz/1⅓ cups wholemeal (whole-wheat) bread flour
25ml/1½ tbsp skimmed milk powder (non fat dry milk)
7.5ml/1½ tsp salt
10ml/2 tsp sugar
5ml/1 tsp easy-blend (rapid-rise) dried yeast

1 Pour the beer and oil into the bread machine pan. Add the mustard. If the instructions for your machine specify that the yeast is to be placed in the pan first, reverse the order in which you add the liquid and dry ingredients.

2 Sprinkle over the white bread flour and wholemeal flour, ensuring that the liquid is completely covered. Add the skimmed milk powder.

3 Add the salt and sugar, placing them in separate corners of the bread pan. Make a small indent in the centre of the flour (but not down as far as the liquid) and add the yeast.

4 Set the bread machine to the white/basic setting, medium crust. Size: 500g for small, or 750g for medium. Press Start.

5 When the baking cycle has finished, remove the cooked bread and turn out on to a wire rack to cool.

Cajun Spiced Bread

The traditional flavours of the Deep South of the USA make this piquant and spicy loaf irresistible.

Makes 1

300ml/½ pint/1¼ cups water
30ml/2 tbsp vegetable oil
15ml/1 tbsp tomato purée (paste)
500g/1lb 2oz/4½ cups unbleached white bread flour
7.5ml/1½ tsp paprika
5ml/1 tsp cayenne pepper
5ml/1 tsp dried oregano
2.5ml/½ tsp ground black pepper
1 garlic clove, crushed
7.5ml/1½ tsp salt
2.5ml/½ tsp sugar
7.5ml/1½ tsp easy-blend (rapid-rise) dried yeast

For the glaze

1 egg yolk
15ml/1 tbsp water

1 Pour the water and vegetable oil into the bread machine pan, then add the tomato purée. Sprinkle over the flour, ensuring that it covers the liquid. Add the paprika, cayenne, oregano, black pepper and crushed garlic. Place the salt and sugar in separate corners of the bread pan.

2 Make a well in the centre of the flour (but not down as far as the liquid) and add the yeast. Set the bread machine to the basic dough setting. Press Start.

3 Once the dough cycle has finished, place the dough on a floured surface. Knock it back (punch it down) and divide into three. Roll the pieces into equal ropes. Put next to each other. From the centre, braid from left to right, working towards you. Press the ends together and tuck under.

4 Turn the dough around and braid the remaining ropes. Place on an oiled baking sheet, cover with oiled clear film (plastic wrap) and leave in a warm place to rise for 30–45 minutes. Meanwhile, preheat the oven to 200°C/400°F/Gas 6.

5 Mix the egg yolk and water for the glaze together. Remove the clear film and brush the glaze over the braid. Bake for 30–35 minutes, or until golden.

Grainy Mustard and Beer Loaf per loaf Energy 1522kcal/6447kJ; Protein 45.8g; Carbohydrate 293.1g, of which sugars 25.2g; Fat 21.7g, of which saturates 3.2g; Cholesterol 6mg; Calcium 574mg; Fibre 20.5g; Sodium 570mg.

Cajun Spiced Bread per loaf Energy 1945kcal/8239kJ; Protein 48.8g; Carbohydrate 395.7g, of which sugars 12g; Fat 29.5g, of which saturates 3.4g; Cholesterol 0mg; Calcium 723mg; Fibre 15.9g; Sodium 3001mg.

Chilli Bread

There is a warm surprise waiting for anyone who bites into this tasty wholemeal bread: fresh chillies are speckled throughout the crumb.

Makes 1

Small

15ml/1 tbsp sunflower oil
1–2 fresh chillies, chopped
210ml/7½fl oz/scant 1 cup water
250g/9oz/2¼ cups unbleached white bread flour
125g/4½oz/generous 1 cup wholemeal (whole-wheat) bread flour
7.5ml/1½ tsp salt
7.5ml/1½ tsp sugar
25g/1oz/2 tbsp butter
5ml/1 tsp easy-blend (rapid-rise) dried yeast

Medium

15ml/1 tbsp sunflower oil
2–3 fresh chillies, chopped
320ml/11fl oz/generous 1⅓ cups water
350g/12oz/3 cups unbleached white bread flour
150g/5½oz/1⅓ cups wholemeal (whole-wheat) bread flour
10ml/2 tsp salt
10ml/2 tsp sugar
25g/1oz/2 tbsp butter
5ml/1 tsp easy-blend (rapid-rise) dried yeast

1 Heat the oil in a small frying pan. Add the chillies and fry them over medium heat for 3–4 minutes until softened. Set aside to cool.

2 Transfer the chillies and their oil into the bread machine pan. Pour in the water. Reverse the order in which you add the wet and dry ingredients if necessary.

3 Sprinkle over both types of flour, ensuring that the liquid is covered. Place the salt, sugar and butter in separate corners of the bread machine pan. Make an indent in the flour (but not down as far as the liquid) and add the yeast.

4 Set the machine to white/basic. Select light crust, 500g for small; or medium crust, large/750g for medium. Press Start.

5 Remove the bread at the end of the baking cycle. Turn out on to a wire rack to cool.

Wild Rice, Oat & Polenta Bread

Polenta, rolled oats and nutty-tasting wild rice blend perfectly to make this bread.

Makes 1

300ml/½ pint/1¼ cups water
30ml/2 tbsp sunflower oil
325g/11½oz/scant 3 cups unbleached white bread flour
50g/2oz/½ cup strong wholemeal (whole-wheat) flour
50g/2oz/½ cup polenta
50g/2oz/½ cup rolled oats
30ml/2 tbsp skimmed milk powder (non fat dry milk)
30ml/2 tbsp golden (light corn) syrup
10ml/2 tsp salt
5ml/1 tsp easy-blend (rapid-rise) dried yeast
50g/2oz/¼ cup wild rice, cooked

1 Pour the water and the sunflower oil into the bread machine pan. If the instructions for your machine specify that the yeast is to be placed first, reverse the order in which you add the wet and dry ingredients.

2 Sprinkle over both flours, then add the polenta, oats and skimmed milk powder, covering the water completely. Add the golden syrup and the salt, placing them in separate corners of the bread pan. Make a shallow indent in the centre of the flour mixture and add the easy bake dried yeast. Set the bread machine to the dough setting; use basic raisin dough setting (if available). Press Start.

3 Add the cooked rice when the machine beeps or during the last 5 minutes of kneading. Oil a 23 × 13cm/9 × 5in loaf tin (pan).

4 When the dough cycle has finished, remove the dough from the pan and knock back (punch down) gently on a floured surface. Divide the dough into six equal pieces. In turn, shape each piece of dough into an oblong mini loaf, about 13cm/5in in length. Then place the six dough shapes widthways, side by side, in the prepared loaf tin. Cover the dough and leave to rise for about 30–45 minutes.

5 Meanwhile preheat the oven to 220°C/425°F/Gas 7. Bake the loaf for 30–35 minutes. Cool on a wire rack.

Chilli Bread per loaf Energy 1525kcal/6445kJ; Protein 39.8g; Carbohydrate 274.2g, of which sugars 6.4g; Fat 37.5g, of which saturates 15.7g; Cholesterol 58mg; Calcium 405mg; Fibre 19g; Sodium 3147mg.

Wild Rice, Oat and Polenta Bread per loaf Energy 2170kcal/9169kJ; Protein 55.6g; Carbohydrate 427g, of which sugars 35.6g; Fat 35.6g, of which saturates 4.6g; Cholesterol 7mg; Calcium 665mg; Fibre 19.1g; Sodium 4105mg.

Marbled Pesto Bread

Using ready-made pesto sauce means that this bread is very easy to make.

Makes 1

140ml/5fl oz/⅝ cup milk
150ml/¼ pint/⅔ cup water
30ml/2 tbsp extra virgin olive oil
450g/1lb/4 cups unbleached white bread flour
7.5ml/1½ tsp sugar
7.5ml/1½ tsp salt
7.5ml/1½ tsp easy-blend (rapid-rise) dried yeast
100g/3½oz/7 tbsp ready-made pesto sauce

For the topping

15ml/1 tbsp extra virgin olive oil
10ml/2 tsp coarse sea salt

1 Remove the milk from the refrigerator 30 minutes before using, to bring it to room temperature. Pour the water, milk and extra virgin olive oil into the bread machine pan. Sprinkle over the flour, ensuring that it covers the liquid mixture completely.

2 Add the sugar and salt, placing them in separate corners of the bread pan. Make a well in the centre of the flour (but do not go down as far as the liquid) and pour the dried yeast into the hollow. Set the bread machine to the basic dough setting. Press Start. Oil a 25 × 10cm/10 × 4in loaf tin (pan).

3 When the cycle has finished, knock back (punch down) the dough gently, then roll it out to a rectangle about 2cm/¾in thick and 25cm/10in long.

4 Spread the pesto sauce over the dough. Leave a border of 1cm/½in along one long edge. Roll up the dough lengthways, tuck the ends under and place seam down in the prepared tin. Cover and set aside to rise for 45 minutes or until the dough has more than doubled in size and reaches the top of the loaf tin. Meanwhile, preheat the oven to 220°C/425°F/Gas 7.

5 Brush olive oil over the top of the loaf. Score the top with four diagonal cuts. Repeat the cuts in the opposite direction to make a criss-cross pattern. Sprinkle with the sea salt. Bake for 25–30 minutes, or until the bread is golden and sounds hollow when tapped on the base. Turn out on to a wire rack to cool.

Three Cheeses Bread

A tempting trio of Italian cheeses are responsible for the marvellous flavour of this round loaf.

Makes 1

180ml/6½fl oz/generous ¾ cup water
1 egg
100g/3½oz/5 tbsp mascarpone
400g/14oz/3½ cups unbleached white bread flour
50g/2oz/½ cup Granary (whole-wheat) flour
10ml/2 tsp sugar
5ml/1 tsp salt
7.5ml/1½ tsp easy-blend (rapid-rise) dried yeast
75g/3oz Gorgonzola cheese, cut into small dice
75g/3oz/1 cup freshly grated Parmesan cheese
45ml/3 tbsp chopped fresh chives

For the topping

1 egg yolk
15ml/1 tbsp water
15ml/1 tbsp wheat flakes
115g/4oz mature (sharp) Cheddar cheese, diced

1 Add the water, egg and mascarpone to the pan. Sprinkle over both types of flour, covering the water completely. Add the sugar and salt in separate corners. Make a small indent in the flour; add the yeast. Set the machine to the dough setting; use basic raisin dough setting (if available). Press Start.

2 Add the Gorgonzola, Parmesan and chives as the machine beeps or during the last 5 minutes of kneading. Lightly oil a baking sheet.

3 When the dough cycle has finished, place the dough on a floured surface. Knock back (punch down) gently, then shape it into a round loaf, about 20cm/8in in diameter.

4 Cover with oiled clear film (plastic wrap); leave for about 30–45 minutes. Preheat the oven to 200°C/400°F/Gas 6.

5 Mix the egg yolk and water together and brush this glaze over the top of the bread. Sprinkle with wheat flakes. Score the top of the bread into eight equal segments. Bake for 30–35 minutes, or until golden and hollow-sounding. Turn out on to a wire rack to cool.

Marbled Pesto Bread per loaf Energy 2316kcal/9754kJ; Protein 57.4g; Carbohydrate 359.3g, of which sugars 14.9g; Fat 82.2g, of which saturates 14.8g; Cholesterol 26mg; Calcium 1066mg; Fibre 15.7g; Sodium 3205mg.
Three Cheeses Bread per loaf Energy 2425kcal/10227kJ; Protein 105.4g; Carbohydrate 357.5g, of which sugars 21.6g; Fat 73.7g, of which saturates 40.8g; Cholesterol 364mg; Calcium 1978mg; Fibre 19.1g; Sodium 3826mg.

Feta Cheese & Black Olive Loaf

Conjuring up memories of sunny holidays in Greece, this bread has a delicious flavour, thanks to the Mediterranean ingredients.

Makes 1

210ml/7½fl oz/scant 1 cup water
350g/12oz/3 cups unbleached white bread flour
25g/1oz/¼ cup wholemeal (whole-wheat) bread flour
15ml/1 tbsp skimmed milk powder (non fat dry milk)
5ml/1 tsp salt
7.5ml/1½ tsp sugar
5ml/1 tsp easy-blend (rapid-rise) dried yeast
40g/1½oz/scant ½ cup well drained, pitted black olives, chopped
50g/2oz feta cheese, crumbled
15ml/1 tbsp olive oil, for brushing

1 Pour the water into the bread pan. If necessary, according to your machine's instructions, reverse the order in which you add the liquid and dry ingredients. Sprinkle over the flours, covering the water completely. Add the skimmed milk powder. Place the salt and sugar in separate corners of the bread pan. Make an indent in the centre of flour and add the yeast.

2 Set the bread machine to the dough setting; use basic raisin dough setting (if available). Press Start. Lightly oil a 18–20cm/7–8in deep round cake tin (pan).

3 Add the olives and feta cheese when the bread machine beeps or 5 minutes before the end of the kneading cycle.

4 Once the dough cycle has finished, place the dough on a lightly floured surface and knock back (punch it down) gently.

5 Shape into a round, plump ball, the same diameter as the tin. Place in the tin, cover with oiled clear film (plastic wrap) and leave to rise in a warm place for 30–45 minutes. Preheat the oven to 200°C/400°F/Gas 6.

6 Remove the clear film and brush the olive oil over the top of the loaf. Bake for 35–40 minutes, or until golden. Turn the bread out on to a wire rack to cool.

Stromboli

This variation on Italian focaccia takes its name from the volcanic island of Stromboli, near Sicily. The dough is pierced to allow the filling to 'erupt' through the holes during baking.

Makes 1

200ml/7fl oz/scant 1 cup water
350g/12oz/3 cups unbleached white bread flour
2.5ml/½ tsp sugar
5ml/1 tsp salt
5ml/1 tsp easy-blend (rapid-rise) dried yeast

For the filling
175g/6oz mozzarella cheese, grated or finely chopped
75g/3oz/1 cup freshly grated Parmesan cheese
15ml/1 tbsp chopped fresh parsley
30ml/2 tbsp fresh basil leaves
5ml/1 tsp ground black pepper
1 garlic clove, finely chopped

For the topping
15ml/1 tbsp extra virgin olive oil
4–5 small fresh rosemary sprigs, woody stems removed

1 Pour the water into the machine pan. Sprinkle over the flour, covering the water. Add the sugar and salt in separate corners of the pan. Make a well in the centre of the flour, add the yeast. Set the bread machine to the basic dough setting. Press Start.

2 When the dough cycle has ended, remove the dough and place on a lightly floured surface. Knock back (punch down) the dough gently. Roll out into a rectangle 30 × 23cm/12 × 9in. Cover with oiled clear film (plastic wrap) and leave for 5 minutes.

3 Sprinkle over the cheeses leaving a 1cm/½in clear border along each edge. Add the parsley, basil, pepper and garlic. Starting from a shorter side, roll up the dough, Swiss roll (jelly roll) fashion, tucking the side edges under to seal. Place the roll, seam down, on the baking sheet. Cover and leave in a warm place for 30 minutes, or until the dough roll has doubled in size.

4 Preheat the oven to 200°C/400°F/Gas 6. Brush the top of the bread with olive oil, then use a skewer to prick holes in the bread, from the top right through to the base. Sprinkle the rosemary over the bread. Bake for 30–35 minutes, until golden.

Feta Cheese and Black Olive Loaf per loaf Energy 1582kcal/6693kJ; Protein 47.5g; Carbohydrate 293.7g, of which sugars 11.5g; Fat 32.3g, of which saturates 10.8g; Cholesterol 41mg; Calcium 824mg; Fibre 14.3g; Sodium 3651mg.

Stromboli per loaf Energy 2108kcal/8871kJ; Protein 96.5g; Carbohydrate 275.9g, of which sugars 9g; Fat 76.2g, of which saturates 41.7g; Cholesterol 177mg; Calcium 2125mg; Fibre 13.4g; Sodium 1536mg.

Spinach & Parmesan Bloomer

This pretty pale green loaf is flavoured with spinach, onion and Parmesan cheese.

Makes 1

15ml/1 tbsp olive oil
1 onion, chopped
115g/4oz fresh young spinach leaves
120ml/4fl oz/½ cup water
1 egg
450g/1lb/4 cups unbleached white bread flour
2.5ml/½ tsp freshly grated nutmeg
50g/2oz/⅔ cup freshly grated Parmesan cheese
7.5ml/1½ tsp salt
5ml/1 tsp sugar
7.5ml/1½ tsp easy-blend (rapid-rise) dried yeast
30ml/2 tbsp pine nuts

1 Heat the olive oil in a frying pan, add the chopped onion and fry until golden. Add the spinach, stir well to combine and cover. Remove from the heat and leave to stand for 5 minutes. Then stir again and leave the pan uncovered, to cool.

2 Place the spinach mixture into the bread machine pan. Add the water and egg. Sprinkle over the bread flour, covering the liquid. Sprinkle over the grated nutmeg and the Parmesan cheese. Place the salt and sugar in separate corners of the bread pan. Make a well in the centre of the flour and add the yeast. Set the bread machine to the basic raisin dough setting (if available). Press Start. Add the pine nuts to the dough when the machine beeps or during the last 5 minutes of the kneading process.

3 When the dough cycle has finished, knock back (punch down) the dough. Roll it out to a rectangle about 2.5cm/1in thick. Roll up from one long side to form a thick baton shape. Place the baton on a floured baking sheet, seam side up, cover and leave to rest for 15 minutes.

4 Turn the bread over and place on the another floured baking sheet. Cover and leave it to rise in a warm place for 30 minutes. Meanwhile, preheat the oven to 220°C/425°F/Gas 7.

5 Slash the top of the bloomer with five diagonal slashes. Bake for 30–35 minutes, until golden. Cool on a wire rack.

Carrot & Fennel Bread

The distinctive flavour of fennel is the perfect foil for the more subtle carrot taste in this unusual bread. It looks pretty when sliced, thanks to the attractive orange flecks of carrot.

Makes 1

Small

180ml/6½fl oz/generous ¾ cup water
15ml/1 tbsp sunflower oil
5ml/1 tsp clear honey
150g/5oz/1 cup grated carrot
375g/13oz/3¼ cups unbleached white bread flour
15ml/1 tbsp skimmed milk powder (non fat dry milk)
5ml/1 tsp fennel seeds
5ml/1 tsp salt
5ml/1 tsp easy-blend (rapid-rise) dried yeast

Large

260ml/9fl oz/1⅛ cups water
30ml/2 tbsp sunflower oil
15ml/1 tbsp clear honey
250g/9oz/scant 2 cups grated carrot
600g/1lb 5oz/5¼ cups unbleached white bread flour
30ml/2 tbsp skimmed milk powder (non fat dry milk)
10ml/2 tsp fennel seeds
10ml/2 tsp salt
7.5ml/1½ tsp easy-blend (rapid-rise) dried yeast

1 Pour the water, oil and honey into the bread machine pan. Sprinkle over the grated carrot. If the instructions for your machine specify that the yeast is to be placed in the pan first, then simply reverse the order in which you add the liquid and dry ingredients.

2 Sprinkle over the flour, ensuring that it completely covers the liquid in the pan. Add the milk powder and fennel seeds. Add the salt in one corner of the bread pan. Make a small indent in the centre of the flour (but not down as far as the liquid) and add the dried yeast.

3 Set the machine to white/basic, medium crust. Size: 500g for small, or 1kg/2lb for large. Press Start.

4 Remove the cooked bread at the end of the baking cycle and turn out on to a wire rack to cool.

Spinach and Parmesan Bloomer per loaf Energy 2205kcal/9305kJ; Protein 76.4g; Carbohydrate 361.6g, of which sugars 17.2g; Fat 60.4g, of which saturates 15.7g; Cholesterol 240mg; Calcium 1475mg; Fibre 17.8g; Sodium 3739mg.

Carrot and Fennel Bread per loaf Energy 1510kcal/6402kJ; Protein 40.2g; Carbohydrate 315.3g, of which sugars 27.1g; Fat 18.6g, of which saturates 3.3g; Cholesterol 6mg; Calcium 690mg; Fibre 15g; Sodium 2069mg.

Caramelized Onion Bread

The unmistakable mouthwatering flavour of golden fried onions is captured in this coburg-shaped bread. Serve with soup, cheeses or salad.

Makes 1

50g/2oz/¼ cup butter
2 onions, chopped
280ml/10fl oz/1¼ cups water
15ml/1 tbsp clear honey
450g/1lb/4 cups unbleached white bread flour
7.5ml/1½ tsp salt
2.5ml/½ tsp ground black pepper
7.5ml/1½ tsp easy-blend (rapid-rise) dried yeast

1 Melt the butter in a frying pan and cook the onions over low heat until golden. Remove the pan from the heat and let the onions cool slightly.

2 Place a sieve (strainer) over the bread machine pan, then transfer the contents of the frying pan into it, so that the juices fall into the pan. Set the onions aside to cool completely.

3 Add the water and honey to the bread pan. Reverse the order in which you add the wet and dry ingredients, if necessary. Sprinkle over the flour, covering the liquid. Place the salt and pepper in separate corners. Make a shallow indent in the centre of the flour and add in the yeast.

4 Set the bread machine to the dough setting; use basic raisin dough setting (if available). Press Start. Add the onions when the machine beeps or in the last 5 minutes of kneading. Lightly flour a baking sheet.

5 When the cycle has finished, remove the dough from the bread pan and place on a lightly floured surface.

6 Knock back (punch down), then shape into a ball. Place on the baking sheet and cover with oiled clear film (plastic wrap). Leave to rise for 45 minutes. Preheat the oven to 200°C/400°F/Gas 6. Slash a 1cm/½in deep cross in the top of the loaf. Bake for 35–40 minutes. Cool on a wire rack.

Bubble Corn Bread

This recipe brings together two traditional American breads: corn bread and bubble loaf. It has the flavour of corn and is spiked with hot chilli. Chunks or 'bubbles' of bread can be pulled from the bread, for easy eating.

Makes 1

85ml/3fl oz/generous ⅓ cup milk
120ml/4fl oz/½ cup water
1 egg
400g/14oz/3½ cups unbleached white bread flour
100g/3½oz/scant 1 cup yellow cornmeal
5ml/1 tsp sugar
5ml/1 tsp salt
7.5ml/1½ tsp easy-blend (rapid-rise) dried yeast
15ml/1 tbsp chopped fresh green chilli
115g/4oz/⅔ cup drained canned corn kernels
25g/1oz/2 tbsp butter

1 Pour the milk and water into the bread pan. Add the egg. Sprinkle over the flour and cornmeal, covering the liquid. Add the sugar and salt in separate corners. Make a small indent in the flour and add in the yeast.

2 Set the bread machine to the basic raisin dough setting (if available). Press Start. Add the chilli and canned corn when the machine beeps or during the last 5 minutes of kneading.

3 When the dough cycle has finished, remove the dough and gently knock it back (punch it down), then cut it into 20 equal pieces. Shape into balls.

4 Arrange half of the dough balls in the base of a 22cm/8½in non-stick springform cake tin (pan), spacing them slightly apart. Place the remaining balls of dough on top so that they cover the spaces. Cover the tin and leave to rise in a warm place for about 30–45 minutes, or until the dough has almost doubled in size. Meanwhile preheat the oven to 200°C/400°F/Gas 6.

5 Melt the butter in a small pan. Drizzle it over the top of the risen loaf. Bake the bread for 30–35 minutes, or until golden and well risen. Turn the bread out on to a wire rack to cool.

Caramelized Onion Bread per loaf Energy 2054kcal/8675kJ; Protein 46.2g; Carbohydrate 384.8g, of which sugars 35g; Fat 47.3g, of which saturates 27.9g; Cholesterol 115mg; Calcium 714mg; Fibre 18.1g; Sodium 3347mg.

Bubble Corn Bread per loaf Energy 2074kcal/8760kJ; Protein 60g; Carbohydrate 394.7g, of which sugars 16.1g; Fat 36.5g, of which saturates 16.7g; Cholesterol 253mg; Calcium 714mg; Fibre 16.3g; Sodium 3594mg.

Fresh Tomato & Basil Loaf

Sweet plum tomatoes, onions and fresh basil complement each other in this attractively shaped loaf.

Makes 1

15ml/1 tbsp extra virgin olive oil
1 small onion, chopped
3 plum tomatoes, about 200g/7oz, peeled, seeded and chopped
500g/1lb 2oz/4½ cups unbleached white bread flour
2.5ml/½ tsp ground black pepper
7.5ml/1½ tsp salt
10ml/2 tsp sugar
5ml/1 tsp easy-blend (rapid-rise) dried yeast
15ml/1 tbsp chopped fresh basil

For the glaze

1 egg yolk
15ml/1 tbsp water

1 Heat the oil in a pan. Add the chopped onion and fry for 3–4 minutes. Add the plum tomatoes and cook for 2–3 minutes. Drain through a sieve (strainer) over a bowl, pressing with the back of a spoon to extract the juices. Set aside. Make the cooking juices up to 280ml/10fl oz/1¼ cups with water. Set aside. When cold, pour it into the bread machine pan.

2 Sprinkle over the flour, ensuring that it covers the tomato and onion liquid. Add the ground black pepper, then place the salt and sugar in separate corners of the bread machine pan. Make a small indent in the centre of the flour and add the yeast. Set the bread machine to the basic dough setting. Press Start. Then lightly oil a 23 × 13cm/9 × 5in bread tin (pan).

3 When finished, remove from the bread machine and knock back (punch down) gently. Knead in the reserved tomato and onion mixture and the basil. Shape it into a 2.5cm/1in thick rectangle. Fold the sides to the middle and press to seal. Make a hollow along the centre and fold in half again. Gently roll it into a loaf about 40cm/16in long. Shape into an 'S' shape and place in the prepared tin. Cover and leave for 30–45 minutes.

4 Preheat the oven to 200°C/400°F/Gas 6. Make the glaze by mixing the egg yolk and water together. Brush the glaze over the bread. Bake for 35–40 minutes, or until golden.

Pumpkin & Tomato Bread

The pumpkin purée gives this loaf a rich golden crumb, a soft crust and a beautifully moist light texture, as well as a delightful flavour.

Makes 1

Small

150g/5½oz cooked pumpkin, cooled
90ml/6 tbsp buttermilk
60ml/4 tbsp water
15ml/1 tbsp extra virgin olive oil
325g/11½oz/scant 3 cups unbleached white bread flour
50g/2oz/½ cup cornmeal
15ml/1 tbsp golden (light corn) syrup
5ml/1 tsp salt
4ml/¾ tsp easy-blend (rapid-rise) dried yeast
15ml/1 tbsp pumpkin seeds

Medium

200g/7oz cooked pumpkin, cooled
110ml/scant 4fl oz/scant ½ cup buttermilk
45ml/3 tbsp water
30ml/2 tbsp extra virgin olive oil
425g/15oz/3¾ cups unbleached white bread flour
75g/3oz/¾ cup cornmeal
25ml/1½ tbsp golden (light corn) syrup
7.5ml/1½ tsp salt
5ml/1 tsp easy-blend (rapid-rise) dried yeast
25ml/1½ tbsp pumpkin seeds

1 Mash the pumpkin and put it in the bread machine pan. Add the buttermilk, water and oil. If the instructions for your machine specify that the dried yeast is to be placed in the pan first, reverse the order in which you add the liquid mixture and dry ingredients.

2 Sprinkle over the flour and cornmeal, ensuring that the liquid is completely covered. Add the golden syrup and salt in separate corners of the bread machine pan. Make an indent in the centre of the flour (but not down as far as the liquid) and add the yeast.

3 Set the machine to white/basic, raisin setting (if available), medium crust. Size: 500g for small, or large/750g for medium. Add the pumpkin seeds to the automatic dispenser, if available (if adding manually, add when the machine beeps during the kneading cycle). Press Start. Remove at the end of the baking cycle. Turn out on to a wire rack to cool.

Fresh Tomato and Basil Loaf per loaf Energy 1904kcal/8082kJ; Protein 49.6g; Carbohydrate 410.3g, of which sugars 27.9g; Fat 18.4g, of which saturates 2.7g; Cholesterol 0mg; Calcium 764mg; Fibre 19.1g; Sodium 40mg.

Pumpkin and Tomato Bread per loaf Energy 1574kcal/6657kJ; Protein 43.1g; Carbohydrate 311g, of which sugars 23.9g; Fat 24.5g, of which saturates 3.7g; Cholesterol 2mg; Calcium 617mg; Fibre 18g; Sodium 2068mg.

Sun-dried Tomato Bread

The dense texture and highly concentrated flavour of sun-dried tomatoes makes them perfect for flavouring bread dough, and when Parmesan cheese is added, the result is an exceptionally tasty loaf.

Makes 1

25g/1oz/½ cup sun-dried tomatoes
190ml/6¾fl oz/scant ⅞ cup water
115ml/4fl oz/½ cup milk
30ml/2 tbsp extra virgin olive oil
425g/15oz/3¾ cups unbleached white bread flour
75g/3oz/¾ cup wholemeal (whole-wheat) bread flour
50g/2oz/⅔ cup freshly grated Parmesan cheese
7.5ml/1½ tsp salt
10ml/2 tsp sugar
5ml/1 tsp easy-blend (rapid-rise) dried yeast

1 Place the sun-dried tomatoes in a small bowl and pour over enough warm water to cover them. Leave to soak for 15 minutes, then transfer into a sieve (strainer) placed over a bowl. Allow to drain thoroughly, then chop finely.

2 Check the quantity of tomato water against the amount of water required for the loaf, and add more water if this is necessary. Pour it into the bread machine pan, then add the milk and olive oil.

3 Sprinkle over both types of flour, ensuring that the liquid is completely covered. Sprinkle over the Parmesan, then add the salt and sugar, placing them in separate corners of the bread pan. Make a small indent in the centre of the flour (but not down as far as the liquid) and add the yeast.

4 Set the machine to white/basic; use the raisin setting (if available), medium crust. Size: 750g for medium. Press Start.

5 Add the tomatoes when the machine beeps during the kneading cycle, or after the first kneading. Remove the bread at the end of the baking cycle. Turn on to a wire rack to cool.

Sun-dried Tomato & Cep Loaf

The flavours of ceps and sun-dried tomatoes exude from this unusual bread.

Makes 1

Small
10g/⅓oz dried cep mushrooms
200ml/7fl oz/scant 1 cup warm water
375g/13oz/3¼ cups unbleached white bread flour
7.5ml/1½ tsp salt
15ml/1 tbsp sugar
25g/1oz/2 tbsp butter
5ml/1 tsp easy-blend (rapid-rise) dried yeast
25g/1oz/¼ cup well-drained sun-dried tomatoes in olive oil

Medium
15g/½oz dried cep mushrooms
200ml/7fl oz/scant 1 cup warm water
500g/1lb 2oz/4½ cups unbleached white bread flour
7.5ml/1½ tsp salt
15ml/1 tbsp sugar
25g/1oz/2 tbsp butter
5ml/1 tsp easy-blend (rapid-rise) dried yeast
40g/1½oz/⅓ cup well-drained sun-dried tomatoes in olive oil

1 Place the dried mushrooms in a small bowl and pour over the warm water. Leave to soak for about 30 minutes.

2 Strain the mushrooms over a bowl. Drain thoroughly, reserving the soaking liquid. Set the mushrooms aside. Make up the soaking liquid to 225ml/8fl oz/scant 1 cup if you a making a small loaf, 320ml/11fl oz/1⅓ cups for medium, or 370ml/13fl oz/generous 1½ cups for large.

3 Pour the liquid into the bread pan. Sprinkle over the flour, covering the water. Add the salt, sugar and butter, placing them in separate corners. Make a small indent in the flour; add the yeast. Set the bread machine to the white/basic setting; use raisin setting (if available), light or medium crust. Size: 500g for small, or 750g for medium. Press Start.

4 Chop the reserved mushrooms and the tomatoes. Add to the dough when the machine beeps during the kneading cycle.

5 Remove the bread at the end of the baking cycle. Turn out on to a wire rack to cool.

Sun-dried Tomato Bread per loaf Energy 1469kcal/6185kJ; Protein 31.2g; Carbohydrate 228.1g, of which sugars 23.6g; Fat 54.3g, of which saturates 9.1g; Cholesterol 9mg; Calcium 576mg; Fibre 8.8g; Sodium 1656mg.

Sun-dried Tomato and Cep Loaf per loaf Energy 1544kcal/6540kJ; Protein 37g; Carbohydrate 311g, of which sugars 25.1g; Fat 25.4g, of which saturates 14.3g; Cholesterol 58mg; Calcium 552mg; Fibre 12.6g; Sodium 3220mg.

Rye Bread with Roasted Vegetables

The roasted peppers and onion add a sweetness to this loaf, which complements the rich, slightly sour flavour of the rye flour.

Makes 1

Small

½ red (bell) pepper, seeded
½ onion
30ml/2 tbsp olive oil
225ml/8fl oz/scant 1 cup water
5ml/1 tsp dried oregano
100g/3¾oz/scant 1 cup rye flour
280g/10oz/2½ cups unbleached white bread flour
5ml/1 tsp salt
10ml/2 tsp sugar
5ml/1 tsp easy-blend (rapid-rise) dried yeast

Medium

½ red (bell) pepper, seeded
½ yellow (bell) pepper, seeded
1 small onion
45ml/3 tbsp olive oil
280ml/10fl oz/1¼ cups water
5ml/1 tsp dried oregano
150g/5½oz/1⅓ cups rye flour
350g/12½oz/3 cups unbleached white bread flour
7.5ml/1½ tsp salt
15ml/1 tbsp sugar
6.5ml/1⅓ tsp easy-blend (rapid-rise) dried yeast

1 Chop the peppers and onion into 1cm/½in pieces. Mix the peppers and onion with the oil and place in a shallow roasting pan. Roast them in a preheated oven at 210°C/425°F/Gas 7 for 20 minutes or until starting to brown at the edges. Cool for 10 minutes.

2 Add the water and vegetables, with any remaining oil to the bread pan. Sprinkle over the flours, ensuring they cover the water and vegetables.

3 Add the salt and sugar in separate corners of the bread pan. Make a small indent in the centre of the flour (but not down as far as the liquid), and add the yeast.

4 Set the machine to white/basic, medium crust. Size: 500g for small, or 750g for medium. Press Start.

5 Remove the bread when finished. Turn the loaf out on to a wire rack and leave to cool.

Mixed Pepper Bread

Colourful and full of flavour, this bread looks good when sliced, showing the pretty pepper studs inside.

Makes 1

½ red (bell) pepper, cored and seeded
½ green (bell) pepper, cored and seeded
½ yellow (bell) pepper, cored and seeded
200ml/7fl oz/scant 1 cup milk
120ml/4fl oz/½ cup water
500g/1lb 2oz/4½ cups unbleached white bread flour
10ml/2 tsp sugar
7.5ml/1½ tsp salt
7.5ml/1½ tsp easy-blend (rapid-rise) dried yeast
milk, for brushing
5ml/1 tsp cumin seeds

1 Cut the peppers into fine dice. Pour the milk and water into the bread pan. Reverse the order in which you add the wet and dry ingredients if necessary. Sprinkle over the flour, ensuring that it covers the liquid. Add the sugar and salt in separate corners of the pan.

2 Make a small indent in the centre of the flour and add the yeast. Set the bread machine to the basic raisin dough setting (if available). Press Start. Lightly oil a baking sheet.

3 Add the mixed peppers when the machine beeps or during the last 5 minutes of kneading.

4 When the dough cycle has finished, remove the dough from the machine and place it on a lightly floured surface. Gently knock it back (punch it down) and shape it into a plump ball. Roll gently into an oval. Place on the prepared baking sheet, cover and leave for 30–45 minutes, or until doubled in size.

5 Preheat the oven to 200°C/400°F/Gas 6. Brush the loaf top with the milk and sprinkle with the cumin seeds. Use a sharp knife to cut a lengthways slash.

6 Bake for 35–40 minutes, or until golden and the bottom sounds hollow when tapped. Turn on to a wire rack to cool.

Rye Bread with Roasted Vegetables per loaf Energy 1581kcal/6693kJ; Protein 36.3g; Carbohydrate 315.1g, of which sugars 24.1g; Fat 28.1g, of which saturates 4g; Cholesterol 0mg; Calcium 453mg; Fibre 22.8g; Sodium 1981mg.

Mixed Pepper Bread per loaf Energy 1994kcal/8470kJ; Protein 60.4g; Carbohydrate 436.3g, of which sugars 54.3g; Fat 13g, of which saturates 4.3g; Cholesterol 18mg; Calcium 1093mg; Fibre 21.1g; Sodium 3142mg.

Potato Bread

This golden crusty loaf has a moist soft centre and is perfect for sandwiches. Use the water in which the potatoes have been cooked to make the bread. If you haven't got enough, you can make up the remainder with ordinary water.

Makes 1

Medium

240ml/8½fl oz/generous 1 cup potato cooking water, at room temperature
30ml/2 tbsp sunflower oil
500g/1lb 2oz/4½ cups unbleached white bread flour
175g/6oz/2 cups cold mashed potato
25ml/1½ tbsp skimmed milk powder (non fat dry milk)
7.5ml/1½ tsp salt
10ml/2 tsp sugar
7.5ml/1½ tsp easy-blend (rapid-rise) dried yeast
milk, for glazing

Large

290ml/generous ½ pint/scant 1¼ cups potato cooking water, at room temperature
45ml/3 tbsp sunflower oil
600g/1lb/5¼ cups unbleached white bread flour
200g/7oz/scant 2½ cups cold cooked mashed potato
30ml/2 tbsp skimmed milk powder (non fat dry milk)
7.5ml/1½ tsp salt
15ml/1 tbsp sugar
7.5ml/1½ tsp easy-blend (rapid-rise) dried yeast
milk, for glazing

1 Pour the water and sunflower oil into the bread machine pan. However, if the instructions for your machine specify that the yeast is to be placed in the pan first, reverse the order in which you add the liquid and dry ingredients.

2 Sprinkle over the flour, ensuring that it covers the water. Add the potato and milk powder. Add the salt and sugar in separate corners of the bread pan. Make a small indent in the centre of the flour (but not down as far as the liquid) and add the yeast.

3 Set the bread machine to the white/basic setting, medium or light crust. Size: 750g for medium, or 1kg/2lb for large. Press Start. To glaze the loaf, brush with the top of the milk halfway through the cooking time. Remove the bread at the end of the baking cycle. Turn out on to a wire rack.

Potato & Saffron Bread

A dough that includes potato produces a moist loaf with a springy texture and good keeping qualities. Saffron adds an aromatic flavour and rich golden colour to this loaf.

Makes 1

1 large potato, about 225g/8oz, peeled
5ml/1 tsp saffron threads
1 egg
450g/1lb/4 cups unbleached white bread flour
30ml/2 tbsp skimmed milk powder (non fat dry milk)
25g/1oz/2 tbsp butter
15ml/1 tbsp clear honey
7.5ml/1½ tsp salt
7.5ml/1½ tsp easy-blend (rapid-rise) dried yeast

1 Place the potato in a pan of boiling water, reduce the heat and simmer until tender. Drain the potato, reserving 200ml/7fl oz/scant 1 cup of the cooking water. Add the saffron to the hot water; leave to stand for 30 minutes. Mash the potato (without adding butter or milk) and leave to cool.

2 Add the saffron water to the bread pan. Add the mashed potato and the egg. Sprinkle over the flour, ensuring that it covers the ingredients already placed in the pan. Spoon over the milk powder. Add the butter, honey and salt in separate corners of the bread pan. Make a well in the centre of the flour and add the yeast. Set the bread machine to the basic dough setting. Press Start. Lightly flour a baking sheet.

3 When the dough cycle has finished, remove the dough from the machine and place on a lightly floured surface. Gently knock back (punch down).

4 Shape the dough into a plump ball. Place on the baking sheet, cover with oiled clear film (plastic wrap) and leave to rise for 30–45 minutes. Preheat the oven to 200°C/400°F/Gas 6.

5 Slash the top of the loaf with three or four diagonal cuts, then rotate and repeat to make a criss-cross effect. Bake the bread for 35–40 minutes, or until the bottom sounds hollow when tapped. Turn out on to a wire rack to cool.

Potato Bread per loaf Energy 1643kcal/6953kJ; Protein 38g; Carbohydrate 319.3g, of which sugars 15.5g; Fat 32.5g, of which saturates 7g; Cholesterol 16mg; Calcium 564mg; Fibre 13g; Sodium 2039mg.

Potato and Saffron Bread per loaf Energy 2039kcal/8639kJ; Protein 55.9g; Carbohydrate 402.3g, of which sugars 26.1g; Fat 34.2g, of which saturates 17.2g; Cholesterol 254mg; Calcium 797mg; Fibre 16.2g; Sodium 3261mg.

Sweet Potato Bread

Adding sweet potato to the dough creates a loaf with a rich golden crust, and the crumb is beautifully moist.

Makes 1

225g/8oz sweet potatoes, peeled
210ml/7½fl oz/scant 1 cup water
500g/1lb 2oz/4½ cups unbleached white bread flour
45ml/3 tbsp rolled oats
30ml/2 tbsp skimmed milk powder (non fat dry milk)
7.5ml/1½ tsp salt
25ml/1½ tbsp muscovado (molasses) sugar
40g/1½oz/3 tbsp butter
7.5ml/1½ tsp easy-blend (rapid-rise) dried yeast

For the topping

15ml/1 tbsp water
10ml/2 tsp rolled oats
10ml/2 tsp wheat grain

1 Cook the sweet potato in plenty of boiling water for 40 minutes or until very tender. Drain, and when cool enough to handle, peel off the skin. Place the sweet potato in a large bowl and mash well, but do not add any butter or milk.

2 Pour the water into the bread machine pan. Sprinkle the white bread flour, rolled oats and skimmed milk powder over the water, covering it completely. Weigh or measure the cooked sweet potatoes to ensure the quantity matches the amount given in the variation. Then add the potatoes to the bread pan.

3 Place the salt, sugar and butter in three separate corners of the bread machine pan. Make a shallow indent in the flour (but not down as far as the liquid underneath) and add the dried yeast. Set the bread machine to the white/basic setting, medium crust. Size: 750g for medium. Press Start.

4 When the rising cycle is almost complete, just before the bread begins to bake, add the topping: brush the top of the loaf with the water and sprinkle the rolled oats and wheat grain over the top of the bread.

5 Remove the bread at the end of the baking cycle. Turn out on to a wire rack to cool.

Parsnip & Nutmeg Bread

The moment you cut into this loaf, the irresistible aroma of nutmeg and parsnips fills the air.

Makes 1

Small

225ml/7fl oz/scant 1 cup water
125g/4½oz/1½ cups mashed cooked parsnips
375g/13oz/3¼ cups unbleached white bread flour
15ml/1 tbsp skimmed milk powder (non fat dry milk)
2.5ml/½ tsp freshly grated nutmeg
25g/1oz/2 tbsp butter
5ml/1 tsp salt
5ml/1 tsp sugar
5ml/1 tsp easy-blend (rapid-rise) dried yeast

Medium

225ml/8fl oz/scant 1 cup water
175g/6oz/2 cups mashed cooked parsnips
500g/1lb 2oz/4½ cups unbleached white bread flour
30ml/2 tbsp skimmed milk powder (non fat dry milk)
5ml/1 tsp freshly grated nutmeg
40g/1½oz/3 tbsp butter
7.5ml/1½ tsp salt
7.5ml/1½ tsp sugar
7.5ml/1½ tsp easy-blend (rapid-rise) dried yeast

1 Pour the water into the bread machine pan and add the mashed parsnips. If the instructions for your machine specify that the yeast is to be placed in the pan first, reverse the order in which you add the liquid mixture and dry ingredients.

2 Sprinkle over the flour, ensuring it covers the ingredients already placed in the pan. Add the milk powder and freshly grated nutmeg.

3 Place the butter, salt and sugar in separate corners of the bread machine pan. Make a small indent in the centre of the flour (but do not go down as far as the liquid) and add in the dried yeast.

4 Set the bread machine to the basic/normal setting, medium crust. Size: 500g for small, or large/750g for medium. Press Start.

5 Remove the bread at the end of the baking cycle. Turn out on to a wire rack to cool.

Sweet Potato Bread per loaf Energy 1816kcal/7695kJ; Protein 44.1g; Carbohydrate 362.7g, of which sugars 35.9g; Fat 31.1g, of which saturates 15.4g; Cholesterol 63mg; Calcium 689mg; Fibre 18.1g; Sodium 2304mg.

Parsnip and Nutmeg Bread per loaf Energy 1607kcal/6805kJ; Protein 40.7g; Carbohydrate 316.7g, of which sugars 22.2g; Fat 28.5g, of which saturates 15.5g; Cholesterol 63mg; Calcium 714mg; Fibre 17.5g; Sodium 2224mg.

Beetroot Bread

This spectacular bread takes on the colour of the beetroot juice. It is also flecked with beetroot flesh, which gives the finished loaf a slightly sweet flavour and delightful consistency.

Makes 1

Small

150ml/¼ pint/⅔ cup water
140g/5oz/1 cup grated raw beetroot (beets)
2 spring onions (scallions), chopped
375g/13oz/3¼ cups unbleached white bread flour
15g/½oz/1 tbsp butter
7.5ml/1½ tsp salt
5ml/1 tsp sugar
5ml/1 tsp easy-blend (rapid-rise) dried yeast

Medium

170ml/6fl oz/¾ cup water
225g/8oz/1½ cups grated raw beetroot (beets)
3 spring onions (scallions), chopped
500g/1lb 2oz/4½ cups unbleached white bread flour
25g/1oz/2 tbsp butter
10ml/2 tsp salt
5ml/1 tsp sugar
5ml/1 tsp easy-blend (rapid-rise) dried yeast

1 Pour the water into the bread pan. Sprinkle over the grated beetroot. If the instructions for your machine specify that the yeast is to be placed in the pan first, reverse the order in which you add the liquid mixture and dry ingredients.

2 Add the chopped spring onions. However, if your bread machine offers you the option of adding any extra ingredients during the kneading cycle, set the spring onions aside so that you may add them later on.

3 Sprinkle the flour over the beetroot and water, ensuring it covers them both. Add the butter, salt and sugar in separate corners. Make a small well in the flour and add the yeast.

4 Set the bread machine to the white/basic setting, medium crust. Size: 500g for small, or large/750g for medium. Press Start.

5 Remove the bread at the end of the baking cycle. Turn it out on to a wire rack to cool.

Chickpea & Peppercorn Bread

Bread may be a basic food, but this recipe contains an exciting combination of ingredients. Chickpeas help to keep the dough light, while pink and green peppercorns add colour and explosions of flavour.

Makes 1

265ml/9½fl oz/1⅛ cup water
30ml/2 tbsp extra virgin olive oil
175g/6oz/1 cup canned chickpeas
500g/1lb 2oz/4½ cups unbleached white bread flour
10ml/2 tsp drained fresh pink peppercorns in brine
10ml/2 tsp drained fresh green peppercorns in brine
25ml/1½ tbsp skimmed milk powder (non fat dry milk)
7.5ml/1½ tsp salt
10ml/2 tsp sugar
7.5ml/1½ tsp easy-blend (rapid-rise) dried yeast
milk, for brushing (optional)

1 Pour the water and extra virgin olive oil into the bread machine pan. Add the well-drained chickpeas. If the instructions for your bread machine specify that the yeast is to be placed in the pan first, then simply reverse the order in which you add the liquid and dry ingredients to the bread pan.

2 Sprinkle over the flour, ensuring that it covers the ingredients already placed in the pan. Add the pink and green peppercorns and milk powder.

3 Place the salt and sugar in separate corners of the pan. Make a small indent in the centre of the flour (but not down as far as the liquid) and add the yeast.

4 Set the machine to white/basic. Select light crust, 750g for medium; or medium crust. Press Start. Brush the top of the loaf with milk just before it starts to bake, if you like.

5 Remove the bread at the end of the baking cycle. Turn out on to a wire rack.

Beetroot Bread per loaf Energy 1444kcal/6127kJ; Protein 38.1g; Carbohydrate 302.6g, of which sugars 16g; Fat 17.4g, of which saturates 8.9g; Cholesterol 35mg; Calcium 564mg; Fibre 14.6g; Sodium 3165mg.

Chickpea and Peppercorn Bread per loaf Energy 1597kcal/6774kJ; Protein 47.6g; Carbohydrate 324.3g, of which sugars 19g; Fat 21.2g, of which saturates 3.7g; Cholesterol 6mg; Calcium 703mg; Fibre 16.8g; Sodium 2307mg.

Sage & Sausage Loaf

When this tasty loaf is sliced, the sausage filling is revealed. It is perfect for picnics, parties or at lunchtime.

Makes 1

15ml/1 tbsp sunflower oil
200g/7oz spicy sausages
3 eggs
30ml/2 tbsp water
350g/12½oz/generous 3 cups unbleached white bread flour
30ml/2 tbsp skimmed milk powder (non fat dry milk)
10ml/2 tsp sugar
7.5ml/1½ tsp salt
50g/2oz/¼ cup butter, melted
5ml/1 tsp easy-blend (rapid-rise) dried yeast
5ml/1 tsp dried sage
1 egg yolk, to glaze
15ml/1 tbsp water, to glaze

1 Heat the oil in a frying pan. Add the sausages. Fry them over medium heat for 7–10 minutes or until cooked. Cool.

2 Add the eggs and water to the bread pan. Sprinkle over the flour, covering the liquid. Add the milk powder. Place the sugar, salt and butter in separate corners of the pan. Make a small indent in the centre of the flour; add the yeast.

3 Set the bread machine to the dough setting; use basic raisin dough setting (if available). Press Start. Add the sage when the machine beeps or during the last 5 minutes of kneading. Lightly oil a 23 × 13cm/9 × 5in loaf tin (pan).

4 When the dough cycle has finished, place the dough on a floured surface. Knock back (punch down) gently. Roll into a rectangle 2.5cm/1in × 23cm/9in.

5 Place the sausages down the centre and roll the dough tightly around the sausages. Place in the loaf tin. Cover with lightly oiled clear film (plastic wrap) and leave to rise in a warm place for 30–45 minutes.

6 Preheat the oven to 190°C/375°F/Gas 5. To glaze, mix the yolk and water; brush over the bread and bake for 30–35 minutes, or until golden. Turn out on to a wire rack to cool.

Leek & Pancetta Tray Bread

Serve this bread sliced, with a simple salad of dressed leaves for a tasty snack.

Makes 1

90ml/6 tbsp water
1 egg
225g/8oz/2 cups unbleached white bread flour
5ml/1 tsp salt
25g/1oz butter
5ml/1 tsp easy-blend (rapid-rise) dried yeast

For the filling

575g/1¼lb/4–5 leeks
30ml/2 tbsp sunflower oil
75g/3oz sliced pancetta or streaky (fatty) bacon, cut into strips
140ml/5fl oz/⅝ cup sour cream
75ml/2½fl oz/5 tbsp milk
2 eggs, lightly beaten
15ml/1 tbsp chopped fresh basil leaves
salt and ground black pepper

1 Pour the water and egg into the bread machine pan. Sprinkle over the flour, ensuring that it covers the liquid. Place the salt and butter in separate corners. Make a well in the centre of the flour and add the yeast. Set the bread machine to the basic or pizza dough setting. Press Start. Then lightly oil a 20 × 30cm/8 × 12in Swiss roll tin (jelly roll pan) that is about 1cm/½in deep.

2 Slice the leeks thinly. Heat the sunflower oil in a large frying pan and cook the leeks over a low heat for about 5 minutes, until they have softened slightly. Set them aside to cool.

3 When the dough cycle has finished, place the dough on a lightly floured surface. Knock back (punch down) the dough gently, then roll it out to a rectangle measuring 23 × 33cm/9 × 13in. Place in the prepared tin and press the edges outwards and upwards, so that the dough covers the base and sides evenly. Preheat the oven to 190°C/375°F/Gas 5.

4 Sprinkle the leeks over the dough. Arrange the pancetta slices on top. Mix the sour cream, milk and eggs together. Add the basil and season with salt and pepper. Pour over the leeks.

5 Bake for 30–35 minutes, or until the filling has set and the base is golden around the edges. Serve the bread hot or warm.

Sage and Sausage Loaf per loaf Energy 2701kcal/11318kJ; Protein 76.5g; Carbohydrate 306.4g, of which sugars 23.5g; Fat 138.9g, of which saturates 59.1g; Cholesterol 786mg; Calcium 791mg; Fibre 11.9g; Sodium 4136mg.

Leek and Pancetta Tray Bread per loaf Energy 2022kcal/8462kJ; Protein 67.4g; Carbohydrate 200.3g, of which sugars 24.8g; Fat 111.6g, of which saturates 46.2g; Cholesterol 765mg; Calcium 761mg; Fibre 19.6g; Sodium 3422mg.

Salami & Peppercorn Bread

This loaf, marbled with salami and crushed black pepper, makes a great accompaniment to hot soup. For a quick snack, try it toasted with a cheese topping.

Makes 1

210ml/7½fl oz/scant 1 cup water
15ml/1 tbsp olive oil
350g/12oz/3 cups unbleached white flour
50g/2oz/½ cup grated mature (sharp) Cheddar cheese
2.5ml/½ tsp salt
5ml/1 tsp sugar
5ml/1 tsp easy-blend (rapid-rise) dried yeast
5ml/1 tsp black peppercorns, coarsely crushed
50g/2oz salami, chopped
milk, for brushing

1 Pour the water and oil into the bread machine pan. If the instructions for your bread machine specify that the yeast is to be placed in the pan first, then simply reverse the order in which you add the liquid and dry ingredients.

2 Sprinkle over the flour, ensuring that it covers the liquid. Add half the cheese. Add the salt in one corner of the bread pan and the sugar in another corner. Make a well in the centre of the flour (but not down as far as the liquid) and add the yeast.

3 Set the bread machine to the basic or pizza dough setting. Press Start. Meanwhile, lightly oil a baking sheet.

4 Once the dough cycle has finished, remove the dough from the machine and place it on a lightly floured surface. Knock it back (punch it down) gently and flatten it slightly. Sprinkle over the peppercorns and salami and knead gently.

5 Shape into a round loaf; place on the baking sheet. Cover with an oiled bowl and leave in a warm place for 30 minutes. Preheat the oven to 200°C/400°F/Gas 6.

6 Uncover the bread, brush it with milk and sprinkle with the remaining cheese. Bake for about 30–35 minutes, until golden.

Venison Tordu

This pretty twisted bread is punctuated with strips of smoked venison, pepper and crushed juniper berries.

Makes 1

230ml/8fl oz/1 cup water
350g/12oz/3 cups unbleached white bread flour
5ml/1 tsp sugar
5ml/1 tsp salt
5ml/1 tsp easy-blend (rapid-rise) dried yeast
40g/1½oz smoked venison, cut into strips
5ml/1 tsp ground black pepper
5ml/1 tsp juniper berries, crushed
unbleached white bread flour, for dusting

1 Pour the water into the bread machine pan. Sprinkle over the white bread flour, ensuring that it covers the water. Add the sugar and salt, placing them in separate corners of the bread pan. Make a well in the centre of the flour and add the yeast. Set the bread machine to the basic dough setting. Press Start.

2 When the dough cycle has finished, knock it back (punch it down) gently. Shape the dough into a ball and flatten the top.

3 Roll the dough out to a round, about 2cm/¾in thick. Sprinkle the top of the dough with venison strips, black pepper and juniper berries. Leave a 1cm/½in clear border around the edge. Fold one side of the dough to the centre, then repeat on the other side. Press the folds gently with a rolling pin to seal them, then fold again along the centre line. Press the seam gently to seal, then roll the dough backwards and forwards to make a loaf about 65cm/26in long.

4 Using the side of your hand, press across the centre of the loaf to make an indentation. Bring both ends towards each other to make an upside down 'U' shape and twist together.

5 Place on an oiled baking sheet. Cover and leave to rise in a warm place for 30 minutes, or until it has almost doubled in size. Meanwhile, preheat the oven to 220°C/425°F/Gas 7. Dust the top of the loaf with white bread flour. Bake for 25–30 minutes, or until golden. Cool on a wire rack.

Salami and Peppercorn Bread per loaf Energy 1762kcal/7427kJ; Protein 55.3g; Carbohydrate 277.1g, of which sugars 9.5g; Fat 54.5g, of which saturates 13.1g; Cholesterol 88mg; Calcium 867mg; Fibre 10.9g; Sodium 2280mg.

Venison Tordu per loaf Energy 1265kcal/5377kJ; Protein 42.5g; Carbohydrate 277.9g, of which sugars 9.4g; Fat 6.1g, of which saturates 1.1g; Cholesterol 20mg; Calcium 504mg; Fibre 10.9g; Sodium 1999mg.

Pitta Breads

These well-known flatbreads are easy to make and extremely versatile. Serve them warm with dips, or split them in half and fill with your favourite filling.

Makes 6–10

210ml/7½fl oz/scant 1 cup water
15ml/1 tbsp olive oil
350g/12oz/3 cups unbleached white bread flour, plus extra for sprinkling
7.5ml/1½ tsp salt
5ml/1 tsp sugar
5ml/1 tsp easy-blend (rapid-rise) dried yeast

1 Pour the water and oil into the bread machine pan. Add the flour, ensuring it covers the water. Add the salt and sugar in separate corners. Make a shallow indent in the centre of the flour and add the yeast. Set to the dough setting; use basic or pizza dough setting (if available). Start.

2 When the dough cycle has finished, remove the dough from the machine. Place it on a lightly floured surface and knock it back (punch it down) gently.

3 Divide the dough into six or ten equal pieces, depending on whether you want large or small pitta breads. Shape each piece into a ball.

4 Cover the balls with oiled clear film (plastic wrap) and leave for about 10 minutes. Preheat the oven to 230°C/450°F/Gas 8. Place three baking sheets in the oven to heat.

5 Flatten each piece of dough slightly, and then roll out into an oval or round, about 5mm/¼in thick.

6 Lightly sprinkle each pitta with flour. Cover with oiled clear film and leave to rest for 10 minutes.

7 Place the pittas on the baking sheets and bake for 5–6 minutes, or until they are puffed up and lightly browned. Transfer the pitta breads on to wire racks to cool.

Lavash

These Middle Eastern flatbreads puff up slightly during cooking, to make a bread which is crispy, but not as dry and crisp as a cracker. Serve warm straight from the oven, or cold, with a little butter, if wished.

Makes 10

250ml/8fl oz/1 cup water
45ml/3 tbsp natural (plain) yogurt
350g/12oz/3 cups unbleached white bread flour
115g/4oz/1 cup wholemeal (whole-wheat) bread flour
5ml/1 tsp salt
5ml/1 tsp easy-blend (rapid-rise) dried yeast

For the topping

30ml/2 tbsp milk
30ml/2 tbsp millet seeds

1 Pour the water and yogurt into the bread machine pan. Sprinkle over both types of flour, ensuring that the liquid is completely covered. Add the salt in one corner of the bread pan. Make an indent in the centre of the flour; add the yeast.

2 Set the bread machine to the dough setting; use basic or pizza dough setting (if available). Press Start.

3 When the dough cycle has finished, place the dough on a lightly floured surface. Knock back gently (punch down) and divide it into 10 equal pieces.

4 Shape each piece into a ball, then flatten into a disc with your hand. Cover with oiled clear film (plastic wrap); leave to rest for 5 minutes. Preheat the oven to 230°C/450°F/Gas 8. Place three or four baking sheets in the oven.

5 Roll each ball of dough out very thinly, then stretch it over the backs of your hands, to make the lavash. If the dough starts to tear, leave it to rest for a few minutes after rolling. Stack the lavash between layers of oiled clear film and cover.

6 Place the lavash on baking sheets, brush with milk and sprinkle with millet seeds. Bake for 5–8 minutes, or until puffed. Transfer to a wire rack and cook the remaining lavash.

Pitta Breads Energy 150kcal/638kJ; Protein 3.9g; Carbohydrate 32.4g, of which sugars 0.6g; Fat 1.5g, of which saturates 0.2g; Cholesterol 0mg; Calcium 58mg; Fibre 1.3g; Sodium 492mg

Lavash Energy 151kcal/644kJ; Protein 5.1g; Carbohydrate 33g, of which sugars 1.2g; Fat 0.8g, of which saturates 0.1g; Cholesterol 0mg; Calcium 57mg; Fibre 2.4g; Sodium 203mg.

Moroccan Ksra

This leavened flatbread is made with semolina and spiced with aniseed. It is the traditional accompaniment to tagine, a spicy Moroccan stew, but is equally good with salad, cheeses or dips.

Makes 2

200ml/7fl oz/⅞ cup water
250g/9oz/2¼ cups unbleached white bread flour
75g/3oz/¾ cup semolina
5ml/1 tsp aniseed
7.5ml/1½ tsp salt
2.5ml/½ tsp sugar
5ml/1 tsp easy-blend (rapid-rise) dried yeast
olive oil, for brushing
sesame seeds, for sprinkling

1 Pour the water into the machine pan. Reverse the order in which you add the wet and dry ingredients if necessary.

2 Add the flour, semolina and aniseed, covering the water. Place the salt and sugar in separate corners. Make an indent in the flour; add the yeast. Set the machine to the basic dough setting.

3 Press Start on your bread machine, then lightly flour two baking sheets. When the cycle has finished, place the dough on a lightly floured surface.

4 Knock the dough back (punch it down) gently, shape into two balls, then flatten into 2cm/¾in thick discs. Place each dough disc on a baking sheet.

5 Cover the dough discs with oiled clear film (plastic wrap) and leave to rise for 30 minutes, or until doubled in size.

6 Preheat the oven to 200°C/400°F/Gas 6. Brush the top of each piece of dough with olive oil and sprinkle with sesame seeds. Prick the surface with a skewer.

7 Bake for about 20–25 minutes, or until the ksra are golden and sound hollow when tapped underneath. Turn out on to a wire rack to cool.

Carta di Musica

This crunchy crispbread originated in Sardinia, and can be found throughout southern Italy, where it is eaten not only as a bread, but as a substitute for pasta in lasagne. It also makes a good pizza base.

Makes 8

280ml/10fl oz/1¼ cups water
450g/1lb/4 cups unbleached white bread flour
7.5ml/1½ tsp salt
5ml/1 tsp sugar
5ml/1 tsp easy-blend (rapid-rise) dried yeast

1 Pour the water into the bread machine pan. Sprinkle over the white bread flour, ensuring that it covers the water. Add the salt in one corner of the bread pan and the sugar in another corner. Make a small indent in the centre of the flour (but not down as far as the liquid) and add the easy-blend dried yeast. Set the bread machine to the dough setting; use basic dough setting (if available). Press Start.

2 When the dough cycle has finished, remove the dough from the machine and place it on a lightly floured surface. Knock it back (punch it down) gently and divide it into four equal pieces. Shape each piece of dough into a ball, then roll a piece out until about 3mm/⅛in thick.

3 Now roll out the other three pieces. If the dough starts to tear, cover it with oiled clear film (plastic wrap) and leave it to rest for 2–3 minutes.

4 When all the dough has been rolled out, cover with oiled clear film and leave to rest on the floured surface for about 10–15 minutes. Preheat the oven to 230°C/450°F/Gas 8. Place two baking sheets in the oven to heat.

5 Keeping the other dough rounds covered, place one round on each baking sheet. Bake for 5 minutes, until puffed up. Remove from the oven and cut each round in half horizontally to make two thinner breads. Place these cut side up on the baking sheets and bake for 5–8 minutes, until crisp. Turn out on to a wire rack and cook the remaining breads.

Moroccan Ksra per ksra Energy 563kcal/2392kJ; Protein 15.8g; Carbohydrate 127.5g, of which sugars 3.2g; Fat 2.3g, of which saturates 0.3g; Cholesterol 0mg; Calcium 183mg; Fibre 4.7g; Sodium 1482mg.

Carta di Musica per loaf Energy 194kcal/824kJ; Protein 5.3g; Carbohydrate 44.2g, of which sugars 1.4g; Fat 0.7g, of which saturates 0.1g; Cholesterol 0mg; Calcium 79mg; Fibre 1.7g; Sodium 370mg.

Pide

A traditional Turkish ridged flatbread, this is often baked plain, but can also be sprinkled with aromatic black nigella seeds, which taste rather like oregano. If you can't find nigella seeds, use poppy seeds instead.

Makes 3

260ml/8½fl oz/generous 1 cup water
30ml/2 tbsp olive oil
450g/1lb/4 cups unbleached white bread flour
5ml/1 tsp salt
5ml/1 tsp sugar
5ml/1 tsp easy-blend (rapid-rise) dried yeast
1 egg yolk mixed with 10ml/2 tsp water, for glazing
nigella or poppy seeds, for sprinkling

1 Pour the water and oil into the machine pan. Sprinkle over the flour, ensuring that it covers the liquid. Add the salt in one corner of the bread pan and the sugar in another corner. Make a small indent in the centre of the flour; add the yeast. Set the bread machine to the dough setting; use basic dough setting (if available). Press Start.

2 When finished, remove the pide dough from the bread machine and place it on a surface lightly dusted with flour. Knock the dough back (punch down) gently and divide it into three equal pieces. Shape each piece of dough into a ball.

3 Roll each ball of dough into a round, about 15cm/6in in diameter. Cover with oiled clear film (plastic wrap) and leave for 20 minutes. Preheat the oven to 230°C/450°F/Gas 8.

4 Using your fingers, ridge the bread, while enlarging it until it is 5mm/¼in thick. Start from the top of the round, pressing your fingers down and away from you, into the bread. Repeat a second row, and continue down the bread.

5 Turn the bread by 90 degrees and repeat the pressing to give a criss-cross ridged effect. Place the pide on floured baking sheets, brush with egg glaze and sprinkle with nigella or poppy seeds. Bake for 9–10 minutes, or until puffy and golden. Serve.

Olive Fougasse

A French hearth bread, fougasse is traditionally baked on the floor of the hot bread oven, just after the fire has been raked out.

Makes 1

210ml/7½fl oz/scant 1 cup water
15ml/1 tbsp olive oil, plus extra for brushing
350g/12oz/3 cups unbleached white bread flour
5ml/1 tsp salt
5ml/1 tsp sugar
5ml/1 tsp easy-blend (rapid-rise) dried yeast
50g/2oz/½ cup pitted black olives, chopped
425g/15oz/3¾ cups wholemeal (whole-wheat) bread flour
175g/6oz/generous 1½ cups white bread flour
30ml/2 tbsp skimmed milk powder (non fat dry milk)
10ml/2 tsp salt
15ml/1 tbsp sugar
25g/1oz/2 tbsp butter
7.5ml/1½ tsp easy-blend (rapid-rise) dried yeast

1 Pour the water and the oil into the machine pan. Sprinkle over the flour, ensuring that it covers the liquid. Add the salt in one corner of the bread pan and the sugar in another corner. Make a well in the centre of the flour and add the yeast. Set the bread machine to the basic or pizza dough setting. Press Start. When the cycle has finished, remove the dough from the machine and place it on a lightly floured surface.

2 Knock the dough back (punch it down) gently and flatten it slightly. Sprinkle over the olives and fold over the dough two or three times to incorporate them. Flatten the dough and roll it into an oblong, about 30cm/12in long. With a sharp knife, make four or five parallel cuts diagonally through the body of the dough, but leaving the edges intact. Gently stretch the fougasse dough so that it resembles a ladder.

3 Place the shaped dough on an oiled baking sheet. Cover and leave for about 30 minutes, until doubled in size.

4 Preheat the oven to 220°C/425°F/Gas 7. Brush the top of the fougasse with olive oil, place in the oven and bake for 20–25 minutes, or until golden. Cool on a wire rack.

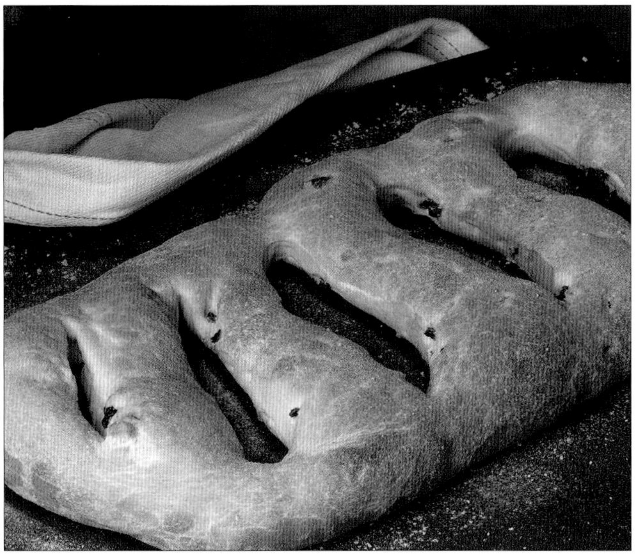

Pide Energy 603kcal/2553kJ; Protein 15.1g; Carbohydrate 117.9g, of which sugars 3.6g; Fat 11.1g, of which saturates 1.8g; Cholesterol 67mg; Calcium 219mg; Fibre 4.6g; Sodium 663mg.

Olive Fougasse Energy 1360kcal/5760kJ; Protein 33.4g; Carbohydrate 276.1g, of which sugars 9.4g; Fat 21g, of which saturates 3.1g; Cholesterol 0mg; Calcium 523mg; Fibre 12.3g; Sodium 3101mg.

Haman Pockets

These delicate tricorn-shaped pockets are properly known as *Hamantaschel*, and are traditionally eaten at the Jewish festival of Esther.

Makes 10–12

100ml/3½fl oz/7 tbsp milk
1 egg
250g/9oz/2¼ cups unbleached white bread flour
25g/1oz/2 tbsp caster (superfine) sugar
2.5ml/½ tsp salt
25g/1oz/2 tbsp butter, melted
5ml/1 tsp easy-blend (rapid-rise) dried yeast
50g/2oz/4 tbsp poppy seeds
40g/1½oz/3 tbsp butter
25g/1oz/¼ cup ground almonds
15ml/1 tbsp clear honey
15ml/1 tbsp chopped mixed (candied) peel
15ml/1 tbsp sultanas (golden raisins), chopped
beaten egg, to glaze

1 Pour the milk and egg into the bread machine pan. Sprinkle over the flour, ensuring that it covers the milk and egg mixture. Add the sugar, salt and butter, placing them in separate corners of the bread pan. Make a small indent in the centre of the flour (but not down as far as the liquid) and add the yeast. Set the bread machine to the basic dough setting. Press Start.

2 Make the filling. Put the poppy seeds in a heatproof bowl, pour over boiling water to cover, cool, then strain. Melt 15g/½oz/1 tbsp of the butter in a pan, add the poppy seeds and cook, stirring, for 1–2 minutes. Remove from the heat and stir in the almonds, honey, mixed peel and sultanas. Cool.

3 When the dough cycle has finished, knock back (punch down) the dough gently and shape into a ball. Roll out to a thickness of about 5mm/¼in. Cut out 10cm/4in circles, re-rolling the trimmings. Melt the remaining butter. Brush each circle with the butter and place a spoonful of filling in the centre. Bring up the edges over the filling to make tricorn shapes.

4 Transfer the shaped pastries to greased baking sheets, cover them and leave for 30 minutes or until doubled in size. Preheat the oven to 190°C/375°F/Gas 5. Brush the pastries with the beaten egg and bake for 15 minutes, or until golden.

Onion Focaccia

This tasty version of focaccia has a red onion and fresh sage topping.

Makes 1

210ml/7½fl oz/scant 1 cup water
15ml/1 tbsp olive oil
350g/12oz/3 cups unbleached white bread flour
2.5ml/½ tsp salt
5ml/1 tsp sugar
5ml/1 tsp easy-blend (rapid-rise) dried yeast
15ml/1 tbsp chopped fresh sage
15ml/1 tbsp chopped red onion

For the topping
30ml/2 tbsp olive oil
½ red onion, thinly sliced
5 fresh sage leaves
10ml/2 tsp coarse sea salt
coarsely ground black pepper

1 Pour the water and oil into the bread pan. Sprinkle over the flour, covering the liquid. Add the salt and sugar in separate corners. Make a well in the flour and add the yeast. Set the bread machine to the basic or pizza dough setting. Press Start.

2 Lightly oil a 25–28cm/10–11in pizza pan. When the cycle has finished, remove the dough from the bread pan and place it on a surface lightly dusted with flour. Knock the dough back (punch down) and flatten it slightly. Sprinkle over the sage and red onion and knead gently to incorporate.

3 Shape the dough into a ball, flatten it, then roll it into a round of about 25–28cm/10–11in. Place in the pizza pan. Cover with oiled clear film (plastic wrap) and leave to rise in a warm place for 20 minutes.

4 Meanwhile, preheat the oven to 200°C/400°F/Gas 6. Uncover the focaccia, and, using your fingertips, poke the dough to make deep dimples over the surface. Cover and leave to rise for 10–15 minutes, or until the dough has doubled in size.

5 Drizzle over the olive oil and sprinkle with the onion, sage leaves, sea salt and black pepper. Bake for 20–25 minutes, or until golden in colour. Turn out on to a wire rack to cool slightly. Serve warm.

Haman Pockets Energy 156kcal/653kJ; Protein 2.8g; Carbohydrate 18.7g, of which sugars 9.1g; Fat 8.3g, of which saturates 3.6g; Cholesterol 52mg; Calcium 46mg; Fibre 0.7g; Sodium 42mg.

Onion Focaccia Energy 1508kcal/6362kJ; Protein 32.1g; Carbohydrate 264.6g, of which sugars 6.7g; Fat 42.9g, of which saturates 6.2g; Cholesterol 0mg; Calcium 481mg; Fibre 10.9g; Sodium 2959mg.

Tomato & Prosciutto Pizza

This combination of fresh plum tomatoes, sun-dried tomatoes, garlic and prosciutto with three cheeses is truly delightful.

Makes 1

140ml/5fl oz/⅝ cup water
15ml/1 tbsp extra virgin olive oil
225g/8oz/2 cups unbleached white bread flour
5ml/1 tsp salt
2.5ml/½ tsp sugar
2.5ml/½ tsp easy-blend (rapid-rise) dried yeast

For the filling

45ml/3 tbsp sun-dried tomato paste
150g/5½oz mozzarella cheese, sliced
4 fresh plum tomatoes, about 400g/14oz, roughly chopped
1 small yellow (bell) pepper, halved, seeded and cut into thin strips
50g/2oz prosciutto, torn into pieces
8 fresh basil leaves
4 large garlic cloves, halved
50g/2oz feta cheese, crumbled
30ml/2 tbsp extra virgin olive oil
30ml/2 tbsp freshly grated Parmesan cheese
salt and ground black pepper

1 Pour the water and olive oil into the bread machine pan. Sprinkle over the flour. Add the salt in one corner of the bread pan and the sugar in another corner. Make a small well in the flour, then add the yeast. Set the bread machine to the basic or pizza dough setting. Press Start. Lightly oil a baking sheet.

2 When the dough cycle has finished, remove the dough from the machine and knock back (punch down) gently. Preheat the oven to 220°C/425°F/Gas 7.

3 Roll out the pizza dough into one 30cm/12in rounds. Place on the baking sheet. Spread the sun-dried tomato paste over the pizza base and arrange two-thirds of the mozzarella slices on top. Sprinkle with the chopped tomatoes, pepper strips, prosciutto, whole basil leaves, garlic, remaining mozzarella and feta. Drizzle over the olive oil and sprinkle with the Parmesan. Season with salt and pepper. Bake the pizza for 15–20 minutes, or until golden and sizzling. Serve immediately.

Pissaladière

This French version of an Italian pizza is typical of Niçoise dishes, with anchovies and olives providing the distinctive flavour typical of the region.

Makes 1

100ml/3½fl oz/7 tbsp water
1 egg
225g/8oz/2 cups unbleached white bread flour
5ml/1 tsp salt
25g/1oz/2 tbsp butter
5ml/1 tsp easy-blend (rapid-rise) dried yeast

For the filling

60ml/4 tbsp olive oil
575g/1¼lb onions, thinly sliced
15ml/1 tbsp Dijon mustard
3–4 tomatoes, about 280g/10oz, peeled and sliced
10ml/2 tsp chopped fresh basil
12 drained canned anchovies
12 black olives
salt and ground black pepper

1 Pour the water and egg into the machine pan. Sprinkle over the white bread flour, covering the water and the egg. Add the salt in one corner of the pan and the butter in another corner. Make a well in the flour and add the yeast. Set the bread machine to the basic or pizza dough setting. Press Start.

2 Make the filling. Heat the olive oil in a large frying pan and cook the onions over low heat for about 20 minutes, until very soft. Set aside to cool. Lightly oil a 27 × 20cm/11 × 8in Swiss roll tin (jelly roll pan) that is about 1cm/½in deep.

3 When the dough cycle has finished, remove the dough from the machine and knock back (punch down) gently, then roll it out to a rectangle measuring about 30 × 23cm/12 × 9in. Place in the prepared tin, and press so it covers the base and sides.

4 Spread the mustard over the dough. Arrange the tomato slices on top. Season the onions with salt, pepper and basil and spread the mixture over the tomatoes. Arrange the anchovies in a lattice and dot with the olives. Cover with oiled clear film (plastic wrap) and leave to rise for 10–15 minutes. Preheat the oven to 200°C/400°F/Gas 6. Bake the pissaladière for 25–30 minutes, or until the base is cooked and golden.

Tomato and Prosciutto Pizza per pizza Energy 1928kcal/8090kJ; Protein 84.5g; Carbohydrate 208.1g, of which sugars 36g; Fat 89.9g, of which saturates 39.8g; Cholesterol 181mg; Calcium 1467mg; Fibre 15g; Sodium 4362mg.

Pissaladière Energy 431kcal/1797kJ; Protein 9.9g; Carbohydrate 51.6g, of which sugars 10g; Fat 21.7g, of which saturates 3.1g; Cholesterol 8mg; Calcium 138mg; Fibre 3.8g; Sodium 825mg.

Sicilian Sfincione

Sfincione is the Sicilian equivalent of pizza. The Sicilians insist they were making these tasty snacks long before pizzas were made in mainland Italy.

Makes 4

200ml/7fl oz/⅞ cup water
30ml/2 tbsp extra virgin olive oil
350g/12oz/3 cups unbleached white bread flour
7.5ml/1½ tsp salt
2.5ml/½ tsp sugar
5ml/1 tsp easy-blend (rapid-rise) dried yeast

For the topping

6 tomatoes
2 garlic cloves, chopped
45ml/3 tbsp olive oil
15ml/1 tbsp sunflower oil
2 onions, chopped
8 pitted black olives, chopped
10ml/2 tsp dried oregano
90ml/6 tbsp grated Pecorino cheese
salt and ground black pepper
15ml/1 tbsp sugar
25g/1oz/2 tbsp butter
7.5ml/1¼ tsp easy-blend (rapid-rise) dried yeast

1 Pour the water and oil into the bread pan. Sprinkle over the flour, covering the liquid. Add the salt and sugar in different corners of the pan. Make a well in the centre of the flour; add the yeast. Set the bread machine to the basic or pizza dough setting. Press Start. Then lightly oil two baking sheets.

2 Peel and chop the tomatoes. Put in a bowl, add the garlic and 15ml/1 tbsp of the olive oil and mix. Heat the sunflower oil in a small pan and fry the onions until softened. Set aside to cool.

3 When the dough cycle has finished, remove the dough from the machine and knock back (punch down) gently and divide into four pieces. Roll each piece of dough out to a round, each about 15–18cm/6–7in in diameter. Space the rounds well apart on the prepared baking sheets, then push up the dough edges on each to make a thin rim. Cover and leave to rise for 10 minutes. Meanwhile, preheat the oven to 220°C/425°F/Gas 7.

4 Sprinkle the topping over the bases, ending with the Pecorino. Season, then drizzle with the remaining olive oil. Bake for 15–20 minutes or until the base of each sfincione is cooked.

Calzone

Calzone is an enclosed pizza, with the filling inside. It originates from Naples, and was made from a rectangular piece of dough.

Makes 2

130ml/4½fl oz/½ cup water
30ml/2 tbsp extra virgin olive oil, plus extra for brushing
225g/8oz/2 cups unbleached white bread flour
5ml/1 tsp salt
2.5ml/½ tsp sugar
5ml/1 tsp easy-blend (rapid-rise) dried yeast

For the filling

75g/3oz salami, in one piece
50g/2oz/½ cup drained sun-dried tomatoes in olive oil, chopped
100g/4oz/⅔ cup mozzarella cheese, cut into small cubes
50g/2oz/⅔ cup freshly grated Parmesan cheese
50g/2oz Gorgonzola cheese, cubed
75g/3oz/scant ½ cup ricotta cheese
30ml/2 tbsp chopped fresh basil
2 egg yolks
salt and ground black pepper

1 Pour the water and olive oil into the bread pan. Sprinkle over the white bread flour, ensuring that it covers the liquid. Add the salt and sugar in separate corners of the bread pan. Make a well in the centre of the flour and add the yeast. Set the bread machine to the basic or pizza dough setting. Press Start.

2 To make the topping, cut the salami into 5mm/¼in dice. Put the dice in a bowl and add the sun-dried tomatoes, the cheeses, basil and egg yolks. Mix well and season.

3 When the cycle has finished, knock back (punch down) gently then divide the dough into two equal pieces. Roll each piece of dough into a flat round, about 5mm/¼in thick.

4 Preheat the oven to 220°C/425°F/Gas 7. Divide the filling between the two pieces of dough, placing it on one half only, in each case. Leave a 1.5cm/½in border of the dough all round. Dampen the edges of each dough round with water, fold the remaining dough over the filling and then seal with your fingers. Place on an oiled baking sheet, brush with olive oil and bake for 20 minutes, or until golden and well risen.

Sicilian Sfincione Energy 610kcal/2562kJ; Protein 19.1g; Carbohydrate 79.7g, of which sugars 10.7g; Fat 26.2g, of which saturates 7.3g; Cholesterol 23mg; Calcium 429mg; Fibre 5.3g; Sodium 1138mg.

Calzone Energy 625kcal/2626kJ; Protein 22.5g; Carbohydrate 75.1g, of which sugars 7.3g; Fat 28.2g, of which saturates 9.8g; Cholesterol 39mg; Calcium 305mg; Fibre 4g; Sodium 1053mg.

Wholemeal Baps

There's nothing nicer than the aroma of fresh bread. The wholemeal flour adds extra flavour to these soft rolls.

Makes 10

140ml/5fl oz/scant ⅔ cup milk
140ml/5fl oz/scant ⅔ cup water
225g/8oz/2 cups stoneground wholemeal (whole-wheat) bread flour, plus extra for dusting
225g/8oz/2 cups unbleached white bread flour
7.5ml/1½ tsp salt
10ml/2 tsp caster (superfine) sugar
5ml/1 tsp easy-blend (rapid-rise) dried yeast
milk, for glazing

1 Pour the milk and water into the pan. Reverse the order in which you add the wet and dry ingredients if necessary. Sprinkle over the flours, covering the liquid. Add the salt and sugar in separate corners. Make a well in the centre of the flour and add the yeast. Set the bread machine to the dough setting; use basic dough setting (if available). Press Start.

2 When the dough cycle has finished, remove the dough and place it on a lightly floured surface. Knock back (punch down) gently, then divide it into ten pieces and cover with lightly oiled clear film (plastic wrap).

3 Take one piece of dough, leaving the rest covered, and cup your hands around it to shape it into a ball. Place it on the lightly floured surface and roll it into a flat oval measuring 10 × 7.5cm/4 × 3in. Repeat with the remaining dough so that you have ten flat oval dough pieces. Lightly oil two baking sheets.

4 Place the baps on the prepared baking sheets. Cover with oiled clear film and leave to rise in a warm place for about 30 minutes, or until the baps are almost doubled in size. Meanwhile, preheat the oven to 200°C/400°F/Gas 6.

5 Press each bap in the centre to help disperse any large air bubbles. Brush with milk and dust lightly with wholemeal flour. Bake for 15–20 minutes, or until the baps are lightly browned.

Parker House Rolls

These stylish rolls were first made in a hotel in Boston, after which they are named.

Makes 10

180ml/6½fl oz/generous ¾ cup milk
1 egg
450g/1lb/4 cups unbleached white bread flour
10ml/2 tsp caster (superfine) sugar
7.5ml/1½ tsp salt
75g/3oz/6 tbsp butter, melted
5ml/1 tsp easy-blend (rapid-rise) dried yeast

1 Pour the milk and egg into the bread machine pan. Sprinkle over the flour, ensuring that it covers the liquid. Add the sugar, salt and 25g/1oz/2 tbsp of the melted butter, placing them in separate corners of the bread pan. Make a small indent in the centre of the flour (but do not go down as far as the liquid underneath) and add the yeast. Set the machine to the basic dough setting. Press Start. Lightly oil two baking sheets.

2 When the dough cycle has finished, remove the dough from the machine, place it on a lightly floured surface and knock back (punch down) gently, then roll out to a 1cm/½in thickness.

3 Use a 7.5cm/3in cookie cutter to make ten rounds, then use a small rolling pin to roll or flatten each across the centre in one direction, to create a valley about 5mm/¼in thick.

4 Brush with a little remaining melted butter to within 1cm/½in of the edge. Fold over, ensuring the top piece of dough overlaps the bottom. Press down lightly on the folded edge.

5 Place the rolls on the prepared baking sheets, just overlapping, brush them with more melted butter and cover with oiled clear film (plastic wrap). Leave in a warm place for 30 minutes, until doubled in size.

6 Preheat the oven to 200°C/400°F/Gas 6. Bake the rolls for 15–18 minutes, or until they are golden. Brush the hot rolls with the last of the melted butter and transfer them to a wire rack to cool.

Wholemeal Baps Energy 157kcal/667kJ; Protein 5.4g; Carbohydrate 33.6g, of which sugars 2.6g; Fat 1g, of which saturates 0.3g; Cholesterol 1mg; Calcium 58mg; Fibre 2.7g; Sodium 304mg.

Parker House Rolls Energy 221kcal/932kJ; Protein 4.9g; Carbohydrate 36.9g, of which sugars 2.6g; Fat 7g, of which saturates 4.3g; Cholesterol 18mg; Calcium 86mg; Fibre 1.4g; Sodium 362mg.

Bridge Rolls

Milk and egg flavour these small soft-textured finger rolls. Use them for canapés.

Makes 12

1 egg
100ml/3½fl oz/7 tbsp milk
225g/8oz/2 cups unbleached white bread flour
5ml/1 tsp salt
2.5ml/½ tsp caster (superfine) sugar
50g/2oz/¼ cup butter
5ml/1 tsp easy-blend (rapid-rise) dried yeast
30ml/2 tbsp milk, for glazing (optional)

1 Pour the egg and milk into the bread pan. If necessary for your machine, place the dry ingredients in the pan before the liquid. Sprinkle over the flour, ensuring that it covers the liquid.

2 Add the salt, sugar and butter, placing them in separate corners of the bread machine pan. Then make a small indent in the centre of the flour (but do not go down as far as the liquid) and add the yeast. Set the bread machine to the basic dough setting. Press Start. Lightly oil two baking sheets.

3 When the dough cycle has finished, remove the dough from the machine and place it on a lightly floured surface. Knock back (punch down) gently, then divide it into 12 pieces and cover with a piece of oiled clear film (plastic wrap).

4 Take one piece of dough, leaving the rest covered, and shape it on the floured surface into a tapered long roll. Repeat with the remaining dough until you have 12 evenly shaped rolls.

5 Place six rolls in a row, keeping them fairly close to each other, on each baking sheet. Cover with oiled clear film and leave in a warm place for about 30 minutes, or until the rolls have doubled in size and are touching each other. Meanwhile, preheat the oven to 220°C/425°F/Gas 7.

6 Brush the bridge rolls with milk, if you like, and bake them for 15–18 minutes, or until lightly browned. Transfer the batch to a wire rack to cool, then separate into rolls.

Partybrot

These are traditional Swiss-German rolls.

Makes 19

For the milk rolls
145ml/5fl oz/scant ⅔ cup milk
225g/8oz/2 cups unbleached white bread flour
7.5ml/1½ tsp sugar
5ml/1 tsp salt
15g/½oz/1 tbsp butter
2.5ml/½ tsp easy-blend (rapid-rise) dried yeast

For the wholemeal rolls
175ml/6fl oz/¾ cup water
175g/6oz/1½ cups wholemeal (whole-wheat) bread flour
75g/3oz/¾ cup unbleached white bread flour
7.5ml/1½ tsp sugar
5ml/1 tsp salt
25g/1oz/2 tbsp butter
2.5ml/½ tsp easy-blend (rapid-rise) dried yeast

For the topping
1 egg yolk, mixed with 15ml/1 tbsp cold water
15ml/1 tbsp rolled oats
15ml/1 tbsp poppy seeds

1 For the milk rolls, pour the milk into the bread pan. Sprinkle the flour. Add the sugar, salt and butter, placing them in separate corners of the pan. Make a small indent in the flour and add the yeast. Set to the basic dough setting. Press Start.

2 When the dough cycle has finished, transfer to an oiled mixing bowl. Cover and chill while you make the wholemeal dough. Follow the instructions for the milk rolls but use water. Remove the milk roll dough from the refrigerator 20 minutes before the end of the wholemeal dough cycle.

3 When the wholemeal dough is ready, knock it back (punch down). Do the same with the milk roll dough. Divide the milk roll dough into nine balls and the wholemeal dough into ten. Alternate 12 balls around the outer edge of an oiled 25cm/10in springform cake tin (pan). Add an inner circle with six balls and place the last ball in the centre. Cover for 30–45 minutes.

4 Brush the wholemeal rolls with the egg yolk and water glaze. Sprinkle with rolled oats. Glaze the white rolls and sprinkle with poppy seeds. Bake for 35–40 minutes at 200°C/400°F/Gas 6.

Bridge Rolls Energy 113kcal/476kJ; Protein 2.6g; Carbohydrate 17.2g, of which sugars 2.9g; Fat 4.3g, of which saturates 2.5g; Cholesterol 26mg; Calcium 40mg; Fibre 0.6g; Sodium 42mg.

Partybrot Energy 104kcal/441kJ; Protein 2.9g; Carbohydrate 19.4g, of which sugars 1.7g; Fat 2.2g, of which saturates 1.3g; Cholesterol 5mg; Calcium 33mg; Fibre 1.2g; Sodium 228mg.

Wholemeal & Rye Pistolets

Unless your bread maker has a setting for wholemeal dough, it is worth the extra effort of the double rising.

Makes 12

300ml/½ pint/1¼ cups water
280g/10oz/2½ cups wholemeal (whole-wheat) bread flour
50g/2oz/½ cup unbleached white bread flour, plus extra for dusting
115g/4oz/1 cup rye flour
30ml/2 tbsp skimmed milk powder (non fat dry milk)
10ml/2 tsp salt
10ml/2 tsp caster (superfine) sugar
25g/1oz/2 tbsp butter
7.5ml/1½ tsp easy-blend (rapid-rise) dried yeast

For the glaze
5ml/1 tsp salt
15ml/1 tbsp water

1 Pour the water into the bread pan and sprinkle over all three types of flour, covering the water completely. Add the skimmed milk powder. Then add the salt, sugar and buttein separate corners of the pan. Make a small indent in the centre of the flour and add the dried yeast.

2 Set the machine to the dough setting; use wholewheat dough setting (if available), otherwise repeat the programme to allow sufficient rising time. Start. Lightly oil two baking sheets.

3 When the dough cycle has finished, remove the dough and place it on a floured surface Knock back (punch down) gently, then divide it into 12. Cover with oiled clear film (plastic wrap). Shape each piece into a ball and roll into an oval. Place the rolls on the baking sheets. Cover with oiled clear film and leave in a warm place for about 30–45 minutes, or until almost doubled in size. Preheat the oven to 220°C/425°F/Gas 7.

4 Mix the salt and water for the glaze and brush over the rolls. Dust the tops with flour. Using the oiled handle of a wooden spoon held horizontally, split each roll almost in half, along its length. Replace the clear film and leave for 10 minutes. Bake the rolls for 15–20 minutes, until the bases sound hollow when tapped. Turn out on to a wire rack to cool.

Mixed-grain Onion Rolls

These crunchy rolls, flavoured with golden onions, are perfect for sandwiches or with soup.

Makes 12

50g/2oz/¼ cup butter
1 large onion, finely chopped
280ml/10fl oz/1¼ cups water
280g/10oz/2½ cups unbleached white bread flour
115g/4oz/1 cup Granary (whole-wheat) bread flour
25g/1oz/¼ cup oat bran
10ml/2 tsp salt
10ml/2 tsp clear honey
7.5ml/1½ tsp easy-blend (rapid-rise) dried yeast
cornmeal, for dusting
30ml/2 tbsp millet grain
15ml/1 tbsp coarse oatmeal
15ml/1 tbsp sunflower seeds

1 Melt half the butter in a frying pan. Add the chopped onions and sauté for 8–10 minutes, or until softened. Set aside to cool.

2 Pour the water into the machine pan. Sprinkle over the flours and oat bran, covering the water. Add the salt, honey and remaining butter, placing them in separate corners of the bread pan. Make a well in the flour, and add the yeast. Set the bread machine to the basic raisin dough setting. Press Start. Lightly oil two baking sheets and sprinkle them with cornmeal.

3 Add the millet grain, coarse oatmeal, sunflower seeds and cooked onion when the machine beeps or 5 minutes before the end of the kneading cycle. When the dough cycle has finished, remove the dough from the bread machine and knock the dough back (punch down), then divide into 12 balls.

4 Flatten the balls slightly with the palm of your hand and place the rolls on the prepared baking sheets and dust them with more cornmeal. Cover with oiled clear film (plastic wrap) and leave them for 30–45 minutes. Meanwhile, preheat the oven to 200°C/400°F/Gas 6.

5 Using a pair of lightly floured sharp scissors snip each roll in five places, cutting inwards from the edge, almost to the centre. Bake for 18–20 minutes, or until the rolls are golden. Turn them out on to a wire rack to cool.

Wholemeal and Rye Pistolets Energy 142kcal/601kJ; Protein 4.5g; Carbohydrate 26.8g, of which sugars 1.9g; Fat 2.6g, of which saturates 1.3g; Cholesterol 5mg; Calcium 31mg; Fibre 3.4g; Sodium 186mg.

Mixed-grain Onion Rolls Energy 178kcal/750kJ; Protein 4.8g; Carbohydrate 28.7g, of which sugars 3.2g; Fat 5.7g, of which saturates 2.5g; Cholesterol 10mg; Calcium 51mg; Fibre 3g; Sodium 362mg.

Cashew & Olive Scrolls

These attractively shaped rolls have a crunchy texture, and ooze with the combined flavours of olives and fresh herbs.

Makes 12

140ml/5fl oz/⅝ cup milk
120ml/4fl oz/½ cup water
30ml/2 tbsp extra virgin olive oil
450g/1lb/4 cups unbleached white bread flour
5ml/1 tsp salt
2.5ml/½ tsp caster (superfine) sugar
7.5ml/1½ tsp easy-blend (rapid-rise) dried yeast
5ml/1 tsp finely chopped fresh rosemary or thyme
50g/2oz/½ cup salted cashew nuts, finely chopped
50g/2oz/½ cup pitted green olives, finely chopped
45ml/3 tbsp freshly grated Parmesan cheese, for sprinkling

1 Pour the milk, water and oil into the pan. Sprinkle over the flour, ensuring that it covers the liquid. Add the salt and sugar, placing them in separate corners of the bread pan. Make a small indent in the centre of the flour (but not down as far as the liquid) and add the yeast.

2 Set the machine to the dough setting; use basic raisin dough setting (if available). Press Start. Add the herbs, cashew nuts and olives when the machine beeps, or five minutes before the end of the kneading period. Lightly oil two baking sheets.

3 When the dough cycle has finished, remove it from the machine and place it on a lightly floured surface. Knock it back gently, then divide into 12 pieces of equal size and cover with oiled clear film.

4 Take one piece, leaving the rest covered, and roll into a rope about 23cm/9in long, tapering the ends. Shape this into an 'S' shape. Repeat with the reamining 11 rolls. Leave to rise in a warm place for 30 minues, until doubled in size.

5 Preheat the oven to 200°C/400°F/Gas 6. Sprinkle the rolls with Parmesan and bake for 18–20 minutes, or until risen and golden. Cool on a wire rack.

Ricotta & Oregano Knots

Ricotta adds a wonderful moistness to these rolls. They are best served warm.

Makes 12

60ml/4 tbsp ricotta cheese
225ml/8fl oz/scant 1 cup water
450g/1lb/4 cups unbleached white bread flour
45ml/3 tbsp skimmed milk powder (non fat dry milk)
10ml/2 tsp dried oregano
5ml/1 tsp salt
10ml/2 tsp caster (superfine) sugar
25g/1oz/2 tbsp butter
5ml/1 tsp easy-blend (rapid-rise) dried yeast

For the topping
1 egg yolk
15ml/1 tbsp water
freshly ground black pepper

1 Spoon the cheese into the bread machine pan and add the water. (Reverse the order in which you add the liquid and dry ingredients if the instructions for your machine specify this.)

2 Sprinkle over the flour to cover the cheese and water. Add the milk powder and oregano. Place the salt, sugar and butter in separate corners of the pan. Make a well in the flour; add the yeast. Set the machine to the basic dough setting. Start.

3 Oil two baking sheets. When the dough cycle has finished, remove the dough and place it on a lightly floured surface. Knock back (punch down) gently, then divide it into 12 pieces and cover these with oiled clear film (plastic wrap).

4 Roll each piece of dough on a floured surface into a rope 25cm/10in long. Lift one end over the other to make a loop. Push the end through the hole in the loop to make a knot.

5 Place the knots on the baking sheets, cover them with oiled clear film and leave in a warm place for about 30 minutes, or until doubled in size. Preheat the oven to 220°C/425°F/Gas 7.

6 Mix the egg yolk and water for the topping and brush over the rolls. Sprinkle some with pepper and leave the rest plain. Bake for about 15–18 minutes, or until golden brown.

Cashew and Olive Scrolls Energy 196kcal/828kJ; Protein 6.3g; Carbohydrate 30.5g, of which sugars 1.3g; Fat 6.3g, of which saturates 1.7g; Cholesterol 4mg; Calcium 116mg; Fibre 1.4g; Sodium 153mg.
Ricotta and Oregano Knots Energy 160kcal/678kJ; Protein 4.3g; Carbohydrate 30.7g, of which sugars 2.1g; Fat 3.1g, of which saturates 1.8g; Cholesterol 7mg; Calcium 65mg; Fibre 1.2g; Sodium 186mg.

Chinese-style Chicken Buns

These sesame-seeded buns are perfect for picnics.

Makes 8

140ml/5fl oz/⅝ cup semi-skimmed (low-fat) milk
225g/8oz/2 cups unbleached white bread flour
2.5ml/½ tsp salt
2.5ml/½ tsp sugar
15g/½oz/1 tbsp butter
5ml/1 tsp easy-blend (rapid-rise) dried yeast

For the filling

30ml/2 tbsp sunflower oil
5cm/2in piece of fresh root ginger, grated
30ml/2 tbsp soy sauce
15ml/1 tbsp clear honey
225g/8oz chicken breast fillets, chopped
3 spring onions (scallions), chopped
15ml/1 tbsp chopped fresh coriander (cilantro)
salt and ground black pepper

For the topping

1 egg yolk
15ml/1 tbsp water
sesame seeds

1 Pour the milk into the bread machine pan. Sprinkle over the flour, covering the milk. Add the salt, sugar and butter in separate corners of the bread pan. Make a well in the flour and add the yeast. Set to the basic dough setting. Press Start.

2 Make the filling. Mix half the oil with the ginger, soy sauce and honey. Add the chicken and toss to coat. Heat a frying pan and add the remaining oil. Add the chicken mixture and stir-fry over medium heat for 5–6 minutes. Add the spring onions and cook until the chicken is cooked. Stir in the coriander and seasoning.

3 When the dough cycle has finished, remove the dough and knock back (punch down) gently. Divide it into eight 13cm/5in rounds. Spoon the filling to the centre of each round.

4 Beat the egg yolk and water in a bowl and brush a little around the edge of each round. Bring up the sides to cover the filling and seal. Place the buns on a greased baking sheet. Cover and leave for about 30 minutes. Brush the tops of the buns with the remaining egg glaze and sprinkle with the sesame seeds. Bake for about 18–20 minutes at 200°C/400°F/Gas 6.

Spanish Picos

These small knotted bread shapes, dusted with salt and sesame seeds, are popular in Spain, where they are often eaten with drinks, but they can also be served with an appetizer or soup.

Makes 70

200ml/7fl oz/scant 1 cup water
45ml/3 tbsp extra virgin olive oil
350g/12½oz/3 cups unbleached white bread flour
5ml/1 tsp salt
2.5ml/½ tsp sugar
5ml/1 tsp easy-blend (rapid-rise) dried yeast

For the topping

30ml/2 tbsp water
15ml/1 tbsp sea salt
15ml/1 tbsp sesame seeds

1 Pour the water and oil into the pan and sprinkle over the flour, ensuring that it covers the liquid. (If necessary, reverse the order in which you add the liquid and dry ingredients.) Add the salt and sugar, in separate corners of the pan. Make a small indent in the centre of the flour and add the yeast.

2 Set the machine to the dough setting, using the basic dough setting if available, and start. Lightly oil two baking sheets.

3 When the cycle has finished, place the dough on a floured surface. Knock back (punch down) gently, then roll it out to a rectangle measuring 30 × 23cm/12 × 9in. Cut lengthways into three strips, then cut each strip into 2.5cm/1in wide ribbons.

4 Preheat the oven to 200°C/400°F/Gas 6. Tie each ribbon into a loose knot and space well apart on the prepared baking sheets. Cover with oiled clear film (plastic wrap) and leave in a warm place for 10–15 minutes to rise. Leave the picos plain, or brush with water and sprinkle with salt or sesame seeds. Bake for 10–15 minutes, or until golden.

Cook's Tip

Make these tasty nibbles up to a day in advance. Re-heat in a medium oven for a few minutes, to refresh.

Chinese-style Chicken Buns per bun Energy 168kcal/709kJ; Protein 9.8g; Carbohydrate 25g, of which sugars 3.2g; Fat 3.9g, of which saturates 1.6g; Cholesterol 17mg; Calcium 70mg; Fibre 1g; Sodium 383mg.

Spanish Picos per pico Energy 23kcal/95kJ; Protein 0.5g; Carbohydrate 4.2g, of which sugars 0.1g; Fat 0.5g, of which saturates 0.1g; Cholesterol 0mg; Calcium 8mg; Fibre 0.2g; Sodium 28mg.

Saffron Braids

Delicately scented and coloured with saffron, these deep-fried braids are favourite coffee-time treats in Scandinavia.

Makes 8

200ml/7fl oz/scant 1 cup milk
3.5ml/¾ tsp saffron threads
2 eggs
450g/1lb/4 cups unbleached white bread flour
2.5ml/½ tsp salt
50g/2oz/¼ cup caster (superfine) sugar, plus extra for sprinkling
50g/2oz/¼ cup butter
5ml/1 tsp easy-blend (rapid-rise) dried yeast
sunflower oil, for deep-frying

1 Heat the milk until hot but not boiling. Pour over the saffron in a bowl. Leave for 45 minutes or until cold.

2 Pour the saffron milk into the bread machine pan, then add the eggs. Sprinkle over the flour, ensuring that it covers the saffron milk completely. Add the salt, sugar and butter, placing them in separate corners of the bread machine pan. Make a small indent in the centre of the flour and add the yeast. Set the bread machine to the basic dough setting. Press Start.

3 When the cycle has finished, remove the dough from the bread machine and place it on a lightly floured surface. Knock back (punch down) gently, then divide the dough into eight pieces. Cover with a piece of oiled clear film (plastic wrap).

4 Take one piece of dough and divide into three. Roll out each small piece into a 20cm/8in rope. Place the ropes next to each other, pinch the ends together and braid them from left to right. When you reach the other end, press the ends together and tuck them under. Repeat with the remaining dough. Place the braids on oiled baking sheets. Cover and set aside for 30–45 minutes.

5 Preheat the oil for deep-frying to 180°C/360°F or until a cube of dried bread turns golden brown in 30–60 seconds. Fry the saffron braids, two at a time, for 4–5 minutes, until golden in colour. Drain on kitchen paper and sprinkle with caster sugar.

Wholemeal English Muffins

After a long walk on a wintry afternoon, come home to warm muffins that are carefully torn apart and spread thickly with butter.

Makes 9

350ml/12fl oz/1½ cups milk
225g/8oz/2 cups unbleached white bread flour
225g/8oz/2 cups stoneground wholemeal (whole-wheat) bread flour
5ml/1 tsp caster (superfine) sugar
7.5ml/1½ tsp salt
15g/½oz/1 tbsp butter
7.5ml/1½ tsp easy-blend (rapid-rise) dried yeast
rice flour or fine semolina, for dusting

1 Pour the milk into the bread machine pan. Sprinkle over each type of flour in turn, making sure that the milk is completely covered. Add the caster sugar, salt and butter, placing each of them in separate corners of the bread pan. Then make a small indent in the centre of the flour (but do not go down as far as the liquid underneath) and add the easy-blend dried yeast.

2 Set the machine to the basic dough setting. Press Start. Sprinkle a baking sheet with rice flour or semolina.

3 When the dough cycle has finished, place the dough on a floured surface. Knock it back (punch it down) gently. Roll out the dough until it is about 1cm/½in thick.

3 Using a floured 7.5cm/3in plain cookie cutter, cut out nine muffins. If you like, you can re-roll the trimmings, knead them together and let the dough rest for a few minutes before rolling it out again and cutting out an extra muffin or two.

4 Place the muffins on the baking sheet. Dust with rice flour or semolina. Cover with oiled clear film (plastic wrap) and leave in a warm place for 20 minutes, or until almost doubled in size.

5 Heat a griddle over medium heat. You should not need any oil if the griddle is well seasoned; if not, add the merest trace of oil. Cook the muffins slowly, three at a time, for about 7 minutes on each side. Serve warm.

Saffron Braids Energy 379kcal/1591kJ; Protein 7.7g; Carbohydrate 51.5g, of which sugars 8.6g; Fat 17.3g, of which saturates 5.3g; Cholesterol 63mg; Calcium 120mg; Fibre 1.7g; Sodium 203mg.

Wholemeal English Muffins Energy 235kcal/997kJ; Protein 7.4g; Carbohydrate 48.2g, of which sugars 3.2g; Fat 2.8g, of which saturates 0.7g; Cholesterol 2mg; Calcium 121mg; Fibre 2.5g; Sodium 351mg.

Brioche Loaf

This rich buttery bread can be eaten with both sweet and savoury foods.

Makes 1

Small

150ml/5fl oz/$\frac{2}{3}$ cup milk
1 egg
75g/3oz/6 tbsp melted butter
375g/13oz/3$\frac{1}{4}$ cups unbleached white bread flour
2.5ml/$\frac{1}{2}$ tsp salt
25g/1oz/2 tbsp sugar
7.5ml/1$\frac{1}{2}$ tsp easy-blend (rapid-rise) dried yeast
15ml/1 tbsp milk, for glazing

Medium

200ml/7fl oz/$\frac{7}{8}$ cup milk
2 eggs
115g/4oz/$\frac{1}{2}$ cup melted butter
500g/1lb 2oz/4$\frac{1}{2}$ cups unbleached white bread flour
5ml/1 tsp salt
40g/1$\frac{1}{2}$oz/3 tbsp sugar
7.5ml/1$\frac{1}{2}$ tsp easy-blend (rapid-rise) dried yeast
15ml/1 tbsp milk, for glazing

1 Pour the milk into the bread machine pan.

2 Add the egg(s) and melted butter. If the instructions for your machine specify that the yeast is to be placed in first, reverse the order in which you add the liquid and the dry ingredients.

3 Sprinkle over the flour, ensuring that it covers the water. Add the salt and sugar in separate corners of the bread pan.

4 Make a small indent in the centre of the flour (but not down as far as the liquid) and add the yeast.

5 Set the bread machine to the sweet/sweet bread or (if not available) basic setting, light crust. Size: 500g for small, or 750g for medium. Press Start.

6 Just before the bread is ready to cook brush the top of the bread with milk.

7 When the baking cycle has finished. Remove the bread and transfer on to a wire rack to cool.

Easy Peanut Butter Loaf

Peanut butter gives this teabread a distinctive flavour and an interesting texture.

Makes 1

115g/4oz/$\frac{1}{3}$ cup crunchy peanut butter
75g/3oz/scant $\frac{1}{2}$ cup caster (superfine) sugar
1 egg, lightly beaten
175ml/6fl oz/$\frac{3}{4}$ cup milk
300g/11oz/generous 2$\frac{1}{2}$ cups self-raising (self-rising) flour

1 Remove the kneading blade from the bread machine pan, if it is detachable, then line the base of the bread machine pan with baking parchment.

2 Cream the peanut butter and sugar in a bowl together until light and fluffy, then gradually beat in the egg. Add the milk and flour and mix with a wooden spoon.

3 Spoon the mixture into the prepared bread pan and set the machine to the bake/bake only setting.

4 Set the timer, if possible for the recommended time. If, on your bread machine, the minimum time on this setting is for longer than the time here, set the timer and check the loaf after the shortest recommended time. Bake for 55–60 minutes. Use the light bake setting if available.

5 The teabread should be well risen and just firm to the touch. Test by inserting a skewer in the centre of the loaf. It should come out completely clean. If necessary, bake for a few minutes more.

6 Remove the bread pan from the bread machine. Leave to stand for 5 minutes, then turn on to a wire rack to cool.

Cook's Tip

Leave a rough finish on the top of the loaf before baking, to add rustic character to the finished teabread.

Brioche Loaf per loaf Energy 2134kcal/8924kJ; Protein 41.2g; Carbohydrate 227g, of which sugars 25.9g; Fat 124.6g, of which saturates 75.8g; Cholesterol 737mg; Calcium 518mg; Fibre 8.2g; Sodium 1923mg.

Easy Peanut Butter Loaf per loaf Energy 1527kcal/6439kJ; Protein 45.8g; Carbohydrate 238.4g, of which sugars 81.2g; Fat 48.8g, of which saturates 11.8g; Cholesterol 196mg; Calcium 497mg; Fibre 10.3g; Sodium 400mg.

Mango & Banana Bread

Tropical fruit juice, fresh banana and dried mango give this light-textured loaf its Caribbean flavour.

Makes 1

60ml/2fl oz/¼ cup orange and mango juice
200ml/7fl oz/⅞ cup buttermilk
175g/6oz/1 large banana, peeled and mashed
45ml/3 tbsp clear honey
500g/1lb 2oz/4½ cups unbleached white bread flour
5ml/1 tsp salt
40g/1½oz/3 tbsp butter
5ml/1 tsp easy-blend (rapid-rise) dried yeast
40g/1½oz/⅓ cup dried mango, chopped

1 Pour the fruit juice and buttermilk into the bread machine pan. Add the mashed banana to the bread pan, with the honey. If necessary for your machine, reverse the order in which you add the liquid and dry ingredients.

2 Sprinkle over the flour, ensuring that it covers all the liquid. Place the salt and butter in separate corners of the bread pan. Make a shallow indent in the centre of the flour and add the yeast.

4 Set the machine to sweet/basic, raisin setting (if available), light crust. Size: 750g for medium.

5 Add the mango pieces to the automatic dispenser, if available. Press Start. If adding them manually, add when the machine beeps during the kneading cycle.

6 Remove the bread at the end of the baking cycle. Turn out on to a wire rack.

Cook's Tip
The small loaf may be cooked before the end of the programme. Check 5–10 minutes before the end, and remove if well browned. Leave to stand for 5 minutes before turning out.

Hazelnut & Fig Bread

This healthy high-fibre bread is flavoured with roasted hazelnuts and dried figs.

Makes 1

280ml/10fl oz/1¼ cups water
7.5ml/1½ tsp lemon juice
350g/12oz/3 cups unbleached white bread flour
100g/3¾oz/scant 1 cup brown bread flour
60ml/4 tbsp toasted wheatgerm
30ml/2 tbsp skimmed milk powder (non fat dry milk)
7.5ml/1½ tsp salt
15ml/1 tbsp sugar
25g/1oz/2 tbsp butter
7.5ml/1½ tsp easy-blend (rapid-rise) dried yeast
40g/1½oz/⅓ cup skinned hazelnuts, roasted and chopped
40g/1½oz/¼ cup ready-to-eat dried figs

1 Pour the water and the lemon juice into the bread machine pan. If the instructions for your machine specify that the yeast is to be placed in the pan first, reverse the order in which you add the liquid and dry ingredients.

2 Sprinkle the white bread flour and the brown bread flour over the water, then the wheatgerm, making sure the water is completely covered.

3 Add the milk powder. Add the salt, sugar and butter in separate corners. Make an indent in the flour; add the yeast. Coarsely chop the figs.

4 Set the bread machine to white/basic, raisin setting (if available), medium crust. Size: 750g for medium. Add the hazelnuts and figs to the automatic dispenser, if available. Press Start. If adding manually, do so when the machine beeps during the kneading cycle, or after the first kneading.

5 Remove the bread from the bread machine pan at the end of the baking cycle and turn out on to a wire rack to allow to cool. Serve sliced.

Mango and Banana Bread per loaf Energy 1859kcal/7880kJ; Protein 44.2g; Carbohydrate 385.3g, of which sugars 88.5g; Fat 26.4g, of which saturates 14.6g; Cholesterol 63mg; Calcium 750mg; Fibre 14.6g; Sodium 2257mg.

Hazelnut and Fig Bread per loaf Energy 1799kcal/7610kJ; Protein 54.1g; Carbohydrate 318.1g, of which sugars 36.9g; Fat 43.4g, of which saturates 14.4g; Cholesterol 52mg; Calcium 793mg; Fibre 44.1g; Sodium 254mg.

Gingerbread

This teatime favourite can be baked easily in your bread machine. Store it in an airtight tin for a couple of days to allow the moist sticky texture to develop.

Makes 1

225g/8oz/2 cups plain (all-purpose) flour
5ml/1 tsp ground ginger
7.5ml/1½ tsp baking powder
2.5ml/½ tsp bicarbonate of soda (baking soda)
2.5ml/½ tsp mixed (apple pie) spice
115g/4oz/½ cup light muscovado (brown) sugar
75g/3oz/6 tbsp butter, cut into pieces
100g/3¾oz/generous ⅓ cup golden (light corn) syrup
50g/2oz black treacle (molasses)
150ml/5fl oz/⅔ cup milk
1 egg, lightly beaten
50g/2oz/⅓ cup drained preserved stem ginger, thinly sliced

1 Remove the kneading blade from the bread pan, if it is detachable, then line the base of the bread machine pan with baking parchment.

2 Sift the flour, ginger, baking powder, bicarbonate of soda and mixed spice together into a large bowl.

3 Place the sugar, butter, syrup and treacle in a pan over low heat until melted.

4 Make a well in the centre of the dry ingredients and pour in the melted mixture. Add the milk, egg and stem ginger and mix together thoroughly.

5 Pour the mixture into the bread pan and set the machine to the bake/bake only setting. Set the timer, if possible, for the recommended time. If, on your machine, the minimum time on this setting is for longer than suggested here, set the timer and check the loaf after the shortest recommended time. Bake the loaf for 50–55 minutes, or until well risen.

6 Remove the bread pan. Leave to stand for 5 minutes, then turn on to a wire rack to cool.

Cranberry & Orange Bread

The distinctive tart flavour of cranberries is intensified when these American fruits are dried. They combine well here with orange rind and pecan nuts.

Makes 1

120ml/4fl oz/½ cup water
120ml/4fl oz/½ cup orange juice
1 egg
500g/1lb 2oz/4½ cups unbleached white bread flour
30ml/2 tbsp skimmed milk powder (non fat dry milk)
50g/2oz/¼ cup caster (superfine) sugar
3.5ml/¾ tsp salt
40g/1½oz/3 tbsp butter
7.5ml/1½ tsp easy-blend (rapid-rise) dried yeast
15ml/1 tbsp grated orange rind
50g/2oz/scant ½ cup dried cranberries
40g/1½oz/3 tbsp pecan nuts, chopped

1 Pour the water, orange juice and egg into the bread machine pan. If the instructions for your machine specify that the yeast is to be placed in the pan first, reverse the order in which you add the liquid and dry ingredients.

2 Sprinkle over the flour, ensuring that it covers the water. Add the milk powder. Place the sugar, salt and butter in separate corners of the bread pan.

3 Make a small indent in the centre of the flour (but not down as far as the liquid). Add the yeast.

4 Set the machine to sweet/basic, raisin setting (if available). Use medium crust, large/750g for medium. Press Start.

5 Add the rind, cranberries and nuts when the machine beeps during the kneading cycle.

6 Remove the bread from the pan at the end of the baking cycle and turn out on to a wire rack.

7 Mix the orange juice and caster sugar in a small pan. Heat, stirring continuously, until all the sugar dissolves, then bring to the boil until syrupy. Brush over the loaf. Leave to cool.

Gingerbread per loaf Energy 1721kcal/7215kJ; Protein 14g; Carbohydrate 222g, of which sugars 221.4g; Fat 92.7g, of which saturates 57g; Cholesterol 401mg; Calcium 1154mg; Fibre 0g; Sodium 1048mg.
Cranberry and Orange Bread per loaf Energy 2004kcal/8475kJ; Protein 42.6g; Carbohydrate 381.3g, of which sugars 95.2g; Fat 44.8g, of which saturates 16.7g; Cholesterol 63mg; Calcium 716mg; Fibre 13.9g; Sodium 1277mg.

Blueberry & Oatmeal Bread

The blueberries add a subtle fruitiness, while the oatmeal contributes texture and a nutty flavour. This is best eaten on the day it is baked.

Makes 1

110ml/scant 4fl oz/scant ½ cup water
120ml/4fl oz/½ cup milk
1 egg
450g/1lb/4 cups unbleached white bread flour, plus 30ml/2 tbsp for coating the blueberries
50g/2oz/½ cup coarse oatmeal
7.5ml/1½ tsp mixed (apple pie) spice
50g/2oz/¼ cup caster (superfine) sugar
3.5ml/¾ tsp salt
40g/1½oz/3 tbsp butter
7.5ml/1½ tsp easy-blend (rapid-rise) dried yeast
75g/3oz/¾ cup blueberries

1 Pour the water, milk and egg into the bread machine pan. If the instructions for your machine specify that the yeast is to be placed in the pan first, reverse the order in which you add the liquid and dry ingredients.

2 Sprinkle over the flour, ensuring it covers the liquid. Add the oatmeal and spice. Add the sugar, salt and butter in separate corners. Make a small indent in the centre of the flour (but not as far down as the liquid) and add the yeast.

3 Set the bread machine to sweet/basic, raisin setting (if available). Use medium crust, large/750g for medium. Press Start. Toss the berries with the extra flour and add when the machine beeps during the kneading cycle.

4 Remove the bread at the end of the baking cycle. Turn out on to a wire rack to cool.

Cook's Tip
Use the light crust setting on the bread machine to avoid a rich, dark crust on this sweet loaf.

Lemon & Macadamia Bread

Originally from Australia, macadamia nuts have a buttery taste that combines well with the tangy flavour of lemon rind and yogurt in this delicious bread.

Makes 1

1 egg
175ml/6fl oz/¾ cup lemon yogurt
115ml/4fl oz/½ cup milk
500g/1lb 2oz/4½ cups unbleached white bread flour
50g/2oz/¼ cup caster (superfine) sugar
3.5ml/¾ tsp salt
40g/1½oz/3 tbsp butter
7.5ml/1½ tsp easy-blend (rapid-rise) dried yeast
40g/1½oz/⅓ cup macadamia nuts, chopped
15ml/1 tbsp grated lemon rind

1 Pour the egg, yogurt and milk into the pan. If necessary, reverse the order of adding the wet and dry ingredients.

2 Sprinkle over the white bread flour, ensuring that it covers the water completely.

3 Add the caster sugar, salt and butter, placing them in separate corners of the bread pan. Make a small indent in the flour (but not down as far as the liquid) and add the yeast.

4 Set the machine to white/basic, raisin setting (if available), medium crust. Size: 750g for medium. Press Start.

5 Add the nuts and lemon rind when the machine beeps during the kneading cycle.

6 Remove the cooked lemon and macadamia bread from the bread pan at the end of the baking cycle. Turn out on to a wire rack to cool.

Cook's Tip
Select the light crust setting if your bread machine tends to produce a rich crust when you make a sweet bread.

Blueberry and Oatmeal Bread per loaf Energy 1549kcal/6551kJ; Protein 43.6g; Carbohydrate 285.1g, of which sugars 13.6g; Fat 34.1g, of which saturates 16.4g; Cholesterol 252mg; Calcium 594mg; Fibre 13.1g; Sodium 1301mg.

Lemon and Macadamia Bread per loaf Energy 2021kcal/8539kJ; Protein 50.9g; Carbohydrate 359.8g, of which sugars 73.8g; Fat 52.1g, of which saturates 19.7g; Cholesterol 256mg; Calcium 850mg; Fibre 12.9g; Sodium 454mg.

Finnish Festive Wreath

This sweet bread is scented with saffron and cardamom.

Makes 1

5ml/1 tsp saffron threads
200ml/7fl oz/⅞ cup milk
2 eggs
500g/1lb 2oz/4½ cups unbleached white bread flour
5ml/1 tsp ground cardamom seeds
2.5ml/½ tsp salt
50g/2oz/¼ cup caster (superfine) sugar
55g/2oz/¼ cup butter, melted
5ml/1 tsp easy-blend (rapid-rise) dried yeast
1 egg yolk, to glaze
15ml/1 tbsp water, to glaze

For the topping
45ml/3 tbsp flaked (sliced) almonds
40g/1½oz/3 tbsp sugar
15ml/1 tbsp rum
15ml/1 tbsp candied lime peel, chopped (optional)

1 Place the saffron threads in a bowl. Heat half the milk and pour it over the saffron and leave to infuse (steep) until the milk is at room temperature. Pour the saffron milk into the bread machine pan, then add the remaining milk and the eggs. Sprinkle over the flour, covering the liquid, then add the cardamom seeds. Add the salt, caster sugar and butter, placing them in separate corners of the bread pan. Make a well in the flour; add the yeast. Set to the basic dough setting. Press Start.

2 When the dough cycle has finished, remove the dough and knock back (punch down) gently. Divide it into three pieces. Roll each piece of dough into a rope, about 65cm/26in long and place them next to each other. Starting from the centre, braid the pieces together, working from left to right. Turn around and repeat the process. Bring the ends of the braid together to form a circular wreath. Place on an oiled baking sheet. Cover and leave for 45–60 minutes, or until almost doubled in size. Preheat the oven to 190°C/375°F/Gas 5.

3 Mix the egg yolk and water in a bowl. In a separate bowl, mix the almonds, sugar, rum and peel for the topping. Brush the glaze over the loaf and sprinkle the topping over it. Bake for 20 minutes, then reduce the oven temperature to 180°C/350°F/Gas 4 and bake for 10–15 minutes more, until golden.

Banana & Pecan Teabread

This moist, light teabread is flavoured with banana, lightly spiced with nutmeg and studded with sultanas and pecan nuts. Weigh the bananas after peeling them – it is important to use the precise quantities given.

Makes 1

100g/3¾oz/7 tbsp butter, softened
175g/6oz/⅞ cup caster (superfine) sugar
2 large eggs, lightly beaten
200g/7oz/1¾ cups self-raising (self-rising) flour, sifted
200g/7oz peeled ripe bananas
85ml/3fl oz/6 tbsp buttermilk
2.5ml/½ tsp baking powder
5ml/1 tsp freshly grated nutmeg
125g/4¼oz/⅔ cup sultanas (golden raisins)
75g/3oz/¾ cup pecan nuts, chopped
30ml/2 tbsp banana or apricot jam, melted
30ml/2 tbsp banana chips

1 Remove the kneading blade from the bread pan, if detachable. Line the base of the pan with baking parchment.

2 Cream the butter and caster sugar in a bowl until fluffy. Gradually beat in the eggs, beating well after each addition, adding a little of the flour if the mixture starts to curdle.

3 Mash the bananas until completely smooth. Beat into the creamed mixture with the buttermilk.

4 Sift the remaining flour and the baking powder into the bowl. Add the nutmeg, sultanas and pecans; beat until smooth.

5 Spoon the mixture into the prepared pan and set the bread machine to the bake/bake only setting. Set the timer, if possible, for the recommended time. If not, check the teabread after the shortest recommended time. Bake the loaf for 50–60 minutes. Use the light crust setting, if available.

6 Remove the pan from the bread machine. Leave it to stand for about 5 minutes, then turn the loaf out on to a wire rack. While the teabread is still warm, brush the top with the melted jam and sprinkle over the banana chips. Cool before serving.

Finnish Festive Wreath Energy 298kcal/1257kJ; Protein 7.6g; Carbohydrate 49.6g, of which sugars 11.3g; Fat 9.1g, of which saturates 3.8g; Cholesterol 52mg; Calcium 116mg; Fibre 1.9g; Sodium 167mg.

Banana and Pecan Teabread per loaf Energy 3277kcal/13745kJ; Protein 52.8g; Carbohydrate 413.7g, of which sugars 239.9g; Fat 168.2g, of which saturates 69.2g; Cholesterol 1263mg; Calcium 1056mg; Fibre 13.1g; Sodium 1701mg.

Maple & Pecan Gluten-free Bread

This delicious teatime bread can be served sliced and buttered, or toasted first. Use other dried fruits and nuts instead of sultanas and pecan nuts, if you like.

Makes 1

170ml/6fl oz/¾ cup milk
180ml/6½fl oz/generous ¾ cup water
2 eggs
45ml/3 tbsp maple syrup
75ml/5 tbsp sunflower oil
5ml/1 tsp cider vinegar
500g/1lb 2oz/4½ cups gluten- and wheat-free white bread flour blend
5ml/1 tsp salt
15ml/1 tbsp sugar
10ml/2 tsp easy-blend (rapid-rise) dried yeast
50g/2oz/⅔ cup pecan nuts, chopped
50g/2oz/⅓ cup sultanas (golden raisins)

1 Pour the milk and water into the bread machine pan. Add the eggs, maple syrup, sunflower oil and vinegar. If the instructions for your machine specify that the yeast is to be placed in the pan first, reverse the order in which you add the liquid and the dry ingredients.

2 Sprinkle over the flour, ensuring that it covers the water. Add the salt and sugar in separate corners of the bread pan. Make a small indent in the centre of the flour (but not down as far as the liquid) and add the yeast.

3 Add the pecan nuts and sultanas, if using the gluten-free setting. If using the basic setting, add them to the automatic dispenser, if available. If adding them manually, add them when the machine beeps during the kneading cycle.

4 Set the bread machine to the gluten-free or white/basic setting, medium crust, if available. Select size: 750g for medium. The weight setting is not available on some gluten-free cycles. Check the amount of gluten-free mix your machine handles. You may need to scrape down the mixture after 5 minutes.

5 Remove the bread at the end of the baking cycle. Turn out on to a wire rack to cool.

Strawberry Teabread

Perfect for a summertime treat, this hazelnut-flavoured teabread is laced with luscious fresh strawberries.

Makes 1

175g/6oz/1½ cups strawberries
150g/5oz/⅔ cup butter, softened
150g/5oz/¾ cup caster (superfine) sugar
2 eggs, beaten
15ml/1 tbsp milk
165g/5½oz/1⅓ cups self-raising (self-rising) flour, sifted
40g/1½oz/⅓ cup ground hazelnuts

1 Remove the kneading blade from the bread machine pan, if it is detachable, then line the base of the pan with baking parchment.

2 Hull the strawberries and chop them roughly. Set them aside. Cream the butter and sugar in a mixing bowl.

3 Gradually beat in the eggs and milk (if you are making the medium cake), beating well after each addition to combine quickly without curdling.

4 Mix the self-raising flour and the ground hazelnuts together and gradually fold into the creamed mixture.

5 Fold in the strawberries and spoon the mixture into the pan. Set the bread machine to the bake/bake only setting. Set the timer, if possible, for the recommended time. If, on your machine, the minimum time on this setting is for longer than the time suggested here, set the timer and check the loaf after the shortest recommended time. Bake the small teabread for 40–45 minutes, medium for 50–55 minutes, or large for 55–60 minutes. Use the light bake setting if available.

6 Test by inserting a skewer in the centre of the teabread. It should come out clean. If necessary, bake the loaf for a few minutes more.

7 Remove the bread pan. Leave the teabread to stand for 5 minutes, then turn out on to a wire rack to cool.

Maple and Pecan Gluten-free Bread per loaf Energy 2400kcal/10108kJ; Protein 53.6g; Carbohydrate 378.5g, of which sugars 73.1g; Fat 85.3g, of which saturates 11.3g; Cholesterol 199mg; Calcium 962mg; Fibre 15.1g; Sodium 2161mg.

Strawberry Teabread per loaf Energy 2119kcal/8862kJ; Protein 31.3g; Carbohydrate 237.4g, of which sugars 130.2g; Fat 122.9g, of which saturates 66.7g; Cholesterol 645mg; Calcium 385mg; Fibre 7.2g; Sodium 1022mg.

Malted Loaf

A malt and sultana loaf makes the perfect breakfast or teatime treat. Serve it sliced with butter.

Makes 1

Medium

280ml/10fl oz/1¼ cups water
25ml/1½ tbsp golden (light corn) syrup
30ml/2 tbsp malt extract
500g/1lb 2oz/4½ cups unbleached white bread flour
30ml/2 tbsp skimmed milk powder (non fat dry milk)
5ml/1 tsp salt
50g/2oz/¼ cup butter
5ml/1 tsp easy-blend (rapid-rise) dried yeast
100g/3¾oz/generous ½ cup sultanas (golden raisins)

Large

320ml/11fl oz/generous 1⅓ cups water
30ml/2 tbsp golden (light corn) syrup
45ml/3 tbsp malt extract
600g/1lb 5oz/5¼ cups unbleached white bread flour
30ml/2 tbsp skimmed milk powder (non fat dry milk)
5ml/1 tsp salt
50g/2oz/¼ cup butter
7.5ml/1½ tsp easy-blend (rapid-rise) dried yeast
125g/4¼oz/generous ⅔ cup sultanas (golden raisins)

1 Pour the water, golden syrup and malt extract into the bread machine pan. If the instructions for your machine specify that the yeast is to be placed in the pan first, reverse the order.

2 Sprinkle over the flour so that it covers the liquid. Add the milk powder. Add the salt and butter in separate corners. Make a shallow indent in the centre of the flour and add the yeast.

3 Set the machine to the white/basic setting, raisin setting if available. Select light crust 500g for small, medium crust large/750g for medium, or medium crust 1kg/2lb for large. Add the sultanas to the automatic dispenser, if available, or when the machine beeps during the kneading cycle. Press Start.

4 Remove the loaf at the end of the baking cycle and turn out on to a wire rack. Glaze the bread immediately, if you like, by dissolving 15ml/1 tbsp caster (superfine) sugar in 15ml/1 tbsp milk and brushing over the top. Allow to cool.

Muesli & Date Bread

This chewy, fruity loaf makes the perfect breakfast or brunch bread. Use your own favourite unsweetened muesli to ring the changes.

Makes 1

260ml/9fl oz/1⅛ cups water
30ml/2 tbsp sunflower oil
15ml/1 tbsp clear honey
300g/10½oz/2⅔ cups unbleached white bread flour
75g/3oz/¾ cup wholemeal (whole-wheat) bread flour
150g/5oz/1½ cups unsweetened fruit and nut muesli (granola)
45ml/3 tbsp skimmed milk powder (non fat dry milk)
7.5ml/1½ tsp salt
7.5ml/1½ tsp easy-blend (rapid-rise) dried yeast
65g/2½oz/scant ½ cup stoned (pitted) dates, chopped

1 Pour the water, oil and honey into the bread pan. Reverse the order in which you add the wet and dry ingredients if necessary. Sprinkle over the flours, covering the water. Add the muesli and milk powder, then the salt, in a corner.

2 Make a small indent in the flour; add the yeast. Set to the dough setting; use basic raisin dough setting (if available). Press Start. Add the dates at the beep or during the last 5 minutes of kneading. Lightly oil a baking sheet.

3 When the dough cycle has finished, remove from the machine and place it on a surface dusted with wholemeal flour. Knock back (punch down) gently.

4 Shape the dough into a round and place it on the prepared baking sheet. Using a sharp knife make three cuts on the top about 1cm/½in deep, to divide the bread into six sections.

5 Cover the loaf with lightly oiled clear film (plastic wrap) and leave for 30–45 minutes, or until almost doubled in size.

6 Preheat the oven to 200°C/400°F/Gas 6. Bake the loaf for 30–35 minutes until it is golden and hollow sounding. Transfer it to a wire rack to cool.

Malted Loaf per loaf Energy 1876kcal/7938kJ; Protein 37.5g; Carbohydrate 368.9g, of which sugars 83.1g; Fat 37.9g, of which saturates 22.4g; Cholesterol 92mg; Calcium 676mg; Fibre 13.1g; Sodium 1401mg.

Muesli and Date Bread per loaf Energy 2852kcal/12101kJ; Protein 65.9g; Carbohydrate 587.6g, of which sugars 197.4g; Fat 42.6g, of which saturates 7.4g; Cholesterol 9mg; Calcium 807mg; Fibre 31.6g; Sodium 3136mg.

Rum & Raisin Loaf

Juicy raisins plumped up with dark rum flavour this teatime loaf. Serve just as it is, or toasted and buttered.

Makes 1

90g/3¼oz/⅔ cup raisins
30ml/2 tbsp dark rum
1 egg, lightly beaten
250ml/9fl oz/generous 1 cup milk
500g/1lb 2oz/4½ cups unbleached white bread flour
2.5ml/½ tsp ground ginger
40g/1½oz/3 tbsp caster (superfine) sugar
3.5ml/¾ tsp salt
50g/2oz/¼ cup butter
7.5ml/1½ tsp easy-blend (rapid-rise) dried yeast
15ml/1 tbsp clear honey, warmed

1 Place the raisins and dark rum in a small bowl and leave to soak for 2 hours. Drain any remaining liquid into the bread machine pan.

2 Add the beaten egg and milk to the bread machine pan. If necessary for your machine, according to manufacturer's instructions, reverse the order in which you add the liquid and dry ingredients.

3 Sprinkle over the white bread flour, ensuring that the flour covers the liquid completely.

4 Add the ground ginger. Add the caster sugar, salt and butter, placing them in separate corners of the bread machine pan.

5 Make a small indent in the centre of the flour (but not down as far as the liquid) and pour in the dried yeast.

6 Set the machine to sweet/basic, with raisin setting (if available), light crust. Size: 750g for medium. Press Start.

7 Add the raisins to the dough when the machine beeps during the kneading cycle.

8 Remove the bread at the end of the baking cycle and turn out on to a wire rack. Brush the top with honey to glaze and leave the loaf to cool.

Schiacciata Con Uva

This Tuscan loaf is baked to celebrate the grape harvest.

Makes 1

For the starter
200ml/7fl oz/scant 1 cup water
175g/6oz/1½ cups strong white bread flour
1.5ml/¼ tsp easy-blend (rapid-rise) dried yeast

For the schiacciata dough
200g/7oz/generous 1 cup raisins
150ml/5fl oz/⅔ cup red wine
45ml/3 tbsp extra virgin olive oil
45ml/3 tbsp water
280g/10oz/2½ cups unbleached white bread flour
50g/2oz/¼ cup sugar
7.5ml/1½ tsp salt
5ml/1 tsp easy-blend (rapid-rise) dried yeast

For the topping
280g/10oz small black grapes
30ml/2 tbsp demerara (raw) sugar

1 Pour the water for the starter into the bread machine pan. Sprinkle the flour over the water. Make a small indent in the centre of the flour and add the yeast. Set the bread machine to the basic dough setting. Press Start. Mix for 5 minutes, then switch off the machine and transfer the starter to a bowl, cover it with a damp dish towel and leave it for 24 hours.

2 Place the raisins for the dough in a small pan. Add the wine and heat gently until warm. Cover and set aside. Return the starter to the machine pan with the oil and water. Sprinkle over the flour. Add the sugar and salt in separate corners. Make a shallow indent in the centre of the flour and add the yeast.

3 Set the bread machine to the basic dough setting. Press Start. Once finished, knock back (punch down) the dough gently, then divide it in half. Roll each piece out into a circle, about 1cm/½in thick. Place one circle on an oiled baking sheet. Spread the raisins over the dough. Place the other piece of dough on top and press together. Cover and leave for 30–45 minutes.

4 Press the grapes into the dough. Sprinkle with the sugar. Preheat the oven to 190°C/375°F/Gas 5. Bake for 40 minutes, or until the bread is golden and sounds hollow when tapped on the base. Turn out on to a wire rack to cool before serving.

Rum and Raisin Loaf per loaf Energy 1939kcal/8198kJ; Protein 41.1g; Carbohydrate 357.7g, of which sugars 91g; Fat 43.1g, of which saturates 23.9g; Cholesterol 282mg; Calcium 573mg; Fibre 12.4g; Sodium 428mg.

Schiacciata Con Uva per loaf Energy 2977kcal/12625kJ; Protein 48.8g; Carbohydrate 619.3g, of which sugars 272.6g; Fat 40g, of which saturates 5.5g; Cholesterol 0mg; Calcium 818mg; Fibre 20.1g; Sodium 159mg.

Tropical Fruit Loaf

There's a tropical taste in every slice of this loaf.

Makes 1

175g/6oz/1½ cup plain (all-purpose) flour
5ml/1 tsp baking powder
50g/2oz/⅔ cup desiccated (dry unsweetened shredded) coconut
100g/3¾oz/7 tbsp butter, diced
100g/3¾oz/7 tbsp caster (superfine) sugar
150g/5oz/scant 1 cup ready-to-eat dried tropical fruits, chopped
130ml/4½fl oz/½ cup plus 1 tbsp milk
1 egg, lightly beaten
grated rind and juice of ½ lime

For the icing

125g/4½oz/½ cup full-fat soft white (farmer's) cheese
60ml/4 tbsp icing (confectioners') sugar
juice of ½ lime

For the decoration

pared lime rind and fresh coconut shreds

1 Remove the kneading blade from the bread pan, if detachable. Line the base of the pan with baking parchment.

2 Sift the flour and baking powder into a large bowl. Then mix in the desiccated coconut. Add the butter and rub in with your fingers until the mixture resembles fine breadcrumbs. Stir in the sugar and dried tropical fruits. Gradually add the milk, egg, grated lime rind and juice, beating well after each addition.

3 Spoon the mixture into the prepared pan and set the bread machine to the bake/bake only setting. Set the timer, if possible for the recommended time. Bake for 40–50 minutes. Use the light crust setting, if available. The fruit loaf should be well risen. Test by inserting a skewer into the loaf. It should come out clean. Remove the bread pan from the bread machine. Leave for 5 minutes, then cool on a wire rack.

4 Make the icing. Cream the soft cheese, icing sugar and lime juice in a bowl. Spread the mixture over the top of the loaf. Lightly toast the coconut shreds. Leave to cool for 2–3 minutes, then decorate the top of the loaf with the pared lime rind.

Goji Berry & Yogurt Teabread

Packed full of fruit and nuts, this healthy teabread is equally delicious served as a mid-morning snack or a teatime treat. Goji berries are vitamin-rich, and are becoming more popular and widely available.

Makes 1

200ml/7fl oz/⅞ cup natural (plain) live yogurt
1 egg
275g/10oz/2½ cups plain (all-purpose) flour
12.5ml/2½ tsp baking powder
4ml/⅖ tsp ground nutmeg
75g/3oz/6 tbsp butter, softened
45g/1¾oz/3 tbsp light muscovado (brown) sugar
30g/1¼oz/2¼ tbsp caster (superfine) sugar
50g/2oz/⅝ cup goji berries
50g/2oz/⅝ cup walnuts, chopped
75g/3oz/⅞ cup ready-to-eat dried apricots, chopped

1 Mix the yogurt and egg together in a measuring jug (cup) and pour into the bread machine pan.

2 Sift the flour and baking powder together. Stir in the nutmeg. Add the butter and rub in with your fingers until the mixture resembles fine breadcrumbs. Stir in the sugars. Mix in the goji berries, walnuts and apricots. Add to the bread machine pan.

3 Set the machine to the cake setting, light crust, 500g, if available. Remove the bread pan at the end of the cycle. Leave to stand for 5 minutes, then turn out the teabread on to a wire rack to cool.

Cook's Tip

If your machine does not have a cake setting, or if you prefer, you can mix the loaf by hand, then bake it in the machine. Mix the yogurt and egg into the dry mixture. Stir in the nuts and fruits. Remove the kneading blade from the bread pan, line the pan with baking parchment and place the mixture in the pan. Cook on the bake setting for 50 minutes, or until risen and firm to the touch. Test it is cooked by inserting a skewer into the centre; it should come out clean.

Tropical Fruit Loaf per loaf Energy 2024kcal/8461kJ; Protein 26.8g; Carbohydrate 218.1g, of which sugars 122.9g; Fat 122.4g, of which saturates 81.5g; Cholesterol 417mg; Calcium 496mg; Fibre 10.3g; Sodium 882mg.

Goji Berry and Yogurt Teabread per loaf Energy 1928kcal/8097kJ; Protein 34.3g; Carbohydrate 274.4g, of which sugars 121.7g; Fat 84.8g, of which saturates 38.3g; Cholesterol 151mg; Calcium 642mg; Fibre 11.6g; Sodium 631mg.

Three-chocolate Bread

If you like chocolate, you'll adore this bread. The recipe suggests three specific types of chocolate, but you can combine your own favourites.

Makes 1

240ml/8½fl oz/generous 1 cup water
1 egg
500g/1lb 2oz/4½ cups unbleached white bread flour
25g/1oz/2 tbsp caster (superfine) sugar
5ml/1 tsp salt
25g/1oz/2 tbsp butter
7.5ml/1½ tsp easy-blend (rapid-rise) dried yeast
50g/2oz plain (semisweet) chocolate with raisins and almonds
50g/2oz plain (semisweet) chocolate with ginger
75g/3oz Belgian milk chocolate

1 Pour the water into the bread pan and add the egg. If necessary for your machine, reverse the order in which you add the liquid and dry ingredients.

2 Sprinkle over the flour, ensuring that it covers the water. Add the sugar, salt and butter, placing them in separate corners of the bread pan.

3 Make a small indent in the centre of the flour (but not down as far as the liquid) and add the yeast.

4 Set the bread machine to sweet/basic, raisin setting (if available). Use medium crust, large/750g for medium. Press Start. Coarsely chop all the chocolate. Add to the bread pan when the machine beeps during the kneading cycle.

5 Remove the bread at the end of the baking cycle. Turn out on to a wire rack to cool.

Cook's Tip
Add the chocolate to the bread machine pan gradually, making sure that it is mixing into the dough before adding more.

Mocha Panettone

This tall domed loaf from Milan is flavoured with coffee and chocolate.

Makes 1

30ml/2 tbsp instant coffee powder
140ml/5fl oz/scant ⅔ cup milk
1 egg, plus 2 egg yolks
400g/14oz/3½ cups unbleached white bread flour
15ml/1 tbsp unsweetened cocoa powder
5ml/1 tsp ground cinnamon
2.5ml/½ tsp salt
75g/3oz/6 tbsp caster (superfine) sugar
75g/3oz/6 tbsp butter, softened
7.5ml/1½ tsp easy-blend (rapid-rise) dried yeast
115g/4oz plain (semisweet) chocolate, coarsely chopped
45ml/3 tbsp pine nuts, lightly toasted
melted butter, for glazing

1 In a bowl, dissolve the coffee in 30ml/2 tbsp hot water. Pour into the bread machine pan. Add the milk, egg and egg yolks. Sift the flour and cocoa powder together. Sprinkle the mixture over the liquid, covering the liquid. Add the ground cinnamon. Place the salt, sugar and butter in separate corners of the bread pan. Make a well in the flour and add the yeast. Set the bread machine to the basic dough setting. Press Start.

2 Oil a 15cm/6in deep cake tin (pan). Using a double sheet of baking parchment that is 7.5cm/3in wider than the depth of the tin, line the container so that the excess paper creates a collar. Remove the dough when finished and knock back (punch down) gently. Gently knead in the chocolate and pine nuts and shape into a ball. Cover and leave it to rest for 5 minutes.

3 Shape the dough into a plump round loaf which has the same diameter as the cake tin, and place in the base of the container. Cover and leave for 45–60 minutes, until the dough has almost reached the top of the parchment collar. Preheat the oven to 200°C/400°F/Gas 6.

4 Brush the top of the loaf with the melted butter and cut a deep cross in the top. Bake for about 10 minutes. Reduce the oven temperature to 180°C/350°F/Gas 4 and continue to bake the panettone for 30–35 minutes more, or until it is golden.

Three-chocolate Bread per loaf Energy 2245kcal/9473kJ; Protein 51.1g; Carbohydrate 386.4g, of which sugars 96g; Fat 65.7g, of which saturates 35.9g; Cholesterol 267mg; Calcium 778mg; Fibre 11.6g; Sodium 1327mg.
Mocha Panettone Energy 336kcal/1412kJ; Protein 6.7g; Carbohydrate 47.3g, of which sugars 16.5g; Fat 14.7g, of which saturates 6.8g; Cholesterol 57mg; Calcium 90mg; Fibre 1.8g; Sodium 76mg.

Mini Brioches

These tiny breads have a characteristic fluted shape.

Makes 12

30ml/2 tbsp milk
2 eggs
225g/8oz/2 cups unbleached white bread flour
2.5ml/½ tsp salt
15ml/1 tbsp caster (superfine) sugar
50g/2oz butter, melted
7.5ml/1½ tsp easy-blend (rapid-rise) dried yeast
1 egg yolk, to glaze
15ml/1 tbsp milk, to glaze

1 Pour the milk and eggs into the bread machine pan. If the instructions for your bread machine specify that the yeast is to be placed in the pan first, reverse the order in which you add the liquid and dry ingredients. Sprinkle over the flour, ensuring that it covers the liquid. Add the salt, sugar and butter, placing them in separate corners. Make a small indent in the centre of the flour (but not down as far as the liquid) and add the easy-blend dried yeast.

2 Set the bread machine to the dough setting. Press Start. Lightly oil 12 small brioche moulds. When the dough cycle has finished, remove from the machine and place on a floured surface. Knock it back (punch it down) gently. Slice off a quarter of the dough, cover with oiled clear film (plastic wrap) and set aside. Divide the remaining dough into 12 pieces.

3 Knead each piece of dough into a small round. Place each round in an oiled mould. Divide the reserved piece of dough into 12 and shape into small pear shapes. To shape each mini brioche, make a small hole or cut a cross in the top of each large piece of dough. Place the pear-shaped pieces of dough on top, narrow end down. Cover with lightly oiled clear film and leave in a warm place for 30–45 minutes, or until well risen. Meanwhile, preheat the oven to 220°C/425°F/Gas 7.

4 Make the glaze by mixing the egg yolk and milk together. Brush the mixture over each brioche. Bake for 15 minutes, or until the brioche are golden and have risen well. Transfer them to a wire rack to cool. Serve warm or cold.

Coconut Milk Sugar Buns

A hint of coconut flavours these spiral-shaped rolls. Serve them warm or cold, with butter and preserves.

Makes 12

115ml/4fl oz/½ cup canned coconut milk
115ml/4fl oz/½ cup milk
1 egg
2.5ml/½ tsp natural vanilla extract
450g/1lb/4 cups unbleached white bread flour
25g/1oz/⅓ cup desiccated (dry unsweetened shredded) coconut
2.5ml/½ tsp salt
50g/2oz/¼ cup caster (superfine) sugar
40g/1½oz/3 tbsp butter
5ml/1 tsp easy-blend (rapid-rise) dried yeast
50g/2oz/¼ cup butter, melted
30ml/2 tbsp demerara (raw) sugar

1 Pour the coconut milk, milk, egg and vanilla extract into the bread machine pan. Sprinkle over the flour, then the coconut, covering the liquid completely. Add the salt, caster sugar and butter, placing them in separate corners of the bread pan. Make a small indent in the centre of the flour and add the yeast. Set the bread machine to the basic dough setting. Press Start.

2 When the dough cycle has finished, remove the dough and place it on a lightly floured surface. Knock back (punch down) gently. Divide the dough into 12 equal pieces and cover these with oiled clear film (plastic wrap).

3 Take one piece of dough, leaving the rest covered; roll it into a rope about 38cm/15in long. Curl the rope into a loose spiral shape and place on an oiled baking sheet. Tuck the end under to seal. Repeat with the remaining pieces of dough, spacing the spirals well apart.

4 Cover with oiled clear film and leave to rise in a warm place for 30 minutes, or until doubled in size. Preheat the oven to 220°C/425°F/Gas 7.

5 Brush the buns with the melted butter and sprinkle them with the demerara sugar. Bake for 12–15 minutes, or until the buns are golden. Turn out on to a wire rack to cool.

Mini Brioches Energy 89kcal/378kJ; Protein 3.3g; Carbohydrate 16g, of which sugars 1.7g; Fat 1.8g, of which saturates 0.6g; Cholesterol 40mg; Calcium 36mg; Fibre 0.8g; Sodium 100mg.

Coconut Milk Sugar Buns Energy 210kcal/887kJ; Protein 4.6g; Carbohydrate 37.2g, of which sugars 8.6g; Fat 5.8g, of which saturates 3.7g; Cholesterol 26mg; Calcium 74mg; Fibre 1.5g; Sodium 137mg.

Yorkshire Teacakes

Serve these treats split and buttered – either warm from the oven or toasted.

Makes 8–10

280ml/10fl oz/1¼ cups milk
450g/1lb/4 cups unbleached white bread flour
5ml/1 tsp salt
40g/1½oz/3 tbsp caster (superfine) sugar
40g/1½oz/3 tbsp lard or butter
5ml/1 tsp easy-blend (rapid-rise) dried yeast
50g/2oz/¼ cup currants
50g/2oz/⅓ cup sultanas (golden raisins)
milk, for glazing

1 Pour the milk into the bread machine pan. Sprinkle over the flour, covering the milk completely. Add the salt, sugar and lard or butter, placing them in separate corners of the bread pan. Make a well in the centre of the flour and add the yeast. Set the bread machine to the basic raisin dough setting. Press Start. Add the currants and sultanas when the machine beeps, or simply add the dried fruits 5 minutes before the end of the kneading period.

2 When the dough cycle has finished, remove the dough from the machine and place it on a lightly floured surface. Knock back (punch down) gently. Then divide the dough into eight or ten portions, depending on how large you like your Yorkshire teacakes, and shape into balls. Flatten out each ball into a disc about 1cm/½in thick.

3 Place the discs on greased baking sheets, about 2.5cm/1in apart. Cover them with oiled clear film (plastic wrap) and leave in a warm place for 30–45 minutes, or until they are almost doubled in size. Preheat the oven to 200°C/400°F/Gas 6.

4 Brush the top of each teacake with the milk, then bake in the oven for 15–18 minutes, or until golden. Turn the teacakes out on to a wire rack to cool.

5 To serve, split open while still warm and spread with lashings of butter, or let the buns cool, then split and toast them before adding butter.

Hot Cross Buns

The tasty currant and sultana buns are traditionally eaten at Easter time.

Makes 12

210ml/7½fl oz/scant 1 cup milk
1 egg
450g/1lb/4 cups unbleached white bread flour
7.5ml/1½ tsp mixed (apple pie) spice
2.5ml/½ tsp ground cinnamon
2.5ml/½ tsp salt
50g/2oz/¼ cup caster (superfine) sugar
50g/2oz/¼ cup butter
7.5ml/1½ tsp easy-blend (rapid-rise) dried yeast
75g/3oz/scant ½ cup currants
25g/1oz/3 tbsp sultanas (golden raisins)
25g/1oz/3 tbsp cut mixed (candied) peel

For the pastry crosses

50g/2oz/½ cup plain (all-purpose) flour
25g/1oz/2 tbsp margarine

For the glaze

30ml/2 tbsp milk
25g/1oz/2 tbsp caster sugar

1 Pour the milk and egg into the bread pan. Sprinkle over the flour, ensuring that it covers the liquid. Add the mixed spice and cinnamon. Place the salt, sugar and butter in separate corners of the pan. Make a well in the flour and add the yeast. Set the bread machine to the basic raisin dough setting. Press Start. Add the dried fruit and peel when the machine beeps, or 5 minutes before the end of the kneading period.

2 When the dough cycle has finished, remove the dough and knock back (punch down) gently, then divide it into 12 balls. Place on greased baking sheets, cover with oiled clear film (plastic wrap) and leave for 30–45 minutes to rise.

3 Preheat the oven to 200°C/400°F/Gas 6. In a bowl, rub the flour and margarine together until the mixture resembles fine breadcrumbs. Bind with enough water to make a soft pastry, then spoon into a piping bag fitted with a plain nozzle and pipe a cross on each bun. Bake the buns for 15–18 minutes.

4 Heat the milk and sugar for the glaze in a small pan until the sugar dissolves. Brush the glaze over the top of the hot buns.

Yorkshire Teacakes Energy 239kcal/1011kJ; Protein 5.4g; Carbohydrate 47.4g, of which sugars 13.1g; Fat 4.4g, of which saturates 2.5g; Cholesterol 11mg; Calcium 107mg; Fibre 1.6g; Sodium 245mg.

Hot Cross Buns Energy 155kcal/657kJ; Protein 3.7g; Carbohydrate 29.3g, of which sugars 11.7g; Fat 3.4g, of which saturates 1.1g; Cholesterol 16mg; Calcium 55mg; Fibre 0.9g; Sodium 60mg.

Chelsea Buns

These sweet buns make a perfect accompaniment to a cup of coffee or tea.

Makes 12

225ml/8fl oz/scant 1 cup milk
1 egg
500g/1lb 2oz/4½ cups unbleached white bread flour
2.5ml/½ tsp salt
75g/3oz/6 tbsp caster (superfine) sugar
50g/2oz/¼ cup butter, softened
5ml/1 tsp easy-blend (rapid-rise) dried yeast
50g/2oz/¼ cup caster (superfine) sugar, to glaze
5ml/1 tsp orange flower water, to glaze

For the filling

25g/1oz/2 tbsp butter, melted
115g/4oz/⅔ cup sultanas (golden raisins)
25g/1oz/3 tbsp mixed chopped (candied) peel
25g/1oz/2 tbsp currants
25g/1oz/2 tbsp soft light brown sugar
5ml/1 tsp mixed (apple pie) spice

1 Pour the milk into the bread machine pan. Add the egg. Sprinkle over the flour, covering the liquid. Add the salt, sugar and butter in three separate corners of the pan. Make a well in the flour; add the yeast. Set the machine to the basic dough setting. Press Start. Grease a 23cm/9in square cake tin (pan).

2 When the dough cycle has finished, remove the dough and knock back (punch down) gently, then roll it out to form a 30cm/12in square. Brush with the melted butter and sprinkle on the filling ingredients, leaving a 1cm/½in border along one edge. Roll the dough up and seal. Cut the roll into 12 slices and then place these cut side uppermost in the prepared tin.

3 Cover and leave for 30–45 minutes, until doubled. Preheat the oven to 200°C/400°F/Gas 6. Bake for 15–20 minutes.

4 Make the glaze. Mix the caster sugar with 60ml/4 tbsp water in a small pan. Heat gently, stirring occasionally, until the sugar is completely dissolved. Then increase the heat and boil the mixture rapidly for 1–2 minutes without stirring, until syrupy. Stir the orange flower water into the glaze and brush the mixture over the warm buns. Serve slightly warm.

Devonshire Splits

A summer afternoon, a scrumptious cream tea – Devonshire splits are an essential part of this British tradition.

Makes 8

140ml/5fl oz/⅝ cup milk
225g/8oz/2 cups unbleached white bread flour
25g/1oz/2 tbsp caster (superfine) sugar
2.5ml/½ tsp salt
5ml/1 tsp easy-blend (rapid-rise) dried yeast
icing (confectioners') sugar, for dusting

For the filling

clotted cream or whipped double (heavy) cream
raspberry or strawberry jam

1 Pour the milk into the bread pan. Sprinkle over the flour, covering the liquid completely. Add the caster sugar and salt, placing them in separate corners of the bread machine pan.

2 Make a small indent in the centre of the flour (do not go down as far as the milk underneath) and pour the yeast into the hollow. Set the bread machine to the basic dough setting. Press Start. Lightly grease two baking sheets.

3 When the dough cycle has finished, remove the dough and place it on a lightly floured surface. Knock back (punch down) gently, then divide into eight portions.

4 Shape each portion of dough into a ball, using cupped hands. Place on the prepared baking sheets, and flatten the top of each ball slightly. Cover with oiled clear film (plastic wrap). Leave the dough to rise for 30–45 minutes or until it has doubled in size.

5 Meanwhile, preheat the oven to 220°C/425°F/Gas 7. Bake the buns for 15–18 minutes, or until they are light golden in colour. Turn out on to a wire rack to cool.

6 Split the buns open and fill them with cream and jam. Dust them with icing sugar just before serving.

Chelsea Buns Energy 287kcal/1208kJ; Protein 6.1g; Carbohydrate 43.5g, of which sugars 16.6g; Fat 11.1g, of which saturates 2.3g; Cholesterol 26mg; Calcium 85mg; Fibre 1.3g; Sodium 243mg.

Devonshire Splits Energy 116kcal/495kJ; Protein 3.2g; Carbohydrate 26g, of which sugars 4.6g; Fat 0.7g, of which saturates 0.2g; Cholesterol 1mg; Calcium 62mg; Fibre 0.9g; Sodium 134mg.

Jam Doughnuts

The main thing to remember about doughnuts is the speed with which they disappear, so make plenty!

Makes 16

90ml/6 tbsp water
140ml/5fl oz/scant ⅔ cup milk
1 egg
450g/1lb/4 cups unbleached white bread flour
50g/2oz/¼ cup caster (superfine) sugar
5ml/1 tsp salt
50g/2oz/¼ cup butter
7.5ml/1½ tsp easy-blend (rapid-rise) dried yeast
oil for deep-frying
caster (superfine) sugar, for sprinkling

For the filling
45ml/3 tbsp red jam
5ml/1 tsp lemon juice

1 Pour the water and milk into the bread machine pan. Break in the egg. Sprinkle over the flour, covering the liquid. Add the sugar, salt and butter, placing them in separate corners of the pan. Make a well in the centre of the flour and add the yeast. Set the bread machine to the basic dough setting. Press Start.

2 When the dough cycle has finished, remove the dough and knock back (punch down) gently. Divide the dough into 16 equal portions and roll them into smooth balls. Place the balls oiled baking sheets. Cover and leave for about 30 minutes.

3 Heat the oil for deep-frying to 180°C/350°F, or until a cube of dried bread, added to the oil, turns golden brown in 30–60 seconds. Add the doughnuts, three or four at a time and cook for about 4–5 minutes, or until they are golden. Remove from the oil using a slotted spoon and drain on kitchen paper. Then toss them in caster sugar. Set aside to cool.

4 Heat the jam and lemon juice in a small pan until warm, stirring to combine. Leave to cool, then spoon the mixture into a piping (pastry) bag fitted with a small plain nozzle. When the round doughnuts have cooled, use a skewer to make a small hole in each. Insert the piping nozzle and squeeze a little of the jam mixture into each doughnut.

Calas

These tasty morsels are a Creole speciality, made from a rice-based yeast dough which is then deep-fried.

Makes 25

50g/2oz/generous ⅓ cup pudding rice
280ml/10fl oz/1¼ cups milk
140ml/5fl oz/⅝ cup water
2 eggs
125g/4½oz/generous 1 cup unbleached white bread flour
5ml/1 tsp grated lemon rind
2.5ml/½ tsp ground ginger
2.5ml/½ tsp freshly grated nutmeg
50g/2oz/¼ cup caster (superfine) sugar
1.5ml/¼ tsp salt
5ml/1 tsp easy-blend (rapid-rise) dried yeast
oil, for deep-frying
icing (confectioners') sugar, for dusting

1 Place the rice, milk and water in a pan and slowly bring to the boil. Lower the heat, cover and simmer for 20 minutes, stirring occasionally, until the rice is soft. Leave to cool.

2 Add the eggs to the bread machine pan. Reverse the order in which you add the wet and dry ingredients if necessary. Add the rice. Sprinkle over the flour, then the lemon rind, ginger and nutmeg. Add the sugar and salt, placing them in separate corners of the bread pan. Make a small indent in the centre of the flour (but not down as far as the liquid) and add the yeast.

3 Set the bread machine to the basic dough setting. Press Start. When the dough cycle has finished, lift out the pan containing the batter from the machine.

4 Preheat the oven to 140°C/275°F/Gas 1. Heat the oil for deep-frying to 180°C/350°F or until a cube of dried bread, added to the oil, turns golden in 45 seconds. Add tablespoons of batter a few at a time and fry for 3–4 minutes, turning occasionally, until golden.

5 Remove the calas from the oil and drain on kitchen paper. Keep them warm in the oven while you cook the remainder. Dust them with icing sugar and serve warm.

Jam Doughnuts Energy 192kcal/802kJ; Protein 2.5g; Carbohydrate 22.6g, of which sugars 8.3g; Fat 10.8g, of which saturates 1.4g; Cholesterol 16mg; Calcium 37mg; Fibre 0.6g; Sodium 11mg.

Calas Energy 80kcal/335kJ; Protein 1.6g; Carbohydrate 8.3g, of which sugars 2.7g; Fat 4.8g, of which saturates 0.7g; Cholesterol 16mg; Calcium 25mg; Fibre 0.2g; Sodium 12mg.

American Breakfast Pancakes

These thick, succulent breakfast pancakes are often served with a sauce made from wild cranberries, also known as lingonberries. They are equally delicious served with maple syrup.

Makes 15

2 eggs
280ml/10fl oz/1¼ cups milk
225g/8oz/2 cups unbleached white bread flour
5ml/1 tsp salt
15ml/1 tbsp caster (superfine) sugar
15g/½oz/1 tbsp butter, melted
5ml/1 tsp easy-blend (rapid-rise) dried yeast
maple syrup or wild cranberry sauce, to serve

1 Separate 1 egg and set the white aside. Place the yolk in the machine pan and add the whole egg and the milk. Sprinkle over the flour, ensuring that it covers the liquid. Add the salt, sugar and butter, placing them in separate corners of the bread pan. Make a small indent in the centre of the flour (but not down as far as the liquid) and add the easy-blend dried yeast.

2 Set the bread machine to the dough setting; use basic dough setting (if available). Press Start.

3 When the dough cycle has finished pour the batter into a large measuring jug. Whisk the reserved egg white; fold it into the batter. Preheat the oven to 140°C/275°F/Gas 1.

4 Lightly oil a large heavy frying pan or griddle and place over a medium heat. Add about 45ml/3 tbsp batter, letting it spread out to form a pancake about 10cm/4in wide.

5 Cook each pancake until the surface begins to dry out, then turn over using a fish slice or metal spatula and cook the other side for about 1 minute, or until golden.

6 Stack the pancakes between sheets of baking parchment on a warm plate and keep them warm in the oven while you cook the rest of the batter. Serve the pancakes with the syrup or sauce.

Pikelets

These are similar to crumpets, and have the same distinctive holey tops. Serve them warm with butter and fruit preserves.

Makes 20

140ml/5fl oz/⅝ cup water
140ml/5fl oz/⅝ cup milk
15ml/1 tbsp sunflower oil
225g/8oz/2 cups unbleached white bread flour
5ml/1 tsp salt
5ml/1 tsp caster (superfine) sugar
7.5ml/1½ tsp easy-blend (rapid-rise) dried yeast
1.5ml/¼ tsp bicarbonate of soda (baking soda)
60ml/4 tbsp water
1 egg white

1 Pour the water into the bread machine pan, then add the milk and sunflower oil. Sprinkle over the white bread flour, ensuring that it covers the liquid completely. Add the salt and caster sugar, placing them in separate corners of the bread pan. Make a shallow indent in the centre of the flour (but not down as far as the liquid) and add the easy-blend dried yeast.

2 Set the bread machine to the basic dough setting. Press Start. Then lightly oil two baking sheets. When the dough cycle has finished, lift the bread pan out of the machine and pour the batter for the pikelets into a bowl.

3 Dissolve the bicarbonate of soda in the remaining water and stir it into the batter. Whisk the egg white in a bowl until it forms soft peaks, then fold it into the batter. Cover with oiled clear film (plastic wrap) and leave the mixture to rise for 30 minutes. Preheat the oven to 140°C/275°F/Gas 1.

4 Lightly grease a griddle and heat it gently. When it is hot, pour generous tablespoonfuls of batter on to the hot surface, spacing them well apart to allow for spreading, and cook until the tops no longer appear wet and have acquired lots of tiny holes.

5 When the base of each pikelet is golden, turn it over and cook until pale golden. Remove the cooked pikelets and layer them in a folded dish towel. Place in the oven to keep them warm while you cook the remaining batter. Serve immediately.

American Breakfast Pancakes Energy 81kcal/342kJ; Protein 2.9g; Carbohydrate 13.6g, of which sugars 2.2g; Fat 2.1g, of which saturates 1g; Cholesterol 29mg; Calcium 48mg; Fibre 0.5g; Sodium 159mg.

Pikelets Energy 48kcal/204kJ; Protein 1.4g; Carbohydrate 9.4g, of which sugars 0.8g; Fat 0.8g, of which saturates 0.2g; Cholesterol 0mg; Calcium 24mg; Fibre 0.4g; Sodium 106mg.

Cherry Foldovers

These Danish pastries contain a sweet cherry filling spiked with Kirsch.

Makes 12

For the pastry

1 egg
75ml/2½fl oz/⅓ cup water
225g/8oz/2 cups unbleached white bread flour
2.5ml/½ tsp ground cinnamon
15ml/1 tbsp caster (superfine) sugar
2.5ml/½ tsp salt
125g/4½oz/generous ½ cup butter, softened
7.5ml/1½ tsp easy-blend (rapid-rise) dried yeast

For the filling and topping

225g/8oz drained pitted morello cherries in syrup, plus 15ml/1 tbsp syrup from the jar or can
25g/1oz/2 tbsp caster (superfine) sugar
15ml/1 tbsp cornflour (cornstarch)
30ml/2 tbsp Kirsch
1 egg, separated
30ml/2 tbsp water
30ml/2 tbsp apricot jam

1 Pour the egg and water into the bread machine pan. Sprinkle over the flour and cinnamon, covering the liquid. Add the sugar, salt and 25g/1oz/2 tbsp of the butter, placing them in separate corners. Make a well in the flour and add the yeast.

2 Set the bread machine to the basic or pizza dough setting. Press Start. When the cycle has finished, remove the dough and knock back (punch down) gently, then roll out to a rectangle about 1cm/½in thick.

3 Divide the remaining butter into three and dot one portion over the top two-thirds of the dough, leaving the edges clear. Fold the unbuttered portion of dough over half the buttered area and fold the remaining portion on top. Seal the edges.

4 Give the dough a quarter turn and repeat the buttering and folding. Wrap in clear film (plastic wrap) and chill for 30 minutes. Repeat the folding and chilling with the remaining butter, then repeat again, this time without any butter. Wrap and chill the dough for 30 minutes.

5 Make the filling. Put the cherries, cherry syrup, caster sugar, cornflour and Kirsch in a pan and toss. Cook over a medium heat for 3–4 minutes, stirring until thickened. Leave to cool.

6 Roll out the dough to a rectangle measuring 40 × 30cm/16 × 12in. Cut into 10cm/4in squares. Place a tablespoon of filling in the middle of each square. Brush one corner of each pastry square with lightly beaten egg white, then bring the opposite corner over to meet it, setting it back slightly to leave some of the cherry filling exposed. Press down to seal.

7 Place the foldovers on lightly greased baking sheets. Cover with oiled clear film and leave to rise for 30 minutes. Preheat the oven to 200°C/400°F/Gas 6.

8 Mix the egg yolk with half the water and brush over the dough. Bake for 15 minutes, or until golden. Mix the jam and remaining water in a pan; heat until warm. Brush over the pastries and turn out on to a wire rack to cool.

Ginger & Raisin Whirls

Tasty spirals of buttery pastry, studded with dried fruit and crystallized ginger.

Makes 12

1 quantity pastry dough (see Cherry Foldovers, left)

For the filling

40g/1½oz/3 tbsp butter, softened
40g/1½oz/3 tbsp caster (superfine) sugar
2.5ml/½ tsp grated nutmeg
25g/1oz/2 tbsp crystallized (candied) ginger
25g/1oz/2 tbsp candied orange peel
75g/3oz/½ cup raisins

For the glaze and icing

1 egg yolk, beaten with 15ml/1 tbsp water
30ml/2 tbsp icing (confectioners') sugar, sifted
15ml/1 tbsp orange juice

1 On a lightly floured surface, roll out the pastry dough into a 30 × 23cm/12 × 9in rectangle.

2 Cream the butter, sugar and nutmeg together and then spread over the dough. Finely chop the ginger and peel. Sprinkle over the dough with the raisins. Lightly oil two baking sheets.

3 Tightly roll up the dough from one long side, as far as the centre. Repeat with the remaining long side, so the two rolls meet at the centre. Brush the edges where the rolls meet with the beaten egg yolk.

4 Cut into 12 equal slices and place, spaced well apart, on the prepared baking sheets. Cover with oiled clear film (plastic wrap) and leave to rise for 30 minutes.

5 Preheat the oven to 200°C/400°F/Gas 6. Brush the whirls with the remaining egg glaze and bake for 12–15 minutes, or until golden.

6 Turn out on to a wire rack to cool. Mix the icing sugar and orange juice together and use to ice the pastries.

Cherry Foldovers Energy 196kcal/820kJ; Protein 3g; Carbohydrate 24.4g, of which sugars 9g; Fat 9.7g, of which saturates 5.9g; Cholesterol 56mg; Calcium 38mg; Fibre 0.7g; Sodium 93mg.

Ginger and Raisin Whirls Energy 221kcal/926kJ; Protein 2.5g; Carbohydrate 27.5g, of which sugars 13.3g; Fat 12g, of which saturates 7.6g; Cholesterol 47mg; Calcium 40mg; Fibre 0.8g; Sodium 120mg.

Petits Pains au Chocolat

These little pastries have a delectable chocolate filling.

Makes 9
125ml/4½fl oz/½ cup water
250g/9oz/2¼ cups unbleached white bread flour
30ml/2 tbsp skimmed milk powder (non fat dry milk)
15ml/1 tbsp caster (superfine) sugar
2.5ml/½ tsp salt
140g/5oz/⅔ cup butter, softened
7.5ml/1½ tsp easy-blend (rapid-rise) dried yeast
225g/8oz plain (semisweet) chocolate, broken into pieces

For the glaze
1 egg yolk
15ml/1 tbsp milk

1 Pour the water into the bread machine pan. Sprinkle over the flour, then the milk powder, covering the water. Add the sugar, salt and 25g/1oz/2 tbsp of the butter, placing in separate corners of the pan. Make a well in the flour and add the yeast. Set the machine to the basic dough setting. Press Start.

2 When finished, knock back (punch down) and shape into a ball. Cut a cross halfway through the top of the dough. Roll out around the cross, leaving a risen centre. Place the remaining butter in the centre. Fold the dough over the butter to enclose. Roll to a rectangle 2cm/¾in thick. Fold the bottom third up and the top down; seal the edges. Wrap in oiled clear film (plastic wrap) and chill for 20 minutes. Repeat twice more, giving a quarter turn and chilling each time. Chill for 30 minutes.

3 Roll out the dough to a rectangle measuring 52 × 30cm/21 × 12in. Cut the dough into nine rectangles. Divide the chocolate among the rectangles, placing the pieces lengthways at one short end. Preheat the oven to 200°C/400°F/Gas 6.

4 Mix the egg yolk and milk for the glaze together. Brush over the edges of the dough. Roll up each piece to completely enclose the chocolate, then press the edges together. Place on greased baking sheets. Cover and leave for 30 minutes. Brush with the remaining glaze and bake for about 15 minutes. Turn out on to a wire rack to cool just slightly, and serve warm.

Apple & Sultana Danish Pastries

These Danish pastries are beautifully light and flaky.

Makes 12
For the pastry
1 egg
75ml/5 tbsp milk
225g/8oz/2 cups unbleached white bread flour
15g/½oz/1 tbsp caster (superfine) sugar
2.5ml/½ tsp salt
140g/5oz/⅔ cup butter, softened
7.5ml/1½ tsp easy-blend (rapid-rise) dried yeast

For the filling
25g/1oz/2 tbsp butter
350g/12oz cooking apples, diced
15ml/1 tbsp cornflour (cornstarch)
25g/1oz/2 tbsp caster (superfine) sugar
30ml/2 tbsp water
5ml/1 tsp lemon juice
25g/1oz/3 tbsp sultanas (golden raisins)

To finish
1 egg, separated
flaked (sliced) almonds, for sprinkling

1 Place the egg and milk in the bread pan. Sprinkle over the flour, covering the liquid. Add the sugar, salt and 25g/1oz/2 tbsp of the butter in separate corners. Make a well in the flour; add the yeast. Set to the basic dough setting. Press Start.

2 Shape the remaining butter into a block 2cm/¾in thick. When the dough cycle has finished, remove the dough and knock back (punch down) gently, then roll it out into a rectangle that is slightly wider than the butter block, and twice as long. Place the butter on one half, fold the pastry over it, then seal the edges.

3 Roll the butter-filled pastry into a rectangle 2cm/¾in thick, making it twice as long as it is wide. Fold the top third down and the bottom third up, seal the edges, wrap in clear film (plastic wrap) and chill for 15 minutes. Repeat the folding and sealing process twice more, giving the pastry a quarter turn each time. Wrap in clear film and chill for 20 minutes.

4 Melt the butter in a pan. Add the apples, cornflour and sugar to a bowl and toss. Then add to the pan. Add the water and lemon juice. Cook over medium heat for 3–4 minutes, stirring. Stir in the sultanas. Leave to cool.

5 Roll out the pastry into a rectangle measuring 40 × 30cm/16 × 12in. Cut into 10cm/4in squares. Divide the filling among the squares, spreading it over half of each piece of pastry, so that when they are folded they will make rectangles.

6 Brush the pastry edges on each square with the lightly beaten egg white, then fold the pastry over the filling to make a rectangle measuring 10 × 5cm/4 × 2in, and press the edges together firmly. Make a few cuts along the long joined edge of each pastry.

7 Place the pastries on the baking sheets, cover them with oiled clear film (plastic wrap) and leave to rise for 30 minutes.

8 Preheat the oven to 200°C/400°F/Gas 6. Mix the egg yolk with 15ml/1 tbsp water and brush over the pastries. Sprinkle with a few flaked almonds and bake for 15 minutes, or until golden. Transfer to a wire rack to cool.

Petits Pains au Chocolat Energy 352kcal/1473kJ; Protein 4.2g; Carbohydrate 40.1g, of which sugars 17.6g; Fat 20.6g, of which saturates 12.8g; Cholesterol 39mg; Calcium 65mg; Fibre 0.9g; Sodium 126mg.

Apple and Sultana Danish Pastries Energy 208kcal/869kJ; Protein 2.7g; Carbohydrate 23.6g, of which sugars 8.1g; Fat 12.1g, of which saturates 7.7g; Cholesterol 48mg; Calcium 42mg; Fibre 1.1g; Sodium 116mg. 105mg.

Marzipan & Almond Twists

Amaretto liqueur, marzipan and almonds make up these delicious pastry twists.

Makes 9

90ml/6 tbsp water
1 egg
60ml/4 tbsp Amaretto liqueur
350g/12oz/3 cups unbleached white bread flour
30ml/2 tbsp skimmed milk powder (non fat dry milk)
40g/1½oz/3 tbsp caster (superfine) sugar
2.5ml/½ tsp salt
50g/2oz/¼ cup butter, melted
7.5ml/1½ tsp easy-blend (rapid-rise) dried yeast
115g/4oz/1 cup ground almonds
50g/2oz/½ cup icing (confectioners') sugar
2–3 drops of almond extract
1 egg, separated
10ml/2 tsp milk
flaked (sliced) almonds, for sprinkling

1 Pour the water, egg and Amaretto into the bread machine pan. Sprinkle over the flour, covering the liquid. Add the milk powder. Place the sugar, salt and butter in separate corners of the bread pan. Make a well in the the flour and add the yeast. Set the machine to the basic dough setting. Press Start.

2 Mix the ground almonds, icing sugar, almond extract, egg white and 15ml/3 tsp water in a bowl and set aside. In a separate bowl, beat the egg yolk with 10ml/2 tsp water.

3 When the dough cycle has finished, remove and knock back (punch down). Roll into a 45 × 23cm/18 × 9in rectangle. Cut in half to make two squares. Spread the filling over one of the squares. Brush beaten egg yolk mixture over the other square and place it egg side down on top of the marzipan filling.

4 Cut nine strips. Cut a lengthways slit near the end of the strip. Twist the strip, starting from the uncut end, then pass the end through the slit and seal together, with egg mixture. Repeat. Place the twists on oiled baking sheets and cover and leave for 30 minutes. Preheat the oven to 200°C/400°F/Gas 6. Mix the remaining egg yolk mixture with the milk and brush over the twists. Sprinkle with flaked almonds. Bake for 12–15 minutes.

Apricot Stars

These mouthwatering light and flaky pastries can be decorated with fresh apricots, when in season.

Makes 12

1 quantity pastry dough (see Apple and Sultana Danish Pastries, page 244)

For the filling
50g/2oz/½ cup ground almonds
50g/2oz/½ cup icing (confectioners') sugar
1 egg, lightly beaten
12 drained canned apricot halves

For the glaze
1 egg yolk
30ml/2 tbsp water
60ml/4 tbsp apricot jam

1 Roll out the pastry into a rectangle measuring 40 × 30cm/16 × 12in. Cut into 10cm/4in squares. On each square, make a 2.5cm/1in diagonal cut with a sharp knife from each corner towards the centre.

2 Make the filling. Mix the ground almonds, icing sugar and egg together in a bowl. Divide the mixture equally among the pastry squares, using a spoon to place in the centre of each dough square.

3 Beat the egg yolk for the glaze with half the water. On each square, fold one corner of each cut section to the centre. Secure with the glaze. Place an apricot half, round side up on top in the centre.

4 Lightly oil two baking sheets. Place the pastries on them and cover with oiled clear film (plastic wrap). Leave to rise for 30 minutes or until doubled in size. Preheat the oven to 200°C/400°F/Gas 6.

5 Brush the pastries with the remaining egg glaze and bake for 15 minutes, until golden. While the stars are cooking, heat the apricot jam in a small pan with the remaining water.

6 Transfer the cooked pastries on to a wire rack, brush them with the warm apricot glaze and leave to cool.

Marzipan and Almond Twists Energy 331kcal/1389kJ; Protein 8.2g; Carbohydrate 44.3g, of which sugars 14.4g; Fat 13.6g, of which saturates 4.1g; Cholesterol 56mg; Calcium 113mg; Fibre 2.2g; Sodium 68mg.

Apricot Stars Energy 220kcal/920kJ; Protein 4.1g; Carbohydrate 22.8g, of which sugars 8.4g; Fat 13.2g, of which saturates 6.9g; Cholesterol 59mg; Calcium 58mg; Fibre 1.1g; Sodium 105mg.

Madeira Cake

Delicately flavoured with vanilla, this classic plain cake has a firm yet light texture. Serve the traditional way, with a glass of its namesake.

Makes 1

150g/5oz/⅔ cup butter, cut into pieces
150g/5oz/¾ cup caster (superfine) sugar
1.5ml/¼ tsp vanilla extract
165g/5½oz/generous 1¼ cups self-raising (self-rising) flour
40g/1½oz/6 tbsp plain (all-purpose) flour
3 eggs, lightly beaten
15–30ml/1–2 tbsp milk

1 Remove the kneading blade from the bread machine pan, if it is detachable, then line the base of the bread pan with baking parchment.

2 Cream the butter and sugar together in a large bowl until the mixture is very light and fluffy, then beat in the vanilla extract.

3 Sift the flours together. Gradually beat the eggs into the creamed mixture, beating well after each addition, and adding a little flour if the mixture starts to curdle.

4 Fold in the remaining flour mixture, using a metal spoon, then add enough of the milk to give a dropping consistency.

5 Spoon the mixture into the prepared pan and set the bread machine to the bake/bake only setting. Set the timer, if possible, for the recommended time. If, on your bread machine, the minimum time on this setting is for longer than the time suggested here, set the timer and check the cake after the shortest recommended time. Bake the cake for 50–55 minutes. Use the light crust setting, if available.

6 The cake should be well risen and firm to the touch. Test by inserting a skewer into the centre. It should come out clean. If necessary, bake for a few minutes more.

7 Remove the pan from the machine. Leave to stand for 5 minutes, then turn the cake out on to a wire rack to cool.

Coconut Cake

Desiccated coconut gives this simple and speedy cake a wonderfully moist texture and delectable aroma.

Makes 1

100g/3¾oz/7 tbsp butter or margarine, softened
150g/5oz/¾ cup caster (superfine) sugar
2 large eggs, lightly beaten
150g/5oz/1⅔ cups desiccated (dry unsweetened shredded) coconut
100g/3¾oz/scant 1 cup self-raising (self-rising) flour
75ml/2½fl oz/⅓ cup sour cream
7.5ml/1½ tsp grated lemon rind

1 Remove the kneading blade from the bread pan, if detachable. Line the base of the pan with baking parchment.

2 In a bowl, cream the butter or margarine and sugar until pale and fluffy. Beat in the eggs a little at a time. Add the desiccated coconut, flour, sour cream and lemon rind. Gradually mix together.

3 Spoon into the pan and set to the bake/bake only setting. If, on your bread machine, the minimum time on this setting is longer than suggested here, set the timer and check after the shortest recommended time. Bake for 40–50 minutes.

4 Test if the cake is cooked by inserting a skewer into the centre. It should come out clean. If necessary, bake the cake for a few minutes more. Remove the bread pan from the machine. Leave the cake to stand for 5 minutes, then turn the cake out on to a wire rack to cool.

Cook's Tip

This cake is delicious with a lemon syrup drizzled over the top once it is cooked. Heat 30ml/2 tbsp lemon juice with 100g/3¾oz/scant ½ cup sugar and 85ml/3fl oz/6 tbsp water in a small pan, stirring constantly until the sugar has dissolved. Bring to the boil, then simmer for 2–3 minutes before drizzling the syrup over the warm cake.

Madeira Cake per cake Energy 2264kcal/9472kJ; Protein 30.4g; Carbohydrate 257.1g, of which sugars 149.9g; Fat 131.3g, of which saturates 77.4g; Cholesterol 776mg; Calcium 368mg; Fibre 4.4g; Sodium 1040mg.

Coconut Cake per cake Energy 2205kcal/9244kJ; Protein 30.4g; Carbohydrate 277.5g, of which sugars 220.5g; Fat 116.3g, of which saturates 82.4g; Cholesterol 611mg; Calcium 313mg; Fibre 16.2g; Sodium 506mg.

Lemon & Ginger Cake

This cake is quick to make, as your machine will mix as well as bake it for you. Just add the liquid ingredients followed by the dry ones, press start, and the machine will do the rest.

Makes 1

Small

125g/4¼oz/generous ½ cup butter, melted and cooled
2 eggs
10ml/2 tsp lemon juice
25g/1oz/2 tbsp candied lemon peel, chopped
40g/1½oz/3 tbsp crystallized ginger, chopped
175g/6oz/generous 1½ cups plain (all-purpose) flour
7.5ml/1½ tsp baking powder
125g/4¼oz/½ cup plus 1 tbsp caster (superfine) sugar

Medium

150g/5oz/⅔ cup butter, melted and cooled
3 eggs
10ml/2 tsp lemon juice
35g/1¼oz/3 tbsp candied lemon peel, chopped
50g/2oz/4 tbsp crystallized ginger, chopped
215g/7½oz/1⅞ cups plain (all-purpose) flour
10ml/2 tsp baking powder
150g/5oz/⅔ cup caster (superfine) sugar

For the lemon icing

10ml/2 tsp lemon juice
40–50g/1½–2oz icing (confectioners') sugar

1 Mix the butter, eggs and lemon juice together in a bowl and pour into the bread machine pan. Add the candied peel and crystallized ginger.

2 In another bowl, sift the plain flour and baking powder together. Stir in the caster sugar and add to the bread machine pan. Set the bread machine to the cake setting, light crust, 500g, if available.

3 Remove the bread pan at the end of the cycle. Leave to stand for 5 minutes, then turn out the cake on to a wire rack to cool.

4 Mix the lemon juice and icing sugar together and drizzle over the cake. Leave to set.

Passion Cake

Don't be misled into assuming this cake contains passion fruit. It is actually a carrot and walnut cake. Topped with a tangy lemon cheese icing, it makes the perfect teatime treat.

Makes 1

150g/5oz/scant ⅔ cup butter
150g/5oz/scant ⅔ cup soft light brown sugar
2 eggs, separated
10ml/2 tsp lemon juice, plus 5ml/1 tsp for the topping
15ml/1 tbsp milk
150g/5oz/1¼ cups self-raising (self-rising) flour
3.5ml/¾ tsp baking powder
40g/1¼oz/⅓ cup ground almonds
75g/3oz/¾ cup walnut pieces, chopped
200g/7oz/scant 1¼ cups grated carrot
150g/5oz/⅔ cup mascarpone cheese
40g/1½oz/3 tbsp icing (confectioners') sugar
30ml/2 tbsp walnut pieces, to decorate

1 Remove the kneading blade from the bread machine pan, if it is detachable. Line the base with baking parchment.

2 Place the butter and sugar together in a bowl and cream until light and fluffy. Beat in the egg yolks, one at a time, then beat in the lemon juice. Beat in the milk. Sift the flour and baking powder together and fold in. Add the ground almonds and chopped walnut pieces.

3 Meanwhile, whisk the egg whites in a grease-free bowl until stiff. Then fold into the creamed cake mixture, together with the grated carrot and mix. Spoon the mixture into the prepared pan and set the machine to the bake/bake only setting. Set the timer, if possible, for the recommended time. If, on your bread machine, the minimum time on this setting is for longer than the time suggested here, set the timer and check after the shortest recommended time. Bake the cake for 40–50 minutes.

4 Remove the pan from the machine. Leave the cake to stand for 5 minutes, then turn out on to a wire rack. Beat the icing sugar with the mascarpone cheese and lemon juice, then spread over the top of the cake and sprinkle with the walnut pieces.

Lemon and Ginger Cake per cake Energy 2367kcal/9931kJ; Protein 30.5g; Carbohydrate 320.7g, of which sugars 187.3g; Fat 116.1g, of which saturates 70.9g; Cholesterol 668mg; Calcium 479mg; Fibre 8.5g; Sodium 1273mg.

Passion Cake per cake Energy 2643kcal/11041kJ; Protein 31.2g; Carbohydrate 279.3g, of which sugars 184.2g; Fat 163.7g, of which saturates 88.2g; Cholesterol 545mg; Calcium 488mg; Fibre 9g; Sodium 1088mg.

Treacle, Date & Walnut Cake

Layered with a tasty date purée and finished with a crunchy sugar and walnut topping, this cake is absolutely irresistible.

Makes 1

150g/5oz/scant 1 cup pitted dates
grated rind and juice of 1 lemon
175g/6oz/1½ cups self-raising (self-rising) flour
3.5ml/¾ tsp each ground cinnamon, ginger and grated nutmeg
75g/3oz/6 tbsp butter
75g/3oz/6 tbsp light muscovado (brown) sugar
25ml/1½ tbsp treacle (molasses)
45ml/3 tbsp golden (light corn) syrup
60ml/4 tbsp milk
1 large egg
50g/2oz/½ cup chopped walnuts

1 Remove the kneading blade from the bread pan, if it is detachable. Line the base of the pan with baking parchment. Place the dates, lemon rind and juice in a pan, add 60ml/4 tbsp water and bring to the boil. Simmer until soft. Purée in a blender or food processor until smooth.

2 Sift the flour and spices together. Cream the butter and sugar until pale and fluffy. Warm the treacle, golden syrup and milk in a pan, until just melted then beat into the creamed butter mixture. Add the egg and beat in the flour mixture, then stir in the chopped walnuts.

3 Place half the mixture in the bread pan. Spread over the date purée, leaving a thin border of cake mix all round. Top with the remaining cake mixture, spreading it evenly over the date purée.

4 Set the bread machine to the bake/bake only setting. Set the timer, if possible for the recommended time. If not, set the timer and check after the shortest recommended time. Bake for 40 minutes. Use the light bake setting if available.

5 Mix the topping ingredients together, sprinkle over the nearly baked cake and cook for 15–20 minutes more, until the topping starts to bubble. Remove the bread pan from the machine. Leave for 15 minutes, then cool on a wire rack.

Crunchy Pear & Cherry Cake

Made from quick all-in-one cake mixture, this cake is filled with juicy pears and cherries, and has a crunchy demerara sugar topping.

Makes 1

100g/3¾oz/7 tbsp soft margarine
100g/3¾oz/½ cup caster (superfine) sugar
2 eggs
60ml/4 tbsp milk
225g/8oz/2 cups plain (all-purpose) flour
10ml/2 tsp baking powder
65g/2½oz/generous ½ cup ready-to-eat dried pears, chopped
65g/2½oz/generous ¼ cup glacé (candied) cherries, quartered
40g/1½oz/3 tbsp crystallized (candied) ginger, chopped
30ml/2 tbsp demerara sugar (raw)

1 Remove the kneading blade from the bread pan, if it is detachable, then line the base of the bread machine pan with baking parchment.

2 Mix the margarine and caster sugar in a large mixing bowl. Add the eggs, milk, flour and baking powder. Beat the mixture together for 1–2 minutes. Fold in the pears, cherries and ginger, using a metal spoon.

3 Spoon the mixture into the prepared pan. Sprinkle half the demerara sugar over the top.

4 Set the machine to the bake/bake only setting. Set the timer, if possible, for the recommended time. If, on your bread machine, the minimum time on this setting is for longer than suggested here, set the timer and check the cake after the shortest recommended time. Bake the cake for 50–55 minutes.

5 Sprinkle the remaining sugar over after 30 minutes. Insert a skewer into the centre of the cake to test if it is cooked; it should come out clean.

6 Remove the pan from the bread machine. Leave the cake to stand for 5 minutes, then turn out on to a wire rack and leave to cool.

Treacle, Date and Walnut Cake per cake Energy 1771kcal/7445kJ; Protein 29.7g; Carbohydrate 256.9g, of which sugars 169g; Fat 76.6g, of which saturates 31.4g; Cholesterol 457mg; Calcium 447mg; Fibre 9.6g; Sodium 573mg.

Crunchy Pear and Cherry Cake per cake Energy 1905kcal/8019kJ; Protein 31.4g; Carbohydrate 295.6g, of which sugars 166.1g; Fat 74.8g, of which saturates 3.4g; Cholesterol 381mg; Calcium 422mg; Fibre 9g; Sodium 775mg.

Hazelnut Twist Cake

Easy to make yet impressive, this sweet bread consists of layers of ground nuts topped with a maple icing.

Makes 1

230ml/8fl oz/1 cup water
1 egg
450g/1lb/4 cups unbleached white bread flour
45ml/3 tbsp skimmed milk powder (non fat dry milk)
grated rind of 1 orange
2.5ml/½ tsp salt
50g/2oz/¼ cup caster (superfine) sugar
75g/3oz/6 tbsp butter, melted
7.5ml/1½ tsp easy-blend (rapid-rise) dried yeast
flaked (sliced) almonds or slivered hazelnuts, to decorate

For the filling

115g/4oz/1 cup ground hazelnuts
100g/3¾oz/1 cup ground almonds
100g/3¾oz/scant ½ cup light muscovado (brown) sugar
2.5ml/½ tsp freshly grated nutmeg
2 egg whites
15ml/1 tbsp brandy

For the topping

60ml/4 tbsp icing (confectioners') sugar
15ml/1 tbsp hot water
30ml/2 tbsp natural maple syrup

1 Pour the water and egg into the bread pan. Sprinkle over the flour. Add the milk powder and orange rind. Place the salt, sugar and butter in separate corners. Make a well in the flour; add the yeast. Set the machine to the basic dough setting. Press Start. Oil a 23cm/9in springform ring cake tin (pan). When finished, knock back (punch down) the dough. Roll it out to a 65 × 45cm/26 × 18in rectangle. Cut in half lengthways.

2 Mix the filling ingredients in a bowl. Spread half over each piece of dough, leaving a border along one long edge of each. Roll up and twist together. Brush the ends with a little water. Place in the tin. Cover and leave for 30–45 minutes, or until it has risen and is puffy. Preheat the oven to 200°C/400°F/Gas 6.

3 Bake for 30–35 minutes. Leave to cool, then place on a wire rack. Mix the icing sugar, hot water and maple syrup in a bowl. Drizzle over the warm cake. Sprinkle with a few flaked almonds or slivered hazelnuts, and leave to cool completely.

Strawberry Chocolate Savarin

This light, spongy cake is soaked in a wine and brandy syrup before being filled with succulent fresh strawberries.

Makes 1

100ml/3½fl oz/7 tbsp milk
4 eggs
225g/8oz/2 cups unbleached white bread flour
40g/1½oz/3 tbsp unsweetened cocoa powder
2.5ml/½ tsp salt
25g/1oz/2 tbsp caster (superfine) sugar
100g/3¾oz/7 tbsp butter, melted
5ml/1 tsp easy-blend (rapid-rise) dried yeast
115g/4oz/½ cup sugar
75ml/2½fl oz/⅓ cup white wine
45ml/3 tbsp brandy
physalis and strawberry leaves, to decorate

For the filling

150ml/5fl oz/⅔ cup double (heavy) cream, whipped, or crème fraîche
225g/8oz/2 cups strawberries, halved
115g/4oz/1 cup raspberries

1 Pour the milk and eggs into the bread pan. Sift the flour and cocoa powder together. Sprinkle the mixture over the liquid in the pan, covering it completely. Place the salt, sugar and butter in separate corners. Make a shallow indent in the centre of the flour; add the yeast. Set the machine to the basic dough setting. Press Start. Oil a 1.5 litre/2½ pint/6¼ cup savarin or ring mould.

2 When the machine has finished mixing the ingredients, leave it on the dough setting for 20 minutes, then stop the machine.

3 Pour the mixture into the mould, cover and leave for 45–60 minutes, until the dough almost reaches the top of the tin. Preheat the oven to 200°C/400°F/Gas 6. Bake for 25–30 minutes, until well risen. Cool on a wire rack.

4 Place the sugar, wine and 75ml/2½fl oz/⅓ cup water in a pan. Heat gently, stirring until the sugar dissolves. Bring to the boil, then lower the heat and simmer for 2 minutes. Remove from the heat and stir in the brandy. Spoon over the savarin. Transfer to a serving plate and leave to cool. To serve, fill the centre with the cream and top with the strawberries and raspberries.

Hazelnut Twist Cake Energy 557kcal/2337kJ; Protein 12.3g; Carbohydrate 73.8g, of which sugars 30.3g; Fat 25.3g, of which saturates 6.7g; Cholesterol 46mg; Calcium 171mg; Fibre 3.6g; Sodium 233mg.

Strawberry Chocolate Savarin Energy 335kcal/1396kJ; Protein 4.9g; Carbohydrate 25.6g, of which sugars 21.7g; Fat 22.4g, of which saturates 13.1g; Cholesterol 146mg; Calcium 66mg; Fibre 0.8g; Sodium 116mg.

Easter Tea Ring

This is ideal for a teatime treat or coffee break.

Makes 1

90ml/6 tbsp milk
1 egg
225g/8oz/2 cups unbleached white bread flour
2.5ml/½ tsp salt
25g/1oz/2 tbsp caster (superfine) sugar
25g/1oz/2 tbsp butter
5ml/1 tsp easy-blend (rapid-rise) dried yeast
50g/2oz/½ cup ready-to-eat dried apricots
15g/½oz/1 tbsp butter
50g/2oz/¼ cup light muscovado (brown) sugar
7.5ml/1½ tsp ground cinnamon
2.5ml/½ tsp allspice
50g/2oz/⅓ cup sultanas (golden raisins)
milk, for brushing

For the decoration

45ml/3 tbsp icing (confectioners') sugar
15–30ml/1–2 tbsp orange liqueur or orange juice
pecan nuts and candied fruits

1 Pour the milk and egg into the bread machine pan. Sprinkle over the flour, covering the liquid. Add the salt, sugar and butter in separate corners of the bread pan. Make a well in the flour; add the yeast. Set to the basic dough setting. Press Start. When finished, remove and knock back (punch down) the dough gently, then roll it out into a 30 × 45cm/12 × 18in rectangle.

2 Chop the dried apricots into small pieces. Melt the butter for the filling and brush it over the dough. Sprinkle the dough with the muscovado sugar, ground cinnamon, allspice, sultanas and chopped apricots. Starting from one long edge, roll up the rectangle of dough then curl into a circle, brush the ends with a little milk and seal. Place on an oiled baking sheet.

3 Snip through the circle at 4cm/1½in intervals, each time cutting two-thirds of the way through the dough. Twist the sections so they start to fall sideways. Cover and leave for about 30 minutes. Preheat the oven to 200°C/400°F/Gas 6. Bake for 20–25 minutes.. While the tea ring is still warm, mix together the icing sugar and liqueur or orange juice. Drizzle over the ring, then arrange pecan nuts and candied fruit on top.

Spiced Fruit Kugelhopf

Juicy sultanas steeped in spiced rum flavour this brioche-style bread.

Makes 1

100ml/3½fl oz/7 tbsp dark rum
5ml/1 tsp ground ginger
3 whole cloves
1 cinnamon stick
5ml/1 tsp freshly grated nutmeg
115g/4oz/⅔ cup sultanas (golden raisins)
30ml/2 tbsp milk
5 eggs
500g/1lb 2oz/4½ cups unbleached white bread flour
2.5ml/½ tsp salt
75g/3oz/6 tbsp caster (superfine) sugar
10ml/2 tsp easy-blend (rapid-rise) dried yeast
75g/3oz/6 tbsp butter, melted
75g/3oz/½ cup cut mixed (candied) peel
icing (confectioners') sugar, for dusting

1 Mix the rum, ginger, cloves, cinnamon stick and nutmeg in a pan and heat until hot, but not bubbling. Remove from the heat, add the sultanas and set aside for 30 minutes. Pour the milk into the machine pan. Add three of the eggs, then separate the remaining eggs, setting the whites aside, and add the egg yolks to the pan.

2 Remove the cloves and cinnamon from the pan and discard. Place a sieve (strainer) over the bread pan and drain the sultanas in it. Set the sultanas aside. Sprinkle over the flour, covering the liquid. Add the salt and sugar in separate corners of the bread pan. Make a well in the flour and add the yeast. Set the bread machine to the basic dough setting. Press Start. Mix for 5 minutes, then gradually add the melted butter.

3 When the dough cycle has finished, put the dough in a large mixing bowl. In a separate bowl, whisk the egg whites to soft peaks. Add the reserved sultanas and cut mixed peel to the dough and fold in. Gradually fold in the egg whites. Spoon the dough into an oiled kugelhopf tin in three or four batches, making sure it is evenly distributed. Cover and leave for 1–1½ hours, until the dough is almost at the top of the tin. Preheat the oven to 190°C/375°F/Gas 5. Bake the kugelhopf for 50–60 minutes or until it has browned. Dust with icing sugar.

Easter Tea Ring Energy 244kcal/1028kJ; Protein 4.4g; Carbohydrate 38.6g, of which sugars 18.2g; Fat 9.1g, of which saturates 4.5g; Cholesterol 44mg; Calcium 87mg; Fibre 1.1g; Sodium 65mg.

Spiced Fruit Kugelhopf per loaf Energy 3635kcal/15330kJ; Protein 83.3g; Carbohydrate 592.5g, of which sugars 211.5g; Fat 97.2g, of which saturates 49.5g; Cholesterol 1126mg; Calcium 1101mg; Fibre 21.4g; Sodium 1180mg.

Polish Babka

Vodka is the surprise ingredient in this classic Polish cake.

Makes 1

60ml/4 tbsp vodka
2.5ml/½ tsp saffron threads
15ml/1 tbsp grated orange rind
15ml/1 tbsp grated lemon rind
115g/4oz/½ cup butter, softened
75g/3oz/6 tbsp caster (superfine) sugar
3 eggs
30ml/2 tbsp water
400g/14oz/3½ cups unbleached white bread flour
2.5ml/½ tsp salt
10ml/2 tsp easy-blend (rapid-rise) dried yeast
75g/3oz/½ cup raisins
75g/3oz/½ cup dried sour cherries
115g/4oz/1 cup icing (confectioners') sugar
15ml/1 tbsp lemon juice

For the decoration
toasted flaked (sliced) almonds
pared orange rind or candied orange peel

1 Steep the vodka, saffron and citrus rinds together for 30 minutes. Beat the butter and sugar in a bowl. Add the saffron mixture into the bread pan, then add the eggs and water. Add the flour, covering the liquid. Add the salt in a corner. Make an indent in the flour; add the yeast. Set to the basic raisin dough setting. Press Start. Mix for 5 minutes, then add the butter and sugar mixture. Add in the raisins and cherries when the machine beeps, or 5 minutes before the end of the kneading cycle.

2 When the cycle has finished, remove the dough and knock back (punch down) gently, and shape into a plump round ball. Place in an oiled brioche tin, cover and leave for about 2 hours, or until it has risen almost to the top of the tin.

3 Preheat the oven to 200°C/400°F/Gas 6. Bake the babka for 20 minutes. Reduce the oven temperature to 190°C/375°F/Gas 5 and continue to bake for 15–20 minutes more, until golden. Turn out on to a wire rack to cool. Meanwhile, make the icing. Place the icing sugar in a bowl and add the lemon juice and 15ml/1 tbsp hot water. Mix well, then drizzle the icing over the cake. Sprinkle over the almonds and orange to decorate.

Peach Brandy Babas

These light, delicate sponges are moistened with a syrup flavoured with peach brandy before being filled with whipped cream and fruit.

Makes 8

100ml/3½fl oz/7 tbsp milk
4 eggs
225g/8oz/2 cups unbleached white bread flour
5ml/1 tsp ground cinnamon
2.5ml/½ tsp salt
25g/1oz/2 tbsp caster (superfine) sugar
5ml/1 tsp easy-blend (rapid-rise) dried yeast
100g/3¾oz/7 tbsp butter, melted
115g/4oz/½ cup sugar
150ml/5fl oz/⅔ cup water
90ml/6 tbsp peach brandy

For the decoration
150ml/5fl oz/⅔ cup double (heavy) cream
15ml/1 tbsp caster (superfine) sugar
3–4 drops natural vanilla extract
fresh fruits, to decorate

1 Pour the milk and eggs into the bread pan. Sprinkle over the flour, covering the liquid. Add the cinnamon, then place the salt and sugar in separate corners. Make a well in the flour and add the yeast. Set to the basic dough setting. Press Start. Lightly oil eight small savarin tins, each with a diameter of 10cm/4in.

2 When the machine has finished mixing the dough, let the dough cycle continue for a further 15 minutes, then stop the machine and scrape the dough into a measuring jug (cup). Beat in the melted butter. Pour the batter into the prepared tins, half filling them. Cover and leave in a warm place until the batter reaches the tin tops. Preheat the oven to 190°C/375°F/Gas 5. Bake for 20 minutes, or until golden and well risen. Turn out on to a wire rack to cool. Slide a large tray under the rack.

3 Place the sugar and water in a small pan and heat gently, stirring occasionally, until the sugar has dissolved. Bring to the boil and boil hard for 2 minutes without stirring. Remove from the heat and stir in the peach brandy. Spoon over the babas. When the babas are cold, whip the cream, sugar and vanilla extract in a bowl. Fill the babas with the flavoured cream and decorate them with fresh fruits of your choice.

Polish Babka Energy 349kcal/1473kJ; Protein 4.2g; Carbohydrate 61.2g, of which sugars 30.7g; Fat 10g, of which saturates 6.3g; Cholesterol 26mg; Calcium 78mg; Fibre 1.5g; Sodium 94mg.

Peach Brandy Babas per cake Energy 415kcal/1735kJ; Protein 6.7g; Carbohydrate 43.2g, of which sugars 21.8g; Fat 23.6g, of which saturates 13.3g; Cholesterol 149mg; Calcium 90mg; Fibre 0.9g; Sodium 145mg.

Lemon & Pistachio Strudel

This superb strudel is made up of thin layers of dough interleaved with a tasty curd and goat's cheese filling.

Makes 1
90ml/6 tbsp milk
1 egg
225g/8oz/2 cups unbleached white bread flour
2.5ml/½ tsp salt
15ml/1 tbsp caster (superfine) sugar
50g/2oz/¼ cup butter
5ml/1 tsp easy-blend (rapid-rise) dried yeast
icing (confectioners') sugar, for dusting

For the filling
115g/4oz/½ cup montrachet or soft goat's cheese
115g/4oz/½ cup curd (farmers') cheese, strained
2 egg yolks
50g/2oz/¼ cup caster (superfine) sugar
grated rind of 1 lemon
2.5ml/½ tsp vanilla extract
50g/2oz/⅓ cup raisins
50g/2oz/⅓ cup pistachio nuts, peeled
50g/2oz/¼ cup ready-to-eat dried apricots, chopped
50g/2oz/¼ cup butter, melted
50g/2oz/½ cup ground almonds

1 Pour the milk and egg into the bread machine pan. Sprinkle over the flour, ensuring that it covers the liquid. Add the salt, sugar and butter, placing them in separate corners of the bread pan. Make a well in the flour and add the yeast. Set the to the basic dough setting. Press Start. Lightly oil a baking sheet.

2 Make the filling. Put both types of cheese, the egg yolks, sugar, lemon rind and vanilla in a bowl. Mix well. Stir in the raisins, pistachios and apricots.

3 When the dough cycle has finished, place the dough on a lightly floured surface. Knock back (punch down) gently. Roll out to a rectangle 35 × 25cm/14 × 10in. Brush with melted butter and sprinkle with the ground almonds. Spread the filling over, leaving a narrow border around the edges. Fold in the edges along both long sides. Roll up the dough from a short side.

4 Place on the baking sheet, seam side down. Cover for 30 minutes. Preheat the oven to 190°C/375°F/Gas 5. Bake for 25–30 minutes, until golden. Dust with icing sugar.

Peach Streuselkuchen

This peach-filled German yeast cake is finished with a crunchy almond and cinnamon topping.

Makes 1
100ml/3½fl oz/7 tbsp milk
1 egg
250g/9oz/2¼ cups unbleached white bread flour
2.5ml/½ tsp salt
40g/1½oz/3 tbsp caster (superfine) sugar
25g/1oz/2 tbsp butter, melted
5ml/1 tsp easy-blend (rapid-rise) dried yeast
4 peaches, halved and stoned (pitted)

For the topping
75g/3oz/¾ cup plain (all-purpose) flour
40g/1½oz/⅓ cup ground almonds
50g/2oz/¼ cup butter, diced and softened
40g/1½oz/4 tbsp caster sugar
5ml/1 tsp ground cinnamon

1 Pour the milk and egg into the bread pan. Sprinkle over the flour, covering the milk and egg completely. Add the salt, sugar and butter, placing them in three separate corners of the bread pan. Make a well in the flour and add the easy-blend dried yeast.

2 Set the bread machine to the basic dough setting. Press Start. Lightly oil a 25cm/10in springform cake tin (pan).

3 When the dough cycle has finished, remove the dough from the pan and place it on a lightly floured surface. Knock back (punch down) gently, then roll it out and fit in the tin.

4 Slice the peaches and arrange them on top of the dough. Next, make the topping. Rub the flour, ground almonds and butter together until the mixture resembles breadcrumbs. Stir in the sugar and cinnamon. Sprinkle over the peaches.

5 Cover the dough and leave for about 20–25 minutes, to rise slightly. Meanwhile, preheat the oven to 190°C/375°F/Gas 5.

6 Bake the cake for 25–30 minutes, or until evenly golden. Leave it to cool in the tin for a few minutes and serve warm, or turn out on to a wire rack to allow to cool completely.

Lemon and Pistachio Strudel Energy 400kcal/1670kJ; Protein 12.5g; Carbohydrate 34.6g, of which sugars 12.8g; Fat 24.7g, of which saturates 11.6g; Cholesterol 120mg; Calcium 129mg; Fibre 2.1g; Sodium 300mg.

Peach Streuselkuchen Energy 313kcal/1319kJ; Protein 6.8g; Carbohydrate 47.7g, of which sugars 16.7g; Fat 12g, of which saturates 5.7g; Cholesterol 46mg; Calcium 99mg; Fibre 2.6g; Sodium 89mg.

Bavarian Plum Cake

As this dish bakes, the juices from the plums trickle through to the base, making a deliciously succulent, fruity cake. Serve it with crème fraîche or ice cream.

Makes 1

90ml/6 tbsp milk
1 egg
225g/8oz/2 cups unbleached white bread flour
5ml/1 tsp ground cinnamon
2.5ml/½ tsp salt
40g/1½oz/3 tbsp caster (superfine) sugar
25g/1oz/2 tbsp butter, melted
5ml/1 tsp easy-blend (rapid-rise) dried yeast
675g/1½lb plums
icing (confectioners') sugar, for dusting

1 Pour the milk into the bread machine pan and add the egg. Sprinkle over the flour, ensuring that it covers the milk and egg completely. Add the ground cinnamon. Place the salt, sugar and butter in separate corners of the bread pan.

2 Make a small indent in the centre of the flour (but not down as far as the liquid), and add the yeast.

3 Set the bread machine to the dough setting; use basic dough setting (if available). Press Start. Lightly oil a 27 × 18cm/10½ × 7in rectangular baking tin (pan) that is about 4cm/1½in deep.

4 When the dough cycle has finished, remove the dough and place it on a lightly floured surface. Knock it back (punch it down) gently, then roll it out to fit the tin. Ease it into position.

5 Cut the plums into quarters and remove the stones (pits). Arrange on the dough, so that they overlap slightly.

6 Cover with lightly oiled clear film (plastic wrap) and leave in a warm place for 30–45 minutes, to rise. Meanwhile, preheat the oven to 190°C/375°F/Gas 5.

7 Bake the cake for 30–35 minutes, or until golden and well risen. Dust with icing sugar and serve warm.

Swiss Pear & Redcurrant Tart

Juicy pears and redcurrants in a nutmeg cream custard provide an unforgettable filling for this Swiss tart.

Makes 1

85ml/3fl oz/⅜ cup milk
1 egg
225g/8oz/2 cups unbleached white bread flour
2.5ml/½ tsp salt
25g/1oz/2 tbsp caster (superfine) sugar
25g/1oz/2 tbsp butter, melted
5ml/1 tsp easy-blend (rapid-rise) dried yeast
icing (confectioners') sugar, to dust

For the filling
120ml/4fl oz/½ cup single (light) cream
2 eggs
25g/1oz/2 tbsp caster (superfine) sugar
2.5ml/½ tsp freshly grated nutmeg
3 pears, peeled, halved and cored
50g/2oz/⅓ cup redcurrants

1 Pour the milk and egg into the bread machine pan. Sprinkle over the flour, ensuring that it covers the liquid completely. Add the salt, sugar and butter, placing them in separate corners of the bread pan. Make a well in the flour and add the yeast.

2 Set the bread machine to the basic dough setting. Press Start. Lightly oil a 25cm/10in pizza pan, shallow pie pan or flan tin.

3 When the dough cycle has finished, remove the dough from the machine and knock back (punch down) gently.

4 Roll out the dough to a 28cm/11in round. Place it in the oiled pizza pan or pie or flan tin. With your fingers, press the dough outwards and upwards so that it covers the base and sides of the tin evenly. Preheat the oven to 190°C/375°F/Gas 5.

5 Make the filling by beating the cream with the eggs, sugar and nutmeg in a bowl. Pour it into the dough-lined tin. Arrange the pears on top, placing them cut side down. Sprinkle the redcurrants in the centre.

6 Bake the tart for 35–40 minutes, until crust is golden. Let it cool for a few minutes in the tin, then sprinkle with icing sugar.

Bavarian Plum Cake Energy 311kcal/1307kJ; Protein 6.4g; Carbohydrate 44.5g, of which sugars 15.9g; Fat 13.2g, of which saturates 7.4g; Cholesterol 89mg; Calcium 86mg; Fibre 2.4g; Sodium 102mg.

Swiss Pear and Redcurrant Tart Energy 212kcal/892kJ; Protein 4.4g; Carbohydrate 35.6g, of which sugars 14.1g; Fat 6.7g, of which saturates 3.8g; Cholesterol 40mg; Calcium 83mg; Fibre 2.3g; Sodium 171mg.

Index

Hand-made and bread-machine recipes with similar recipe titles are indicated with '(HM)' or '(BM)' after the title.